Collins

Primary Illustrated

French Dictionary

D0376934

HarperCollins Publishers
Westerhill Road
Bishopbriggs
Glasgow
G64 2QT
Great Britain

www.collinsdictionary.com
www.collins.co.uk

First Edition 2014
Previously published as Collins First Time
French Dictionary 2003, 2006, 2012

10 9 8 7 6 5 4

© HarperCollins Publishers 2014

ISBN   978-0-00-757874-0

A catalogue record for this book is available
from the British Library

Art direction by Mark Thomson
Designed by Wolfgang Homola
Typeset by Davidson Pre-Press, Glasgow

Printed in Italy by Grafica Veneta SpA.

Acknowledgements
We would like to thank those authors and
publishers who kindly gave permission for
copyright material to be used in the Collins
Corpus. We would also like to thank Times
Newspapers Ltd for providing valuable data.

PUBLISHING DIRECTOR
Rob Scriven

MANAGING EDITOR
Gaëlle Amiot-Cadey

PROJECT MANAGEMENT
Alex Hepworth
Susanne Reichert

CONTRIBUTORS
Maree Airlie
Cécile Aubinière-Robb
Daphne Day
Morven Dooner
Genevieve Gerrard
Sandy Hamilton
Cordelia Lilly

ILLUSTRATIONS
Q2A Media

ILLUSTRATED SUPPLEMENT
Marcella Grassi
© Boroli Editore 2008

We would like to give special thanks to Simon
Green and Helen Morrison for their invaluable
contribution to the first edition of this
dictionary. We would also like to thank the
many teachers who provided us with
invaluable information and advice.

Contents

This bilingual dictionary is aimed at primary school children who are starting to learn French.

Access to a dictionary which is pitched at an appropriate level is a vital part of the language-learning process. The content of this dictionary has been carefully selected to reflect current trends in primary education and help children with acquiring basic language-learning skills.

The key aims of this dictionary are:
- to develop both language skills in French and language learning skills in general
- to cover the four key areas of language attainment: listening, speaking, reading and writing
- to reinforce key aspects of the language by the use of notes and feature boxes throughout the entries
- to extend cultural awareness by providing information about France, especially where traditions differ from those in Britain

This dictionary supports language learning in a number of specific ways:
- it develops children's knowledge of how language works by encouraging them to understand, analyse and use simple aspects of grammar
- it develops children's individual learning skills by using a wide range of notes that explain things in a simple but interesting way
- it enables children to make comparisons between French and English by encouraging them to explore the similarities and differences between the two languages and cultures
- it introduces young learners to all the basic elements of a bilingual dictionary and provides detailed instructions on how to get the most out of using the dictionary

The dictionary is presented in an easy-to-use format which is intended to appeal to children of primary school age. It provides lots of simple, relevant examples and tips on how to remember words, and how to avoid some of the pitfalls of translation. It also features key phrases, illustrations and information about life in France, making it an invaluable and exciting resource.

Step one:
Pick the right side

Remember there are two halves to the dictionary. If you want to know what a French word means, look in the **French-English** half. It comes first.

If you want to translate an English word into French, look in the second half, which is **English-French**. It comes after the supplement in the middle of the dictionary.

1 Which of these words would you look up in the **French-English** half?
demain brother horse bonbon

2 Look at page 51 of the dictionary. Is this the French side or the English side? How can you tell?

3 Look at page 411 of the dictionary. What is shown at the top of the page, above the row of dots?

4 Is **fish** the first or the last word on page 411?

Remember that you do not read across the whole page in a dictionary – you have to read down the columns.

5 Which word comes immediately after **fireworks** on page 411?

Step two:
Find the right word

A B C D E F G H I J K L M N O P Q R S T U V W X Y Z

Words are in alphabetical order in the dictionary – like names in the phone book, and in a school register. The alphabet is shown down the edge of each page of the dictionary. You can sort words into alphabetical order by looking at the first letter of each word.

6 Can you put these names in alphabetical order?
Chantal, Luc, Sophie, Pierre, Jean-Marie, Hélène

When two words start with the same letter, look at their second letters.

7 In alphabetical order which comes first – **Hermione** or **Harry**?

This is the order of the days of the week on a calendar:
Monday, Tuesday, Wednesday, Thursday, Friday, Saturday, Sunday

8 Which day comes first in a dictionary? Which comes last?

9 **Thursday** comes before **Tuesday** in a dictionary. Why?

10 Put the seven days of the week into alphabetical order. If the first letters are the same, and the second letters are the same, look at the third letters.

11 **June, July, August**: which comes last in the dictionary?

Step three:
Pick the right translation

The translations are easy to spot in this dictionary because they are in red on the **French-English** side and blue on the **English-French** side.

Some French words can be masculine or feminine, or even plural. In the dictionary MASC, FEM, and PL are the abbreviations used for these. The dictionary also shows you the French word for 'the' (this can be **le**, **la**, **l'** or **les**).

doll NOUN
    la **poupée** *fem*

When you look up **doll** you can see that the word for doll in French is **poupée**.

You can tell that the French word for **doll** is feminine because it is given with **la** and the dictionary says that it is *fem* (feminine).

So **the doll** is **la poupée** and **a doll** would be **une poupée**.

penfriend NOUN
    le **correspondant** *masc*
    la **correspondante** *fem*
      I'm Emma, your English penfriend.
      Je suis Emma, ta correspondante anglaise.

Here there are two translations, one masculine, one feminine.
If your penfriend is a boy, you need the French word which is masculine (*masc*) – **le correspondant**.
If your penfriend is a girl, you need the French word which is feminine (*fem*) – **la correspondante**.

12 If you were talking about your penfriend, which would go in the gap, **correspondant** or **correspondante**?

    J'ai un _____.
    Il s'appelle Hugo.

animal NOUN
    l' **animal** *masc* (PL les **animaux**)

Here there are two translations. The second one is plural (PL).

13 If you want to say that you love animals, which translation would go in the gap?

    J'adore les _____.

Sometimes there is more than one translation, and each one has a number. If there is more than one translation, don't just pick the first one! Check to see which is the right one.

ball NOUN
  1 la **balle** *fem* (*for tennis, golf, cricket*)
    Hit the ball!
    Frappe la balle!
  2 le **ballon** *masc* (*for football, rugby*)
    Pass the ball!
    Passe le ballon!

14 Which is the French word for a ball that you kick – **une balle** or **un ballon**? Look for the clue.

Step four:
Parts of speech

Sometimes, to pick the right translation, you need to know the *part of speech* of a word, for example whether a word is a **noun**, an **adjective**, an **adverb** or a **verb**. Other parts of speech are **conjunction**, **exclamation**, **number**, **preposition** and **pronoun**.

NOUNS

Nouns are naming words for things or people. You often use the words 'a' or 'the' with a noun – eg a **girl**, a **boy**, the **school**, the **windows**.

Nouns can be singular, eg an **accident**, the **canteen**, my **dad**, **football** – or plural, eg **sweets**, the **children**, my **friends**.

15 How many nouns are there in the sentence below? What are they?
The car has got a flat tyre and a big dent in the door.

ADJECTIVES

An **adjective** is a describing word which tells you what things are like: **flat** shoes are shoes that don't have high heels. A **flat** tyre is a tyre with no air in it.

16 How many adjectives are there in the sentence below? What are they?
She's got brown hair and blue eyes.

Some words have a **noun** meaning and an **adjective** meaning. In the dictionary there is a box to tell you about this. The different meanings usually have different translations in French.

sweet

sweet *can be a noun or an adjective.*

A NOUN
1 le **bonbon** *masc (candy)*
a bag of sweets
un paquet de bonbons
2 le **dessert** *masc (pudding)*
Sweets: ice cream or chocolate mousse
Desserts: glace ou mousse au chocolat

B ADJECTIVE
1 **sucré** *masc*
sucrée *fem (sugary)*
It's too sweet.
C'est trop sucré.
2 **gentil** *masc*
gentille *fem (kind)*
She's a sweet person.
Elle est gentille.
3 **mignon** *masc*
mignonne *fem (cute)*
Isn't she sweet?
Comme elle est mignonne!

17 You want to ask someone if they would like a sweet. Fill in the gap. How can you be sure this is the right translation?

Tu veux un _____?

ADVERBS

An **adverb** is a word which describes a verb or an adjective:
She writes **neatly**. The film was **very** good.

18 How many adverbs are there in the sentence below? What are they? What do they have in common?
The children sat quietly and played happily.

Some words have an **adjective** meaning and an **adverb** meaning. The different meanings have different translations in French.

hard

> **hard** *can be an adjective or an adverb.*

A ADJECTIVE
1 **difficile** *(difficult)*
   This question's too hard for me.
   Cette question est trop difficile pour moi.
2 **dur** *masc*
   dure *fem (not soft)*
   This cheese is very hard.
   Ce fromage est très dur.
B ADVERB
   dur
   Colette works hard.
   Colette travaille dur.

19 You want to say you work hard. Fill in the gap in the sentence below:

   Je travaille _____.

VERBS
Verbs are sometimes called 'doing words'. They often go with words like 'I' and 'you', and with names, eg I **play** football, What do you **want**?, Hugo **likes** mashed potato.

Verbs tell you about the present: eg I'**m listening**; the past: I **scored** a goal; and the future: eg I'**m going to get** an ice cream.

20 How many verbs are there in the sentence below? What are they?
   School starts at 9.00 and finishes at 3.30.

Some words have an **adjective** meaning and a **verb** meaning. The different meanings have different translations in French.

clean

> **clean** *can be an adjective or a verb.*

A ADJECTIVE
   propre
   a clean shirt
   une chemise propre
B VERB
   nettoyer
   Clean the board please!
   Nettoie le tableau s'il te plaît!

21 If you want to ask for 'a clean glass', how do you know that **propre** is the translation, not **nettoyer**?

Some words have a **noun** meaning and a **verb** meaning.

rain

> **rain** *can be a noun or a verb.*

A NOUN
   la **pluie** *fem*
   in the rain
   sous la pluie
B VERB
   pleuvoir
   It's going to rain.
   Il va pleuvoir.
   It rains a lot here.
   Il pleut beaucoup par ici.

> **It's raining.**
> Il pleut.

22 Is **la pluie** a noun or a verb?

23 Why is **It rains a lot here.** in part **B**?

Learn useful phrases

In the dictionary you'll see phrases that are especially important in orange boxes. Try to learn these when you come across them, and you'll soon know lots of useful things to say in French.

> **What time is it?**
> Quelle heure est-il?
> **It's lunch time.**
> C'est l'heure du déjeuner.
> **How many times?**
> Combien de fois?

Find out interesting things about life in France

There are also boxes which tell you about French customs, and about differences between life in France and Britain.

> **Did you know...?**
> *In France, Easter eggs are said to be brought by the Easter bells or* **cloches de Pâques** *which fly from Rome and drop them in people's gardens.*

Even more words

At school you will learn to talk about subjects such as the time and the weather, your family, your pets, and your clothes. The most important words for talking about these subjects are shown in the dictionary itself, and even more words are given in **Language Plus**, the supplement in the middle part of the dictionary. Have a look!

Answer key

1 demain and bonbon
2 the French side; French words on it; French-English written at the side of the page.
3 fire → fish
4 It's the last word on page 411.
5 first
6 Chantal, Hélène, Jean-Marie, Luc, Pierre, Sophie
7 Harry – because 'a' comes before 'e'
8 Friday comes first and Wednesday comes last.
9 because the second letter of Thursday is 'h', which comes before 'u', the second letter of Tuesday
10 Friday, Monday, Thursday, Tuesday, Saturday, Sunday, Wednesday
11 June
12 correspondant
13 animaux
14 un ballon – the clue is in the example: un ballon de football
15 4 – car, tyre, dent, door
16 2 – brown, blue
17 bonbon – a sweet is a noun, it means candy; the example helps too
18 2 – quietly, happily; they both end in -ly
19 dur
20 2 – starts, finishes
21 because clean has an adjective meaning in this sentence; the example helps too
22 a noun
23 because it's a verb

French – English

A a

a VERB ▷see **avoir**

Language tip
*Don't confuse **a** with the preposition **à**.*

1 has
Elle a beaucoup d'amis.
She has lots of friends.

Language tip
*Sometimes **a** is used to show that something has happened in the past.*

Il a joué au football.
He played football.
2 is
Il a neuf ans.
He is nine years old.
il y a
there is/there are

Language tip
il y a has two translations. Look at the examples.

Il y a un bon film à la télé.
There's a good film on TV.
Il y a beaucoup de monde.
There are lots of people.

Language tip
il y a can also mean ago.

Elle est partie il y a dix minutes.
She left ten minutes ago.

Qu'est-ce qu'il y a?
What's the matter?

à PREPOSITION

Language tip
*Don't confuse **à** with the verb form a. See also **au** (= à + le) and **aux** (= à + les).*

1 at
Je suis à la maison.
I am at home.
Je finis à quatre heures.
I finish at 4 o'clock.
2 in
Il est à Paris.
He is in Paris.
Elle habite au Portugal.
She lives in Portugal.
Mes grands-parents habitent à la campagne.
My grandparents live in the country.
au printemps
in the spring
au mois de juin
in June
3 to
Je vais à Paris.
I'm going to Paris.
Elle va au Portugal.
She's going to Portugal.
Cet été je vais à la campagne.
I'm going to the country this summer.
Il l'a donné à son frère.
He gave it to his brother.
Je n'ai rien à faire.
I've got nothing to do.
Ce livre est à Paul.
This book is Paul's.
4 by
Il est arrivé à bicyclette.
He arrived by bicycle.

à pied
on foot
Je vais à l'école à pied.
I walk to school.
à … d'ici
… from here
C'est à dix kilomètres d'ici.
It's 10 kilometres from here.
… à l'heure
… an hour
cent kilomètres à l'heure
100 kilometres an hour
À samedi!
See you on Saturday!
À tout à l'heure!
See you later!

À bientôt!
See you soon!
À demain!
See you tomorrow!

abandonner VERB
1 **to abandon**
2 **to give up**
   Je veux abandonner la natation.
   I want to give up swimming.

l' **abeille** FEM NOUN
bee

abominable ADJECTIVE
awful

l' **abord** MASC NOUN
   d'abord
   first
   Je vais rentrer chez moi d'abord.
   I'll go home first.

l' **abricot** MASC NOUN
   apricot

absent MASC ADJECTIVE
(FEM **absente**)
   absent

absolument ADVERB
absolutely

l' **accent** MASC NOUN
   accent
   un accent aigu
   an acute accent
   un accent grave
   a grave accent
   un accent circonflexe
   a circumflex

Language tip

French vowels sometimes have an accent to change their sound. There are three kinds of accents: the acute (**é**cole), the grave (m**è**re) and the circumflex (h**ô**tel). See also **aigu**, **grave**, **circonflexe**.

accepter VERB
to accept

l' **accident** MASC NOUN
accident

accompagner VERB
to accompany

Language tip

There is the word **accompany** in English, but it is quite a formal word and we will often use something different, such as **take**.

Elle m'accompagne à l'école.
She takes me to school.

l' **accord** MASC NOUN
être d'accord
to agree
Tu es d'accord avec moi?
Do you agree with me?

D'accord!
OK!

l' **accordéon** MASC NOUN
accordion
Ray joue de l'accordéon.
Ray plays the accordion.

l' **accueil** MASC NOUN
reception

acheter VERB
to buy

l' **acné** FEM NOUN
acne

l' **acteur** MASC NOUN
actor
un acteur de cinéma
a film actor

actif MASC ADJECTIVE
(FEM **active**)
active

l' **activité** FEM NOUN
activity

l' **actrice** FEM NOUN
actress
une actrice de cinéma
a film actress

les **actualités** FEM PL NOUN
news
Je regarde les actualités tous les soirs.
I watch the news every night.

l' **addition** FEM NOUN
1 **sum**
2 **bill**
L'addition, s'il vous plaît!
Can we have the bill, please?

adhésif MASC ADJECTIVE
(FEM **adhésive**)
le ruban adhésif
sticky tape

l' **adjectif** MASC NOUN
adjective
'grand' est un adjectif.
'grand' is an adjective.

admettre VERB
1 **to admit**
J'admets que j'ai eu tort.
I admit I was wrong.
2 **to allow**
Les chiens ne sont pas admis dans le restaurant.
Dogs are not allowed in the restaurant.

l' **adolescent** MASC NOUN
l' **adolescente** FEM NOUN
teenager

French English

a
b
c
d
e
f
g
h
i
j
k
l
m
n
o
p
q
r
s
t
u
v
w
x
y
z

3

French English

a
b
c
d
e
f
g
h
i
j
k
l
m
n
o
p
q
r
s
t
u
v
w
x
y
z

adorable ADJECTIVE
lovely

adorer VERB
to love
> **Elle adore le chocolat.**
> She loves chocolate.
> **J'adore jouer au tennis.**
> I love playing tennis.

l' **adresse** FEM NOUN
address

Language tip

The French word has only one **d***, and an extra* **e***.*

> **mon adresse électronique**
> my email address

l' **adulte** MASC/FEM NOUN
adult
> **une chambre pour deux adultes et un enfant**
> a room for two adults and a child

l' **adverbe** MASC NOUN
adverb
> **'Beaucoup' est un adverbe.**
> 'Beaucoup' is an adverb.

l' **adversaire** MASC/FEM NOUN
opponent

l' **aérobic** MASC NOUN
aerobics
> **Je fais de l'aérobic.**
> I do aerobics.

l' **aéroport** MASC NOUN
airport

les **affaires** FEM PL NOUN
1 things
> **Va chercher tes affaires!**
> Go and get your things!
> **Rangez vos affaires!**
> Put your things away!

2 business
> **un homme d'affaires**
> a businessman

l' **affiche** FEM NOUN
poster

affreux MASC ADJECTIVE
(FEM **affreuse**)
awful

africain MASC ADJECTIVE
(FEM **africaine**)
African

l' **Africain** MASC NOUN
l' **Africaine** FEM NOUN
African

l' **Afrique** FEM NOUN
Africa

agacer VERB
to get on somebody's nerves
> **Tu m'agaces!**
> You're getting on my nerves!

l' **âge** MASC NOUN
age
> **Écrivez votre nom et votre âge.**
> Write down your name and age.

Tu as quel âge?
How old are you?
Quel âge a-t-elle?
How old is she?

âgé MASC ADJECTIVE (FEM **âgée**)
old

l' **agence** FEM NOUN
agency
> **une agence de voyages**
> a travel agency
> **une agence immobilière**
> an estate agent's

l' **agenda** MASC NOUN
diary

**Elle note tous ses rendez-
vous dans son agenda.**
She makes a note of all her
appointments in her diary.

Language tip

*Be careful! The French word
agenda does not mean the same as
the English word **agenda**.*

---

l' **agent** MASC NOUN
un agent de police
a policeman

l' **agneau** MASC NOUN
(PL les **agneaux**)
lamb
un gigot d'agneau
a leg of lamb

l' **agrafeuse** FEM NOUN
stapler

agréable MASC ADJECTIVE
(FEM **agréable**)
nice

l' **agriculteur** MASC NOUN
farmer

ai VERB ▷see **avoir**
J'ai deux chats.
I have two cats.

Language tip

*Sometimes **ai** is used to show that
something has happened in the past.*

J'ai oublié mon livre.
I've forgotten my book.

l' **aide** FEM NOUN
help

aider VERB
to help
Tu peux m'aider?
Can you help me?

aïe EXCLAMATION
Ouch!

aigu MASC ADJECTIVE
un accent aigu
an acute accent

l' **aiguille** FEM NOUN
needle

l' **ail** MASC NOUN
garlic
Je n'aime pas l'ail.
I don't like garlic.

l' **aile** FEM NOUN
wing
une aile de poulet
a chicken wing

aimable MASC ADJECTIVE
(FEM **aimable**)
nice

l' **aimant** MASC NOUN
magnet

aimer VERB
1 to love
Elle aime ses enfants.
She loves her children.
Je t'aime.
I love you.
2 to like
Tu aimes le chocolat?
Do you like chocolate?
J'aime bien ce garçon.
I like this boy.

J'aime bien jouer au tennis.
I like playing tennis.

aîné MASC ADJECTIVE (FEM **aînée**)
C'est mon frère aîné.
He's my big brother.

l' **aîné** MASC NOUN
l' **aînée** FEM NOUN
oldest child
C'est l'aîné.
He's the oldest child.
C'est l'aînée.
She's the oldest child.

l' **air** MASC NOUN
air
Tu as l'air fatiguée.
You look tired.

l' **aire de jeux** FEM NOUN
playground

ajouter VERB
to add

l' **alarme** FEM NOUN
alarm

l' **alcool** MASC NOUN
alcohol
Je ne bois pas d'alcool.
I don't drink alcohol.

l' **Algérie** FEM NOUN
Algeria

algérien MASC ADJECTIVE
(FEM **algérienne**)
Algerian

l' **Algérien** MASC NOUN
l' **Algérienne** FEM NOUN
Algerian

l' **alimentation** FEM NOUN
groceries
le rayon alimentation
the grocery department

l' **allée** FEM NOUN
1 path
les allées du parc
the paths in the park
2 drive
5, allée Saint-Exupéry
5 Saint-Exupéry Drive

l' **Allemagne** FEM NOUN
Germany

allemand MASC NOUN, MASC
ADJECTIVE (FEM **allemande**)
German

l' **Allemand** MASC NOUN
l' **Allemande** FEM NOUN
German

aller

aller *can be a verb or a noun.*

A VERB
to go
Je vais à Londres.
I'm going to London.
Nous allons visiter un château.
We're going to visit a castle.
Allez! Dépêche-toi!
Come on! Hurry up!
Comment vas-tu? —
Je vais bien.
How are you? — I'm fine.
Je vais mieux.
I'm feeling better.

Comment ça va? — Ça va bien.
How are you? — I'm fine.

B MASC NOUN
single
Je voudrais un aller pour Angers.
I'd like a single to Angers.
un aller simple
a single
un aller retour
a return ticket

allergique ADJECTIVE
allergique à
allergic to
Je suis allergique aux chats.
I'm allergic to cats.

allez VERB ▷ see **aller**
Vous allez où?
Where are you going?

allô EXCLAMATION
hello!
Allô! Je voudrais parler à Monsieur Simon.
Hello! I'd like to speak to Mr Simon.

> *Language tip*
>
> **allô** *is only used when talking to someone on the phone.*

allons VERB ▷ see **aller**
Nous allons nous coucher.
We're going to bed.

allumer VERB
1 **to put on**
Tu peux allumer la lumière?
Can you put the light on?
2 **to switch on**
Allume l'ordinateur.
Switch on the computer.
3 **to light**
Tu peux allumer cette bougie?
Can you light this candle?

l' **allumette** FEM NOUN
match
une boîte d'allumettes
a box of matches

alors ADVERB
1 **then**
Alors, tu viens?
Are you coming, then?
2 **so**
Alors tu habites ici?
So you live here?
Et alors?
So what?

les **Alpes** FEM PL NOUN
Alps
dans les Alpes
in the Alps

l' **alphabet** MASC NOUN
alphabet

alphabétique ADJECTIVE
alphabetical
par ordre alphabétique
in alphabetical order

l' **amande** FEM NOUN
almond
la pâte d'amandes
marzipan

l' **ambulance** FEM NOUN
ambulance
Appelez une ambulance!
Call an ambulance!

l' **amende** FEM NOUN
fine
    une amende de trente euros
    a 30 euro fine

amener VERB
to bring
    Je peux amener un ami?
    Can I bring a friend?

américain MASC ADJECTIVE
(FEM **américaine**)
American

l' **Américain** MASC NOUN
l' **Américaine** FEM NOUN
American

l' **Amérique** FEM NOUN
America

l' **ami** MASC NOUN
l' **amie** FEM NOUN
friend

J'ai beaucoup d'amis.
I have lots of friends.
mon meilleur ami
my best friend
ma meilleure amie
my best friend
un petit ami
a boyfriend
une petite amie
a girlfriend

amical MASC ADJECTIVE
(FEM **amicale**)
friendly

amicalement ADVERB
    Amicalement, Pierre.
    Best wishes, Pierre.

l' **amitié** FEM NOUN
friendship
    Amitiés, Christelle.
    Best wishes, Christelle.

l' **amour** MASC NOUN
love
    une histoire d'amour
    a love story

amoureux MASC ADJECTIVE
(FEM **amoureuse**)
in love
    Il est amoureux de Naïma.
    He's in love with Naïma.

l' **ampoule** FEM NOUN
1 light bulb
    Tu peux changer l'ampoule?
    Can you change the light bulb?
2 blister
    J'ai une ampoule au pied.
    I've got a blister on my foot.

amusant MASC ADJECTIVE
(FEM **amusante**)
amusing

s' **amuser** VERB
1 to play
    Les enfants s'amusent dehors.
    The children are playing outside.
2 to enjoy oneself
    Amuse-toi bien!
    Enjoy yourself!

l' **an** MASC NOUN
year
    Elle a douze ans.
    She's twelve years old.
    le premier de l'an
    New Year's Day

le nouvel an
New Year

J'ai dix ans.
I'm ten years old.

l' **ananas** MASC NOUN
pineapple

l' **ancêtre** MASC/FEM NOUN
ancestor

l' **anchois** MASC NOUN
anchovy

ancien MASC ADJECTIVE
(FEM **ancienne**)
1 former
C'est une ancienne élève.
She's a former pupil.
2 old
notre ancienne voiture
our old car
3 antique
un fauteuil ancien
an antique chair

l' **âne** MASC NOUN
donkey

l' **ange** MASC NOUN
angel

l' **angine** FEM NOUN
throat infection
J'ai une angine.
I've got a throat
infection.

anglais MASC NOUN, MASC
ADJECTIVE (FEM **anglaise**)
English
Je suis anglais.
I'm English.

l' **Anglais** MASC NOUN
Englishman
les Anglais
the English

l' **Anglaise** FEM NOUN
Englishwoman

l' **Angleterre** FEM NOUN
England
J'habite en Angleterre.
I live in England.

l' **animal** MASC NOUN
(PL les **animaux**)
animal

un animal
domestique
a pet
Tu as un animal domestique?
Have you got a pet?

l' **animateur** MASC NOUN
l' **animatrice** FEM NOUN
host
Il est animateur à la télé.
He's a TV host.

animé MASC ADJECTIVE
(FEM **animée**)
lively
Cette ville est très animée.
This is a very lively town.
un dessin animé
a cartoon
J'adore les dessins animés.
I love cartoons.

l' **année** FEM NOUN
year
Cette année, j'apprends le
français.
I'm learning French this year.

l'année dernière
last year
l'année prochaine
next year

Bonne année!
Happy New Year!

l' **anniversaire** MASC NOUN
  1 birthday
    Aujourd'hui, c'est mon anniversaire.
    It's my birthday today.

Quelle est la date de ton anniversaire?
When is your birthday?
Mon anniversaire, c'est le douze février.
My birthday is on the twelfth of February.
Joyeux anniversaire!
Happy birthday!

  2 anniversary
    leur anniversaire de mariage
    their wedding anniversary

l' **annonce** FEM NOUN
  advert
    J'ai vu une annonce dans le journal.
    I saw an advert in the newspaper.
    les petites annonces
    the small ads

annuler VERB
  to cancel

l' **anorak** MASC NOUN
  anorak

l' **antenne** FEM NOUN
  aerial

les **Antilles** FEM PL NOUN
  West Indies

l' **antiquité** FEM NOUN
  antique
    un magasin d'antiquités
    an antique shop

anxieux MASC ADJECTIVE
(FEM **anxieuse**)
  anxious

août MASC NOUN
  August
    en août
    in August
    le trois août
    the third of August

apercevoir VERB
  to see

l' **apéritif** MASC NOUN
    En été, on prend l'apéritif dans le jardin.
    In the summer we have drinks in the garden.

Did you know...?
*An **apéritif** is a drink that you have before dinner. You usually have a snack to go with it. Adults have something alcoholic and children have juice.*

l' **appareil** MASC NOUN
    un appareil dentaire
    a brace
    Je dois porter un appareil dentaire.
    I have to wear a brace.

un **appareil photo**
a camera
J'ai perdu mon appareil photo.
I've lost my camera.

l' **appartement** MASC NOUN
flat

appartenir VERB
Ça m'appartient.
This belongs to me.

l' **appel** MASC NOUN
1 **phone call**
un appel d'Italie
a phone call from Italy
2 **register**
faire l'appel
to call the register
Silence! Je fais l'appel.
Quiet! I'm calling the register.

appeler VERB
to call
Elle appelle le médecin.
She's calling the doctor.
■ **s'appeler**
to be called
Elle s'appelle Muriel.
Her name's Muriel.
Comment ça s'appelle?
What is it called?

Comment tu t'appelles?
What's your name?
Je m'appelle Alice.
My name's Alice.

l' **appendicite** FEM NOUN
appendicitis

l' **appétit** MASC NOUN

Bon appétit!
Enjoy your meal!

apporter VERB
to bring
Je vais apporter un gâteau.
I'm going to bring a cake.

apprendre VERB
to learn
J'apprends le français.
I'm learning French.
J'apprends à faire la cuisine.
I'm learning to cook.

appris VERB ▷see **apprendre**
Qu'est-ce que tu as appris aujourd'hui?
What have you learned today?

s' **approcher** VERB
to come closer
Approchez-vous.
Come closer.

appuyer VERB
to press
Il faut appuyer sur ce bouton.
You have to press this button.

après PREPOSITION, ADVERB
1 **after**
après le déjeuner
after lunch
2 **afterwards**
aussitôt après
immediately afterwards

après-demain ADVERB
the day after tomorrow

l' **après-midi** MASC/FEM NOUN
afternoon
L'après-midi, je vais à la piscine.
In the afternoon, I go to the swimming pool.

French English

a
b
c
d
e
f
g
h
i
j
k
l
m
n
o
p
q
r
s
t
u
v
w
x
y
z

cet après-midi
this afternoon

arabe

arabe *can be an adjective or a noun.*

A ADJECTIVE
Arab
les pays arabes
the Arab countries

B MASC NOUN
Arabic
Il parle arabe.
He speaks Arabic.

l' **araignée** FEM NOUN
spider

Il y a une araignée dans la baignoire!
There's a spider in the bath!

l' **arbitre** MASC NOUN
referee

l' **arbre** MASC NOUN
tree
un arbre généalogique
a family tree

l' **arc** MASC NOUN
bow
un arc et des flèches
a bow and arrows

l' **arc-en-ciel** MASC NOUN
rainbow

l' **argent** MASC NOUN
1 money
Je n'ai pas d'argent.
I haven't got any money.
l'argent de poche
pocket money
2 silver
une médaille d'argent
a silver medal

l' **arme** FEM NOUN
weapon

l' **armée** FEM NOUN
army

l' **armoire** FEM NOUN
wardrobe

l' **arobase** FEM NOUN
at symbol
mon adresse e-mail, c'est 'lola arobase europost point fr'
my email address is 'lola@europost.fr'

arranger VERB
1 to arrange
Elle arrange des fleurs dans un vase.
She's arranging flowers in a vase.
2 to suit
Ça m'arrange de partir plus tôt.
It suits me to leave earlier.

l' **arrêt** MASC NOUN
stop
un arrêt de bus
a bus stop

arrêter VERB
1 **to stop**
Tu peux arrêter la cassette?
Can you stop the tape?
Arrête!
Stop it!
Arrête de copier!
Stop copying!
2 **to switch off**
Il a arrêté le moteur.
He switched the engine off.

arrière

> **arrière** *can be a noun or an adjective.*

A MASC NOUN
back
l'arrière de la maison
the back of the house
B MASC, FEM, PL ADJECTIVE
back
le siège arrière
the back seat
les roues arrière
the rear wheels

l' **arrière-grand-mère**
FEM NOUN
great-grandmother

l' **arrière-grand-père**
MASC NOUN
great-grandfather

l' **arrivée** FEM NOUN
arrival

arriver VERB
1 **to arrive**
J'arrive à l'école à huit heures.
I arrive at school at 8 o'clock.
2 **to come**
J'arrive!
I'm coming!
3 **to happen**

Qu'est-ce qui est arrivé à Christian?
What happened to Christian?

l' **arrondissement** MASC NOUN
district

> **Did you know…?**
> *Paris, Lyons, and Marseilles are divided into numbered districts called* **arrondissements***.*

arroser VERB
to water
Daphne arrose ses tomates.
Daphne is watering her tomatoes.

l' **arrosoir** MASC NOUN
watering can

l' **artichaut** MASC NOUN
artichoke

l' **article** MASC NOUN
article
un article de journal
a newspaper article

l' **artiste** MASC/FEM NOUN
artist
Paul est un véritable artiste.
Paul is a real artist.

les **arts plastiques** MASC PL NOUN
art

as

> **as** *can be part of the verb* **avoir** *or a noun.*

A VERB ▷*see* **avoir**
Tu as de beaux cheveux.
You've got nice hair.

> **Language tip**
> *Sometimes* **as** *is used to show that something has happened in the past.*

Tu as aimé le film?
Did you like the film?

B MASC NOUN
ace
l'as de cœur
the ace of hearts

l' **ascenseur** MASC NOUN
lift

Il n'y a pas d'ascenseur dans mon immeuble.
There's no lift in my building.

asiatique ADJECTIVE
Asian
la cuisine asiatique
Oriental cooking

l' **Asie** FEM NOUN
Asia

l' **asperge** FEM NOUN
asparagus

l' **aspirateur** MASC NOUN
vacuum cleaner
passer l'aspirateur
to vacuum
Je déteste passer l'aspirateur!
I hate vacuuming!

l' **aspirine** FEM NOUN
aspirin
Prenez de l'aspirine.
Take some aspirin.

l' **assassin** MASC NOUN
murderer

assassiner VERB
to murder

s' **asseoir** VERB
to sit down
Je peux m'asseoir ici?
Can I sit here?

Asseyez-vous, tout le monde!
Sit down everybody!
Assieds-toi, Nicole!
Sit down Nicole!

assez ADVERB
1 enough
Nous n'avons pas assez de temps.
We don't have enough time.
Est-ce qu'il y a assez de pain?
Is there enough bread?
J'en ai assez!
I've had enough!
2 quite
Il faisait assez beau.
The weather was quite nice.

l' **assiette** FEM NOUN
plate

une assiette creuse
a soup plate
une assiette à dessert
a dessert plate

assis MASC ADJECTIVE (FEM **assise**)
sitting
Il est assis par terre.
He's sitting on the floor.

French English
a b c d e f g h i j k l m n o p q r s t u v w x y z

l' **assistant** MASC NOUN
l' **assistante** FEM NOUN
assistant
> **Il est assistant d'anglais à Tourcoing.**
> He is an English assistant in Tourcoing.
> **Elle est assistante de français à Oxford.**
> She's a French assistant in Oxford.
> **une assistante sociale**
> a social worker

l' **asthme** MASC NOUN
asthma
> **une crise d'asthme**
> an asthma attack

l' **atelier** MASC NOUN
1 workshop
> **un atelier de poterie**
> a pottery workshop
2 studio
> **L'artiste est dans son atelier.**
> The artist is in his studio.

l' **athlète** MASC/FEM NOUN
athlete

l' **athlétisme** MASC NOUN
athletics
> **Je fais de l'athlétisme.**
> I do athletics.

l' **Atlantique** MASC NOUN
Atlantic

l' **atlas** MASC NOUN
atlas

attacher VERB
to tie up
> **Elle attache ses cheveux avec un élastique.**
> She ties her hair up with an elastic band.

attaquer VERB
to attack

attendre VERB
to wait
> **J'attends ma copine.**
> I'm waiting for my friend.
> **Attends-moi!**
> Wait for me!

> *Language tip*
> *Be careful! The French word* **attendre** *does not mean the same as the English word* **to attend**.

l' **attente** FEM NOUN
wait
> **deux heures d'attente**
> two hours' wait
> **la salle d'attente**
> the waiting room

l' **attention** FEM NOUN
> **Attention!**
> Watch out!
> **faire attention**
> to be careful
> **Il ne fait pas attention.**
> He's not careful.

atterrir VERB
to land

l' **attraction** FEM NOUN
> **un parc d'attractions**
> an amusement park

attraper VERB
to catch

French
English

a
b
c
d
e
f
g
h
i
j
k
l
m
n
o
p
q
r
s
t
u
v
w
x
y
z

15

a b c d e f g h i j k l m n o p q r s t u v w x y z

au PREPOSITION ▷ see **à**

> **Language tip**
> **au** is made up of **à** + **le**.

Je vais au cinéma.
I am going to the cinema.
au printemps
in the spring

l' **aube** FEM NOUN
dawn
Il se lève à l'aube.
He gets up at dawn.

l' **auberge de jeunesse**
FEM NOUN
youth hostel

aucun

> **aucun** can be an adjective or a
> pronoun.

A MASC ADJECTIVE (FEM **aucune**)
no
Il n'a aucun ami.
He's got no friends.
B MASC PRONOUN (FEM **aucune**)
none
**Aucune d'elles n'aime le
football.**
None of them like football.

au-dessous ADVERB
downstairs
Ils habitent au-dessous.
They live downstairs.
au-dessous de
under

au-dessous du pont
under the bridge

au-dessus ADVERB
upstairs

J'habite au-dessus.
I live upstairs.
au-dessus de
above
au-dessus de la table
above the table

aujourd'hui ADVERB
today
**Aujourd'hui, c'est le onze
juillet.**
Today is the eleventh of July.

**aura, aurai, auras,
aurez, aurons, auront**
VERB ▷ see **avoir**
Demain, il y aura du soleil.
It will be sunny tomorrow.
**J'aurai mon nouveau vélo
mardi.**
I'm getting my new bike on
Tuesday.
Tu auras quel âge en juillet?
How old will you be next July?
Vous n'aurez pas le temps.
You won't have time.
**Nous aurons une semaine
de vacances.**
We'll have one week off.
**Ils n'auront pas le temps de
venir nous voir.**
They won't have time to visit us.

aussi ADVERB

1 too

Dors bien. — Toi aussi.
Sleep well. — You too.

Moi aussi!
Me too!

2 also

Je parle anglais et aussi français.
I speak English and also French.
aussi ... que
as ... as
Michael est aussi grand que moi.
Michael is as tall as me.

aussitôt ADVERB

aussitôt après son retour
straight after his return
aussitôt que
as soon as
aussitôt que possible
as soon as possible

l' **Australie** FEM NOUN
Australia

australien MASC ADJECTIVE
(FEM **australienne**)
Australian

autant ADVERB

Language tip

autant de *can either mean* **so much** *or* **so many.**

Je ne veux pas autant de gâteau.
I don't want so much cake.
Je n'ai jamais vu autant de monde.
I've never seen so many people.

Language tip

autant ... que *can either mean* **as much ... as** *or* **as many ... as.**

J'ai autant d'argent que toi.
I've got as much money as you have.
J'ai autant d'amis que lui.
I've got as many friends as he has.

l' **auteur** MASC NOUN
author

l' **auto** FEM NOUN
car

l' **autobus** MASC NOUN
bus

Je vais à l'école en autobus.
I go to school by bus.

l' **autocar** MASC NOUN
coach

l' **autocollant** MASC NOUN
sticker

l' **auto-école** FEM NOUN
driving school

l' **automne** MASC NOUN
autumn

en automne
in autumn

automobile

automobile *can be a noun or an adjective.*

A FEM NOUN
car
une vieille automobile
an old car

B ADJECTIVE
une course automobile
a motor race

l' **automobiliste** MASC/FEM NOUN
  motorist

l' **autoradio** MASC NOUN
  car radio

l' **autoroute** FEM NOUN
  motorway

l' **auto-stop** MASC NOUN
    C'est dangereux de faire de l'auto-stop.
    Hitchhiking is dangerous.

autour ADVERB
  around
    autour de la maison
    around the house

autre ADJECTIVE, PRONOUN
  other
    Je viendrai un autre jour.
    I'll come some other day.
    J'ai d'autres projets.
    I've got other plans.
    autre chose
    something else
    Tu veux autre chose?
    Would you like something else?
    autre part
    somewhere else
    Je voudrais aller autre part.
    I'd like to go somewhere else.
    un autre
    another
    Tu veux un autre morceau de gâteau?
    Would you like another piece of cake?

  l'autre
  the other
    Non, pas celui-ci, l'autre.
    No, not that one, the other one.
    d'autres
    others
    Je t'en apporterai d'autres.
    I'll bring you some others.
    les autres
    the others
    Les autres sont arrivés plus tard.
    The others arrived later.
    ni l'un ni l'autre
    neither of them
    Je n'aime ni l'un ni l'autre.
    I like neither of them.

autrefois ADVERB
  in the old days

autrement ADVERB
  1 differently
    Fais-le autrement.
    Do it differently.
  2 otherwise
    Je n'ai pas pu faire autrement.
    I couldn't do otherwise.

l' **Autriche** FEM NOUN
  Austria

autrichien MASC ADJECTIVE
  (FEM **autrichienne**)
  Austrian

l' **Autrichien** MASC NOUN
l' **Autrichienne** FEM NOUN
  Austrian

l' **autruche** FEM NOUN
  ostrich

aux PREPOSITION ▷ see **à**

Il va aux États-Unis.
He's going to the United States.

avaler VERB
to swallow

l' **avance** FEM NOUN
être en avance
to be early
Je suis en avance.
I am early.
à l'avance
beforehand
Il faut réserver longtemps à l'avance.
You need to book well beforehand.
d'avance
in advance
Elle a payé d'avance.
She paid in advance.

avancer VERB
to go forward
Avance de trois cases.
Go forward three squares.

avant

avant *can be a preposition, an adjective or a noun.*

A PREPOSITION
before
avant de partir
before leaving

B MASC, FEM, PL ADJECTIVE
front
la roue avant
the front wheel
le siège avant
the front seat
C MASC NOUN
front
l'avant de la voiture
the front of the car
à l'avant
in front
J'aime m'asseoir à l'avant.
I like to sit in the front.
en avant
forward
Fais un pas en avant.
Take a step forward.

l' **avantage** MASC NOUN
advantage

avant-dernier MASC ADJECTIVE
(FEM **avant-dernière**)
last but one
l'avant-dernière page
the last page but one
Ils sont arrivés avant-derniers.
They arrived last but one.

avant-hier ADVERB
the day before yesterday

avec PREPOSITION
with
Je joue avec mes copains.
I am playing with my friends.

Et avec ça?
Anything else?

l' **avenir** MASC NOUN
future
> à l'avenir
> in future

l' **aventure** FEM NOUN
adventure

l' **avenue** FEM NOUN
avenue
> **J'habite au 3, avenue Pasteur.**
> I live at 3 Pasteur Avenue.

l' **averse** FEM NOUN
shower
> **Il y a des averses sur toute la France.**
> There are showers all over France.

aveugle ADJECTIVE
blind

avez VERB ▷see avoir
> **Vous avez des frères et sœurs?**
> Have you got any brothers or sisters?

Language tip

Sometimes **avez** *is used to show that something has happened in the past.*

> **Vous avez aimé le film?**
> Did you like the film?

l' **avion** MASC NOUN
plane

> **Tu préfères y aller en avion ou en train?**
> Would you rather go by plane or by train?

Il va en Italie en avion.
He is flying to Italy.
par avion
by airmail

l' **avis** MASC NOUN
opinion
> **à mon avis**
> in my opinion
> **J'ai changé d'avis.**
> I've changed my mind.

l' **avocat** MASC NOUN
1 lawyer
> **Il est avocat.**
> He's a lawyer.
2 avocado
> **Tu aimes les avocats?**
> Do you like avocados?

l' **avocate** FEM NOUN
lawyer
> **Elle est avocate.**
> She's a lawyer.

l' **avoine** FEM NOUN
oats
> **les flocons d'avoine**
> porridge oats

avoir VERB
1 to have
> **Ils ont deux enfants.**
> They have two children.
> **Il a les yeux bleus.**
> He's got blue eyes.

Language tip

avoir *is used to make the past tense of most verbs.*

> **Qu'est-ce que tu as fait hier?**
> What did you do yesterday?
2 to be
> **Il a trois ans.**
> He's three.
> **J'ai faim.**
> I'm hungry.

French English

a
b
c
d
e
f
g
h
i
j
k
l
m
n
o
p
q
r
s
t
u
v
w
x
y
z

3 to get
J'ai des devoirs de maths deux fois par semaine.
I get maths homework twice a week.
Qu'est-ce que tu as eu pour Noël?
What did you get for Christmas?
il y a
there is/there are

Language tip
il y a *has two translations. Look at the examples.*

Il y a quelqu'un à la porte.
There's somebody at the door.
Il y a des chocolats sur la table.
There are some chocolates on the table.

Language tip
il y a *can also mean* **ago**.

Je l'ai rencontré il y a deux ans.
I met him two years ago.

Qu'est-ce qu'il y a?
What's the matter?

avons VERB ▷*see* **avoir**
Nous avons une grande maison.
We have a big house.

Language tip
Sometimes **avons** *is used to show that something has happened in the past.*

Nous avons regardé la télévision.
We watched television.

avouer VERB
to admit

avril MASC NOUN
April
en avril
in April
le deux avril
the second of April

French English

a
b
c
d
e
f
g
h
i
j
k
l
m
n
o
p
q
r
s
t
u
v
w
x
y
z

B b

le **babillard** MASC NOUN (*Canada*)
bulletin board

le **baby-foot** MASC NOUN
table football

le **baby-sitting** MASC NOUN
**Ma sœur fait du baby-sitting
le week-end.**
My sister babysits at the weekend.

le **bac** MASC NOUN
= baccalauréat

le **baccalauréat** MASC NOUN
A levels
**Ma sœur passe son
baccalauréat cette année.**
My sister is doing her A levels
this year.

> **Did you know...?**
> The **baccalauréat** or **bac** *is an
> exam taken at the end of* **lycée**,
> *when French students are 17 and
> 18 years old.*

les **bagages** MASC PL NOUN
luggage
**Les bagages sont dans la
voiture.**
The luggage is in the car.
Je déteste faire les bagages!
I hate packing!

la **bague** FEM NOUN
ring
J'ai une belle bague.
I have a beautiful ring.

la **baguette** FEM NOUN
stick of French bread

se **baigner** VERB
to swim

J'aime me baigner.
I like swimming.

la **baignoire** FEM NOUN
bath
**Il y a une araignée dans
la baignoire!**
There's a spider in the bath!

le **bain** MASC NOUN
bath
Je prends un bain.
I'm having a bath.

le **baiser** MASC NOUN
kiss
donner un baiser
to give a kiss
Donne-moi un baiser!
Give me a kiss!

la **balade** FEM NOUN
walk
Tu veux faire une balade?
Do you want to go for a walk?

le **baladeur** MASC NOUN
Walkman®
un baladeur numérique
an MP3 player

le **balai** MASC NOUN
broom

la **balançoire** FEM NOUN
swing

le **balcon** MASC NOUN
balcony

la **baleine** FEM NOUN
whale

la **balle** FEM NOUN
ball
> Le chien joue avec une
> balle.
> The dog is playing with a ball.
> **une balle de ping-pong**
> a ping-pong ball
> **une balle de tennis**
> a tennis ball

le **ballon** MASC NOUN
1 ball
> **un ballon de football**
> a football
2 balloon
> **Je veux
> un ballon!**
> I want a
> balloon!

la **banane** FEM NOUN
banana

le **banc** MASC NOUN
bench

la **bande dessinée**
FEM NOUN
comic strip
> **J'adore les bandes
> dessinées!**
> I love comic strips!

Did you know…?

Les bandes dessinées or **comic
strips** are very popular with people
of all ages in France.

la **banlieue** FEM NOUN
suburbs
> **J'habite en banlieue.**
> I live in the suburbs.

la **banque** FEM NOUN
bank

le **banquier** MASC NOUN
la **banquière** FEM NOUN
banker

le **baptême** MASC NOUN
christening

le **bar** MASC NOUN
bar

barbant MASC ADJECTIVE
(FEM **barbante**)
boring
> **Il est vraiment barbant!**
> He's so boring!

la **barbe** FEM NOUN
beard
> **Il porte la barbe.**
> He's got a beard.
> **la barbe à papa**
> candyfloss

le **barbecue** MASC NOUN
barbecue

la **barque** FEM NOUN
rowing boat

la **barrière** FEM NOUN
fence

le **bar-tabac** MASC NOUN

Did you know…?

A **bar-tabac** is a café which also
sells cigarettes and stamps. It has a
red diamond-shaped sign outside it.

le **bas** MASC NOUN
bottom

French | English

a
b
c
d
e
f
g
h
i
j
k
l
m
n
o
p
q
r
s
t
u
v
w
x
y
z

le bas de la page
the bottom of the page
en bas
downstairs
La salle de bains est en bas.
The bathroom is downstairs.

le **basilic** MASC NOUN
basil

le **basket** MASC NOUN
basketball
Je joue au basket.
I play basketball.

les **baskets** FEM PL NOUN
trainers

une paire de baskets
a pair of trainers

le **bassin** MASC NOUN
pond

le **bateau** MASC NOUN
(PL les **bateaux**)
boat
Je vais en France en bateau.
I'm going to France by boat.

le **bateau-mouche**
MASC NOUN
pleasure boat

le **bâtiment** MASC NOUN
building

la **batterie** FEM NOUN
drums
Je joue de la batterie.
I play the drums.

battre VERB
to beat

bavard MASC ADJECTIVE
(FEM **bavarde**)
talkative

bavarder VERB
to chat

le **bazar** MASC NOUN
mess

Quel bazar!
What a mess!
Va ranger ton bazar!
Go and tidy up your mess!

la **BD** FEM NOUN
comic strip
Rose adore les BD.
Rose loves comic strips.

beau MASC ADJECTIVE (MASC **bel**,
FEM **belle**)

Language tip
beau *changes to* **bel** *before a vowel
sound.*

1 **lovely**
un beau cadeau
a lovely present
une belle journée
a lovely day
2 **beautiful**
une belle femme
a beautiful woman
3 **good-looking**
un beau garçon
a good-looking boy
4 **handsome**
un bel homme
a handsome man

Il fait beau aujourd'hui.
It's a nice day today.

beaucoup ADVERB
1 **a lot**
  Il mange beaucoup.
  He eats a lot.
  beaucoup de
  a lot of
  J'ai beaucoup de devoirs.
  I have a lot of homework.
  J'ai beaucoup de chance.
  I am very lucky.
2 **much**
  Je n'ai pas beaucoup d'argent.
  I haven't got much money.

le **beau-fils** MASC NOUN
1 **son-in-law**
2 **stepson**

le **beau-frère** MASC NOUN
  brother-in-law

le **beau-père** MASC NOUN
1 **father-in-law**
2 **stepfather**

le **bébé** MASC NOUN
  baby

beige ADJECTIVE, MASC NOUN
  beige

le **beignet** MASC NOUN
  fritter
  des beignets aux pommes
  apple fritters

bel MASC ADJECTIVE ▷ *see* **beau**
  un bel été
  a beautiful summer

belge ADJECTIVE
  Belgian

le/la **Belge** MASC/FEM NOUN
  Belgian

la **Belgique** FEM NOUN
  Belgium

belle FEM ADJECTIVE ▷ *see* **beau**
  une belle statue
  a beautiful statue

la **belle-fille** FEM NOUN
1 **daughter-in-law**
2 **stepdaughter**

la **belle-mère** FEM NOUN
1 **mother-in-law**
2 **stepmother**

la **belle-sœur** FEM NOUN
  sister-in-law

le **berceau** MASC NOUN
  (PL les **berceaux**)
  cradle

le **berger** MASC NOUN
  shepherd

le **besoin** MASC NOUN
  Je vais avoir besoin d'aide.
  I will need some help.
  J'ai besoin d'un stylo.
  I need a pen.

bête ADJECTIVE
  stupid

les **bêtises** FEM PL NOUN
  faire des bêtises
  to misbehave
  Ma sœur fait toujours des bêtises.
  My sister is always misbehaving.
  dire des bêtises
  to talk nonsense
  Tu dis des bêtises!
  You're talking nonsense!

la **betterave** FEM NOUN
beetroot

le **beurre** MASC NOUN
butter

le **biberon** MASC NOUN
bottle
>**Ma maman donne le biberon
à ma sœur.**
>My mum is giving my baby sister
>her bottle.

la **bibliothèque** FEM NOUN
1 library
2 bookcase

le **bic**® MASC NOUN
Biro®
>**J'ai deux bics dans ma
trousse.**
>I've got two Biros in my pencil
>case.

la **biche** FEM NOUN
doe

la **bicyclette** FEM NOUN
bicycle

>**J'ai une nouvelle bicyclette.**
>I've got a new bicycle.

bien ADJECTIVE, ADVERB
1 well
>**Daphné travaille bien.**
>Daphné works well.
2 good
>**Ce livre est vraiment bien.**
>This book is really good.

J'aime bien les maths.
I like maths.
**Comment ça va? — Ça va bien,
merci.**
How are you? — Fine, thanks.

bien sûr ADVERB
of course
>**Tu aimes les frites? —
Oui, bien sûr!**
>Do you like chips? —
>Yes, of course!

bientôt ADVERB
soon

À bientôt!
See you soon!

la **bienvenue** FEM NOUN
welcome
>**Bienvenue à Paris!**
>Welcome to Paris!

la **bière** FEM NOUN
beer

le **bijou** MASC NOUN
jewel

le **billard** MASC NOUN
billiards

le **bifteck** MASC NOUN
steak

la **bille** FEM NOUN
marble
>**J'aime jouer aux billes.**
>I like playing with marbles.

le **billet** MASC NOUN
1 ticket
>**un billet d'avion**
>a plane ticket
2 banknote
>**un billet de 10€**
>a €10 note

bio ADJECTIVE
organic
> **Ma maman achète des produits bio.**
> My mum buys organic produce.

la **biologie** FEM NOUN
biology

la **biscotte** FEM NOUN
toasted bread

le **biscuit** MASC NOUN
biscuit

la **bise** FEM NOUN
kiss
> **Grosses bises de Bretagne.**
> Love and kisses from Brittany.
> **Viens me faire la bise.**
> Come and give me a kiss.
> **Je fais la bise à mes copines tous les matins.**
> Every morning I give my friends a kiss.

Did you know...?

Between girls and boys, and between girls, the normal French way of saying hello and goodbye is with kisses, usually one on each cheek. Boys shake hands with each other instead.

le **bisou**
MASC NOUN
kiss
> **Viens faire un bisou à maman!**
> Come and give Mummy a little kiss!

bizarre ADJECTIVE
strange

la **blague** FEM NOUN
joke

blanc

> **blanc** *can be an adjective or a noun.*

A MASC ADJECTIVE (FEM **blanche**)
white
> **un chemisier blanc**
> a white blouse
> **une chemise blanche**
> a white shirt

B MASC NOUN
white
> **Vous avez ce T-shirt en blanc?**
> Do you have this T-shirt in white?

blanche FEM ADJECTIVE
▷ *see* **blanc**
> **de la peinture blanche**
> white paint

le **blé** MASC NOUN
wheat

blessé MASC ADJECTIVE
(FEM **blessée**)
injured

la **blessure** FEM NOUN
injury

bleu

> **bleu** *can be an adjective or a noun.*

A MASC ADJECTIVE (FEM **bleue**)
blue
> **une veste bleue**
> a blue jacket
> **Mon uniforme est bleu et blanc.**
> My uniform is blue and white.

B MASC NOUN
blue
> **La couleur préférée de ma sœur, c'est le bleu.**
> Blue is my sister's favourite colour.

le **bleuet** MASC NOUN (*Canada*)
blueberry

> **Did you know…?**
> *The Saguenay-Lac-St-Jean region of Quebec is famous for its blueberries. The people who live there are also known as* **les Bleuets**.

blond MASC ADJECTIVE
(FEM **blonde**)
blond
> **Andrew a les cheveux blonds.**
> Andrew has blond hair.

le **blouson** MASC NOUN
jacket
> **un blouson en cuir**
> a leather jacket

le **bocal** MASC NOUN
(PL les **bocaux**)
jar

le **bœuf** MASC NOUN
beef
> **un rôti de bœuf**
> a joint of beef

bof EXCLAMATION
> **Comment ça va? —**
> **Bof! Pas terrible.**
> How is it going? —
> Oh … not too well actually.

boire VERB
to drink
> **Je bois du jus d'orange au petit déjeuner.**
> I drink orange juice with my breakfast.

le **bois** MASC NOUN
wood
> **en bois**
> wooden

une table en bois
a wooden table

la **boisson** FEM NOUN
drink
> **une boisson chaude**
> a hot drink

la **boîte** FEM NOUN
box
> **une boîte d'allumettes**
> a box of matches
> **une boîte aux lettres**
> a letter box
> **une boîte de conserve**
> a tin
> **une boîte de nuit**
> a night club

le **bol** MASC NOUN
bowl
> **un bol de céréales**
> a bowl of cereal

bon MASC ADJECTIVE (FEM **bonne**)
1 good
> **un bon restaurant**
> a good restaurant
> **Je suis bon en maths.**
> I'm good at maths.

> **Bonne journée!**
> Have a nice day!
> **Bonne nuit!**
> Good night!
> **Bon anniversaire!**
> Happy birthday!

Bon courage!
Good luck!
Bon voyage!
Have a good trip!
Bon week-end!
Have a nice weekend!
Bonne chance!
Good luck!
Bonne année!
Happy New Year!

2 right
C'est la bonne réponse.
That's the right answer.
Ah bon?
Really?
Bon, d'accord.
OK then.

le **bonbon** MASC NOUN
sweet

Ma sœur aime les bonbons.
My sister likes sweets.

le **bonhomme de neige**
MASC NOUN
snowman

bonjour EXCLAMATION
1 hello!
Bonjour madame!
Hello Miss!
2 Good morning!
Bonjour, tout le monde!
Good morning everyone!
3 Good afternoon!

Language tip
bonjour *is used in the morning and*
in the afternoon; in the evening
bonsoir *is used instead.*

bonne FEM ADJECTIVE ▷*see* **bon**
Elle est bonne en français.
She's good at French.

le **bonnet** MASC NOUN
hat
un bonnet de laine
a woolly hat

bonsoir EXCLAMATION
good evening!

le **bord** MASC NOUN
j'habite au bord de la mer.
I live at the seaside.
**Cet été, je vais au bord
de la mer.**
This summer, I'm going to
the seaside.

bordeaux

bordeaux can be a noun or an
adjective.

A MASC NOUN
Bordeaux wine
B MASC, FEM, PL ADJECTIVE
maroon
une jupe bordeaux
a maroon skirt

la **bosse** FEM NOUN
bump

le **bossu** MASC NOUN
la **bossue** FEM NOUN
hunchback

la **botte** FEM NOUN
boot
une paire de bottes
a pair of boots
des bottes en caoutchouc
wellington boots

French English

a
b
c
d
e
f
g
h
i
j
k
l
m
n
o
p
q
r
s
t
u
v
w
x
y
z

29

la **bouche** FEM NOUN
mouth

le **boucher** MASC NOUN
la **bouchère** FEM NOUN
butcher

la **boucherie** FEM NOUN
butcher's
Où est la boucherie?
Where is the butcher's?

le **bouchon** MASC NOUN
1 top
un bouchon en plastique
a plastic top
2 cork
un bouchon de champagne
a champagne cork
3 hold-up
Il y a beaucoup de bouchons sur l'autoroute.
There are a lot of hold-ups on the motorway.

la **boucle d'oreille** FEM NOUN
earring
des boucles d'oreille en or
gold earrings

bouclé MASC ADJECTIVE
(FEM **bouclée**)
curly
J'ai les cheveux bouclés.
I've got curly hair.

bouder VERB
to sulk

le **boudin** MASC NOUN
le boudin noir
black pudding
le boudin blanc
white pudding

la **boue** FEM NOUN
mud

la **bouée** FEM NOUN
buoy
une bouée de sauvetage
a life buoy

bouger VERB
to move

la **bougie** FEM NOUN
candle

la **bouillabaisse** FEM NOUN
fish soup

bouillant MASC ADJECTIVE
(FEM **bouillante**)
boiling
de l'eau bouillante
boiling water

bouillir VERB
to boil

la **bouilloire** FEM NOUN
kettle

la **bouillotte** FEM NOUN
hot-water bottle

le **boulanger** MASC NOUN
la **boulangère** FEM NOUN
baker

la **boulangerie** FEM NOUN
baker's
Je vais à la boulangerie.
I'm going to the baker's.

la **boule** FEM NOUN
ball
> **une boule de neige**
> a snowball
> **jouer aux boules**
> to play bowls
> **Mon grand-père aime jouer aux boules.**
> My grandad likes playing bowls.

Did you know...?

boules *is played on rough ground, not smooth grass. The balls are slightly smaller than tennis balls, and are made of metal.*

le **boulevard** MASC NOUN
boulevard

la **boum** FEM NOUN
party
> **Je vais à une boum ce week-end.**
> I'm going to a party this weekend.

le **bouquet** MASC NOUN
bunch of flowers
> **un bouquet de roses**
> a bunch of roses

la **Bourgogne** FEM NOUN
Burgundy

la **boussole** FEM NOUN
compass

le **bout** MASC NOUN
1 **end**
> **Elle habite au bout de la rue.**
> She lives at the end of the street.
2 **tip**
> **le bout du nez**
> the tip of the nose

la **bouteille** FEM NOUN
bottle

> **une bouteille de limonade**
> a bottle of lemonade

la **boutique** FEM NOUN
shop

le **bouton** MASC NOUN
1 **button**
> **Appuie sur le bouton.**
> Press the button.
2 **spot**
> **Elle a des boutons.**
> She's got spots.

le **bowling** MASC NOUN
1 **tenpin bowling**
> **J'aime aller au bowling.**
> I like going bowling.
2 **bowling alley**
> **Il y a un bowling près de chez moi.**
> There's a bowling alley near my house.

le **bracelet** MASC NOUN
bracelet

la **branche** FEM NOUN
branch

branché MASC ADJECTIVE
(FEM **branchée**)
trendy

le **bras** MASC NOUN
arm
> **J'ai mal au bras.**
> My arm hurts.

la **brasserie** FEM NOUN
café-restaurant

bravo EXCLAMATION
well done!

le **Brésil** MASC NOUN
Brazil

la **Bretagne** FEM NOUN
Brittany

les **bretelles** FEM PL NOUN
braces
> Il porte des bretelles.
> He's wearing braces.

breton MASC ADJECTIVE
(FEM **bretonne**)
Breton

le **brevet des collèges**
MASC NOUN
> Mon frère passe son brevet
> des collèges.
> My brother is taking his GCSEs.

Did you know…?
The **brevet des collèges** *is an
exam you take at the end of*
collège, *at the age of 15.*

le **bricolage** MASC NOUN
DIY
> Elle aime le bricolage.
> She likes doing DIY.

bricoler VERB
to do DIY
> Pascal aime bricoler.
> Pascal loves doing DIY.

brillant MASC ADJECTIVE
(FEM **brillante**)
1 brilliant
> une idée brillante
> a brilliant idea
2 shiny

> des cheveux brillants
> shiny hair

briller VERB
to shine

la **brioche** FEM NOUN
brioche
> Je mange une brioche au
> petit déjeuner.
> I have a brioche for breakfast.

Did you know…?
brioche *is a kind of sweet bread.*

la **brique** FEM NOUN
brick

le **briquet** MASC NOUN
cigarette lighter

britannique ADJECTIVE
British
> Je suis britannique.
> I am British.

la **brochette** FEM NOUN
skewer

la **brochure** FEM NOUN
brochure

la **bronchite** FEM NOUN
bronchitis

le **bronze** MASC NOUN
bronze
> la médaille de bronze
> the bronze medal

bronzer VERB
to get a tan

French English

a
b
c
d
e
f
g
h
i
j
k
l
m
n
o
p
q
r
s
t
u
v
w
x
y
z

la **brosse** FEM NOUN
brush
 une brosse à cheveux
 a hairbrush
 une brosse à dents
 a toothbrush

brosser VERB
to brush
 se brosser les dents
 to brush one's teeth
 Je me brosse les dents tous les soirs.
 I brush my teeth every night.

le **brouillard** MASC NOUN
fog

 Demain il y aura du brouillard.
 It will be foggy tomorrow.

 Il y a du brouillard.
 It's foggy.

la **brouette** FEM NOUN
wheelbarrow

le **bruit** MASC NOUN
noise
 Il y a trop de bruit!
 There's too much noise!
 faire du bruit
 to make a noise
 Cette voiture fait beaucoup de bruit.
 This car makes a lot of noise.
 sans bruit
 without a sound

brûlant MASC ADJECTIVE
(FEM **brûlante**)
1 blazing
 un soleil brûlant
 a blazing sun
2 boiling
 La soupe est brûlante.
 The soup is boiling.

brûler VERB
to burn
 Ne te brûle pas!
 Don't burn yourself!

la **brûlure** FEM NOUN
burn
 des brûlures d'estomac
 heartburn

la **brume** FEM NOUN
mist

brun MASC ADJECTIVE (FEM **brune**)
brown
 J'ai les cheveux bruns.
 I've got brown hair.

Bruxelles NOUN
Brussels

bruyant MASC ADJECTIVE
(FEM **bruyante**)
noisy

la **bruyère** FEM NOUN
heather

bu VERB ▷see **boire**
 J'ai bu du jus d'orange.
 I drank some orange juice.

la **bûche** FEM NOUN
 la bûche de Noël
 the Yule log
 Le vingt-cinq décembre, on mange de la bûche de Noël.
 On the twenty-fifth of December we eat Yule log.

Did you know…?
la bûche de Noël *is what is usually eaten in France as a Christmas pudding.*

le **buffet** MASC NOUN
1 **sideboard**
un buffet en chêne
an oak sideboard
2 **buffet**
un buffet de gare
a station buffet

le **buisson** MASC NOUN
bush

la **bulle** FEM NOUN
bubble

le **bulletin** MASC NOUN
report
un bulletin scolaire
a school report

le **bureau** MASC NOUN
(PL les **bureaux**)
1 **desk**
Il y a un bureau dans ma chambre.
There's a desk in my room.

2 **office**
Ma mère travaille dans un bureau.
My mum works in an office.
un bureau de change
a bureau de change
le bureau de poste
the post office
le bureau de tabac
the tobacconist's

le **bus** MASC NOUN
bus
en bus
by bus
Je vais à l'école en bus.
I go to school by bus.

le **but** MASC NOUN
goal
marquer un but
to score a goal
J'ai marqué un but.
I scored a goal.

C c

c' PRONOUN ▷ *see* **ce**
C'est lui!
That's him!

ça PRONOUN
1 this
Je voudrais un peu de ça.
I'd like a bit of this.
2 that
Ne fais pas ça.
Don't do that.
3 it
Ça ne fait rien.
It doesn't matter.

Ça va? — Oui, ça va, merci.
How are you? — I'm fine thanks.
Ça alors!
Well, well!
C'est ça.
That's right.
Ça y est!
That's it!

la **cabane** FEM NOUN
hut
une cabane à sucre (*Canada*)
a sugar shack

la **cabine** FEM NOUN
cabin
une cabine d'essayage
a fitting room
une cabine téléphonique
a phone box

le **cabinet** MASC NOUN
surgery

la **cacahuète** FEM NOUN
peanut

le **cacao** MASC NOUN
cocoa

cache-cache MASC NOUN
hide-and-seek
Tu veux jouer à cache-cache?
Do you want to play hide-and-seek?

le **cache-nez** MASC NOUN
long woollen scarf

> *Language tip*
> **cacher** *means 'hide' and* **nez**
> *means 'nose', so this scarf covers*
> *your nose.*

cacher VERB
to hide

■ **se cacher**
to hide
Elle s'est cachée sous la table.
She's hiding under the table.

le **cachet** MASC NOUN
tablet
un cachet d'aspirine
an aspirin

la **cachette** FEM NOUN
hiding place

le **cadavre exquis**
MASC NOUN
consequences

a b c d e f g h i j k l m n o p q r s t u v w x y z

This is a game where one player writes something on a piece of paper, folds it over and passes it on to the next player to continue the story.

le **Caddie**® MASC NOUN
supermarket trolley

le **cadeau** MASC NOUN
(PL les **cadeaux**)
present

un cadeau d'anniversaire
a birthday present
un cadeau de Noël
a Christmas present
Je vais faire un cadeau à ma mère.
I'm going to give my mum a present.

le **cadenas** MASC NOUN
padlock

cadet MASC ADJECTIVE
(FEM **cadette**)
1 **younger**
2 **youngest**

le **cadet** MASC NOUN
la **cadette** FEM NOUN
youngest

Luc est le cadet de la famille.
Luc is the youngest in the family.
Muriel est la cadette de la famille.
Muriel is the youngest in the family.

le **cafard** MASC NOUN
cockroach

J'ai le cafard.
I'm feeling down.

le **café** MASC NOUN
1 **coffee**
un café
au lait
a white
coffee
un café crème
a strong white coffee

Did you know...?
*If you have asked for **un café**, it will not have milk in it. If you want a coffee with milk, you must ask for **un café au lait**.*

2 **café**
Rendez-vous au café à trois heures.
Let's meet at the café at three o'clock.

le **café-tabac** MASC NOUN

Did you know...?
*A **café-tabac** is a café which also sells cigarettes and stamps; you can tell a **café-tabac** by the red diamond-shaped sign outside it.*

la **cafétéria** FEM NOUN
cafeteria

la **cage** FEM NOUN
cage

la **cagoule**
FEM NOUN
balaclava

Language tip
*une **cagoule** is something you wear on your head. It's not an anorak as it is in English.*

le **cahier** MASC NOUN
jotter
>   **mon cahier de français**
>   my French jotter

le **caillou** MASC NOUN
(PL les **cailloux**)
pebble

la **caisse** FEM NOUN
1 checkout
>   **Payez à la caisse.**
>   Pay at the checkout.
2 box
>   **une caisse à outils**
>   a tool box

le **caissier** MASC NOUN
la **caissière** FEM NOUN
cashier

la **calculatrice** FEM NOUN
calculator

calculer VERB
to work out
>   **Calculez combien ça va
>   coûter.**
>   Work out how much it's going
>   to cost.

la **calculette** FEM NOUN
pocket calculator

le **caleçon** MASC NOUN
boxer shorts

le **calendrier** MASC NOUN
calendar

le **câlin** MASC NOUN
cuddle

calme

> **calme** *can be an adjective or a
> noun.*

A ADJECTIVE
1 quiet

>   **un endroit calme**
>   a quiet place
2 calm
>   **La mer est calme.**
>   The sea is calm.
B MASC NOUN
peace and quiet
>   **J'ai besoin de calme pour
>   travailler.**
>   I need peace and quiet to work.

se **calmer** VERB
to calm down
>   **Calme-toi!**
>   Calm down!

le/la **camarade** MASC/FEM
NOUN
friend
>   **un camarade de classe**
>   a school friend

la **caméra** FEM NOUN
camera
>   **une caméra de télévision**
>   a television camera

le **caméscope**® MASC NOUN
camcorder

le **camion** MASC NOUN
lorry

la **camionnette** FEM NOUN
van

le **camp** MASC NOUN
camp

la **campagne** FEM NOUN
country
>   **à la campagne**
>   in the country

camper VERB
to camp

le **camping** MASC NOUN
camping

Je n'aime pas le camping.
I don't like camping.
Je vais faire du camping.
I'm going camping.
un terrain de camping
a campsite

le **Canada** MASC NOUN
Canada

canadien MASC ADJECTIVE
(FEM **canadienne**)
Canadian

le **Canadien** MASC NOUN
la **Canadienne** FEM NOUN
Canadian

le **canapé** MASC NOUN
sofa

le **canard** MASC NOUN
duck

le **canari** MASC NOUN
canary

le **caniche** MASC NOUN
poodle

le **canif** MASC NOUN
penknife

la **canne** FEM NOUN
walking stick
une canne à pêche
a fishing rod

la **cannelle** FEM NOUN
cinnamon

le **canoë** MASC NOUN

canoe
Je vais faire du canoë.
I'm going canoeing.

la **cantine** FEM NOUN
canteen
Je mange à la cantine.
I eat in the canteen.

le **caoutchouc** MASC NOUN
rubber
des bottes en caoutchouc
Wellington boots

le **capitaine** MASC NOUN
captain

la **capitale** FEM NOUN
capital
Paris est la capitale de la France.
Paris is the capital of France.

la **capuche** FEM NOUN
hood

car
A MASC NOUN
coach
On va en France en car.
We're going to France by coach.

Language tip
The French car holds a lot more people than the English car.

B CONJUNCTION
because
Écoutez, car c'est très important.
Listen, because it's very important.

le **caractère** MASC NOUN
personality
Il a le même caractère que son père.
He's got the same personality as his father.

Il a bon caractère.
He's good-natured.
Elle a mauvais caractère.
She's bad-tempered.

la **carafe** FEM NOUN
jug

les **Caraïbes** FEM PL NOUN
Caribbean Islands

le **caramel** MASC NOUN
toffee

la **caravane** FEM NOUN
caravan

le **carême** MASC NOUN
Lent

la **caresse** FEM NOUN
faire des caresses
to stroke
Elle fait des caresses au chat.
She's stroking the cat.

caresser VERB
to stroke

la **carie** FEM NOUN
J'ai une carie.
I've got a hole in my tooth.

le **carnaval** MASC NOUN
carnival

Did you know...?
French children usually celebrate
carnaval *on Shrove Tuesday, when
they often go to school in fancy
dress. There is a procession in the
streets, and at the end of the day,
a man made of papier mâché,
called* **bonhomme carnaval** *is
burnt on a bonfire.*

le **carnet** MASC NOUN
1 notebook
2 book

un carnet d'adresses
an address book
un carnet de timbres
a book of stamps
un carnet de tickets
a book of tickets

Did you know...?
*It is cheaper to buy tickets for the
Paris Metro in a book of ten.*

un carnet de notes
a school report

la **carotte** FEM NOUN
carrot

carré

carré can be an adjective or a noun.

A MASC ADJECTIVE (FEM **carrée**)
square
un mètre carré
a square metre
B MASC NOUN
un carré de chocolat
a square of chocolate

le **carreau** MASC NOUN
(PL les **carreaux**)
1 check
une chemise à carreaux
a checked shirt
2 window
Maxime a cassé un carreau.
Maxime has broken a window.

3 diamonds
l'as de carreau
the ace of diamonds

le **carrefour** MASC NOUN
junction
Tournez à gauche au carrefour.
Turn left at the junction.

le **cartable** MASC NOUN
satchel

la **carte** FEM NOUN
1 card
une carte d'anniversaire
a birthday card

une carte postale
a postcard
une carte de vœux
a Christmas card

une carte de crédit
a credit card
une carte d'identité
an identity card
une carte téléphonique
a phonecard
un jeu de cartes
a pack of cards/a card game

J'ai acheté un nouveau jeu de cartes.
I've bought a new pack of cards.
Tu connais ce jeu de cartes?
Do you know this card game?
2 map
une carte de France
a map of France
une carte routière
a road map
3 menu
Je voudrais la carte, s'il vous plaît.
I'd like the menu, please.

le **carton** MASC NOUN
1 cardboard
un morceau de carton
a piece of cardboard
2 cardboard box
un carton à chaussures
a shoe box

le **cas** MASC NOUN (PL les **cas**)
case
en tout cas
in any case
au cas où
just in case
Prends de l'argent au cas où.
Take some money just in case.
en cas de
in case of

En cas d'incendie, appelez ce numéro.
In case of fire, call this number.

le **casier** MASC NOUN
locker

le **casque** MASC NOUN
1 helmet
2 headphones
J'ai cassé mon casque.
I've broken my headphones.

la **casquette** FEM NOUN
cap

le **casse-croûte** MASC NOUN
snack

casse-pieds MASC, FEM, PL
ADJECTIVE
Il est vraiment casse-pieds!
He's a real pain in the neck!

casser VERB
to break
J'ai cassé un verre.
I've broken a glass.
■ **se casser**
to break
Je me suis cassé la jambe au ski.
I broke my leg when I was skiing.

la **casserole** FEM NOUN
saucepan

le **cassis** MASC NOUN
blackcurrant

le **castor** MASC NOUN
beaver

la **catastrophe** FEM NOUN
disaster
C'est une catastrophe!
It's a disaster!

le **catéchisme** MASC NOUN
catechism

la **cathédrale** FEM NOUN
cathedral

catholique ADJECTIVE, MASC/FEM NOUN
Catholic

le **cauchemar** MASC NOUN
nightmare
J'ai fait un cauchemar.
I had a nightmare.

la **cause** FEM NOUN
à cause de
because of
Il n'y a pas de courrier à cause de la grève.
There's no post because of the strike.

la **cave** FEM NOUN
cellar

Did you know…?
une cave *is dark and underground, like a cave in English, but it often contains bottles of wine.*

le **CD** MASC NOUN (PL les **CD**)
CD

ce

ce can be an adjective or a pronoun.

A MASC ADJECTIVE (MASC **cet**, FEM **cette**, PL **ces**)

Language tip
ce *changes to* **cet** *before a vowel sound.*

French English

a b **c** d e f g h i j k l m n o p q r s t u v w x y z

a
b
c
d
e
f
g
h
i
j
k
l
m
n
o
p
q
r
s
t
u
v
w
x
y
z

1 this

Tu peux prendre ce livre.
You can take this book.
cet hiver
this winter
cette année
this year
cette semaine
this week

2 that

Je n'aime pas du tout ce film.
I don't like that film at all.
ce livre-là
that book
cette nuit
tonight/last night

Language tip

cette nuit *has two translations.*
Look at the examples.

Il va neiger cette nuit.
It's going to snow tonight.
Je n'ai pas beaucoup dormi
cette nuit.
I didn't sleep much last night.

B PRONOUN

it
Ce n'est pas facile.
It's not easy.

Language tip

ce *changes to* **c'** *in* **c'est***.*

c'est
it is/he is/she is

Language tip

c'est *has three translations. Look at*
the examples.

C'est trop cher.
It's too expensive.
C'est un véritable artiste.
He's a real artist.
C'est une actrice très célèbre.
She's a very famous actress.

C'est super!
It's great!
C'est moi!
It's me!

ce sont
they are
Ce sont des amis à mes
parents.
They're friends of my parents.
ce qui
what
C'est ce qui compte.
That's what matters.
ce que
what
Je vais lui dire ce que je pense.
I'm going to tell him what I think.

le **CE1** MASC NOUN
Year 3

le **CE2** MASC NOUN
Year 4

ceci PRONOUN
this
Prends ceci, tu en auras
besoin.
Take this, you'll need it.

céder VERB
to give in
Elle ne veut pas céder.
She won't give in.

céder à
to give in to
Je ne veux pas céder à ses caprices.
I'm not going to give in to her demands.

la **cédille** FEM NOUN
cedilla
c cédille
c with a cedilla

Language tip

The cedilla looks like the number 5 with the top missing. It's attached to the bottom of the letter C as in the word **garçon**. It makes a **c** sound like an **s** rather than a **k**.

---

la **ceinture** FEM NOUN
belt
une ceinture en cuir
a leather belt

une ceinture de sécurité
a seatbelt

cela PRONOUN
1 **it**
Cela dépend.
It depends.
2 **that**
Je n'aime pas cela.
I don't like that.

célèbre ADJECTIVE
famous

célébrer VERB
to celebrate

le **céleri** MASC NOUN
le céleri-rave
celeriac
le céleri en branche
celery

célibataire

célibataire can be an adjective or a noun.

A ADJECTIVE
not married
Ma tante est célibataire.
My aunt isn't married.
B MASC NOUN
bachelor
un célibataire de quarante ans
a 40 year-old bachelor
C FEM NOUN
single woman
une célibataire de trente-cinq ans
a 35 year-old single woman

celle PRONOUN ▷ see **celui**

celles PRONOUN ▷ see **ceux**

celui MASC PRONOUN (FEM **celle**)
the one
Prends celui que tu préfères.
Take the one you like best.
Ne prends pas mon appareil photo; prends celui de ma sœur!
Don't take my camera, take my sister's!
Ce n'est pas ma platine laser, c'est celle de mon frère.
This isn't my CD player, it's my brother's.
celui-ci
this one
celle-ci
this one
celui-là
that one
celle-là
that one

le **cendrier** MASC NOUN
ashtray

cent NUMBER
a hundred
cent euros
a hundred euros
trois cents ans
three hundred years
cent deux kilomètres
a hundred and two kilometres
**trois cent cinquante
kilomètres**
three hundred and fifty
kilometres

la **centaine** FEM NOUN
about a hundred
**Il y a une centaine de
personnes dans la salle.**
There are about a hundred
people in the hall.
des centaines de
hundreds of
**J'ai des centaines de timbres
dans ma collection.**
I've got hundreds of stamps in
my collection.

centième ADJECTIVE
hundredth

le **centilitre** MASC NOUN
centilitre

le **centime** MASC NOUN
1 cent
un centime d'euro
a euro cent

Did you know…?
*There are 100 **centimes** in a euro.*

2 centime
**une pièce de cinquante
centimes**
a 50-centime coin

le **centimètre** MASC NOUN
centimetre

le **centre** MASC NOUN
centre
un centre commercial
a shopping centre

le **centre-ville** MASC NOUN
town centre

le **cercle** MASC NOUN
circle

la **céréale** FEM NOUN
cereal
un bol de céréales
a bowl of cereal

la **cérémonie** FEM NOUN
ceremony

le **cerf** MASC NOUN
stag

le **cerf-volant**
MASC NOUN
kite

la **cerise**
FEM NOUN
cherry

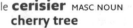

le **cerisier** MASC NOUN
cherry tree

certain MASC ADJECTIVE
(FEM **certaine**)
1 certain
Ce n'est pas certain.
It's not certain.

2 some
Les chiens sont interdits sur certaines plages.
Dogs are forbidden on some beaches.

certainement ADVERB
1 definitely
C'est certainement le meilleur film de l'année.
It's definitely the best film of the year.
2 of course
Est-ce que je peux t'emprunter ton stylo? — Mais certainement!
Can I borrow your pen? — Of course!

certains PRONOUN
1 some
certains de ses amis
some of his friends
2 some people
Certains pensent que c'est difficile.
Some people think it's difficult.

le **certificat** MASC NOUN
certificate

le **cerveau** MASC NOUN
(PL les **cerveaux**)
brain

le **CES** MASC NOUN
secondary school
Elle est au CES.
She's in secondary school.

Did you know...?
*In France, pupils go to a **CES** between the ages of 11 and 15, and then to a **lycée** until the age of 18.*

ces PL ADJECTIVE
1 these

Tu peux prendre ces photos si tu veux.
You can have these photos if you like.
ces photos-ci
these photos
2 those
Ces montagnes sont dangereuses en hiver.
Those mountains are dangerous in winter.
ces livres-là
those books

c'est ▷ see **ce**

c'est-à-dire ADVERB
that is
Est-ce que tu peux venir lundi prochain, c'est-à-dire le quinze?
Can you come next Monday, that's the fifteenth?

cet MASC ADJECTIVE ▷ see **ce**

cette FEM ADJECTIVE ▷ see **ce**

ceux MASC PL PRONOUN
(FEM PL **celles**)
the ones
Prends ceux que tu préfères.
Take the ones you like best.
Ne prends pas mes skis; prends ceux de ma sœur!
Don't take my skis, take my sister's!
Ce ne sont pas mes baskets, ce sont celles de mon frère.
They're not my trainers, they're my brother's.
ceux-ci
these ones
celles-ci
these ones

ceux-là
those ones
celles-là
those ones

chacun PRONOUN
1 each
Nous avons chacun donné deux euros.
We each gave two euros.
2 everyone
Chacun fait ce qu'il veut.
Everyone does what they like.

la **chaîne** FEM NOUN
1 chain
une chaîne en or
a gold chain
2 channel
Le film passe sur quelle chaîne?
Which channel is the film on?
une chaîne hi-fi
a hi-fi system
une chaîne laser
a CD player
une chaîne stéréo
a music centre

la **chair** FEM NOUN
flesh
la chair de poule
goose pimples
J'ai la chair de poule!
I've got goose pimples!

> ### Language tip
> *The French actually means 'I've got hen's flesh'!*

la **chaise**
FEM NOUN
chair
une chaise longue
a deckchair

la **chaleur** FEM NOUN
heat
Quelle chaleur!
Phew! It's hot!

la **chambre** FEM NOUN
bedroom

C'est la chambre de Camille.
This is Camille's bedroom.
une chambre à coucher
a bedroom
une chambre d'amis
a spare room
une chambre à un lit
a single room
une chambre pour une personne
a single room
une chambre pour deux personnes
a double room
'Chambres d'hôte'
'Bed and Breakfast'

le **chameau** MASC NOUN
(PL les **chameaux**)
camel

le **champ** MASC NOUN
field

le **champignon** MASC NOUN
mushroom

le **champion** MASC NOUN
la **championne** FEM NOUN
champion

le **championnat** MASC NOUN
championship
  le championnat du monde
  the world championship

la **chance** FEM NOUN
  1 luck
    Tu as de la chance!
    You're lucky!
    Je n'ai pas de chance.
    I'm unlucky.

> **Bonne chance!**
> Good luck!

  2 chance
    Il n'a aucune chance.
    He's got no chance.

le **changement** MASC NOUN
change
    **Est-ce qu'il y a un
    changement? —
    Non, c'est direct.**
    Do you have to change? —
    No, it's a through train.

changer VERB
to change
    Tu peux changer les draps?
    Can you change the sheets?
    Je vais me changer.
    I'm going to get changed.
    Tu vas te changer?
    Are you going to get changed?

la **chanson** FEM NOUN
song

le **chant** MASC NOUN
singing
    des cours de chant
    singing lessons
    un chant de Noël
    a Christmas carol

chanter VERB
to sing

le **chanteur** MASC NOUN
la **chanteuse** FEM NOUN
singer

la **Chantilly** FEM NOUN
whipped cream

le **chapeau** MASC NOUN
(PL les **chapeaux**)
hat

le **chapitre** MASC NOUN
chapter

chaque ADJECTIVE
every
    chaque année
    every year

la **charade** FEM NOUN
riddle

le **charbon** MASC NOUN
coal

la **charcuterie** FEM NOUN
  1 delicatessen
  2 cold meats
    **Comme entrée, je voudrais
    de la charcuterie.**
    As a starter, I would like a plate
    of cold meats.

le **chariot** MASC NOUN
trolley

charmant MASC ADJECTIVE
(FEM **charmante**)
charming

la **chasse** FEM NOUN
  1 hunting

un chien de chasse
a hunting dog

2 shooting
la chasse au canard
duck shooting

chasser VERB
to hunt

le **chasseur** MASC NOUN
hunter

le **chat** MASC NOUN
cat
J'ai deux chats.
I've got two cats.

la **châtaigne** FEM NOUN
chestnut

le **châtaignier** MASC NOUN
chestnut tree

châtain MASC, FEM, PL ADJECTIVE
brown
J'ai les cheveux châtain.
I've got brown hair.

le **château** MASC NOUN
(PL les **châteaux**)

1 castle
2 palace
le château de Versailles
the palace of Versailles
un château de sable
a sandcastle

le **chaton** MASC NOUN
kitten

chatouiller VERB
to tickle

la **chatte** FEM NOUN
cat

> **Language tip**
> **te** *added to the word* **chat** *shows you that the cat is female.*

chaud MASC ADJECTIVE
(FEM **chaude**)
1 warm
des vêtements chauds
warm clothes
2 hot
de l'eau chaude
hot water

Il fait chaud.
It's hot.
J'ai chaud!
I'm hot!

le **chauffage** MASC NOUN
heating
le chauffage central
central heating

le **chauffeur** MASC NOUN
driver
un chauffeur de taxi
a taxi driver

> **Language tip**
> *In English, a chauffeur drives a car for another person, but* **chauffeur** *in French means any kind of driver.*

la **chaussette** FEM NOUN
sock

le **chausson** MASC NOUN
slipper
un chausson aux pommes
an apple turnover

la **chaussure** FEM NOUN
shoe
les chaussures de ski
ski boots

chauve ADJECTIVE
bald

la **chauve-souris** FEM NOUN
bat

> **Language tip**
>
> *The French actually means 'bald mouse'!*

le **chef** MASC NOUN
1 boss
  C'est toi le chef!
  You're the boss!
2 chef

  la spécialité du chef
  the chef's speciality
  un chef d'orchestre
  a conductor

le **chef-d'œuvre** MASC NOUN
masterpiece

le **chemin** MASC NOUN
1 path
2 way
  Montre-moi le chemin.
  Show me the way.
  en chemin
  on the way
  les chemins de fer
  the railways

la **cheminée** FEM NOUN
1 chimney
2 fireplace

la **chemise** FEM NOUN
1 shirt
  **une chemise
  à carreaux**
  a checked shirt
  une chemise de nuit
  a nightdress
2 folder

le **chemisier** MASC NOUN
blouse

le **chêne** MASC NOUN
oak

la **chenille** FEM NOUN
caterpillar

le **chèque** MASC NOUN
cheque
  les chèques de voyage
  traveller's cheques

cher

> **cher** *can be an adjective or an adverb.*

A MASC ADJECTIVE (FEM **chère**)
1 dear
  Chère Mélusine ...
  Dear Mélusine ...
2 expensive
  C'est trop cher.
  It's too expensive.
B ADVERB
  coûter cher
  to be expensive
  Cet ordinateur coûte cher.
  This computer is expensive.

chercher VERB
1 to look for
  Je cherche mes clés.
  I'm looking for my keys.
2 to look up
  Cherche 'apple' dans le dictionnaire.
  Look up 'apple' in the dictionary.

aller chercher
to go to get
Je vais chercher du pain pour le déjeuner.
I'm going to get some bread for lunch.

le **chercheur** MASC NOUN
la **chercheuse** FEM NOUN
scientist

chère FEM ADJECTIVE ▷see cher

chéri MASC NOUN, MASC ADJECTIVE
(FEM **chérie**)
darling

le **cheval** MASC NOUN
(PL les **chevaux**)
horse

un cheval de course
a racehorse
à cheval
on horseback
Je fais du cheval le samedi.
I go riding on Saturdays.

le **chevalier** MASC NOUN
knight

les **chevaux** MASC PL NOUN
horses

les **cheveux** MASC PL NOUN
hair
Elle a les cheveux courts.
She's got short hair.

la **cheville** FEM NOUN
ankle

la **chèvre** FEM NOUN
goat
le fromage de chèvre
goat's cheese

le **chevreuil** MASC NOUN
1 roe deer
2 venison
On va manger du chevreuil à Noël.
We'll eat venison at Christmas.

chez PREPOSITION

Language tip
chez *means either* at *or* to *someone's house.*

On va chez moi?
Shall we go to my house?
Je vais chez Marc.
I'm going to Marc's house.
Je rentre chez moi à quatre heures.
I go home at four.
Nicole va chez elle.
Nicole is going home.
Jean-Claude reste chez lui.
Jean-Claude is staying at home.
Tu rentres chez toi?
Are you going home?

Language tip
chez le dentiste *means either* at the dentist's *or* to the dentist's.

J'ai rendez-vous chez le dentiste.
I've got an appointment at the dentist's.
Je vais chez le dentiste.
I'm going to the dentist's.

Je suis chez moi.
I'm at home.
Je vais chez moi.
I'm going home.

chic MASC, FEM, PL ADJECTIVE
smart
une tenue chic
a smart outfit

le **chien** MASC NOUN
dog

la **chienne** FEM NOUN
bitch
    **C'est un chien ou une
    chienne?**
    Is it a dog or a bitch?

le **chiffon** MASC NOUN
cloth

le **chiffre** MASC NOUN
figure
    Écris ce nombre en chiffres.
    Write this number in figures.

la **chimie** FEM NOUN
chemistry

la **Chine** FEM NOUN
China

chinois MASC NOUN, MASC
ADJECTIVE (FEM **chinoise**)
Chinese

le **Chinois** MASC NOUN
Chinese man
    les Chinois
    the Chinese

la **Chinoise** FEM NOUN
Chinese woman

le **chiot** MASC NOUN
puppy

les **chips**
FEM PL NOUN
crisps
    **un paquet
    de chips**
    a packet
    of crisps

Language tip

Be careful! The French word **chips**
*does not mean the same as the
English word* **chips***.*

le **chirurgien** MASC NOUN
surgeon

le **chocolat** MASC NOUN
chocolate
    **un chocolat
    chaud**
    a hot
    chocolate

le **chœur** MASC NOUN
choir

choisir VERB
to choose

le **choix** MASC NOUN
1 choice
    Je n'ai pas le choix.
    I don't have a choice.
2 selection
    **Il n'y a pas beaucoup de
    choix dans ce magasin.**
    There's not much of a selection
    in this shop.

le **chômage** MASC NOUN
unemployment
    au chômage
    unemployed
    Mon père est au chômage.
    My dad is unemployed.

le **chômeur** MASC NOUN
la **chômeuse** FEM NOUN
    Il est chômeur.
    He's unemployed.
    Elle est chômeuse.
    She's unemployed.

la **chorale** FEM NOUN
choir

la **chose** FEM NOUN
thing
    **J'ai fait beaucoup de choses
    pendant les vacances.**
    I did lots of things in the holidays.

French English

a
b
c
d
e
f
g
h
i
j
k
l
m
n
o
p
q
r
s
t
u
v
w
x
y
z

French English

a
b
c
d
e
f
g
h
i
j
k
l
m
n
o
p
q
r
s
t
u
v
w
x
y
z

le **chou** MASC NOUN
(PL les **choux**)
cabbage
les choux de Bruxelles
Brussels sprouts

le **chouchou** MASC NOUN
la **chouchoute** FEM NOUN
teacher's pet

la **choucroute** FEM NOUN
sauerkraut with sausages and ham

Did you know…?
Sauerkraut *is a kind of pickled cabbage.*

chouette

chouette can be an adjective or a noun.

A ADJECTIVE
brilliant
Chouette alors!
Brilliant
B FEM NOUN
owl

le **chou-fleur** MASC NOUN
cauliflower

chrétien MASC ADJECTIVE
(FEM **chrétienne**)
Christian

le **chronomètre** MASC NOUN
stopwatch

le **chrysanthème** MASC NOUN
chrysanthemum

Did you know…?
People in France put bunches of chrysanthemum flowers on graves, and wouldn't give them to someone as a present.

chuchoter VERB
to whisper

chut EXCLAMATION
shh!

-ci ADVERB
ce livre-ci
this book
ces bottes-ci
these boots

la **ciboulette** FEM NOUN
chives

la **cicatrice** FEM NOUN
scar

ci-contre ADVERB
opposite
la page ci-contre
the opposite page

ci-dessous ADVERB
below
la photo ci-dessous
the picture below

ci-dessus ADVERB
above

le **cidre** MASC NOUN
cider

le **ciel** MASC NOUN
sky
un ciel nuageux
a cloudy sky

le **cigare** MASC NOUN
cigar

la **cigarette** FEM NOUN
cigarette

le **cil** MASC NOUN
eyelash

le **cimetière** MASC NOUN
cemetery

le **cinéma** MASC NOUN
cinema

cinq NUMBER
five
> **Il est cinq heures du matin.**
> It's five in the morning.
> **Il a cinq ans.**
> He's five.

le cinq février
the fifth of February

la **cinquantaine** FEM NOUN
about fifty
> **Il y a une cinquantaine de personnes dans la salle.**
> There are about fifty people in the hall.
> **Il a la cinquantaine.**
> He's in his fifties.

cinquante NUMBER
fifty
> **Il a cinquante ans.**
> He's fifty.

cinquante et un
fifty-one
cinquante-deux
fifty-two

cinquième

> **cinquième** *can be an adjective or a noun.*

A ADJECTIVE
fifth
> **au cinquième étage**
> on the fifth floor

B FEM NOUN
Year 8
> **Mon frère est en cinquième.**
> My brother's in Year 8.

Did you know…?

*In French secondary schools and sixth form colleges, years are counted from the **sixième** (youngest) to the **première** and the **terminale** (oldest).*

circonflexe ADJECTIVE
> **un accent circonflexe**
> a circumflex

la **circulation** FEM NOUN
traffic
> **Il y a beaucoup de circulation.**
> There is a lot of traffic.

le **cirque** MASC NOUN
circus

les **ciseaux** MASC PL NOUN
> **une paire de ciseaux**
> a pair of scissors

la **cité** FEM NOUN
estate
> **J'habite dans une cité.**
> I live on an estate.

French English

a b **c** d e f g h i j k l m n o p q r s t u v w x y z

le **citron** MASC NOUN
lemon

un citron vert
a lime
un citron pressé
a fresh lemon juice

la **citrouille** FEM NOUN
pumpkin

clair MASC ADJECTIVE (FEM **claire**)
light
vert clair
light green
C'est une pièce très claire.
It's a very light room.

clairement ADVERB
clearly

la **claque** FEM NOUN
slap

claquer VERB
to slam

les **claquettes** FEM PL NOUN
faire des claquettes
to tap-dance
Je fais des claquettes le samedi.
I do tap on Saturdays.

la **clarinette**
FEM NOUN
clarinet
Élodie joue de la clarinette.
Élodie plays the clarinet.

la **classe** FEM NOUN
1 class
C'est la meilleure élève de la classe.
She's the best pupil in the class.
un aller simple en première classe
a first class single
2 classroom

classer VERB
to arrange

le **classeur** MASC NOUN
ring binder

classique ADJECTIVE
1 classical
la musique classique
classical music
2 classic

le **clavier** MASC NOUN
keyboard

la **clé** FEM NOUN
key

la **clef** FEM NOUN
key

le **client** MASC NOUN
la **cliente** FEM NOUN
customer

le **climat** MASC NOUN
climate

le **clin d'œil** MASC NOUN
wink

la **clinique** FEM NOUN
private hospital

cliquer VERB
to click
> **Clique sur une icône.**
> Click on an icon.

la **cloche** FEM NOUN
bell
> **les cloches de Pâques**
> Easter bells

Did you know…?
*In France, Easter eggs are said to be brought by the Easter bells (**cloches de Pâques**) that fly from Rome and drop them in people's gardens.*

le **clocher** MASC NOUN
1 church tower
2 steeple

le **club** MASC NOUN
club

le **CM1** MASC NOUN
Year 5

le **CM2** MASC NOUN
Year 6

le **cobaye** MASC NOUN
guinea pig

le **coca** MASC NOUN
Coke®

la **coccinelle**
FEM NOUN
ladybird

cocher VERB
to tick
> **Cochez la bonne réponse.**
> Tick the right answer.

le **cochon** MASC NOUN
pig

un cochon d'Inde
a guinea pig

le **coco** MASC NOUN
> **une noix de coco**
> a coconut

cocorico EXCLAMATION
1 Cock-a-doodle-doo!
2 Three cheers for France!

Did you know…?
*The symbol of France is the cockerel and so **cocorico!** is sometimes used as an expression of French national pride.*

le **cœur** MASC NOUN
heart
> **la dame de cœur**
> the queen
> of hearts
> **J'ai mal au cœur!**
> I feel sick!
> **Il faut l'apprendre par cœur.**
> You must learn it by heart.
> **Apprenez ce petit poème par cœur.**
> Learn this little poem by heart.

le **coffre** MASC NOUN
car boot
> **un coffre à jouets**
> a toybox

le **coffret** MASC NOUN
> **un coffret à bijoux**
> a jewellery box

coiffé MASC ADJECTIVE
(FEM **coiffée**)
> **Tu es bien coiffée.**
> Your hair looks nice.

se **coiffer** VERB
> **Maman se coiffe.**
> Mum is doing her hair.

le **coiffeur** MASC NOUN
la **coiffeuse** FEM NOUN
hairdresser

la **coiffure** FEM NOUN
hairstyle
Cette coiffure te va bien.
That hairstyle suits you.
un salon de coiffure
a hairdresser's

le **coin** MASC NOUN
corner
au coin de la rue
on the corner of the street

le **col** MASC NOUN
collar

la **colère** FEM NOUN
anger
en colère
angry
Je suis en colère.
I'm angry.
Il va se mettre en colère.
He's going to get angry.

le **colin-maillard** MASC NOUN
blind man's buff

le **colis** MASC NOUN
parcel

collant

> **collant** can be an adjective or a noun.

A MASC ADJECTIVE (FEM **collante**)
sticky

B MASC NOUN
tights
un collant en laine
woollen tights

la **colle** FEM NOUN
glue

la **collection** FEM NOUN
collection
une collection d'autocollants
a sticker collection

collectionner VERB
to collect

le **collège** MASC NOUN
secondary school

> ### Did you know…?
> In France, pupils go to a **collège** between the ages of 11 and 15, and then to a **lycée** until the age of 18.

le **collégien** MASC NOUN
la **collégienne** FEM NOUN
secondary school pupil

le/la **collègue** MASC/FEM NOUN
colleague

coller VERB
1 **to stick**
Colle cette feuille dans ton cahier.
Stick this piece of paper in your book.
2 **to be sticky**
Elle a les mains qui collent.
Her hands are sticky.

le **collier** MASC NOUN
1 **necklace**
un collier de perles
a pearl necklace
2 **collar**
Où est le collier du chien?
Where's the dog's collar?

la **colline** FEM NOUN
hill

la **colonie de vacances** FEM NOUN
summer camp
> Je n'aime pas partir en colonie de vacances.
> I don't like going to summer camp.

> *Did you know...?*
> French schoolchildren often go to a **colonie de vacances** for a fortnight in the summer holidays.

la **colonne** FEM NOUN
column

colorier VERB
to colour in

combien ADVERB
1 how much
> Vous en voulez combien? Un kilo?
> How much do you want? One kilo?
> Combien est-ce que ça coûte?
> How much does it cost?
> Ça fait combien?
> How much does it come to?

> C'est combien?
> How much is that?

2 how many
> Tu en veux combien? Deux?
> How many do you want? Two?
> combien de
> how much/how many

> *Language tip*
> **combien de** has two translations. Look at the examples.

> Tu reçois combien d'argent de poche?
> How much pocket money do you get?

> Tu as combien de frères et sœurs?
> How many brothers and sisters have you got?
> combien de temps
> how long
> Combien de temps est-ce que ça dure?
> How long does it last?

> On est le combien aujourd'hui?
> What's the date today?

la **combinaison** FEM NOUN
> une combinaison de plongée
> a wetsuit
> une combinaison de ski
> a ski suit

la **comédie** FEM NOUN
comedy

le **comédien** MASC NOUN
la **comédienne** FEM NOUN
actor

> *Language tip*
> Be careful! **comédien** does not mean the same as **comedian**.

comique

> **comique** can be an adjective or a noun.

A ADJECTIVE
comical
B MASC NOUN
comedian

commander VERB
to order
> J'ai commandé un steak frites.
> I ordered steak and chips.

comme CONJUNCTION, ADVERB
1 like

Il est comme son père.
He's like his father.
comme ça
like this
Ça se plie comme ça.
You fold it like this.
C'était un poisson grand comme ça.
The fish was this big.

2 for
Qu'est-ce que tu veux comme dessert?
What would you like for pudding?

3 as
Elle travaille comme serveuse.
She works as a waitress.
Fais comme tu veux.
Do as you like.

4 how
Comme tu as grandi!
How you've grown!
Regarde comme c'est beau!
Look, isn't it lovely!

Comment ça va? — Comme ci comme ça.
How are you? — Okay, I suppose.

commencer VERB
to start

comment ADVERB
how
Comment dit-on 'apple' en français?
How do you say 'apple' in French?

Comment tu t'appelles?
What's your name?
Comment s'appelle-t-il?
What's his name?
Comment ça va?
How are you?

Comment?
What did you say?
Comment ça s'écrit?
How do you spell it?

le **commerce** MASC NOUN
business
Il fait des études de commerce.
He's studying business.

commercial MASC ADJECTIVE
un centre commercial
a shopping centre

le **commissariat** MASC NOUN
police station

les **commissions** FEM PL NOUN
shopping
J'ai quelques commissions à faire.
I've got some shopping to do.

commode FEM NOUN
chest of drawers

commun MASC ADJECTIVE
(FEM **commune**)
en commun
in common
Ils n'ont rien en commun.
They've got nothing in common.
les transports en commun
public transport

compact MASC ADJECTIVE
(FEM **compacte**)
compact
un disque compact
a compact disc

la **compagnie** FEM NOUN
company
une compagnie aérienne
an airline

comparer VERB
to compare

le **compartiment** MASC NOUN
compartment

le **compas** MASC NOUN
compasses
Je peux emprunter ton compas?
Can I borrow your compasses?

la **compétition** FEM NOUN
competition
une compétition de natation
a swimming competition

complet MASC ADJECTIVE
(FEM **complète**)
full
L'hôtel est complet.
The hotel is full.
'complet'
'no vacancies'
le pain complet
wholemeal bread

complètement ADVERB
completely

compléter VERB
to complete

compliqué MASC ADJECTIVE
(FEM **compliquée**)
complicated

composter VERB
to punch
Tu as composté ton billet?
Have you punched your ticket?

Did you know…?
In France, you have to punch your ticket before you get on the train. If you don't you might get a fine.

la **compote** FEM NOUN
stewed fruit
la compote de pommes
stewed apple

comprendre VERB
to understand
Tu comprends?
Do you understand?

Je ne comprends pas!
I don't understand!

le **comprimé** MASC NOUN
tablet

compris

compris *can be part of a verb or an adjective.*

A VERB ▷*see* **comprendre**
Je n'ai pas compris.
I don't understand.
B MASC ADJECTIVE (FEM **comprise**)
included
Le service n'est pas compris.
Service is not included.

le/la **comptable** MASC/FEM NOUN
accountant

le **compte** MASC NOUN
account
> **un compte bancaire**
> a bank account
> **Ma mère travaille à son compte.**
> My mum is self-employed.

compter VERB
to count

se **concentrer** VERB
to concentrate
> **Il faut te concentrer!**
> You've got to concentrate!

le **concert** MASC NOUN
concert

le/la **concierge** MASC/FEM NOUN
caretaker

le **concombre** MASC NOUN
cucumber

le **concours** MASC NOUN
competition
> **un concours de chant**
> a singing competition

la **condition** FEM NOUN
condition
> **Je vais le faire à une condition.**
> I'll do it, on one condition.

le **conducteur** MASC NOUN
la **conductrice** FEM NOUN
driver

conduire VERB
to drive
> **Ma grand-mère ne sait pas conduire.**
> My grandma can't drive.

> **Ma mère me conduit à l'école.**
> My mum drives me to school.
- **se conduire**
  to behave
  > **Il se conduit mal en classe.**
  > He behaves badly in class.

les **confettis** MASC PL NOUN
confetti

la **confiance** FEM NOUN
trust
> **Tu peux avoir confiance en moi.**
> You can trust me.
> **Je n'ai pas confiance en lui.**
> I don't trust him.

la **confiserie** FEM NOUN
sweet shop

confit MASC ADJECTIVE
(FEM **confite**)
> **des fruits confits**
> crystallized fruits

la **confiture** FEM NOUN
jam

> **la confiture de fraises**
> strawberry jam
> **la confiture d'oranges**
> marmalade

confortable
ADJECTIVE
comfortable
> **des chaussures confortables**
> comfortable shoes

le **congé** MASC NOUN
holiday
une semaine de congé
a week's holiday
en congé
on holiday

le **congélateur** MASC NOUN
freezer

congeler VERB
to freeze

connaître VERB
to know
Je ne la connais pas.
I don't know her.

se connecter VERB
to log on
Comment est-ce qu'on se connecte sur internet?
How do you log on to the internet?

connu MASC ADJECTIVE
(FEM **connue**)
well-known
C'est un acteur connu.
He's a well-known actor.

le **conseil** MASC NOUN
advice
Est-ce que je peux te demander conseil?
Can I ask you for some advice?
un conseil
a piece of advice

conseiller VERB
1 to advise

Qu'est-ce que tu me conseilles de faire?
What do you advise me to do?
2 to recommend
Je te conseille ce livre.
I recommend this book.

le **conseiller** MASC NOUN
la **conseillère** FEM NOUN
adviser
le conseiller d'orientation
the careers adviser

le **conservatoire** MASC NOUN
school of music

la **conserve** FEM NOUN
tin
une boîte de conserve
a tin
en conserve
tinned
des petits pois en conserve
tinned peas

la **consigne** FEM NOUN
left-luggage office
une consigne automatique
a left-luggage locker

la **console de jeu** FEM NOUN
games console

constamment ADVERB
constantly

construire VERB
to build

contacter VERB
to get in touch with
Tu peux me contacter par courrier électronique.
You can get in touch with me by email.

le **conte de fées** MASC NOUN
fairy tale

content MASC ADJECTIVE
(FEM **contente**)
happy
> **Je suis content pour toi.**
> I'm happy for you.
> **content de**
> pleased with
> **Elle est contente de mon travail.**
> She is pleased with my work.

continuer VERB
to carry on
> **Continuez sans moi!**
> Carry on without me!

le **contraire** MASC NOUN
opposite
> **Il fait le contraire de ce que je lui demande.**
> He does the opposite of what I ask him to.
> **au contraire**
> on the contrary

contre PREPOSITION
against
> **Ne mets pas ton vélo contre le mur.**
> Don't put your bike against the wall.
> **Je suis contre cette idée.**
> I'm against this idea.
> **par contre**
> on the other hand

la **contrebasse** FEM NOUN
double bass
> **Je joue de la contrebasse.**
> I play the double bass.

le **contrôle** MASC NOUN
1 control
> **le contrôle des passeports**
> passport control
2 check

> **un contrôle d'identité**
> an identity check
> **le contrôle des billets**
> ticket inspection

contrôler VERB
to check

le **contrôleur** MASC NOUN
la **contrôleuse** FEM NOUN
ticket inspector

la **conversation** FEM NOUN
conversation

cool MASC, FEM, PL ADJECTIVE
cool
> **J'adore le français. C'est vraiment cool.**
> I love French. It's really cool.

le **copain** MASC NOUN
1 friend
> **C'est un bon copain.**
> He's a good friend.
2 boyfriend
> **Elle a un nouveau copain.**
> She's got a new boyfriend.

la **copie** FEM NOUN
1 copy
2 paper
> **Rendez vos copies!**
> Hand in your papers!

copier VERB
to copy
> **copier-coller**
> to copy and paste

la **copine** FEM NOUN
1 friend
> **C'est une bonne copine.**
> She's a good friend.
2 girlfriend
> **Il a une nouvelle copine.**
> He's got a new girlfriend.

le **coq** MASC NOUN
cockerel

Did you know…?
The cockerel is the symbol of France.

la **coque** FEM NOUN
  un œuf à la coque
  a soft-boiled egg

le **coquelicot** MASC NOUN
poppy

le **coquillage** MASC NOUN
shell

la **coquille** FEM NOUN
shell
  une coquille Saint-Jacques
  a scallop

coquin MASC ADJECTIVE
(FEM **coquine**)
cheeky

le **corbeau** MASC NOUN
(PL les **corbeaux**)
crow

la **corbeille** FEM NOUN
basket

  une corbeille à papier
  a wastepaper basket

la **corde** FEM NOUN
rope

la **cordonnerie** FEM NOUN
shoe repair shop

le **cordonnier** MASC NOUN
cobbler

la **cornemuse** FEM NOUN
bagpipes
  Je joue de la cornemuse.
  I play the bagpipes.

le **cornet**
MASC NOUN
  un cornet
  de frites
  a bag of
  chips
  un cornet
  de glace
  an ice cream
  cone

le **cornichon** MASC NOUN
gherkin

la **Cornouailles** FEM NOUN
Cornwall

le **corps** MASC NOUN
body

correct MASC ADJECTIVE
(FEM **correcte**)
correct
  Est-ce que cette phrase est
  correcte?
  Is this sentence correct?

la **correspondance** FEM
NOUN
connection
  Il y a une correspondance
  pour Toulouse à dix heures.
  There's a connection for
  Toulouse at ten o'clock.

le **correspondant** MASC
NOUN
la **correspondante** FEM
NOUN
penfriend

correspondre VERB
to correspond

corriger VERB
to mark
Vous pouvez corriger cet exercice?
Could you mark this exercise?

corse ADJECTIVE
Corsican

le/la **Corse** MASC/FEM NOUN
Corsican

la **Corse** FEM NOUN
Corsica

le **costume** MASC NOUN
1 **man's suit**
Fabien ne porte pas souvent de costume.
Fabien doesn't often wear a suit.

2 **costume**
Je prépare mon costume pour le carnaval.
I'm making my costume for the carnival.

la **côte** FEM NOUN
1 **coastline**
La route longe la côte.
The road follows the coastline.
la Côte d'Azur
the French Riviera

2 **hill**
La maison est en haut d'une côte.
The house is at the top of a hill.

3 **rib**
Elle a une côte cassée.
She has a broken rib.

4 **chop**

une côte de porc
a pork chop
une côte de bœuf
a rib of beef

côte à côte
side by side

le **côté** MASC NOUN
side
de l'autre côté
on the other side
La pharmacie est de l'autre côté de la rue.
The chemist's is on the other side of the street.
à côté de
next to/next door to

Language tip
à côté de has two translations. Look at the examples.

La poste est à côté du supermarché.
The post office is next to the supermarket.
Il habite à côté de chez moi.
He lives next door to me.

la **côtelette** FEM NOUN
chop
une côtelette d'agneau
a lamb chop

le **coton** MASC NOUN
cotton
une chemise en coton
a cotton shirt
le coton hydrophile
cotton wool

le **coton-tige**® MASC NOUN
cotton bud

le **cou** MASC NOUN
neck

couchant MASC ADJECTIVE
le soleil couchant
the setting sun

la **couche** FEM NOUN
nappy

couché MASC ADJECTIVE
(FEM **couchée**)
1 **lying down**
Le chien est couché sur le tapis.
The dog is lying down on the rug.
2 **in bed**
Tu es déjà couché?
Are you in bed already?

le **coucher** MASC NOUN
un coucher de soleil
a sunset

se **coucher** VERB
1 **to go to bed**
Il faut se coucher tôt ce soir.
You must go to bed early tonight.
Tu te couches à quelle heure?
What time do you go to bed?
Je me couche à neuf heures.
I go to bed at nine.
2 **to set**
Le soleil se couche vers neuf heures.
The sun sets at around 9 o'clock.

la **couchette** FEM NOUN
berth

le **coude** MASC NOUN
elbow

coudre VERB
to sew
Tu sais coudre?
Can you sew?

la **couette** FEM NOUN
duvet

les couettes
bunches
Ma petite sœur a des couettes.
My little sister has bunches.

couler VERB
1 **to run**
J'ai le nez qui coule.
My nose is running.
2 **to flow**
La rivière coule lentement.
The river flows slowly.
3 **to leak**
Mon stylo coule.
My pen's leaking.
4 **to sink**
Un bateau a coulé pendant la tempête.
A boat sank during the storm.

la **couleur** FEM NOUN
colour
De quelle couleur est ton stylo?
What colour is your pen?
Elle a les yeux de quelle couleur?
What colour eyes has she got?

C'est de quelle couleur?
What colour is it?

le **couloir** MASC NOUN
corridor

le **coup** MASC NOUN
1 **knock**
2 **blow**

un coup sur la tête
a blow to the head
du premier coup
first time
Il a eu son permis du premier coup.
He passed his driving test first time.

Language tip

*There are lots of **coup de** combinations of words. Look through this list to find the one you need.*

un coup de pied
a kick
un coup de poing
a punch
un coup de feu
a shot
un coup de fil
a ring
Donne-moi un coup de fil ce soir.
Give me a ring this evening.
Tu peux me donner un coup de main?
Can you give me a hand?
Tu vas prendre un coup de soleil!
You'll get sunburnt!
un coup de téléphone
a phone call
un coup de tonnerre
a clap of thunder

coupable

coupable *can be an adjective or a noun.*

A ADJECTIVE
guilty
B MASC/FEM NOUN
culprit

la **coupe** FEM NOUN
cup
la coupe du monde
the World Cup
une coupe de cheveux
a haircut
une coupe de champagne
a glass of champagne

couper VERB
to cut
Attention! Tu vas te couper!
Careful! You're going to cut yourself!
Je vais me faire couper les cheveux.
I'm going to get my hair cut.

le **couple** MASC NOUN
couple

le **couplet** MASC NOUN
verse
le premier couplet
the first verse

la **coupure** FEM NOUN
cut
une coupure de courant
a power cut

la **cour** FEM NOUN
yard
la cour de l'école
the playground

courageux MASC ADJECTIVE
(FEM **courageuse**)
brave

couramment ADVERB
fluently
> Elle parle couramment
> japonais.
> She speaks Japanese fluently.

courant

> **courant** *can be an adjective or a noun.*

A MASC ADJECTIVE
(FEM **courante**)
common
> 'Marie' est un prénom
> courant.
> 'Marie' is a common name.

B MASC NOUN
1 current
> Le courant est fort.
> The current is strong.
> un courant d'air
> a draught
2 power
> une panne de courant
> a power cut
> Tu es au courant?
> Have you heard about it?

le **coureur** MASC NOUN
la **coureuse** FEM NOUN
runner
> un coureur à pied
> a runner
> un coureur cycliste
> a racing cyclist
> un coureur automobile
> a racing driver

courir VERB
to run

> Ne courez pas dans le
> couloir.
> Don't run in the corridor.
> J'ai couru jusqu'à l'école.
> I ran all the way to school.

la **couronne**
FEM NOUN
crown

courons, courez VERB
▷ *see* **courir**
> Courons jusqu'à la barrière!
> Let's run as far as the gate!
> Vous courez trop vite!
> You're running too fast!

le **courriel** MASC NOUN
email

le **courrier** MASC NOUN
mail
> Le facteur apporte le courrier
> à huit heures.
> The postman brings the mail at
> 8 o'clock.
> le courrier électronique
> email

le **cours** MASC NOUN
1 lesson
> un cours d'espagnol
> a Spanish lesson
2 class
> un cours du soir
> an evening class
3 rate
> le cours du change
> the exchange rate

la **course** FEM NOUN
1 running
> la course de fond
> long-distance running
2 race
> une course hippique
> a horse race

French English

a
b
c
d
e
f
g
h
i
j
k
l
m
n
o
p
q
r
s
t
u
v
w
x
y
z

a b **c** d e f g h i j k l m n o p q r s t u v w x y z

3 shopping
J'ai juste une course à faire.
I've just got a bit of shopping to do.
faire les courses
to shop
Je n'aime pas faire les courses au supermarché.
I don't like shopping in supermarkets.

court

> court *can be an adjective or a noun.*

A MASC ADJECTIVE (FEM **courte**)
short
B MASC NOUN
un court de tennis
a tennis court

couru VERB ▷see **courir**
J'ai couru jusqu'à la maison.
I ran all the way home.

le **couscous** MASC NOUN
couscous

> *Did you know…?*
>
> **couscous** *is a grain from North Africa which is often eaten with spicy food.*

le **cousin** MASC NOUN
la **cousine** FEM NOUN
cousin

le **coussin** MASC NOUN
cushion

le **couteau** MASC NOUN
(PL les **couteaux**)
knife

coûter VERB
to cost
Est-ce que ça coûte cher?
Does it cost a lot?

Combien ça coûte?
How much is it?

la **couture** FEM NOUN
sewing
Je n'aime pas la couture.
I don't like sewing.

le **couvercle** MASC NOUN
1 lid
le couvercle de la casserole
the lid of the pan
2 top
le couvercle du pot de confiture
the top of the jam jar

couvert

> couvert *can be an adjective, a noun or part of the verb* **couvrir**.

A MASC ADJECTIVE
(FEM **couverte**)
overcast
Le ciel est couvert.
The sky is overcast.
couvert de
covered with
un arbre couvert de fleurs
a tree covered with blossom
B MASC NOUN
les couverts
cutlery
Les couverts sont dans le tiroir de gauche.
The cutlery is in the left-hand drawer.

c VERB ▷*see* **couvrir**
Il est couvert de boutons.
He's covered with spots.

la **couverture** FEM NOUN
blanket

le **couvre-lit** MASC NOUN
bedspread

couvrir VERB
to cover
Le chien est revenu couvert de boue.
The dog came back covered in mud.
- **se couvrir**
to wrap up/to cloud over

Language tip

se couvrir *has two translations. Look at the examples.*

Couvre-toi bien: il fait froid dehors.
Wrap up well: it's cold outside.
Le ciel se couvre.
The sky's clouding over.

le **CP** MASC NOUN
Year 2

le **crabe** MASC NOUN
crab

cracher VERB
to spit

la **craie** FEM NOUN
chalk

craindre VERB
to fear
Tu n'as rien à craindre.
You've got nothing to fear.

craintif MASC ADJECTIVE
(FEM **craintive**)
timid

la **crampe** FEM NOUN
cramp
J'ai une crampe au pied.
I've got cramp in my foot.

le **crapaud** MASC NOUN
toad

la **cravate**
FEM NOUN
tie

le **crayon**
MASC NOUN
pencil
un crayon de couleur
a coloured pencil
un crayon feutre
a felt-tip pen

la **crèche** FEM NOUN
1 nursery
Ma petite sœur va à la crèche.
My little sister goes to nursery.
2 nativity scene

créer VERB
to create

la **crème** FEM NOUN
cream
la crème anglaise
custard
la crème Chantilly
whipped cream
une crème caramel
a crème caramel
une crème au chocolat
a chocolate dessert

French English

a
b
c
d
e
f
g
h
i
j
k
l
m
n
o
p
q
r
s
t
u
v
w
x
y
z

le **crème** MASC NOUN
white coffee
    un grand crème
    a large white coffee

la **crêpe** FEM NOUN
pancake

la **crêperie** FEM NOUN
pancake restaurant

le **cresson** MASC NOUN
watercress

la **Crète** FEM NOUN
Crete

creuser VERB
to dig

crevé MASC ADJECTIVE
(FEM **crevée**)
  1 punctured
    un pneu crevé
    a puncture
  2 knackered
    Je suis complètement crevé!
    I'm really knackered!

crever VERB
  1 to burst
    Il a crevé mon ballon!
    He's burst my balloon!
  2 to have a puncture
    On a crevé en route.
    We had a puncture on the way.

la **crevette** FEM NOUN
prawn

le **cri** MASC NOUN
scream

crier VERB
to shout

le **crime** MASC NOUN
  1 crime
  2 murder

le **criquet** MASC NOUN
grasshopper

la **crise** FEM NOUN
attack
    une crise d'asthme
    an asthma attack
    une crise de foie
    an upset stomach

critiquer VERB
to criticize

le **crocodile** MASC NOUN
crocodile

croire VERB
to believe
    Je ne te crois pas.
    I don't believe you.
    Tu l'as cru?
    Did you believe him?
    croire que
    to think that
    Tu crois que c'est vrai?
    Do you think that's true?
    Il croit en Dieu.
    He believes in God.

crois VERB ▷*see* **croire**
    Je crois que tu as raison.
    I think you're right.

le **croisement** MASC NOUN
crossroads
    Tournez à gauche au croisement.
    Turn left at the crossroads.

croiser VERB
croiser les bras
to fold one's arms
croiser les jambes
to cross one's legs
- **se croiser**
to pass each other
Nous nous croisons dans la rue tous les matins.
We pass each other on the street every morning.

le **croissant** MASC NOUN
croissant

croit VERB ▷see **croire**
Il croit encore au Père Noël!
He still believes in Santa!

la **croix** FEM NOUN
cross

le **croque-madame** MASC NOUN
le **croque-monsieur** MASC NOUN

Did you know…?

A **croque-monsieur** *is a toasted ham and cheese sandwich.*
A **croque-madame** *has an added fried egg.*

croquer VERB
to munch

la **croûte** FEM NOUN
1 crust
en croûte
in pastry
2 rind
Mon chat aime la croûte du fromage.
My cat likes cheese rind.
3 scab
J'ai une croûte sur le genou.
I've got a scab on my knee.

le **croûton** MASC NOUN
1 end of a baguette
2 crouton
Tu veux des croûtons dans ta soupe?
Would you like some croutons in your soup?

cru

cru *can be an adjective or part of the verb* **croire**.

A MASC ADJECTIVE (FEM **crue**)
raw
la viande crue
raw meat
le jambon cru
Parma ham
B VERB ▷see **croire**
Je l'ai cru.
I believed him.

la **cruche** FEM NOUN
jug

les **crudités** FEM PL NOUN
assorted raw vegetables

cruel MASC ADJECTIVE (FEM **cruelle**)
cruel

les **crustacés** MASC PL NOUN
shellfish

le **cube** MASC NOUN
cube

cueillir VERB
to pick
J'ai cueilli des fleurs dans le jardin.
I picked some flowers in the garden.

la **cuiller** FEM NOUN
la **cuillère**
spoon

une cuiller à café
a teaspoon
une cuiller à soupe
a tablespoon

la **cuillerée** FEM NOUN
spoonful

le **cuir** MASC NOUN
leather
un sac en cuir
a leather bag

cuire VERB
to cook
faire cuire
to cook
'faire cuire pendant une heure'
'cook for one hour'
bien cuit
well done
trop cuit
overdone

la **cuisine** FEM NOUN
1 kitchen

La cuisine est très grande.
The kitchen is very big.
2 food
Tu aimes la cuisine française?
Do you like French food?

faire la cuisine
to cook
Je ne fais jamais la cuisine.
I never cook.

cuisiner VERB
to cook
J'aime beaucoup cuisiner.
I love cooking.

le **cuisinier** MASC NOUN
cook

la **cuisinière** FEM NOUN
1 cook
C'est une bonne cuisinière.
She's a good cook.
2 cooker
une cuisinière à gaz
a gas cooker

la **cuisse** FEM NOUN
thigh
une cuisse de poulet
a chicken leg

la **cuisson** FEM NOUN
cooking
'une heure de cuisson'
'cooking time: one hour'

cuit VERB ▷see **cuire**
Est-ce que c'est cuit?
Is it cooked?

le **cuivre** MASC NOUN
copper

la **culotte** FEM NOUN
knickers

le **cultivateur** MASC NOUN
la **cultivatrice** FEM NOUN
farmer

cultiver VERB
to grow
Il cultive des légumes.
He grows vegetables.

le **curé** MASC NOUN
  parish priest

curieux MASC ADJECTIVE
  (FEM **curieuse**)
  curious

le **curseur** MASC NOUN
  cursor

le **cybercafé** MASC NOUN
  internet café

cyclable ADJECTIVE
  une piste cyclable
  a cycle track

le **cyclisme** MASC NOUN
  cycling

le/la **cycliste** MASC/FEM NOUN
  cyclist

le **cyclone** MASC NOUN
  hurricane

le **cygne** MASC NOUN
  swan

French English

a
b
c
d
e
f
g
h
i
j
k
l
m
n
o
p
q
r
s
t
u
v
w
x
y
z

D d

d'

d' can be an article or a preposition.

Language tip
de changes to **d'** *before a vowel sound. See also* **du (=de+le)** *and* **des (=de+les).**

A ARTICLE
any
Je n'ai pas d'argent.
I haven't got any money.
Je n'ai pas d'animal domestique à la maison.
I haven't got a pet.
B PREPOSITION
1 of
une bouteille d'orangina
a bottle of orangina
la voiture d'Hélène
Hélène's car
un bébé d'un an
a one-year-old baby
2 from
une lettre d'Olivier
a letter from Olivier

le **daim** MASC NOUN
suede
une veste en daim
a suede jacket

la **dame** FEM NOUN
1 lady
une dame de service
a dinner lady
2 queen
la dame de pique
the queen of spades
les dames
draughts

un jeu de dames
a game of draughts

le **Danemark** MASC NOUN
Denmark

dangereux MASC ADJECTIVE
(FEM **dangereuse**)
dangerous

danois MASC NOUN, MASC ADJECTIVE (FEM **danoise**)
Danish

le **Danois** MASC NOUN
la **Danoise** FEM NOUN
Dane

dans PREPOSITION
in
Il est dans sa chambre.
He's in his bedroom.
dans deux mois
in two months

la **danse** FEM NOUN
dance
la danse classique
ballet
Je fais de la danse.
I go to dancing classes.

danser VERB
to dance

le **danseur** MASC NOUN
la **danseuse**
FEM NOUN
dancer

la **date** FEM NOUN
date

Quelle est ta date de naissance?
What's your date of birth?
Quelle est la date de ton anniversaire?
What date is your birthday?

Quelle est la date aujourd'hui?
What's the date today?

le **dauphin** MASC NOUN
dolphin

de

de can be an article or a preposition.

Language tip

de changes to **d'** *before a vowel sound. See also* **du (=de+le)** *and* **des (=de+les).**

A ARTICLE

Language tip

You can use **de** *to mean either* **some** *or* **any.**

Je voudrais de l'eau.
I'd like some water.
du pain et de la confiture
bread and jam
Il n'a pas de frères et sœurs.
He hasn't got any brothers or sisters.
Il n'y a plus de biscuits.
There aren't any more biscuits.

B PREPOSITION

1 of
un paquet de biscuits
a packet of biscuits

la voiture de Paul
Paul's car
la voiture de mes parents
my parents' car
un billet de dix euros
a ten-euro note

2 from
de Londres à Paris
from London to Paris
Il vient de Londres.
He comes from London.
une lettre de Victor
a letter from Victor

3 in
à une heure de l'après-midi
at one o'clock in the afternoon

le **dé** MASC NOUN
dice
Lance le dé.
Throw the dice.

débarrasser VERB
to clear
Tu peux débarrasser la table, s'il te plaît?
Can you clear the table please?

debout ADVERB
Debout!
Get up!

le **début** MASC NOUN
beginning
au début
at the beginning
début mai
in early May

le **débutant** MASC NOUN
la **débutante** FEM NOUN
beginner

le **décalage horaire** MASC NOUN
time difference

French English

a
b
c
d
e
f
g
h
i
j
k
l
m
n
o
p
q
r
s
t
u
v
w
x
y
z

Il y a une heure de décalage horaire entre la France et la Grande-Bretagne.
There's an hour's time difference between France and Britain.

décalquer VERB
to trace
> **Décalquez la carte de France.**
> Trace the map of France.

décapotable ADJECTIVE
> **une voiture décapotable**
> a convertible

décembre MASC NOUN
December
> **en décembre**
> in December
> **le dix décembre**
> the tenth of December

décevoir VERB
to disappoint

déchirer VERB
to tear
> **Le poster est tout déchiré.**
> The poster is all torn.

décider VERB
to decide
> **J'ai décidé d'y aller.**
> I've decided to go.

le **décollage** MASC NOUN
takeoff

décoller VERB
to take off
> **L'avion a décollé avec dix minutes de retard.**
> The plane took off ten minutes late.

se **décontracter** VERB
to relax

Il fait du yoga pour se décontracter.
He goes to yoga to relax.

le **décorateur** MASC NOUN
la **décoratrice** FEM NOUN
interior decorator

les **décorations** FEM PL NOUN
decorations
> **les décorations de Noël**
> the Christmas decorations

décorer VERB
to decorate

découper VERB
to cut out

se **décourager** VERB
> **Ne te décourage pas!**
> Don't give up!

la **découverte** FEM NOUN
discovery

découvrir VERB
to discover
> **Christophe Colomb a découvert l'Amérique en 1492.**
> Christopher Colombus discovered America in 1492.

décrire VERB
to describe
> **Décris quelqu'un de célèbre.**
> Describe somebody famous.

déçu MASC ADJECTIVE
(FEM **déçue**)
disappointed

dedans ADVERB
inside
> **C'est une jolie boîte: qu'est-ce qu'il y a dedans?**
> That's a nice box: what's in it?

French **English**

défendre VERB
1 **to defend**
Il ne sait pas se défendre.
He doesn't know how to defend himself.
2 **to forbid**
Je te défends de lui dire.
I forbid you to tell her.

défendu MASC ADJECTIVE
(FEM **défendue**)
forbidden
C'est défendu.
It's not allowed.

la **défense** FEM NOUN
tusk

une défense d'éléphant
an elephant's tusk
'défense de fumer'
'no smoking'

le **défilé** MASC NOUN
parade
un défilé de mode
a fashion show

dégoûtant MASC ADJECTIVE
(FEM **dégoûtante**)
disgusting

le **degré** MASC NOUN
degree
Il fait trente degrés à l'ombre.
It's thirty degrees in the shade.

le **déguisement** MASC NOUN
dressing-up costume
un déguisement de sorcière
a witch's costume

se **déguiser** VERB
to dress up
J'aime me déguiser.
I like dressing up.

la **dégustation** FEM NOUN
tasting

dehors ADVERB
outside
Je t'attends dehors.
I'll wait for you outside.

déjà ADVERB
1 **already**
J'ai déjà fini.
I've already finished.
2 **before**
Tu es déjà venu en France?
Have you been to France before?

déjeuner

déjeuner can be a noun or a verb.

A MASC NOUN
lunch
Pour le déjeuner, je mange souvent un sandwich.
I often have a sandwich for lunch.
B VERB
to have lunch
Je déjeune à midi et demi.
I have lunch at half past twelve.

le **délégué** MASC NOUN
la **déléguée** FEM NOUN
representative
les délégués de classe
the class representatives

Did you know...?

In French schools, each class elects two délégués de classe, one boy and one girl.

77

délicieux MASC ADJECTIVE
(FEM **délicieuse**)
delicious

le **deltaplane** MASC NOUN
hang-glider
J'aimerais faire du
deltaplane.
I'd like to go hang-gliding.

demain ADVERB
tomorrow

À demain!
See you tomorrow!

demander VERB
to ask for
J'ai demandé la permission.
I've asked for permission.
Je vais demander à mes
parents si je peux sortir.
I'll ask my parents if I can go out.

Language tip
Be careful! **demander** does not
mean the same as **to demand**.

■ se demander
to wonder
Je me demande quelle heure
il est.
I wonder what time it is.

le **déménagement** MASC
NOUN
move
un camion de déménagement
a removal van

déménager VERB
to move house
Nous déménageons dans
un mois.
We're moving house in a
month's time.

le **déménageur** MASC NOUN
removal man

demi MASC ADJECTIVE (FEM **demie**)
half
Il a trois ans et demi.
He's three and a half.
Il est trois heures et demie.
It's half past three.

Il est midi et demi.
It's half past twelve.

la **demi-baguette** FEM NOUN
half a baguette

le **demi-cercle** MASC NOUN
semicircle
en demi-cercle
in a semicircle

la **demi-douzaine** FEM NOUN
half a dozen
une demi-douzaine d'œufs
half a dozen eggs

la **demi-finale** FEM NOUN
semifinal

le **demi-frère** MASC NOUN
half-brother
mon demi-frère
my half brother

la **demi-heure** FEM NOUN
half an hour
dans une demi-heure
in half an hour
toutes les demi-heures
every half an hour

le **demi-litre** MASC NOUN
half a litre
un demi-litre de lait
half a litre of milk

la **demi-livre** FEM NOUN
half a pound
une demi-livre de tomates
half a pound of tomatoes

Did you know...?
A **demi-livre** *is 250g.*

le/la **demi-pensionnaire**
MASC/FEM NOUN

Did you know...?
In French secondary schools, pupils are described as **externe** *if they go home for lunch,* **demi-pensionnaire** *if they have a school lunch, or* **interne** *if they stay at the school as a boarder.*

demi-sel MASC, FEM, PL
ADJECTIVE
    du beurre demi-sel
    slightly salted butter

la **demi-sœur** FEM NOUN
half-sister
    ma demi-soeur
    my half-sister

le **demi-tour** MASC NOUN
    faire demi-tour
    to turn back
    Il est temps de faire demi-tour.
    It's time we turned back.

démodé MASC ADJECTIVE
(FEM **démodée**)
old-fashioned

la **demoiselle** FEM NOUN
young lady
    une demoiselle d'honneur
    a bridesmaid

démolir VERB
to demolish

la **dent** FEM NOUN
tooth
    une dent de lait
    a milk tooth

    une dent de sagesse
    a wisdom tooth

la **dentelle** FEM NOUN
lace

le **dentifrice** MASC NOUN
toothpaste

le/la **dentiste** MASC/FEM NOUN
dentist

le **dépanneur** MASC NOUN
(*Canada*)
convenience store

la **dépanneuse** FEM NOUN
breakdown lorry

le **départ** MASC NOUN
departure
    Le départ est à onze heures quinze.
    The departure is at 11.15.
    Je vais lui téléphoner la veille de son départ.
    I'll phone him the day before he leaves.

le **département**
MASC NOUN
1 administrative region
    le département du Vaucluse
    the Vaucluse département

Did you know...?
France is divided into 96 **départements**, *which are similar to counties in the UK.*

2 department
    le département d'anglais à l'université
    the English department at the university

a b c d e f g h i j k l m n o p q r s t u v w x y z

se **dépêcher** VERB
to hurry

> **Dépêche-toi!**
> Hurry up!

dépendre VERB
> **Ça dépend du temps.**
> It depends on the weather.

dépenser VERB
to spend
> **J'ai dépensé tout mon argent.**
> I've spent all my money.

le **dépliant** MASC NOUN
leaflet

déposer VERB
to drop
> **Tu peux me déposer à la piscine?**
> Can you drop me at the swimming pool?

depuis PREPOSITION
1 **since**
> **J'habite à Paris depuis 2005.**
> I've been living in Paris since 2005.
> **depuis que**
> since
> **Il a plu tous les jours depuis qu'il est arrivé.**
> It's rained every day since he arrived.

2 **for**

> **Il habite Paris depuis cinq ans.**
> He's been living in Paris for five years.
3 **Tu le connais depuis combien de temps?**
> How long have you known him?
> **Tu le connais depuis quand?**
> How long have you known him?

> **Depuis quand?**
> How long?
> **depuis 2006**
> since 2006
> **Depuis combien de temps?**
> How long?
> **depuis cinq ans**
> for five years

déranger VERB
1 **to bother**
> **Excusez-moi de vous déranger.**
> I'm sorry to bother you.
2 **to mess up**
> **Ne dérange pas mes livres, s'il te plaît.**
> Don't mess up my books, please.

dernier MASC ADJECTIVE
(FEM **dernière**)
1 **last**
> **Il est arrivé dernier.**
> He arrived last.
> **la dernière fois**
> the last time
> **en dernier**
> last
> **Ajoutez le lait en dernier.**
> Put the milk in last.
2 **latest**
> **le dernier film de Spielberg**
> Spielberg's latest film

derrière

> **derrière** *can be a preposition, an adverb or a noun.*

French English

a b c d e f g h i j k l m n o p q r s t u v w x y z

A PREPOSITION, ADVERB
behind
derrière moi
behind me
derrière la télévision
behind the television

Devant ou derrière?
In front or behind?

B MASC NOUN
1 back
la porte de derrière
the back door
2 backside
un coup de pied dans le derrière
a kick up the backside

des ARTICLE

Language tip

des *is made up of* de + les.

1 some
Tu veux des chips?
Would you like some crisps?

Language tip

des *is sometimes not translated in English.*

J'ai des cousins en France.
I have cousins in France.
pendant des mois
for months
2 any
Tu as des frères?
Have you got any brothers?
3 of the
la fin des vacances
the end of the holidays

la voiture des Durand
the Durands' car
4 from
Il arrive des États-Unis.
He's arriving from the United States.

dès PREPOSITION
from
dès le mois de novembre
from November
dès le début
right from the start
dès que
as soon as
Appelle-moi dès que tu arrives.
Phone me as soon as you get there.
Je t'appelle dès mon retour.
I'll phone you as soon as I get back.

désagréable ADJECTIVE
unpleasant

le **désastre** MASC NOUN
disaster

descendre VERB
1 to go down
Je suis tombé en descendant l'escalier.
I fell as I was going down the stairs.
2 to come down
Attends en bas; je descends!
Wait downstairs; I'm coming down!
3 to get down
Vous pouvez descendre ma valise, s'il vous plaît?
Can you get my suitcase down, please?
4 to get off
Nous descendons à la prochaine station.
We're getting off at the next station.

French English

a
b
c
d
e
f
g
h
i
j
k
l
m
n
o
p
q
r
s
t
u
v
w
x
y
z

81

French English

a
b
c
d
e
f
g
h
i
j
k
l
m
n
o
p
q
r
s
t
u
v
w
x
y
z

la **descente** FEM NOUN
slope
une descente abrupte
a steep slope

Language tip

descente *is related to the verb*
descendre *which means 'to go
down', so* **une descente** *is a slope
that goes downhill.*

la **description** FEM NOUN
description

désert

désert *can be an adjective or a
noun.*

A MASC ADJECTIVE (FEM **déserte**)
deserted
**Le dimanche, le centre
commercial est désert.**
On Sundays the shopping centre
is deserted.
une île déserte
a desert island
B MASC NOUN
desert
le désert du Sahara
the Sahara desert

déshabiller VERB
to undress
■ se déshabiller
to get undressed
**Déshabille-toi, mets ton
pyjama et vas te coucher.**
Get undressed, put on your
pyjamas and go to bed.

désirer VERB
to want
**Vous désirez? —
Je voudrais un coca.**
What would you like? —
I'd like a coke.

désolé MASC ADJECTIVE
(FEM **désolée**)
sorry
Je suis vraiment désolé.
I'm very sorry.

Désolé!
Sorry!

désordonné MASC ADJECTIVE
(FEM **désordonnée**)
untidy

le **désordre** MASC NOUN
untidiness

**Quel
désordre!**
What a mess!
en désordre
in a mess
**Sa chambre est toujours en
désordre.**
His bedroom is always in a
mess.

le **dessert** MASC NOUN
pudding
**Qu'est-ce que vous désirez
comme dessert?**
What would you like for pudding?

le **dessin** MASC NOUN
drawing
**C'est un dessin de ma petite
sœur.**
It's a drawing my little sister did.
un dessin animé
a cartoon

82

un dessin humoristique
a cartoon

dessiner
VERB
to draw
Dessinez votre animal préféré.
Draw your favourite animal.

dessous

dessous can be an adverb or a noun.

A ADVERB
underneath
Le prix du vase est marqué dessous.
The price of the vase is marked underneath.
ci-dessous
below
Complétez les phrases ci-dessous.
Complete the sentences below.
B MASC NOUN
les voisins du dessous
the downstairs neighbours

dessus

dessus can be an adverb or a noun.

A ADVERB
on top
un gâteau avec des bougies dessus
a cake with candles on top

au-dessus
above
au-dessus du lit
above the bed
ci-dessus
above
l'exemple ci-dessus
the example above
là-dessus
on that
Tu peux écrire là-dessus.
You can write on that.
par-dessus
over
Tu peux sauter par-dessus la barrière?
Can you jump over the gate?
B MASC NOUN
les voisins du dessus
the upstairs neighbours

la **destination** FEM NOUN
destination
les passagers à destination de Paris
passengers travelling to Paris

le **détail** MASC NOUN
detail
en détail
in detail

le **détective** MASC NOUN
detective
un détective privé
a private detective

détendre VERB
to relax
La lecture, ça me détend.
I find reading relaxing.
■ **se détendre**
to relax
J'écoute de la musique pour me détendre.
I listen to music to relax.

détester VERB
to hate
>Je déteste les épinards.
>I hate spinach.

deux NUMBER
two
>Il est deux heures.
>It's two o'clock.
>Elle a deux ans.
>She's two.
>**deux fois**
>twice
>**tous les deux**
>both
>**Allez-y toutes les deux.**
>Go on, both of you.

>**le deux février**
>the second of February

deuxième ADJECTIVE
second
>au deuxième étage
>on the second floor

devant

>devant *can be a preposition,*
>*an adverb or a noun.*

A PREPOSITION
in front of
>Il y a un grand jardin devant
>la maison.
>There's a big garden in front of
>the house.
>**passer devant**
>to go past
>**Nous passons tous les jours**
>**devant chez lui.**
>We go past his house every day.

B ADVERB
in front
>Il marche toujours devant.
>He always walks in front.

>Allez-y, passez devant.
>Come on, you go in front.

C MASC NOUN
front
>**le devant de la maison**
>the front of the house
>**les pattes de devant**
>the front legs

développer VERB
to develop

devenir VERB
to become
>Ça devient de plus en plus
>difficile.
>It's becoming more and more
>difficult.

devez VERB ▷*see* devoir
>Vous devez attendre ici.
>You've got to wait here.

deviner VERB
to guess
>**Devine à quel animal je**
>**pense.**
>Guess which animal I'm thinking
>of.

la **devinette** FEM NOUN
riddle

devoir VERB
1 to have to
>Je dois partir.
>I've got to go.
2 must
>Tu dois être fatigué.
>You must be tired.

les **devoirs** MASC PL NOUN
homework
>Quand je rentre de l'école,
>je fais mes devoirs.
>When I get home from school I
>do my homework.

devons VERB ▷*see* devoir
Nous devons partir tôt.
We have to leave early.

diabétique ADJECTIVE
diabetic

le **diable** MASC NOUN
devil

le **diabolo** MASC NOUN
fruit cordial and lemonade
un diabolo menthe
a mint cordial and lemonade

le **dialogue** MASC NOUN
dialogue

le **diamant** MASC NOUN
diamond

la **diapositive** FEM NOUN
slide

la **diarrhée** FEM NOUN
diarrhoea
J'ai la diarrhée.
I've got diarrhoea.

la **dictée** FEM NOUN
dictation
La maîtresse nous fait faire une dictée tous les samedis matins.
The teacher gives us a dictation every Saturday morning.

Did you know…?

French pupils do a lot of dictation exercises, to help them learn to spell. French is difficult to spell because there are a lot of letters that are not pronounced – such as the 's' on the end of plural words.

dicter VERB
to dictate

le **dictionnaire** MASC NOUN
dictionary
Cherchez le mot 'piscine' dans le dictionnaire.
Look up the word 'piscine' in the dictionary.

diététique ADJECTIVE
un magasin diététique
a health food shop

le **dieu** MASC NOUN (PL les **dieux**)
god
Dieu
God

la **différence** FEM NOUN
difference
Quelle est la différence entre les écoles françaises et anglaises?
What's the difference between French and British schools?

différent MASC ADJECTIVE
(FEM **différente**)
1 different
Je n'aime pas le bleu. Je voudrais une couleur différente.
I don't like blue. I'd like a different colour.

French English

a
b
c
d
e
f
g
h
i
j
k
l
m
n
o
p
q
r
s
t
u
v
w
x
y
z

2 various
différents parfums de glace
various flavours of ice cream

difficile ADJECTIVE
difficult
Son accent est difficile à comprendre.
His accent is difficult to understand.

le **dimanche** MASC NOUN
1 Sunday
Aujourd'hui, nous sommes dimanche.
It's Sunday today.
2 on Sunday
Dimanche, nous allons déjeuner chez mes grands-parents.
On Sunday we're having lunch at my grandparents'.
Le dimanche, je fais la grasse matinée.
I have a lie-in on Sundays.

tous les dimanches
every Sunday
le dimanche
on Sundays
dimanche dernier
last Sunday
dimanche prochain
next Sunday
À dimanche!
See you on Sunday!

le **diminutif** MASC NOUN
pet name
Loulou est le diminutif de Louise.
Loulou is Louise's pet name.

la **dinde** FEM NOUN
turkey
la dinde de Noël
the Christmas turkey

Language tip
le dindon *is a live turkey;* **la dinde** *is the bird you eat.*

le **dindon** MASC NOUN
turkey

dîner

dîner can be a verb or a noun.

A VERB
to have dinner
Le soir, nous dînons à sept heures.
We have dinner at seven o'clock in the evening.
B MASC NOUN
dinner
Le dîner est à quelle heure?
What time is dinner?

le **diplôme** MASC NOUN
qualification
Il n'a aucun diplôme.
He hasn't got any qualifications.

dire VERB
1 to say
Comment est-ce qu'on dit 'dog' en français?
How do you say 'dog' in French?
2 to tell
Je vais te dire un secret.
I'm going to tell you a secret.
Elle me dit toujours la vérité.
She always tells me the truth.

Ma mère me dit toujours de ranger ma chambre.
My mother is always telling me to tidy up my room.
Beaucoup de gens me disent que je ressemble à ma mère.
Lots of people tell me I look like my mother.
dire des bêtises
to talk nonsense

le **directeur** MASC NOUN
la **directrice** FEM NOUN
1 headteacher
Elle est directrice.
She's a headteacher.
2 manager
Il est directeur du personnel.
He's a personnel manager.

dis VERB ▷ see **dire**
Dis-moi la vérité!
Tell me the truth!

la **discothèque** FEM NOUN
club
Florence aime aller danser dans les discothèques.
Florence likes going clubbing.

discuter VERB
to talk

Nous discutons toujours à la récréation.
We always talk at break time.

disent VERB ▷ see **dire**
Qu'est-ce qu'ils disent?
What are they saying?

disons VERB ▷ see **dire**
Nous disons des bêtises.
We're talking nonsense.

disparaître VERB
to disappear
Il peut faire disparaître le lapin.
He can make the rabbit disappear.

la **disparition** FEM NOUN
disappearance
une espèce en voie de disparition
an endangered species

dispensé MASC ADJECTIVE
(FEM **dispensée**)
Elle est dispensée de gymnastique.
She's excused from gym.

la **dispute** FEM NOUN
argument
Depuis notre dispute, elle ne me parle plus.
She hasn't been speaking to me since our argument.

se **disputer** VERB
to argue
Je me dispute souvent avec ma sœur.
I often argue with my sister.
se faire disputer
to get a telling-off
Je vais me faire disputer par ma mère si je ne rentre pas tout de suite.
I'll get a telling-off from my mother if I don't go home now.

French English

a
b
c
d
e
f
g
h
i
j
k
l
m
n
o
p
q
r
s
t
u
v
w
x
y
z

le **disque** MASC NOUN
record
   un disque compact
   a compact disc

la **distance** FEM NOUN
distance
   **Ton école est à quelle
   distance d'ici?**
   How far is your school from
   here?

distrait MASC ADJECTIVE
(FEM **distraite**)
absent-minded

distribuer VERB
  1 **to give out**
   **Distribue les livres, s'il te
   plaît.**
   Give out the books please.
  2 **to deal**
   **Distribue les cartes, s'il
   te plaît.**
   Deal the cards please.

le **distributeur** MASC NOUN
   un distributeur automatique
   a vending machine
   un distributeur de billets
   a cash dispenser

dit VERB ▷see **dire**
   Elle ne me dit jamais rien.
   She never tells me anything.
   Je te l'ai dit hier.
   I told you yesterday.

dites VERB ▷see **dire**
   Dites-moi ce que vous pensez.
   Tell me what you think.

diviser VERB
  to divide
   **Quatre divisé par deux égale
   deux.**
   Four divided by two equals two.

divorcé MASC ADJECTIVE
(FEM **divorcée**)
divorced
   Mes parents sont divorcés.
   My parents are divorced.

divorcer VERB
  to get divorced
   Ils ont décidé de divorcer.
   They've decided to get
   divorced.

dix NUMBER
  ten
   Elle a dix ans.
   She's ten.
   Il est dix heures.
   It's ten o'clock.

le dix février
the tenth of February

dix-huit NUMBER
  eighteen
   Elle a dix-huit ans.
   She's eighteen.
   Il est dix-huit heures.
   It's six o'clock.

le dix-huit mars
the eighteenth of March

Did you know…?
*The 24-hour clock is used in France
for travel times, appointments and
other formal situations.*

dixième ADJECTIVE
  tenth
   au dixième étage
   on the tenth floor

dix-neuf NUMBER
  nineteen
   Elle a dix-neuf ans.
   She's nineteen.

Il est dix-neuf heures.
It's seven o'clock.

le dix-neuf avril
the nineteenth of April

dix-sept NUMBER
seventeen
Elle a dix-sept ans.
She's seventeen.
Il est dix-sept heures.
It's five o'clock.

le dix-sept avril
the seventeenth of April

la **dizaine** FEM NOUN
about ten
une dizaine de jours
about ten days

le **docteur** MASC NOUN
doctor
Je vais chez le docteur.
I'm going to the doctor's.

le **documentaire** MASC NOUN
documentary

le/la **documentaliste** MASC/
FEM NOUN
librarian

le **doigt** MASC NOUN
finger
les doigts de pied
the toes

dois, doit, doivent VERB
▷ see **devoir**
Je dois mettre la table.
I have to lay the table.
Il doit être tard.
It must be late.
Ils doivent rentrer à huit heures.
They have to be home at eight
o'clock.

domestique

domestique *can be an adjective
or a noun.*

A ADJECTIVE
les animaux domestiques
pets
B MASC/FEM NOUN
servant

le **domicile** MASC NOUN
à domicile
at home
Il travaille à domicile.
He works at home.

les **dominos** MASC PL NOUN
dominoes
**Je joue aux dominos avec
ma sœur.**
I play dominoes with my sister.

le **dommage** MASC NOUN
C'est dommage.
It's a shame.

Quel dommage!
What a shame!

donc CONJUNCTION
so
**Il fait beau, donc nous
pouvons faire un pique-
nique.**
The weather's nice, so we can
have a picnic.

donner VERB
to give
**Elle me donne toujours des
bonbons.**
She always gives me sweets.
Ça me donne faim.
That makes me feel hungry.

dont PRONOUN
1 of which

deux livres, dont l'un est en anglais
two books, one of which is in English
le prix dont il est si fier
the prize he's so proud of
2 **of whom**
dix blessés, dont deux grièvement
ten people injured, two of them seriously
la fille dont je t'ai parlé
the girl I told you about

doré MASC ADJECTIVE (FEM **dorée**)
golden

dormir VERB
1 **to sleep**
Tu as bien dormi?
Did you sleep well?
2 **to be asleep**
Ne faites pas de bruit, il dort.
Don't make a noise, he's asleep.

le **dortoir** MASC NOUN
dormitory

le **dos** MASC NOUN
back
dos à dos
back to back
J'ai mal au dos.
I've got backache.
dans mon dos
behind my back
Elle me critique dans mon dos.
She criticizes me behind my back.

le dos crawlé
the backstroke

le **dossier** MASC NOUN
1 **file**
une pile de dossiers
a stack of files
2 **report**
un bon dossier scolaire
a good school report
3 **back**
le dossier de la chaise
the back of the chair

la **douane** FEM NOUN
customs
un contrôle de douane
a customs inspection

le **douanier** MASC NOUN
customs officer

le **double** MASC NOUN
le double
twice as much
Il gagne le double.
He earns twice as much.
le double du prix normal
twice the normal price
en double
in duplicate
Garde cette photo, je l'ai en double.
Keep this photo, I've got a copy of it.

doublé MASC ADJECTIVE
(FEM **doublée**)
dubbed
un film doublé
a dubbed film

douce FEM ADJECTIVE ▷ see **doux**
une peau douce
soft skin

doucement ADVERB
  1 **gently**
    Il a frappé doucement à la porte.
    He knocked gently at the door.
  2 **slowly**
    Je ne comprends pas, parle plus doucement.
    I don't understand, speak more slowly.

la **douche** FEM NOUN
  shower

    Je prends une douche tous les matins.
    I have a shower every morning.

se **doucher** VERB
  to have a shower
    Je me douche le matin.
    I have a shower in the morning.

doué MASC ADJECTIVE (FEM **douée**)
  talented
    Il est doué en maths.
    He's good at maths.

la **douleur** FEM NOUN
  pain

le **doute** MASC NOUN
  doubt
    sans doute
    probably

se **douter** VERB
  se douter de
    to suspect

Elle ne se doute de rien.
She doesn't suspect anything.
Je m'en doutais.
I thought as much.

Douvres NOUN
  Dover

doux MASC ADJECTIVE
(FEM **douce**)
  1 **soft**
    un tissu doux
    soft material
  2 **sweet**
    du cidre doux
    sweet cider
  3 **mild**
    Il fait doux aujourd'hui.
    It's mild today.
  4 **gentle**
    C'est quelqu'un de très doux.
    He's a very gentle person.

la **douzaine** FEM NOUN
  dozen
    une douzaine d'œufs
    a dozen eggs
    une douzaine de personnes
    about twelve people

douze NUMBER
  twelve
    Il a douze ans.
    He's twelve.

le douze février
the twelfth of February

douzième ADJECTIVE
  twelfth
    au douzième étage
    on the twelfth floor

la **dragée** FEM NOUN
  sugared almond

Did you know…?
French people give **dragées** *to family and friends at weddings and christenings.*

le **drap** MASC NOUN
sheet

le **drapeau** MASC NOUN
(PL les **drapeaux**)
flag

dressé MASC ADJECTIVE
(FEM **dressée**)
trained
un chien bien dressé
a well-trained dog

la **droguerie** FEM NOUN
hardware shop

droit

droit can be an adjective or a noun.

A MASC ADJECTIVE (FEM **droite**)
1 right
la jambe droite
the right leg
le côté droit
the right-hand side
2 straight
une ligne droite
a straight line
Tiens-toi droite sur ta chaise!
Sit up straight on your chair!
Allez tout droit.
Go straight on.

tout droit
straight on

B MASC NOUN
law
un étudiant en droit
a law student
Tu as le droit de sortir?
Are you allowed to go out?

Je n'ai pas le droit d'aller en ville toute seule.
I'm not allowed to go into town by myself.

la **droite** FEM NOUN
right
sur votre droite
on your right
à droite
right/on the right

Language tip
à droite *has two translations. Look at the examples.*

Tournez à droite.
Turn right.
Prenez la troisième rue à droite.
Take the third street on the right.

C'est à droite.
It's on your right.
la deuxième rue à droite
the second street on the right

droitier MASC ADJECTIVE
(FEM **droitière**)
right-handed
Elle est droitière.
She's right-handed.

drôle ADJECTIVE
funny

Ça n'est pas drôle.
It's not funny.
un drôle de temps
funny weather

le **dromadaire**
MASC NOUN
camel

du ARTICLE

Language tip
du *is made up of* **de** + **le**.

1 **some**
Tu veux du fromage?
Would you like some cheese?

2 **any**
Tu as du chocolat?
Have you got any chocolate?

3 **of the**
la porte du garage
the door of the garage
la femme du directeur
the headmaster's wife

4 **from**
Il rentre du Canada.
He's back from Canada.
à sept heures du soir
at seven o'clock in the evening

le **duc** MASC NOUN
duke

la **duchesse** FEM NOUN
duchess

dur

dur *can be an adjective or an adverb.*

A MASC ADJECTIVE (FEM **dure**)
hard
Il est dur avec moi.
He's hard on me.

B ADVERB
hard
Elle travaille dur à l'école.
She works hard at school.

durant PREPOSITION

1 **during**
durant la nuit
during the night

2 **for**
durant des années
for years

durer VERB
to last
La leçon dure une heure.
The lesson lasts an hour.

dyslexique ADJECTIVE
dyslexic

French English

a
b
c
d
e
f
g
h
i
j
k
l
m
n
o
p
q
r
s
t
u
v
w
x
y
z

l' **eau** FEM NOUN
water
>**Je voudrais de l'eau.**
>I'd like some water.
>**Qu'est-ce que tu veux boire?**
>**— De l'eau.**
>What would you like to drink?
>– Water.
>**l'eau minérale**
>mineral water
>**l'eau plate**
>still water
>**l'eau gazeuse**
>fizzy water

l' **écart** MASC NOUN
>**Je sais faire le grand écart.**
>I can do the splits.

l' **échalote** FEM NOUN
shallot

l' **échange** MASC NOUN
exchange
>**en échange de**
>in exchange for

échanger VERB
to swap
>**Je t'échange cet autocollant**
>**contre celui-là.**
>I'll swap you this sticker for that
>one.

s' **échapper** VERB
to escape

l' **écharpe** FEM NOUN
scarf

s' **échauffer** VERB
to warm up
>**Nous allons faire quelques**
>**exercices pour nous**
>**échauffer.**
>We're going to do some
>exercises to warm up.

les **échecs** MASC PL NOUN
chess
>**Je joue aux échecs.**
>I play chess.

l' **échelle** FEM NOUN
ladder

l' **éclair** MASC NOUN
flash of lightning
>**un éclair au chocolat**
>a chocolate éclair

l' **école** FEM NOUN
school
>**aller à l'école**
>to go to school
>**Je vais à l'école avec ma**
>**sœur.**
>I go to school with my sister.
>**une école privée**
>a private school
>**une école publique**
>a state school
>**une école maternelle**
>a nursery school
>**une école primaire**
>a primary school

Did you know…?

French children go to l'école
maternelle *when they are three,*
and stay there until they are six.
They then go to l'école primaire
and stay there until they are 11.

l' **écolier** MASC NOUN
schoolboy

l' **écolière** FEM NOUN
schoolgirl

les **économies** FEM PL NOUN
savings
Je dois faire des économies.
I must save up.

économiser VERB
to save up
J'économise pour m'acheter une nouvelle raquette de tennis.
I'm saving up to buy a new tennis racquet.

écossais MASC ADJECTIVE
(FEM **écossaise**)
1 Scottish
Elle est écossaise.
She's Scottish.
2 tartan
une jupe écossaise
a tartan skirt

l' **Écossais** MASC NOUN
l' **Écossaise** FEM NOUN
Scot
les Écossais
the Scots

l' **Écosse** FEM NOUN
Scotland

écouter VERB
to listen to
J'aime écouter de la musique.
I like listening to music.

Écoute-moi, Bruno!
Listen Bruno!
Écoutez tout le monde!
Listen everybody!

écraser VERB
1 to crush
Écrasez une gousse d'ail.
Crush a clove of garlic.
2 to run over
Attention, tu vas te faire écraser!
Be careful or you'll get run over!

écrire VERB
to write
Nous nous écrivons régulièrement.
We write to each other regularly.

Ça s'écrit comment?
How do you spell that?

l' **écriture** FEM NOUN
handwriting
J'aime bien ton écriture.
I like your handwriting.

l' **écrivain** MASC NOUN
writer

écru MASC ADJECTIVE (FEM **écrue**)
off-white

l' **écureuil** MASC NOUN
squirrel

Édimbourg NOUN
Edinburgh

French English

a
b
c
d
e
f
g
h
i
j
k
l
m
n
o
p
q
r
s
t
u
v
w
x
y
z

éducatif MASC ADJECTIVE
(FEM **éducative**)
educational
un jeu éducatif
an educational game

l' **éducation** FEM NOUN
education
l'éducation physique
physical education

effacer VERB
to rub out
Efface la dernière lettre.
Rub out the last letter.

l' **effort** MASC NOUN
effort
Il faut faire un effort.
You've got to make an effort.

effrayant MASC ADJECTIVE
(FEM **effrayante**)
frightening

égal MASC ADJECTIVE (FEM **égale**)
equal
**une quantité égale de farine
et de sucre**
equal quantities of flour and
sugar
Ça m'est égal.
I don't mind./I don't care.

> **Language tip**
>
> **ça m'est égal** *has two
> translations. Look at the examples.*

**Tu préfères du riz ou des
pâtes? — Ça m'est égal.**
Would you rather have rice or
pasta? — I don't mind.
**Fais ce que tu veux, ça m'est
égal.**
Do what you like, I don't care.

égaler VERB
to equal

Deux plus trois égalent cinq.
Two plus three equals five.

l' **église** FEM NOUN
church
**Nous allons à l'église tous
les dimanches.**
We go to church every Sunday.

égoïste ADJECTIVE
selfish

l' **Égypte** FEM NOUN
Egypt

égyptien MASC ADJECTIVE
(FEM **égyptienne**)
Egyptian

l' **Égyptien** MASC NOUN
l' **Égyptienne** FEM NOUN
Egyptian

l' **élastique** MASC NOUN
rubber band

l' **électricien** MASC NOUN
electrician

élégant MASC ADJECTIVE
(FEM **élégante**)
smart
**une robe
élégante**
a smart dress

l' **éléphant** MASC NOUN
elephant

élevé MASC ADJECTIVE
(FEM **élevée**)

Elle est bien élevée.
She has good manners.
Il est très mal élevé.
He has very bad manners.

l' **élève** MASC/FEM NOUN
pupil
Il y a un nouvel élève dans ma classe.
There's a new boy in my class.

éliminer VERB
to eliminate
Tu es éliminé!
You're out!

elle PRONOUN
1 **she**
Elle est institutrice.
She is a primary school teacher.
Elle, elle est toujours en retard!
Oh, SHE's always late!
2 **her**
C'est ma copine; je joue toujours avec elle.
She's my friend; I always play with her.
Lui ou elle?
Him or her?
Elle l'a choisi elle-même.
She chose it herself.

elle-même
herself

3 **it**
Prends cette chaise: elle est plus confortable.
Take this chair: it's more comfortable.

elles PRONOUN
1 **they**
Où sont Anne et Rachel? — Elles sont dans le jardin.
Where are Anne and Rachel? — They're in the garden.

2 **them**
Julie et Aurélie ont emmené le chien avec elles.
Julie and Aurélie have taken the dog with them.

elles-mêmes
themselves

l' **Élysée** MASC NOUN
Élysée Palace

Did you know...?
The **Élysée** is the home of the French president.

l' **e-mail** MASC NOUN
email

Je vais envoyer un e-mail à ma copine.
I'm going to email my friend.

embarrassant MASC
ADJECTIVE (FEM **embarrassante**)
embarrassing

embêtant MASC ADJECTIVE
(FEM **embêtante**)
annoying

embêter VERB
to pester
Il n'arrête pas de m'embêter.
He's always pestering me.
■ **s'embêter**
to be bored
Qu'est-ce qu'on s'embête ici!
It's so boring here!

French English

a
b
c
d
e
f
g
h
i
j
k
l
m
n
o
p
q
r
s
t
u
v
w
x
y
z

l' **embouteillage** MASC NOUN
traffic jam

embrasser VERB
to kiss

Il l'a embrassée.
He kissed her.
■ **s'embrasser**
to kiss each other
Ils se sont embrassés.
They kissed each other.

l' **émission** FEM NOUN
programme
une émission de télévision
a TV programme

emménager VERB
to move in
**Nous venons d'emménager
dans une nouvelle maison.**
We've just moved into a new
house.

emmener VERB
to take
**Ma grand-mère m'emmène
à l'école le matin.**
My granny takes me to school
in the morning.

empêcher VERB
to stop
Tu m'empêches de travailler!
You're stopping me doing my
work.

l' **emploi** MASC NOUN
1 **use**

le mode d'emploi
instructions for use
un emploi du temps
a timetable
2 **job**
Il recherche un emploi.
He's looking for a job.

l' **employé** MASC NOUN
l' **employée** FEM NOUN
employee
un employé de bureau
an office worker
une employée de banque
a bank clerk

employer VERB
to employ

empoisonner VERB
to poison

emporter VERB
to take
des plats à emporter
take-away meals

l' **empreinte** FEM NOUN
footprint
une empreinte digitale
a fingerprint

emprunter VERB
to borrow
Je peux emprunter ta gomme?
Can I borrow your rubber?

en

*en can be a preposition or a
pronoun.*

A PREPOSITION
1 **in**
Il habite en France.
He lives in France.
2 **to**
Je vais en France cet été.
I'm going to France this summer.

French English

3 **by**
en vélo
by bike
C'est plus rapide en voiture.
It's quicker by car.
4 **made of**
C'est en verre.
It's made of glass.
un bracelet en or
a gold bracelet
5 **while**
Il s'est coupé le doigt en ouvrant une boîte de conserve.
He cut his finger while opening a tin.
B PRONOUN
of it
Il a un beau jardin et il en est très fier.
He's got a beautiful garden and is very proud of it.
Si tu as un problème, tu peux m'en parler.
If you've got a problem, you can talk to me about it.
Tu peux me rendre ce livre? J'en ai besoin.
Can you give me back that book? I need it.

Language tip

When **en** is used with **avoir** and **il y a**, it is not translated in English. Please see below for an example.

Tu as un dictionnaire? — Oui, j'en ai un.
Have you got a dictionary? — Yes, I've got one.
Il y a combien d'élèves dans ta classe? — Il y en a trente.
How many pupils are there in your class? — There are 30.

J'en ai assez.
I've had enough.

enceinte FEM ADJECTIVE
pregnant
Ma tante est enceinte de six mois.
My aunt is six months pregnant.

enchanté MASC ADJECTIVE
(FEM **enchantée**)
delighted
Ma mère est enchantée de sa nouvelle voiture.
My mother's delighted with her new car.

Enchanté!
Pleased to meet you!

encore ADVERB
1 **still**
Il est encore au travail.
He's still at work.
Il reste encore deux morceaux de gâteau.
There are two bits of cake left.
2 **even**
C'est encore mieux.
That's even better.
3 **again**
Nous allons encore en Espagne cet été.
We're going to Spain again this summer.

encore une fois
once again
pas encore
not yet
Je n'ai pas encore fini.
I haven't finished yet.

l' **encre** FEM NOUN
ink

a b c d e f g h i j k l m n o p q r s t u v w x y z

l' **encyclopédie** FEM NOUN
encyclopaedia

l' **endive** FEM NOUN
chicory

Did you know...?

endive *is a leafy vegetable which is eaten raw in a salad, boiled, or baked with ham and cheese.*

s' **endormir** VERB
to go to sleep
Je m'endors vers neuf heures du soir.
I go to sleep at about nine o'clock.

l' **endroit** MASC NOUN
place
C'est un endroit très tranquille.
It's a very quiet place.
à l'endroit
the right way out/the right way up

Language tip

à l'endroit *has two translations. Look at the examples.*

Remets ton pull à l'endroit.
Turn your jumper the right way out.
Tu ne tiens pas le livre à l'endroit.
You're not holding the book the right way up.

l' **énergie** FEM NOUN
energy

énerver VERB
to get on someone's nerves
Il m'énerve!
He gets on my nerves!

Ne t'énerve pas!
Take it easy!

l' **enfant** MASC/FEM NOUN
child
Ils ont trois enfants.
They've got three children.

l' **enfer** MASC NOUN
hell

enfin ADVERB
at last
Tu arrives enfin!
Here you are at last!

enflé MASC ADJECTIVE
(FEM **enflée**)
swollen
J'ai la cheville enflée.
I have a swollen ankle.

enlever VERB
to take off
Enlève ton manteau!
Take off your coat!

enneigé MASC ADJECTIVE
(FEM **enneigée**)
blocked with snow
Les routes sont encore enneigées.
The roads are still blocked with snow.

l' **ennemi** MASC NOUN
l' **ennemie** FEM NOUN
enemy

ennuyer VERB
J'espère que ça ne t'ennuie pas.
I hope this isn't a problem for you.
Ça t'ennuie?
Do you mind?
■ **s'ennuyer**
to be bored

Je m'ennuie quand Laura n'est pas là.
I get bored when Laura isn't here.

ennuyeux MASC ADJECTIVE
(FEM **ennuyeuse**)
boring

énorme ADJECTIVE
huge
un énorme gâteau
a huge cake

énormément ADVERB
Il y a énormément de neige.
There's a huge amount of snow.
Il a énormément grossi.
He's got terribly fat.

l' **enquête** FEM NOUN
investigation

enquêter VERB
to investigate

l' **enregistrement** MASC
NOUN
recording
un mauvais enregistrement
a bad recording
l'enregistrement des bagages
baggage check-in

enregistrer VERB
1 to record

Ils viennent d'enregistrer un nouvel album.
They've just recorded a new album.

2 to check in
Combien de valises voulez-vous enregistrer?
How many bags do you want to check in?

enrhumé MASC ADJECTIVE
(FEM **enrhumée**)
Je suis enrhumé.
I've got a cold.

l' **enseignant** MASC NOUN
l' **enseignante** FEM NOUN
teacher

enseigner VERB
to teach
Mon père enseigne les maths dans un lycée.
My father teaches maths in a secondary school.

ensemble

ensemble *can be an adverb or a noun.*

A ADVERB
together
tous ensemble
all together
B MASC NOUN
outfit
Elle porte un nouvel ensemble.
She's wearing a new outfit.

ensoleillé MASC ADJECTIVE
(FEM **ensoleillée**)
sunny
une matinée ensoleillée
a sunny morning

ensuite ADVERB
then
> **Nous sommes allés au cinéma et ensuite au restaurant.**
> We went to the cinema and then to a restaurant.

entendre VERB
to hear
> **Je ne t'entends pas.**
> I can't hear you.
- **s'entendre**
to get on
> **Il s'entend bien avec sa sœur.**
> He gets on well with his sister.

entendu MASC ADJECTIVE
bien entendu
of course

l' **enterrement** MASC NOUN
funeral

entier MASC ADJECTIVE
(FEM **entière**)
whole
> **Il a mangé une quiche entière.**
> He ate a whole quiche.
> **Je n'ai pas lu le livre en entier.**
> I haven't read the whole book.
> **dans le monde entier**
> in the whole wide world
> **le lait entier**
> full fat milk

entièrement ADVERB
completely

l' **entorse** FEM NOUN
sprain

entourer VERB
to surround
> **Le jardin est entouré d'un mur de pierres.**
> The garden is surrounded by a stone wall.

l' **entraînement** MASC NOUN
training

s' **entraîner** VERB
to train

> **Il s'entraîne au foot tous les samedis matins.**
> He does football training every Saturday morning.

l' **entraîneur** MASC NOUN
trainer
> **l'entraîneur d'une équipe de rugby**
> the trainer of a rugby team

entre PREPOSITION
between
> **Il est assis entre son père et son oncle.**
> He's sitting between his father and his uncle.

l' **entrecôte** FEM NOUN
rib steak

l' **entrée** FEM NOUN
1 **starter**
> **Que voulez-vous comme entrée?**
> What would you like as a starter?
2 **hall**
> **Il y a un grand placard dans l'entrée.**
> There's a big cupboard in the hall.

French English
a b c d e f g h i j k l m n o p q r s t u v w x y z

3 **entrance**
l'entrée du tunnel
the tunnel entrance

l' **entreprise** FEM NOUN
firm

entrer VERB
1 **to come in**
Entrez!
Come in!
2 **to go in**
**Ils sont tous entrés dans
la maison.**
They all went into the house.

l' **enveloppe** FEM NOUN
envelope

l' **envers** MASC NOUN
à l'envers
inside out
Ton pull est à l'envers.
Your jumper is inside out.

l' **envie** FEM NOUN
J'ai envie de pleurer.
I feel like crying.
J'ai envie de dormir.
I want to go to sleep.
J'ai envie de faire pipi.
I need a wee.

envier VERB
to envy
Je t'envie.
I envy you.

environ ADVERB
about
**C'est à soixante kilomètres
environ.**
It's about 60 kilometres.

l' **environnement** MASC
NOUN
environment

les **environs** MASC PL NOUN
area
les environs de Nantes
the Nantes area
**Il y a beaucoup de choses
intéressantes à voir dans les
environs.**
There are a lot of interesting
things to see in the area.
aux environs de
around
**aux environs de dix-neuf
heures**
around 7 p.m.

s' **envoler** VERB
1 **to fly away**
**Le papillon
s'est envolé.**
The butterfly
flew away.
2 **to blow away**
**Attention, tes dessins vont
s'envoler!**
Be careful, your drawings are
going to blow away!

envoyer VERB
to send
**Ma tante m'a envoyé une
carte pour mon anniversaire.**
My aunt sent me a card for my
birthday.
Je vais t'envoyer un e-mail.
I'm going to email you.

épais MASC ADJECTIVE
(FEM **épaisse**)
thick

l' **épaule** FEM NOUN
shoulder

l' **épée** FEM NOUN
sword

épeler VERB
to spell
> **Tu peux épeler ton nom s'il te plaît?**
> Can you spell your name please?

épicé MASC ADJECTIVE
(FEM **épicée**)
spicy
> **Ce n'est pas assez épicé.**
> It's not spicy enough.

l' **épicerie** FEM NOUN
shop

l' **épicier** MASC NOUN
l' **épicière** FEM NOUN
grocer

les **épinards** MASC PL NOUN
spinach
> **Je n'aime pas les épinards.**
> I don't like spinach.

éplucher VERB
to peel

l' **éponge** FEM NOUN
sponge

épouvantable ADJECTIVE
awful

l' **EPS** FEM NOUN
PE

épuisé MASC ADJECTIVE
(FEM **épuisée**)
exhausted

l' **équilibre** MASC NOUN
balance
> **J'ai failli perdre l'équilibre.**
> I nearly lost my balance.

l' **équipe** FEM NOUN
team

l' **équipement** MASC NOUN
equipment

l' **équitation** FEM NOUN
riding
> **Je fais de l'équitation.**
> I go riding.

l' **erreur**
FEM NOUN
mistake

es VERB ▷ see **être**
> **Tu es très gentille.**
> You're very kind.

Language tip

*Sometimes **es** is used to show that something has happened in the past.*

> **Tu es parti à quelle heure?**
> What time did you leave?

l' **escalade** FEM NOUN
climbing
> **Il fait de l'escalade.**
> He goes climbing.

l' **escalier** MASC NOUN
stairs

l' **escargot** MASC NOUN
snail

l' **escrime** FEM NOUN
fencing
> **Il fait de l'escrime.**
> He does fencing.

les **espadrilles** FEM PL NOUN
rope-soled sandals

French English

a b c d e f g h i j k l m n o p q r s t u v w x y z

Did you know...?

A lot of French people wear **espadrilles** *in the summer. They are cheap and colourful fabric sandals with soles made of rope.*

l' **Espagne** FEM NOUN
Spain

espagnol MASC NOUN, MASC ADJECTIVE (FEM **espagnole**)
Spanish

l' **Espagnol** MASC NOUN
l' **Espagnole** FEM NOUN
Spaniard

l' **espèce** FEM NOUN
sort
> **Elle porte une espèce de cape en velours.**
> She's wearing a sort of velvet cloak.

Espèce d'idiot!
You idiot!

espérer VERB
to hope
> **J'espère que tu passes de bonnes vacances.**
> I hope you're having a nice holiday.

J'espère bien!
I hope so!
J'espère que non.
I hope not.

l' **esquimau**® MASC NOUN
(PL les **esquimaux**)
choc ice on a stick

l' **Esquimau** MASC NOUN
l' **Esquimaude** FEM NOUN
Eskimo
> **les Esquimaux**
> the Eskimos

essayer VERB
1 to try
> **Essaie de compter jusqu'à cent en français.**
> Try to count up to 100 in French.
2 to try on
> **Je peux l'essayer?**
> Can I try it on?

l' **essence** FEM NOUN
petrol

essentiel

> **essentiel** *can be an adjective or a noun.*

A MASC ADJECTIVE
(FEM **essentielle**)
essential
B MASC NOUN
> **Tu es là: c'est l'essentiel.**
> You're here: that's the main thing.

essuyer VERB
to wipe
> **Tu peux essuyer la table?**
> Could you wipe the table?
> **Il essuie la vaisselle.**
> He's drying the dishes.
> **Essuie-toi les mains avec cette serviette.**
> Dry your hands on this towel.

est

> **est** *can be part of the verb* **être**, *an adjective or a noun.*

A VERB ▷ *see* **être**
> **Elle est merveilleuse.**
> She's marvellous.

Language tip

Sometimes **est** *is used to show that something has happened in the past.*

105

Hier soir, il est allé au cinéma.
He went to the cinema last night.

B MASC, FEM, PL ADJECTIVE
east
la côte est des États-Unis
the east coast of the United States

C MASC NOUN
east
Je vis dans l'est de la France.
I live in the east of France.
à l'est de Paris
east of Paris

est-ce que ADVERB

Language tip
One way of asking a question in French is to use **est-ce que**.

Comment est-ce que tu t'appelles?
What's your name?
Est-ce que c'est cher?
Is it expensive?

l' **estomac** MASC NOUN
stomach

et CONJUNCTION
and

l' **étage** MASC NOUN
floor
au premier étage
on the first floor

l' **étagère** FEM NOUN
shelf

étaient VERB ▷ *see* être
J'ai trouvé mes baskets: elles étaient sous mon lit.
I've found my trainers: they were under my bed.

étais, était VERB ▷ *see* être
J'étais dans le jardin.
I was in the garden.

C'était super!
It was great!

l' **étang** MASC NOUN
pond

l' **état** MASC NOUN
condition
en bon état
in good condition
en mauvais état
in poor condition

les **États-Unis** MASC PL NOUN
United States

été

été can be a noun or part of the verb être.

A MASC NOUN
summer
cet été
this summer
en été
in the summer

B VERB ▷ *see* être
Il a été puni.
He has been punished.

éteindre VERB
to switch off
Éteins la lumière s'il te plaît
Switch off the light please.

étendre VERB
étendre le linge
to hang out the washing

a b c d e f g h i j k l m n o p q r s t u v w x y z

éternuer VERB
to sneeze

Did you know…?
*When you sneeze in France people say '**À tes souhaits!**', which means '**May your wishes come true!**'.*

êtes VERB ▷ see **être**
Vous êtes en retard.
You're late.

Language tip
*Sometimes **êtes** is used to show that something has happened in the past.*

Vous êtes partis de bonne heure.
You left early.

l' **étiquette** FEM NOUN
label

l' **étoile** FEM NOUN
star
une étoile de mer
a starfish
une étoile filante
a shooting star

étonnant MASC ADJECTIVE
(FEM **étonnante**)
amazing
une nouvelle étonnante
amazing news

étonner VERB
to surprise
Ça t'étonne?
Does that surprise you?

étourdi MASC ADJECTIVE
(FEM **étourdie**)
scatterbrained

étrange MASC, FEM ADJECTIVE
strange

étranger MASC ADJECTIVE
(FEM **étrangère**)
foreign
un pays étranger
a foreign country

l' **étranger** MASC NOUN
l' **étrangère** FEM NOUN
1 foreigner
Il y a beaucoup d'étrangers ici.
There are lots of foreigners here.
à l'étranger
abroad
2 stranger
Il ne faut pas parler aux étrangers.
You mustn't speak to strangers.

être

être *can be a verb or a noun.*

A VERB
1 to be
Je suis heureux.
I'm happy.
Mon père est instituteur.
My father's a primary school teacher.
Il est dix heures.
It's 10 o'clock.
2 to have

Language tip
être *is used to make the past tense of some verbs.*

Il n'est pas encore arrivé.
He hasn't arrived yet.
B MASC NOUN
being
un être humain
a human being

French English

a
b
c
d
e
f
g
h
i
j
k
l
m
n
o
p
q
r
s
t
u
v
w
x
y
z

les **étrennes** FEM PL NOUN

> *Did you know…?*
> **les étrennes** *are like a Christmas box, but one that is given after Christmas, to people like the postman and the dustmen. Children sometimes get money or a gift too.*

les **études** FEM PL NOUN
> **Mon frère va faire des études de droit.**
> My brother is going to study law.

l' **étudiant** MASC NOUN
l' **étudiante** FEM NOUN
student

étudier VERB
to study

l' **étui** MASC NOUN
case
> **un étui à lunettes**
> a glasses case

eu VERB ▷ *see* **avoir**
> **J'ai eu une bonne note.**
> I got a good mark.

euh EXCLAMATION
er
> **Euh … je ne sais pas.**
> Er … I don't know.

l' **euro** MASC NOUN
euro
> **Ça coûte vingt-cinq euros.**
> It costs 25 euros.
> **50 €**
> €50

l' **Europe** FEM NOUN
Europe

européen MASC ADJECTIVE
(FEM **européenne**)
European

l' **européen** MASC NOUN
l' **européenne** FEM NOUN
European

eux PRONOUN
them
> **Je pense souvent à eux.**
> I often think of them.

eux-mêmes
themselves

évident MASC ADJECTIVE
(FEM **évidente**)
obvious
> **Elle est jalouse, c'est évident.**
> It's obvious she's jealous.

l' **évier** MASC NOUN
sink

exactement ADVERB
exactly

ex aequo MASC, FEM, PL
ADJECTIVE
> **Huit points partout: vous êtes ex aequo.**
> Eight points each: it's a tie.

> *Language tip*
> **ex aequo** *sounds like 'ex-echo'.*

exagérer VERB
to exaggerate
> **Il exagère toujours.**
> He always exaggerates.
> **Ça fait trois fois que tu arrives en retard: tu exagères!**
> That's three times you've been late: it's not good enough!

108

l' **examen** MASC NOUN
exam
un examen de français
a French exam

excellent MASC ADJECTIVE
(FEM **excellente**)
excellent

excitant MASC ADJECTIVE
(FEM **excitante**)
exciting

l' **excuse** FEM NOUN
excuse
un mot d'excuse
a note
**C'est un mot d'excuse de
mes parents.**
This is a note from my parents.

excuser VERB
excusez-moi
sorry/excuse me

Language tip

excusez-moi *is used to apologize
and to attract someone's attention.*

Excusez-moi!
Sorry!
Excusez-moi, je suis en retard.
Sorry I'm late.
Excusez-moi!
Excuse me!
**Excusez-moi, je cherche
la poste.**
Excuse me, I'm looking for the
post office.
■ **s'excuser**
to apologize
Je m'excuse.
I apologize.

l' **exemple** MASC NOUN
example
par exemple
for example

l' **exercice** MASC NOUN
exercise

exister VERB
to exist
Ça n'existe pas.
It doesn't exist.

exotique ADJECTIVE
exotic
une plante exotique
an exotic plant
**un yaourt aux fruits
exotiques**
a tropical fruit yoghurt

l' **expéditeur** MASC NOUN
sender

l' **expérience** FEM NOUN
1 experience
2 experiment
une expérience de chimie
a chemistry experiment

l' **explication** FEM NOUN
explanation

expliquer VERB
to explain
**Je vais expliquer en
anglais.**
I'm going to explain in
English.

l' **exposition** FEM NOUN
exhibition

exprès ADVERB
1 **on purpose**
Je suis sûr qu'il l'a fait exprès.
I'm sure he did it on purpose.

2 specially
J'ai fait ce gâteau exprès pour toi.
I made this cake specially for you.

l' **extérieur** MASC NOUN
outside
à l'extérieur
outside
Les toilettes sont à l'extérieur.
The toilet is outside.

l' **externe** MASC/FEM NOUN

> ### Did you know...?
>
> In French secondary schools, pupils are described as **externe** if they go home for lunch, **demi-pensionnaire** if they have a school lunch, or **interne** if they stay at the school as boarders.

extra MASC, FEM, PL ADJECTIVE
excellent
Ce fromage est extra!
This cheese is excellent!

l' **extrait** MASC NOUN
extract

extraordinaire ADJECTIVE
extraordinary

extrêmement ADVERB
extremely

l' **Extrême-Orient** MASC NOUN
the Far East

F f

fabriquer VERB
to make
    fabriqué en France
    made in France

la **face** FEM NOUN
    en face de
    opposite
    Le bus s'arrête en face de chez moi.
    The bus stops opposite my house.

Pile ou face? — Face.
Heads or tails? — Heads.

fâché

MASC ADJECTIVE
(FEM **fâchée**)
angry

Elle est fâchée contre moi.
She's angry with me.
Elle est fâchée avec sa sœur.
She's fallen out with her sister.

se **fâcher** VERB
    to get angry
    Je vais me fâcher.
    I'm going to get angry.
    Il s'est fâché avec son frère.
    He's fallen out with his brother.

facile ADJECTIVE
easy
    C'est facile à faire.
    It's easy to do.

facilement ADVERB
easily

la **façon** FEM NOUN
way

Il a une drôle de façon de parler.
He has a funny way of talking.
de toute façon
anyway

le **facteur** MASC NOUN
postman

faible ADJECTIVE
weak
    Je me sens encore faible.
    I still feel a bit weak.
    Il est faible en maths.
    He's not very good at maths.

la **faim** FEM NOUN
hunger
    Tu as faim?
    Are you hungry?

J'ai faim.
I'm hungry.

faire VERB
1 **to make**
    Je vais faire un gâteau.
    I'm going to make a cake.
    Ils font trop de bruit.
    They're making too much noise.
2 **to do**
    Qu'est-ce que tu fais?
    What are you doing?
    Il fait de l'italien.
    He's doing Italian.
    Elle fait la vaisselle.
    She's doing the dishes.
3 **to play**
    Il fait du piano.
    He plays the piano.
    Je fais du basket.
    I play basketball.

a
b
c
d
e
f
g
h
i
j
k
l
m
n
o
p
q
r
s
t
u
v
w
x
y
z

4 to be
Il fait chaud.
It's hot.
Ça fait combien? —
Ça fait dix euros.
How much is that? —
It's ten euros.
5 to go
Tu veux faire du vélo?
Do you want to go cycling?
Je fais du vélo.
I go cycling.
Ça fait trois ans qu'ils
habitent à Paris.
They've lived in Paris for three
years.

Ça ne fait rien.
It doesn't matter.

fais, faisaient, faisais, faisait VERB ▷see faire

Language tip
Look at the entry **faire** *to see all the*
meanings it can have.

Ne fais pas ça!
Don't do that!
Ils faisaient beaucoup de
bruit.
They were making a lot of noise.
Qu'est-ce que tu faisais?
What were you doing?
Il faisait très froid.
It was very cold.

le **faisan** MASC NOUN
pheasant

faisiez, faisions, faisons, fait VERB ▷see faire

Language tip
Look at the entry **faire** *to see all the*
meanings it can have.

Vous faisiez du bruit.
You were making a noise.
Qu'est-ce que nous faisions
hier?
What were we doing yesterday?
Nous faisons du vélo le
week-end.
We go cycling at the weekend.
Il fait des bêtises.
He does silly things.

faites VERB ▷see faire

Language tip
Look at the entry **faire** *to see all the*
meanings it can have.

Qu'est-ce que vous faites?
What are you doing?

la **falaise** FEM NOUN
cliff

falloir VERB ▷see faut
Il va falloir se dépêcher.
We'll have to hurry up.

familier MASC ADJECTIVE
(FEM **familière**)
familiar
les animaux familiers
pets

la **famille** FEM NOUN
1 family
une famille nombreuse
a big family
2 relatives
Il a de la famille à Paris.
He's got relatives in Paris.

fantastique ADJECTIVE
fantastic

le **fantôme** MASC NOUN
ghost

la **farce** FEM NOUN
practical joke

French English

farci MASC ADJECTIVE (FEM **farcie**)
stuffed
> **des tomates farcies**
> stuffed tomatoes

la **farine** FEM NOUN
flour

fatigant MASC ADJECTIVE
(FEM **fatigante**)
tiring

fatigué MASC ADJECTIVE
(FEM **fatiguée**)
tired
> **Je suis fatigué.**
> I'm tired.

fausse FEM ADJECTIVE ▷*see* **faux**
> **Cette réponse est fausse.**
> This answer's wrong.

faut VERB

> *Language tip*
> **faut** *is the present tense of* **falloir**.

> **Il faut faire attention.**
> You've got to be careful.

la **faute** FEM NOUN
1 mistake
> **J'ai fait une faute.**
> I've made a mistake.
2 fault
> **Ce n'est pas de ma faute.**
> It's not my fault.

le **fauteuil** MASC NOUN
armchair
> **un fauteuil roulant**
> a wheelchair

faux MASC ADJECTIVE (FEM **fausse**)
1 untrue
> **C'est entièrement faux.**
> It's totally untrue.
2 wrong
> **Ce mot est faux.**
> The word is wrong.

> **Vrai ou faux?**
> True or false?

favori MASC ADJECTIVE
(FEM **favorite**)
favourite
> **Quel est ton sport favori?**
> What's your favourite sport?

la **fée** FEM NOUN
fairy

> **un conte de fées**
> a fairy tale

les **félicitations** FEM PL NOUN
congratulations

féliciter VERB
to congratulate
> **Je te félicite pour tes bons résultats.**
> Congratulations on your good results!

la **femelle** FEM NOUN
female

féminin MASC ADJECTIVE
(FEM **féminine**)
feminine

la **femme** FEM NOUN
1 woman
> **une jeune femme**
> a young woman
> **une femme de ménage**
> a cleaning woman
2 wife
> **C'est la femme du directeur.**
> She's the headmaster's wife.

une femme au foyer
a housewife

la **fenêtre** FEM NOUN
window

Regardez par la fenêtre.
Look out of the window.

le **fenouil** MASC NOUN
fennel

Did you know…?

fenouil *is white, looks a bit like celery but has a rounded shape. It tastes of aniseed.*

le **fer** MASC NOUN
iron
un fer à repasser
an iron
un fer à cheval
a horseshoe

fera, ferai, feras, ferez
VERB ▷*see* **faire**

Language tip

Look at the entry **faire** *to see all the meanings it can have.*

Marc fera la vaisselle.
Marc will do the washing up.
Je te ferai un gâteau.
I'll make you a cake.
Qu'est-ce que tu feras l'année prochaine?
What are you going to do next year?

Vous ferez du cheval pendant les vacances?
Will you go horse-riding during the holidays?

férié MASC ADJECTIVE
un jour férié
a public holiday

la **ferme** FEM NOUN
farm

fermé MASC ADJECTIVE
(FEM **fermée**)
closed
La pharmacie est fermée.
The chemist's is closed.

fermer VERB
1 **to close**
Ferme la fenêtre s'il te plaît.
Close the window please.
2 **to turn off**
Ferme le robinet.
Turn the tap off.
N'oublie pas de fermer la porte à clef!
Don't forget to lock the door!

la **fermeture** FEM NOUN
les heures de fermeture
closing times
une fermeture éclair®
a zip

le **fermier** MASC NOUN
farmer

la **fermière** FEM NOUN
1 **woman farmer**
2 **farmer's wife**

féroce ADJECTIVE
fierce
un animal féroce
a fierce animal

ferons, feront VERB
▷*see* **faire**

Nous le ferons si nous avons le temps.
We'll do it if we have time.
Ils feront des quiches pour la fête.
They're going to make quiches for the party.

les **fesses** FEM PL NOUN
bottom

la **fête** FEM NOUN
1 **party**
Tu fais une fête pour ton anniversaire?
Are you having a party for your birthday?
faire la fête
to party
2 **name day**
C'est ma fête aujourd'hui.
It's my name day today.

une fête foraine
a funfair
les fêtes de fin d'année
the festive season
la Fête Nationale
Bastille Day

fêter VERB
to celebrate
Aujourd'hui, ma mère fête ses quarante ans.
My mum's celebrating her fortieth birthday today.

le **feu** MASC NOUN (PL les **feux**)
1 **fire**
Au feu!
Fire!
un feu d'artifice
a firework display
2 **traffic light**
un feu rouge
a red light
le feu vert
the green light
Tournez à gauche aux feux.
Turn left at the lights.

la **feuille** FEM NOUN
1 **leaf**

des feuilles mortes
dead leaves
2 **sheet**
une feuille de papier
a sheet of paper

le **feuilleton** MASC NOUN
soap
Tu regardes les feuilletons à la télé?
Do you watch soaps on telly?

le **feutre** MASC NOUN
felt-tip pen
un stylo-feutre
a felt-tip pen

la **fève** FEM NOUN
broad bean

> **Did you know…?**
> **la fève** *can also be a little figure which is baked in the cake traditionally eaten at Epiphany (the sixth of January). If you find* **la fève** *in your slice of cake you are king (or queen) for the day.*

février MASC NOUN
February
en février
in February
au mois de février
in February
le six février
the sixth of February

les **fiançailles** FEM PL NOUN
engagement
une bague de fiançailles
an engagement ring

fiancé MASC ADJECTIVE
(FEM **fiancée**)
être fiancé
to be engaged
Elle est fiancée.
She's engaged.

se **fiancer** VERB
to get engaged
Luc et Claire vont se fiancer.
Luc and Claire are going to get engaged.

la **ficelle** FEM NOUN
string

la **fiche** FEM NOUN
form
Remplissez cette fiche s'il vous plaît.
Fill in this form please.

le **fichier** MASC NOUN
file

fier MASC ADJECTIVE (FEM **fière**)
proud
Il est fier de toi.
He's proud of you.

la **fièvre** FEM NOUN
fever
J'ai de la fièvre.
I've got a temperature.

la **figue** FEM NOUN
fig

la **figure** FEM NOUN
face
Va te laver la figure!
Go and wash your face!

le **fil** MASC NOUN
thread
le fil de fer
wire
un coup de fil
a phone call

la **file** FEM NOUN
line
une file de gens
a line of people
en file indienne
in single file

le **filet** MASC NOUN
net

la **fille** FEM NOUN
1 girl
une petite fille
a little girl

une grande fille
a big girl
une jeune fille
a young girl
2 daughter
C'est leur fille aînée.
She's their oldest daughter.

la **fillette** FEM NOUN
little girl

le **filleul** MASC NOUN
godson

la **filleule** FEM NOUN
goddaughter

le **film** MASC NOUN
film
un film policier
a thriller
un film d'aventures
an adventure film
un film d'horreur
a horror film

le **fils** MASC NOUN
(PL les **fils**)
son
Ils ont deux fils et une fille.
They have two sons and one daughter.

fin

fin *can be a noun or an adjective.*

A FEM NOUN
end
à la fin de la leçon
at the end of the lesson
'Fin'
'The End'
fin juin
at the end of June
la fin de semaine (*Canada*)
the weekend

B MASC ADJECTIVE (FEM **fine**)
slim
Elle est fine.
She's slim.

la **finale** FEM NOUN
final
Ils sont en finale.
They're through to the final.
les quarts de finale
the quarter finals

finalement ADVERB
1 in the end
Finalement, ils ont perdu.
They lost in the end.
2 after all
Finalement, tu avais raison.
You were right after all.

fini MASC ADJECTIVE (FEM **finie**)
finished

finir VERB
to finish
Le cours finit à onze heures.
The lesson finishes at 11 o'clock.
J'ai fini!
I've finished!

finlandais MASC NOUN, MASC ADJECTIVE (FEM **finlandaise**)
Finnish

le **Finlandais** MASC NOUN
la **Finlandaise** FEM NOUN
Finn

la **Finlande** FEM NOUN
Finland

le **flacon** MASC NOUN
bottle

les **flageolets** MASC PL NOUN
small haricot beans

flamand MASC NOUN, MASC ADJECTIVE (FEM **flamande**)
Flemish

117

a
b
c
d
f
g
h
i
j
k
l
m
n
o
p
q
r
s
t
u
v
w
x
y
z

Did you know…?
French is one of the languages spoken in Belgium. The other is Flemish; it is similar to Dutch.

le **Flamand** MASC NOUN
la **Flamande** FEM NOUN
Fleming

Did you know…?
A Flamand or a Flamande is a Belgian person who speaks Flemish.

la **flamme** FEM NOUN
flame
en flammes
on fire

le **flan** MASC NOUN
baked custard

la **flaque** FEM NOUN
puddle

la **flèche** FEM NOUN
arrow

les **fléchettes** FEM PL NOUN
darts
J'aime jouer aux fléchettes.
I like playing darts.

la **fleur** FEM NOUN
flower
un bouquet de fleurs
a bunch of flowers
Les arbres sont en fleurs.
The trees are in blossom.

le/la **fleuriste** MASC/FEM NOUN
florist

le **fleuve** MASC NOUN
river

Did you know…?
In France, only big rivers are called **fleuves***: the Seine, the Loire, the Garonne, the Rhône, and the Rhine.*

le **flipper** MASC NOUN
pinball machine

le **flocon** MASC NOUN
flake
un flocon de neige
a snow flake
des flocons d'avoine
oat flakes

flotter VERB
to float

la **flûte** FEM NOUN
flute
Je joue de la flûte.
I play the flute.
une flûte à bec
a recorder

le **foie** MASC NOUN
liver
une crise de foie
a stomach upset

le **foin** MASC NOUN
hay
le rhume des foins
hay fever

la **foire** FEM NOUN
fair

la **fois** FEM NOUN
time
la première fois
the first time
à chaque fois
each time
deux fois deux font quatre
two times two is four
une fois
once

deux fois
twice

folklorique ADJECTIVE
folk
la musique folklorique
folk music

folle FEM ADJECTIVE
mad
Elle est folle!
She's mad!

foncé MASC ADJECTIVE
(FEM **foncée**)
dark
une couleur très foncée
a very dark colour
des rideaux bleu foncé
dark blue curtains

le/la **fonctionnaire** MASC/FEM
NOUN
civil servant

le **fond** MASC NOUN
1 bottom
Mon porte-monnaie est au fond de mon sac.
My purse is at the bottom of my bag.
2 end
Les toilettes sont au fond du couloir.
The toilets are at the end of the corridor.

fondre VERB
to melt
La neige fond.
The snow is melting.

fondu MASC ADJECTIVE
(FEM **fondue**)
melted
Ma glace est toute fondue.
My ice cream is all melted.

la **fondue** FEM NOUN
fondue

> **Did you know...?**
> A **fondue** is a Swiss dish. Guests around a table dip bits of dried bread into a pot of melted cheese. If you lose your bread in the cheese, you can be given a forfeit!

font VERB ▷see **faire**
Elles font leur devoirs ensemble.
They do their homework together.

la **fontaine** FEM NOUN
fountain

le **foot** MASC NOUN
football
Je fais du foot avec mes copains.
I play football with my friends.

> **Did you know...?**
> le **foot** is a slang way of saying le **football**. A slang term for 'football' in English is 'footy'.

le **football**
MASC NOUN
football
Tu veux jouer au football?
Do you want to play football?

le **footballeur** MASC NOUN
footballer

le **footing** MASC NOUN
jogging
Tu veux faire du footing?
Do you want to go jogging?

forain

forain can be an adjective or a noun.

A MASC ADJECTIVE (FEM **foraine**)
une fête foraine
a funfair
B MASC NOUN
fairground worker

la **force** FEM NOUN
strength
Je n'ai pas beaucoup de force dans les bras.
I haven't got much strength in my arms.

la **forêt** FEM NOUN
forest

la **forme** FEM NOUN
être en forme
to be fit
Ça va? Tu es en forme?
How are you? Are you fit?
Je ne suis pas en forme aujourd'hui.
I'm not feeling too good today.

formidable ADJECTIVE
great
Vous avez fini? Formidable!
Have you finished? That's great!

le **formulaire** MASC NOUN
form
Tu dois remplir le formulaire.
You have to fill in the form.

fort

fort can be an adjective or an adverb.

A MASC ADJECTIVE (FEM **forte**)
1 strong
Le café est trop fort.
The coffee's too strong.
2 good
Il est très fort en maths.
He's very good at maths.
B ADVERB
1 loud
Tu peux parler plus fort?
Can you speak louder?
2 hard
Tu dois le frapper fort.
You've got to hit it hard.

fou MASC ADJECTIVE (FEM **folle**)
mad
Tu es fou?
Are you mad?

la **foudre** FEM NOUN
lightning

le **foulard** MASC NOUN
scarf

la **foule** FEM NOUN
crowd

le **four** MASC NOUN
oven
un four à micro-ondes
a microwave oven

la **fourchette** FEM NOUN
fork

la **fourmi** FEM NOUN
ant

J'ai des fourmis dans les jambes.
I've got pins and needles in my legs.

Language tip
The French actually means 'I've got ants in my legs'!

les **fournitures** FEM PL NOUN
les fournitures scolaires
school stationery

la **fourrure** FEM NOUN
fur

frais MASC ADJECTIVE (FEM **fraîche**)
1 **fresh**
des œufs frais
fresh eggs
2 **chilly**
Il fait un peu frais ce soir.
It's a bit chilly this evening.
3 **cool**
des boissons fraîches
cool drinks

la **fraise** FEM NOUN
strawberry
les fraises des bois
wild strawberries

la **framboise** FEM NOUN
raspberry

franc

franc can be an adjective or a noun.

A MASC ADJECTIVE (FEM **franche**)
frank
Pour être franc, je le trouve méchant.
To be frank, I think he's horrible.
B MASC NOUN
franc

Did you know...?
The euro replaced the franc as the unit of currency in France, Belgium and Luxembourg in 2002.

français MASC NOUN, MASC
ADJECTIVE (FEM **française**)
French
J'apprends le français.
I'm learning French.

le **Français** MASC NOUN
Frenchman
les Français
the French

la **Française** FEM NOUN
Frenchwoman

la **France** FEM NOUN
France

franche FEM ADJECTIVE
▷*see* **franc**
frank

francophone ADJECTIVE
French-speaking

la **frange** FEM NOUN
fringe
J'ai une frange.
I've got a fringe.

frapper VERB
Frappez dans vos mains.
Clap your hands.
On frappe à la porte.
Somebody's knocking at the door.

le **frère** MASC NOUN
brother
mon grand frère
my big brother
mon petit frère
my little brother

French English

a b c d e f g h i j k l m n o p q r s t u v w x y z

French English

a
b
c
d
e
f
g
h
i
j
k
l
m
n
o
p
q
r
s
t
u
v
w
x
y
z

le **frigidaire**® MASC NOUN
refrigerator

le **frigo** MASC NOUN
fridge

frisé MASC ADJECTIVE (FEM **frisée**)
curly
J'ai les cheveux frisés.
I've got curly hair.

frit MASC ADJECTIVE (FEM **frite**)
fried
du poisson frit
fried fish

les **frites** FEM PL NOUN
chips
J'adore le steak-frites.
I love steak and chips.

froid MASC NOUN, MASC ADJECTIVE
(FEM **froide**)
cold
La soupe est froide!
The soup is cold!

J'ai froid.
I'm cold.
Il fait froid.
It's cold.

le **fromage** MASC NOUN
cheese
Tu veux du fromage ou un dessert?
Would you like some cheese or a pudding?
un sandwich au fromage
a cheese sandwich

le **front** MASC NOUN
forehead

la **frontière** FEM NOUN
border

le **fruit** MASC NOUN
fruit
J'aime les fruits.
I like fruit.
un fruit
a piece of fruit
les fruits de mer
seafood

fumé MASC ADJECTIVE
(FEM **fumée**)
smoked
du saumon fumé
smoked salmon

la **fumée** FEM NOUN
smoke

fumer VERB
to smoke
Il fume la pipe.
He smokes a pipe.

le **fumeur** MASC NOUN
smoker
un compartiment fumeurs
a smoking compartment

le **furet** MASC NOUN
ferret

furieux MASC ADJECTIVE
(FEM **furieuse**)
furious

la **fusée** FEM NOUN
rocket

le **fusil** MASC NOUN
gun

le **futur** MASC NOUN
future

G g

le **gage** MASC NOUN
forfeit

le **gagnant** MASC NOUN
la **gagnante** FEM NOUN
winner

gagner VERB
to win
Qui a gagné?
Who won?
J'ai gagné!
I've won!

la **galerie** FEM NOUN
gallery
une galerie de peinture
an art gallery
une galerie marchande
a shopping arcade

le **galet** MASC NOUN
pebble

la **galette** FEM NOUN
1 cake
2 biscuit
des galettes pur beurre
shortbread biscuits
la galette des Rois

> **Did you know...?**
>
> *A **galette des Rois** is a cake eaten at Epiphany (the sixth of January) which contains a little figure. The person who finds it is the king (or queen) and gets a paper crown. They then choose someone to be their queen (or king).*

Galles FEM NOUN
le pays de Galles
Wales

gallois MASC NOUN, MASC ADJECTIVE (FEM **galloise**)
Welsh

le **Gallois** MASC NOUN
Welshman
les Gallois
the Welsh

la **Galloise** FEM NOUN
Welshwoman

le **gant** MASC NOUN
glove
des gants en laine
woollen gloves
un gant de toilette
a face cloth

le **garage** MASC NOUN
garage

le **garagiste** MASC NOUN
garage owner

le **garçon** MASC NOUN
boy
Les garçons, levez-vous!
Stand up, boys!

garder VERB
1 to keep
Tu peux garder ce crayon.
You can keep this pencil.
2 to look after
Aujourd'hui, je garde ma nièce.
I'm looking after my niece today.

la **garderie** FEM NOUN
nursery

le **gardien** MASC NOUN
la **gardienne** FEM NOUN

a b c d e f **g** h i j k l m n o p q r s t u v w x y z

caretaker
un gardien de musée
a museum attendant
un gardien de but
a goalkeeper

la **gare** FEM NOUN
station

Où est la gare?
Where's the station?
la gare routière
the bus station

garer VERB
to park
Où as-tu garé la voiture?
Where have you parked the car?
- **se garer**
to park
Gare-toi devant la maison.
Park in front of the house.

garni MASC ADJECTIVE
(FEM **garnie**)
un plat garni
a main course

Did you know...?
A **plat garni** is a dish served with vegetables, salad, chips, or rice.

les **gars** MASC PL NOUN
guys
Salut, les gars!
Hi guys!

gaspiller VERB
to waste

le **gâteau** MASC NOUN
(PL les **gâteaux**)

cake
un gâteau d'anniversaire
a birthday cake
un gâteau sec
a biscuit

gauche

gauche can be a noun or an adjective.

A FEM NOUN
left
sur votre gauche
on your left
à gauche
left/on the left

Language tip
à gauche has two translations. Look at the examples.

Tournez à gauche.
Turn left.
Prenez la troisième rue à gauche.
Take the third street on the left.

C'est à gauche.
It's on your left.
la deuxième rue à gauche
the second street on the left

B ADJECTIVE
left
Levez le bras gauche!
Put up your left arm!

gaucher MASC ADJECTIVE
(FEM **gauchère**)
left-handed

la **gaufre** FEM NOUN
waffle

la **gaufrette** FEM NOUN
wafer

le **Gaulois** MASC NOUN
la **Gauloise** FEM NOUN
Gaul
> **J'aime les bandes dessinées d'Astérix le Gaulois.**
> I like Asterix the Gaul comic strips.

le **gaz** MASC NOUN
gas

gazeux MASC ADJECTIVE
(FEM **gazeuse**)
> **une boisson gazeuse**
> a fizzy drink
> **de l'eau gazeuse**
> sparkling water

géant MASC NOUN, MASC ADJECTIVE
(FEM **géante**)
giant

la **gelée** FEM NOUN
jelly

geler VERB
to freeze

> **Il gèle.**
> It's freezing.

le **gendarme** MASC NOUN
policeman

la **gendarmerie** FEM NOUN
police station

général MASC ADJECTIVE
(FEM **générale**)
general
> **en général**
> usually

généralement ADVERB
generally

généreux MASC ADJECTIVE
(FEM **généreuse**)
generous

génial MASC ADJECTIVE
(FEM **géniale**)
great
> **C'est génial.**
> That's great.

le **génie** MASC NOUN
genius
> **C'est un vrai génie.**
> She's a real genius.

le **genou** MASC NOUN
(PL les **genoux**)
knee
> **Mettez-vous à genoux.**
> Kneel down.

le **genre** MASC NOUN
1 **kind**
> **C'est un genre de gâteau à la crème.**
> It's a kind of cream cake.
2 **gender**
> **De quel genre est 'chien'?**
> What's the gender of 'chien'?

les **gens** MASC PL NOUN
people

gentil MASC ADJECTIVE
(FEM **gentille**)
1 **nice**
> **Nos voisins sont très gentils.**
> Our neighbours are very nice.
2 **kind**
> **C'est gentil.**
> That's kind.

la **géographie** FEM NOUN
geography

la **géométrie** FEM NOUN
geometry

germain MASC ADJECTIVE
(FEM **germaine**)
Hugues est mon cousin germain.
Hugues is my first cousin.
Delphine est ma cousine germaine.
Delphine is my first cousin.

le **gigot** MASC NOUN
leg of lamb

le **gilet** MASC NOUN
1 cardigan
2 waistcoat

la **girafe** FEM NOUN
giraffe

le **gîte** MASC NOUN
holiday home
Nous avons loué un gîte pour cet été.
We've rented a holiday home for this summer.

la **glace** FEM NOUN
1 ice cream
Je voudrais une glace à la fraise.
I'd like a strawberry ice cream.
2 ice
Elle a glissé sur la glace.
She slipped on the ice.

3 mirror
Il se regarde souvent dans la glace.
He often looks at himself in the mirror.

glacé MASC ADJECTIVE
(FEM **glacée**)
1 icy
un vent glacé
an icy wind
2 iced
un thé glacé
an iced tea

le **glaçon** MASC NOUN
ice cube

glisser VERB
1 to slip
Elle a glissé sur une peau de banane.
She slipped on a banana skin.
2 to be slippery
Attention, ça glisse!
Watch out, it's slippery!

le **goéland** MASC NOUN
seagull

le **golf** MASC NOUN
1 golf
Il joue au golf.
He plays golf.
2 golf course
C'est un golf dix-huit trous.
It's an 18-hole golf course.

la **gomme**
FEM NOUN
rubber

gommer VERB
to rub out

la **gorge** FEM NOUN
throat
J'ai mal à la gorge.
I've got a sore throat.

le **gorille** MASC NOUN
gorilla

gourmand MASC ADJECTIVE
(FEM **gourmande**)
greedy

le **goût** MASC NOUN
taste

> **Ça a mauvais goût.**
> It has a horrible taste.
> **Ça a un goût sucré.**
> It tastes sweet.
> **Ça a bon goût.**
> It tastes nice.

goûter

> **goûter** *can be a noun or a verb.*

A MASC NOUN
afternoon snack

> **C'est l'heure du goûter.**
> It's time for an afternoon
> snack.

B VERB

1 **to taste**
> **Tu veux goûter?**
> Do you want to taste it?

2 **to have an afternoon
snack**
> **Je goûte généralement vers
> quatre heures.**
> I usually have a snack around
> four o'clock.

la **graine** FEM NOUN
seed

la **grammaire** FEM NOUN
grammar

le **gramme** MASC NOUN
gramme

> **trois cents grammes de
> fromage**
> three hundred grammes of
> cheese

grand MASC ADJECTIVE
(FEM **grande**)

1 **tall**
> **Il est grand.**
> He's tall.

2 **big**
> **C'est sa grande sœur.**
> She's his big sister.

> **les grandes vacances**
> the summer holidays
> **un grand magasin**
> a department store

grand-chose NOUN
> **pas grand-chose**
> not much

la **Grande-Bretagne**
FEM NOUN
Britain
> **J'habite en Grande-Bretagne.**
> I live in Britain.

> *Language tip*
>
> **Bretagne** *means 'Brittany'. Britain
> is bigger than Brittany, which is why
> its French name is* **Grande-
> Bretagne***.*

grandir VERB
to grow
> **Il a beaucoup grandi.**
> He's grown a lot.

la **grand-mère** FEM NOUN
grandmother

le **grand-père** MASC NOUN
grandfather

les **grands-parents** MASC PL
NOUN
grandparents

gras MASC ADJECTIVE (FEM **grasse**)
1 **fatty**

a b c d e f **g** h i j k l m n o p q r s t u v w x y z

127

French English

a b c d e **f g** h i j k l m n o p q r s t u v w x y z

Évitez les aliments gras.
Avoid fatty foods.
2 greasy
J'ai les cheveux gras.
I've got greasy hair.
3 oily
J'ai une peau grasse.
I've got oily skin.

le **gratte-ciel** MASC NOUN
skyscraper

gratter VERB
1 to scratch
Ne gratte pas tes piqûres
de moustiques!
Don't scratch your mosquito
bites!
2 to be itchy
Ce pull me gratte!
This jumper's itchy.

gratuit MASC ADJECTIVE
(FEM **gratuite**)
free
entrée gratuite
admission free

grave ADJECTIVE
serious
C'est grave?
Is it serious?
Ce n'est pas grave.
It doesn't matter.
un accent grave
a grave accent

gravement ADVERB
seriously
Il est gravement blessé.
He is seriously injured.

grec MASC NOUN, MASC ADJECTIVE
(FEM **grecque**)
Greek

le **Grec** MASC NOUN
la **Grecque** FEM NOUN
Greek

la **Grèce** FEM NOUN
Greece

grêler VERB
to hail
Il grêle.
It's hailing.

la **grenadine** FEM NOUN
grenadine

Did you know...?

grenadine *is a popular drink with
children in France. It is very pink!*

le **grenier** MASC NOUN
attic

la **grenouille**
FEM NOUN
frog

la **grève** FEM NOUN
strike
en grève
on strike
Les profs sont en grève.
The teachers are on strike.

griffer VERB
to scratch
Le chat m'a griffé.
The cat scratched me.

la **grillade** FEM NOUN
grilled food
une grillade d'agneau
grilled lamb

le **grille-pain** MASC NOUN
toaster

griller VERB
1 to toast
du pain grillé
toast
2 to grill
des saucisses grillées
grilled sausages

la **grimace** FEM NOUN
faire des grimaces
to make faces
Arrête de faire des grimaces.
Stop making faces.

grimper VERB
to climb

grincheux MASC ADJECTIVE
(FEM grincheuse)
grumpy

la **grippe** FEM NOUN
flu

Carol a la grippe.
Carol has got flu.

gris MASC ADJECTIVE (FEM grise)
grey

grogner VERB
to growl

gronder VERB
se faire gronder
to get a telling off
Tu vas te faire gronder par
ton père!
You're going to get a telling off
from your father!

gros MASC ADJECTIVE (FEM grosse)
1 big
une grosse pomme
a big apple
2 fat
Il est un peu gros.
He's quite fat.

la **groseille** FEM NOUN
redcurrant

la **grotte** FEM NOUN
cave

le **groupe** MASC NOUN
group
Mettez-vous en groupes
de quatre.
Get into groups of four.

la **guêpe** FEM NOUN
wasp

guérir VERB
to recover
Il est complètement guéri.
He's fully recovered.

la **guerre** FEM NOUN
war

la **gueule** FEM NOUN
mouth
Regarde, le chat a une souris
dans sa gueule!
Look, the cat has a mouse in
its mouth!

le **guichet** MASC NOUN
counter

le **guide** MASC NOUN
guide

guider VERB
to guide

la **guirlande** FEM NOUN
tinsel
> **Nous allons décorer le sapin de Noël avec des guirlandes.**
> We're going to decorate the Christmas tree with tinsel.
> **une guirlande en papier**
> a paper chain

la **guitare** FEM NOUN
guitar
> **Je joue de la guitare.**
> I play the guitar.

la **gym** FEM NOUN
PE

le **gymnase** MASC NOUN
gym
> **L'école a un nouveau gymnase.**
> The school's got a new gym.

la **gymnastique** FEM NOUN
gymnastics
> **Je fais de la gymnastique le mercredi.**
> I do gymnastics on Wednesdays.

H h

s' **habiller** VERB
to get dressed
Je m'habille rapidement.
I get dressed quickly.

l' **habitant** MASC NOUN
l' **habitante** FEM NOUN
inhabitant

habiter VERB
to live
Il habite à Montpellier.
He lives in Montpellier.

les **habits** MASC PL NOUN
clothes

l' **habitude** FEM NOUN
habit
une mauvaise habitude
a bad habit
J'ai l'habitude.
I'm used to it.
d'habitude
usually
D'habitude, je vais à la piscine le mardi.
I usually go to the pool on Tuesdays.
comme d'habitude
as usual

le **hachis** MASC NOUN
le hachis Parmentier
shepherd's pie

la **haie** FEM NOUN
hedge

haïr VERB
to hate
Je la hais.
I hate her.

les **halles** FEM PL NOUN
covered market

le **hamster**
MASC NOUN
hamster

la **hanche**
FEM NOUN
hip

le **handball** MASC NOUN
handball
Le lundi, je joue au handball.
I play handball on Mondays.

Did you know...?
handball *is a very popular game in French schools. It is played on a similar pitch to football but players throw the ball instead of kicking it.*

handicapé MASC ADJECTIVE
(FEM **handicapée**)
disabled

les **handicapés** MASC PL NOUN
disabled people

les **haricots** MASC PL NOUN
beans
les haricots verts
green beans
les haricots blancs
haricot beans

l' **harmonica** MASC NOUN
mouth organ

la **harpe** FEM NOUN
harp

le **hasard** MASC NOUN
au hasard
at random
Choisis un numéro au hasard.
Choose a number at random.
par hasard
by chance
Je l'ai rencontrée par hasard au supermarché.
I met her at the supermarket by chance.

hausser VERB
hausser les épaules
to shrug one's shoulders

haut

haut *can be an adjective or a noun.*

A MASC ADJECTIVE (FEM **haute**)
high
La fenêtre est trop haute.
The window is too high.
B MASC NOUN
en haut
upstairs/at the top

Language tip

en haut *has two translations. Look at the examples.*

La salle de bain est en haut.
The bathroom is upstairs.
Le nid est tout en haut de l'arbre.
The nest is right at the top of the tree.
trois mètres de haut
three metres high

la **hauteur** FEM NOUN
height

hein? EXCLAMATION
eh?
Hein? Qu'est-ce que tu dis?
Eh? What did you say?

l' **hélicoptère** MASC NOUN
helicopter

l' **herbe** FEM NOUN
grass
les herbes de Provence
mixed herbs
les fines herbes
mixed herbs

le **hérisson** MASC NOUN
hedgehog

l' **héroïne** FEM NOUN
heroine
l'héroïne du roman
the heroine of the novel

le **héros** MASC NOUN
hero
C'est le héros du film.
He's the hero of the film.

hésiter VERB
to hesitate
J'hésite.
I can't decide.
J'hésite entre un hamster et un lapin.
I don't know whether to choose a hamster or a rabbit.

l' **heure** FEM NOUN
1 hour
Le trajet dure six heures.
The journey lasts six hours.
2 time
Vous avez l'heure?
Have you got the time?
À quelle heure?
What time?

À quelle heure arrivons-nous?
What time do we arrive?
Elle est toujours à l'heure.
She's always on time.
3 o'clock
à deux heures du matin
at two o'clock in the morning
4 period
une heure de français
a period of French

Quelle heure est-il?
What time is it?
Il est sept heures dix.
It's ten past seven.
à dix-neuf heures
at seven o'clock

Did you know...?
The 24-hour clock is used in France for travel times, appointments, and other formal situations.

heureusement ADVERB
luckily

heureux MASC ADJECTIVE
(FEM **heureuse**)
happy

l' **hexagone** MASC NOUN
hexagon
l'Hexagone
France

Did you know...?
A hexagon has six sides. France is often called **l'Hexagone** because of its six-sided shape.

le **hibou** MASC NOUN
(PL les **hiboux**)
owl

hier ADVERB
yesterday

avant-hier
the day before yesterday

la **hi-fi** FEM NOUN
une chaîne hi-fi
a hifi

hippique ADJECTIVE
un club hippique
a riding centre
un concours hippique
a horse show

l' **hippopotame** MASC NOUN
hippopotamus

Language tip
hippopotame *is never shortened to 'hippo' in French as it is in English.*

l' **hirondelle** FEM NOUN
swallow

l' **histoire** FEM NOUN
1 history
un cours d'histoire
a history lesson
2 story

l' **hiver** MASC NOUN
winter
en hiver
in winter

le **hockey**
MASC NOUN
hockey
Il joue au hockey.
He plays hockey.
le hockey sur glace
ice hockey

hollandais MASC NOUN, MASC
ADJECTIVE (FEM **hollandaise**)
Dutch

le **Hollandais** MASC NOUN
Dutch man
    les Hollandais
    the Dutch

la **Hollandaise** FEM NOUN
Dutch woman

la **Hollande** FEM NOUN
Holland

le **homard** MASC NOUN
lobster

l' **homme** MASC NOUN
man
    un homme d'affaires
    a businessman

la **Hongrie** FEM NOUN
Hungary

honnête ADJECTIVE
honest

la **honte** FEM NOUN
    avoir honte
    to be ashamed
    J'ai un peu honte.
    I'm a bit ashamed.

l' **hôpital** MASC NOUN
(PL les **hôpitaux**)
hospital

le **hoquet** MASC NOUN
    J'ai le hoquet.
    I've got hiccups.

l' **horaire** MASC NOUN
timetable

    les horaires de train
    the train timetable

l' **horloge**
FEM NOUN
clock

l' **horreur** FEM NOUN
    J'ai horreur du chou.
    I hate cabbage.

horrible ADJECTIVE
horrible

le **hors-d'œuvre** MASC NOUN
starter
    Comme hors-d'œuvre, il y a des carottes râpées.
    As a starter there's carrot salad.

l' **hôtel** MASC NOUN
hotel
    Nous passons une semaine à l'hôtel.
    We are spending a week at a hotel.
    l'hôtel de ville
    the town hall

l' **hôtesse** FEM NOUN
    une hôtesse de l'air
    an air hostess

le **houx** MASC NOUN
holly

l' **huile** FEM NOUN
oil

huit NUMBER
eight
    Il est huit heures.
    It's eight o'clock.

Il a huit ans.
He's eight.
dans huit jours
in a week's time

le huit février
the eighth of February

la **huitaine** FEM NOUN
une huitaine de jours
about a week
Nous rentrons dans une huitaine de jours.
We'll be back in about a week.

huitième ADJECTIVE
eighth
au huitième étage
on the eighth floor

l' **huître** FEM NOUN
oyster

humain MASC NOUN, MASC ADJECTIVE (FEM **humaine**)
un être humain
a human being

l' **humeur** FEM NOUN
mood

Il est de bonne humeur.
He's in a good mood.
Elle est de mauvaise humeur.
She's in a bad mood.

humide ADJECTIVE
damp

l' **humour** MASC NOUN
avoir le sens de l'humour
to have a sense of humour
Il n'a pas le sens de l'humour.
He has no sense of humour.

hurler VERB
1 **to howl**
Le chien des voisins hurle tous les soirs.
The neighbours' dog howls every evening.
2 **to yell**
Arrête de hurler comme ça!
Stop yelling like that!

hygiénique MASC ADJECTIVE
le papier hygiénique
toilet paper

l' **hypermarché** MASC NOUN
hypermarket

French English

a
b
c
d
e
f
g
h
i
j
k
l
m
n
o
p
q
r
s
t
u
v
w
x
y
z

135

I i

ici ADVERB
here
> **Viens ici.**
> Come here.

l' **idée** FEM NOUN
idea
> **C'est une bonne idée.**
> It's a good idea.

idéal MASC ADJECTIVE (FEM idéale)
ideal
> **Décrivez votre chambre idéale.**
> Describe your ideal bedroom.

identique ADJECTIVE
identical

l' **identité** FEM NOUN
identity

idiot MASC ADJECTIVE (FEM idiote)
stupid
> **C'est vraiment une plaisanterie idiote!**
> It's really a stupid joke!

l' **idiot** MASC NOUN
l' **idiote** FEM NOUN
idiot

il PRONOUN
1 he
> **Il habite à Paris.**
> He lives in Paris.

2 it
> **Il pleut.**
> It's raining.
> **Attention à ce chien: il mord.**
> Watch that dog: it bites.

l' **île** FEM NOUN
island
> **les îles Anglo-Normandes**
> the Channel Islands
> **l'île de Man**
> the Isle of Man
> **l'île de Wight**
> the Isle of Wight

ils PRONOUN
they
> **Ils sont à la piscine.**
> They are at the swimming pool.

l' **image** FEM NOUN
picture
> **Regardez les images.**
> Look at the pictures.

imaginaire ADJECTIVE
imaginary
> **C'est un personnage imaginaire.**
> He's an imaginary character.

l' **imagination** FEM NOUN
imagination
> **Elle a beaucoup d'imagination.**
> She's got a vivid imagination.

imaginer VERB
to imagine

l' **imbécile** MASC/FEM NOUN
idiot
> **C'est une imbécile.**
> She's an idiot.

Il fait l'imbécile dans la classe.
He plays the fool in the class.

imiter VERB
to imitate

immédiatement ADVERB
immediately

immense ADJECTIVE
huge
une maison immense
a huge house

l' **immeuble** MASC NOUN
block of flats
J'habite dans un immeuble.
I live in a block of flats.

les **immigrés** MASC PL NOUN
immigrants

immobilier MASC ADJECTIVE
(FEM **immobilière**)
une agence immobilière
an estate agent's

impair MASC ADJECTIVE
un nombre impair
an odd number

l' **impasse** FEM NOUN
cul-de-sac
Ma maison est au bout d'une impasse.
My house is at the end of a cul-de-sac.

impeccable ADJECTIVE
1 **immaculate**
Elle est toujours impeccable.
She's always immaculate.
2 **perfect**
C'est impeccable!
That's perfect!

l' **imper** MASC NOUN
raincoat

l' **imperméable** MASC NOUN
raincoat

impoli MASC ADJECTIVE
(FEM **impolie**)
rude

l' **importance** FEM NOUN
Ça n'a pas d'importance.
It doesn't matter.

important MASC ADJECTIVE
(FEM **importante**)
1 **important**
une lettre importante
an important letter
2 **large**
un nombre important
a large number

importer VERB
Peu importe.
It doesn't matter.

impossible ADJECTIVE
impossible

l' **impression** FEM NOUN
impression
Ce n'est qu'une impression.
It's only an impression.
avoir l'impression que
to have a feeling that
J'ai l'impression qu'il va neiger.
I have a feeling that it's going to snow.

impressionnant MASC
ADJECTIVE (FEM **impressionnante**)
impressive

impressionné MASC ADJECTIVE
(FEM **impressionnée**)
impressed
Je suis très impressionné.
I'm very impressed.

l' **imprimante** FEM NOUN
printer

imprimer VERB
to print

l' **incendie** MASC NOUN
fire
> un incendie de forêt
> a forest fire

l' **incident** MASC NOUN
incident

l' **inconnu** MASC NOUN
l' **inconnue** FEM NOUN
stranger
> Ne parle pas à des
> inconnus.
> Don't speak to strangers.

l' **inconvénient** MASC NOUN
disadvantage

incorrect MASC ADJECTIVE
(FEM **incorrecte**)
incorrect
> une réponse incorrecte
> an incorrect answer

incroyable ADJECTIVE
incredible

l' **Inde** FEM NOUN
India

indépendant MASC ADJECTIVE
(FEM **indépendante**)
independent

l' **index**
MASC NOUN
index finger

les **indications** FEM PL NOUN
instructions
> Suivez les indications.
> Follow the instructions.

l' **indice** MASC NOUN
clue

> Je te donne un indice?
> Shall I give you a clue?

indien MASC ADJECTIVE
(FEM **indienne**)
Indian

l' **Indien** MASC NOUN
l' **Indienne** FEM NOUN
Indian
> les Indiens
> Indians

l' **industrie** FEM NOUN
industry

infirme ADJECTIVE
disabled

l' **infirmerie** FEM NOUN
medical room
> Elle est à l'infirmerie.
> She's in the medical room.

l' **infirmier**
MASC NOUN
l' **infirmière**
FEM NOUN
nurse

l' **informaticien** MASC NOUN
l' **informaticienne** FEM NOUN
computer scientist

les **informations** FEM PL
NOUN
1 news
> J'aime regarder les
> informations à la télé.
> I like watching the news on the TV.

2 information
Je voudrais quelques informations, s'il vous plaît.
I'd like some information, please.
une information
a piece of information

l' **informatique** FEM NOUN
1 ICT
mon prof d'informatique
my ICT teacher
2 computing
Il travaille dans l'informatique.
He works in computing.

l' **infusion** FEM NOUN
herbal tea

l' **ingénieur** MASC NOUN
engineer

l' **inhalateur** MASC NOUN
inhaler

les **initiales** FEM PL NOUN
initials
Quelles sont tes initiales?
What are your initials?

l' **initiation** FEM NOUN
introduction
un stage d'initiation au karaté
an introductory course in karate

injuste ADJECTIVE
unfair
C'est vraiment trop injuste.
It is really quite unfair.

innocent MASC ADJECTIVE
(FEM **innocente**)
innocent

l' **inondation** FEM NOUN
flood

inquiet MASC ADJECTIVE
(FEM **inquiète**)
worried

s' **inquiéter** VERB
to worry
Ne t'inquiète pas!
Don't worry!

l' **insecte** MASC NOUN
insect

insolent MASC ADJECTIVE
(FEM **insolente**)
cheeky

l' **inspecteur** MASC NOUN
l' **inspectrice** FEM NOUN
inspector
Il y a une inspectrice à l'école.
There's an inspector in the school.

l' **instant** MASC NOUN
moment
Attendez un instant.
Wait a moment.

l' **instituteur** MASC NOUN
l' **institutrice** FEM NOUN
primary school teacher

l' **instrument** MASC NOUN
instrument
un instrument de musique
a musical instrument

insupportable ADJECTIVE
unbearable

intelligent MASC ADJECTIVE
(FEM **intelligente**)
intelligent
Mon chien est très intelligent.
My dog is very intelligent.

French English

a
b
c
d
e
f
g
h
i
j
k
l
m
n
o
p
q
r
s
t
u
v
w
x
y
z

l' **interdiction** FEM NOUN
'interdiction de fumer'
'no smoking'
'interdiction de stationner'
'no parking'

interdire VERB
to forbid
Ses parents lui ont interdit de sortir.
His parents have forbidden him to go out.

interdit MASC ADJECTIVE
(FEM **interdite**)
forbidden
C'est interdit.
It's forbidden.
Il est interdit de courir dans les couloirs.
Running in the corridors is forbidden.

intéressant MASC ADJECTIVE
(FEM **intéressante**)
interesting

intéresser VERB
to interest
L'histoire, ça m'intéresse.
I'm interested in history.
Je m'intéresse aux dinosaures.
I'm interested in dinosaurs.

l' **intérêt** MASC NOUN
Tu as intérêt à te dépêcher.
You'd better hurry up.
C'est un film sans intérêt.
It's not a very interesting film.

l' **intérieur**
MASC NOUN
à l'intérieur
inside
Il fait plus frais à l'intérieur.
It's cooler inside.

l' **internat** MASC NOUN
boarding school

international MASC ADJECTIVE
(FEM **internationale**)
international

l' **interne** MASC/FEM NOUN
boarder

Did you know…?

In French secondary schools, pupils can be described as **externe** *if they go home for lunch,* **demi-pensionnaire** *if they have a school lunch, or* **interne** *if they stay as boarders at the school.*

l' **internet** MASC NOUN
internet
sur internet
on the internet

l' **interprète** MASC/FEM NOUN
interpreter

l' **interrogation** FEM NOUN
test
une interrogation écrite
a written test
une interrogation orale
an oral test

interroger VERB
to ask questions

interrompre VERB
to interrupt
Ne m'interrompez pas.
Don't interrupt me.

intime ADJECTIVE
un journal intime
a diary

inutile ADJECTIVE
useless

inventer VERB
1 to invent
J'ai inventé une machine.
I have invented a machine.

2 to make up
Elle a inventé une excuse.
She made up an excuse.

l' **inventeur** MASC NOUN
inventor

inverse

> **inverse** *can be an adjective or a noun.*

A ADJECTIVE
dans le sens inverse des aiguilles d'une montre
anti-clockwise
B MASC NOUN
C'est l'inverse.
It's the other way round.

l' **invité** MASC NOUN
l' **invitée**
FEM NOUN
guest

inviter VERB
to invite

l' **iPod**® MASC NOUN
iPod®

irai VERB ▷*see* aller
J'irai demain au supermarché.
I'll go to the supermarket tomorrow.

l' **Irak** MASC NOUN
Iraq

l' **Iran** MASC NOUN
Iran

irlandais MASC ADJECTIVE
(FEM **irlandaise**)
Irish

l' **Irlandais** MASC NOUN
Irishman
les Irlandais
the Irish

l' **Irlandaise** FEM NOUN
Irishwoman

l' **Irlande** FEM NOUN
Ireland
la République d'Irlande
the Irish Republic
l'Irlande du Nord
Northern Ireland

l' **ironie** FEM NOUN
irony

ironique ADJECTIVE
ironical

irons VERB ▷*see* aller
Nous irons à la plage cet après-midi.
We'll go to the beach this afternoon.

irrégulier MASC ADJECTIVE
(FEM **irrégulière**)
irregular
un verbe irrégulier
an irregular verb

irriter VERB
to irritate
Elle m'irrite.
She's irritating me.

islamique ADJECTIVE
Islamic

l' **Islande** FEM NOUN
Iceland

isolé MASC ADJECTIVE (FEM **isolée**)
isolated
une ferme isolée
an isolated farm

Israël MASC NOUN
Israel

israélien MASC ADJECTIVE
(FEM **israélienne**)
Israeli

l' **Israélien** MASC NOUN
l' **Israélienne** FEM NOUN
Israeli

l' **issue** FEM NOUN
'issue de secours'
'emergency exit'
une voie sans issue
a dead end

l' **Italie** FEM NOUN
Italy

italien MASC NOUN, MASC
ADJECTIVE (FEM **italienne**)
Italian

l' **Italien** MASC NOUN
l' **Italienne** FEM NOUN
Italian

J j

j' PRONOUN

> **Language tip**
> *je changes to* **j'** *before a vowel sound.*

I
> **J'arrive!**
> I'm coming!
> **J'habite à Calais.**
> I live in Calais.

la **jalousie** FEM NOUN
jealousy

jaloux MASC ADJECTIVE
(FEM **jalouse**)
jealous

jamais ADVERB
never
> **Tu vas souvent au cinéma?
> — Non, jamais.**
> Do you go to the cinema often?
> — No, never.
> **Elle ne fait jamais la vaisselle.**
> She never does the washing-up.

la **jambe** FEM NOUN
leg

le **jambon** MASC NOUN
ham
> **le jambon cru**
> Parma ham

janvier MASC NOUN
January
> **en janvier**
> in January
> **au mois de janvier**
> in January
> **le vingt-quatre janvier**
> the twenty-fourth of January

le **Japon** MASC NOUN
Japan

japonais MASC NOUN, MASC
ADJECTIVE (FEM **japonaise**)
Japanese

le **Japonais** MASC NOUN
Japanese man
> **les Japonais**
> the Japanese

la **Japonaise** FEM NOUN
Japanese woman

le **jardin** MASC NOUN
garden
> **Nous avons un grand jardin
> derrière la maison.**
> We have a big garden at the
> back of the house.
> **un jardin d'enfants**
> a kindergarten

le **jardinage** MASC NOUN
gardening
> **Le passe-temps préféré de
> mon père, c'est le jardinage.**
> My dad's favourite hobby is
> gardening.

le **jardinier** MASC NOUN
gardener

jaune

> **jaune** *can be an adjective or a noun.*

A ADJECTIVE
yellow
> **une robe jaune**
> a yellow dress
B MASC NOUN
yellow

Ma couleur préférée, c'est le jaune.
My favourite colour is yellow.
un jaune d'œuf
an egg yolk

le **jazz** MASC NOUN
jazz

je PRONOUN

I
Je déteste les araignées.
I hate spiders.

le **jean** MASC NOUN
jeans
Elle porte un jean.
She is wearing jeans.
une veste en jean
a denim jacket

la **jeannette** FEM NOUN
Brownie

jeter VERB
1 **to throw**
Jette ton chewing-gum à la poubelle.
Throw your chewing gum in the bin.
2 **to throw away**
J'ai jeté mes vieux jouets.
I've thrown away my old toys.

le **jeton** MASC NOUN
counter
Je vous donne six jetons chacun.
I'm giving you six counters each.

le **jeu** MASC NOUN (PL les **jeux**)
game
C'est un jeu qui s'appelle 'le Pendu'.
It's a game called 'Hangman'.
un jeu de mots
a pun
un jeu de société
a board game

un jeu électronique
an electronic game
un jeu vidéo
a video game
un jeu de cartes
a pack of cards/a card game

J'ai acheté un nouveau jeu de cartes.
I've bought a new pack of cards.
Tu connais ce jeu de cartes?
Do you know this card game?

le **jeudi** MASC NOUN
1 **Thursday**
Aujourd'hui, nous sommes jeudi.
It's Thursday today.
2 **on Thursday**
Il va venir jeudi.
He's coming on Thursday.
Le musée est fermé le jeudi.
The museum is closed on Thursdays.

tous les jeudis
every Thursday
le jeudi
on Thursdays
jeudi dernier
last Thursday
jeudi prochain
next Thursday
À jeudi!
See you on Thursday!

jeune ADJECTIVE
young
  un jeune homme
  a young man
  une jeune femme
  a young woman
  une jeune fille
  a girl

les **jeunes** MASC PL NOUN
young people

la **jeunesse** FEM NOUN
youth

le **jogging** MASC NOUN
  1 jogging
    Il fait du jogging.
    He goes jogging.
  2 tracksuit
    Clémentine porte un jogging rose.
    Clémentine's wearing a pink tracksuit.

joli MASC ADJECTIVE (FEM **jolie**)
pretty

la **jonquille** FEM NOUN
daffodil

la **joue** FEM NOUN
cheek
  Elle a les joues roses.
  She's got pink cheeks.

jouer VERB
to play
  Le soir, je joue avec ma petite sœur.
  I play with my little sister in the evening.
  jouer de
  to play
  Il joue de la guitare et du piano.
  He plays the guitar and the piano.
  jouer à
  to play
  Elle joue au tennis.
  She plays tennis.
  Ils jouent aux cartes.
  They are playing cards.

le **jouet** MASC NOUN
toy

  Range tes jouets!
  Tidy up your toys!

le **joueur** MASC NOUN
la **joueuse** FEM NOUN
player

le **jour** MASC NOUN
day
  On est quel jour aujourd'hui?
  What day is it today?
  Il fait jour.
  It's daylight.
  le jour de l'An
  New Year's Day
  un jour de congé
  a day off
  le jour de Noël
  Christmas Day

un jour férié
a public holiday

dans huit jours
in a week
dans quinze jours
in a fortnight

le **journal** MASC NOUN
(PL les **journaux**)
1 newspaper
Mon père aime lire le journal.
My dad likes to read the
newspaper.
le journal télévisé
the television news
2 diary
**J'écris tous les jours dans
mon journal.**
I write in my diary every day.

le/la **journaliste** MASC/FEM
NOUN
journalist

la **journée** FEM NOUN
day
**Nous allons passer la journée
au bord de la mer.**
We are going to spend the day at
the seaside.
toute la journée
all day long

joyeux MASC ADJECTIVE
(FEM **joyeuse**)
happy

des enfants joyeux
happy children

Joyeux Noël!
Merry Christmas!
Joyeux anniversaire!
Happy birthday!
Joyeuses Pâques!
Happy Easter!

le **judo** MASC NOUN
judo
Le mercredi, je fais du judo.
I do judo on Wednesdays.

juif MASC ADJECTIVE (FEM **juive**)
Jewish

juillet MASC NOUN
July
en juillet
in July
le onze juillet
the eleventh of July

juin MASC NOUN
June
en juin
in June
au mois de juin
in June
le vingt-trois juin
the twenty-third of June

jumeau MASC ADJECTIVE
(FEM **jumelle**)
twin
C'est mon frère jumeau.
He's my twin brother.
C'est ma sœur jumelle.
She's my twin sister.
Marcel et Léon sont jumeaux.
Marcel and Léon are twins.

les **jumeaux** MASC PL NOUN
twins

Les jumeaux s'appellent Jean et Marc.

The twins are called Jean and Marc.

jumeler VERB
  to twin
  Hastings est jumelée avec Béthune.
  Hastings is twinned with Béthune.

les **jumelles** FEM PL NOUN
  1 **twins**
  Les jumelles s'appellent Anna et Louise.
  The twins are called Anna and Louise.
  2 **binoculars**

la **jungle** FEM NOUN
  jungle

la **jupe** FEM NOUN
  skirt

jurer VERB
  to swear
  Je jure que c'est vrai!
  I swear it's true!

le **jus** MASC NOUN
  juice
  un jus de fruit
  a fruit juice
  du jus d'orange
  orange juice

jusqu'à PREPOSITION
  1 **as far as**
  Allez jusqu'à la mairie et tournez à droite.
  Go as far as the town hall, then turn right.
  2 **until**
  On est en vacances jusqu'à dimanche.
  We're on holiday until Sunday.

juste ADJECTIVE
  fair
  Il est sévère, mais juste.
  He's strict but fair.

K k

a
b
c
d
e
f
g
h
i
j
k
l
m
n
o
p
q
r
s
t
u
v
w
x
y
z

kaki ADJECTIVE
khaki
> **des chaussures kaki**
> khaki shoes

le **kangourou**
MASC NOUN
kangaroo

le **karaté** MASC NOUN
karate
> **Le lundi, je fais du karaté.**
> I do karate on Mondays

la **kermesse** FEM NOUN
fête
> **Au mois de juin, il y a une kermesse à mon école.**
> There's a fête at our school in June.

le **kilo** MASC NOUN
kilo
> **un kilo d'oranges**
> a kilo of oranges

le **kilogramme** MASC NOUN
kilogramme

le **kilomètre** MASC NOUN
kilometre
> **Mon école est à deux kilomètres de chez moi.**
> My school is two kilometres from my house.

le/la **kinésithérapeute**
MASC/FEM NOUN
physiotherapist

le **kiosque** MASC NOUN
> **un kiosque à journaux**
> a news stand

le **koala** MASC NOUN
koala

le **K-way**® MASC NOUN
cagoule

l'

l' can be an article or a pronoun.

Language tip

le and la both change to l' before a vowel sound.

A ARTICLE
the
l'arbre
the tree

B PRONOUN

1 **him**
C'est un homme intelligent: je l'admire beaucoup.
He's an intelligent man: I admire him very much.

2 **her**
Ma maîtresse est gentille et je l'aime bien.
My teacher is nice and I like her.

3 **it**
J'aime bien ce T-shirt. Je l'achète.
I like this T-shirt. I'm going to buy it.

la

la can be an article or a pronoun.

A ARTICLE
the
la maison
the house

B PRONOUN

1 **her**
C'est ma voisine: je la vois tous les jours.
This is my neighbour: I see her every day.

2 **it**
Prends la gomme et mets-la dans la trousse.
Take the rubber and put it in the pencil case.

là ADVERB

1 **there**
Ton livre est là, sur la table.
Your book's there, on the table.

2 **here**
Elle n'est pas là.
She isn't here.

là-bas ADVERB
over there
Va t'asseoir là-bas.
Go and sit over there.

le **laboratoire** MASC NOUN
laboratory

le **labyrinthe** MASC NOUN
maze

le **lac** MASC NOUN
lake

le **lacet** MASC NOUN
lace
des chaussures à lacets
lace-up shoes

là-haut ADVERB
up there
Le ballon est là-haut sur le toit.
The ball is up there on the roof.

French English

a b c d e f g h i j k l m n o p q r s t u v w x y z

laid MASC ADJECTIVE (FEM **laide**)
ugly
Elle est très laide.
She's very ugly.

la **laine** FEM NOUN
wool
un pull en laine
a woolly jumper

laisser VERB
1 to leave
Laisse ton cahier sur la table.
Leave your jotter on the table.
2 to let
Laisse-le parler.
Let him speak.

le **lait** MASC NOUN
milk
Je voudrais du lait.
I'd like some milk.
un café au lait
a white coffee

la **laitue** FEM NOUN
lettuce

la **lampe** FEM NOUN
lamp
une lampe de poche
a torch

lancer VERB
to throw
Lance-moi le ballon!
Throw me the ball!

le **landau** MASC NOUN
pram

la **langouste** FEM NOUN
crayfish

Did you know…?
A **langouste** is a popular kind of seafood in France and is similar to a lobster.

la **langue** FEM NOUN
1 tongue
Elle m'a tiré la langue!
She stuck her tongue out at me!
2 language
une langue étrangère
a foreign language

le **lapin** MASC NOUN
rabbit

le **lard** MASC NOUN
streaky bacon

les **lardons** MASC PL NOUN
chunks of bacon

large ADJECTIVE
wide

la **largeur** FEM NOUN
width

le **lavabo** MASC NOUN
washbasin

la **lavande** FEM NOUN
lavender

laver VERB
to wash
Tu peux laver la voiture?
Could you wash the car?
■ se laver
to wash
Je me lave le matin.
I get washed in the morning.
se laver les mains
to wash one's hands
Lave-toi les mains.
Wash your hands.

le **lave-vaisselle** MASC NOUN
dishwasher

le

> *le can be an article or a pronoun.*

> **Language tip**
> **le** *changes to* **l'** *before a vowel sound.*

A ARTICLE
the
le livre
the book
Aujourd'hui nous sommes le douze mai.
Today is the twelfth of May.

B PRONOUN

1 him
C'est mon voisin: je le vois tous les jours.
He's my neighbour: I see him every day.

2 it
Où est mon stylo? Je ne le trouve pas.
Where's my pen? I can't find it.

lécher VERB
to lick

la **leçon** FEM NOUN
lesson
une leçon de piano
a piano lesson

le **lecteur** MASC NOUN
un lecteur de cassettes
a cassette player
un lecteur de CD
a CD player
un lecteur MP3
an MP3 player

la **lecture** FEM NOUN
reading
J'aime la lecture.
I love reading.

> **Language tip**
> *Be careful! The French word* **lecture** *does not mean the same as the English word* **lecture**.

léger MASC ADJECTIVE (FEM **légère**)
light
un déjeuner léger
a light lunch

légèrement ADVERB
slightly

les **légumes**
MASC PL NOUN
vegetables

Je n'aime pas les légumes.
I don't like vegetables.

le **lendemain** MASC NOUN
next day
Il est parti le lendemain.
He left the next day.

lent MASC ADJECTIVE (FEM **lente**)
slow

lentement ADVERB
slowly
Parle plus lentement s'il te plaît.
Please speak more slowly.

les **lentilles** FEM PL NOUN

1 contact lenses
Je porte des lentilles.
I wear contact lenses.

2 lentils
un rôti de porc aux lentilles
roast pork with lentils

le **léopard** MASC NOUN
leopard

les

les can be an article or a pronoun.

A ARTICLE
the
les arbres
the trees

B PRONOUN
them
J'ai deux chiens et je les promène tous les jours.
I've got two dogs and I walk them every day.

la **lessive** FEM NOUN
1 **washing powder**
2 **washing**
Maman n'aime pas faire la lessive.
Mum doesn't like doing the washing.

la **lettre** FEM NOUN
letter
J'écris une lettre à ma meilleure copine.
I'm writing a letter to my best friend.

leur

leur can be an adjective or a pronoun.

A ADJECTIVE
their
leur ami
their friend

B PRONOUN
them
Donnez-leur le ballon.
Give them the ball.

leurs PL ADJECTIVE
their
leurs amis
their friends

lever VERB
to raise
Levez la jambe gauche.
Raise your left leg.
Levez la main!
Put your hand up!
■ **se lever**
to get up/to stand up

Language tip

se lever *has two translations. Look at the examples.*

Il se lève souvent à six heures.
He often gets up at six o'clock.
Levez-vous!
Stand up!

la **lèvre** FEM NOUN
lip

le **lézard** MASC NOUN
lizard

la **liberté**
FEM NOUN
freedom

le/la **libraire** MASC/FEM NOUN
bookseller

la **librairie** FEM NOUN
bookshop
J'aime acheter des livres à la librairie.
I like to buy books in the bookshop.

Language tip

Be careful! **librairie** *does not mean the same as* **library**.

libre ADJECTIVE
free

Tu es libre de faire ce que tu veux.
You are free to do as you wish.
Avez-vous une chambre de libre?
Have you got a free room?

la **licence** FEM NOUN
degree
une licence de droit
a law degree

le **lièvre** MASC NOUN
hare

la **ligne** FEM NOUN
line
Tracez deux lignes verticales.
Draw two vertical lines.
Mettez-vous en ligne.
Line up.

le **lilas** MASC NOUN
lilac

la **limace** FEM NOUN
slug

la **limonade** FEM NOUN
lemonade

le **linge** MASC NOUN
linen
le linge sale
dirty linen
Je vais étendre le linge.
I'm going to hang out the washing.

le **lion** MASC NOUN
lion

la **lionne** FEM NOUN
lioness

lire VERB
to read

Le soir, je lis dans mon lit.
At night I read in bed.

lis, lisent, lisez VERB ▷see **lire**
Je lis beaucoup.
I read a lot.
Qu'est-ce que tu lis?
What are you reading?
Ils lisent des BD.
They read comics.
Lisez la première phrase.
Read the first sentence.

la **liste** FEM NOUN
list

lit

lit *can be a noun or part of the verb* **lire**.

A MASC NOUN
bed
aller au lit
to go to bed
Je vais au lit à sept heures.
I go to bed at seven.
faire son lit
to make one's bed
Je fais mon lit tous les matins.
I make my bed every morning.
un grand lit
a double bed
un lit de camp
a campbed

B VERB ▷see **lire**
Il lit des magazines.
He reads magazines.

le **litre** MASC NOUN
litre
un litre de lait
a litre of milk

la **littérature** FEM NOUN
literature

le **livre** MASC NOUN
book

un livre de poche
a paperback

la **livre** FEM NOUN
pound
> **Le guide coûte trois livres.**
> The guide book costs £3.

Did you know...?
une livre *is also a weight – 500 grams, which is nearly the same as a British pound (450 grams).*

le **livret** MASC NOUN
> **le livret scolaire**
> the school report book

logique ADJECTIVE
logical

loin ADVERB
far
> **La gare n'est pas très loin d'ici.**
> The station is not very far from here.
> **C'est un peu plus loin.**
> It's a little further on.

lointain MASC ADJECTIVE
(FEM **lointaine**)
distant
> **un pays lointain**
> a distant country

les **loisirs** MASC PL NOUN
1 free time
> **Qu'est-ce que tu fais d'habitude pendant tes loisirs?**
> What do you usually do in your free time?
2 hobbies
> **Le ski et l'équitation sont des loisirs coûteux.**
> Skiing and riding are expensive hobbies.

Londres NOUN
London
> **J'habite à Londres.**
> I live in London.
> **Je vais à Londres.**
> I'm going to London.

long MASC ADJECTIVE (FEM **longue**)
long
> **une longue promenade**
> a long walk
> **Elle a les cheveux longs.**
> She has long hair.

la **longueur** FEM NOUN
length

la **loterie** FEM NOUN
lottery
> **la loterie nationale**
> the National Lottery

le **lotissement** MASC NOUN
housing estate

le **loto** MASC NOUN
1 lottery
> **Mes parents jouent au loto toutes les semaines.**
> My parents play the lottery every week.
> **le loto sportif**
> the pools
2 bingo
> **On va jouer au loto.**
> We're going to play bingo.

la **louche** FEM NOUN
ladle

louer VERB
1 to let
> **Ils louent des chambres à des étudiants.**
> They let rooms to students.
> **'à louer'**
> 'to let'

2 to rent
L'été, nous louons un petit appartement au bord de la mer.
In the summer we rent a little flat by the sea.

3 to hire
Est-ce que vous louez des vélos?
Do you hire bikes?

le **loup** MASC NOUN
wolf

la **loupe** FEM NOUN
magnifying glass

lourd MASC ADJECTIVE
(FEM **lourde**)
heavy

la **loutre** FEM NOUN
otter

la **luge** FEM NOUN
sledge
J'aime bien faire de la luge.
I like sledging.
Quand il neige, je fais de la luge.
I go sledging when it snows.

lui PRONOUN

1 him
Voilà ton père: demande-lui!
Here's your dad – ask him!
Je pense beaucoup à lui.
I think about him a lot.
Lui, il est toujours en retard!
Oh, HE's always late!
Il a construit son bateau lui-même.
He built his boat himself.

lui-même
himself

2 to him
Michael m'énerve, alors je ne lui parle pas en ce moment.
Michael's getting on my nerves so I'm not speaking to him at the moment.

3 her
Voilà ta mère: demande-lui!
Here's your mum – ask her!

4 to her
C'est Julie au téléphone. Tu veux lui parler?
Julie's on the phone. Do you want to speak to her?

5 it
Cette plante ne pousse pas vite; je vais lui donner plus d'eau.
This plant isn't growing well; I'm going to give it more water.

la **lumière** FEM NOUN
light
Sylvia, allume la lumière s'il te plaît.
Sylvia, turn on the light please.

lunatique ADJECTIVE
temperamental

le **lundi** MASC NOUN

1 Monday
Aujourd'hui, nous sommes lundi.
It's Monday today.

2 on Monday
Nous partons lundi.
We're leaving on Monday.
Le lundi, je vais à la piscine.
I go swimming on Mondays.

tous les lundis
every Monday

le lundi
on Mondays
lundi dernier
last Monday
lundi prochain
next Monday
À lundi!
See you on Monday!

la **lune** FEM NOUN
moon

les **lunettes** FEM PL NOUN
glasses
> **Je porte des lunettes.**
> I wear glasses.
> **des lunettes de soleil**
> sunglasses
> **des lunettes de plongée**
> swimming goggles

la **lutte** FEM NOUN
wrestling

le **luxe** MASC NOUN
luxury
> **de luxe**
> luxury
> **un hôtel de luxe**
> a luxury hotel

luxueux MASC ADJECTIVE
(FEM **luxueuse**)
luxurious

le **lycée** MASC NOUN
secondary school

Did you know...?

*In France, pupils go to a **collège** between the ages of 11 and 15, and then to a **lycée** until the age of 18.*

> **un lycée technique**
> a technical college

le **lycéen** MASC NOUN
la **lycéenne** FEM NOUN
secondary school pupil

M m

M. ABBREVIATION
Mr
> **M. Bernard**
> Mr Bernard

m' PRONOUN
me

> **Language tip**
> *The French word* **me** *changes to* **m'** *before a vowel sound.*

> **Dominique m'invite chez elle ce week-end.**
> Dominique has invited me to her house this weekend.
> **Il m'attend depuis une heure.**
> He's been waiting for me for an hour.

> **Language tip**
> **m'** *is often not translated.*

> **Je m'habille à sept heures tous les matins.**
> I get dressed at seven every morning.

ma FEM ADJECTIVE ▷ *see* **mon**
my
> **ma mère**
> my mother

les **macaronis** MASC PL NOUN
macaroni

le **machin** MASC NOUN
thingy

> **Passe-moi le machin pour râper les carottes.**
> Pass me the thingy for grating carrots.

la **machine** FEM NOUN
machine
> **une machine à sous**
> a fruit machine
> **une machine à laver**
> a washing machine

le **maçon** MASC NOUN
bricklayer

madame FEM NOUN
(PL **mesdames**)
1 Mrs
> **Madame Legall**
> Mrs Legall
2 Madam
> **Madame, ...**
> Dear Madam, ...

> **Language tip**
> **madame** *is a useful way of attracting a woman's attention.*

> **Madame! Vous avez oublié votre parapluie!**
> Excuse me! You've forgotten your umbrella!

mademoiselle FEM NOUN
(PL **mesdemoiselles**)
Miss
> **Mademoiselle Martin**
> Miss Martin

> **Language tip**
> **mademoiselle** *is a useful way of attracting a young or unmarried woman's attention.*

a
b
c
d
e
f
g
h
i
j
k
l
m
n
o
p
q
r
s
t
u
v
w
x
y
z

Mademoiselle! L'addition, s'il vous plaît!
Excuse me, could I have the bill?

le **magasin** MASC NOUN
shop
Les magasins ouvrent à huit heures.
The shops open at eight o'clock.
J'aime faire les magasins.
I like going shopping.

magasiner VERB (*Canada*)
to shop

le **magazine** MASC NOUN
magazine

le **magicien**
MASC NOUN
la **magicienne**
FEM NOUN
magician

la **magie** FEM NOUN
magic
un tour de magie
a magic trick

magique ADJECTIVE
magic
une baguette magique
a magic wand

le **magnétophone** MASC NOUN
tape recorder

le **magnétoscope** MASC NOUN
video recorder

magnifique ADJECTIVE
superb

mai MASC NOUN
May
en mai
in May

le trente mai
the thirtieth of May

le premier mai
the first of May

Did you know...?
le premier mai (*May 1st*) *is a holiday in France. People give friends little bunches of lily of the valley (***muguet***) for good luck.*

maigre ADJECTIVE
skinny

le **mail** MASC NOUN
email

le **maillot de bain** MASC NOUN
1 **swimsuit**
J'adore le maillot de bain de Jacqueline.
I love Jacqueline's swimsuit.
2 **swimming trunks**
Paul a un nouveau maillot de bain.
Paul has new swimming trunks.

la **main** FEM NOUN
hand
Donne-moi la main!
Give me your hand!
se serrer la main
to shake hands
Les garçons se serrent la main en arrivant à l'école le matin.
The boys shake hands when they get to school in the morning.

maintenant ADVERB
now

le **maire** MASC NOUN
mayor

la **mairie** FEM NOUN
town hall

mais CONJUNCTION
but
> J'aime bien les maths mais c'est difficile.
> I like maths, but it's difficult.

le **maïs** MASC NOUN
1 sweetcorn
> J'adore le maïs.
> I love sweetcorn.
2 maize

la **maison**
FEM NOUN
house

> Ils habitent dans une grande maison.
> They live in a big house.
> Viens à la maison si tu veux.
> Come to the house if you want.
> Je vais rester à la maison pendant les vacances.
> I'm going to stay at home in the holidays.
> rentrer à la maison
> to go home
> Rentrons à la maison.
> Let's go home.

le **maître** MASC NOUN
la **maîtresse** FEM NOUN
1 teacher
> Cette année, j'ai un maître au lieu d'une maîtresse.
> This year I have a male teacher instead of a female one.
> Maîtresse!
> Miss!

2 master
> Ce chien suit son maître partout.
> This dog follows his master everywhere.
> un maître nageur
> a lifeguard

Majorque FEM NOUN
Majorca

majuscule

> **majuscule** can be an adjective or a noun.

A ADJECTIVE
capital
> un M majuscule
> a capital M
B FEM NOUN
capital letter
> Les jours de la semaine ne prennent pas de majuscule en français.
> In French the days of the week don't start with a capital letter.

mal

> **mal** can be a noun, an adjective or an adverb.

A MASC NOUN (PL les **maux**)
ache
> J'ai mal aux dents.
> I've got toothache.
> J'ai mal au dos.
> My back hurts.
> Ça fait mal.
> It hurts.
> Où est-ce que tu as mal?
> Where does it hurt?

> **J'ai mal à la tête.**
> I've got a headache.

B MASC, FEM, PL ADJECTIVE
pas mal
not bad

Ça va? — Oui, pas mal.
How are you? — Not bad.

c ADVERB
   badly
   C'est mal fait.
   It's badly done.

malade ADJECTIVE
   ill

la **maladie** FEM NOUN
   illness

mâle ADJECTIVE
   male

malheureusement ADVERB
   unfortunately

malin MASC ADJECTIVE
   (FEM **maligne**)
   cunning

la **maman** FEM NOUN
   mum

la **mamie** FEM NOUN
   granny

la **manche** FEM NOUN
   sleeve
   un T-shirt à manches longues
   a long-sleeved T-shirt
   la Manche
   the Channel

la **mandarine** FEM NOUN
   mandarin

le **manège** MASC NOUN
   merry-go-round

manger VERB
   to eat
   **Pour le petit déjeuner,
   je mange des céréales.**
   I have cereal for breakfast.

la **mangue** FEM NOUN
   mango

la **manifestation** FEM NOUN
   demonstration

le **mannequin** MASC NOUN
   model

manquer VERB
   to miss
   **Il manque des pages à ce
   livre.**
   There are some pages missing
   from this book.
   Mes parents me manquent.
   I miss my parents.
   Ma sœur me manque.
   I miss my sister.

le **manteau** MASC NOUN
   (PL les **manteaux**)
   coat

manuel MASC ADJECTIVE
   (FEM **manuelle**)
   les travaux manuels
   arts and crafts

le **maquereau** MASC NOUN
   (PL les **maquereaux**)
   mackerel

la **maquette** FEM NOUN
   model

le **maquillage** MASC NOUN
   make-up

French   English

se **maquiller** VERB
  to put on one's make-up
    J'adore me maquiller.
    I love to put on make-up.

le **marchand** MASC NOUN
la **marchande** FEM NOUN
  1 shopkeeper
    un marchand de journaux
    a newsagent
    un marchand de fruits et
    légumes
    a greengrocer
  2 stallholder

la **marche** FEM NOUN
  step
    Fais attention à la marche!
    Mind the step!

le **marché** MASC NOUN
  market

marcher VERB
  1 to walk
    Marchez deux par deux.
    Walk in twos.
  2 to work
    L'ascenseur ne marche pas.
    The lift isn't working.
    Ça marche?
    How are you getting on?

le **mardi** MASC NOUN
  1 Tuesday
    Aujourd'hui, nous sommes
    mardi.
    Today is Tuesday.

    Mardi gras
    Shrove Tuesday
  2 on Tuesday
    Ils reviennent mardi.
    They're coming back on Tuesday.
    Le mardi, je vais à la gym.
    I go to the gym on Tuesdays.

tous les mardis
every Tuesday
le mardi
on Tuesdays
mardi dernier
last Tuesday
mardi prochain
next Tuesday
À mardi!
See you on Tuesday!

la **marelle** FEM NOUN
  hopscotch

la **margarine** FEM NOUN
  margarine

la **marge** FEM NOUN
  margin
    Laissez une marge à droite
    de la page.
    Leave a margin on the right-
    hand side of the page.

le **mari** MASC NOUN
  husband
    son mari
    her husband

le **mariage** MASC NOUN
  wedding
    Samedi, je vais à un mariage.
    I'm going to a wedding on
    Saturday.

marié MASC ADJECTIVE
(FEM **mariée**)
  married
    Ma sœur est mariée.
    My sister is married.

le **marié** MASC NOUN
bridegroom
les mariés
the bride and groom

la **mariée** FEM NOUN
bride

se **marier** VERB
to get married
Mon frère se marie ce week-end.
My brother is getting married this weekend.

marin MASC NOUN
sailor

marine MASC, FEM, PL ADJECTIVE
bleu marine
navy-blue
des chaussettes bleu marine
navy-blue socks

la **marionnette**
FEM NOUN
puppet

la **marmelade** FEM NOUN
la marmelade d'oranges
marmalade

le **Maroc** MASC NOUN
Morocco

marocain MASC ADJECTIVE
(FEM **marocaine**)
Moroccan

le **Marocain** MASC NOUN
la **Marocaine** FEM NOUN
Moroccan

la **marque** FEM NOUN
1 mark
des marques de doigts
fingermarks

2 make
De quelle marque est ton jean?
What make are your jeans?
3 brand
une marque de lessive
a brand of washing powder

À vos marques! prêts! partez!
Ready, steady, go!

marquer VERB
1 to mark
Tu peux marquer où se trouve ton village sur la carte?
Can you mark where your village is on the map?
2 to score
L'équipe irlandaise a marqué dix points.
The Irish team scored ten points.

la **marraine** FEM NOUN
godmother

marrant MASC ADJECTIVE
(FEM **marrante**)
funny

marron

marron can be an adjective or a noun.

A MASC, FEM, PL ADJECTIVE
brown
J'ai les yeux marron.
I have brown eyes.
B MASC NOUN
1 chestnut
la crème de marrons
chestnut purée
2 brown
Je n'aime pas le marron.
I don't like the colour brown.

Mars NOUN
Mars

la planète Mars
Mars

mars MASC NOUN
March
en mars
in March
le dix-huit mars
the eighteenth of March

le **marteau** MASC NOUN
(PL les **marteaux**)
hammer

le **martien** MASC NOUN
la **martienne** FEM NOUN
Martian

masculin MASC ADJECTIVE
(FEM **masculine**)
masculine

le **masque** MASC NOUN
mask

masser VERB
to massage

le **match** MASC NOUN
match
un match de football
a football match
Match nul!
It's a draw!

le **matelas** MASC NOUN
mattress
un matelas pneumatique
an air bed

maternel MASC ADJECTIVE
(FEM **maternelle**)
ma grand-mère maternelle
my mother's mother
l'école maternelle
nursery school

la **maternelle** FEM NOUN
nursery school

Did you know...?
The **maternelle** *is a state school for three to six year-olds.*

les **mathématiques** FEM PL NOUN
mathematics

les **maths** FEM PL NOUN
maths
J'adore les maths.
I love maths.

le **matin** MASC NOUN
morning
à trois heures du matin
at three o'clock in the morning
ce matin
this morning

la **matinée** FEM NOUN
toute la matinée
all morning

mauvais

mauvais *can be an adjective or an adverb.*

A MASC ADJECTIVE (FEM **mauvaise**)
1 bad
une mauvaise note
a bad mark
Je suis mauvais en maths.
I'm bad at maths.

Il fait mauvais.
The weather's bad.

2 wrong
Vous avez fait le mauvais numéro.
You've dialled the wrong number.
B ADVERB
sentir mauvais
to smell
Ça sent mauvais ici!
It smells in here!

la **mayonnaise** FEM NOUN
mayonnaise

me PRONOUN
1 me
Elle me téléphone tous les jours.
She phones me every day.

> **Language tip**
> **me** *changes to* **m'** *before a vowel sound.*

Tu peux m'aider?
Can you help me?
2 to me
Il me parle en allemand.
He talks to me in German.

> **Language tip**
> **me** *is often not translated.*

Je me lève à sept heures tous les matins.
I get up at seven every morning.

le **mécanicien** MASC NOUN
mechanic

méchant MASC ADJECTIVE
(FEM **méchante**)
nasty
Elle est méchante avec moi.
She's nasty to me.

la **médaille** FEM NOUN
medal
la médaille de bronze
the bronze medal

le **médecin**
MASC NOUN
doctor
aller chez le médecin
to go to the doctor's
Ce soir, je vais chez le médecin.
I'm going to the doctor's this evening.

le **médicament** MASC NOUN
medicine
Tu as pris tes médicaments?
Have you taken your medicine?

la **Méditerranée** FEM NOUN
Mediterranean

méditerranéen MASC
ADJECTIVE
(FEM **méditerranéenne**)
Mediterranean

la **méduse** FEM NOUN
jellyfish

meilleur MASC ADJECTIVE
(FEM **meilleure**)
better
C'est meilleur avec du fromage râpé.
It's better with grated cheese.
Le livre est meilleur que le film.
The book is better than the film.

le **meilleur** MASC NOUN
la **meilleure** FEM NOUN
the best
C'est la meilleure en sport.
She's the best at sport.

le **mélange** MASC NOUN
mixture

French English
a b c d e f g h i j k l m n o p q r s t u v w x y z

mélanger VERB
to mix
> **Mélangez le tout.**
> Mix everything together.

la **mélodie** FEM NOUN
melody

le **melon** MASC NOUN
melon

le **membre** MASC NOUN
member

la **mémé** FEM NOUN
granny

même

> **même** *can be an adjective or an adverb.*

A ADJECTIVE
same
> **J'ai la même robe.**
> I've got the same dress.
> **en même temps**
> at the same time
> **Paul et moi, on arrive toujours en même temps à l'école.**
> Paul and I always get to school at the same time.

B ADVERB
even
> **Je sais faire l'équilibre, et je sais même faire la roue.**
> I can do a handstand, and I can even do a cartwheel.

le/la **même** MASC/FEM NOUN
same one

> **Tiens, c'est curieux j'ai le même!**
> That's funny, I've got the same one!

la **mémoire** FEM NOUN
memory

menacer VERB
to threaten

le **ménage** MASC NOUN
housework
> **faire le ménage**
> to do the housework
> **C'est mon père qui fait le ménage à la maison.**
> My father is the one who does the housework.
> **une femme de ménage**
> a cleaning lady

le **mensonge** MASC NOUN
lie
> **Il ne faut pas dire de mensonges.**
> You shouldn't tell lies.

le **menteur** MASC NOUN
la **menteuse** FEM NOUN
liar
> **C'est une menteuse.**
> She's a liar.

la **menthe** FEM NOUN
mint
> **des bonbons à la menthe**
> mints

mentir VERB
to lie
> **Tu mens!**
> You're lying!

le **menton** MASC NOUN
chin

le **menu** MASC NOUN
menu
  le menu du jour
  today's menu

le **menuisier** MASC NOUN
joiner

la **mer** FEM NOUN
sea
  la mer du Nord
  the North Sea
  au bord de la mer
  at the seaside

merci EXCLAMATION
thank you

  merci beaucoup
  thank you very much

le **mercredi** MASC NOUN
1 **Wednesday**
  Aujourd'hui, nous sommes le
  mercredi vingt-deux février.
  Today's Wednesday the twenty-
  second of February.
2 **on Wednesday**
  Nous partons mercredi.
  We're leaving on Wednesday.
  Le musée est fermé le
  mercredi.
  The museum is shut on
  Wednesdays.

  tous les mercredis
  every Wednesday
  le mercredi
  on Wednesdays
  mercredi dernier
  last Wednesday
  mercredi prochain
  next Wednesday
  À mercredi!
  See you on Wednesday!

la **mère** FEM NOUN
mother

Ma mère s'appelle Laura.
My mother is called Laura.

la **merguez** FEM NOUN
spicy sausage

mériter VERB
to deserve

le **merlan** MASC NOUN
whiting

le **merle** MASC NOUN
blackbird

merveilleux MASC ADJECTIVE
(FEM **merveilleuse**)
marvellous

mes
PL ADJECTIVE
▷ see **mon**
my
  mes parents
  my parents

mesdames FEM PL NOUN
ladies
  Bonjour, mesdames.
  Good morning, ladies.

mesdemoiselles FEM PL
NOUN
ladies
  Bonjour, mesdemoiselles.
  Good morning, ladies.

le **message** MASC NOUN
message
  un message SMS
  a text message

la **messe** FEM NOUN
mass
  la messe de minuit
  midnight mass

messieurs MASC PL NOUN
gentlemen

Bonjour, messieurs.
Good morning, gentlemen.

mesurer VERB
to measure
> **Mesurez la longueur et la largeur.**
> Measure the length and the width.
> **Il mesure un mètre quatre-vingts.**
> He's six foot tall.

Did you know...?

In France, people use metres and centimetres to say how tall someone is, not feet and inches.

---

met VERB ▷ *see* mettre
> **Il met la table.**
> He is laying the table.

le **métal** MASC NOUN
(PL les **métaux**)
metal

la **météo** FEM NOUN
weather forecast
> **Qu'est-ce que dit la météo pour cet après-midi?**
> What's the weather forecast for this afternoon?

le **métier** MASC NOUN
job
> **Quel métier est-ce que tu aimerais faire plus tard?**
> What job would you like to do when you're older?

le **mètre** MASC NOUN
metre
> **La piscine fait vingt-cinq mètres de long.**
> The pool is 25 metres long.
> **un mètre ruban**
> a tape measure

le **métro** MASC NOUN
underground
> **prendre le métro**
> to take the underground
> **Je prends toujours le métro pour aller en ville.**
> I always take the underground into town.

mets VERB ▷ *see* mettre
> **Je ne mets jamais de jupe.**
> I never wear a skirt.

mettre VERB
1 **to put**
> **Mets les jouets dans le placard s'il te plaît.**
> Put the toys in the cupboard please.
2 **to put on**
> **Je mets mon manteau et j'arrive.**
> I'll put on my coat and then I'll be ready.
3 **to wear**
> **Qu'est-ce que tu vas mettre pour la boum?**
> What are you going to wear to the party?
> **mettre la table**
> to set the table
> **Tu peux mettre la table?**
> Could you set the table?

les **meubles**
MASC PL NOUN
furniture

le **Mexique** MASC NOUN
Mexico

French English

a
b
c
d
e
f
g
h
i
j
k
l
m
n
o
p
q
r
s
t
u
v
w
x
y
z

miauler VERB
to mew
Mon chat miaule quand
il a faim.
My cat mews when he's hungry.

le **micro** MASC NOUN
microphone

le **micro-ondes** MASC NOUN
microwave oven

le **midi** MASC NOUN
1 **midday**
On déjeune
à midi.
We have
lunch at
midday.

Il est midi et demi.
It's half past twelve.

Il est midi.
It's midday.

2 **lunchtime**
Je rentre à la maison le midi.
I go home at lunchtime.
le Midi
the South of France

le **miel** MASC NOUN
honey

le **mien** MASC PRONOUN
la **mienne** FEM PRONOUN
mine
Ce vélo-là, c'est le mien.
That bike's mine.
Ces baskets-là, ce sont les
miennes.
Those trainers are mine.

mieux

mieux *can be an adverb, an
adjective or a noun.*

A ADVERB
better
Elle va mieux.
She's better.
Je la connais mieux que son
frère.
I know her better than her
brother.
B MASC, FEM, PL ADJECTIVE
Il est mieux avec la
moustache.
He looks better with a
moustache.
C MASC NOUN
best
C'est la région que je connais
le mieux.
It's the region I know best.

mignon MASC ADJECTIVE
(FEM **mignonne**)
sweet
Qu'est-ce qu'il est mignon!
Isn't he sweet!

le **milieu** MASC NOUN
(PL les **milieux**)
middle
au milieu de
in the middle of
Mets le vase au milieu de la
table.
Put the vase in the middle of the
table.

mille NUMBER
a thousand
mille euros
a thousand euros
deux mille personnes
two thousand people

le **millénaire** MASC NOUN
millennium
> **le troisième millénaire**
> the third millennium

le **milliard** MASC NOUN
thousand million

milliardaire MASC/FEM NOUN,
ADJECTIVE
multimillionaire

le **millier** MASC NOUN
thousand
> **des milliers de personnes**
> thousands of people

le **million** MASC NOUN
million
> **deux millions de personnes**
> two million people

millionnaire MASC/FEM NOUN,
ADJECTIVE
millionaire

mimer VERB
to mimic

mince ADJECTIVE
slim
> **Il est grand et mince.**
> He's tall and slim.
> **Mince!**
> Sugar!

minéral MASC ADJECTIVE
(FEM **minérale**)
mineral
> **l'eau minérale**
> mineral water

mineur MASC ADJECTIVE
(FEM **mineure**)
under 18
> **Elle est mineure.**
> She's under 18.
> **les mineurs**
> the under-18s

la **minijupe** FEM NOUN
miniskirt

le **minimessage** MASC NOUN
text message

le **minimum** MASC NOUN
minimum
> **au minimum**
> at the very least

le **ministre** MASC NOUN
minister
> **le Premier ministre**
> the Prime Minister

le **Minitel**® MASC NOUN

> ***Did you know…?***
> **Minitel** *is a mini-computer plugged into your phone. You can use it instead of a phone directory, and to book train tickets, etc.*

la **minorité** FEM NOUN
minority

Minorque FEM NOUN
Minorca

minuit MASC NOUN
midnight
> **L'avion arrive à minuit.**
> The plane lands at midnight.
> **Il est minuit et demi.**
> It's half past twelve.

> **Il est minuit.**
> It's midnight.

French English

a
b
c
d
e
f
g
h
i
j
k
l
m
n
o
p
q
r
s
t
u
v
w
x
y
z

minuscule

minuscule can be an adjective or a noun.

A ADJECTIVE
1 tiny
 un poisson minuscule
 a tiny fish
2 small
 un m minuscule
 a small m
B FEM NOUN
 small letter
 Ça s'écrit avec une minuscule, pas une majuscule.
 You spell it with a small letter, not a capital.

la **minute** FEM NOUN
minute

le **miracle** MASC NOUN
miracle

le **miroir**
MASC NOUN
mirror

mis VERB
 ▷ *see* **mettre**
 Tu as mis le lait au frigo?
 Have you put the milk in the fridge?

la **mi-temps** FEM NOUN
half-time
 La mi-temps dure quinze minutes.
 Half-time lasts fifteen minutes.
 à mi-temps
 part-time
 Elle travaille à mi-temps.
 She works part-time.

Mlle ABBREVIATION (PL **Mlles**)
Miss
 Mlle Renoir
 Miss Renoir

Mme ABBREVIATION (PL **Mmes**)
Mrs
 Mme Leroy
 Mrs Leroy

le **mobile** MASC NOUN
mobile phone
 Tu me donnes ton numéro de mobile?
 Can you give me your mobile number?

la **mobylette**® FEM NOUN
moped

moche ADJECTIVE
horrible
 Cette couleur est vraiment moche.
 That colour's really horrible.

la **mode** FEM NOUN
fashion
 à la mode
 fashionable
 J'aime être à la mode.
 I like to be fashionable.
 Ce jean n'est pas vraiment à la mode.
 These jeans aren't really fashionable.

le **modèle** MASC NOUN
model
 C'est le nouveau modèle.
 It's the new model.
 Suivez le modèle.
 Follow the example.

moderne ADJECTIVE
modern

moi PRONOUN
me

Coucou, c'est moi!
Hello, it's me!
à moi
mine/my turn

Language tip

à moi *has two translations. Look at the examples.*

Ce livre n'est pas à moi.
This book isn't mine.
un ami à moi
a friend of mine
C'est à moi.
It's my turn.

moi-même PRONOUN
myself
Je l'ai fait moi-même.
I did it myself.

moins

moins *can be an adverb, a preposition or a noun.*

A ADVERB
1 less
Deux cents euros? —
Non, beaucoup moins.
Two hundred euros? —
No, much less.
Moins de bruit, s'il vous plaît.
Less noise please.

Language tip

When **moins de** *is followed by a number it means 'less than'.*

Ça coûte moins de deux cents euros.
It costs less than two hundred euros.

Language tip

de moins *is used when talking about how many years younger someone is.*

Il a trois ans de moins que moi.
He's three years younger than me.
2 fewer
Il y a moins de gens aujourd'hui.
There are fewer people today.
le moins
the least

Language tip

le moins *changes to* **la moins** *before a feminine adjective, and* **les moins** *before a plural adjective.*

C'est le modèle le moins cher.
It's the least expensive model.
C'est la plage la moins polluée.
It's the least polluted beach.
La musique, c'est la matière que j'aime le moins.
Music is my least favourite subject.
B PREPOSITION
1 minus
quatre moins trois
four minus three
Il fait moins cinq dehors.
It's minus five outside.
2 to
Il est onze heures moins cinq.
It's five to eleven.
Il est onze heures moins le quart.
It's quarter to eleven.
C MASC NOUN
au moins
at least
Il reste au moins dix bonbons dans le paquet.
There are at least ten sweets left in the packet.

a b c d e f g h i j k l **m** n o p q r s t u v w x y z

le **mois** MASC NOUN
month
au mois de juillet
in July

la **moitié** FEM NOUN
half
une moitié de pomme
half an apple

molle FEM ADJECTIVE
soft
La margarine est plus molle que le beurre.
Margarine is softer than butter.

le **moment** MASC NOUN
1 moment
Attendez un moment.
Wait a moment.
en ce moment
at the moment
Nous avons beaucoup de travail en ce moment.
We have a lot of work to do at the moment.
2 time
C'est le moment de partir.
It's time to go.

mon MASC ADJECTIVE (FEM **ma**, PL **mes**)
my
mon frère
my brother
mon ami
my friend
ma tante
my aunt
mes parents
my parents

le **monde** MASC NOUN
world
Je voudrais faire le tour du monde.
I'd like to go round the world.

Il y a du monde.
There are a lot of people.
beaucoup de monde
a lot of people
Il y a beaucoup de monde sur la plage.
There are a lot of people on the beach.

mondial MASC ADJECTIVE
(FEM **mondiale**)
world
un nouveau record mondial
a new world record

le **moniteur** MASC NOUN
1 instructor
un moniteur de voile
a sailing instructor
2 monitor
le moniteur de mon ordinateur
my computer monitor

la **monitrice** FEM NOUN
instructor
une monitrice de ski
a ski instructor

la **monnaie** FEM NOUN
change
Voici la monnaie.
Here's the change.
une pièce de monnaie
a coin

le **monsieur** MASC NOUN
man
Il y a un monsieur qui veut te voir.
There's a man wanting to see you.

monsieur MASC NOUN
(PL **messieurs**)
1 Mr
Monsieur Dupont
Mr Dupont

2 Sir
Monsieur, ...
Dear Sir, ...

Monsieur! Vous avez laissé tomber votre billet!
Excuse me! You've dropped your ticket!

le **monstre**
MASC NOUN
monster

la **montagne** FEM NOUN
mountain
les montagnes russes
the roller coaster

montagneux MASC ADJECTIVE
(FEM **montagneuse**)
mountainous
une région montagneuse
a mountainous area

monter VERB
to go up
Montez au deuxième étage.
Go up to the second floor.

la **montre** FEM NOUN
watch

montrer VERB
to show
Montre la carte.
Show the card.

le **monument** MASC NOUN
les monuments de Paris
the sights of Paris

la **moquette** FEM NOUN
fitted carpet

le **morceau** MASC NOUN
(PL les **morceaux**)
piece
un morceau de pain
a piece of bread

mordre VERB
to bite
Je me suis fait mordre par un chien.
I was bitten by a dog.

mort MASC ADJECTIVE (FEM **morte**)
dead

la **mosquée** FEM NOUN
mosque

le **mot** MASC NOUN
1 word
C'est un mot de six lettres.
It's a six-letter word.
des mots croisés
a crossword
le mot de passe
the password
2 note
J'écris un mot à Pierrot.
I'm writing a note to Pierrot.

la **moto** FEM NOUN
motorbike

mou MASC ADJECTIVE (FEM **molle**)
soft
Mon matelas est trop mou.
My mattress is too soft.

la **mouche**
FEM NOUN
fly

French English

a
b
c
d
e
f
g
h
i
j
k
l
m
n
o
p
q
r
s
t
u
v
w
x
y
z

le **mouchoir** MASC NOUN
handkerchief
   un mouchoir en papier
   a tissue

la **mouette** FEM NOUN
seagull

mouillé MASC ADJECTIVE
(FEM **mouillée**)
wet

le **moule** MASC NOUN
tin
   un moule à gâteaux
   a cake tin

les **moules** FEM PL NOUN
mussels

le **moulin** MASC NOUN
mill
   un moulin à vent
   a windmill

mourir VERB
to die
   Elle est morte.
   She's dead.

la **mousse** FEM NOUN
   une mousse au chocolat
   a chocolate mousse

la **moustache** FEM NOUN
moustache
   les moustaches
   whiskers

le **moustique** MASC NOUN
mosquito

la **moutarde** FEM NOUN
mustard

le **mouton**
MASC NOUN
1 sheep

2 mutton
   un gigot de mouton
   a leg of mutton

moyen MASC ADJECTIVE
(FEM **moyenne**)
1 average
   Je suis plutôt moyen en maths.
   I'm just average at maths.
2 medium
   Elle est de taille moyenne.
   She's of medium height.
   le moyen âge
   the Middle Ages

la **moyenne** FEM NOUN
average
   la moyenne d'âge
   the average age
   J'espère avoir la moyenne en maths.
   I hope to get a pass mark in maths.

le **Moyen-Orient** MASC NOUN
Middle East

le **muguet** MASC NOUN
lily of the valley

Did you know…?

People give friends little bunches of lily of the valley on May 1st, which is a holiday in France. **Le muguet** is lucky – like white heather.

---

municipal MASC ADJECTIVE
(FEM **municipale**)
   la bibliothèque municipale
   the public library

le **mur** MASC NOUN
wall

mûr MASC ADJECTIVE (FEM **mûre**)
1 ripe
   Ces pêches ne sont pas mûres.
   These peaches aren't ripe.

2 mature
Elle est très mûre pour son âge.
She's very mature for her age.

les **mûres** FEM PL NOUN
blackberries

murmurer VERB
to whisper
Pense à un mot et murmure le mot à ton voisin.
You think of a word and whisper the word to the person next to you.

musclé MASC ADJECTIVE
(FEM **musclée**)
muscular

le **musée** MASC NOUN
museum
J'adore faire les musées.
I love going round museums.

le **musicien** MASC NOUN
la **musicienne** FEM NOUN
musician

la **musique** FEM NOUN
music
J'aime écouter de la musique.
I like listening to music.

musulman MASC NOUN, MASC
ADJECTIVE (FEM **musulmane**)
Muslim

myope ADJECTIVE
short-sighted

le **mystère** MASC NOUN
mystery

mystérieux MASC ADJECTIVE
(FEM **mystérieuse**)
mysterious

a
b
c
d
e
f
g
h
i
j
k
l
m
n
o
p
q
r
s
t
u
v
w
x
y
z

N n

n' ADVERB

> *Language tip*
> **ne** *is changed to* **n'** *before a vowel sound.*

> **Je n'ai pas d'argent.**
> I haven't got any money.

nager VERB
to swim
> **Tu sais nager?**
> Can you swim?

le **nageur** MASC NOUN
la **nageuse** FEM NOUN
swimmer
> **C'est une très bonne nageuse.**
> She's a very good swimmer.

la **naissance** FEM NOUN
birth
> **Quelle est ta date de naissance?**
> What's your date of birth?

naître VERB
to be born
> **Il est né en 1982.**
> He was born in 1982.
> **Elle est née le cinq octobre.**
> She was born on the fifth of October.

la **natation** FEM NOUN
swimming
> **Je fais de la natation tous les mercredis.**
> I go swimming every Wednesday.

national MASC ADJECTIVE
(FEM **nationale**)
national
> **Aujourd'hui, c'est le quatorze juillet: c'est la fête nationale.**
> Today is the fourteenth of July, the national holiday.

la **nationalité** FEM NOUN
nationality
> **Tu es de quelle nationalité?**
> What nationality are you?

nature

> **nature** *can be a noun or an adjective.*

A FEM NOUN
nature
B ADJECTIVE
plain
> **un yaourt nature**
> a plain yoghurt

naturel MASC ADJECTIVE
(FEM **naturelle**)
natural

naturellement ADVERB
of course
> **Naturellement, il est encore en retard.**
> He's late again, of course.

nautique ADJECTIVE
water
> **les sports nautiques**
> water sports
> **le ski nautique**
> water-skiing

le **navet** MASC NOUN
turnip
> **Je n'aime pas les navets.**
> I don't like turnips.

la **navette** FEM NOUN
shuttle
> **une navette spatiale**
> a space shuttle

ne ADVERB

> *Language tip*
>
> **ne** *goes with* **pas, personne, plus**
> *and* **jamais** *in negatives.*

> **Je ne peux pas venir.**
> I can't come.
> **Ils ne vont jamais à la piscine.**
> They never go to the swimming
> pool.
> **Je ne connais personne ici.**
> I don't know anyone here.
> **Elle ne fait plus d'équitation.**
> She doesn't go riding any more.

> *Language tip*
>
> **ne** *changes to* **n'** *before a vowel*
> *sound.*

> **Je n'aime pas les maths.**
> I don't like maths.

né VERB ▷*see* **naître**
born
> **Elle est née en 1990.**
> She was born in 1990.

nécessaire ADJECTIVE
necessary

néerlandais MASC ADJECTIVE
(FEM **néerlandaise**)
Dutch

la **neige** FEM NOUN
snow
> **une boule de neige**
> a snowball

**un bonhomme
de neige**
a snowman

neiger VERB
to snow

> **Il neige.**
> It's snowing.

néo-zélandais MASC
ADJECTIVE (FEM **néo-zélandaise**)
New Zealand
> **Elle est néo-zélandaise.**
> She's from New Zealand.

le **Néo-Zélandais** MASC NOUN
la **Néo-Zélandaise** FEM
NOUN
New Zealander

nerveux MASC ADJECTIVE
(FEM **nerveuse**)
nervous

n'est-ce pas ADVERB

> *Language tip*
>
> **n'est-ce pas** *is used to check that*
> *something is true.*

> **Nous sommes le douze
> aujourd'hui, n'est-ce pas?**
> It's the 12th today, isn't it?
> **Elle a un chien, n'est-ce pas?**
> She's got a dog, hasn't she?

le **Net** MASC NOUN
the Net

nettoyer VERB
to clean
> **Nettoie la table, s'il te plaît.**
> Clean the table please.

French English

a
b
c
d
e
f
g
h
i
j
k
l
m
n
o
p
q
r
s
t
u
v
w
x
y
z

neuf

neuf can be a number or an adjective.

A NUMBER
nine
Il est neuf heures.
It's nine o'clock.
Claire a neuf ans.
Claire's nine.

le neuf février
the ninth of February

B MASC ADJECTIVE (FEM **neuve**)
new
des chaussures neuves
new shoes

neuvième ADJECTIVE
ninth
au neuvième étage
on the ninth floor

le **neveu** MASC NOUN
(PL les **neveux**)
nephew
mon neveu
my nephew

le **nez** MASC NOUN
nose

ni CONJUNCTION
ni ... ni ...
neither ... nor ...
Je n'aime ni Marie ni Luc.
I like neither Marie nor Luc.

la **nièce** FEM NOUN
niece
ma nièce
my niece

le **Noël** MASC NOUN
Christmas
Qu'est-ce que tu a eu pour Noël?
What did you get for Christmas?

le père Noël
Father Christmas
les cadeaux de Noël
Christmas presents

Joyeux Noël!
Merry Christmas!

le **nœud** MASC NOUN
knot
Fais un nœud à la corde.
Tie a knot in the rope.
un nœud papillon
a bow tie

Language tip

The French actually means 'butterfly knot'!

noir

noir can be an adjective or a noun.

A MASC ADJECTIVE (FEM **noire**)
1 black
une robe noire
a black dress
Elle est noire.
She's black.
2 dark
Il fait noir dehors.
It's dark outside.

B MASC NOUN

1 **black**
J'aime le noir.
I like the colour black.

2 **dark**
J'ai peur du noir.
I'm afraid of the dark.

le **Noir** MASC NOUN
black man
les Noirs
black people

la **Noire** FEM NOUN
black woman

la **noisette** FEM NOUN
hazelnut

la **noix** FEM NOUN (PL les **noix**)
walnut
une noix de coco
a coconut
les noix de cajou
cashew nuts

le **nom** MASC NOUN

1 **name**
Écrivez votre nom en haut de la feuille.
Write your name at the top of the sheet.
mon nom de famille
my surname

2 **noun**
'la banane' est un nom féminin.
'la banane' is a feminine noun.

le **nombre** MASC NOUN
number

un nombre pair
an even number
un nombre impair
an odd number

nombreux MASC ADJECTIVE
(FEM **nombreuse**)
Nous sommes trop nombreux.
There are too many of us.
Nous sommes peu nombreux.
There aren't many of us.
une famille nombreuse
a large family

le **nombril** MASC NOUN
navel

non ADVERB
no
Tu connais Jean-Pierre? — Non.
Do you know Jean-Pierre? — No.
Je n'aime pas les hamburgers. — Moi non plus.
I don't like burgers. — Neither do I.

nord

nord *can be a noun or an adjective.*

A MASC NOUN
north
Ils vivent dans le nord de l'île.
They live in the north of the island.
au nord de Paris
north of Paris
l'Afrique du Nord
North Africa

B MASC, FEM, PL ADJECTIVE
le pôle Nord
the North Pole

le **nord-est** MASC NOUN
north-east
J'habite au nord-est de Paris.
I live in north-east Paris.

French English

a
b
c
d
e
f
g
h
i
j
k
l
m
n
o
p
q
r
s
t
u
v
w
x
y
z

le **nord-ouest** MASC NOUN
north-west
> **J'habite au nord-ouest de Paris.**
> I live in north-west Paris.

normal MASC ADJECTIVE
(FEM **normale**)
normal
> **une journée normale**
> a normal day

> **C'est normal.**
> It's only natural.
> **Ce n'est pas normal!**
> That's not right!

normalement
ADVERB
normally
> **Normalement, il mange à midi.**
> He normally eats at midday.

normand MASC ADJECTIVE
(FEM **normande**)
from Normandy
> **Ma grand-mère est
> normande.**
> My grandmother is from
> Normandy.

la **Normandie** FEM NOUN
Normandy

la **Norvège** FEM NOUN
Norway

norvégien MASC NOUN, MASC
ADJECTIVE (FEM **norvégienne**)
Norwegian

le **Norvégien** MASC NOUN
la **Norvégienne** FEM NOUN
Norwegian

nos PL ADJECTIVE ▷see **notre**
our
> **Où sont nos affaires?**
> Where are our things?

le **notaire** MASC NOUN
solicitor

la **note** FEM NOUN
1 **mark**
> **Vincent a de bonnes notes
> en maths.**
> Vincent gets good marks in maths.
2 **bill**
> **La note, s'il vous plaît!**
> The bill please!
3 **note**
> **Écoutez et prenez des notes.**
> Listen and take notes.

notre ADJECTIVE (PL **nos**)
our
> **Voici notre maison.**
> This is our house.

le/la **nôtre** MASC/FEM PRONOUN
ours
> **À qui est ce chien? —
> C'est le nôtre.**
> Whose dog is it? — It's ours.
> **Leur voiture est rouge, la
> nôtre est bleue.**
> Their car is red, ours is blue.
> **Ces places-là sont les nôtres.**
> Those seats are ours.

les **nouilles** FEM PL NOUN
noodles

le **nounours**
MASC NOUN
teddy

la **nourriture**
FEM NOUN
food

nous PRONOUN
1 **we**
> **Nous avons deux chiens.**
> We have two dogs.

2 us
Viens avec nous.
Come with us.

nous-mêmes
ourselves

nouveau MASC ADJECTIVE
(FEM **nouvelle**)
new
Je voudrais un nouveau vélo.
I'd like a new bike.
**Nous avons une nouvelle
voiture.**
We've got a new car.

Language tip

nouveau *changes to* **nouvel**
before a vowel sound.

**Il y a un nouvel élève dans
ma classe.**
There's a new boy in my class.
le nouvel an
New Year

le **nouveau** MASC NOUN
la **nouvelle** FEM NOUN
new person
**Il y a plusieurs nouveaux
dans la classe.**
There are several new people
in the class.

nouvel, nouvelle ADJECTIVE
▷ *see* **nouveau**
new

la **nouvelle** FEM NOUN
1 news
C'est une bonne nouvelle.
That's good news.
les nouvelles
the news
**J'écoute les nouvelles à la
radio.**
I listen to the news on the radio.

2 short story
un livre de nouvelles
a book of short stories

la **Nouvelle-Zélande**
FEM NOUN
New Zealand

novembre MASC NOUN
November
en novembre
in November
le vingt-deux novembre
the twenty-second of November

nu MASC ADJECTIVE (FEM **nue**)
naked
tout nu
stark naked

le **nuage** MASC NOUN
cloud
un gros nuage noir
a big black cloud

Il y a des nuages.
It's cloudy.

nuageux MASC ADJECTIVE
(FEM **nuageuse**)
cloudy
Il fait un temps nuageux.
It's cloudy.

la **nuit** FEM NOUN
night

La nuit est belle.
It's a beautiful night.

French English

a
b
c
d
e
f
g
h
i
j
k
l
m
n
o
p
q
r
s
t
u
v
w
x
y
z

la nuit
at night
Tout est calme la nuit.
Everything is quiet at night.
cette nuit
tonight
Il va rentrer cette nuit.
He'll be back tonight.

Bonne nuit!
Good night!
Il fait nuit.
It's dark.

nul MASC ADJECTIVE (FEM **nulle**)
rubbish
  Ce film est nul.
  This film's rubbish.
  Je suis nul en maths.
  I'm rubbish at maths.

un match nul
a draw
Ils ont fait match nul.
It was a draw.
nulle part
nowhere
Je ne le vois nulle part.
I can't see it anywhere.

numérique ADJECTIVE
digital

le **numéro** MASC NOUN
number
  J'habite au numéro trois.
  I live at number three.
  mon numéro de téléphone
  my phone number

O o

l' objet MASC NOUN
object
> les objets dans la classe
> classroom objects

obligé MASC ADJECTIVE
(FEM **obligée**)
> Je suis obligé de rester.
> I have to stay.

observer VERB
to watch
> J'aime bien observer les
> fourmis à la loupe.
> I like watching ants with my
> magnifying glass.

l' occasion FEM NOUN
> d'occasion
> second-hand
> une voiture d'occasion
> a second-hand car

occupé MASC ADJECTIVE
(FEM **occupée**)
1 busy
> Il est très occupé.
> He's very busy.
2 taken
> Est-ce que cette place est
> occupée?
> Is this seat taken?
3 engaged
> Les toilettes sont occupées.
> The toilet's engaged.

s' **occuper** VERB
> s'occuper de
> to be in charge of
> Elle s'occupe d'un club de
> sport.
> She's in charge of a sports club.

l' océan MASC NOUN
ocean

octobre MASC NOUN
October
> en octobre
> in October
> le quinze octobre
> the fifteenth of October

l' odeur FEM NOUN
smell
> Il y a une drôle d'odeur ici.
> There's a funny smell round here.

l' œil MASC NOUN (PL les **yeux**)
eye
> J'ai les yeux marron.
> I've got brown eyes.
> Est-ce que j'ai quelque chose
> dans l'œil?
> Have I got something in my eye?

l' œuf MASC NOUN
egg

> un œuf à la coque
> a soft-boiled egg
> un œuf dur
> a hard-boiled egg
> un œuf au plat
> a fried egg
> les œufs brouillés
> scrambled eggs
> un œuf de Pâques
> an Easter egg

a
b
c
d
e
f
g
h
i
j
k
l
m
n
o
p
q
r
s
t
u
v
w
x
y
z

French English

Did you know...?

*In France, Easter eggs are said to be brought by the Easter bells (***cloches de Pâques***) which fly from Rome and drop them in people's gardens.*

offert VERB ▷see **offrir**
Elle m'a offert un CD pour mon anniversaire.
She gave me a CD for my birthday.

l' **office** MASC NOUN
l' office du tourisme
the tourist office

offrir VERB
to give
Je vais offrir des fleurs à ma mère.
I'm going to give my mum some flowers.
Elle m'a offert un appareil photo.
She gave me a camera.

l' **oie** FEM NOUN
goose

l' **oignon**
MASC NOUN
onion

l' **oiseau**
MASC NOUN
(PL les **oiseaux**)
bird

l' **olive** FEM NOUN
olive
l'huile d'olive
olive oil

olympique ADJECTIVE
les Jeux olympiques
the Olympic Games

l' **omelette** FEM NOUN
omelette

on PRONOUN
1 **we**
On va à la plage demain.
We're going to the beach tomorrow.
2 **someone**
On m'a volé mon porte-monnaie.
Someone has stolen my purse.
3 **you**
On peut visiter le parc en été.
You can visit the park in the summer.

l' **oncle** MASC NOUN
uncle
mon oncle
my uncle

l' **ongle** MASC NOUN
nail

ont VERB ▷see **avoir**
Ils ont beaucoup d'argent.
They have got lots of money.

Language tip

*Sometimes ***ont*** shows that something has happened in the past.*

Ils ont passé de bonnes vacances.
They had a good holiday.

onze NUMBER
eleven
Elle a onze ans.
She's eleven.
Il est onze heures.
It's eleven o'clock.

le onze février
the eleventh of February

onzième ADJECTIVE
eleventh
au onzième étage
on the eleventh floor

opérer VERB
> **se faire opérer**
> to have an operation
> **Je dois me faire opérer.**
> I need to have an operation.
> **Elle s'est fait opérer de l'appendicite.**
> She's had her appendix out.

l' **opticien** MASC NOUN
l' **opticienne** FEM NOUN
optician

l' **or** MASC NOUN
gold
> **en or**
> gold
> **un bracelet en or**
> a gold bracelet

l' **orage** MASC NOUN
thunderstorm

orageux MASC ADJECTIVE
(FEM **orageuse**)
stormy
> **Le temps est orageux.**
> It's stormy.

orange

> **orange** *can be a noun or an adjective.*

A FEM NOUN
orange
> **J'adore les oranges.**
> I love oranges.

B MASC NOUN
orange
> **Vous avez ce T-shirt en orange?**
> Do you have this T-shirt in orange?

C MASC, FEM, PL ADJECTIVE
orange
> **des rideaux orange**
> orange curtains

l' **orchestre** MASC NOUN
> **1** orchestra
> **un orchestre symphonique**
> a symphony orchestra
> **2** band
> **un orchestre de jazz**
> a jazz band

l' **ordinateur**
MASC NOUN
computer

l' **ordre** MASC NOUN
order
> **par ordre alphabétique**
> in alphabetical order
> **dans l'ordre**
> in order
> **Remettez les images dans l'ordre.**
> Put the pictures in order.

l' **oreille** FEM NOUN
ear
> **J'ai mal à l'oreille.**
> I've got earache.

l' **oreiller** MASC NOUN
pillow

organiser VERB
to organize
> **Nous organisons une tombola.**
> We're organizing a raffle.

a
b
c
d
e
f
g
h
i
j
k
l
m
n
o
p
q
r
s
t
u
v
w
x
y
z

l' **orgue** MASC NOUN
organ

l' **orphelin** MASC NOUN
l' **orpheline** FEM NOUN
orphan

l' **orteil** MASC NOUN
toe

l' **orthographe** FEM NOUN
spelling
Je suis bon en orthographe.
I'm good at spelling.

l' **os** MASC NOUN
bone

oser VERB
Je n'ose pas demander.
I daren't ask.

ou CONJUNCTION
or
**Tu veux une limonade ou
un coca?**
Would you like a lemonade or
a coke?

où

où can be an adverb or a pronoun.

A ADVERB
where
Où est Nick?
Where's Nick?
Où vas-tu?
Where are you going?
Je sais où il est.
I know where he is.

B PRONOUN
that
**Le jour où il est parti, tout le
monde a pleuré.**
The day that he left, everyone
cried.

oublier VERB
1 to forget
**N'oublie pas de fermer la
porte.**
Don't forget to shut the door.
2 to leave
**J'ai oublié mon sac chez
Sabine.**
I left my bag at Sabine's.

ouest

*ouest can be a noun or an
adjective.*

A MASC NOUN
west
**Elle vit dans l'ouest de
l'Angleterre.**
She lives in the West of
England.
à l'ouest de Paris
west of Paris
l'Europe de l'Ouest
Western Europe
B MASC, FEM, PL ADJECTIVE
west
la côte ouest de l'Écosse
the west coast of Scotland

ouf EXCLAMATION
thank heavens for that!
**Ouf! J'ai retrouvé mes
lunettes!**
Thank heavens for that! I've
found my glasses!

oui ADVERB
yes
Tu aimes les fraises? — Oui.
Do you like strawberries? — Yes.

l' **ours** MASC NOUN
bear
un ours en
peluche
a teddy bear

les **outils** MASC PL NOUN
tools
une boîte à outils
a tool box

ouvert MASC ADJECTIVE
(FEM **ouverte**)
open
Le magasin est ouvert.
The shop's open.

l' **ouverture** FEM NOUN
les heures d'ouverture
opening hours

l' **ouvrier** MASC NOUN
l' **ouvrière** FEM NOUN
worker

ouvrir VERB
to open
Ouvre la porte s'il te plaît.
Open the door please.
Je peux ouvrir la fenêtre?
Can I open the window?

l' **ovni** MASC NOUN
UFO

Pp

Pacifique ADJECTIVE, MASC NOUN
Pacific

paf EXCLAMATION
wham!

la **pagaille** FEM NOUN
mess
> **Quelle pagaille!**
> What a mess!

la **page** FEM NOUN
page
> **Tournez la page.**
> Turn the page.

la **paille** FEM NOUN
straw

le **pain** MASC NOUN
bread
> **un morceau de pain**
> a piece of bread
> **le pain complet**
> wholemeal bread
> **le pain d'épice**
> gingerbread
> **le pain grillé**
> toast

pair MASC ADJECTIVE (FEM **paire**)
even
> **un nombre pair**
> an even number
> **une jeune fille au pair**
> an au pair

la **paire** FEM NOUN
pair
> **une paire de chaussures**
> a pair of shoes

la **paix** FEM NOUN
peace
> **J'espère qu'ils vont faire la paix.**
> I hope they're going to make up.

le **palais** MASC NOUN
palace

pâle ADJECTIVE
pale
> **bleu pâle**
> pale blue

la **palme** FEM NOUN
flipper
> **Tu as tes palmes?**
> Have you got your flippers?

le **palmier** MASC NOUN
palm tree

le **pamplemousse** MASC NOUN
grapefruit

pané MASC ADJECTIVE (FEM **panée**)
fried in breadcrumbs
> **du poisson pané**
> fish fried in breadcrumbs

le **panier** MASC NOUN
basket

la **panique** FEM NOUN
panic
> **Pas de panique!**
> Don't panic!

la **panne** FEM NOUN
> **en panne**
> out of order
> **L'ascenseur est en panne.**
> The lift's not working.
> **tomber en panne**
> to break down

une panne de courant
a power cut

le **panneau** MASC NOUN
(PL les **panneaux**)
sign

le **pansement** MASC NOUN
1 **dressing**
2 **sticking plaster**
**J'ai mis un pansement sur
ma coupure.**
I put a plaster on my cut.

le **pantalon** MASC NOUN
trousers
Son pantalon est trop court.
His trousers are too short.

la **panthère** FEM NOUN
panther

les **pantoufles** FEM PL NOUN
slippers

le **paon** MASC NOUN
peacock

le **papa** MASC NOUN
dad

la **papeterie** FEM NOUN
stationer's
**On peut acheter un cahier à
la papeterie.**
You can buy an exercise book at
the stationer's.

le **papi** MASC NOUN
granddad

le **papier** MASC NOUN
paper
une feuille de papier
a sheet of paper
le papier cadeau
wrapping paper
le papier hygiénique
toilet paper

le **papier peint**
wallpaper

le **papillon**
MASC NOUN
butterfly

Pâques FEM PL NOUN
Easter
les vacances de Pâques
Easter holidays
un œuf de Pâques
an Easter egg

Did you know...?

*In France, Easter eggs are said to be
brought by the Easter bells (**cloches
de Pâques**) which fly from Rome
and drop them in people's gardens.*

Joyeuses Pâques!
Happy Easter!

---

le **paquet** MASC NOUN
1 **packet**
2 **parcel**
Il y a un paquet pour toi.
There's a parcel for you.

par PREPOSITION
1 **by**
**Il s'est fait disputer par
sa mère.**
He was told off by his mum.
Rangez-vous deux par deux.
Get into twos.
2 **with**
**Son nom commence par
un H.**
His name begins with H.
3 **out of**
Regardez par la fenêtre.
Look out of the window.

4 per
Le voyage coûte trois cents euros par personne.
The trip costs three hundred euros per person.

5 via
Nous passons par Paris.
We're going via Paris.

6 through
Il faut passer par la salle à manger pour aller dans la cuisine.
You have to go through the dining room to get to the kitchen.
par ici
this way/near here

Language tip

par ici *has two translations. Look at the examples.*

Venez par ici.
Come this way.
Il y a une boulangerie par d'ici?
Is there a baker's near here?

paraître VERB

1 to seem
Ça paraît incroyable.
It seems incredible.

2 to look
Elle paraît plus jeune que son mari.
She looks younger than her husband.

le **parapluie**
MASC NOUN
umbrella

le **parasol** MASC NOUN
umbrella

le **parc** MASC NOUN
park

un parc d'attractions
an amusement park

parce que CONJUNCTION
because
Paul pleure parce qu'il a mal à la jambe.
Paul is crying because his leg is hurting.

pardon EXCLAMATION

1 sorry!
Pardon.
I'm sorry.

2 excuse me!
Pardon, madame! Je cherche la poste.
Excuse me, I'm looking for the post office.

3 pardon?
Pardon? Vous pouvez répéter?
Pardon? Could you say that again?

pardonner VERB
to forgive
Je te pardonne.
I forgive you.

pareil MASC ADJECTIVE
(FEM **pareille**)
the same
Ces images ne sont pas pareilles.
These pictures aren't the same.

les **parents** MASC PL NOUN
parents
mes parents
my parents

paresseux MASC ADJECTIVE
(FEM **paresseuse**)
lazy

parfait MASC ADJECTIVE
(FEM **parfaite**)
perfect

parfaitement ADVERB
perfectly
> **Il parle parfaitement l'arabe.**
> He speaks perfect Arabic.

parfois ADVERB
sometimes

le **parfum** MASC NOUN
1 perfume
2 flavour

Paris NOUN
Paris
> **J'habite à Paris.**
> I live in Paris.
> **Je vais à Paris.**
> I'm going to Paris.

parisien MASC ADJECTIVE
(FEM **parisienne**)
from Paris
> **Elle est parisienne.**
> She's from Paris.

les **Parisiens** MASC PL NOUN
people from Paris

le **parking** MASC NOUN
car park

> **Language tip**
>
> *Be careful! The French word*
> **parking** *does not mean the same*
> *as The English word* **parking**.

parler VERB
1 to speak
> **Vous parlez français?**
> Do you speak French?

> **Je parle français.**
> I speak French.

2 to talk

> **Arrêtez de parler!**
> Stop talking!

parmi PREPOSITION
among

les **paroles** FEM PL NOUN
lyrics
> **J'aime les paroles de cette**
> **chanson.**
> I like the lyrics of this song.

le **parquet** MASC NOUN
wooden floor

le **parrain** MASC NOUN
godfather

parrainer VERB
to sponsor
> **Tu veux me parrainer?**
> Will you sponsor me?

pars, part VERB ▷see **partir**
> **Je pars demain.**
> I'm going tomorrow.
> **Le train part à quelle heure?**
> What time does the train leave?

la **part** FEM NOUN
piece
> **une part de gâteau**
> a piece of cake
> **à part**
> except
> **Tout le monde va au pique-**
> **nique, à part Sandra.**
> Everyone except Sandra is going
> to the picnic.

partager VERB
1 to share
> **Ils partagent un**
> **appartement.**
> They share a flat.

2 to divide
> **Partage le gâteau en quatre.**
> Divide the cake into four.

a
b
c
d
e
f
g
h
i
j
k
l
m
n
o
p
q
r
s
t
u
v
w
x
y
z

le/la **partenaire** MASC/FEM NOUN
partner

la **partie** FEM NOUN
1 **game**
une partie de cartes
a game of cards
2 **part**
une partie de la classe
part of the class
Je fais partie d'une chorale.
I belong to a choir.

partir VERB
1 **to go**
Je dois partir.
I've got to go.
Il part travailler à sept heures.
He goes to work at seven o'clock.
partir en vacances
to go on holiday
Nous partons en vacances lundi prochain.
We're going on holiday next Monday.
2 **to go away**
Je pars demain et je rentre lundi.
I'm going away tomorrow and coming back on Monday.

Language tip

partir is related to the English word 'to depart'.

à partir de maintenant
from now on

partout ADVERB
everywhere

pas

pas can be an adverb or a noun.

A ADVERB
ne ... pas
not
Il ne pleut pas.
It's not raining.
Ils n'ont pas de voiture.
They haven't got a car.
pas du tout
not at all
Je n'aime pas du tout ça.
I don't like that at all.
pas toi
not you
pas mal
not bad

Ça va? — Oui, pas mal.
How are you? — Not bad.

B MASC NOUN
step
Faites trois pas en avant.
Take three steps forward.
un pas en arrière
a step backwards

le **passager** MASC NOUN
la **passagère** FEM NOUN
passenger

le **passé** MASC NOUN
past

le **passeport** MASC NOUN
passport

passer VERB
1 **to go**
Passez devant l'école et tournez à gauche.
Go past the school and turn left.

Nous passons par Paris pour aller à Tours.
We go through Paris on our way to Tours.

2 to have
Je passe de bonnes vacances.
I'm having a nice holiday.
Vous avez passé de bonnes vacances?
Did you have a nice holiday?

3 to spend
Ils passent toujours leurs vacances au Danemark.
They always spend their holidays in Denmark.

4 to pass
Passe-moi le sel, s'il te plaît.
Pass me the salt please.

5 to take
Gordon passe ses examens la semaine prochaine.
Gordon is taking his exams next week.

> **Language tip**
>
> *Be careful!* **passer un examen** *does not mean the same as* **to pass an exam**.

■ **se passer**
to take place/to go/ to happen

> **Language tip**
>
> **se passer** *has several translations. Look at the examples.*

Cette histoire se passe à New York.
This story takes place in New York.
Tout se passe bien.
Everything's going well.
Qu'est-ce qu'il s'est passé?
What happened?

Qu'est-ce qu'il se passe?
What's the matter?

le **passe-temps** MASC NOUN
hobby
Quel est ton passe-temps préféré?
What's your favourite hobby?

passionnant MASC ADJECTIVE
(FEM **passionnante**)
gripping

la **pastèque** FEM NOUN
watermelon

la **pastille** FEM NOUN
cough sweet

la **pâte** FEM NOUN
1 pastry
2 dough
3 cake mixture
la pâte à crêpes
pancake batter
la pâte à modeler
Plasticine®
la pâte d'amandes
marzipan

le **pâté** MASC NOUN
pâté

les **pâtes** FEM PL NOUN
pasta

J'adore les pâtes.
I love pasta.

le **patin** MASC NOUN
    le patin à glace
    ice skating
    Je fais du patin à glace tous les samedis.
    I go ice skating every Saturday.
    les patins à glace
    ice skates
    le patin à roulettes
    roller skating
    Je fais du patin à roulettes avec mes copains.
    I go roller skating with my friends.
    les patins à roulettes
    roller skates

le **patinage** MASC NOUN
    le patinage artistique
    figure skating

la **patinoire** FEM NOUN
  ice rink

la **pâtisserie** FEM NOUN
  cake shop

le **pâtissier** MASC NOUN
la **pâtissière** FEM NOUN
    aller chez le pâtissier
    to go to the cake shop

la **patte**
FEM NOUN
1 **paw**
    la patte du chat
    the cat's paw
2 **leg**
    Cet oiseau a une patte cassée.
    This bird has a broken leg.

pauvre ADJECTIVE
poor
    Sa famille est pauvre.
    His family is poor.

    Pauvre Jean-Pierre!
    Poor Jean-Pierre!

payant MASC ADJECTIVE
(FEM **payante**)
    C'est payant.
    You have to pay.

payer VERB
to pay

le **pays** MASC NOUN
country

le **paysage** MASC NOUN
landscape

les **Pays-Bas** MASC PL NOUN
Netherlands

le **pays de Galles** MASC NOUN
Wales
    J'habite au pays de Galles.
    I live in Wales.
    Cet été, je vais au pays de Galles.
    I'm going to Wales this summer.

la **pêche** FEM NOUN
1 **peach**
2 **fishing**
    aller à la pêche
    to go fishing
    Il va à la pêche tous les dimanches.
    He goes fishing every Sunday.

le **pêcheur** MASC NOUN
fisherman

le **peigne** MASC NOUN
comb

peigner VERB
to comb
    Elle peigne sa poupée.
    She's combing her doll's hair.
    ■ **se peigner**
    to comb one's hair

Je vais me peigner.
I'm going to comb my hair.

peindre VERB
to paint

la **peine** FEM NOUN
Ce n'est pas la peine.
Don't bother.
Ce n'est pas la peine de téléphoner.
There's no point phoning.

le **peintre** MASC NOUN
painter

la **peinture** FEM NOUN
paint

la **pelle** FEM NOUN
1 shovel
2 spade

la **pellicule** FEM NOUN
film
une pellicule couleur
a colour film

la **pelouse** FEM NOUN
lawn

la **peluche** FEM NOUN
soft toy
un ours en peluche
a teddy bear

pendant PREPOSITION
in
Pendant les vacances, je fais de l'équitation.
I go riding in the holidays.
pendant que
while

Ma petite sœur joue pendant que je fais mes devoirs.
My little sister plays while I do my homework.

le **pendu** MASC NOUN
hangman
On va jouer au pendu.
We're going to play hangman.

la **pendule** FEM NOUN
clock

penser VERB
to think
Je pense que Yann a raison.
I think Yann is right.
Je pense à mes vacances.
I'm thinking about my holidays.

la **pension** FEM NOUN
boarding school
Elle est en pension.
She is at boarding school.

la **Pentecôte** FEM NOUN
Whitsun
le dimanche de Pentecôte
Whit Sunday
le lundi de Pentecôte
Whit Monday

Did you know...?

Whit Sunday always occurs seven weeks after Easter, and the following Monday, Whit Monday, is a holiday in France.

le **perdant** MASC NOUN
la **perdante** FEM NOUN
loser
Il est mauvais perdant.
He's a bad loser.

perdre VERB
to lose
Tu vas perdre!
You're going to lose!

perdu VERB ▷see **perdre**
> J'ai perdu ma trousse.
> I've lost my pencil case.

le **père** MASC NOUN
father
> mon père
> my father
> le père Noël
> Father Christmas

le **perroquet**
MASC NOUN
parrot

la **perruche** FEM NOUN
budgie

le **persil** MASC NOUN
parsley

le **personnage** MASC NOUN
character
> le personnage principal du film
> the main character in the film

la **personnalité** FEM NOUN
personality

personne

> personne *can be a noun or a pronoun.*

A FEM NOUN
person
la même personne
the same person
deux personnes
two people
une grande personne
an adult
une table pour quatre personnes
a table for four

B PRONOUN
1 **nobody**
> Qui est là? — **Personne.**
> Who's there? — Nobody.
> **Personne ne la connaît.**
> Nobody knows her.
2 **anybody**
> **Elle ne veut voir personne.**
> She doesn't want to see anybody.

peser VERB
to weigh
> **Elle pèse cent kilos.**
> She weighs 100 kilos.

la **pétanque** FEM NOUN

> *Did you know...?*
> **pétanque** *is a kind of bowls game played on rough ground.*

le **pétard** MASC NOUN
banger

> *Did you know...?*
> *There is a certain kind of* **pétard** *firework that children in France throw at the pavement to make a bang.*

petit MASC ADJECTIVE
(FEM **petite**)
1 **small**
> **Je suis petite.**
> I'm small.
2 **little**
> **Phyllis a une jolie petite maison.**
> Phyllis has got a nice little house.
> **le petit déjeuner**
> breakfast

Je prends mon petit déjeuner à sept heures.
I have my breakfast at seven o'clock.

des petits pois
garden peas
un petit copain
a boyfriend
une petite copine
a girlfriend

la **petite-fille** FEM NOUN
granddaughter

le **petit-fils** MASC NOUN
grandson

les **petits-enfants** MASC PL NOUN
grandchildren

peu ADVERB
   un peu
   a bit
   Elle est un peu timide.
   She's a bit shy.
   un peu de gâteau
   a bit of cake
   à peu près
   about
   Le voyage prend à peu près deux heures.
   The journey takes about two hours.

la **peur** FEM NOUN
   Tu as peur?
   Are you scared?

J'ai peur!
I'm scared!

peut VERB ▷see **pouvoir**
   Il ne peut pas venir.
   He can't come.

peut-être ADVERB
perhaps

Tu viens? — Peut-être.
Are you coming? — Perhaps.
Je vais peut-être aller en Corse.
I may go to Corsica.

peuvent, peux VERB
   ▷see **pouvoir**
   Ils ne peuvent pas venir.
   They can't come.
   Je ne peux pas le faire.
   I can't do it.

le **phare** MASC NOUN
lighthouse

la **pharmacie** FEM NOUN
chemist's

Did you know…?
In France, chemists have a big green cross outside the shop.

le **pharmacien** MASC NOUN
la **pharmacienne** FEM NOUN
pharmacist
   aller chez le pharmacien
   to go to the chemist

le **phoque** MASC NOUN
seal

la **photo** FEM NOUN
photo
   Tu peux m'envoyer ta photo?
   Could you send me your photo?
   Je veux prendre une photo.
   I want to take a photo.
   Je vais te prendre en photo.
   I'm going to take a photo of you.

la **photocopie** FEM NOUN
photocopy

photocopier VERB
to photocopy

la **photocopieuse** FEM NOUN
photocopier

a b c d e f g h i j k l m n o **p** q r s t u v w x y z

le/la **photographe** MASC/FEM NOUN
photographer
On va chez le photographe.
We're going to the photographer's.

le **photophone** MASC NOUN
camera phone

la **phrase** FEM NOUN
sentence
Complétez la phrase.
Complete the sentence.

physique

physique can be an adjective or a noun.

A ADJECTIVE
physical
l'éducation physique
physical education
B FEM NOUN
physics
Il est professeur de physique.
He's a physics teacher.

le/la **pianiste** MASC/FEM NOUN
pianist

le **piano** MASC NOUN
piano
Je joue du piano.
I play the piano.

la **pièce** FEM NOUN
1 room

Il y a six pièces dans ma maison.
There are six rooms in my house.

2 coin
une pièce de cinquante centimes
a fifty centime coin

une pièce de théâtre
a play
un maillot une-pièce
a one-piece swimsuit
un maillot deux-pièces
a bikini

le **pied** MASC NOUN
foot
J'ai mal aux pieds.
My feet are hurting.
à pied
on foot
Je vais à l'école à pied.
I walk to school.

la **pierre** FEM NOUN
stone

le **piéton** MASC NOUN
la **piétonne** FEM NOUN
pedestrian

la **pieuvre** FEM NOUN
octopus

le **pigeon** MASC NOUN
pigeon

pile

pile can be a noun or an adverb.

A FEM NOUN
battery
Il faut changer les piles de ma lampe de poche.
I need to change the batteries in my torch.

B ADVERB
on the dot
à deux heures pile
at two o'clock on the dot

Pile ou face?
Heads or tails?

le **pilote** MASC NOUN
pilot
un pilote de ligne
an airline pilot
un pilote de course
a racing driver

le **piment** MASC NOUN
chilli

le **pinceau** MASC NOUN
(PL les **pinceaux**)
paintbrush

le **pingouin**
MASC NOUN
penguin

le **ping-pong**
MASC NOUN
table tennis
Tu veux jouer au ping-pong?
Do you want to play table
tennis?

piquant MASC ADJECTIVE
(FEM **piquante**)
1 prickly
un buisson piquant
a prickly bush
2 spicy
une sauce très piquante
a very spicy sauce

le **pique** MASC NOUN
spades
l'as de pique
the ace of spades

le **pique-nique** MASC NOUN
picnic

pique-niquer VERB
to picnic

piquer VERB
1 to bite
J'ai été piqué par un
moustique.
I have been bitten by a mosquito.
2 to burn
Cette sauce me pique
la langue.
This sauce is burning my tongue.

la **piqûre** FEM NOUN
1 injection
Je n'aime pas les piqûres.
I don't like injections.
2 bite
une piqûre de moustique
a mosquito bite
3 sting
une piqûre d'abeille
a bee sting

le **pirate** MASC NOUN
pirate

pire

pire can be an adjective or a noun.

A ADJECTIVE
worse
C'est encore pire qu'avant.
It's even worse than before.
B MASC/FEM NOUN
the worst
Ce garçon est le pire de la
bande.
That boy is the worst in the group.

la **piscine** FEM NOUN
swimming pool

French English

a
b
c
d
e
f
g
h
i
j
k
l
m
n
o
P
q
r
s
t
u
v
w
x
y
z

199

Tu veux aller à la piscine?
Do you want to go to the swimming pool?
Je vais à la piscine le samedi.
I go to the swimming pool on Saturdays.

la **pistache** FEM NOUN
pistachio
une glace à la pistache
a pistachio ice cream

Did you know...?
Pistachio ice cream is green.

la **piste** FEM NOUN
la piste de danse
the dance floor
une piste cyclable
a cycle lane
une piste de ski
a ski slope

le **pistolet** MASC NOUN
pistol

le **placard** MASC NOUN
cupboard

la **place** FEM NOUN
1 **place**
Vincent a eu la troisième place.
Vincent is in third place.
2 **square**
la place du village
the village square
3 **room**
Ça prend de la place.
It takes up a lot of room.

4 **seat**
Il reste une place.
There's one seat left.
sur place
on the spot
Courez sur place.
Run on the spot.
à la place
instead
Je n'ai pas de bonbons; tu veux une pomme à la place?
I haven't got any sweets, do you want an apple instead?

le **plafond** MASC NOUN
ceiling

la **plage** FEM NOUN
beach

se **plaindre**
VERB
Arrête de te plaindre!
Stop complaining!
Elle se plaint tout le temps.
She's always complaining.

plaire VERB
Mon cadeau me plaît beaucoup.
I like my present a lot.
Elle lui plaît.
He fancies her.
Entrez, s'il vous plaît!
Come in, please!

plaisanter VERB
to joke
Je plaisante!
I'm joking!

la **plaisanterie** FEM NOUN
joke

le **plaisir** MASC NOUN
pleasure
> **Ça te fait plaisir?**
> Are you happy?
> **Cette photo va faire très plaisir à ma mère.**
> My mum will love this photo.

plaît VERB ▷ *see* **plaire**
> **Ça te plaît?**
> Do you like it?
> **Ferme la porte, s'il te plaît.**
> Close the door please.

s'il te plaît
please
s'il vous plaît
please

le **plan** MASC NOUN
1 map
> **un plan de la ville**
> a street map
2 plan
> **Voici le plan de ma maison.**
> This is a plan of my house.

la **planche** FEM NOUN
board
> **une planche à repasser**
> an ironing board
> **une planche à roulettes**
> a skateboard
> **une planche à voile**
> a windsurfer

le **plancher** MASC NOUN
floor

la **planète**
FEM NOUN
planet

la **plante**
FEM NOUN
plant

planter VERB
to plant

la **plaque** FEM NOUN
> **une plaque de chocolat**
> a slab of chocolate
> **une plaque d'immatriculation**
> a number plate

la **plaquette** FEM NOUN
> **une plaquette de chocolat**
> a bar of chocolate
> **une plaquette de beurre**
> a pack of butter

le **plastique** MASC NOUN
plastic
> **un sac en plastique**
> a carrier bag

plat

plat *can be a noun or an adjective.*

A MASC NOUN
1 dish
> **un plat en verre**
> a glass dish
> **le plat du jour**
> the dish of the day
2 course
> **le plat principal**
> the main course
> **le plat de résistance**
> the main course
B MASC ADJECTIVE (FEM **plate**)
flat
> **La Hollande est un pays plat.**
> Holland is a flat country.

le **plateau** MASC NOUN
(PL les **plateaux**)
tray
  un plateau d'argent
  a silver tray
  le plateau de fromages
  the cheeseboard

la **platine** FEM NOUN
  une platine laser
  a CD player

le **plâtre** MASC NOUN
  plaster
    J'ai le bras dans
    le plâtre.
    I've got my arm in plaster.

plein MASC ADJECTIVE (FEM **pleine**)
  full
    Ton verre est encore plein.
    Your glass is still full.
    à plein temps
    full-time
    Elle travaille à plein temps.
    She works full-time.
    en plein jour
    in broad daylight
    en pleine nuit
    in the middle of the night
    en plein air
    in the open air
    plein de
    lots of
    un gâteau avec plein de
    crème
    a cake with lots of cream

pleurer VERB
  to cry
    Pourquoi tu pleures?
    Why are you crying?

pleut VERB ▷*see* **pleuvoir**
  Il ne pleut plus.
  It's not raining any more.

pleuvoir VERB
  to rain

  Il pleut.
  It's raining.

plier VERB
  to fold
    Pliez la feuille en deux.
    Fold the paper in two.

le **plombier** MASC NOUN
  plumber

la **plongée** FEM NOUN
  diving

plonger VERB
  to dive
    Tu sais plonger?
    Can you dive?

plouf EXCLAMATION
  splash!

plu VERB ▷*see* **plaire, pleuvoir**
    La photo lui a plu.
    She loved the photo.
    Il a plu toute la journée.
    It rained all day.

la **pluie**
FEM
NOUN
rain
  sous
  la pluie
  in the
  rain

la **plume** FEM NOUN
  feather
    un stylo à plume
    a fountain pen

plupart PRONOUN
    la plupart
    most of them

French English
a b c d e f g h i j k l m n o p q r s t u v w x y z

Il y a quinze filles dans ma classe et la plupart sont sympas.

There are fifteen girls in my class and most of them are nice.

la plupart de
most

La plupart des gens ont peur des serpents.

Most people are afraid of snakes.

la plupart du temps
most of the time

le **pluriel** MASC NOUN
plural

  au pluriel
  in the plural

plus

> plus *can be an adverb or a conjunction.*

A ADVERB
more

C'est plus difficile.
It's more difficult.

Il fait plus chaud aujourd'hui.
It's warmer today.

ne ... plus
not ... any more

Je ne veux plus le voir.
I don't want to see him any more.

Je n'en ai plus.
I haven't any left.

Je n'ai plus d'argent.
I've got no money left.

plus ... que
more ... than

Elle est plus gaie que sa sœur.
She's more cheerful than her sister.

Elle est plus grande que moi.
She's bigger than me.

C'est le plus grand de la classe.
He's the tallest in the class.

plus de
more/more than

> *Language tip*
>
> **plus de** *has two translations. Look at the examples.*

Il nous faut plus de pain.
We need more bread.

Le voyage dure plus de six heures.

The journey takes more than six hours.

en plus
as well

Il est bête, et en plus il est méchant.

He's stupid and nasty as well.

de plus en plus
more and more

Il y a de plus en plus de touristes par ici.

There are more and more tourists round here.

Il fait de plus en plus chaud.
It's getting hotter and hotter.

B CONJUNCTION
plus

Quatre plus deux égalent six.
Four plus two is six.

plusieurs PRONOUN
several

  plusieurs personnes
  several people

plutôt ADVERB

1 **quite**

  Elle est plutôt jolie.
  She's quite pretty.

2 **rather**

  L'eau est plutôt froide.
  The water's rather cold.

3 **instead**
Demande-lui plutôt de rester.
Ask her to stay instead.
plutôt que
instead of
Invite Marie plutôt que Nathalie.
Invite Marie instead of Nathalie.

la **poche** FEM NOUN
pocket
l'argent de poche
pocket money
un livre de poche
a paperback

la **poêle** FEM NOUN
frying pan

le **poème** MASC NOUN
poem

le **poids** MASC NOUN
weight

le **poids lourd** MASC NOUN
lorry

le **poignet** MASC NOUN
wrist

le **poil** MASC NOUN
1 **hair**
Il y a des poils de chat partout sur la moquette.
There are cat hairs all over the carpet.
2 **fur**
Ton chien a un beau poil.
Your dog's got lovely fur.

le **poing** MASC NOUN
fist
un coup de poing
a punch

le **point** MASC NOUN
full stop
un point d'exclamation
an exclamation mark
un point d'interrogation
a question mark

la **pointe** FEM NOUN
sur la pointe des pieds
on tiptoe

la **pointure** FEM NOUN
size
Quelle est ta pointure?
What size shoes do you take?

la **poire** FEM NOUN
pear

le **poireau** MASC NOUN
(PL les **poireaux**)
leek

les **pois** MASC PL NOUN
les petits pois
peas
les pois chiches
chickpeas
à pois
spotted
une robe à pois
a spotted dress

le **poison** MASC NOUN
poison

le **poisson**
MASC NOUN
fish

Je n'aime pas le poisson.
I don't like fish.
un poisson rouge
a goldfish
Poisson d'avril!
April fool!

French English
a b c d e f g h i j k l m n o p q r s t u v w x y z

a
b
c
d
e
f
g
h
i
j
k
l
m
n
o
p
q
r
s
t
u
v
w
x
y
z

Did you know…?

Pinning a paper fish to somebody's back is a traditional April fool's joke in France.

la **poissonnerie** FEM NOUN
fish shop

le **poissonnier** MASC NOUN
fishmonger

le **poivre** MASC NOUN
pepper

le **poivron** MASC NOUN
pepper
  un poivron rouge
  a red pepper

le **pôle** MASC NOUN
pole
  le pôle Nord
  the North Pole
  le pôle Sud
  the South Pole

poli MASC ADJECTIVE (FEM **polie**)
polite

la **police** FEM NOUN
police

policier

policier can be a noun or an adjective.

A MASC NOUN
  policeman
B MASC ADJECTIVE
  (FEM **policière**)
  un roman policier
  a detective novel

pollué MASC ADJECTIVE
(FEM **polluée**)
polluted

la **pollution** FEM NOUN
pollution

le **polo** MASC NOUN
polo shirt

la **Pologne** FEM NOUN
Poland

polonais MASC NOUN, MASC
ADJECTIVE (FEM **polonaise**)
Polish

le **Polonais** MASC NOUN
la **Polonaise** FEM NOUN
Pole

la **Polynésie** FEM NOUN
Polynesia

la **pomme** FEM NOUN
apple
  les pommes
  de terre
  potatoes
  les pommes
  frites
  chips
  les pommes vapeur
  boiled potatoes

le **pompier** MASC NOUN
fireman

le **poney**
MASC NOUN
pony

le **pont**
MASC NOUN
bridge

populaire ADJECTIVE
popular

le **porc** MASC NOUN
1 pig
  Ils élèvent des porcs.
  They breed pigs.

2 pork
du rôti de porc
roast pork

le **port** MASC NOUN
harbour

le **portable** MASC NOUN
1 mobile phone
Je vais appeler Marie sur mon portable.
I'll phone Marie on my mobile.
2 laptop
Je vais te montrer sur mon portable.
I'll show you on my laptop.

le **portail** MASC NOUN
gate

la **porte** FEM NOUN
door
Ferme la porte, s'il te plaît.
Close the door, please.

le **porte-clés** MASC NOUN
key ring

le **portefeuille** MASC NOUN
wallet

le **portemanteau** MASC NOUN
(PL les **portemanteaux**)
1 coat hanger
2 coat rack

le **porte-monnaie**
MASC NOUN
purse

porter VERB
1 to carry
Tu peux me porter? —
Non, tu es trop lourde!
Can you carry me? —
No, you're too heavy!
2 to wear
Elle porte une jolie robe bleue.
She's wearing a lovely blue dress.

portugais MASC NOUN, MASC
ADJECTIVE (FEM **portugaise**)
Portuguese

le **Portugais** MASC NOUN
la **Portugaise** FEM NOUN
Portuguese

le **Portugal** MASC NOUN
Portugal

poser VERB
1 to put down
Posez vos crayons.
Put your pencils down.
2 to ask
Je peux te poser une question?
Can I ask you a question?

possible ADJECTIVE
possible
Ça n'est pas possible.
It's not possible.
le plus vite possible
as quickly as possible

la **poste** FEM NOUN
post office

poster

poster *can be a noun or a verb.*

A MASC NOUN
poster
un poster de Madonna
a poster of Madonna

Language tip

When **poster** *is a noun, the ending sounds like 'air'.*

B VERB
to post
Je vais poster ce colis.
I'm going to post this parcel.

le **pot** MASC NOUN
  pot
      un pot de confiture
      a pot of jam
      un pot de yaourt
      a yogurt

le **potage** MASC NOUN
  soup

le **potager** MASC NOUN
  vegetable garden

le **pot-au-feu** MASC NOUN
  beef stew

la **poterie** FEM NOUN
  pottery

la **poubelle** FEM NOUN
  bin
      **Mets ton chewing-gum à la
      poubelle.**
      Put your chewing gum in the bin.

le **pouce** MASC NOUN
  thumb

la **poule** FEM NOUN
  hen

le **poulet** MASC NOUN
  chicken
      J'adore le poulet.
      I love chicken.

la **poupée**
  FEM NOUN
  doll

pour PREPOSITION
  for
      C'est un cadeau pour toi.
      It's a present for you.

**Qu'est-ce que tu veux pour
ton petit déjeuner?**
What would you like for
breakfast?
**Pour aller à la gare, s'il vous
plaît?**
Which way is it to the station,
please?

pourquoi ADVERB
  why
      Pourquoi tu pleures?
      Why are you crying?
      Pourquoi pas?
      Why not?

**pourra, pourrai,
pourras, pourrez,
pourrons, pourront**
VERB ▷ see **pouvoir**
Quand est-ce qu'il pourra venir?
When can he come?
Je ne pourrai pas venir.
I won't be able to come.
**Tu pourras me téléphoner
ce soir?**
Can you ring me tonight?
**Vous pourrez arrêter à cinq
heures.**
You can stop at five o'clock.
Nous pourrons faire du vélo.
We can go for bike rides.
**Ils ne pourront pas faire de
natation.**
They won't be able to go swimming.

pousser VERB
1 **to push**
      Arrêtez de pousser.
      Stop pushing.
      Pousse-toi, je ne vois rien.
      Move over, I can't see a thing.
2 **to grow**
      Mes cheveux poussent vite.
      My hair grows quickly.

la **poussette** FEM NOUN
pushchair

le **poussin** MASC NOUN
chick

la **poutine** FEM NOUN (*Canada*)

Did you know…?

poutine *is a type of fast food popular in Quebec. It is French fries topped with cheese curds and gravy.*

pouvoir VERB
can
Je peux lui téléphoner si tu veux.
I can phone her if you want.
Il ne peut pas venir.
He can't come.

pratique ADJECTIVE
handy
Ce sac est très pratique.
This bag's very handy.

précieux MASC ADJECTIVE
(FEM **précieuse**)
precious

préféré MASC ADJECTIVE
(FEM **préférée**)
favourite
Quel est ton sport préféré?
What's your favourite sport?

préférer VERB
to prefer
Je préfère manger à la cantine.
I prefer to eat in the canteen.
Tu préfères le riz ou les pâtes?
Would you prefer rice or pasta?

préhistorique ADJECTIVE
prehistoric

premier

premier *can be an adjective or a noun.*

A MASC ADJECTIVE
(FEM **première**)
first
au premier étage
on the first floor
C'est la première fois que je viens ici.
This is the first time I've been here.

le premier avril
the first of April
le premier mai
the first of May

B MASC NOUN
first
Tu veux être le premier?
Do you want to be first?

la **première** FEM NOUN
1 first
Elle est arrivée la première.
She came first.
2 year 12
Ma sœur est en première.
My sister's in year 12.

Did you know…?

*In French secondary schools the years are counted from the **sixième** (youngest) to the **première** and the **terminale** (oldest).*

prendre VERB
1 to take
Prends le plus gros!
Take the biggest!

2 to get
Nous prenons le train de huit heures.
We're getting the eight o'clock train.

3 to have
Je prends mon petit déjeuner à huit heures.
I have breakfast at eight.

le **prénom** MASC NOUN
first name
Quel est ton prénom?
What's your first name?

préparer VERB
to prepare
Elle prépare le dîner.
She's preparing dinner.

près ADVERB
près de
near
C'est près d'ici?
Is it near here?
tout près
nearby
J'habite tout près.
I live nearby.

présent

présent *can be an adjective or a noun.*

A MASC ADJECTIVE (FEM **présente**)
present
Je vais faire l'appel; les garçons, répondez 'présent', et les filles, répondez 'présente'.
I'm going to call the register. Boys, say 'présent', and girls, say 'présente'.
B MASC NOUN
present
à présent
now

présenter VERB
to present
Il va présenter le spectacle.
He's going to present the show.
Marc, je te présente Anaïs.
Marc, this is Anaïs.

presque ADVERB
nearly
Il est presque six heures.
It's nearly six o'clock.

pressé MASC ADJECTIVE
(FEM **pressée**)
in a hurry
Je ne peux pas rester, je suis pressé.
I can't stay, I'm in a hurry.
une orange pressée
a glass of freshly squeezed orange juice

se **presser** VERB
to hurry up
Allez, presse-toi, on va être en retard!
Come on, hurry up, we're going to be late!

prêt MASC ADJECTIVE (FEM **prête**)
ready
Vous êtes prêts?
Are you ready?

prêter VERB
to lend
Tu peux me prêter ta gomme?
Could you lend me your rubber?

prévenir VERB
Je te préviens, il est de mauvaise humeur.
I'm warning you, he's in a bad mood.

la **prière** FEM NOUN
prayer

primaire ADJECTIVE
l'école primaire
primary school

le **prince** MASC NOUN
prince

la **princesse**
FEM NOUN
princess

principal

> **principal** *can be an adjective or a noun.*

A MASC ADJECTIVE (FEM **principale**)
main
le personnage principal
the main character

B MASC NOUN
1 **headmaster**

> **Did you know…?**
> **le principal** *is the headmaster of a* **collège** – *a secondary school for pupils aged 11 to 15.*

2 **main thing**
Personne n'a été blessé; c'est le principal.
Nobody was injured; that's the main thing.

le **printemps** MASC NOUN
spring
au printemps
in spring

pris VERB ▷see **prendre**
Il a pris le plus gros!
He took the biggest!

la **prison** FEM NOUN
prison

prisonnier MASC ADJECTIVE
(FEM **prisonnière**)
captive

le **prix** MASC NOUN
1 price
Je n'arrive pas à lire le prix de ce livre.
I can't see the price of this book.
2 prize
Cécile a eu le prix de la meilleure actrice.
Cécile got the prize for best actress.

le **problème** MASC NOUN
problem

prochain MASC ADJECTIVE
(FEM **prochaine**)
next
la prochaine fois
next time

> **À la semaine prochaine!**
> See you next week!

le **produit** MASC NOUN
product

le/la **prof** MASC/FEM NOUN
teacher
Elle est prof de maths.
She's a maths teacher.

> **Did you know…?**
> **prof** *is a secondary school teacher.*

le **professeur**
MASC NOUN
teacher
Christine est professeur d'histoire.
Christine's a history teacher.

un professeur des écoles
a primary school teacher

la **profession** FEM NOUN
profession

professionnel MASC ADJECTIVE
(FEM **professionnelle**)
professional

profond MASC ADJECTIVE
(FEM **profonde**)
deep

le **programmeur** MASC NOUN
la **programmeuse** FEM
NOUN
programmer

le **progrès** MASC NOUN
progress
Tu fais des progrès!
You're making progress!

progresser VERB
to progress

le **projet** MASC NOUN
plan
des projets de vacances
holiday plans

la **promenade** FEM NOUN
1 walk
Il y a de belles promenades par ici.
There are some nice walks round here.
Tu veux faire une promenade?
Do you want to go for a walk?
2 ride
Il va faire une promenade à vélo.
He's going to go for a bike ride.
Je voudrais faire une promenade en voiture.
I'd like to go for a drive.

promener VERB
to take for a walk
Cordelia promène son chien tous les jours.
Cordelia takes her dog for a walk every day.
■ **se promener**
to go for a walk
Chantal veut se promener.
Chantal wants to go for a walk.

la **promesse** FEM NOUN
promise
Il m'a fait une promesse.
He made me a promise.

promettre VERB
to promise
Je te promets de venir.
I promise I'll come.
Je viendrai, c'est promis.
I'll come, it's a promise.

prononcer VERB
to pronounce
Le russe est difficile à prononcer.
Russian is difficult to pronounce.

la **prononciation** FEM NOUN
pronunciation

propre ADJECTIVE
clean
Ce verre n'est pas propre.
This glass isn't clean.

le **prospectus** MASC NOUN
leaflet

protéger VERB
to protect

protestant MASC ADJECTIVE
(FEM **protestante**)
Protestant

le **proverbe** MASC NOUN
proverb

a b c d e f g h i j k l m n o **p** q r s t u v w x y z

la **province** FEM NOUN
province
Ils habitent en province.
They don't live in Paris.

le **proviseur** MASC NOUN
headteacher

> **Did you know…?**
> **le proviseur** *is the headmaster of a* **lycée** *– a secondary school for pupils aged 15 to 18.*

prudent MASC ADJECTIVE
(FEM **prudente**)
1 careful
Soyez prudents!
Be careful!
2 wise
Laisse ton passeport à la maison, c'est plus prudent.
It would be wiser to leave your passport at home.

la **prune** FEM NOUN
plum

> **Did you know…?**
> *In English, a* **prune** *is a dried plum, but a French* **prune** *is a fresh plum.*

le **pruneau** MASC NOUN
(PL les **pruneaux**)
prune

le/la **psychiatre** MASC/FEM
NOUN
psychiatrist

le/la **psychologue** MASC/FEM
NOUN
psychologist

pu VERB ▷ see **pouvoir**
Je n'ai pas pu venir.
I couldn't come.

la **pub** FEM NOUN
1 advertising

Il y a trop de pub à la télé.
There's too much advertising on TV.
2 advert
J'aime regarder les pubs à la télé.
I like watching the adverts on the telly.

> **Language tip**
> **la pub** *is a slang word for* **la publicité**.

public MASC ADJECTIVE
(FEM **publique**)
public
un jardin public
a public park

une école publique
a state school

la **publicité** FEM NOUN
1 advertising
Muriel travaille dans la publicité.
Muriel works in advertising.
2 advert
Il y a trop de publicités dans ce journal.
There are too many adverts in this newspaper.

publique FEM ADJECTIVE
▷ see **public**
public

puer VERB
to stink
> **Ça pue le tabac ici!**
> It stinks of tobacco in here!

puis ADVERB
then
> **Faites dorer le poulet, puis ajoutez le vin blanc.**
> Fry the chicken till golden, then add white wine.

puisque CONJUNCTION
since
> **Puisque c'est si cher, nous irons manger ailleurs.**
> Since it's so expensive, we'll eat somewhere else.

puissant MASC ADJECTIVE
(FEM **puissante**)
powerful

le **puits** MASC NOUN
well

le **pull** MASC NOUN
jumper

le **pull-over** MASC NOUN
jumper

la **punaise** FEM NOUN
drawing pin

punir VERB
> **être puni**
> to be grounded
> **Il est puni.**
> He's grounded.

la **punition** FEM NOUN
punishment

la **purée** FEM NOUN
mashed potatoes

le **puzzle** MASC NOUN
jigsaw puzzle

le **pyjama** MASC NOUN
pyjamas

la **pyramide** FEM NOUN
pyramid

les **Pyrénées** FEM PL NOUN
Pyrenees
> **dans les Pyrénées**
> in the Pyrenees

French English

a
b
c
d
e
f
g
h
i
j
k
l
m
n
o
P
q
r
s
t
u
v
w
x
y
z

Q q

quand CONJUNCTION
when
> **Quand est-ce que tu pars en vacances?**
> When are you going on holiday?

la **quarantaine** FEM NOUN
about forty
> **une quarantaine de personnes**
> about forty people
> **Elle a la quarantaine.**
> She's in her forties.

quarante NUMBER
forty
> **Elle a quarante ans.**
> She's forty.
> **quarante et un**
> forty-one
> **quarante-deux**
> forty-two

le **quart** MASC NOUN
quarter
> **un quart d'heure**
> a quarter of an hour

Il est deux heures et quart.
It's a quarter past two.
Il est dix heures moins le quart.
It's a quarter to ten.

le **quartier** MASC NOUN
area
> **un quartier tranquille**
> a quiet area

quatorze NUMBER
fourteen
> **Il a quatorze ans.**
> He's fourteen.
> **à quatorze heures**
> at 2 p.m.

Did you know...?
The 24-hour clock is used in France for travel times, appointments and other formal situations.

le quatorze février
the fourteenth of February

quatre NUMBER
four
> **Il est quatre heures.**
> It's four o'clock.
> **Il a quatre ans.**
> He's four.

le quatre février
the fourth of February

quatre-vingts NUMBER
eighty
> **quatre-vingts euros**
> eighty euros
> **Elle a quatre-vingt-deux ans.**
> She's eighty-two.
> **quatre-vingt-dix**
> ninety
> **quatre-vingt-onze**
> ninety-one
> **quatre-vingt-quinze**
> ninety-five
> **quatre-vingt-dix-huit**
> ninety-eight

quatrième

quatrième can be an adjective or a noun.

A ADJECTIVE
fourth
> **au quatrième étage**
> on the fourth floor

B FEM NOUN
year 9
Mon frère est en quatrième.
My brother's in year 9.

Did you know…?

*In French secondary schools, years are counted from the **sixième** (youngest) to the **première** and the **terminale** (oldest).*

que

que can be a conjunction or a pronoun.

A CONJUNCTION
that
J'espère que tu passes de bonnes vacances.
I hope that you're having a nice holiday.
plus … que
more … than
Il a plus d'argent que moi.
He's got more money than me.
Il est plus grand que moi.
He's taller than me.
aussi … que
as … as
Elle est aussi grande que moi.
She's as tall as me.
ne … que
only
Il ne boit que de l'eau.
He only drinks water.

B PRONOUN
what
Que fais-tu?
What are you doing?
Qu'est-ce que …?
What …?
Qu'est-ce que tu fais?
What are you doing?

Qu'est-ce que c'est?
What's that?

quel MASC ADJECTIVE (FEM quelle)
1 **who**
Quel est ton chanteur préféré?
Who's your favourite singer?
2 **what**
Quelle est ta couleur préférée?
What's your favourite colour?
3 **which**
C'est quel jumeau celui-là?
Which twin is that?

Quelle heure est-il?
What time is it?

quelque ADJECTIVE
1 **some**
Il a quelques amis à Paris.
He has some friends in Paris.
2 **a few**
Il y a quelques tulipes dans le jardin.
There are a few tulips in the garden.
quelque chose
something/anything

Language tip

quelque chose *has two translations. Look at the examples.*

a
b
c
d
e
f
g
h
i
j
k
l
m
n
o
p
q
r
s
t
u
v
w
x
y
z

J'ai quelque chose pour toi.
I've got something for you.

Je voudrais quelque chose de moins cher.
I'd like something cheaper.
Tu veux quelque chose d'autre?
Would you like anything else?

quelquefois ADVERB
sometimes

quelqu'un PRONOUN
1 somebody
  Il y a quelqu'un à la porte.
  There's somebody at the door.
2 anybody
  Il y a quelqu'un?
  Is there anybody there?

qu'est-ce que ▷ see **que**
what

qu'est-ce qui ▷ see **qui**
what

la **question** FEM NOUN
question

le **questionnaire** MASC NOUN
questionnaire

la **queue** FEM NOUN
tail
  Il faut faire la queue.
  You have to queue.

une queue de cheval
a ponytail

> ***Language tip***
> *Word for word this means 'horse's tail'.*

qui PRONOUN
1 who
  Qui a téléphoné?
  Who phoned?
2 that
  J'aime bien les chaussures noires qui sont dans la vitrine.
  I like the black shoes that are in the window.
  Qu'est-ce qui ...?
  What ...?
  Qu'est-ce qui est sur la table?
  What's on the table?
  à qui
  whose
  À qui est ce sac?
  Whose bag is this?

la **quille** FEM NOUN
  un jeu de quilles
  skittles

la **quinzaine** FEM NOUN
about fifteen
  une quinzaine de personnes
  about fifteen people
  une quinzaine de jours
  a fortnight

quinze NUMBER
fifteen
  Elle a quinze ans.
  She's fifteen.
  quinze jours
  a fortnight
  à quinze heures
  at three p.m.

French English

Did you know...?

The 24-hour clock is used in France for travel times, appointments, and other formal situations

le quinze avril
the fifteenth of April

quitter VERB
to leave

Je quitte la maison à huit heures du matin.
I leave the house at eight o'clock in the morning.

quoi PRONOUN
what?
À quoi tu penses?
What are you thinking about?

a
b
c
d
e
f
g
h
i
j
k
l
m
n
o
p
q
r
s
t
u
v
w
x
y
z

R r

raccompagner VERB
to take home
Tu peux me raccompagner?
Can you take me home?

le **raccourci** MASC NOUN
shortcut

la **race** FEM NOUN
1 **race**
la race humaine
the human race
2 **breed**
De quelle race est ton chat?
What breed is your cat?

la **racine** FEM NOUN
root

le **racisme** MASC NOUN
racism

raciste ADJECTIVE
racist

raconter VERB
to tell
Je vais te raconter une histoire.
I'm going to tell you a story.

le **radiateur** MASC NOUN
radiator
un radiateur électrique
an electric heater

la **radio** FEM NOUN
1 **radio**
J'écoute la radio.
I listen to the radio.
une radio numérique
a digital radio
2 **X-ray**
une radio des poumons
an X-ray of the lungs

le **radio-réveil** MASC NOUN
clock radio

le **radis** MASC NOUN
radish

> **Did you know...?**
> In France, people often eat radishes
> with bread and butter as a starter.

le **ragoût** MASC NOUN
stew

raide ADJECTIVE
1 **straight**
Laure a les cheveux raides.
Laure has got straight hair.
2 **steep**
Cette côte est raide.
This is a steep hill.
3 **stiff**
Son bras est encore raide.
His arm's still stiff.

le **raisin** MASC NOUN
grapes

le raisin noir
black grapes
le raisin blanc
green grapes
un grain de raisin
a grape
des raisins secs
raisins

la **raison** FEM NOUN
reason

Tu as raison.
You're right.

raisonnable ADJECTIVE
sensible

ramasser VERB
1 **to pick up**
Ramasse le crayon, s'il te plaît.
Pick up the pencil please.
2 **to collect**
Paul, ramasse les cahiers s'il te plaît.
Paul, collect the books please.

ramener VERB
1 **to bring back**
Ramène-moi un souvenir!
Bring me back a souvenir!
2 **to take home**
Tu me ramènes?
Will you take me home?

la **randonnée** FEM NOUN
une randonnée pédestre
a ramble
une randonnée à vélo
a bike ride

le **rang** MASC NOUN
row
au premier rang
in the front row
Mettez-vous en rang.
Line up.

la **rangée** FEM NOUN
row
une rangée de chaises
a row of chairs

ranger VERB
1 **to put away**
Rangez vos affaires.
Put your things away.
2 **to tidy up**
Va ranger ta chambre.
Go and tidy up your room.

Rangez-vous deux par deux.
Get into twos.

râper VERB
to grate
le fromage râpé
grated cheese

rapide ADJECTIVE
fast

rapidement ADVERB
quickly

rappeler VERB
1 **to call back**
Je te rappelle dans cinq minutes.
I'll call you back in five minutes.
2 **to remind**
Rappelle-moi de prendre mon maillot de bain.
Remind me to take my swimming costume.
Cette chanson me rappelle mes vacances.
This song reminds me of my holiday.
Tu te rappelles?
Do you remember?
Je ne me rappelle plus.
I can't remember.

rapporter VERB
to bring back
N'oublie pas de rapporter la clé.
Don't forget to bring back the key.

la **raquette** FEM NOUN
  1 racket
    une raquette de tennis
    a tennis racket
  2 bat
    une raquette de ping-pong
    a table tennis bat

se **raser** VERB
  to shave
    Il se rase tous les matins.
    He shaves every morning.

le **rasoir** MASC NOUN
  razor

rassembler VERB
  to gather
    Rassemblez vos affaires!
    Gather up your things!
    Rassemblez-vous!
    Gather round!
    Il faut se rassembler demain à huit heures devant l'école.
    We've got to meet at eight tomorrow in front of the school.

rassurer VERB
  to reassure
    Je suis rassuré.
    I don't need to worry any more.

le **rat** MASC NOUN
  rat

raté MASC ADJECTIVE (FEM **ratée**)
    Mes photos sont ratées.
    My photos are no good.
    Le gâteau est raté.
    The cake's a failure.

le **râteau** MASC NOUN
  (PL les **râteaux**)
  rake

rater VERB
  1 to miss
    Je ne veux pas rater mon train.
    I don't want to miss my train.
  2 to fail
    J'ai peur de rater mon examen de maths.
    I'm afraid I'm going to fail my maths exam.
    Elle rate toujours ses gâteaux.
    Her cakes are never any good.

rayé MASC ADJECTIVE (FEM **rayée**)
  striped
    une chemise rayée
    a striped shirt

le **rayon** MASC NOUN
  1 ray
    un rayon de soleil
    a ray of sunshine
  2 department
    le rayon des jouets
    the toy department

la **rayure** FEM NOUN
  stripe
    un T-shirt à rayures rouges et blanches
    a T-shirt with red and white stripes

le/la **réceptionniste** MASC/FEM NOUN
  receptionist

la **recette** FEM NOUN
  recipe

recevoir VERB
  to get
    Je suis contente quand je reçois une lettre.
    I'm pleased when I get a letter.

réchauffer VERB
to warm up
Un bon café va te réchauffer.
A nice cup of coffee will warm
you up.
■ se réchauffer
to get warm
Je vais me réchauffer près
du feu.
I'll go and get warm by the fire.

le **récipient** MASC NOUN
container

la **récitation** FEM NOUN
recitation

Did you know…?

A **récitation** is a poem which
pupils have to learn off by heart and
recite in front of the whole class.

réciter VERB
to recite

reçois, reçoit, reçoivent
VERB ▷see recevoir
Tu reçois combien d'argent de
poche?
How much pocket money do you
get?
Il reçoit toujours des tas de
lettres.
He always gets loads of letters.
Ils ne reçoivent jamais rien.
They never get anything.

recommencer VERB
to start again

Il recommence à pleuvoir.
It's started raining again.

la **récompense** FEM NOUN
reward

reconnaître VERB
to recognize
Elle ne va peut-être pas me
reconnaître.
She might not recognize me.
Je ne l'ai pas reconnue.
I didn't recognize her.

le **record** MASC NOUN
record
J'essaie de battre le record.
I'm trying to break the record.

la **récréation** FEM NOUN
break
Les élèves sont en récréation.
The pupils are having their break.
la cour de récréation
the playground

le **rectangle** MASC NOUN
rectangle

reçu VERB ▷see recevoir
J'ai reçu un colis ce matin.
I got a parcel this morning.
être reçu à un examen
to pass an exam

reculer VERB
to step back
Reculez de trois cases.
Go back three spaces.

reculons ADVERB
à reculons
backwards
Marchez à reculons.
Walk backwards.

la **rédaction** FEM NOUN
essay

redoubler VERB
to repeat a year

refaire VERB
1 to do again
Je dois refaire mon dessin.
I'll have to do my drawing again.
2 to start doing again
Je voudrais refaire de la gym.
I'd like to start doing gymnastics again.

réfléchir VERB
to think
Il est en train de réfléchir.
He's thinking.

la **réflexion** FEM NOUN
remark

le **refrain** MASC NOUN
chorus

refroidir VERB
to cool
Laissez le gâteau refroidir.
Leave the cake to cool.

regarder VERB
1 to look at
Regardez l'image: qu'est-ce que c'est?
Look at the picture: what is it?
2 to watch
Je regarde la télévision.
I'm watching television.

le **régime** MASC NOUN
diet
Il est au régime.
He's on a diet.

la **région** FEM NOUN
region

la **règle** FEM NOUN
ruler

regretter VERB
to be sorry
Je regrette, je ne peux pas venir.
I'm sorry, I can't come.

régulier MASC ADJECTIVE
(FEM **régulière**)
regular

régulièrement ADVERB
regularly

le **rein** MASC NOUN
kidney

la **reine** FEM NOUN
queen

le **relais** MASC NOUN
relay race

se **relaxer** VERB
to relax

la **religieuse** FEM NOUN
1 nun
Marie est religieuse.
Marie is a nun.
2 choux cream bun
une religieuse au chocolat
a choux bun with chocolate cream and chocolate icing

la **religion** FEM NOUN
religion

relire VERB
to read again

remarquable ADJECTIVE
remarkable

la **remarque** FEM NOUN
remark

remarquer VERB
to notice
**Regardez les deux dessins:
que remarquez-vous?**
Look at the two pictures: what
do you notice?

remercier VERB
to thank
**Je te remercie pour ton
cadeau.**
Thank you for your present.

remettre VERB
1 to put back
**Remettez les boîtes dans le
placard, s'il vous plaît.**
Put the boxes back in the
cupboard please.
2 to put back on
Remets ton pull, il fait froid.
Put your sweater back on, it's
cold.
■ se remettre
to get better
**J'espère que tu vas vite te
remettre.**
I hope you will get better soon.

le **remonte-pente** MASC
NOUN
ski tow

les **remparts** MASC PL NOUN
city walls

le **remplaçant** MASC NOUN
la **remplaçante** FEM NOUN
supply teacher

remplacer VERB
to replace

remplacer par
to replace with
**Le premier avril, j'ai
remplacé le sel par du sucre.**
On April Fool's Day, I replaced
the salt with sugar.
Il remplace le prof de maths.
He's covering for the maths
teacher.

remplir VERB
to fill in
Remplissez la grille.
Fill in the grid.

remuer VERB
to stir

le **renard**
MASC NOUN
fox

rencontrer VERB
to meet
**Je la rencontre souvent au
marché.**
I often meet her at the market.
**Ils se sont rencontrés il y a
deux ans.**
They met two years ago.

le **rendez-vous** MASC NOUN
appointment
**J'ai rendez-vous chez le
coiffeur.**
I've got an appointment at the
hairdresser's.

rendre VERB
1 to give back
Rends-moi ma gomme.
Give me back my rubber.
2 to take back
**Je vais rendre mes livres à la
bibliothèque.**
I'm going to take my books back
to the library.

French English

a
b
c
d
e
f
g
h
i
j
k
l
m
n
o
p
q
r
s
t
u
v
w
x
y
z

223

renifler VERB
to sniff

le **renne** MASC NOUN
reindeer

le **renseignement** MASC NOUN
piece of information
Il me manque un renseignement.
There's one piece of information I still need.
des renseignements
information
Je cherche des renseignements sur l'Écosse.
I'm looking for information about Scotland.

la **rentrée** FEM NOUN
la rentrée (des classes)
the start of the new school year
le jour de la rentrée
the day the schools go back

rentrer VERB
1 **to come in**
Rentre, tu vas prendre froid.
Come in, you'll catch cold.
2 **to get home**
Il rentre à sept heures du soir.
He gets home at seven o'clock in the evening.

réparer VERB
to repair

le **repas** MASC NOUN
meal
le repas de midi
lunch

le repas du soir
dinner

le **repassage** MASC NOUN
ironing
Ma mère déteste le repassage.
My mum hates ironing.

repasser VERB
to iron

répéter VERB
to repeat
Écoutez et répétez après moi.
Listen and repeat after me.

la **répétition** FEM NOUN
rehearsal

le **répondeur** MASC NOUN
answering machine

répondre VERB
to answer
Répondez par oui ou par non.
Answer yes or no.

la **réponse** FEM NOUN
answer
C'est la bonne réponse.
That's the right answer.

se **reposer** VERB
to have a rest
Le week-end, je me repose.
I have a rest at the weekend.

le **représentant** MASC NOUN
la **représentante** FEM NOUN
rep

le **requin** MASC NOUN
shark

réservé MASC ADJECTIVE
(FEM **réservée**)
reserved

réserver VERB
to book

la **résidence** FEM NOUN
block of flats
   une résidence secondaire
   a second home

respirer VERB
to breathe

responsable ADJECTIVE
responsible
   Elle est responsable de
   l'accident.
   She's responsible for the
   accident.

ressembler VERB
   ressembler à
   to look like
   Elle ressemble à sa sœur.
   She looks like her sister.
   On se ressemble.
   We look alike.

le **restaurant** MASC NOUN
restaurant

le **reste** MASC NOUN
rest
   Tu peux manger le reste des
   pâtes.
   You can eat the rest of the pasta.
   les restes
   the left-overs

rester VERB
1 to stay
   Je reste à la maison ce week-
   end.
   I'm staying at home this
   weekend.

2 to be left
   Il reste du pain.
   There's some bread left.

le **résultat** MASC NOUN
result
   les résultats des examens
   the exam results

le **retard** MASC NOUN
   Je suis en retard!
   I'm late!
   Tu ne dois pas être en
   retard.
   You mustn't be late.

la **retenue** FEM NOUN
detention
   Gerry est en retenue.
   Gerry's in detention.

retirer VERB
to take off
   Retire ton manteau.
   Take your coat off.

le **retour** MASC NOUN
return
   Il est de retour.
   He's back.

retourner VERB
1 to go back
   Je dois retourner chez le
   dentiste la semaine
   prochaine.
   I have to go back to the dentist
   next week.

2 to turn over
   Retourne la carte.
   Turn the card over.
   Retourne-toi.
   Turn round.

la **retraite** FEM NOUN
   être à la retraite
   to be retired

Mon grand-père est à la retraite.
My granddad's retired.
prendre sa retraite
to retire
Il prend sa retraite l'année prochaine.
He's retiring next year.

retraité MASC ADJECTIVE
(FEM **retraitée**)
retired

retrouver VERB
to find
Je n'arrive pas à retrouver mes gants.
I can't find my gloves.

la **réunion** FEM NOUN
meeting

réussi MASC ADJECTIVE
(FEM **réussie**)
successful
une soirée très réussie
a very successful party

réussir VERB
réussir à un examen
to pass an exam

le **rêve** MASC NOUN
dream
la maison de mes rêves
my dream house

le **réveil**
MASC NOUN
alarm
clock

réveiller
VERB
to wake up

Ma mère me réveille à sept heures.
My mum wakes me up at seven o'clock.
■ **se réveiller**
to wake up
Je me réveille à sept heures.
I wake up at seven o'clock.

le **réveillon** MASC NOUN
le réveillon du jour de l'An
New Year's Eve celebrations
le réveillon de Noël
Christmas Eve celebrations

> **Did you know...?**
>
> In France, people celebrate Christmas Eve and New Year's Eve with special meals in the evening. They eat delicacies such as oysters, smoked salmon, caviar, and quails cooked with white grapes.
> The special Christmas cake is **la bûche de Noël**.

réveillonner VERB
1 to celebrate New Year's Eve
2 to celebrate Christmas Eve

revenez VERB ▷see revenir
Revenez vite!
Come back soon!

revenir VERB
to come back
Reviens vite!
Come back soon!

rêver VERB
to dream

reviens, revient VERB
▷see revenir
Tu reviens l'année prochaine?
Are you coming back next year?

Antoine revient souvent nous voir.
Antoine often comes back to see us.

réviser VERB
to revise
> **Je dois réviser mon anglais.**
> I've got to revise my English.

revoir VERB
to see again
> **J'aimerais bien la revoir.**
> I'd really like to see her again.

au revoir
goodbye

la **révolution** FEM NOUN
revolution
> **la Révolution française**
> the French Revolution

le **revolver** MASC NOUN
revolver

le **rez-de-chaussée**
MASC NOUN
ground floor
> **au rez-de-chaussée**
> on the ground floor

le **Rhin** MASC NOUN
Rhine

le **rhinocéros** MASC NOUN
rhinoceros

le **Rhône** MASC NOUN
Rhone

la **rhubarbe** FEM NOUN
rhubarb

le **rhum** MASC NOUN
rum

le **rhume** MASC NOUN
cold
> **J'ai le rhume.**
> I've got a cold.

le rhume des foins
hay fever

riche ADJECTIVE
1 **well-off**
> **Sa famille est très riche.**
> His family's very well-off.
2 **rich**
> **riche en vitamines**
> rich in vitamins

le **rideau**
MASC NOUN
(PL les **rideaux**)
curtain
> **Tire les rideaux.**
> Draw the curtains.

ridicule ADJECTIVE
ridiculous
> **Je trouve ça complètement ridicule.**
> I think that's absolutely ridiculous.

rien PRONOUN
1 **nothing**
> **Qu'est-ce que tu veux boire? — Rien, merci.**
> What would you like to drink? — Nothing, thanks.
> **rien d'intéressant**
> nothing interesting
> **rien d'autre**
> nothing else
> **rien du tout**
> nothing at all
2 **anything**
> **Il ne fait rien ce soir.**
> He's not doing anything tonight.
> **Elle ne mange rien.**
> She's not eating anything.
> **De rien!**
> Not at all!

French English

a
b
c
d
e
f
g
h
i
j
k
l
m
n
o
p
q
r
s
t
u
v
w
x
y
z

Merci beaucoup! — De rien!
Thank you very much! — Not at all!

rigolo MASC ADJECTIVE
(FEM **rigolote**)
funny

rire VERB
to laugh
Il me fait toujours rire.
He always makes me laugh.

le **risque** MASC NOUN
risk

la **rivière** FEM NOUN
river

le **riz** MASC NOUN
rice
le riz au lait
rice pudding

la **robe** FEM NOUN
dress
une robe de mariée
a wedding dress
une robe de chambre
a dressing gown

le **robinet** MASC NOUN
tap
Ferme le robinet.
turn off the tap.

le **robot** MASC NOUN
robot

le **rocher**
MASC NOUN
rock

le **rock**
MASC NOUN
rock
un chanteur
de rock
a rock singer

le **roi** MASC NOUN
king
les Rois mages
the Three Wise Men
la fête des Rois
Epiphany

Did you know...?

The sixth of January is **la fête des Rois**, *when the Three Wise Men, or Three Kings, are said to have come to visit baby Jesus. This day is also called Twelfth Night, because it is the twelfth day after Christmas.*

les **rollers** MASC PL NOUN
Rollerblades®

romain MASC ADJECTIVE
(FEM **romaine**)
Roman
des ruines romaines
Roman remains

le **roman** MASC NOUN
novel

rond

rond *can be an adjective or a noun.*

A MASC ADJECTIVE (FEM **ronde**)
round
La Terre est ronde.
The earth is round.
B MASC NOUN
circle
Dessinez un rond.
Draw a circle.
en rond
in a circle
Asseyez-vous en rond.
Sit in a circle.

la **rondelle** FEM NOUN
slice
une rondelle de citron
a slice of lemon

le **rond-point** MASC NOUN
roundabout

ronfler VERB
to snore

le **rosbif** MASC NOUN
roast beef

rose

> **rose** *can be an adjective or a noun.*

A ADJECTIVE
pink
des chaussettes roses
pink socks

B FEM NOUN
rose
une rose rouge
a red rose

C MASC NOUN
pink
Ma couleur préférée, c'est le rose.
Pink is my favourite colour.

le **rosier** MASC NOUN
rosebush

rôti

> **rôti** *can be a noun or an adjective.*

A MASC NOUN
roast meat
un rôti de bœuf
a joint of beef

B MASC ADJECTIVE (FEM **rôtie**)
roast
un poulet rôti
a roast chicken

la **roue** FEM NOUN
wheel
une roue de secours
a spare wheel
Je sais faire la roue.
I can do cartwheels.

rouge

> **rouge** *can be an adjective or a noun.*

A ADJECTIVE
red
des chaussettes rouges
red socks

B MASC NOUN
red
Ma couleur préférée, c'est le rouge.
Red is my favourite colour.
un rouge à lèvres
a lipstick

Language tip
rouge à lèvres *means 'red for lips'.*

la **rougeole** FEM NOUN
measles

rougir VERB
to blush
Tu rougis!
You're blushing!

la **rouille** FEM NOUN
rust

rouillé MASC ADJECTIVE
(FEM **rouillée**)
rusty

roulant MASC ADJECTIVE
(FEM **roulante**)
une table roulante
a trolley
un fauteuil roulant
a wheelchair

French **English**

a
b
c
d
e
f
g
h
i
j
k
l
m
n
o
p
q
r
s
t
u
v
w
x
y
z

a
b
c
d
e
f
g
h
i
j
k
l
m
n
o
p
q
r
s
t
u
v
w
x
y
z

rouler VERB
1 **to drive**
Il roule trop vite.
He drives too fast.
2 **to roll up**
Aide-moi à rouler le tapis.
Help me to roll up the mat.
Roulez la pâte.
Roll out the pastry.

roumain MASC ADJECTIVE
(FEM **roumaine**)
Romanian

le **Roumain** MASC NOUN
la **Roumaine** FEM NOUN
Romanian

la **Roumanie** FEM NOUN
Romania

rousse

rousse *can be an adjective or a noun.*

A FEM ADJECTIVE
red
une poule rousse
a red hen
Elle est rousse.
She's red-haired.
B FEM NOUN
redhead

la **route** FEM NOUN
1 **road**
une route nationale
an A road
au bord de la route
at the roadside
2 **way**
Je ne connais pas la route.
I don't know the way.
en route
on the way
On s'arrête toujours en route.
We always stop on the way.

3 **journey**
Bonne route!
Have a good journey!
Il y a trois heures de route.
It's a three-hour journey.

le **routier** MASC NOUN
lorry driver

roux

roux *can be an adjective or a noun.*

A MASC ADJECTIVE (FEM **rousse**)
red
Harry a les cheveux roux.
Harry has red hair.
Il est roux.
He's red-haired.
B MASC NOUN
redhead

royal MASC ADJECTIVE (FEM **royale**)
royal
la famille royale
the Royal Family

le **royaume** MASC NOUN
kingdom
le Royaume-Uni
the United Kingdom

le **ruban** MASC NOUN
ribbon

la **rubéole** FEM NOUN
German measles

la **rue** FEM NOUN
street

le **rugby** MASC NOUN
rugby
> **Yann joue au rugby.**
> Yann plays rugby.

la **ruine** FEM NOUN
ruin
> **les ruines de la cathédrale**
> the ruins of the cathedral

le **ruisseau** MASC NOUN
(PL les **ruisseaux**)
stream

rusé MASC ADJECTIVE (FEM **rusée**)
cunning

russe MASC NOUN, ADJECTIVE
Russian

le/la **Russe** MASC/FEM NOUN
Russian

la **Russie** FEM NOUN
Russia

le **rythme** MASC NOUN
rhythm

S s

' PRONOUN

Language tip

s' is what **se** changes to before a vowel sound.

Ils s'aiment.
They love each other.

sa FEM ADJECTIVE ▷ see **son**
1 **his**
Benjamin est chez sa grand-mère.
Benjamin is at his grandmother's.
2 **her**
Elle attend sa mère.
She's waiting for her mother.
3 **its**
Remets la télécommande à sa place.
Put the remote control back in its place.

le **sable** MASC NOUN
sand

le **sac** MASC NOUN
bag
un sac à main
a handbag
un sac à dos
a rucksack
un sac de couchage
a sleeping bag

sage ADJECTIVE
well-behaved
Fatima est très sage.
Fatima is very well-behaved.

Sois sage.
Be good.

saignant MASC ADJECTIVE
(FEM **saignante**)
rare
Saignant ou à point?
Rare or medium?

saigner VERB
to bleed
Il saigne du nez.
His nose is bleeding.

saint MASC ADJECTIVE (FEM **sainte**)
holy
la Saint-Jean-Baptiste (Canada)
Midsummer's Day

Did you know...?

La Saint-Jean-Baptiste is a national holiday in Quebec. It is celebrated on the twenty-fourth of June.

la Saint-Sylvestre
New Year's Eve
le vendredi saint
Good Friday

le **saint** MASC NOUN
la **sainte** FEM NOUN
saint
Aujourd'hui, c'est la sainte Louise.
Today is Saint Louise's day.

Did you know...?

Every day on a French calendar belongs to a saint. For example, on the fifteenth of March, St Louise's day, people say 'Bonne fête Louise!' to anyone with that name. Girls called Louise might get presents too.

sais VERB ▷ see **savoir**
  Je ne sais pas.
  I don't know.

la **saison** FEM NOUN
  season

sait VERB ▷ see **savoir**
  Il sait que ...
  He knows that ...
  On ne sait jamais!
  You never know!

la **salade** FEM NOUN
  1 lettuce
  Les tortues aiment la salade.
  Tortoises like lettuce.
  2 salad
  une salade de fruits
  a fruit salad

le **saladier** MASC NOUN
  salad bowl

sale ADJECTIVE
  dirty

salé MASC ADJECTIVE (FEM **salée**)
  1 salty
  La soupe est trop salée.
  The soup's too salty.
  2 salted
  du beurre salé
  salted butter
  3 savoury
  des biscuits salés
  savoury biscuits

la **salle** FEM NOUN
  room
    la salle à manger
    the dining room
    la salle de séjour
    the living room
    la salle de bains
    the bathroom
    la salle d'attente
    the waiting room

  une salle de classe
  a classroom

  la salle des professeurs
  the staffroom

le **salon** MASC NOUN
  lounge
    un salon de thé
    a tearoom
    un salon de beauté
    a beauty salon

la **salopette** FEM NOUN
  dungarees

salut EXCLAMATION
  Hi!

le **samedi** MASC NOUN
  1 Saturday
  **Aujourd'hui, nous sommes
  samedi.**
  It's Saturday today.
  2 on Saturday
  Je suis allé au cinéma samedi.
  I went to the cinema on Saturday.
  **Le magasin ferme à dix-huit
  heures le samedi.**
  The shop closes at six p.m. on
  Saturdays.

---

tous les samedis
every Saturday
le samedi
on Saturdays
samedi dernier
last Saturday
samedi prochain
next Saturday
À samedi!
See you on Saturday!

French English

a
b
c
d
e
f
g
h
i
j
k
l
m
n
o
p
q
r
s
t
u
v
w
x
y
z

les **sandales** FEM PL NOUN
sandals

le **sandwich**
MASC NOUN
sandwich
un sandwich
au jambon
a ham sandwich

le **sang** MASC NOUN
blood

le **sanglier** MASC NOUN
wild boar

sans PREPOSITION
without
Elle est venue sans son frère.
She came without her brother.

la **santé** FEM NOUN
health
en bonne santé
in good health
Santé!
Cheers!

le **sapin** MASC NOUN
fir tree
un sapin de Noël
a Christmas tree

la **sauce** FEM NOUN
1 sauce
la sauce tomate
tomato sauce
2 gravy

la **saucisse** FEM NOUN
sausage

le **saucisson** MASC NOUN
salami

Did you know…?
le saucisson sec *is a hard sausage
that is eaten cold.*

sauf PREPOSITION
except
Tout le monde est venu sauf
lui.
Everyone came except him.
sauf si
unless
Je n'irai pas sauf si tu viens.
I won't go unless you come too.

le **saumon** MASC NOUN
salmon

le **saut** MASC NOUN
jump

sauter VERB
to jump
sauter à la corde
to skip

sauvage ADJECTIVE
wild
les animaux sauvages
wild animals

sauver VERB
to save
Il m'a sauvé la vie.
He saved my life.

le **savant** MASC NOUN
scientist

savent, savez VERB
▷ *see* **savoir**
Ils ne savent pas ce qu'ils
veulent.
They don't know what they want.
Est-ce que vous savez où elle
habite?
Do you know where she lives?

savoir VERB
to know

> **Je ne sais pas où il est allé.**
> I don't know where he's gone.

> **Nous ne savons pas quoi faire.**
> We don't know what to do.
> **Tu savais que Canberra était la capitale de l'Australie?**
> Did you know that Canberra is the capital of Australia?

> **Tu sais nager?**
> Can you swim?

le **savon** MASC NOUN
soap

la **savonnette** FEM NOUN
bar of soap

savons VERB ▷ *see* savoir
> **Nous savons où tu es caché.**
> We know where you're hiding.

la **Scandinavie** FEM NOUN
Scandinavia

la **science** FEM NOUN
science

> **Elle est forte en sciences.**
> She is good at science.

scolaire ADJECTIVE
school

> **l'année scolaire**
> the school year
> **les vacances scolaires**
> the school holidays

mon livret scolaire
my school report

le **Scotch**® MASC NOUN
adhesive tape

se PRONOUN

> **Language tip**
>
> **se** *changes to* **s'** *before a vowel sound.*

1 **himself**
> **Il se regarde dans la glace.**
> He's looking at himself in the mirror.

2 **herself**
> **Elle se regarde dans la glace.**
> She's looking at herself in the mirror.
> **Elle s'admire dans sa nouvelle robe.**
> She's admiring herself in her new dress.

3 **itself**
> **Le chat se regarde dans la glace.**
> The cat's looking at itself in the mirror.

4 **themselves**
> **Ils se sont regardés dans la glace.**
> They looked at themselves in the mirror.

5 **each other**
> **Ils se détestent.**
> They hate each other.

> **Language tip**
>
> *Sometimes* **se** *is not translated.*

> **Il s'appelle Paul.**
> His name is Paul.
> **Elle se brosse les dents trois fois par jour.**
> She brushes her teeth three times a day.

French English

a
b
c
d
e
f
g
h
i
j
k
l
m
n
o
p
q
r
s
t
u
v
w
x
y
z

le **seau** MASC NOUN (PL les **seaux**)
bucket

sec MASC ADJECTIVE (FEM **sèche**)
1 **dry**
Mon jean n'est pas encore sec.
My jeans aren't dry yet.
2 **dried**
des figues sèches
dried figs

le **sèche-cheveux** MASC NOUN
hair dryer

le **sèche-linge** MASC NOUN
tumble dryer

sécher VERB
to dry

second MASC ADJECTIVE
(FEM **seconde**)
second

la **seconde** FEM NOUN
1 **second**
Attends une seconde!
Wait a second!
2 **year 11**
Ma sœur est en seconde.
My sister's in year 11.

Did you know...?
In French secondary schools the years are counted from the **sixième** (youngest) to the **première** and the **terminale** (oldest).

le **secours** MASC NOUN
help
Il est allé chercher du secours.
He went to get help.
une sortie de secours
an emergency exit

Au secours!
Help!

le **secret**

secret can be a noun or an adjective.

A MASC NOUN
secret
J'ai un secret à te dire.
I have a secret to tell you.
B MASC ADJECTIVE (FEM **secrète**)
secret

la **secrétaire** FEM NOUN
secretary

le **secrétariat** MASC NOUN
secretary's office

la **sécurité** FEM NOUN
safety
une ceinture de sécurité
a seatbelt

seize NUMBER
sixteen
Elle a seize ans.
She's sixteen.
Il est seize heures.
It's four p.m.

Did you know...?
The 24-hour clock is used in France for travel times, appointments, and other formal situations.

le seize novembre
the sixteenth of November

seizième ADJECTIVE
sixteenth

le **sel** MASC NOUN
salt

le **self** MASC NOUN
self-service restaurant

selon PREPOSITION
according to
> **Ils sont répartis selon leur âge.**
> They're divided up according to age.

la **semaine** FEM NOUN
week
> **en semaine**
> on weekdays

le **semblant** MASC NOUN
> **faire semblant**
> to pretend
> **Il fait semblant de dormir.**
> He's pretending to be asleep.

sembler VERB
to seem
> **Le temps semble s'améliorer.**
> The weather seems to be improving.

la **semoule** FEM NOUN
semolina

le **sens** MASC NOUN
1 sense
> **Il a le sens de l'humour.**
> He has a sense of humour.
> **Je n'ai pas le sens de l'orientation.**
> I've got no sense of direction.
> **Ça n'a pas de sens.**
> It doesn't make sense.

2 direction
> **Elle est partie dans le mauvais sens.**
> She set off in the wrong direction.

> **dans le sens des aiguilles d'une montre**
> clockwise
> **dans le sens contraire des aiguilles d'une montre**
> anticlockwise
> **sens dessus dessous**
> upside down

sensible ADJECTIVE
sensitive
> **Elle est très sensible.**
> She's very sensitive.

> **Language tip**
>
> *Be careful! The French word* **sensible** *does not mean the same as the English word* **sensible**.

sentir VERB
1 to smell
> **Ça sent bon.**
> That smells good.

> **Ça sent mauvais.**
> It smells horrible.

2 to smell of
> **Ça sent les frites ici.**
> It smells of chips in here.

3 to feel
> **Ça t'a fait mal? — Non, je n'ai rien senti.**
> Did it hurt? — No, I didn't feel a thing.
> **Je ne me sens pas bien.**
> I don't feel well.

séparé MASC ADJECTIVE
(FEM **séparée**)
separated

séparer VERB
to separate
> **Séparez le blanc du jaune.**
> Separate the yolk from the white.
- **se séparer**
  to separate
  > **Mes parents se sont séparés l'année dernière.**
  > My parents separated last year.

sept NUMBER
seven
> **Je me lève à sept heures.**
> I get up at seven o'clock.
> **Elle a sept ans.**
> She's seven.

le sept février
the seventh of February

septembre MASC NOUN
September
> **en septembre**
> in September
> **le six septembre**
> the sixth of September

septième ADJECTIVE
seventh
> **au septième étage**
> on the seventh floor

sera, serai, seras, serez
VERB ▷ *see* **être**
> **Il sera là demain.**
> He'll be here tomorrow
> **Je serai de retour à dix heures.**
> I'll be back at 10 o'clock.
> **Tu ne seras pas toute seule.**
> You won't be alone.
> **Vous serez chez vous demain?**
> Will you be at home tomorrow?

la série FEM NOUN
series
> **une série télévisée américaine**
> an American TV series

sérieux MASC ADJECTIVE
(FEM **sérieuse**)
1 **serious**
> **Il plaisante? — Non, il est sérieux.**
> Is he joking? — No, he's serious.
2 **responsible**
> **C'est un employé très sérieux.**
> He's a very responsible employee.

serons, seront VERB
▷ *see* **être**
> **Nous serons en vacances demain.**
> We'll be on holiday tomorrow.
> **Ils seront contents de te revoir.**
> They'll be happy to see you again.

le serpent MASC NOUN
snake

se **serrer** VERB
> **se serrer la main**
> to shake hands
> **Allez, serrez-vous la main!**
> Come on, shake hands!

la serrure FEM NOUN
lock

sers, sert VERB ▷ *see* **servir**
> **Sers-toi.**
> Help yourself.
> **Ça ne sert à rien.**
> That's no use.

le serveur MASC NOUN
waiter

la serveuse FEM NOUN
waitress

la **serviette** FEM NOUN
1 **towel**
une serviette de bain
a bath towel
2 **napkin**

servir VERB
À quoi ça sert?
What's it for?
Ça ne sert à rien.
It's no use.
■ **se servir de**
to use
Tu te sers souvent de ton vélo?
Do you use your bike a lot?
Servez-vous.
Help yourself.

ses PL ADJECTIVE ▷ *see* **son**
1 **his**
Il est chez ses grands-parents.
He's at his grandparents'.
2 **her**
Delphine joue avec ses copines.
Delphine's playing with her friends.
3 **its**
la chatte et ses petits
the cat and its kittens

seul

seul *can be an adjective or an adverb.*

A MASC ADJECTIVE (FEM **seule**)
1 **only**
Il reste une seule nectarine.
There's only one nectarine left.
C'est la seule chose que je n'aime pas.
It's the only thing I don't like.
2 **alone**
Elle vit seule.
She lives alone.

B ADVERB
tout seul
by oneself
Elle a fait ça toute seule?
Did she do it by herself?

seulement ADVERB
only
non seulement ... mais
not only ... but
Non seulement il pleut, mais en plus il fait froid.
Not only is it raining, but it's cold as well.

sévère ADJECTIVE
strict

le **shampooing** MASC NOUN
shampoo

le **short** MASC NOUN
shorts
Il est en short.
He's wearing shorts.

si

si *can be a conjunction or an adverb.*

A CONJUNCTION
if
si tu veux
if you like
Je me demande si elle va venir.
I wonder if she'll come.
si seulement
if only

French English

a b c d e f g h i j k l m n o p q r **s** t u v w x y z

B ADVERB

1 so
Elle est si gentille.
She's so kind.

2 yes actually
Tu n'es pas allé à l'école habillé comme ça? — Si.
You didn't go to school dressed like that? — Yes I did, actually.

la **Sicile** FEM NOUN
Sicily

le **siècle** MASC NOUN
century

le **siège** MASC NOUN
seat

le **sien** MASC PRONOUN
la **sienne** FEM PRONOUN

> *Language tip*
> **le sien, la sienne, les siens,** *and* **les siennes** *can either mean* **his** *or* **hers.**

C'est le vélo de Paul? — Oui, c'est le sien.
Is this Paul's bike? — Yes, it's his.
C'est le vélo d'Isabelle? — Oui, c'est le sien.
Is this Isabelle's bike? — Yes, it's hers.
C'est la montre de Paul? — Oui, c'est la sienne.
Is this Paul's watch? — Yes, it's his.
Ce sont les baskets de Christian? — Oui, ce sont les siennes.
Are these Christian's trainers? — Yes, they're his.

la **sieste** FEM NOUN
nap
faire la sieste
to have a nap

siffler VERB
to whistle

le **sifflet** MASC NOUN
whistle

signifier VERB
to mean
Que signifie ce mot?
What does this word mean?

le **silence** MASC NOUN
silence
Silence!
Be quiet!

silencieux MASC ADJECTIVE
(FEM silencieuse)
silent

simple ADJECTIVE
simple

simplement ADVERB
simply

le **singe** MASC NOUN
monkey

le **singulier** MASC NOUN
singular
au singulier
in the singular

sinon CONJUNCTION
otherwise
Dépêche-toi, sinon je pars sans toi.
Hurry up, otherwise I'll leave without you.

la **sirène** FEM NOUN
mermaid
 la sirène d'alarme
 the fire alarm

le **sirop** MASC NOUN
cordial
 du sirop de framboise
 raspberry cordial

Did you know…?
*You dilute **le sirop** with water, rather like squash. There are all kinds of flavours.*

 le sirop contre la toux
 cough mixture

le **site** MASC NOUN
 un site Web
 a website

six NUMBER
six
 Il est rentré à six heures.
 He got back at six o'clock.
 Il a six ans.
 He's six.

le six février
the sixth of February

sixième

sixième *can be an adjective or a noun.*

A ADJECTIVE
 sixth
 au sixième étage
 on the sixth floor
B FEM NOUN
 year 7
 Mon frère est en sixième.
 My brother's in year 7.

Did you know…?
*In French secondary schools the years are counted from the **sixième** (youngest) to the **première** and the **terminale** (oldest).*

le **ski** MASC NOUN
 1 ski
 Mes skis sont trop petits.
 My skis are too small.
 2 skiing
 J'adore le ski.
 I love skiing.
 faire du ski
 to go skiing
 En hiver, je fais du ski.
 In winter I go skiing.
 le ski nautique
 water-skiing

skier VERB
to ski

le **skieur** MASC NOUN
la **skieuse** FEM NOUN
skier

le **slip** MASC NOUN
pants
 un slip de bain
 swimming trunks

le **SMS** MASC NOUN
text message

la **SNCF** FEM NOUN

Did you know…?
*You will see **SNCF** on trains and stations in France. It's the name of the French railways, which are owned by the government.*

la **société** FEM NOUN
 1 society
 2 company

a
b
c
d
e
f
g
h
i
j
k
l
m
n
o
p
q
r
s
t
u
v
w
x
y
z

la **sœur** FEM NOUN
  sister
    ma grande sœur
    my big sister
    ma petite sœur
    my little sister

soi PRONOUN
  oneself
    rester chez soi
    to stay at home

la **soie** FEM NOUN
  silk

la **soif** FEM NOUN
  thirst
    Tu as soif?
    Are you thirsty?
    J'ai soif.
    I'm thirsty.

soi-même PRONOUN
  oneself
    Il vaut mieux le faire soi-même.
    It's better to do it oneself.

le **soin** MASC NOUN
  care
    Prends bien soin de ce livre.
    Take good care of this book.

le **soir** MASC NOUN
  evening
    ce soir
    this evening
    le soir
    in the evening

demain soir
tomorrow night
hier soir
last night

la **soirée** FEM NOUN
  evening

    en tenue de soirée
    in evening dress

sois VERB ▷see **être**
    Sois sage!
    Be good!

soit CONJUNCTION
    soit ..., soit ...
    either ... or ...
    soit lundi, soit mardi
    either Monday or Tuesday

la **soixantaine** FEM NOUN
  about sixty
    une soixantaine de personnes
    about sixty people
    Elle a la soixantaine.
    She's in her sixties.

soixante NUMBER
  sixty
    Il a soixante ans.
    He's sixty.
    soixante et un
    sixty-one
    soixante-deux
    sixty-two
    soixante et onze
    seventy-one
    soixante-quinze
    seventy-five

soixante-dix NUMBER
  seventy
    Il a soixante-dix ans.
    He's seventy.

solaire ADJECTIVE
  solar
    le système solaire
    the solar system
    la crème solaire
    sun cream

le **soldat** MASC NOUN
  soldier

le **solde** MASC NOUN
en solde
reduced
Les baskets sont en solde.
The trainers are reduced.
les soldes
the sales

le **soleil** MASC NOUN
sun

au soleil
in the sun

Il y a du soleil.
It's sunny.

solide ADJECTIVE
strong

sombre ADJECTIVE
dark
Il fait un peu sombre ici.
It's a little dark in here.

le **sommeil** MASC NOUN
sleep

J'ai sommeil.
I'm sleepy.

sommes VERB ▷see être
Nous sommes en vacances.
We're on holiday.

Language tip

*Sometimes **sommes** shows that something has happened in the past.*

Nous sommes arrivés à une heure.
We arrived at 1 o'clock.

son

son *can be an adjective or a noun.*

A MASC ADJECTIVE (FEM **sa**, PL **ses**)
1 his
Il est chez son grand-père.
He's at his granddad's.
2 her
Elle joue avec son frère.
She's playing with her brother.
3 its
Le chien est dans son panier.
The dog's in its basket.
B MASC NOUN
sound
Le son n'est pas très bon.
The sound's not very good.

le **sondage** MASC NOUN
survey

sonner VERB
to ring
Le téléphone sonne.
The phone's ringing.

la **sonnerie** FEM NOUN
1 bell
2 ringtone

la **sonnette** FEM NOUN
bell
la sonnette d'alarme
the alarm bell

sont VERB ▷see être
Ils sont en vacances.
They're on holiday.

Language tip

*Sometimes **sont** shows that something has happened in the past.*

Ils sont allés en France.
They went to France.

la **sorcière**
FEM NOUN
witch

le **sort** MASC NOUN
spell
La sorcière lui a jeté un sort.
The witch cast a spell on him.
tirer au sort
to draw lots

la **sorte** FEM NOUN
sort
C'est une sorte de gâteau.
It's a sort of cake.

la **sortie** FEM NOUN
way out
Où est la sortie?
Where's the way out?
la sortie de secours
the emergency exit
Attends-moi à la sortie de l'école.
Meet me after school.

sortir VERB
1 **to go out**
Il est sorti.
He's gone out.
2 **to come out**
Il sort de l'hôpital aujourd'hui.
He's coming out of hospital today.
3 **to take out**
Sortez vos affaires.
Take out your things.

la **soucoupe** FEM NOUN
saucer

une soucoupe volante
a flying saucer

soudain

> **soudain** *can be an adjective or an adverb.*

A MASC ADJECTIVE (FEM **soudaine**)
sudden
une douleur soudaine
a sudden pain
B ADVERB
suddenly
Soudain, il s'est fâché.
Suddenly, he got angry.

souffler VERB
1 **to blow**
Le vent souffle fort.
The wind's blowing hard.
2 **to blow out**
Souffle les bougies!
Blow out the candles!

le **souhait** MASC NOUN
wish
faire un souhait
to make a wish

> **Atchoum! — À tes souhaits!**
> Atchoo! — Bless you!

> *Did you know...?*
> *When you sneeze in France people say* **'À tes souhaits!'**, *which means* **'May your wishes come true!'**.

souhaiter VERB
to wish
Nous te souhaitons un bon Noël.
We wish you a happy Christmas.

le **soulier** MASC NOUN
shoe

souligner VERB
to underline

la **soupe** FEM NOUN
soup

le **sourcil** MASC NOUN
eyebrow

sourd MASC ADJECTIVE
(FEM **sourde**)
deaf

souriant MASC ADJECTIVE
(FEM **souriante**)
cheerful

sourire

> **sourire** can be a verb or a noun.

A VERB
to smile
Elle ne sourit jamais.
She never smiles.

B MASC NOUN
smile
Elle a un joli sourire.
She has a nice smile.

la **souris** FEM NOUN
mouse

la petite souris
the tooth fairy

> **Did you know...?**
> French children believe that a little
> mouse (**la petite souris**) comes at
> night to take their tooth from under
> the pillow and replace it with money.

sous PREPOSITION
under

Le chat est sous la chaise.
The cat's under the chair.
sous la pluie
in the rain

le **sous-marin** MASC NOUN
submarine

le **sous-sol** MASC NOUN
basement

les **sous-titres** MASC PL NOUN
subtitles

sous-titré MASC ADJECTIVE
(FEM **sous-titrée**)
with subtitles
un film sous-titré
a film with subtitles

la **soustraction** FEM NOUN
subtraction

souvenir

> **souvenir** can be a noun or a verb.

A MASC NOUN
1 memory
2 souvenir
un souvenir de Paris
a souvenir of Paris

B VERB
■ **se souvenir**
to remember
Je ne me souviens pas de son adresse.
I can't remember his address.
Je me souviens qu'il neigeait ce jour-là.
I remember it was snowing that day.

souvent ADVERB
often
Tu vas souvent au cinéma?
Do you go to the cinema often?

French English

a
b
c
d
e
f
g
h
i
j
k
l
m
n
o
p
q
r
s
t
u
v
w
x
y
z

a b c d e f g h i j k l m n o p q r s t u v w x y z

soyez VERB ▷see **être**
Soyez sages!
Be good!

la **SPA** FEM NOUN
RSPCA

spécialement ADVERB
1 **specially**
Il est venu spécialement pour te parler.
He came specially to speak to you.
2 **particularly**
Ce n'est pas spécialement difficile.
It's not particularly difficult.

le **spectacle** MASC NOUN
show
un spectacle de Noël
a Christmas show

splendide ADJECTIVE
magnificent
Il fait un temps splendide.
The weather is magnificent.

sport

sport *can be a noun or an adjective.*

A MASC NOUN
sport
Quel est ton sport préféré?
What's your favourite sport?
Qu'est-ce que tu fais comme sport?
What sport do you do?
Il fait beaucoup de sport.
He does a lot of sport.

aller aux sports d'hiver
to go on a skiing holiday
Je vais aux sports d'hiver en février.
I'm going on a skiing holiday in February.
B ADJECTIVE
casual
une veste sport
a casual jacket
des vêtements sport
casual clothes

sportif MASC ADJECTIVE
(FEM **sportive**)
1 **sporty**
Elle est très sportive.
She's very sporty.
2 **sports**
un club sportif
a sports club

le **squelette** MASC NOUN
skeleton

le **stade** MASC NOUN
stadium

la **station** FEM NOUN
une station de métro
an underground station
une station de ski
a ski resort

le **steak** MASC NOUN
steak
un steak frites
steak and chips
un steak haché
a hamburger

stressé MASC ADJECTIVE
(FEM **stressée**)
stressed out

le **studio** MASC NOUN
studio flat

stupide ADJECTIVE
stupid

le **stylo** MASC NOUN
pen
    un stylo bille
    a ballpoint pen
    un stylo-feutre
    a felt-tip pen

su VERB ▷see **savoir**
    Si j'avais su ...
    If I'd known ...

le **succès** MASC NOUN
success
    Ce film a beaucoup de succès en ce moment.
    This film is very successful at the moment.

la **sucette** FEM NOUN
lollipop

le **sucre** MASC NOUN
sugar
    un sucre
    a sugar-lump
    Je prends deux sucres dans mon café.
    I take two lumps of sugar in my coffee.

sucré MASC ADJECTIVE (FEM **sucrée**)
sweet
    Ce gâteau est un peu trop sucré.
    This cake is a bit too sweet.

les **sucreries** FEM PL NOUN
sweet things

sud

> **sud** can be a noun or an adjective.

A MASC NOUN
    south

    Ils vivent dans le sud de la France.
    They live in the South of France.
    au sud de Paris
    south of Paris
    l'Amérique du Sud
    South America
B ADJECTIVE
    south
    le pôle sud
    the South Pole

le **sud-est** MASC NOUN
south-east
    au sud-est
    in the south-east

le **sud-ouest** MASC NOUN
south-west
    au sud-ouest
    in the south-west

la **Suède** FEM NOUN
Sweden

suédois MASC NOUN, MASC ADJECTIVE (FEM **suédoise**)
Swedish

le **Suédois** MASC NOUN
la **Suédoise** FEM NOUN
Swede

suffire VERB
to be enough
    Tiens, voilà cinq euros. Ça te suffit?
    Here's five euros. Is that enough for you?

Ça suffit!
That's enough!

suffisamment ADVERB
enough

suis VERB ▷see **être**
    Je suis écossais.
    I'm Scottish.

Language tip

*Sometimes **suis** shows that something has happened in the past.*

Je suis restée chez moi.
I stayed at home.

suisse ADJECTIVE
Swiss

le **Suisse** MASC NOUN
Swiss man

la **Suisse** FEM NOUN
1 **Swiss woman**
2 **Switzerland**

la **suite** FEM NOUN
rest

Je vous raconterai la suite de l'histoire demain.
I'll tell you the rest of the story tomorrow.

J'y vais tout de suite.
I'll go straightaway.

tout de suite
straightaway

suivre VERB
to follow

Suivez-moi, tout le monde!
Follow me, everybody!

Suis-moi, Alice!
Follow me, Alice!

Il me suit partout.
He follows me everywhere.

super MASC, FEM, PL ADJECTIVE
great

C'est super!
It's great!

le **supermarché** MASC NOUN
supermarket

superposé MASC ADJECTIVE
des lits superposés
bunk beds

supplémentaire ADJECTIVE
additional

supporter VERB
to stand

Je ne supporte pas le golf.
I can't stand golf.

Je ne peux pas la supporter.
I can't stand her.

Language tip

*Be careful! **supporter** does not mean **to support**.*

sur PREPOSITION
1 **on**
Pose-le sur la table.
Put it down on the table.
une émission sur les ours polaires
a programme on polar bears
2 **in**
une personne sur dix
one person in ten
3 **out of**
J'ai eu quatorze sur vingt en maths.
I got 14 out of 20 in maths.

Did you know...?

In French schools, tests and homework are usually marked out of 20.

sûr MASC ADJECTIVE (FEM **sûre**)
sure
Tu es sûr?
Are you sure?

sûrement ADVERB
certainly
Sûrement pas!
Certainly not!

le **surnom** MASC NOUN
nickname

surpris MASC ADJECTIVE
(FEM **surprise**)
surprised
> **Il était surpris de me voir.**
> He was surprised to see me.

la **surprise** FEM NOUN
surprise

surtout ADVERB
especially
> **Il est assez timide, surtout avec les filles.**
> He's rather shy, especially with girls.

surveiller VERB
1 to keep an eye on
> **Tu peux surveiller mes bagages?**
> Can you keep an eye on my luggage?
2 to supervise
> **Nous sommes toujours surveillés pendant la récréation.**
> We're always supervised during break.

le **survêtement** MASC NOUN
tracksuit

SVP ABBREVIATION
please

le **sweat** MASC NOUN
sweatshirt

sympa ADJECTIVE
nice
> **Elle est très sympa.**
> She's a really nice person.

sympathique ADJECTIVE
nice
> **Ce sont des gens très sympathiques.**
> They're very nice people.

Language tip
Be careful! **sympathique** *does not mean the same as* **sympathetic**.

le **syndicat** MASC NOUN
> **le syndicat d'initiative**
> the tourist information office

French English

a
b
c
d
e
f
g
h
i
j
k
l
m
n
o
p
q
r
s
t
u
v
w
x
y
z

T t

t' PRONOUN

> **Language tip**
>
> **te** *is changed to* **t'** *before a vowel sound.*

Je ne t'entends pas.
I can't hear you.
Comment tu t'appelles?
What's your name?

ta FEM ADJECTIVE ▷ *see* **ton**
your
Quel âge a ta sœur?
How old is your sister?

le **tabac** MASC NOUN
tobacco

> **Did you know…?**
>
> **tabac** *is also the name for a shop that sells cigarettes and stamps.*

la **table** FEM NOUN
table
une table de nuit
a bedside table

Mets la table, s'il te plaît.
Lay the table please.
À table!
Dinner's ready!

le **tableau** MASC NOUN
(PL les **tableaux**)
1 **painting**
2 **blackboard**
C'est écrit au tableau.
It's on the blackboard.
3 **whiteboard**

la **tablette** FEM NOUN
une tablette de chocolat
a bar of chocolate

le **tablier** MASC NOUN
apron

le **tabouret** MASC NOUN
stool

la **tache** FEM NOUN
mark
Tu as une tache sur ton T-shirt.
You've got a mark on your T-shirt.
des taches de rousseur
freckles

la **taille** FEM NOUN
1 **waist**
Elle a la taille fine.
She has a slim waist.
2 **height**
un homme de taille moyenne
a man of average height
3 **size**
Avez-vous ma taille?
Have you got my size?

le **taille-crayon** MASC NOUN
pencil sharpener

se **taire** VERB
to stop talking
Taisez-vous!
Stop talking!

le **tambour** MASC NOUN
drum
Il joue du tambour.
He is playing the drum.

la **Tamise** FEM NOUN
Thames

tant ADVERB
so much
> **Je l'aime tant!**
> I love him so much!
> **tant de**
> so much/so many

> *Language tip*
>
> **tant de** *has two translations. Look at the examples.*

> **tant de nourriture**
> so much food
> **tant de livres**
> so many books

> **Tant mieux!**
> So much the better!
> **Tant pis!**
> Never mind!

la **tante** FEM NOUN
aunt
> **ma tante**
> my aunt

taper VERB
to bang
> **Arrêtez de taper sur la table.**
> Stop banging on the table.
> **Maman, il m'a tapé!**
> Mum, he hit me!
> **taper des pieds**
> to stamp one's feet
> **Ma petite sœur tape des pieds quand elle est en colère.**
> My little sister stamps her feet when she's angry.
> **taper des mains**
> to clap
> **Elle chante et nous tapons des mains.**
> She sings and we clap.

le **tapis** MASC NOUN
rug

la **tapisserie** FEM NOUN
wallpaper

tard ADVERB
late
> **Il est tard.**
> It's late.
> **plus tard**
> later on

la **tarte** FEM NOUN
tart
> **une tarte aux pommes**
> an apple tart

la **tartine** FEM NOUN
slice of bread
> **une tartine de confiture**
> a slice of bread and jam

la **tasse** FEM NOUN
cup
> **une tasse de thé**
> a cup of tea

le **taureau** MASC NOUN
(PL les **taureaux**)
bull

le **taxi** MASC NOUN
taxi

tchèque ADJECTIVE
Czech

te PRONOUN

> *Language tip*
>
> **te** *is often not translated into English.*

1 you
Je te vois.
I can see you.
Il t'a vu?
Did he see you?

2 to you
Est-ce qu'il te parle en français?
Does he talk to you in French?
Elle t'a parlé?
Did she speak to you?

3 yourself
Tu vas te rendre malade.
You'll make yourself sick.
Ne t'en fais pas.
Don't worry yourself.

Language tip

te *is often not translated into English.*

Je compte jusqu'à dix pendant que tu te caches.
I'll count to ten while you hide.

la **techno** FEM NOUN
techno music

la **télé** FEM NOUN
telly
à la télé
on telly

la **télécommande**
FEM NOUN
remote control

le **téléphérique** MASC NOUN
cable car

le **téléphone** MASC NOUN
telephone

Elle est au téléphone.
She's on the phone.
un téléphone portable
a mobile phone
un téléphone appareil photo
a camera phone

téléphoner VERB
to phone
Je vais téléphoner à Claire.
I'll phone Claire.
Je peux téléphoner?
Can I make a phone call?

la **télévision** FEM NOUN
television
à la télévision
on television

tellement ADVERB
1 so
Andrew est tellement gentil.
Andrew's so nice.
2 so much
Il a tellement mangé que ...
He ate so much that ...
3 so many
Il y avait tellement de monde!
There were so many people!

la **température** FEM NOUN
temperature

la **tempête** FEM NOUN
storm

le **temps** MASC NOUN
1 weather
Il fait mauvais temps.
The weather's bad.

Quel temps fait-il?
What's the weather like?

2 time
Je n'ai pas le temps.
I haven't got time.

de temps en temps
from time to time
en même temps
at the same time
Elle travaille à plein temps.
She works full time.
Elle travaille à temps partiel.
She works part-time.

tenir VERB
to hold
> **Tu peux tenir la lampe, s'il te plaît?**
> Can you hold the torch, please?
> **Tiens, voilà un stylo.**
> Here's a pen.

le **tennis** MASC NOUN
1 tennis
> **Elle joue au tennis.**
> She plays tennis.
2 tennis court
> **Il est au tennis.**
> He's at the tennis court.

les **tennis** FEM PL NOUN
trainers

la **tente** FEM NOUN
tent

tenu VERB ▷ see **tenir**
Il n'a pas tenu sa promesse.
He didn't keep his promise.

la **tenue** FEM NOUN
clothes
> **en tenue de soirée**
> in evening dress

la **terminale** FEM NOUN
year 13
> **Elle est en terminale.**
> She's in year 13.

> ### Did you know...?
> In French secondary schools the years are counted from the **sixième**, (youngest), to the **première** and the **terminale**, (oldest).

terminer VERB
to finish
▪ **se terminer**
to end
> **Les vacances se terminent demain.**
> The holidays end tomorrow.

le **terrain** MASC NOUN
> **un terrain de camping**
> a campsite
> **un terrain de football**
> a football pitch
> **un terrain de golf**
> a golf course
> **un terrain de jeu**
> a playground
> **un terrain de sport**
> a sports ground

la **terrasse** FEM NOUN
terrace
> **L'été, il y a beaucoup de gens assis aux terrasses de cafés.**
> In the summer there are a lot of people sitting at pavement cafés.

la **terre** FEM NOUN
earth

French English

a
b
c
d
e
f
g
h
i
j
k
l
m
n
o
p
q
r
s
t
u
v
w
x
y
z

la Terre
the Earth
par terre
on the floor
Asseyez-vous par terre.
Sit on the floor.

terrible ADJECTIVE
terrible
> **Quelque chose de terrible est arrivé.**
> Something terrible has happened.
> **pas terrible**
> nothing special
> **Ce film n'est pas terrible.**
> The film's nothing special.

tes PL ADJECTIVE ▷ *see* **ton**
your
> **J'aime bien tes baskets.**
> I like your trainers.

le **têtard** MASC NOUN
tadpole

la **tête** FEM NOUN
head

têtu MASC ADJECTIVE (FEM **têtue**)
stubborn

le **Texto®** MASC NOUN
text message

le **TGV** MASC NOUN
high-speed train

Did you know…?
French railways are very modern.
TGVs *go so fast that they are a good alternative to planes for long journeys.*

le **thé** MASC NOUN
tea

Did you know…?
French people usually drink tea wih lemon, rather than with milk.

le **théâtre** MASC NOUN
theatre
> **J'aime aller au théâtre.**
> I like going to the theatre.
> **faire du théâtre**
> to act
> **Est-ce que tu as déjà fait du théâtre?**
> Have you ever acted?

la **théière** FEM NOUN
teapot

le **thon** MASC NOUN
tuna
> **un sandwich au thon mayonnaise**
> a tuna mayonnaise sandwich

tiède ADJECTIVE
warm

le **tien** MASC PRONOUN
la **tienne** FEM PRONOUN
yours
> **J'ai oublié mon stylo. Tu peux me prêter le tien?**
> I've forgotten my pen. Can you lend me yours?
> **Ce n'est pas ma raquette, c'est la tienne.**
> It's not my racket, it's yours.
> **Ce ne sont pas mes baskets, ce sont les tiennes.**
> These aren't my trainers, they're yours.

tiens VERB ▷ *see* **tenir**
> **Tiens, prends un biscuit.**
> Go on, have a biscuit.

le **tiers** MASC NOUN
third
> **Un tiers de la classe a un chien.**
> A third of the class own a dog.
> **le tiers monde**
> the Third World

le **tigre** MASC NOUN
tiger

le **timbre** MASC NOUN
stamp

timide ADJECTIVE
shy

le **tire-bouchon** MASC NOUN
corkscrew

la **tirelire** FEM NOUN
money box

tirer VERB
1 **to pull**
Il m'a tiré les cheveux.
He pulled my hair.
'Tirez'
'Pull'
2 **to draw**
Tire les rideaux s'il te plaît.
Draw the curtains please.
tirer au sort
to draw lots
Nous avons tiré au sort et j'ai gagné.
We drew lots and I won.
tirer les rois
to cut the galette des Rois

Did you know…?

A **galette des Rois** is a cake eaten at Epiphany (the sixth of January) which contains a little figure. The person who finds it is the king (or queen) and gets a paper crown. They then choose somebody to be their queen (or king).

le **tiroir** MASC NOUN
drawer

la **tisane** FEM NOUN
herbal tea

le **tissu** MASC NOUN
material
C'est un joli tissu.
It's nice material.

le **titre** MASC NOUN
title

la **TNT** FEM NOUN
digital television

le **toast** MASC NOUN
piece of toast
des toasts beurrés
buttered toast

le **toboggan** MASC NOUN
slide

toi PRONOUN
you
Ça va? — Oui, et toi?
How are you? — Fine, and you?
J'ai faim, pas toi?
I'm hungry, aren't you?
Assieds-toi.
Sit down.
à toi
your turn/yours

Language tip

à toi has two translations. Look at the examples.

C'est à toi de jouer.
It's your turn to play.
Est-ce que ce stylo est à toi?
Is this pen yours?

la **toile** FEM NOUN
canvas
un sac de toile
a canvas bag
une toile d'araignée
a cobweb

la **toilette** FEM NOUN
faire sa toilette
to have a wash
Le matin, je me lève, je fais ma toilette et je m'habille.
In the morning I get up, have a wash and get dressed.

les **toilettes** FEM PL NOUN
toilet

Je peux aller aux toilettes, s'il vous plaît?
May I go to the toilet please?

toi-même PRONOUN
yourself
Tu as fait ça toi-même?
Did you do it yourself?

le **toit** MASC NOUN
roof

la **tomate** FEM NOUN
tomato

tomber VERB
to fall
Attention, tu vas tomber!
Be careful, you'll fall!
laisser tomber
to drop/to give up/to let down

Language tip
laisser tomber *has three translations. Look at the examples.*

Elle a laissé tomber son stylo.
She dropped her pen.
Je vais laisser tomber le piano.
I'm going to give up the piano.
Il ne laisse jamais tomber ses amis.
He never lets his friends down.

ton MASC ADJECTIVE (FEM **ta**, PL **tes**)
your
C'est ton stylo?
Is this your pen?
Ce sont tes feutres?
Are these your felt-tips?

le **tonnerre** MASC NOUN
thunder

tordre VERB
Je me suis tordu la cheville.
I've twisted my ankle.

la **tortue** FEM NOUN
tortoise

une tortue d'eau douce
a terrapin
une tortue de mer
a turtle

tôt ADVERB
early
Il se lève très tôt.
He gets up very early.

totalement ADVERB
totally

toucher VERB
to touch
> **Ne touche pas à mes livres!**
> Don't touch my books!

toujours ADVERB
1 **always**
> **Il est toujours très gentil.**
> He's always very nice.
> **pour toujours**
> forever
2 **still**
> **Quand nous sommes revenus, il était toujours là.**
> When we got back he was still there.

la **tour** FEM NOUN
1 **tower**
> **la Tour Eiffel**
> the Eiffel Tower
2 **tower block**
> **J'habite dans une tour de vingt étages.**
> I live in a twenty-storey tower block.

le **tour** MASC NOUN
turn
> **C'est ton tour de jouer.**
> It's your turn to play.
> **faire un tour**
> to go for a walk
> **Allons faire un tour dans le parc.**
> Let's go for a walk in the park.
> **faire un tour en voiture**
> to go for a drive
> **faire un tour à vélo**
> to go for a bike ride

> **Tu veux aller faire un tour à vélo?**
> Do you want to go for a bike ride?
> **faire le tour du monde**
> to travel round the world

tourner VERB
to turn
> **Tournez à droite au prochain feu.**
> Turn right at the lights.

le **tournesol** MASC NOUN
sunflower

le **tournoi** MASC NOUN
tournament

tous MASC PL ADJECTIVE, MASC PL PRONOUN
1 **all**
> **tous les biscuits**
> all the biscuits
> **Nous y sommes tous allés.**
> We all went.
2 **every**
> **tous les ans**
> every year

la **Toussaint** FEM NOUN
All Saints' Day

> *Did you know…?*
>
> **la Toussaint** *is on the first of November, when people in France traditionally go to the cemetery to visit the graves of their relatives.*

> **les vacances de la Toussaint**
> autumn half term

tousser VERB
to cough

French English

a
b
c
d
e
f
g
h
i
j
k
l
m
n
o
p
q
r
s
t
u
v
w
x
y
z

tout

> **tout** *can be an adjective, an adverb, a pronoun or a noun.*

A MASC ADJECTIVE (FEM **toute**)

1 all

tout le lait
all the milk

tous les livres
all the books

tout le temps
all the time

toute la journée
all day

toute la nuit
all night

tous les deux
both

Aurélie et moi avons toutes les deux un chien.
Aurélie and I both have a dog.

Je les ai invités tous les trois.
I invited all three of them.

2 every

tous les jours
every day

tous les deux jours
every two days

tout le monde
everybody

tout ce qui
everything that

tout ce qui est en face de toi
everything that's in front of you

tout ce que
everything

Tu peux avoir tout ce que tu veux.
You can have everything you want.

B ADVERB

very

Il habite tout près.
He lives very close.

Elle est toute petite.
She's very small.

tout à l'heure
just now/in a moment

Language tip

tout à l'heure *has two translations. Look at the examples.*

Je l'ai vu tout à l'heure.
I saw him just now.
Je finirai ça tout à l'heure.
I'll finish it in a moment.

À tout à l'heure!
See you later!
tout de suite
straight away
tout droit
straight ahead
tout d'abord
first of all
tout à coup
suddenly
tout à fait
absolutely

C PRONOUN

everything

Il a tout organisé.
He organized everything.

D MASC NOUN

pas du tout
not at all

toutes FEM PL ADJECTIVE, FEM PL PRONOUN

1 all

toutes les photos
all the photos

Je les connais toutes.
I know them all.

2 toutes les semaines
every week

le **tracteur**

MASC NOUN

tractor

traduire VERB
to translate

le **train** MASC NOUN
train
> **un train électrique**
> a train set
> **Il est en train de manger.**
> He's eating.
> **Ils sont en train de dormir.**
> They're sleeping.

le **traîneau** MASC NOUN
(PL les **traîneaux**)
sledge

le **trait** MASC NOUN
line

traiter VERB
> **Il m'a traité d'imbécile.**
> He called me an idiot.

le **tramway** MASC NOUN
tram

la **tranche** FEM NOUN
slice

tranquille ADJECTIVE
quiet
> **Cette rue est très tranquille.**
> This is a very quiet street.
> **Tiens-toi tranquille!**
> Behave yourself!
> **Laisse-moi tranquille.**
> Leave me alone.

le **travail** MASC NOUN
1 **work**
> **J'ai beaucoup de travail.**
> I've got a lot of work.
2 **job**
> **Il a un travail intéressant.**
> He's got an interesting job.

> *Language tip*
>
> Be careful! **travail** does not mean
> the same as **travel**.

travailler VERB
to work
> **Elle travaille dans un bureau.**
> She works in an office.

> *Language tip*
>
> Be careful! **travailler** does not
> mean the same as **travel**.

travailleur MASC ADJECTIVE
(FEM **travailleuse**)
hard-working

les **travaux** MASC PL NOUN
roadworks
> **Il y a beaucoup de bruit à
> cause des travaux dans la rue.**
> There's a lot of noise from the
> roadworks.
> **les travaux manuels**
> handicrafts

le **travers** MASC NOUN
> **à travers**
> through
> **Passe à travers la haie.**
> Go through the hedge.

la **traversée** FEM NOUN
crossing
> **La traversée de la Manche
> dure une heure.**
> The Channel crossing takes an hour.

traverser VERB
1 **to cross**
> **Traversez la rue.**
> Cross the street.
2 **to go through**
> **Nous avons traversé la
> France pour aller en Espagne.**
> We went through France on our
> way to Spain.

le **traversier** MASC NOUN
(*Canada*)
ferry

le **trèfle** MASC NOUN
  1 clover
    un trèfle à quatre feuilles
    a four-leaved clover
  2 clubs
    le roi de trèfle
    the king of clubs

treize NUMBER
  thirteen
    Il a treize ans.
    He's thirteen.
    à treize heures
    at one p.m.

> **Did you know...?**
> *The 24-hour clock is used in France for travel times, appointments, and other formal situations.*

> **le treize février**
> the thirteenth of February

treizième ADJECTIVE
  thirteenth

le **tremblement de terre**
  MASC NOUN
  earthquake

trembler VERB
  to shake
    trembler de froid
    to shiver

trempé MASC ADJECTIVE
  (FEM **trempée**)
  soaking wet

la **trentaine** FEM NOUN
  about thirty
    une trentaine de personnes
    about thirty people
    Il a la trentaine.
    He's in his thirties.

trente NUMBER
  thirty

Elle a trente ans.
She's thirty.
trente et un
thirty-one
trente-deux
thirty-two

> **le trente janvier**
> the thirtieth of January

très ADVERB
  very

le **trésor** MASC NOUN
  treasure

tricher VERB
  to cheat
    Tu as triché!
    You cheated!

tricolore ADJECTIVE
  three-coloured
    le drapeau tricolore
    the French tricolour

> **Did you know...?**
> **le drapeau tricolore** *is the French flag: its three colours are blue, white, and red.*

tricoter VERB
  to knit

le **trimestre** MASC NOUN
  term

triste
  ADJECTIVE
  sad

trois NUMBER
three
trois fois
three times
à trois heures du matin
at three in the morning
Elle a trois ans.
She's three years old.

le trois septembre
the third of September

troisième

troisième can be an adjective or a noun.

A ADJECTIVE
third
au troisième étage
on the third floor
B FEM NOUN
year 10
Mon frère est en troisième.
My brother's in year 10.

Did you know…?

In French secondary schools the years are counted from the **sixième** *(youngest) to the* **première** *and the* **terminale** *(oldest).*

les **trois-quarts** MASC PL NOUN
three-quarters
les trois-quarts de la classe
three-quarters of the class

le **trombone** MASC NOUN
1 trombone
Il joue du trombone.
He plays the trombone.
2 paper clip

la **trompe** FEM NOUN
trunk
la trompe d'un éléphant
an elephant's trunk

se **tromper** VERB
to make a mistake
Je me suis trompé.
I've made a mistake.
se tromper de jour
to get the wrong day

la **trompette** FEM NOUN
trumpet
Il joue de la trompette.
He plays the trumpet.

le **tronc** MASC NOUN
trunk
un tronc d'arbre
a tree trunk

trop ADVERB
1 too
Il conduit trop vite.
He drives too fast.
2 too much
J'ai trop mangé.
I've eaten too much.
trop de
too much/too many

Language tip

trop de *has two translations. Look at the examples.*

J'ai trop de devoirs à faire.
I've got too much homework to do.
Il y a trop de monde.
There are too many people.

le **trottoir** MASC NOUN
pavement

le **trou** MASC NOUN
hole

la **trousse** FEM NOUN
pencil case
> **une trousse de toilette**
> a toilet bag

trouver VERB
1 **to find**
> **Je ne trouve pas mes lunettes.**
> I can't find my glasses.
2 **to think**
> **Je trouve que c'est bête.**
> I think it's stupid.
- **se trouver**
to be
> **Où se trouve la poste?**
> Where is the post office?
> **Marseille se trouve dans le sud de la France.**
> Marseilles is in the South of France.

le **truc** MASC NOUN
thing

la **truite** FEM NOUN
trout

le **T-shirt** MASC NOUN
T-shirt

tu PRONOUN
you
> **Tu as un animal?**
> Have you got a pet?

le **tube** MASC NOUN
1 **tube**
> **un tube de dentifrice**
> a tube of toothpaste
2 **hit**
> **Ça va être le tube de l'été.**
> It's going to be this summer's hit.

tuer VERB
to kill

la **Tunisie** FEM NOUN
Tunisia

tunisien MASC ADJECTIVE
(FEM **tunisienne**)
Tunisian

le **Tunisien** MASC NOUN
la **Tunisienne** FEM NOUN
Tunisian

le **tunnel** MASC NOUN
tunnel
> **le tunnel sous la Manche**
> the Channel Tunnel

turc MASC NOUN, MASC ADJECTIVE
(FEM **turque**)
Turkish

le **Turc** MASC NOUN
la **Turque** FEM NOUN
Turk

la **Turquie** FEM NOUN
Turkey

tutoyer VERB
> **tutoyer quelqu'un**
> to call somebody 'tu'
> **On ne doit pas tutoyer la maîtresse.**
> We can't call the teacher 'tu'.

> **Did you know...?**
> There are two words for 'you' in French, **tu** and **vous**. Tu is the less formal one. You would call your teacher 'vous' but your friend 'tu'.

typique ADJECTIVE
typical

U u

l' **UE** FEM NOUN
EU

un

un *can be an article or a number.*

A ARTICLE

Language tip

un *is used in front of a masculine noun.*

1 **a**
  un garçon
  a boy
2 **an**
  un œuf
  an egg
B NUMBER

Language tip

un *is used for masculine nouns.*

one
un citron et deux oranges
one lemon and two oranges
Combien de timbres? — Un.
How many stamps? — One.
un de mes meilleurs copains
one of my best friends
un par un
one by one
Sortez un par un.
Go out one by one.

Elle a un an.
She's one year old.

une

une *can be an article or a number.*

A ARTICLE

Language tip

une *is used in front of a feminine noun.*

1 **a**
  une fille
  a girl
2 **an**
  une pomme
  an apple
B NUMBER

Language tip

une *is used for feminine nouns.*

one
une pomme et deux bananes
one apple and two bananas
Combien de cartes postales? — Une.
How many postcards? — One.
une de mes meilleures copines
one of my best friends
une par une
one by one
Elles sont entrées une par une.
They went in one by one.

Il est une heure.
It's one o'clock.

l' **uniforme** MASC NOUN
uniform

unique ADJECTIVE
unique
  C'est une occasion unique.
  It's a unique opportunity.

Il est fils unique.
He's an only child.

a
b
c
d
e
f
g
h
i
j
k
l
m
n
o
p
q
r
s
t
u
v
w
x
y
z

French English

a
b
c
d
e
f
g
h
i
j
k
l
m
n
o
p
q
r
s
t
u
v
w
x
y
z

Elle est fille unique.
She's an only child.

uniquement ADVERB
only

l' **université** FEM NOUN
university

l' **usine** FEM NOUN
factory
Mon père travaille dans une usine.
My dad works in a factory.

utile ADJECTIVE
useful

utiliser VERB
to use

V v

va VERB ▷*see* **aller**
 Il va à l'école avec ses copains.
 He goes to school with his friends.
 Elle va partir demain.
 She'll leave tomorrow.

les **vacances** FEM PL NOUN
 holidays
 **Je vais passer les vacances
 chez ma grand-mère.**
 I'm going to spend the holidays
 with my grandmother.
 aller en vacances
 to go on holiday
 **Où est-ce que tu vas en
 vacances cet été?**
 Where are you going on holiday
 this summer?
 **Nous partons en vacances
 ce soir.**
 We're setting off on holiday
 this evening.

 en vacances
 on holiday
 les vacances de Noël
 the Christmas holidays
 les vacances de Pâques
 the Easter holidays
 les grandes vacances
 the summer holidays
 Bonnes vacances!
 Have a good holiday!

la **vache**
 FEM NOUN
 cow

la **vague** FEM NOUN
 wave

le **vainqueur** MASC NOUN
 winner

vais VERB ▷*see* **aller**
 Je vais écrire à mes cousins.
 I'm going to write to my cousins.

le **vaisseau** MASC NOUN
 (PL les **vaisseaux**)
 un vaisseau spatial
 a spaceship

la **vaisselle** FEM NOUN
 washing-up
 Je vais faire la vaisselle.
 I'll do the washing-up.

le **valet** MASC NOUN
 jack
 le valet de carreau
 the jack of diamonds

la **valise** FEM NOUN
 suitcase
 faire sa valise
 to pack

la **vallée** FEM NOUN
 valley

valoir VERB
 to be worth
 Ça vaut la peine.
 It's worth it.

French English

a
b
c
d
e
f
g
h
i
j
k
l
m
n
o
p
q
r
s
t
u
v
w
x
y
z

la **vanille** FEM NOUN
vanilla

vas VERB ▷ see **aller**
Tu vas souvent au cinéma?
Do you go to the cinema often?

vaut VERB ▷ see **valoir**
Ça vaut mieux.
That would be better.

le **veau** MASC NOUN
(PL les **veaux**)
1 calf
la vache et son veau
the cow and her calf
2 veal

la **vedette** FEM NOUN
star
une vedette de cinéma
a film star

végétarien MASC ADJECTIVE
(FEM **végétarienne**)
vegetarian

la **veille** FEM NOUN
the day before
la veille de son départ
the day before he left

la veille de Noël
Christmas Eve

le **vélo** MASC NOUN
bike
faire du vélo
to go cycling
un vélo tout-terrain
a mountain bike

les **vendanges** FEM PL NOUN
grape harvest

le **vendeur** MASC NOUN
la **vendeuse** FEM NOUN
shop assistant

vendre VERB
to sell
Il m'a vendu son vélo.
He sold me his bike.
'à vendre'
'for sale'

le **vendredi** MASC NOUN
1 Friday
**Aujourd'hui, nous sommes
vendredi.**
It's Friday today.
2 on Friday
Il est venu vendredi.
He came on Friday.
Je joue au foot le vendredi.
I play football on Fridays.

tous les vendredis
every Friday
le vendredi
on Fridays
vendredi dernier
last Friday
vendredi prochain
next Friday
À vendredi!
See you on Friday!
le Vendredi saint
Good Friday

vénéneux MASC ADJECTIVE
(FEM **vénéneuse**)
poisonous

venimeux MASC ADJECTIVE
(FEM **venimeuse**)
poisonous
un serpent venimeux
a poisonous snake

venir VERB
to come
> **Il viendra demain.**
> He'll come tomorrow.
> **Viens t'asseoir.**
> Come and sit down.
> **venir de**
> to have just
> **Je viens de le voir.**
> I've just seen him.

le **vent** MASC NOUN
wind

> **Il y a du vent.**
> It's windy.

le **ventre** MASC NOUN
stomach
> **J'ai mal au ventre.**
> I've got tummy ache.

venu VERB ▷ *see* **venir**
> **Il est venu nous voir.**
> He came to see us.

le **ver** MASC NOUN
worm
> **un ver de terre**
> an earthworm

le **verbe** MASC NOUN
verb

le **verglas** MASC NOUN
black ice

vérifier VERB
to check

la **vérité** FEM NOUN
truth

le **vernis** MASC NOUN
varnish
> **le vernis à ongles**
> nail varnish

verra, verrai, verras VERB
> ▷ *see* **voir**
> **on verra …**
> we'll see …
> **Je le verrai demain.**
> I'll see him tomorrow.
> **Tu verras, c'est facile.**
> You'll see, it's easy.

le **verre** MASC NOUN
glass
> **une table en verre**
> a glass table
> **un verre d'eau**
> a glass of water

vers PREPOSITION
1 **towards**
> **Il allait vers la poste.**
> He was going towards the post office.
2 **at about**
> **Je me couche vers huit heures.**
> I go to bed at about eight o'clock.

vert

> **vert** *can be an adjective or a noun.*

A MASC ADJECTIVE (FEM **verte**)
green
> **J'ai les yeux verts.**
> I've got green eyes.
B MASC NOUN
green
> **J'aime le vert.**
> I like the colour green.

French English

a b c d e f g h i j k l m n o p q r s t u **v** w x y z

267

la **veste** FEM NOUN
jacket
   une veste en jean
   a denim jacket

le **vestiaire** MASC NOUN
  1 **changing room**
  2 **cloakroom**

les **vêtements** MASC PL NOUN
clothes

le/la **vétérinaire**
MASC/FEM NOUN
vet
   Elle est
   vétérinaire.
   She's a vet.

le **veuf** MASC NOUN
widower

veulent, veut VERB
  ▷ see **vouloir**
   Ils ne veulent pas jouer.
   They don't want to play.
   Qui veut jouer?
   Who wants to play?

la **veuve** FEM NOUN
widow

veux VERB ▷ see **vouloir**
   Tu veux aller au cinéma?
   Do you want to go to the cinema?

la **viande** FEM NOUN
meat
   la viande hachée
   mince

vide ADJECTIVE
empty

vidéo MASC, FEM, PL ADJECTIVE
video
   une cassette vidéo
   a video cassette

   un jeu vidéo
   a video game

le **vidéoclip** MASC NOUN
music video

le **vidéoclub** MASC NOUN
video shop

vider VERB
to empty

la **vie** FEM NOUN
life

vieil MASC ADJECTIVE

Language tip
*When **vieux** in the singular comes*
before a vowel sound, it changes to
***vieil**.*

old
   un vieil arbre
   an old tree
   un vieil homme
   an old man

vieille

vieille *can be an adjective or a*
noun.

A FEM ADJECTIVE
  old
   une vieille dame
   an old lady
   Elle est plus vieille que moi.
   She's older than me.
B FEM NOUN
  old woman
   une petite vieille
   a little old lady

vieillir VERB
to age

viendrai, viens VERB
  ▷ see **venir**
   Je viendrai dès que possible.
   I'll come as soon as possible.

Viens ici!
Come here!

vieux

vieux can be an adjective or a noun.

A MASC, MASC PL ADJECTIVE
(FEM **vieille**)
old
un vieux monsieur
an old gentleman
Il est plus vieux que moi.
He's older than me.

Language tip

vieux in the singular changes to vieil before a vowel sound.

un vieil homme
an old man
B MASC NOUN
old man
un petit vieux
a little old man
les vieux
old people

vif MASC ADJECTIVE (FEM **vive**)
bright
rouge vif
bright red

la **vigne** FEM NOUN
vine
des champs de vigne
vineyards

le **vigneron** MASC NOUN
wine grower

le **vignoble** MASC NOUN
vineyard

vilain MASC ADJECTIVE
(FEM **vilaine**)
1 naughty

C'est très vilain de dire des mensonges.
It's very naughty to tell lies.
2 horrible
Il a de vilaines dents.
He's got horrible teeth.
une vilaine sorcière
an evil witch

le **village** MASC NOUN
village

la **ville** FEM NOUN
town
Je vais en ville.
I'm going into town.
une grande ville
a city

le **vin** MASC NOUN
wine
du vin blanc
white wine
du vin rouge
red wine

le **vinaigre** MASC NOUN
vinegar

la **vinaigrette** FEM NOUN
French dressing

vingt NUMBER
twenty
Elle a vingt ans.
She's twenty.
à vingt heures
at 8 p.m.

French English

a
b
c
d
e
f
g
h
i
j
k
l
m
n
o
p
q
r
s
t
u
v
w
x
y
z

Did you know...?
The 24-hour clock is used in France for travel times, appointments, and other formal situations.

vingt et un
twenty-one
vingt-deux
twenty-two

le vingt février
the twentieth of February

la **vingtaine** FEM NOUN
about twenty
> **une vingtaine de personnes**
> about twenty people
> **Il a une vingtaine d'années.**
> He's about twenty.

vingtième ADJECTIVE
twentieth

violet

violet *can be an adjective or a noun.*

A MASC ADJECTIVE (FEM **violette**)
purple
> **une robe violette**
> a purple dress

B MASC NOUN
purple
> **J'aime le violet.**
> I like the colour purple.

le **violon** MASC NOUN
violin
> **Je joue du violon.**
> I play the violin.

le **violoncelle** MASC NOUN
cello
> **Elle joue du violoncelle.**
> She plays the cello

la **vipère** FEM NOUN
viper

la **virgule** FEM NOUN
comma

vis VERB ▷*see* **vivre**
> **Je vis en Écosse.**
> I live in Scotland.

le **visage** MASC NOUN
face
> **Elle a le visage rond.**
> She's got a round face.

la **visite** FEM NOUN
> **rendre visite à quelqu'un**
> to visit somebody
> **Je vais rendre visite à mon grand-père.**
> I'm going to visit my grandfather.
> **une visite guidée**
> a guided tour

visiter VERB
to visit
> **Nous avons visité des châteaux.**
> We visited some castles.

vit VERB ▷*see* **vivre**
> **Il vit chez ses parents.**
> He lives with his parents.

vite ADVERB
1 quick
> **Vite, ils arrivent!**
> Quick, they're coming!
> **Prenons la voiture, ça ira plus vite.**
> Let's take the car, it'll be quicker.
2 fast
> **Il roule trop vite.**
> He drives too fast.
> **Il court plus vite que moi.**
> He runs faster than me.

3 soon
Il va vite oublier.
He'll soon forget.

la **vitesse** FEM NOUN
1 speed
en vitesse
quickly
2 gear
J'ai un vélo à dix vitesses.
I've got a bike with ten gears.

le **viticulteur** MASC NOUN
wine grower

le **vitrail** MASC NOUN
(PL les **vitraux**)
stained-glass window

la **vitre** FEM NOUN
window

la **vitrine**
FEM NOUN
shop
window

vivant MASC ADJECTIVE
(FEM **vivante**)
living

vive

> **vive** can be an adjective or an
> exclamation.

A FEM ADJECTIVE
bright
les couleurs vives
bright colours
B EXCLAMATION
Vive le roi!
Long live the king!

vivement EXCLAMATION
Vivement les vacances!
Roll on the holidays!

vivre VERB
to live
J'aimerais vivre à l'étranger.
I'd like to live abroad.

le **vocabulaire** MASC NOUN
vocabulary

le **vœu** MASC NOUN
(PL les **vœux**)
wish
faire un vœu
to make a wish
Meilleurs vœux de bonne
année!
Best wishes for the New Year!

voici PREPOSITION
this is
Voici mon frère et voilà ma
sœur.
This is my brother and that's
my sister.

voilà PREPOSITION
1 there is
Tiens! Voilà Paul.
Look! There's Paul.
Les voilà!
There they are!
Voilà!
There you are!
2 that is
Voilà ma sœur.
That's my sister.

la **voile** FEM NOUN
sailing
faire de la voile
to go sailing
un bateau à voile
a sailing boat

le **voilier** MASC NOUN
sailing boat

voir VERB
to see

Venez me voir quand vous serez à Paris.
Come and see me when you're in Paris.
faire voir
to show
Il m'a fait voir sa collection de timbres.
He showed me his stamp collection.

vois VERB ▷see **voir**
Je n'y vois rien sans mes lunettes.
I can't see anything without my glasses.

le **voisin** MASC NOUN
la **voisine** FEM NOUN
neighbour

la **voiture** FEM NOUN
car
une voiture de sport
a sports car

la **voix** FEM NOUN (PL les **voix**)
voice

le **vol** MASC NOUN
flight

voler VERB
1 **to fly**
2 **to steal**
On a volé mon appareil photo.
My camera's been stolen.

le **volet** MASC NOUN
shutter

Did you know…?
Traditional French houses have wooden shutters.

le **voleur** MASC NOUN
la **voleuse** FEM NOUN
thief

Au voleur !
Stop thief!

le **volley** MASC NOUN
volleyball
jouer au volley
to play volleyball

le/la **volontaire** MASC/FEM NOUN
volunteer

vomir VERB
to be sick

vont VERB ▷see **aller**
Ils vont à la piscine.
They're going to the pool.

vos PL ADJECTIVE ▷see **votre**
your
Rangez vos jouets, les enfants!
Put your toys away, children.
J'ai trouvé vos clés, M. Durand.
I've found your keys, Mr Durand.

voter VERB
to vote

votre ADJECTIVE (PL **vos**)
your
C'est votre manteau, Mme Leblanc?
Is this your coat, Mrs Leblanc?
Restez à votre place, les enfants!
Stay in your seats children.

le/la **vôtre** MASC/FEM PRONOUN
yours
À qui est cette écharpe? C'est la vôtre?
Whose is this scarf? Is it yours?
Ce ne sont pas mes clés, ce sont les vôtres.
These aren't my keys, they're yours.

voudrais VERB ▷*see* **vouloir**
**Je voudrais deux litres de lait,
s'il vous plaît.**
I'd like two litres of milk, please.

vouloir VERB
to want
> **Elle veut un vélo pour Noël.**
> She wants a bike for Christmas.
> **Je ne veux pas de dessert.**
> I don't want any pudding.
> **On va au cinéma? — Si tu veux.**
> Shall we go to the cinema? —
> If you like.

voulu VERB ▷*see* **vouloir**
Elle n'a pas voulu venir.
She didn't want to come.

vous PRONOUN
1 you
> **Vous voulez de l'eau,
> monsieur?**
> Would you like some water, sir?
> **Vous devez faire attention,
> les enfants.**
> You must be careful, children.

2 to you
> **Je vous écrirai bientôt.**
> I'll write to you soon.

3 yourself
> **Vous vous êtes fait mal?**
> Have you hurt yourself?

vous-même
yourself
Vous l'avez fait vous-même?
Did you do it yourself?

vouvoyer VERB
> **vouvoyer quelqu'un**
> to call somebody 'vous'
> **Est-ce que je dois vouvoyer
> ta sœur?**
> Should I say 'vous' to your
> sister?

Did you know…?
*There are two words for 'you' in
French,* **tu** *and* **vous**. *Vous is the
formal one. You would call your
teacher 'vous' but your friend 'tu'.*

le **voyage** MASC NOUN
journey
> **Avez-vous fait bon voyage?**
> Did you have a good journey?

Bon voyage!
Have a good trip!

voyager VERB
to travel

voyez VERB ▷*see* **voir**
> **Vous voyez l'arc-en-ciel là-bas?**
> Can you see the rainbow over
> there?

voyons VERB ▷*see* **voir**
> **Nous ne les voyons pas souvent.**
> We don't see them very often.

vrai ADJECTIVE
true
> **une histoire vraie**
> a true story
> **C'est vrai?**
> Is that true?

vraiment ADVERB
really

le **VTT** MASC NOUN
mountain bike

vu VERB ▷*see* **voir**
> **J'ai vu un film au cinéma.**
> I saw a film at the cinema.

la **vue** FEM NOUN
1 eyesight
2 view
> **Il y a une belle vue d'ici.**
> There's a lovely view from here.

W w

wallon MASC NOUN, MASC ADJECTIVE (FEM **wallonne**)
Walloon

le **Wallon** MASC NOUN
la **Wallonne** FEM NOUN
Walloon

les **Wallons** MASC PL NOUN
Walloons

Did you know...?

Walloons are Belgian people who speak French, one of the two languages spoken in Belgium. The other language is Flemish, which is spoken by **les Flamands**.

la **Wallonie** FEM NOUN
French-speaking Belgium

les **WC** MASC PL NOUN
toilet
> **Où sont les WC?**
> Where's the toilet?

Language tip

The French word **WC** *is pronounced 'vay-say'.*

le **Web** MASC NOUN
World Wide Web

la **webcam** FEM NOUN
webcam

le **week-end** MASC NOUN
weekend
> **Ce week-end, nous allons à Paris.**
> We're going to Paris this weekend.
> **Qu'est-ce que tu as fait pendant le week-end?**
> What did you do at the weekend?

Bon week-end!
Have a nice weekend!

le **western** MASC NOUN
western

X x

le **xylophone** MASC NOUN
xylophone
**Elle joue du
xylophone.**
She plays the
xylophone.

Y y

y PRONOUN
1 there
**Nous y sommes allés l'été
dernier.**
We went there last summer.
Vas-y!
Go on!
2 it
Arrête d'y penser!
Stop thinking about it!

le **yaourt** MASC NOUN
yoghurt

un yaourt nature
a plain yoghurt
un yaourt aux fruits
a fruit yoghurt

les **yeux** MASC PL NOUN
eyes
Elle a les yeux bleus.
She's got blue eyes.

le **yoga** MASC NOUN
yoga
Elle fait du yoga.
She does yoga.

youpi EXCLAMATION
Yippee!

le **yoyo** MASC NOUN
yo-yo

Z z

le **zèbre** MASC NOUN
  zebra

le **zéro** MASC NOUN
  zero
>   **Ils ont gagné trois à zéro.**
>   They won three-nil.

la **zone** FEM NOUN
  zone
>   **une zone industrielle**
>   an industrial estate

le **zoo** MASC NOUN
  zoo

zut EXCLAMATION
  Oh heck!

Language plus

Language plus

• Pets

budgie NOUN la **perruche** *fem*

canary NOUN le **canari** *masc*

cat NOUN le **chat** *masc*,
la **chatte** *fem*

dog NOUN le **chien** *masc*,
la **chienne** *fem*

ferret NOUN le **furet** *masc*

gerbil NOUN la **gerbille** *fem*

goldfish NOUN le **poisson rouge** *masc*

guinea pig NOUN le **cochon d'Inde** *masc*

hamster NOUN le **hamster** *masc*

kitten NOUN le **chaton** *masc*

mouse NOUN la **souris** *fem*

parrot NOUN le **perroquet** *masc*

poodle NOUN le **caniche** *masc*

puppy NOUN le **chiot** *masc*

rabbit NOUN le **lapin** *masc*

rat NOUN le **rat** *masc*

stick insect NOUN le **phasme** *masc*

tortoise NOUN la **tortue** *fem*

• Farm animals

bull NOUN le **taureau** *masc*

calf NOUN le **veau** *masc*

chick NOUN le **poussin** *masc*

chicken NOUN la **poule** *fem*

cock NOUN le **coq** *masc*

cow NOUN la **vache** *fem*

donkey NOUN l' **âne** *masc*

duck NOUN le **canard** *masc*

goat NOUN la **chèvre** *fem*

goose NOUN l' **oie** *fem*

hen NOUN la **poule** *fem*

horse NOUN le **cheval** *masc*

lamb NOUN l' **agneau** *masc*

mare NOUN la **jument** *fem*

pig NOUN le **cochon** *masc*

pony NOUN le **poney** *masc*

ram NOUN le **bélier** *masc*

sheep NOUN le **mouton** *masc*

sheepdog NOUN le **chien de berger** *masc*

turkey NOUN le **dindon** *masc*

• Other animals

ant NOUN la **fourmi** *fem*

bat NOUN la **chauve-souris** *fem*

bear NOUN l' **ours** *masc*

bee NOUN l' **abeille** *fem*

beetle NOUN le **scarabée** *masc*

bird NOUN l' **oiseau** *masc*

butterfly NOUN le **papillon** *masc*

camel NOUN le **chameau** *masc*

crab NOUN le **crabe** *masc*

crocodile NOUN le **crocodile** *masc*

cub NOUN le **petit** *masc*

dinosaur NOUN le **dinosaure** *masc*

dolphin NOUN le **dauphin** *masc*

dragon NOUN le **dragon** *masc*

duck NOUN le **canard** *masc*

elephant NOUN l' **éléphant** *masc*

fish NOUN le **poisson** *masc*

fly NOUN la **mouche** *fem*

fox NOUN le **renard** *masc*

frog NOUN la **grenouille** *fem*

giraffe NOUN la **girafe** *fem*

gorilla NOUN le **gorille** *masc*

hare NOUN le **lièvre** *masc*

hedgehog NOUN le **hérisson** *masc*

hippo NOUN l' **hippopotame** *masc*

insect NOUN l' **insecte** *masc*

jellyfish NOUN la **méduse** *fem*

kangaroo NOUN le **kangourou** *masc*

ladybird NOUN la **coccinelle** *fem*

leopard NOUN le **léopard** *masc*

lion NOUN le **lion** *masc*

lizard NOUN le **lézard** *masc*

mammoth NOUN le **mammouth** *masc*

midge NOUN le **moucheron** *masc*

mole NOUN la **taupe** *fem*

monkey NOUN le **singe** *masc*

mosquito NOUN le **moustique** *masc*

moth NOUN le **papillon de nuit** *masc*

octopus NOUN la **pieuvre** *fem*

ostrich NOUN l' **autruche** *fem*

owl NOUN le **hibou** *masc*

panther NOUN la **panthère** *fem*

peacock NOUN le **paon** *masc*

penguin NOUN le **pingouin** *masc*

pheasant NOUN le **faisan** *masc*

pigeon NOUN le **pigeon** *masc*

polar bear NOUN l' **ours blanc** *masc*

red deer NOUN le **cerf** *masc*

reindeer NOUN le **renne** *masc*

rhinoceros NOUN
le **rhinocéros** *masc*

seagull NOUN
la **mouette** *fem*

seal NOUN le **phoque** *masc*

shark NOUN le **requin** *masc*

slug NOUN la **limace** *fem*

snail NOUN l' **escargot** *masc*

snake NOUN le **serpent** *masc*

spider NOUN l' **araignée** *fem*

squirrel NOUN l' **écureuil** *masc*

swan NOUN le **cygne** *masc*

tadpole NOUN le **têtard** *masc*

tiger NOUN le **tigre** *masc*

toad NOUN le **crapaud** *masc*

trout NOUN la **truite** *fem*

turtle NOUN la **tortue** *fem*

wasp NOUN la **guêpe** *fem*

whale NOUN la **baleine** *fem*

wolf NOUN le **loup** *masc*

worm NOUN le **ver** *masc*

zebra NOUN le **zèbre** *masc*

ankle NOUN la **cheville** *fem*

arm NOUN le **bras** *masc*

back NOUN le **dos** *masc*

beard NOUN la **barbe** *fem*

blood NOUN le **sang** *masc*

body NOUN le **corps** *masc*

bottom NOUN le **derrière** *masc*

brain NOUN le **cerveau** *masc*

cheek NOUN la **joue** *fem*

chest NOUN la **poitrine** *fem*

chin NOUN le **menton** *masc*

ear NOUN l' **oreille** *fem*

elbow NOUN le **coude** *masc*

eye NOUN l' **œil** *masc*

eyebrow NOUN le **sourcil** *masc*

eyelash NOUN le **cil** *masc*

eyelid NOUN la **paupière** *fem*

face NOUN la **figure** *fem*

finger NOUN le **doigt** *masc*

fist NOUN le **poing** *masc*

foot NOUN le **pied** *masc*

forehead NOUN le **front** *masc*

freckles NOUN PL les **taches de rousseur** *fem pl*

fringe NOUN la **frange** *fem*

hair NOUN les **cheveux** *masc pl*

hand NOUN la **main** *fem*

head NOUN la **tête** *fem*

heart NOUN le **cœur** *masc*

heel NOUN le **talon** *masc*

hip NOUN la **hanche** *fem*

jaw NOUN la **mâchoire** *fem*

knee NOUN le **genou** *masc*

leg NOUN la **jambe** *fem*

lip NOUN la **lèvre** *fem*

moustache NOUN la **moustache** *fem*

mouth NOUN la **bouche** *fem*

muscle NOUN le **muscle** *masc*

nail NOUN l' **ongle** *masc*

neck NOUN le **cou** *masc*

nose NOUN le **nez** *masc*

palm NOUN la **paume** *fem*

rib NOUN la **côte** *fem*

shin NOUN le **tibia** *masc*

shoulder NOUN l' **épaule** *fem*

skeleton NOUN le **squelette** *masc*

skin NOUN la **peau** *fem*

skull NOUN le **crâne** *masc*

stomach NOUN l' **estomac** *masc*

thigh NOUN la **cuisse** *fem*

throat NOUN la **gorge** *fem*

thumb NOUN le **pouce** *masc*

toe NOUN le **doigt de pied** *masc*

tongue NOUN la **langue** *fem*

tonsils NOUN PL les **amygdales** *fem pl*

tooth NOUN la **dent** *fem*

tummy NOUN le **ventre** *masc*

waist NOUN la **taille** *fem*

wrist NOUN le **poignet** *masc*

anorak NOUN l' **anorak** *masc*

apron NOUN le **tablier** *masc*

ballet shoes NOUN PL
les **chaussons de danse**
masc pl

baseball cap NOUN
la **casquette de base-ball** *fem*

belt NOUN la **ceinture** *fem*

bikini NOUN le **bikini** *masc*

blazer NOUN le **blazer** *masc*

blouse NOUN le **chemisier** *masc*

boots NOUN les **bottes** *fem pl*

bow tie NOUN le **nœud**
papillon *masc*

boxer shorts NOUN PL
le **caleçon** *masc*

bra NOUN le **soutien-gorge** *masc*

cagoule NOUN le **K-way**® *masc*

cap NOUN la **casquette** *fem*

cardigan NOUN le **cardigan**
masc

clothes NOUN PL les **vêtements**
masc pl

coat NOUN le **manteau** *masc*

dinner jacket NOUN
le **smoking** *masc*

dress NOUN la **robe** *fem*

dressing gown NOUN
la **robe de chambre** *fem*

dungarees NOUN la **salopette**
fem

fleece NOUN la **laine polaire**
fem

flippers NOUN PL les **palmes**
fem pl

football boots NOUN
les **chaussures de foot**
fem pl

football shirt NOUN
le **maillot de foot** *masc*

glasses NOUN PL les **lunettes**
fem pl

glove NOUN le **gant** *masc*

goggles NOUN PL les **lunettes**
de plongée *fem pl*

hat NOUN le **chapeau** *masc*

helmet NOUN le **casque** *masc*

hood NOUN la **capuche** *fem*

jacket NOUN la **veste** *fem*

jeans NOUN PL le **jean** *masc*

jersey NOUN le **pull-over**
masc

jumper NOUN le **pull** *masc*

kilt NOUN le **kilt** *masc*

knickers NOUN PL la **culotte**
fem

leather jacket NOUN
la **veste en cuir** *fem*

miniskirt NOUN la **minijupe**
fem

nightdress NOUN la **chemise**
de nuit *fem*

nightie NOUN la **chemise de**
nuit *fem*

nightshirt NOUN la **chemise**
de nuit *fem*

overalls NOUN PL les **bleus de**
travail *masc pl*

panties NOUN PL le **slip** *masc*

pants NOUN PL le **slip** *masc*

plimsolls NOUN PL
les **chaussons de gym** *masc pl*

polo-necked sweater
NOUN le **pull à col roulé** *masc*

polo shirt NOUN le **polo** *masc*

pullover NOUN le **pull** *masc*

pyjamas NOUN PL le **pyjama**
masc

raincoat NOUN l' **imperméable**
masc

sandals NOUN PL les **sandales**
fem pl

scarf NOUN l' **écharpe** *fem*

shirt NOUN la **chemise** *fem*

shoes NOUN PL les **chaussures**
fem pl

shorts NOUN PL le **short** *masc*

ski boots NOUN PL
les **chaussures de ski** *fem pl*

skirt NOUN la **jupe** *fem*

slippers NOUN PL
les **chaussons** *masc pl*

sock NOUN la **chaussette** *fem*

suit NOUN le **costume** *masc*
(*for a man*), le **tailleur** *masc*
(*for a woman*)

sunglasses NOUN PL
les **lunettes de soleil** *fem pl*

sweater NOUN le **pull** *masc*

sweatshirt NOUN le **sweat**
masc

swimming costume NOUN
le **maillot de bain** *masc*

swimming trunks NOUN PL
le **maillot de bain** *masc*

swimsuit NOUN le **maillot de
bain** *masc*

tee-shirt NOUN le **tee-shirt**
masc

tie NOUN la **cravate** *fem*

tights NOUN PL le **collant** *masc*

top NOUN le **haut** *masc*

tracksuit NOUN le **jogging** *masc*

trainers NOUN PL les **baskets**
fem pl

trousers NOUN PL le **pantalon**
masc

trunks NOUN PL le **maillot de
bain** *masc*

T-shirt NOUN le **tee-shirt** *masc*

underpants NOUN PL le **slip**
masc

underskirt NOUN le **jupon**
masc

underwear NOUN
les **sous-vêtements** *masc pl*

uniform NOUN l' **uniforme**
masc

vest NOUN le **maillot de corps**
masc

waistcoat NOUN le **gilet** *masc*

wellingtons NOUN PL
les **bottes en caoutchouc**
fem pl

wetsuit NOUN la **combinaison
de plongée** *fem*

beige ADJECTIVE **beige**

black ADJECTIVE **noir** *masc,* **noire** *fem*

blue ADJECTIVE **bleu** *masc,* **bleue** *fem*

brown ADJECTIVE **marron** *masc, fem, pl*

cream ADJECTIVE **crème** *masc, fem, pl*

green ADJECTIVE **vert** *masc,* **verte** *fem*

grey ADJECTIVE **gris** *masc,* **grise** *fem*

maroon ADJECTIVE **bordeaux** *masc, fem, pl*

navy ADJECTIVE **bleu marine** *masc, fem, pl*

navy blue ADJECTIVE **bleu marine** *masc, fem, pl*

orange ADJECTIVE **orange** *masc, fem, pl*

pink ADJECTIVE **rose**

purple ADJECTIVE **violet** *masc,* **violette** *fem*

red ADJECTIVE **rouge**

turquoise ADJECTIVE **turquoise**

white ADJECTIVE **blanc** *masc,* **blanche** *fem*

yellow ADJECTIVE **jaune**

aunt, aunty NOUN la **tante** *fem*

brother NOUN le **frère** *masc*

brother-in-law NOUN
le **beau-frère** *masc*

cousin NOUN le **cousin** *masc*,
la **cousine** *fem*

dad NOUN le **père** *masc*

daddy NOUN le **papa** *masc*

daughter NOUN la **fille** *fem*

daughter-in-law NOUN
la **belle-fille** *fem*

family NOUN la **famille** *fem*

father NOUN le **père** *masc*

father-in-law NOUN
le **beau-père** *masc*

fiancé NOUN le **fiancé** *masc*

fiancée NOUN la **fiancée** *fem*

godfather NOUN le **parrain**
masc

godmother NOUN la **marraine**
fem

grandchildren NOUN PL
les **petits-enfants** *masc pl*

granddad NOUN le **papi** *masc*

granddaughter NOUN
la **petite-fille** *fem*

grandfather NOUN
le **grand-père** *masc*

grandma NOUN la **mamie** *fem*

grandmother NOUN
la **grand-mère** *fem*

grandpa NOUN le **papi** *masc*

grandparents NOUN PL
les **grands-parents** *masc pl*

grandson NOUN le **petit-fils**
masc

granny NOUN la **mamie** *fem*

half-brother NOUN
le **demi-frère** *masc*

half-sister NOUN
la **demi-sœur** *fem*

husband NOUN le **mari** *masc*

mother NOUN la **mère** *fem*

mother-in-law NOUN
la **belle-mère** *fem*

mum NOUN
la **mère** *fem*

mummy NOUN la **maman** *fem*

nephew NOUN le **neveu** *masc*

niece NOUN la **nièce** *fem*

parent NOUN le **parent** *masc*

sister NOUN la **sœur** *fem*

sister-in-law NOUN
la **belle-sœur** *fem*

son NOUN le **fils** *masc*

son-in-law NOUN le **gendre**
masc

stepbrother NOUN
le **demi-frère** *masc*

stepdaughter NOUN
la **belle-fille** *fem*

stepfather NOUN
le **beau-père** *masc*

stepmother NOUN
la **belle-mère** *fem*

stepsister NOUN
la **demi-sœur** *fem*

stepson NOUN le **beau-fils** *masc*

uncle NOUN l' **oncle** *masc*

wife NOUN la **femme** *fem*

• Days of the week

Monday lundi
Tuesday mardi
Wednesday mercredi
Thursday jeudi
Friday vendredi
Saturday samedi
Sunday dimanche

• Months of the year

January janvier
February février
March mars
April avril
May mai
June juin
July juillet
August août
September septembre
October octobre
November novembre
December décembre

• Special days

April Fool's Day NOUN le **premier avril** *masc*
Boxing Day NOUN le **lendemain de Noël** *masc*
Christmas NOUN **Noël** *masc*
Christmas Day NOUN le **jour de Noël** *masc*
Christmas Eve NOUN la **veille de Noël** *fem*
Easter NOUN **Pâques** *fem pl*
Father's Day NOUN la **fête des Pères** *fem*
Hallowe'en NOUN la **veille de la Toussaint** *fem*
Mother's Day NOUN la **fête des Mères** *fem*
New Year's Day NOUN le **premier de l'An** *masc*
New Year's Eve NOUN la **Saint-Sylvestre** *fem*
Pancake Day NOUN le **mardi gras** *masc*
Passover NOUN la **Pâque juive** *fem*
Ramadan NOUN le **ramadan** *masc*
Remembrance Day NOUN le **jour de l'Armistice** *masc*
Shrove Tuesday NOUN le **mardi gras** *masc*
Valentine's Day NOUN la **Saint-Valentin** *fem*
Whitsun NOUN la **Pentecôte** *fem*

It's chilly. Il fait froid.

It's cloudy. Il fait gris.

It's cold. Il fait froid.

It's dull. Il fait gris.

It's foggy. Il y a du brouillard.

It's freezing. Il gèle.

It's frosty. Il gèle.

It's icy. Il gèle.

It's misty. Le temps est brumeux.

It's nice. Il fait beau.

It's overcast. Le ciel est couvert.

It's raining. Il pleut.

It's snowing. Il neige.

It's stormy. Le temps est orageux.

It's sunny. Il fait du soleil.

It's warm. Il fait chaud.

It's windy. Il fait du vent.

• **Seasons**

winter NOUN l' **hiver** *masc*

spring NOUN le **printemps** *masc*

summer NOUN l' **été** *masc*

autumn NOUN l' **automne** *masc*

• Europe

Alps NOUN PL les **Alpes** *fem pl*

Andorra NOUN **Andorre** *fem*

Atlantic NOUN l' **Atlantique** *masc*

Austria NOUN l' **Autriche** *fem*

Belgium NOUN la **Belgique** *fem*

Britain NOUN la **Grande-Bretagne** *fem*

British Isles NOUN PL les **îles Britanniques** *fem pl*

Brittany NOUN la **Bretagne** *fem*

Brussels NOUN **Bruxelles**

Bulgaria NOUN **Bulgarie** *fem*

Channel NOUN la **Manche** *fem*

Channel Islands NOUN PL les **îles Anglo-Normandes** *fem pl*

Cornwall NOUN la **Cornouailles** *fem*

Corsica NOUN la **Corse** *fem*

Cyprus NOUN **Chypre** *fem*

Czech Republic NOUN la **République tchèque** *fem*

Denmark NOUN le **Danemark** *masc*

Dover NOUN **Douvres**

Edinburgh NOUN **Édimbourg**

Eire NOUN la **République d'Irlande** *fem*

England NOUN l' **Angleterre** *fem*

Europe NOUN l' **Europe** *fem*

Finland NOUN la **Finlande** *fem*

France NOUN la **France** *fem*

French Riviera NOUN la **Côte d'Azur** *fem*

Germany NOUN l' **Allemagne** *fem*

Great Britain NOUN la **Grande-Bretagne** *fem*

Greece NOUN la **Grèce** *fem*

Greenland NOUN le **Groenland** *masc*

Holland NOUN la **Hollande** *fem*

Hungary NOUN la **Hongrie** *fem*

Iceland NOUN l' **Islande** *fem*

Ireland NOUN l' **Irlande** *fem*

Italy NOUN l' **Italie** *fem*

Lapland NOUN la **Laponie** *fem*

Liechtenstein NOUN le **Liechtenstein** *masc*

London NOUN **Londres**

Luxembourg NOUN le **Luxembourg** *masc*

Majorca NOUN **Majorque** *fem*

Malta NOUN **Malte** *fem*

Mediterranean NOUN la **Méditerranée** *fem*

Menorca NOUN **Minorque** *fem*

Monaco NOUN **Monaco** *masc*

Netherlands NOUN PL les **Pays-Bas** *masc pl*

Normandy NOUN la **Normandie** *fem*

Northern Ireland NOUN l' **Irlande du Nord** *fem*

North Sea NOUN la **mer du Nord** *fem*

Norway NOUN la **Norvège** *fem*

Orkneys NOUN PL les **Orcades** *fem pl*

Poland NOUN la **Pologne** *fem*

Portugal NOUN le **Portugal** *masc*

Pyrenees NOUN PL les **Pyrénées** *fem pl*

Romania NOUN la **Roumanie** *fem*

Russia NOUN la **Russie** *fem*

Scandinavia NOUN la **Scandinavie** *fem*

Scotland NOUN l' **Écosse** *fem*

Shetland Islands NOUN PL les **îles Shetland** *fem pl*

Sicily NOUN la **Sicile** *fem*

Spain NOUN l' **Espagne** *fem*

Sweden NOUN la **Suède** *fem*

Switzerland NOUN la **Suisse** *fem*

Turkey NOUN la **Turquie** *fem*

UK NOUN le **Royaume-Uni** *masc*

Ulster NOUN l' **Irlande du Nord** *fem*

United Kingdom NOUN le **Royaume-Uni** *masc*

Wales NOUN le **pays de Galles** *masc*

• Rest of the world

Africa NOUN l' **Afrique** *fem*

Algeria NOUN l' **Algérie** *fem*

America NOUN l' **Amérique** *fem*

Australia NOUN l' **Australie** *fem*

Brazil NOUN le **Brésil** *masc*

Canada NOUN le **Canada** *masc*

Caribbean NOUN les **Caraïbes** *fem pl*

China NOUN la **Chine** *fem*

Egypt NOUN l' **Égypte** *fem*

Ethiopia NOUN l' **Éthiopie** *fem*

India NOUN l' **Inde** *fem*

Iran NOUN l' **Iran** *masc*

Iraq NOUN l' **Iraq** *masc*

Israel NOUN **Israël** *masc*

Japan NOUN le **Japon** *masc*

Jordan NOUN la **Jordanie** *fem*

Korea NOUN la **Corée** *fem*

Lebanon NOUN le **Liban** *masc*

Libya NOUN la **Libye** *fem*

Malaysia NOUN la **Malaisie** *fem*

Mexico NOUN le **Mexique** *masc*

Middle East NOUN le **Moyen-Orient** *masc*

Morocco NOUN le **Maroc** *masc*

New Zealand NOUN la **Nouvelle-Zélande** *fem*

Nigeria NOUN le **Nigéria** *masc*

North America NOUN
l' **Amérique du Nord** *fem*

North Pole NOUN le **pôle
Nord** *masc*

Pacific NOUN le **Pacifique**
masc

Pakistan NOUN le **Pakistan**
masc

Palestine NOUN la **Palestine**
fem

Saudi Arabia NOUN l' **Arabie
Saoudite** *fem*

South Africa NOUN
l' **Afrique du Sud** *fem*

South America NOUN
l' **Amérique du Sud** *fem*

South Pole NOUN le **pôle
Sud** *masc*

Tunisia NOUN la **Tunisie** *fem*

United States NOUN
les **États-Unis** *masc pl*

USA NOUN les **USA** *masc pl*

Vietnam NOUN le **Viêt-Nam**
masc

West Indies NOUN PL
les **Antilles** *fem pl*

• **Savoury**

bacon NOUN le **bacon** *masc*

baked beans NOUN PL
les **haricots blancs à la
sauce tomate** *masc pl*

baked potato NOUN
la **pomme de terre cuite
au four** *fem*

beans NOUN PL les **haricots
blancs à la sauce tomate**
masc pl

beef NOUN le **bœuf** *masc*

boiled egg NOUN l' **œuf à
la coque** *masc*

bread NOUN le **pain** *masc*

breakfast NOUN le **petit
déjeuner** *masc*

brown bread NOUN le **pain
complet** *masc*

bun NOUN le **petit pain** *masc*

burger NOUN le **hamburger**
masc

butter NOUN le **beurre** *masc*

casserole NOUN le **ragoût** *masc*

cereal NOUN les **céréales** *fem pl*

cheese NOUN le **fromage** *masc*

cheeseburger NOUN
le **cheeseburger** *masc*

chicken NOUN le **poulet** *masc*

chips NOUN les **frites** *fem pl*

chop NOUN la **côte** *fem*

cod NOUN le **cabillaud** *masc*

coleslaw NOUN la **salade de
chou cru à la mayonnaise**
fem

cornflakes NOUN PL
les **cornflakes** *masc pl*

cream cheese NOUN
le **fromage à tartiner** *masc*

crisps NOUN PL les **chips** *fem pl*

curry NOUN le **curry** *masc*

dinner NOUN le **dîner** *masc*

egg NOUN l' **œuf** *masc*

fish NOUN le **poisson** *masc*

fish fingers NOUN PL
les **bâtonnets de poisson**
masc pl

flan NOUN la **quiche** *fem*

French fries NOUN PL
les **frites** *fem pl*

fried egg NOUN l' **œuf sur
le plat** *masc*

garlic NOUN l' **ail** *masc*

gravy NOUN la **sauce** *fem*

haddock NOUN l' **églefin**
masc

ham NOUN le **jambon** *masc*

hamburger NOUN
le **hamburger** *masc*

hard-boiled egg NOUN
l' **œuf dur** *masc*

herbs NOUN PL les **fines herbes**
fem pl

hot dog NOUN le **hot-dog** *masc*

jacket potato NOUN
la **pomme de terre cuite au
four** *fem*

ketchup NOUN le **ketchup** *masc*

lamb NOUN l' **agneau** *masc*

lentil NOUN la **lentille** *fem*

liver NOUN le **foie** *masc*

loaf NOUN le **pain** *masc*

lobster NOUN le **homard** *masc*

lunch NOUN le **déjeuner** *masc*

macaroni NOUN les **macaronis** *masc pl*

margarine NOUN la **margarine** *fem*

mashed potatoes NOUN PL la **purée** *fem*

mayonnaise NOUN la **mayonnaise** *fem*

meat NOUN la **viande** *fem*

mince NOUN la **viande hachée** *fem*

muesli NOUN le **muesli** *masc*

mussel NOUN la **moule** *fem*

mustard NOUN la **moutarde** *fem*

noodles NOUN PL les **nouilles** *fem pl*

olive NOUN l' **olive** *fem*

olive oil NOUN l' **huile d'olive** *fem*

omelette NOUN l' **omelette** *fem*

parsley NOUN le **persil** *masc*

pasta NOUN les **pâtes** *fem pl*

pâté NOUN le **pâté** *masc*

peanut butter NOUN le **beurre de cacahuètes** *masc*

pepper NOUN le **poivre** *masc*

pie NOUN la **tourte** *fem*

pizza NOUN la **pizza** *fem*

poached egg NOUN l' **œuf poché** *masc*

pork NOUN le **porc** *masc*

porridge NOUN le **porridge** *masc*

prawn cocktail NOUN le **cocktail de crevettes** *masc*

prawns NOUN PL les **crevettes** *fem pl*

rice NOUN le **riz** *masc*

roll NOUN le **petit pain** *masc*

salad NOUN la **salade** *fem*

salad cream NOUN la **mayonnaise** *fem*

salad dressing NOUN la **vinaigrette** *fem*

salami NOUN le **salami** *masc*

salmon NOUN le **saumon** *masc*

salt NOUN le **sel** *masc*

sandwich NOUN le **sandwich** *masc*

sardine NOUN la **sardine** *fem*

sauce NOUN la **sauce** *fem*

sausage NOUN la **saucisse** *fem*

scampi NOUN PL les **scampi** *masc pl*

scrambled eggs NOUN PL les **œufs brouillés** *masc pl*

seafood NOUN les **fruits de mer** *masc pl*

shepherd's pie NOUN le **hachis Parmentier** *masc*

shrimps NOUN PL les **crevettes** *fem pl*

soft-boiled egg NOUN l' **œuf à la coque** *masc*

soup NOUN la **soupe** *fem*

soy sauce NOUN la **sauce de soja** *fem*

spaghetti NOUN les **spaghettis** *masc pl*

steak NOUN le **steak** *masc*

stew NOUN le **ragoût** *masc*

supper NOUN le **dîner** *masc*

toast NOUN le **pain grillé** *masc*

toastie NOUN le **sandwich chaud** *masc*

tuna NOUN le **thon** *masc*

turkey NOUN la **dinde** *fem*

vinegar NOUN le **vinaigre** *masc*

wholemeal bread NOUN le **pain complet** *masc*

• **Sweet**

afters NOUN PL le **dessert** *masc*

apple tart NOUN la **tarte aux pommes** *fem*

biscuit NOUN le **gâteau sec** *masc*

bubble gum NOUN le **chewing-gum** *masc*

cake NOUN le **gâteau** *masc*

candyfloss NOUN la **barbe à papa** *fem*

caramel NOUN le **caramel** *masc*

chewing gum NOUN le **chewing-gum** *masc*

chocolate NOUN le **chocolat** *masc*

cone NOUN le **cornet** *masc*

cream NOUN la **crème** *fem*

cream cake NOUN le **gâteau à la crème** *masc*

custard NOUN la **crème anglaise** *fem*

dessert NOUN le **dessert** *masc*

doughnut NOUN le **beignet** *masc*

flan NOUN la **tarte** *fem*

fruit salad NOUN la **salade de fruits** *fem*

honey NOUN le **miel** *masc*

ice cream NOUN la **glace** *fem*

ice lolly NOUN la **glace à l'eau** *fem*

jam NOUN la **confiture** *fem*

jelly NOUN la **gelée** *fem*

lollipop NOUN la **sucette** *fem*

marmalade NOUN la **confiture d'oranges** *fem*

marzipan NOUN la **pâte d'amandes** *fem*

meringue NOUN la **meringue** *fem*

mince pie NOUN la **tartelette de Noël** *fem*

mousse NOUN la **mousse** *fem*

pancake NOUN la **crêpe** *fem*

popcorn NOUN le **pop-corn** *masc*

pudding NOUN le **dessert** *masc*

rice pudding NOUN le **riz au lait** *masc*

scone NOUN le **scone** *masc*

sponge cake NOUN le **biscuit de Savoie** *masc*

sugar NOUN le **sucre** *masc*

tart NOUN la **tarte** *fem*

toffee NOUN le **caramel** *masc*

trifle NOUN le **diplomate** *masc*

vanilla NOUN la **vanille** *fem*

whipped cream NOUN la **crème fouettée** *fem*

yoghurt NOUN le **yaourt** *masc*

apple NOUN la **pomme** *fem*

aubergine NOUN l' **aubergine** *fem*

avocado NOUN l' **avocat** *masc*

banana NOUN la **banane** *fem*

beetroot NOUN la **betterave rouge** *fem*

blackberry NOUN la **mûre** *fem*

blackcurrant NOUN le **cassis** *masc*

broccoli NOUN les **brocolis** *masc pl*

Brussels sprouts NOUN PL les **choux de Bruxelles** *masc pl*

cabbage NOUN le **chou** *masc*

carrot NOUN la **carotte** *fem*

cauliflower NOUN le **chou-fleur** *masc*

celery NOUN le **céleri** *masc*

cherry NOUN la **cerise** *fem*

coconut NOUN la **noix de coco** *fem*

corn on the cob NOUN l' **épi de maïs** *masc*

courgette NOUN la **courgette** *fem*

cress NOUN le **cresson** *masc*

cucumber NOUN le **concombre** *masc*

currant NOUN le **raisin sec** *masc*

gooseberry NOUN la **groseille à maquereau** *fem*

grapefruit NOUN le **pamplemousse** *masc*

grapes NOUN PL le **raisin** *masc*

green beans NOUN PL les **haricots verts** *masc pl*

leek NOUN le **poireau** *masc*

lemon NOUN le **citron** *masc*

lettuce NOUN la **salade** *fem*

lime NOUN le **citron vert** *masc*

mango NOUN la **mangue** *fem*

melon NOUN le **melon** *masc*

mushrooom NOUN le **champignon** *masc*

onion NOUN l' **oignon** *masc*

orange NOUN l' **orange** *fem*

parsnip NOUN le **panais** *masc*

pea NOUN le **petit pois** *masc*

peach NOUN la **pèche** *fem*

pear NOUN la **poire** *fem*

pepper NOUN le **poivron** *masc*

pineapple NOUN l' **ananas** *masc*

plum NOUN la **prune** *fem*

potato NOUN la **pomme de terre** *fem*

pumpkin NOUN le **potiron** *masc*

radish NOUN le **radis** *masc*

raisin NOUN le **raisin sec** *masc*

raspberry NOUN la **framboise** *fem*

redcurrant NOUN
la **groseille** *fem*

rhubarb NOUN la **rhubarbe**
fem

satsuma NOUN la **satsuma** *fem*

spinach NOUN les **épinards**
masc pl

sprouts NOUN PL les **choux**
de Bruxelles *masc pl*

strawberry NOUN la **fraise**
fem

sultana NOUN le **raisin sec**
masc

sweetcorn NOUN le **maïs**
masc

tangerine NOUN
la **mandarine** *fem*

tomato NOUN la **tomate** *fem*

turnip NOUN le **navet** *masc*

watermelon NOUN
la **pastèque** *fem*

apple juice NOUN le **jus de pomme** *masc*

beer NOUN la **bière** *fem*

black coffee NOUN le **café** *masc*

champagne NOUN le **champagne** *masc*

cider NOUN le **cidre** *masc*

cocoa NOUN le **cacao** *masc*

coffee NOUN le **café** *masc*

Coke® NOUN le **coca** *masc*

decaffeinated coffee NOUN le **café décaféiné** *masc*

drink NOUN la **boisson** *fem*

fruit juice NOUN le **jus de fruits** *masc*

grapefruit juice NOUN le **jus de pamplemousse** *masc*

hot chocolate NOUN le **chocolat chaud** *masc*

juice NOUN le **jus** *masc*

lager NOUN la **bière blonde** *fem*

lemonade NOUN la **limonade** *fem*

milk NOUN le **lait** *masc*

milkshake NOUN le **milk-shake** *masc*

mineral water NOUN l' **eau minérale** *fem*

orange juice NOUN le **jus d'orange** *masc*

pineapple juice NOUN le **jus d'ananas** *masc*

red wine NOUN le **vin rouge** *masc*

shandy NOUN le **panaché** *masc*

soft drink NOUN la **boisson non alcoolisée** *fem*

sparkling wine NOUN le **mousseau** *masc*

tea NOUN le **thé** *masc*

tomato juice NOUN le **jus de tomate** *masc*

tonic NOUN le **Schweppes**® *masc*

water NOUN l' **eau** *fem*

whisky NOUN le **whisky** *masc*

white coffee NOUN le **café au lait** *masc*

white wine NOUN le **vin blanc** *masc*

wine NOUN le **vin** *masc*

armchair NOUN le **fauteuil** *masc*

bath NOUN la **baignoire** *fem*

bed NOUN le **lit** *masc*

bench NOUN le **banc** *masc*

bookcase NOUN la **bibliothèque** *fem*

bookshelf NOUN l' **étagère à livres** *fem*

bunk beds NOUN les **lits superposés** *masc pl*

CD player NOUN la **platine laser** *fem*

chair NOUN la **chaise** *fem*

chest of drawers NOUN la **commode** *fem*

coffee table NOUN la **table basse** *fem*

cooker NOUN la **cuisinière** *fem*

couch NOUN le **canapé** *masc*

cupboard NOUN le **placard** *masc*

curtain NOUN le **rideau** *masc*

cushion NOUN le **coussin** *masc*

deckchair NOUN la **chaise longue** *fem*

dishwasher NOUN le **lave-vaisselle** *masc*

double bed NOUN le **grand lit** *masc*

DVD player NOUN le **lecteur de DVD** *masc*

easy chair NOUN le **fauteuil** *masc*

freezer NOUN le **congélateur** *masc*

fridge NOUN le **frigo** *masc*

microwave oven NOUN le **four à micro-ondes** *masc*

oven NOUN le **four** *masc*

refrigerator NOUN le **réfrigérateur** *masc*

rug NOUN le **tapis** *masc*

settee NOUN le **canapé** *masc*

sink NOUN l' **évier** *masc*

sofa NOUN le **canapé** *masc*

table NOUN la **table** *fem*

television NOUN la **télévision** *fem*

tumble dryer NOUN le **sèche-linge** *masc*

video recorder NOUN le **magnétoscope**

wardrobe NOUN l' **armoire** *fem*

washing machine NOUN la **machine à laver** *fem*

accordion NOUN l' **accordéon** *masc*

bagpipes NOUN PL la **cornemuse** *fem*

bass drum NOUN la **grosse caisse** *fem*

bass guitar NOUN la **guitare basse** *fem*

bassoon NOUN le **basson** *masc*

cello NOUN le **violoncelle** *masc*

clarinet NOUN la **clarinette** *fem*

cornet NOUN le **cornet à pistons** *masc*

double bass NOUN la **contrebasse** *fem*

drum NOUN le **tambour** *masc*

drums NOUN PL la **batterie** *fem*

electric guitar NOUN la **guitare électrique** *fem*

flute NOUN la **flûte** *fem*

guitar NOUN la **guitare** *fem*

horn NOUN le **cor** *masc*

keyboards NOUN PL le **synthétiseur** *masc*

mouth organ NOUN l' **harmonica** *masc*

oboe NOUN le **hautbois** *masc*

organ NOUN l' **orgue** *masc*

percussion NOUN la **percussion** *fem*

piano NOUN le **piano** *masc*

pipes NOUN PL la **cornemuse** *fem*

recorder NOUN la **flûte à bec** *fem*

saxophone NOUN le **saxophone** *masc*

trombone NOUN le **trombone** *masc*

trumpet NOUN la **trompette** *fem*

tuba NOUN le **tuba** *masc*

viola NOUN l' **alto** *masc*

violin NOUN le **violon** *masc*

accountant NOUN
le/la **comptable** *masc/fem*

actor NOUN l' **acteur** *masc*

actress NOUN l' **actrice** *fem*

architect NOUN l' **architecte**
masc/fem

artist NOUN l' **artiste** *masc/fem*

athlete NOUN l' **athlète**
masc/fem

au pair NOUN la **jeune fille**
au pair *fem*

author NOUN l' **auteur** *masc*

baker NOUN le **boulanger**
masc, la **boulangère** *fem*

barmaid NOUN la **barmaid** *fem*

barman NOUN le **barman** *masc*

builder le **maçon** *masc*

bus driver NOUN
le **conducteur d'autobus** *masc*

butcher NOUN le **boucher**
masc

caretaker NOUN le **gardien**
masc, la **gardienne** *fem*

carpenter NOUN
le **charpentier** *masc*

chef NOUN le **chef** *masc*

child minder NOUN
la **nourrice** *fem*

cleaner NOUN
la **femme de ménage** *fem*,
l' **agent d'entretien** *masc*

computer programmer
NOUN le **programmeur** *masc*,
la **programmeuse** *fem*

conductor NOUN le **chef**
d'orchestre *masc*

cook NOUN le **cuisinier** *masc*,
la **cuisinière** *fem*

dancer NOUN le **danseur** *masc*,
la **danseuse** *fem*

dentist NOUN le/la **dentiste**
masc/fem

detective NOUN l' **inspecteur**
de police *masc*

dinner lady NOUN la **dame**
de service *fem*

disc jockey, DJ NOUN
le **disc-jockey** *masc*

doctor NOUN le **médecin** *masc*

dustman NOUN l' **éboueur**
masc

electrician NOUN
l' **électricien** *masc*

engineer NOUN l' **ingénieur**
masc

farmer NOUN l' **agriculteur**
masc, l' **agricultrice** *fem*

film star NOUN la **vedette**
de cinéma *fem*

firefighter NOUN le **pompier**
masc

fisherman NOUN le **pêcheur**
masc

flight attendant NOUN
l' **hôtesse de l'air** *fem*,
le **steward** *masc*

florist NOUN le/la **fleuriste**
masc/fem

footballer NOUN
le **footballeur** *masc*,
la **footballeuse** *fem*

gardener NOUN le **jardinier**
masc

goalkeeper NOUN le **gardien**
de but *masc*

hairdresser NOUN le **coiffeur**
masc, la **coiffeuse** *fem*

headmaster NOUN
le **directeur** *masc*

headmistress NOUN
la **directrice** *fem*

housewife NOUN la **femme**
au foyer *fem*

imam NOUN l' **imam** *masc*

instructor NOUN le **moniteur**
masc, la **monitrice** *fem*

interior designer NOUN
le/la **designer** *masc/fem*

interpreter NOUN l' **interprète**
masc/fem

janitor NOUN le **concierge** *masc*

jockey NOUN le **jockey** *masc*

joiner NOUN le **menuisier** *masc*

journalist NOUN
le/la **journaliste** *masc/fem*

judge NOUN le **juge** *masc*

lawyer NOUN l' **avocat** *masc*,
l' **avocate** *fem*

lecturer NOUN le **professeur**
d'université *masc*

librarian NOUN
le/la **bibliothécaire**
masc/fem

lorry driver NOUN le **routier**
masc

matron NOUN
l' **infirmière-chef** *fem*

mayor NOUN le **maire** *masc*

mechanic NOUN
le **mécanicien** *masc*

midwife NOUN
la **sage-femme** *fem*

milkman NOUN le **laitier**
masc

miner NOUN le **mineur** *masc*

minister NOUN le **pasteur**
masc

model NOUN le **mannequin**
masc

MP NOUN le **député** *masc*

musician NOUN le **musicien**
masc, la **musicienne** *fem*

nanny NOUN la **garde**
d'enfants *fem*

nurse NOUN
l' **infirmier** *masc*,
l' **infirmière** *fem*

optician NOUN l' **opticien**
masc, l' **opticienne** *fem*

painter NOUN le **peintre** *masc*

paperboy NOUN le **livreur de**
journaux *masc*

papergirl NOUN la **livreuse**
de journaux *fem*

pharmacist NOUN
le **pharmacien** *masc*,
la **pharmacienne** *fem*

physiotherapist NOUN
le/la **kinésithérapeute**
masc/fem

pilot NOUN le **pilote** *masc*

plumber NOUN le **plombier**
masc

policeman NOUN le **policier**
masc

policewoman NOUN
la **femme policier** *fem*

pop star NOUN la **pop star** *fem*

postman NOUN le **facteur** *masc*

priest NOUN le **prêtre** *masc*

professor NOUN le **professeur**
d'université *masc*

programmer NOUN
le **programmeur** *masc*,
la **programmeuse** *fem*

rabbi NOUN le **rabbin** *masc*

receptionist NOUN
le/la **réceptionniste** *masc/fem*

rep NOUN le **représentant**
masc, la **représentante** *fem*

reporter NOUN le **reporter**
masc

sailor NOUN le **marin** *masc*

salesman NOUN
le **représentant** *masc*

saleswoman NOUN
la **répresentante** *fem*

scientist NOUN le **chercheur**
masc, la **chercheuse** *fem*

secretary NOUN
le/la **secrétaire** *masc/fem*

security guard NOUN
l' **agent de sécurité** *masc*

shop assistant NOUN
le **vendeur** *masc*, la **vendeuse**
fem

shopkeeper NOUN
le **commerçant** *masc*,
la **commerçante** *fem*

social worker NOUN
l' **assistante sociale** *fem*
le **travailleur social** *masc*

soldier NOUN le **soldat** *masc*

solicitor NOUN l' **avocat**
masc/fem, le **notaire** *masc*

supply teacher NOUN
le **suppléant** *masc*,
la **suppléante** *fem*

surgeon NOUN le **chirurgien**
masc

surveyor NOUN l' **expert en**
bâtiment *masc*

taxi driver NOUN le **chauffeur**
de taxi *masc*

teacher NOUN le **professeur**
des écoles *masc (in primary*
school), le **professeur** *masc*
(in secondary school)

technician NOUN
le **technicien** *masc*
la **technicienne** *fem*

train driver NOUN
le **conducteur de train** *masc*

translator NOUN
le **traducteur** *masc*,
la **traductrice** *fem*

undertaker NOUN
l' **entrepreneur des**
pompes funèbres *masc*

vet NOUN le/la **vétérinaire**
masc/fem

vicar NOUN le **pasteur** *masc*

waiter NOUN le **serveur** *masc*

waitress NOUN la **serveuse**
fem

writer NOUN l' **écrivain** *masc*

aerobics NOUN l' **aérobic** *fem*

athletics NOUN l' **athlétisme** *masc*

badminton NOUN le **badminton** *masc*

baseball NOUN le **base-ball** *masc*

basketball NOUN le **basket** *masc*

bowling NOUN le **bowling** *masc*

boxing NOUN la **boxe** *fem*

cricket NOUN le **cricket** *masc*

cycling NOUN le **cyclisme** *masc*

dancing NOUN la **danse** *fem*

fishing NOUN la **pêche** *fem*

football NOUN le **football** *masc*

golf NOUN le **golf** *masc*

gymnastics NOUN la **gymnastique** *fem*

handball NOUN le **handball** *masc*

high jump NOUN le **saut en hauteur** *masc*

hockey NOUN le **hockey** *masc*

ice hockey NOUN le **hockey sur glace** *masc*

ice-skating NOUN le **patinage sur glace** *masc*

judo NOUN le **judo** *masc*

karate NOUN le **karaté** *masc*

long jump NOUN le **saut en longueur** *masc*

motor racing NOUN la **course automobile** *fem*

mountaineering NOUN l' **alpinisme** *masc*

netball NOUN le **netball** *masc*

pool NOUN le **billard américain** *masc*

riding NOUN l' **équitation** *fem*

roller-blading NOUN le **roller** *masc*

roller-skating NOUN le **patin à roulettes** *masc*

rugby NOUN le **rugby** *masc*

running NOUN la **course** *fem*

sailing NOUN la **voile** *fem*

skateboarding NOUN le **skateboard** *masc*

skating NOUN le **patin à glace** *masc*

skiing NOUN le **ski** *masc*

snooker NOUN le **billard** *masc*

soccer NOUN le **football** *masc*

squash NOUN le **squash** *masc*

surfing NOUN le **surf** *masc*

swimming NOUN la **natation** *fem*

table tennis NOUN le **ping-pong** *masc*

tennis NOUN le **tennis** *masc*

tenpin bowling NOUN le **bowling** *masc*

trampolining NOUN le **trampoline** *masc*

volleyball NOUN le **volley-ball** *masc*

water-skiing NOUN le **ski nautique** *masc*

windsurfing NOUN la **planche à voile** *fem*

wrestling NOUN la **lutte** *fem*

absent ADJECTIVE **absent** *masc*, **absente** *fem*

assembly hall NOUN la **salle de réunion** *fem*

atlas NOUN l' **atlas** *masc*

bell NOUN la **sonnerie** *fem*

Biro® NOUN le **bic**® *masc*

blackboard NOUN le **tableau** *masc*

board NOUN le **tableau** *masc*

book NOUN le **livre** *masc*

break time NOUN la **récréation** *fem*

calculator NOUN la **calculatrice** *fem*

canteen NOUN la **cantine** *fem*

cassette player NOUN le **lecteur de cassettes** *masc*

CD player NOUN la **platine laser** *fem*

chair NOUN la **chaise** *fem*

chalk NOUN la **craie** *fem*

chart NOUN le **tableau** *masc*

class NOUN la **classe** *fem*

classroom NOUN la **classe** *fem*

classroom assistant NOUN l' **aide-éducateur** *masc*, l' **aide-éducatrice** *fem*

cloakroom NOUN le **vestiaire** *masc*

computer NOUN l' **ordinateur** *masc*

computer room NOUN la **salle d'informatique** *fem*

corridor NOUN le **couloir** *masc*

curriculum NOUN le **programme** *masc*

deputy head NOUN le **directeur adjoint** *masc*, la **directrice adjointe** *fem*

desk NOUN le **pupitre** *masc*

diagram NOUN le **diagramme** *masc*

dictionary NOUN le **dictionnaire** *masc*

dining room NOUN le **réfectoire** *masc*

dormitory NOUN le **dortoir** *masc*

drawing NOUN le **dessin** *masc*

drawing pin NOUN la **punaise** *fem*

essay NOUN le **devoir** *masc*

exam NOUN l' **examen** *masc*

exercise NOUN l' **exercice** *masc*

exercise book NOUN le **cahier** *masc*

felt-tip pen NOUN le **stylo-feutre** *masc*

folder NOUN la **chemise** *fem*

GCSE NOUN le **brevet des collèges** *masc*

general knowledge NOUN les **connaissances générales** *fem pl*

grammar NOUN la **grammaire** *fem*

gym hall NOUN la **salle de gym** *fem*

gym kit NOUN les **affaires de gym** *fem pl*

half term NOUN les **petites vacances** *fem pl*

headmaster NOUN le **directeur** *masc*

headmistress NOUN la **directrice** *fem*

homework NOUN les **devoirs** *masc pl*

interval NOUN la **récréation** *fem*

jotter NOUN le **cahier** *masc*

junior school NOUN l' **école primaire** *fem*

language laboratory NOUN le **laboratoire de langues** *masc*

lesson NOUN la **leçon** *fem*

library NOUN la **bibliothèque** *fem*

lower sixth NOUN la **première** *fem*

mouse NOUN la **souris** *fem*

mouse mat NOUN le **tapis de souris** *masc*

office NOUN le **secrétariat** *masc*

overhead projector NOUN le **rétroprojecteur** *masc*

packed lunch NOUN le **casse-croûte** *masc*

page NOUN la **page** *fem*

pen NOUN le **stylo** *masc*

pencil NOUN le **crayon** *masc*

pencil case NOUN la **trousse** *fem*

pencil sharpener NOUN le **taille-crayon** *masc*

photocopier NOUN la **photocopieuse** *fem*

photocopy NOUN la **photocopie** *fem*

playground NOUN la **cour de récréation** *fem*

playtime NOUN la **récréation** *fem*

poster NOUN le **poster** *masc*

primary school NOUN l' **école primaire** *fem*

printer NOUN l' **imprimante** *fem*

projector NOUN le **projecteur** *masc*

pupil NOUN l' **élève** *masc/fem*

register NOUN le **cahier d'appel** *masc*

registration NOUN l' **appel** *masc*

rubber NOUN la **gomme** *fem*

ruler NOUN la **règle** *fem*

satchel NOUN le **cartable** *masc*

school NOUN l' **école** *fem*

school bag NOUN le **cartable** *masc*

schoolboy NOUN l' **écolier** *masc*

schoolchildren NOUN
les **écoliers** *masc pl*

schoolgirl NOUN l' **écolière**
fem

school holidays NOUN
les **vacances scolaires** *fem pl*

school uniform NOUN
l' **uniforme scolaire** *masc*

secondary school NOUN
le **collège** *masc (for 11-15 year olds)*, le **lycée** *masc (for 15-18 year olds)*

sharpener NOUN
le **taille-crayon** *masc*

teacher NOUN le **professeur
des écoles** *masc (in primary school)*, le **professeur** *masc (in secondary school)*

team NOUN l' **équipe** *fem*

test NOUN le **test** *masc*

textbook NOUN le **manuel**
masc

toilets NOUN les **toilettes**
fem pl

upper sixth NOUN
la **terminale** *fem*

whiteboard NOUN le **tableau**
masc

worksheet NOUN la **feuille
d'exercices** *fem*

• School subjects

art NOUN les **arts plastiques**
masc pl

biology NOUN la **biologie** *fem*

chemistry NOUN la **chimie**
fem

citizenship NOUN
la **citoyenneté** *fem*

design and technology
NOUN la **technologie** *fem*

drama NOUN l' **art
dramatique** *masc*

English NOUN l' **anglais** *masc*

French NOUN le **français** *masc*

games NOUN PL le **sport** *masc*

geography NOUN
la **géographie** *fem*

gym NOUN la **gym** *fem*

history NOUN l' **histoire** *fem*

ICT NOUN l' **informatique** *fem*

literacy NOUN l' **apprentissage
de la lecture** *masc*

literature NOUN
la **littérature** *fem*

maths NOUN les **maths** *fem pl*

music NOUN la **musique** *fem*

PE NOUN l' **EPS** *fem*

physics NOUN la **physique** *fem*

RE NOUN l' **éducation
religieuse** *fem*

science NOUN les **sciences**
fem pl

• **School classes**

Reception year/ Primary 1 NOUN les **moyens** *masc pl*

Year 1/Primary 2 NOUN les **grands** *masc pl*

Year 2/Primary 3 NOUN le **CP** *masc*

Year 3/Primary 4 NOUN le **CE1** *masc*

Year 4/Primary 5 NOUN le **CE2** *masc*

Year 5/Primary 6 NOUN le **CM1** *masc*

Year 6/Primary 7 NOUN le **CM2** *masc*

Year 7/S1 NOUN la **sixième** *fem*

1	un(une)	16	seize	81	quatre-vingt-un(-une)
2	deux	17	dix-sept	82	quatre-vingt-deux
3	trois	18	dix-huit		
4	quatre	19	dix-neuf	90	quatre-vingt-dix
5	cinq	20	vingt	91	quatre-vingt-onze
6	six	21	vingt et un(une)	100	cent
7	sept	22	vingt-deux	101	cent un(une)
8	huit	30	trente	200	deux cents
9	neuf	40	quarante	250	deux cent cinquante
10	dix	50	cinquante		
11	onze	60	soixante		
12	douze	70	soixante-dix		
13	treize	71	soixante et onze	1,000	mille
14	quatorze	72	soixante-douze	2,000	deux mille
15	quinze	80	quatre-vingts	1,000,000	un million

Quelle heure est-il?
What time is it?

Il est...
It's...

une heure
one o'clock

une heure dix
ten past one

une heure et quart
quarter past one

une heure et demie
half past one

deux heures moins vingt
twenty to two

deux heures moins le quart
quarter to two

À quelle heure...?

What time...?

à minuit
at midnight

à midi
at midday

à une heure (de l'après-midi)
at one o'clock
(in the afternoon)

à huit heures
(du soir)
at eight o'clock
(at night)

à 11h15 or **onze heures quinze**
at quarter past eleven
(in the morning)

à 20h45 or **vingt heures quarante-cinq**
at quarter to nine
(at night)

In French, the ending of the verb varies according to the person – ie, the form of the verb that goes with **je** is different from the form that goes with **nous**, **vous** etc.

Here are the present tenses of some common verbs, with the endings highlighted.

We have also shown some useful phrases which require other tenses. As the examples make clear, a French verb may be translated in several different ways, depending on the context.

A verb form that is of particular interest to teachers is the imperative. In English, **Look!**, **Listen!**, **Don't do that!** can be used to a single child, or to the whole class, but in French there are always two different forms of the verb, depending on whether one, or more than one person is being spoken to. The plural form always ends in **-ez**, and this is also the polite form used to an adult. This dictionary contains many examples of imperatives that will be of use to teachers.

The dictionary also contains an explanation of the difference between the two words for **you** (**tu** and **vous**) – see the entry for **you**.

Some examples are given here to illustrate the past tense, and the dictionary includes translations for past tenses that children are very likely to want, such as **I got**, **I went**, **I've broken**, **it was** etc. Translations for these will be found at the entries for **get**, **go**, **break**, **be**.

regarder *to look*

je regard**e**	**Regarde**-moi, Emmanuelle. *Look at me Emmanuelle.*
tu regard**es**	**Regardez**, les enfants! *Look, children!*
il regard**e**	**Regardez** le tableau! *Look at the board.*
elle regard**e**	Je **regarde** la télé le samedi matin. *I watch TV on*
nous regard**ons**	*Saturday morning.*
vous regard**ez**	Il **a regardé** sa montre. *He looked at his watch.*
ils regard**ent**	Elle aime **regarder** des films. *She likes watching films.*
elles regard**ent**	

finir *to finish*

je fin**is**	J'**ai fini**! *I've finished!*
tu fin**is**	**Finis** tes devoirs! *Finish your homework!*
il fin**it**	Elle **a fini** sa soupe. *She's finished her soup.*
elle fin**it**	Il n'**a** pas **fini** le livre. *He hasn't finished the book.*
nous fin**issons**	Elle va **finir** ses devoirs demain. *She's going to finish*
vous fin**issez**	*her homework tomorrow.*
ils fin**issent**	
elles fin**issent**	

attendre *to wait*

j'attend**s**	**Attends**-moi! *Wait for me!*
tu attend**s**	**Attendez** ici, les enfants! *Wait here, children!*
il attend	J'**ai attendu** deux heures. *I waited for two hours.*
elle attend	Il m'**a attendu** à la gare. *He waited for me at the*
nous attend**ons**	*station.*
vous attend**ez**	Je vais **attendre** ici. *I'm going to wait here.*
ils attend**ent**	
elles attend**ent**	

avoir *to have*

j'ai	Je n'**ai** pas d'argent. *I haven't got any money.*
tu as	J'**ai** les cheveux longs. *I've got long hair.*
il a	Elle **a** un vélo. *She's got a bike.*
elle a	Il **a eu** un accident. *He's had an accident.*
nous av**ons**	J'**ai eu** beaucoup de cadeaux. *I got lots of presents.*
vous av**ez**	Quel âge **as**-tu? *How old are you?*
ils ont	Elle **a** cinq ans. *She is five.*
elles ont	Il y **a** un bon film à la télé. *There's a good film on TV.*
	Qu'est-ce qu'il y **a**? *What's the matter?*
	Je n'**ai** pas fait mes devoirs. *I haven't done my homework.*
	J'**ai** faim. *I'm hungry.*
	J'**avais** faim. *I was hungry.*

être *to be*

je suis	Ne **sois** pas effronté! *Don't be cheeky!*
tu es	Je **suis** fatigué. *I'm tired.*
il est	Tu **es** en retard. *You're late.*
elle est	C'**est** moi. *It's me.*
nous sommes	Elle **est** anglaise. *She's English.*
vous êtes	C'**était** difficile. *It was difficult.*
ils sont	J'**étais** content. *I was happy.*
elles sont	Nous **sommes** les gagnants! *We're the winners!*
	Vous **êtes** prêts? *Are you ready?*
	Nous **sommes** le premier mai. *It's the first of May.*
	Mes parents **sont** au travail. *My parents are at work.*
	Je **suis** allé à Paris. *I went to Paris.*
	Où **es-tu** allé? *Where did you go?*

aller *to go*

je vais	Je ne **vais** pas à l'école le samedi. *I don't go to school on Saturday.*
tu vas	
il va	Je **vais** gagner. *I'm going to win.*
elle va	Où **vas**-tu? *Where are you going?*
nous all**ons**	**Vas**-y! *Go on!*
vous all**ez**	Ça **va**? *Are you okay?*
ils vont	Il **va** pleuvoir. *It's going to rain.*
elles vont	Je **suis allé** chez Luc. *I went to Luc's house.*
	Où **es**-tu **allé** hier? *Where did you go yesterday?*
	Nous **sommes allés** en France. *We went to France.*

faire *to do*

je fais	Je **fais** beaucoup de vélo. *I do a lot of cycling.*
tu fais	Ne **fais** pas ça, chéri. *Don't do that, dear.*
il fait	Qu'est-ce que tu **fais**? *What are you doing?*
elle fait	Mon frère **fait** du judo. *My brother does judo.*
nous fais**ons**	Deux et deux **font** quatre. *Two and two make four.*
vous faites	**Faites** les gestes! *Do the actions!*
ils font	Je n'**ai** pas **fait** mes devoirs. *I haven't done my homework.*
elles font	Qui **a fait** ça? *Who did that?*
	Quel temps **fait**-il? *What's the weather like?*
	Il **fait** chaud. *It's hot.*
	Il **faisait** froid. *It was cold.*
	Je **fais** mon lit tous les matins. *I make my bed every morning.*
	Ça ne **fait** rien. *It doesn't matter.*
	Il va **faire** beau demain. *It's going to be nice weather tomorrow.*

313

s'appeler *to be called*

je m'appell**e**	Je **m'appelle** Amélie. *My name is Amélie.*
tu t'appell**es**	Comment ça **s'appelle**? *What is it called?*
il s'appell**e**	Comment tu **t'appelles**? *What are you called?*
elle s'appell**e**	Vous **vous appelez** comment? *What are you called?*
nous nous appel**ons**	Tes frères **s'appellent** comment? *What are your*
vous vous appel**ez**	*brothers called?*
ils s'appell**ent**	
elles s'appell**ent**	

pouvoir *can*

je peux	Je ne **peux** pas venir. *I can't come.*
tu peux	Vous **pouvez** vous asseoir là. *You can sit there.*
il peut	Tu **peux** te pousser un peu? *Could you move over a bit?*
elle peut	Qui **peut** répondre à la question? *Who can answer*
nous pouv**ons**	*the question?*
vous pouv**ez**	Je **peux** avoir un verre d'eau? *Could I have a glass*
ils peuv**ent**	*of water?*
elles peuv**ent**	Tu **pourras** venir? *Will you be able to come?*

vouloir *to want*

je veux	Qu'est-ce que tu **veux**, Marie? *What do you want,*
tu veux	*Marie?*
il veut	Qu'est-ce que vous **voulez**, les garçons? *What do*
elle veut	*you want, boys?*
nous voul**ons**	Vous **voulez** du café, Madame? *Would you like some*
vous voul**ez**	*coffee, Miss?*
ils veul**ent**	Tu **veux** un bonbon, Louis? *Would you like a sweet,*
elles veul**ent**	*Louis?*
	Je **voudrais** une glace. *I'd like an ice cream.*
	Qu'est-ce que ça **veut** dire? *What does that mean?*

la gare

Ma ville

l'hôpital (masc)

la rivière

HÔPITAL

le pont

la poste

le musée

la pharmacie

la place

l'église (fem)

la banque

le marché

le cinéma

ODÉON

la rue

la cour

la cour

le trottoir

l'école (fem)

le supermarché

les feux (masc pl)

ÉCOLE

315

à la maison

l'immeuble (masc)

l'escalier (masc)

le toit

le troisième étage

le deuxième étage

le premier étage

le rez-de-chaussée

la porte

la fenêtre   l'ascenseur (masc)

l'entrée (fem)

le jardin

la clé

la plante

MA CHAMBRE

le balcon

ma chambre

l'armoire (fem)

le rideau

l'ordinateur (masc)

le livre

le bureau

le jouet

la chaise

le tiroir

le jeu électronique

la bibliothèque

le réveil

les magazines (masc pl)

le lit

les chaussons (masc pl)

la couette

l'oreiller (masc)

le pyjama

la guitare

ma fête d'anniversaire

la bougie

le ballon

le gâteau

la barbe à papa

la paille

la fourchette

le verre

la serviette

l'assiette (fem)

la cuillère

le jus de fruits

les chips (fem pl)

la limonade

l'appareil photo (masc)

le cadeau

les bonbons (masc pl)

au parc

le manège
le cerf-volant
le toboggan
la balançoire
l'herbe (fem)
le skateboard
le ballon
la fleur
les rollers (masc pl)
boissons fraîches
la glace
l'étang (masc)
le banc
le cygne
le canard
le vélo

319

le papillon

à la montagne

la piste de ski

la neige

le skieur

la luge

le remonte-pente

le patin à glace

le sac à dos

le bonhomme de neige

la truite

le lac

la biche

les chaussures de marche (fem pl)

la vache

la chèvre

à la plage

le soleil

la mouette

la vague

les palmes (fem pl)

le poisson

le rocher

la nageuse

la mer

le maître nageur

la bouée

le parasol

le sable

l'étoile de mer (fem)

le crabe

les lunettes de soleil (fem pl)

le maillot de bain

la crème solaire

le château de sable

le seau et la pelle

le coquillage

dans la forêt

le hibou

l'écureuil (masc)

l'arbre

le renard

le sapin

la feuille

le cerf

le trèfle

le lapin

le champignon

le ruisseau

la châtaigne

la framboise

la fourmi

le hérisson

322

English - French

A a

a ARTICLE

> *Language tip*
> Use **un** for masculine nouns, **une**
> *for feminine nouns.*

un *masc*
  a book
  un livre
une *fem*
  a girl
  une fille
  ten kilometres an hour
  dix kilomètres à l'heure

able ADJECTIVE
  Will you be able to come?
  Est-ce que tu pourras venir?
  I won't be able to come.
  Je ne pourrai pas venir.

about

> **about** *can be an adverb or a*
> *preposition.*

A ADVERB
  environ *(approximately)*
  about sixteen girls
  environ seize filles
  about fourteen euros
  environ quatorze euros
  at about eleven o'clock
  vers onze heures
B PREPOSITION
  sur *(concerning)*
  about myself
  sur moi
  a letter about yourself
  une lettre sur toi
  a song about animals
  une chanson sur les animaux
  How about a game of cards?
  Tu veux jouer aux cartes?

above PREPOSITION
  1 au-dessus de *(higher than)*
  Hold the ball above your heads.
  Tenez la balle au-dessus de
  votre tête.
  2 plus de *(more than)*
  above thirty degrees
  plus de trente degrés

abroad ADVERB
  à l'étranger
  We're going abroad this year.
  Nous partons à l'étranger cette
  année.

absent ADJECTIVE
  absent *masc*
  absente *fem*
  Who's absent today?
  Qui est absent aujourd'hui?

absurd ADJECTIVE
  absurde
  That's absurd!
  C'est absurde!

academy NOUN
  le **collège** *masc*

accent NOUN
  l' **accent** *masc*
  He's got a good accent.
  Il a un bon accent.

accident NOUN
  l' **accident** *masc*
  It was an accident.
  C'était un accident.

ace NOUN
  l' **as** *masc*
  the ace of
  hearts
  l'as de cœur

ache VERB
My leg's aching.
J'ai mal à la jambe.

across PREPOSITION
de l'autre côté de
It's across the road.
C'est de l'autre côté de la rue.

act VERB
jouer
He's acting in a play.
Il joue dans une pièce.

activity NOUN
l' **activité** fem
outdoor activities
les activités de plein air

actor NOUN
l' **acteur** masc

actress NOUN
l' **actrice** fem

actually ADVERB
en fait
Actually it's good fun.
En fait, c'est bien amusant.

AD ABBREVIATION
ap. J.-C.
in 800 AD
en 800 ap. J.-C.

add VERB
ajouter
Add some sugar.
Ajoutez du sucre.

add up VERB
additionner
Add the figures up.
Additionnez les chiffres.

address NOUN
l' **adresse** fem
What's your address?
Quelle est votre adresse?

What's your address, Charlotte?
Quelle est ton adresse, Charlotte?

Language tip
address in English is spelled with a double **d**. The French word has only one **d**, and an extra **e** on the end.

adjective NOUN
l' **adjectif** masc

admission NOUN
l' **entrée** fem
'admission free'
'entrée gratuite'

adopted ADJECTIVE
adopté masc
adoptée fem

adult NOUN
l' **adulte** masc/fem
two adults and one child
deux adultes et un enfant

advantage NOUN
l' **avantage** masc
It's an advantage to be able to speak French.
C'est un avantage de savoir parler français.

adventure NOUN
l' **aventure** fem
Harry has lots of adventures.
Harry a beaucoup d'aventures.

advice NOUN
les **conseils** masc pl
Could you give me some advice?
Vous pouvez me donner des conseils?

aerobics PL NOUN
l' **aérobic** fem
I'm going to aerobics tonight.
Je vais au cours d'aérobic ce soir.

aeroplane NOUN
l' **avion** masc
on an aeroplane
en avion

this afternoon cet après-midi **in the afternoon** l'après-midi

affectionate ADJECTIVE
affectueux masc
affectueuse fem
My cat is very affectionate.
Mon chat est très affectueux

afraid ADJECTIVE
to be afraid of ...
avoir peur de ...
I'm afraid of spiders.
J'ai peur des araignées.
Are you afraid of the dark?
Tu as peur du noir?

after PREPOSITION
après
after me
après moi
after you
après toi
after lunch
après le déjeuner

afternoon NOUN
l' **après-midi** masc/fem
In the morning or in the afternoon?
Le matin ou l'après-midi?
3 o'clock in the afternoon
trois heures de l'après-midi
I'm playing football on Saturday afternoon.
Je joue au foot samedi après-midi.

afters NOUN
le **dessert** masc
What do you want for afters?
Qu'est-ce que tu veux comme dessert?

again ADVERB
1 encore
Tamsin has won again.
Tamsin a encore gagné.
2 encore une fois
(one more time)
Try again!
Essaie encore une fois!

Language tip
In French, you can also add **re-** to verbs, to show you're doing something again. This is the same as English, for example, **re**paint, **re**write.

Let's begin again.
Recommençons.
Can you tell me again?
Tu peux me le redire?
Do it again!
Refais-le!

against PREPOSITION
contre
Don't put your chair against the wall.
Ne mets pas ta chaise contre le mur.

English French

a
b
c
d
e
f
g
h
i
j
k
l
m
n
o
p
q
r
s
t
u
v
w
x
y
z

age NOUN
l' **âge** *masc*
Age: twelve
Âge: douze ans
your age
ton âge
at the age of thirteen
à l'âge de treize ans
Write your name and age.
Écris ton nom et ton âge.
I am the same age as you.
J'ai le même âge que toi.

ago ADVERB
two days ago
il y a deux jours
a week ago
il y a une semaine
a month ago
il y a un mois
a long time ago
il y a longtemps

agree VERB
être d'accord
I agree!
Je suis d'accord!
I agree with Carol.
Je suis d'accord avec Carol.

ahead ADVERB
devant
Look straight ahead!
Regardez droit devant vous!
The red team is five points ahead.
L'équipe rouge a cinq points d'avance.

air NOUN
l' **air** *masc*
Throw the ball into the air.
Lance le ballon en l'air.
I prefer to travel by air.
Je préfère voyager en avion.

air-conditioned ADJECTIVE
climatisé *masc*
climatisée *fem*

air hostess NOUN
l' **hôtesse de l'air** *fem*

airmail NOUN
by airmail
par avion

airport NOUN
l' **aéroport** *masc*

alarm clock NOUN
le **réveil** *masc*

album NOUN
l' **album** *masc*

alcohol NOUN
l' **alcool** *masc*
I don't like alcohol.
Je n'aime pas l'alcool.

A levels PL NOUN
le **baccalauréat** *masc*
My brother is taking his A levels.
Mon frère passe le baccalauréat.

> **Did you know…?**
> In France, the **baccalauréat** (or **bac** for short) is the equivalent of A levels in the UK.

alien NOUN
l' **extra-terrestre** *masc*

alive ADJECTIVE
vivant *masc*
vivante *fem*
They're still alive.
Ils sont encore vivants.

all ADJECTIVE, PRONOUN, ADVERB
tout *masc*
toute *fem*
> **all the time**
> tout le temps
> **all day**
> toute la journée
> **all my friends**
> tous mes amis
> **all the girls**
> toutes les filles
> **The score is five all**.
> Le score est de cinq partout.

> **Is that all?**
> C'est tout?

allergic ADJECTIVE
allergique
> **I'm allergic to eggs.**
> Je suis allergique aux œufs.

allergy NOUN
l'**allergie** *fem*
> **Have you got any allergies?**
> Tu as des allergies?

allowed ADJECTIVE
> **It's not allowed.**
> Ce n'est pas permis.

all right ADVERB
1 **pas mal** *(not bad)*
> **Great, or just all right?**
> Super, ou seulement pas mal?
> **Do you like school? —
> It's all right.**
> Tu aimes l'école? — C'est pas mal.
2 **d'accord** *(when agreeing)*
> **I'd like a coke. — All right.**
> Je voudrais un coca. — D'accord.

> **Are you all right?**
> Ça va?
> **Is that all right?**
> Ça va?

almost ADVERB
presque
> **Are you ready? — Almost.**
> Tu es prêt? — Presque.

alone ADJECTIVE, ADVERB
seul *masc*
seule *fem*
> **She lives alone.**
> Elle habite seule.
> **Leave my things alone!**
> Ne touche pas à mes affaires!
> **Luc, leave Pierre alone!**
> Luc, laisse Pierre tranquille!

> *Language tip*
> **le** *can mean 'him' and* **la** *can mean 'her'.*

> **Leave him alone!**
> Laisse-le tranquille!
> **Leave her alone!**
> Laisse-la tranquille!

along PREPOSITION
le long de
> **a walk along the beach**
> une promenade le long de
> la plage

aloud ADVERB
à haute voix
> **Read the words aloud,
> children.**
> Lisez les mots à haute voix,
> les enfants.
> **Read the words aloud,
> Marcel.**
> Lis les mots à haute voix, Marcel.

alphabet NOUN
l'**alphabet** *masc*

alphabetical order NOUN
> **in alphabetical order**
> par ordre alphabétique

Alps PL NOUN
les **Alpes** *fem pl*

already ADVERB
déjà
Have you finished already?
Tu as déjà fini?

also ADVERB
aussi

alternate ADJECTIVE
on alternate days
tous les deux jours

alternative NOUN
le **choix** *masc*
You have no alternative.
Tu n'as pas le choix.

altogether ADVERB
en tout
That's £20 altogether.
Ça fait vingt livres en tout.

always ADVERB
toujours
The bus is always late.
Le bus est toujours en retard.

am VERB ▷*see* **be**

a.m. ABBREVIATION
du matin
at 4 a.m.
à quatre heures du matin

amazing ADJECTIVE
1 **incroyable** *(surprising)*
That's amazing!
C'est incroyable!
2 **exceptionnel** *masc*
exceptionnelle *fem*
(excellent)
Vivian's an amazing cook.
Vivian est une cuisinière
exceptionnelle.

amber ADJECTIVE
an amber light
un feu orange

ambition NOUN
l' **ambition** *fem*
It's my ambition.
C'est mon ambition.

ambulance NOUN
l' **ambulance** *fem*

America NOUN
l' **Amérique** *fem*
We're going to America.
Nous allons en Amérique.

American

American *can be an adjective or a noun.*

A ADJECTIVE
américain *masc*
américaine *fem*
American food
la cuisine américaine

He's American.
Il est américain.
She's American.
Elle est américaine.

B NOUN
l' **Américain** *masc*
l' **Américaine** *fem*
the Americans
les Américains

Language tip
américain *is not spelled with a
capital letter except when it means
an American person.*

amount NOUN
1 la **somme** *fem (sum of money)*
a large amount of money
une grosse somme d'argent
2 la **quantité** *fem (quantity)*
a huge amount of rice
une énorme quantité de riz

amusement arcade NOUN
la **salle de jeux électroniques** *fem*

an ARTICLE

> *Language tip*
>
> *Use* **un** *for masculine nouns,* **une** *for feminine nouns.*

un *masc*
an animal
un animal
une *fem*
an apple
une pomme

and CONJUNCTION
et
you and me
toi et moi
Two and two are four.
Deux et deux
font quatre.

angel NOUN
l' **ange** *masc*
You're an angel!
Tu es un ange!

angry ADJECTIVE
to get angry
se fâcher
Mum gets angry if I'm late.
Maman se fâche si je suis en retard.

animal NOUN
l' **animal** *masc* (PL les **animaux**)

anniversary NOUN
l' **anniversaire** *masc*
my parents' wedding anniversary
l'anniversaire de mariage de mes parents

Happy anniversary!
Joyeux anniversaire de mariage!

announcement NOUN
l' **annonce** *fem*
an important announcement
une annonce importante

anorak NOUN
l' **anorak** *masc*
my new anorak
mon nouvel anorak

another ADJECTIVE
un autre *masc*
une autre *fem*
Would you like another sandwich?
Tu veux un autre sandwich?
Do you want another card?
Tu veux une autre carte?

answer

> **answer** *can be a verb or a noun.*

A VERB
répondre
Inès, you have to answer yes or no.
Inès, tu dois répondre par oui ou par non.
Think before you answer.
Réfléchissez avant de répondre.
to answer a question
répondre à une question

Who can answer the question?
Qui peut répondre à la question?
Can you answer my question?
Peux-tu répondre à ma question?
B NOUN
la **réponse** *fem*
the right answer
la bonne réponse

Language tip
The English words 'respond' and 'response' are related to **répondre** and **réponse** in French.

ant NOUN
la **fourmi**
fem

anthem NOUN
the national anthem
l'hymne national

any ADJECTIVE

Language tip
any can be **du**, **de la**, **de l'** or **des**, in the same way that 'the' can be 'le', 'la', 'l' or 'les'.

du
Do you want any bread?
Voulez-vous du pain?
de la
Would you like any salad?
Voulez-vous de la salade?
de l'
Have you got any mineral water?
Avez-vous de l'eau minérale?
des
Have you got any brothers or sisters?
Tu as des frères et sœurs?

Language tip
In negative phrases, the French for **any** is **de** or **d'**.

de
I don't want any bread.
Je ne veux pas de pain.
d'
I haven't got any mineral water.
Je n'ai pas d'eau minérale.
I don't want any more.
Je n'en veux plus.

Have you got any money?
Tu as de l'argent?
Have you got any pets?
Tu as des animaux?
I haven't got any pets.
Je n'ai pas d'animaux.

anybody PRONOUN
1 **quelqu'un** *(in question)*
Does anybody want a sweet?
Quelqu'un veut un bonbon?
2 **personne** *(in negative phrases)*
I can't see anybody.
Je ne vois personne.

anyone PRONOUN
1 **quelqu'un** *(in question)*
Does anyone want to try?
Quelqu'un veut essayer?
2 **personne** *(in negative phrases)*
I can't see anyone.
Je ne vois personne.

anything PRONOUN
1 **quelque chose** *(in question)*
Do you want anything to eat?
Tu veux manger quelque chose?
2 **rien** *(in negative phrases)*
I don't want anything.
Je ne veux rien.

apart ADVERB
Stand with your feet apart.
Tenez-vous debout, les pieds
écartés.

apartment NOUN
l' **appartement** masc

Language tip
What are the two differences in
spelling between the French word
and the English word?

apostrophe NOUN
l' **apostrophe** fem
Don't forget the apostrophe!
N'oubliez pas l'apostrophe!

app NOUN
l'**appli** fem (for phone)

apple NOUN
la **pomme** fem
a big red apple
une grosse pomme rouge

apple juice NOUN
le **jus de pomme** masc

apple tart NOUN
la **tarte aux pommes** fem

appointment NOUN
le **rendez-vous** masc
**I've got a dental
appointment.**
J'ai rendez-vous chez le dentiste.

April NOUN
avril masc
April or May?
Avril ou mai?
My birthday's in April.
Mon anniversaire est en avril.

in April
en avril
the ninth of April
le neuf avril

Language tip
In French, the months are not
spelled with a capital letter.

April Fool NOUN
le **poisson d'avril** masc

Did you know…?
Pinning a paper fish to somebody's
back is a traditional April Fool joke
in France.

April Fool's Day NOUN
le **premier avril** masc

apron NOUN
le **tablier** masc
a white apron
un tablier blanc

are VERB ▷see be

area NOUN
la **région** fem
She lives in the Paris area.
Elle habite dans la région
parisienne.

argue VERB
se disputer
Stop arguing!
Arrêtez de vous disputer!

arm NOUN
le **bras** masc
Swing your arms!
Balancez les bras!

armchair NOUN
le **fauteuil** masc

army NOUN
l' **armée** fem
**He's in the
army.**
Il est dans
l'armée.

around PREPOSITION
1 **vers** (date, time)
I go to bed around ten o'clock.
Je me couche vers vingt-deux heures.
2 (nearby)
around here
près d'ici
Is there a chemist's around here?
Il y a une pharmacie près d'ici?

arrive VERB
arriver
What time does the train arrive?
Le train arrive à quelle heure?

arrow NOUN
la **flèche** fem
Follow the arrows.
Suivez les flèches.

art NOUN
les **arts plastiques** masc pl (at school)
Art is my favourite subject.
Ma matière préférée, c'est les arts plastiques.

art gallery NOUN
le **musée** masc
The art gallery is closed.
Le musée est fermé.

artist
NOUN
l' **artiste**
masc/fem

as CONJUNCTION, PREPOSITION
puisque (since)

Alice, as it's your birthday you can choose.
Alice, tu peux choisir, puisque c'est ton anniversaire.
He works as a waiter in the holidays.
Il travaille comme serveur pendant les vacances.
as ... as
aussi ... que
Pierre's as tall as Michel.
Pierre est aussi grand que Michel.
Write to me as soon as possible.
Écris-moi dès que possible.

ashamed ADJECTIVE
to be ashamed
avoir honte
You should be ashamed of yourself!
Tu devrais avoir honte!

ashtray NOUN
le **cendrier** masc

Asian

Asian can be an adjective or a noun.

A ADJECTIVE
indo-pakistanais masc
indo-pakistanaise fem
He's Asian.
Il est indo-pakistanais.
She's Asian.
Elle est indo-pakistanaise.
B NOUN
l' **Indo-Pakistanais** masc
l' **Indo-Pakistanaise** fem

Language tip

indo-pakistanais is not spelled with a capital letter except when it means an Asian person.

ask VERB

1 demander

If you need help, ask!
Si tu as besoin d'aide, demande!

Ask his name.
Demande-lui son nom.

Ask her age.
Demande-lui son âge.

Language tip

When **ask** is followed by a person, use **demander à**.

Ask your penfriend.
Demande à ton correspondant.

Ask your friends.
Demande à tes amis.

Language tip

to ask for is also **demander**.

Ask for some chips and a drink.
Demandez des frites et une boisson.

Who wants to ask a question?
Qui veut poser une question?

Ask the question.
Pose la question.

2 inviter (invite)

Are you going to ask Matthew to the party?
Tu vas inviter Matthew à la fête?

asleep ADJECTIVE

to be asleep
dormir

Are you asleep?
Tu dors?

assembly NOUN

Did you know...?

There is no assembly in French schools.

assistant NOUN

1 le **vendeur** masc
la **vendeuse** fem (shop assistant)

Ask the assistant.
Demande à la vendeuse.

2 l' **assistant** masc
l' **assistante** fem (helper)

asthma NOUN

l' **asthme** masc

I've got asthma.
J'ai de l'asthme.

astronomy NOUN

l' **astronomie** fem

at

A PREPOSITION

à

at Christmas
à Noël

two at a time
deux à la fois

Language tip

à + **le** becomes **au**, **à** + **les** becomes **aux**.

au

at the café
au café

aux

at the races
aux courses

at night
la nuit

What are you doing at the weekend?
Qu'est-ce que tu fais ce week-end?

B NOUN

l' **arobase** fem
(symbol in email address)

a
b
c
d
e
f
g
h
i
j
k
l
m
n
o
p
q
r
s
t
u
v
w
x
y
z

at four o'clock
à quatre heures
at school
à l'école
at home
à la maison

athlete NOUN
l' **athlète** *masc/fem*
He's a good athlete.
C'est un bon athlète.

Atlantic NOUN
l' **Atlantique** *masc*

atlas NOUN
l' **atlas** *masc*

attention NOUN
l' **attention** *fem*
Pay attention!
Faites attention!
Pay attention, Léon!
Fais attention, Léon!

attic NOUN
le **grenier** *masc*

attractive ADJECTIVE
séduisant *masc*
séduisante *fem*
She's very attractive.
Elle est très séduisante.

August NOUN
août *masc*
August or September?
Août ou septembre?
My birthday's in August.
Mon anniversaire est en août.

in August
en août
the fifth of August
le cinq août

Language tip
The months are not spelled with a capital letter in French.

aunt NOUN
la **tante** *fem*
my aunt
ma tante

au pair NOUN
la **jeune fille au pair** *fem*
She's an au pair.
Elle est jeune fille au pair.

Language tip
You do not translate a *when you say what someone's job is in French.*

Australia NOUN
l' **Australie** *fem*

Austria NOUN
l' **Autriche** *fem*

author NOUN
l' **auteur** *masc*
J. K. Rowling is a famous author.
J. K. Rowling est un auteur connu.

autumn NOUN
l' **automne** *masc*

in autumn
en automne

avenue NOUN
l' **avenue** *fem*

average

> **average** *can be a noun or an adjective.*

A NOUN
la **moyenne** *fem*
on average
en moyenne
above average
au dessus de la moyenne

B ADJECTIVE
moyen *masc*
moyenne *fem*
the average age
l'âge moyen
I'm average height.
Je suis de taille moyenne.

away ADJECTIVE
absent *masc*
absente *fem (not here)*
André's away today.
André est absent aujourd'hui.
He's away for a week.
Il est parti pour une semaine.

> **He's away.**
> Il est absent.
> **She's away.**
> Elle est absente.

awful ADJECTIVE
affreux *masc*
affreuse *fem*
That's awful!
C'est affreux!

B b

baby NOUN
le **bébé** *masc*
We've got a new baby!
On a un nouveau bébé!

babysit VERB
faire du baby-sitting
I babysit at the weekend.
Je fais du baby-sitting le weekend.

babysitter NOUN
le/la **baby-sitter** *masc/fem*

back

> **back** *can be a noun or an adjective.*

A NOUN
1 le **dos** *masc (of person, horse, book)*
Lie on your back!
Couchez-vous sur le dos.
2 le **fond** *masc (of room)*
at the back
au fond
Luc and I sit at the back.
Luc et moi, on s'assoit au fond.
B ADJECTIVE
arrière *masc, fem, pl*
the back seat
le siège arrière
the back wheels of the car
les roues arrière de la voiture
the back door
la porte de derrière

background NOUN
l' **arrière-plan** *masc*
a house in the background
une maison à l'arrière-plan

backstroke NOUN
le **dos crawlé** *masc*
I do the backstroke.
Je fais le dos crawlé.

backwards ADVERB
en arrière
Take a step backwards!
Faites un pas en arrière!

bacon NOUN
le **bacon** *masc*
bacon and eggs
des œufs au bacon

bad ADJECTIVE
1 **mauvais** *masc*
mauvaise *fem (awful)*
a bad film
un mauvais film
bad weather
le mauvais temps
That's not bad.
Ce n'est pas mal.
I'm bad at maths.
Je suis mauvais en maths.

> **Language tip**
>
> *A boy is saying this. How can you tell?*

2 **grave** *(serious)*
a bad accident
un accident grave
3 **vilain** *masc*
vilaine *fem (naughty)*
You bad boy!
Vilain!

> **not bad**
> pas mal
> **Bad luck!**
> Pas de chance!

badge NOUN
le **badge** *masc*

badly ADVERB
mal
> He behaved badly.
> Il s'est mal comporté.

badminton NOUN
le **badminton** *masc*
> I play badminton.
> Je joue au badminton.

bag NOUN
le **sac** *masc*

baggy ADJECTIVE
ample
> baggy trousers
> un pantalon ample

bagpipes PL NOUN
la **cornemuse** *fem*
> Ed plays the bagpipes.
> Ed joue de la cornemuse.

baked beans PL NOUN
les haricots blancs à la sauce tomate *masc pl*

> **Language tip**
> The literal translation of the French means 'white beans in tomato sauce'.

baked potato NOUN
la **pomme de terre cuite au four** *fem*
> two baked potatoes
> deux pommes de terre cuites au four

baker NOUN
le **boulanger** *masc*
la **boulangère** *fem*

bakery NOUN
la **boulangerie** *fem*

balcony NOUN
le **balcon** *masc*

bald ADJECTIVE
chauve
> My grandfather is bald.
> Mon grand-père est chauve.

ball NOUN
1 la **balle** *fem (for tennis, golf, cricket)*
> Hit the ball!
> Frappe la balle!

2 le **ballon** *masc (for football, rugby)*
> Pass the ball!
> Passe le ballon!

ballet NOUN
la **danse classique** *fem*
> I do ballet.
> Je fais de la danse classique.

> **Language tip**
> What's the difference in spelling between the English word **dance** and the French word **danse**?

ballet dancer NOUN
le **danseur classique** *masc*
la **danseuse classique** *fem*

ballet shoes PL NOUN
les **chaussons de danse** *masc pl*

balloon NOUN
le **ballon** *masc*
> a red balloon
> un ballon rouge

English French

a
b
c
d
e
f
g
h
i
j
k
l
m
n
o
p
q
r
s
t
u
v
w
x
y
z

banana NOUN
la **banane** *fem*

band NOUN
1 le **groupe** *masc (rock band)*
2 la **fanfare** *fem (brass band)*

bandage NOUN
le **bandage** *masc*
He's got a bandage round his arm.
Il a un bandage au bras.

bang

bang *can be a noun or a verb.*

A NOUN
Bang! Bang!
Pan! Pan!
B VERB
Don't bang the door!
Ne claque pas la porte!

banger NOUN
1 la **saucisse** *fem (sausage)*
bangers and mash
les saucisses à la purée
2 le **pétard** *masc (firework)*
Phyllis is scared of bangers.
Phyllis a peur des pétards.

bank NOUN
1 la **banque** *fem (for money)*
2 le **bord** *masc (of river, lake)*

bank holiday NOUN
le **jour férié** *masc*

bar NOUN
a bar of chocolate
une barre de chocolat

barbecue NOUN
le **barbecue** *masc*

bare ADJECTIVE
nu *masc*
nue *fem*

bare feet
les pieds nus

bargain NOUN
l' **affaire** *fem*
It's a bargain!
C'est une affaire!

barge NOUN
la **péniche** *fem*

bark VERB
aboyer
My dog barks a lot.
Mon chien aboie beaucoup.

baseball NOUN
le **base-ball** *masc*
I play baseball.
Je joue au base-ball.

baseball cap NOUN
la **casquette de base-ball** *fem*

basement NOUN
le **sous-sol** *masc*

basin NOUN
le **lavabo** *masc*

basket
NOUN
le **panier**
masc

basketball NOUN
le **basket** *masc*
Do you play basketball?
Tu joues au basket?

bat NOUN
1 la **batte** *fem (for cricket, rounders)*
2 la **raquette** *fem (for table tennis)*
3 la **chauve-souris** *fem (animal)*
two bats
deux chauves-souris

Language tip
Make sure you pick the word for the right sort of bat!

bath NOUN
1 le **bain** *masc (wash)*
I have a bath every night.
Je prends un bain tous les soirs.
a hot bath
un bain chaud
2 la **baignoire** *fem (tub)*
There's a spider in the bath!
Il y a une araignée dans la baignoire!

bathroom NOUN
la **salle de bains** *fem*
There are two bathrooms.
Il y a deux salles de bains.

baths PL NOUN
la **piscine** *fem*

battery NOUN
la **pile** *fem (for torch, toy)*
I need a battery.
J'ai besoin d'une pile.

battle NOUN
la **bataille** *fem*
the Battle of Hastings
la bataille de Hastings

battleships NOUN
la **bataille navale** *fem*

BC ABBREVIATION
av. J.-C.
in 200 BC
en 200 av. J.-C.

be VERB
1 **être**
It's me.
C'est moi.
It's easy.
C'est facile.

It's not easy.
Ce n'est pas facile.
I'm tired.
Je suis fatigué.
You're late.
Tu es en retard.
She's English.
Elle est anglaise.
We're the winners!
Nous sommes les gagnants!
Are you ready?
Vous êtes prêts?
My parents are in Paris at the moment.
Mes parents sont à Paris en ce moment.
My name is not Inès, it's Fleur.
Mon nom n'est pas Inès, c'est Fleur.

Language tip
*With certain adjectives, such as 'cold', 'hot', 'hungry' and 'thirsty', you use **avoir** instead of **être**.*

I'm cold.
J'ai froid.
I'm hungry.
J'ai faim.

Language tip
*When talking about ages, you use **avoir**, not **être**.*

I'm eleven.
J'ai onze ans.
My brother is thirteen.
Mon frère a treize ans.

Language tip
*When talking about the weather, you use **fait**.*

It's cold.
Il fait froid.

It's too hot.
Il fait trop chaud.
It's a nice day.
Il fait beau.
It's the twenty-eighth of October today.
Aujourd'hui, nous sommes le vingt-huit octobre.

> **Language tip**
>
> *Another way of saying this date is* **Aujourd'hui c'est le vingt-huit octobre**.

2 égaler *(with totals)*
Two times three is six.
Deux fois trois égalent six.
Ten divided by two is five.
Dix divisé par deux égalent cinq.

beach NOUN
la **plage** *fem*

beans NOUN
1 les **haricots blancs à la sauce tomate** *masc pl (baked beans)*
Would you like some beans?
Tu veux des haricots blancs à la sauce tomate?

> **Language tip**
>
> *Word for word this means 'white beans in tomato sauce'.*

2 les **haricots verts** *masc pl* *(green beans)*

beard NOUN
la **barbe** *fem*

beat VERB
battre

We're going to beat you!
Nous allons vous battre!

beautiful ADJECTIVE
beau *masc*
belle *fem*
Your garden is beautiful.
Votre jardin est beau.
Delphine is very beautiful.
Delphine est très belle.
Your hair is beautiful.
Tes cheveux sont beaux.

because CONJUNCTION
parce que
Yvette is absent because she's ill.
Yvette est absente parce qu'elle est malade.
because of you
à cause de toi
because of the weather
à cause du temps

bed NOUN
le **lit** *masc*
in bed
au lit
It's time to go to bed.
Il est temps de se coucher.
I go to bed at ten o'clock.
Je me couche à dix heures.
What time do you go to bed?
À quelle heure tu te couches?

bed and breakfast NOUN
la **chambre d'hôte** *fem*

bedroom NOUN
la **chambre** *fem*
my bedroom
ma chambre
Alain's bedroom
la chambre d'Alain

bedtime NOUN
Ten o'clock is my usual bedtime.
Je me couche généralement à dix heures.
Bedtime!
Au lit!

bee NOUN
l' **abeille** *fem*

beef NOUN
le **bœuf** *masc*
Would you like beef or chicken?
Tu veux du bœuf ou du poulet?
roast beef
le rôti de bœuf

beefburger NOUN
le **hamburger** *masc*

beer NOUN
la **bière** *fem*
a can of beer
une canette de bière

beetle NOUN
le **scarabée** *masc*

beetroot NOUN
la **betterave rouge** *fem*

before PREPOSITION, CONJUNCTION
avant
before three o'clock
avant trois heures
Think before you answer, Noémie!
Réfléchis avant de répondre, Noémie!

begin VERB
commencer
It begins with 'b'.
Ça commence par un 'b'.

beginner NOUN
le **débutant** *masc*
la **débutante** *fem*
I'm a beginner.
Je suis débutante.

Language tip

*In the example for **beginner**, a girl is speaking. How can you tell?*

beginning NOUN
le **début** *masc*
at the beginning
au début

behave VERB
se comporter
He behaves badly.
Il se comporte mal.
Behave!
Sois sage!

behind PREPOSITION
derrière
behind the television
derrière la télévision
one behind the other
l'un derrière l'autre

beige

beige can be an adjective or a noun.

A ADJECTIVE
beige
a beige skirt
une jupe beige

Language tip

Colour adjectives come after the noun in French.

B NOUN
le **beige** *masc*

Belgian

Belgian can be an adjective or a noun.

English French

a
b
c
d
e
f
g
h
i
j
k
l
m
n
o
p
q
r
s
t
u
v
w
x
y
z

A ADJECTIVE
belge
Belgian chocolate
le chocolat belge

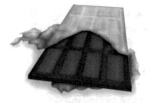

Pauline is Belgian.
Pauline est belge.

Language tip

belge *is not spelled with a capital letter except when it means a Belgian person.*

B NOUN
le/la **Belge** *masc/fem*
the Belgians
les Belges

Belgium NOUN
la **Belgique** *fem*

believe VERB
croire
I don't believe you.
Je ne te crois pas.

bell NOUN
1 la **sonnerie** *fem (at school)*
There's the bell!
C'est la sonnerie!
2 la **clochette**
fem (small bell)
My cat has a bell on its collar.
Mon chat a une clochette à son collier.

belong VERB
That belongs to me.
C'est à moi.

Does this belong to you?
C'est à toi?
Who does it belong to?
C'est à qui?
The ball belongs to Mathieu.
Le ballon est à Mathieu.

below PREPOSITION
au-dessous de
below ground
au-dessous du sol
ten degrees below freezing
moins dix

belt NOUN
la **ceinture** *fem*

bench NOUN
le **banc** *masc*

bend

bend *can be a noun or a verb.*

A NOUN
le **virage** *masc*
a dangerous bend
un virage dangereux
B VERB
plier
Bend your leg!
Pliez la jambe!

beneath PREPOSITION
sous
beneath the table
sous la table

beret NOUN
le **béret** *masc*
a black beret
un béret noir

berth NOUN
la **couchette** *fem*

beside PREPOSITION
à côté de

Sit beside me.
Assieds-toi à côté de moi.

> **Language tip**
>
> *To get the accents right in* **à côté de**,
> *remember that they form a W:* `` `^´``.

best

> **best** *can be an adjective, a noun or
> an adverb.*

A ADJECTIVE
meilleur *masc*
meilleure *fem*
Étienne is my best friend.
Étienne est mon meilleur ami.
**Fleur and Roxanne are my
best friends.**
Fleur et Roxanne sont mes
meilleures amies.
the best team in the world
la meilleure équipe du monde
B NOUN
le **meilleur** *masc*
la **meilleure** *fem*
He's the best in the class.
C'est le meilleur de la classe.
C ADVERB
le **mieux** *masc*
Emma sings best.
C'est Emma qui chante le mieux.

> **Best wishes!**
> Meilleurs vœux!

best man NOUN
le **garçon d'honneur** *masc*

better

> **better** *can be an adjective or an
> adverb.*

A ADJECTIVE
meilleur *masc*
meilleure *fem*

**The ice cream is better than
the cake.**
La glace est meilleure que le
gâteau.
B ADVERB
mieux
That's better!
C'est mieux comme ça.

> **Get better soon!**
> Remets-toi vite!

between PREPOSITION
entre
**a number between one and
twelve**
un nombre entre un et douze

Bible NOUN
la **Bible** *fem*

bicycle NOUN
le **vélo** *masc*
by bicycle
en vélo

big ADJECTIVE
1 **grand** *masc*
grande *fem (garden, glass,
plate, size)*
a big garden
un grand jardin
a big house
une grande maison
my big brother
mon grand frère
her big sister
sa grande sœur
2 **gros** *masc*
grosse *fem (car, animal, book,
parcel)*
a big car
une grosse voiture

bike NOUN
le **vélo** *masc*

by bike
en vélo

bikini NOUN
le **bikini** *masc*

bill NOUN
l' **addition** *fem*
  Can we have the bill, please?
  L'addition, s'il vous plaît.

billion NOUN
le **milliard** *masc*

bin NOUN
la **poubelle** *fem*
  Put your chewing gum in the bin.
  Mets ton chewing-gum à la poubelle.

bingo NOUN
le **loto** *masc*
  We're going to play bingo.
  On va jouer au loto.

biology NOUN
la **biologie** *fem*

bird NOUN
l' **oiseau** *masc* (PL les **oiseaux**)
  My cat catches birds.
  Mon chat attrape des oiseaux.

Biro® NOUN
le **bic**® *masc*

birthday NOUN
l' **anniversaire** *masc*

My birthday is the fifth of May.
Mon anniversaire est le cinq mai.
When's your birthday?
Quelle est la date de ton anniversaire?

Happy Birthday!
Bon anniversaire!

Language tip

anniversaire *is related to* **an**, *which is the French word for 'year', and to English words like 'annual' and 'anniversary'.*

birthday cake NOUN
le **gâteau d'anniversaire** *masc*

birthday card NOUN
la **carte d'anniversaire** *fem*
  I got ten birthday cards.
  J'ai eu dix cartes d'anniversaire.

birthday party NOUN
la **fête d'anniversaire** *fem*
  Would you like to come to my birthday party?
  Tu veux venir à ma fête d'anniversaire?

Language tip

In France, a children's party held in the afternoon is called **un goûter d'anniversaire**.

biscuit NOUN
le **biscuit** *masc*
  Would you like a biscuit?
  Tu veux un biscuit?

bit NOUN
  a bit
  un peu

I'm a bit tired.
Je suis un peu fatigué.
Wait a bit!
Attends un peu!

bite VERB
mordre
My dog doesn't bite.
Mon chien ne mord pas.

black

black *can be an adjective or a noun.*

A ADJECTIVE
noir *masc*
noire *fem*
She's black.
Elle est noire.
a black jacket
une veste noire

Language tip
Colour adjectives come after the noun in French.

B NOUN
le **noir** *masc*
He is wearing black.
Il est habillé en noir.

blackberry NOUN
la **mûre** *fem*
We picked blackberries.
Nous avons cueilli des mûres.

blackboard NOUN
le **tableau** *masc*
(PL les **tableaux**)
Look at the blackboard!
Regardez le tableau!

black coffee NOUN
le **café** *masc*

blackcurrant NOUN
le **cassis** *masc*
blackcurrant jam
la confiture de cassis

blank

blank *can be an adjective or a noun.*

A ADJECTIVE
blanc *masc*
blanche *fem*
a blank sheet of paper
une feuille blanche
B NOUN
le **blanc** *masc*
Fill in the blanks, everyone!
Remplissez les blancs, tout le monde!

blanket NOUN
la **couverture** *fem*

blazer NOUN
le **blazer** *masc*
a navy blazer
un blazer bleu marine

bless VERB
Bless you!
À tes souhaits!

blind

blind *can be an adjective or a noun.*

A ADJECTIVE
aveugle
Are you blind?
Tu es aveugle?
B NOUN
le **store** *masc*
Open the blinds!
Ouvrez les stores!

blindfold VERB
> **I'm going to blindfold you.**
> Je vais te bander les yeux.

block NOUN
> **a block of flats**
> un immeuble

blog NOUN
> le **blog** masc

blonde ADJECTIVE
blond masc
blonde fem
> **She's got blonde hair.**
> Elle a les cheveux blonds.

blood NOUN
> le **sang** masc

blouse NOUN
> le **chemisier** masc
> **a white blouse**
> un chemisier blanc

blow VERB
souffler
> **The wind is blowing.**
> Le vent souffle.
> **Stop when I blow the whistle!**
> Arrêtez-vous quand je siffle!
> **Blow your nose!**
> Mouche-toi!
> **Blow out the candles!**
> Souffle sur les bougies!

blue

> blue can be an adjective or a noun.

A ADJECTIVE
bleu masc
bleue fem
> **a blue dress**
> une robe bleue

> ***Language tip***
> Colour adjectives come after the
> noun in French.

B NOUN
> le **bleu** masc
> **Blue is my favourite colour.**
> Ma couleur préférée, c'est le bleu.

board NOUN
1 le **tableau** masc
(PL les **tableaux**) (blackboard)
> **on the board**
> au tableau
> **Come to the board, Émilie.**
> Viens au tableau, Émilie.
2 le **jeu** masc (PL les **jeux**)
(for board games)

boarder NOUN
> l' **interne** masc/fem

board game NOUN
> le **jeu de société** masc

boarding school NOUN
> **I go to boarding school.**
> Je suis interne dans une école
> privée.

boat NOUN
> le **bateau** masc
> (PL les **bateaux**)

body NOUN
> le **corps** masc

boiled ADJECTIVE
> à l'**eau** masc, fem, pl
> **boiled potatoes**
> des pommes de terre à l'eau

boiled egg NOUN
> l' **œuf à la coque** masc
> **two boiled eggs**
> deux œufs à la coque

bomb NOUN
> la **bombe** fem

bonfire NOUN
> le **feu** masc (PL les **feux**)

Bonfire Night NOUN

Did you know...?

In France, people do not celebrate **Bonfire Night**, *though they have fireworks displays on the fourteenth of July, Bastille Day.*

book

book *can be a noun or a verb.*

A NOUN

1 le **livre** *masc (printed)*
   Open your books at page 10.
   Ouvrez vos livres à la page 10.

2 le **cahier** *masc (exercise book)*
   Write the words in your books.
   Écrivez les mots dans vos cahiers.

B VERB
   réserver
   I want to book a seat.
   Je veux réserver une place.

bookcase NOUN
   la **bibliothèque** *fem*

booklet NOUN
   la **brochure** *fem*

bookshelf NOUN
   l' **étagère à livres** *fem*
   on the bookshelves
   sur les étagères à livres

bookshop NOUN
   la **librairie** *fem*

Language tip

librairie is related to the English word 'library'. Both places contain books, but a **librairie** sells them, and a 'library' lends them.

boot NOUN

1 la **botte** *fem*
   I like your boots!
   J'aime bien tes bottes!
   football boots
   des chaussures de foot
2 le **coffre** *masc (of car)*
   It's in the boot.
   C'est dans le coffre.

border NOUN
   la **frontière** *fem*

bored ADJECTIVE
   I'm bored.
   Je m'ennuie.
   Are you bored?
   Tu t'ennuies?

boring ADJECTIVE
   ennuyeux *masc*
   ennuyeuse *fem*
   a boring programme
   une émission ennuyeuse

born ADJECTIVE
   I was born in 1996.
   Je suis né en 1996.
   She was born in 1998.
   Elle est née en 1998.

borrow VERB
   emprunter
   Can I borrow your pen?
   Je peux emprunter ton stylo?

boss NOUN
   le **patron** *masc*
   la **patronne** *fem*

bossy ADJECTIVE
autoritaire

both PRONOUN
tous les deux masc pl
toutes les deux fem pl
Louis and Daniel, you're both late!
Louis et Daniel, vous êtes tous les deux en retard!
Inès et Nadège have both got a rabbit.
Inès et Nadège ont toutes les deux un lapin.

bother VERB
déranger (disturb)
I'm sorry to bother you.
Je suis désolé de vous déranger.

no bother
aucun problème
Don't bother!
Ça n'est pas la peine!

bottle NOUN
la **bouteille** fem

bottom NOUN
1 le **bas** masc (of page, list)
Look at the bottom of the page.
Regardez le bas de la page.
2 le **fond** masc (of container, bag, sea)
My pen's in the bottom of my bag.
Mon stylo est au fond de mon sac.

bow NOUN
1 le **nœud** masc (in ribbon)
Tie a bow!
Fais un nœud!
2 l' **arc** masc (for archery)
a bow and arrows
un arc et des flèches

bowl NOUN
le **bol** masc
a bowl of soup
un bol de soupe

bowling NOUN
le **bowling** masc
Do you want to come bowling?
Tu veux jouer au bowling?

bowls NOUN
les **boules** fem pl
My grandfather plays bowls.
Mon grand-père joue aux boules.

Did you know…?
boules *is played on rough ground, not smooth grass. The balls are smaller than those used in bowls, and are made of metal.*

box NOUN
1 la **boîte** fem (container)
a box of matches
une boîte d'allumettes
a cardboard box
un carton

2 la **case** fem (in questionnaire)
Tick the boxes.
Cochez les cases.

boxer NOUN
le **boxeur** masc

boxer shorts PL NOUN
le **caleçon** *masc*

> *Language tip*
> **caleçon** *is a singular word.*

boxing NOUN
la **boxe** *fem*
I don't like boxing.
Je n'aime pas la boxe.

Boxing Day NOUN
le **lendemain de Noël** *masc*
on Boxing Day
le lendemain de Noël

> *Language tip*
> *Word for word this means 'the day after Christmas'.*

boy NOUN
le **garçon** *masc*
Well done, boys!
Bravo les garçons!

boyfriend NOUN
le **copain** *masc*
Have you got a boyfriend?
Tu as un copain?

bra NOUN
le **soutien-gorge** *masc*

brace NOUN
l' **appareil** *masc*
She wears a brace.
Elle a un appareil.

bracelet NOUN
le **bracelet** *masc*

brain NOUN
le **cerveau** *masc* (PL les **cerveaux**)

brainy ADJECTIVE
intelligent *masc*
intelligente *fem*

Sabine is very brainy.
Sabine est très intelligente.

branch NOUN
la **branche** *fem*

brand-new ADJECTIVE
tout neuf *masc*
toute neuve *fem*
I've got a brand-new computer.
J'ai un ordinateur tout neuf.

brass band NOUN
la **fanfare** *fem*

brave ADJECTIVE
courageux *masc*
courageuse *fem*
Be brave!
Sois courageux!

bread NOUN
le **pain** *masc*
Would you like some bread?
Tu veux du pain?
bread and butter
les tartines de pain beurrées

break

> **break** *can be a noun or a verb.*

A NOUN
la **récréation** *fem*
during morning break
pendant la récréation du matin
B VERB
casser
Michel has broken a window.
Michel a cassé une fenêtre.
Who broke the window?
Qui a cassé la fenêtre?
I have broken my leg.
Je me suis cassé la jambe.
Richard has broken his arm.
Richard s'est cassé le bras.

English French

a
b
c
d
e
f
g
h
i
j
k
l
m
n
o
p
q
r
s
t
u
v
w
x
y
z

break down VERB
tomber en panne
Our car broke down.
Notre voiture est tombée en panne.

breakfast NOUN
le **petit déjeuner** masc
Breakfast is at eight o'clock.
Le petit déjeuner est à huit heures.
I have cereal for breakfast.
Je prends des
céréales au petit
déjeuner.

break time NOUN
la **récréation** fem
at break time
à la récréation

break up VERB
We break up next Wednesday.
Nos vacances commencent mercredi.

breaststroke NOUN
la **brasse** fem
I can do the breaststroke.
Je sais faire la brasse.

breath NOUN
Take a deep breath!
Respirez à fond!

brick NOUN
la **brique** fem
a brick wall
un mur en brique

bride NOUN
la **mariée** fem

bridegroom NOUN
le **marié** masc

bridesmaid NOUN
la **demoiselle d'honneur** fem
I'm going to be a bridesmaid.
Je vais être demoiselle d'honneur.

bridge NOUN
le **pont** masc

bright ADJECTIVE
vif masc
vive fem
a bright colour
une couleur vive
bright blue
bleu vif
a bright blue shirt
une chemise bleu vif

brilliant ADJECTIVE
génial masc
géniale fem
We're going to Paris. — Brilliant!
On va à Paris. — Génial!

bring VERB
apporter
Bring the money tomorrow.
Apportez l'argent demain.
Could you bring me a glass of water?
Tu peux m'apporter un verre d'eau?

bring back VERB
rapporter
Bring them back!
Rapporte-les!

Britain NOUN
la **Grande-Bretagne** fem
in Britain
en Grande-Bretagne
When are you coming to Britain?
Quand est-ce que tu viens en Grande-Bretagne?

British

British can be an adjective or a noun.

A ADJECTIVE
britannique
I'm British.
Je suis britannique.

Language tip

britannique *is not spelled with a capital letter except when it means a British person. Remember that it has two **n**s.*

B NOUN
the British
les Britanniques

British Isles PL NOUN
les **îles Britanniques** *fem pl*

Brittany NOUN
la **Bretagne** *fem*

Language tip

Brittany *has double* **t**, **Bretagne** *has one* **t**.

broccoli NOUN
les **brocolis** *masc pl*
Would you like some broccoli?
Tu veux des brocolis?

Language tip

What are the two differences in spelling between the French word and the English word?

brochure NOUN
la **brochure** *fem*

broke VERB ▷ *see* **break**

broken ADJECTIVE
cassé *masc*
cassée *fem*

It's broken.
C'est cassé.
a broken leg
une jambe cassée
He's got a broken arm.
Il a le bras cassé.

Language tip

If you want to say, for example, 'I have broken', look at the verb to **break**.

bronze NOUN
le **bronze** *masc*
the bronze medal
la médaille de bronze

brother NOUN
le **frère** *masc*
my big brother
mon grand frère
I've got one brother.
J'ai un frère.
I haven't got a brother.
Je n'ai pas de frère.

Have you got any brothers or sisters?
Tu as des frères et sœurs?

brown

brown can be an adjective or a noun.

A ADJECTIVE
1 **marron** *masc, fem, pl*
I've got brown eyes.
J'ai les yeux marron.
My shoes are brown.
Mes chaussures sont marron.
2 **brun** *masc*
brune *fem (hair)*
I've got brown hair.
J'ai les cheveux bruns.
She's got light brown hair.
Elle a les cheveux châtain.

Language tip
Colour adjectives come after the noun in French.

3 bronzé *masc*
bronzée *fem (tanned)*
Nina is very brown.
Nina est très bronzée.

B NOUN
le **marron** *masc*
Do you have these shoes in brown?
Vous avez ces chaussures en marron?

brown bread NOUN
le **pain complet** *masc*

Brownie NOUN
la **Jeannette** *fem*
I'm a Brownie.
Je suis Jeannette.
I go to Brownies.
Je vais au club des Jeannettes.

Did you know…?
The brownies aren't as common in France as they are in Britain.

bruise NOUN
le **bleu** *masc*
You've got a bruise.
Tu as un bleu.

Language tip
bleu *is also the word for 'blue'. In English 'black and blue' means 'covered with bruises'.*

brush

brush *can be a noun or a verb.*

A NOUN
la **brosse** *fem*
a brush and comb
une brosse et un peigne

B VERB
brosser
I brush my pony.
Je brosse mon poney.
I brush my hair.
Je me brosse les cheveux.
I brush my teeth every night.
Je me brosse les dents tous les soirs.

Brussels sprouts PL NOUN
les **choux de Bruxelles** *masc pl*

Language tip
Brussels *has one* l, **Bruxelles** *has two.*

bubble gum NOUN
le **chewing-gum** *masc*

bucket NOUN
le **seau** *masc*
(PL les **seaux**)
my bucket and spade
mon seau et ma pelle

budgie NOUN
la **perruche** *fem*
I've got a budgie.
J'ai une perruche.

buggy NOUN
la **poussette** *fem*

build VERB
construire
My dad is building a garage.
Mon père construit un garage.

building NOUN
le **bâtiment** *masc*
a tall building
un grand bâtiment

bull NOUN
le **taureau** *masc* (PL les **taureaux**)

There's a bull in the field.
Il y a un taureau dans le champ.

bully NOUN
He's a big bully.
Il joue les caïds.

bum NOUN
le **derrière** masc

bum bag NOUN
la **banane** fem

bun NOUN
le **petit pain au lait** masc (roll)
I'd like a bun.
Je voudrais un petit pain au lait.

bunch NOUN
a bunch of flowers
un bouquet de fleurs

bunches PL NOUN
les **couettes** fem pl
She has bunches.
Elle a des couettes.

bungalow NOUN
le **bungalow** masc

bunk beds PL NOUN
les **lits superposés** masc pl

burger NOUN
le **hamburger** masc
a burger and chips
un hamburger avec des frites

bus NOUN
le **bus** masc
by bus
en bus
I go to school by bus.
Je vais à l'école en bus.
the school bus
le car scolaire

bus driver NOUN
le **conducteur de bus** masc

bus station NOUN
la **gare routière** fem

bus stop NOUN
l' **arrêt de bus** masc

business NOUN
les **affaires** fem pl
He's away on business.
Il est en voyage d'affaires.
a business trip
un voyage d'affaires

busy ADJECTIVE
occupé masc
occupée fem
My mother is always busy.
Ma mère est toujours occupée.

but CONJUNCTION
mais
Thanks, but I'm not hungry.
Merci, mais je n'ai pas faim.

butcher's NOUN
la **boucherie** fem

butter NOUN
le **beurre** masc

butterfly
NOUN
le **papillon**
masc

button NOUN
le **bouton** masc

buy VERB
acheter
What are you going to buy?
Qu'est-ce que tu vas acheter?
I'm going to buy a present for Christophe.
Je vais acheter un cadeau pour Christophe.

by PREPOSITION
1 **par**
  a meal prepared by Pierre
  un repas préparé par Pierre
2 **de** *(done by)*
  a painting by Picasso
  un tableau de Picasso
  a book by J.K. Rowling
  un livre de J.K. Rowling
3 **à côté de** *(next to)*
  **Where's the library? —
  It's by the post office.**
  Où est la bibliothèque? —
  Elle est à côté de la poste.

> ### *Language tip*
> *To get the accents right in* **à côté
> de**, *remember that they form a
> W:* `` ` ``^´.

4 **en**
  We're going by car.
  On y va en voiture.

by car
en voiture
by train
en train
by bus
en bus

bye EXCLAMATION
salut!

C c

cab NOUN
le **taxi** *masc*

cabbage NOUN
le **chou** *masc* (PL les **choux**)

cactus NOUN
le **cactus** *masc*

café NOUN
le **café** *masc*

Did you know...?
Cafés in France sell both alcoholic and non-alcoholic drinks.

cafeteria NOUN
la **cafétéria** *fem*

cage NOUN
la **cage** *fem*

cagoule NOUN
le **K-way®** *masc*

cake NOUN
le **gâteau** *masc*
(PL les **gâteaux**)

calculator NOUN
la **calculatrice** *fem*

calendar NOUN
le **calendrier** *masc*

calf NOUN
le **veau** *masc* (PL les **veaux**)

call

call can be a verb or a noun.

A VERB
appeler
Call this number.
Appelez ce numéro.
Call the police!
Appelez la police!
I am going to call the register.
Je vais faire l'appel.

Language tip
*The **l** of **appeler** doubles when it is followed by **e**, **es** and **ent**.*

Everyone calls him Matt.
Tout le monde l'appelle Matt.
My cat is called Fluffy.
Mon chat s'appelle Fluffy.
What's your cat called?
Ton chat s'appelle comment?

Language tip
*The question word **comment** can come at the beginning or end of a phrase.*

What's she called?
Comment elle s'appelle?
What are your brothers called?
Tes frères s'appellent comment?

What are you called?
Comment tu t'appelles?/
Tu t'appelles comment?
I'm called Helen.
Je m'appelle Helen.

B NOUN
l' **appel** *masc*
Thanks for your call.
Merci de votre appel.
Give me a call.
Appelle-moi.

call back VERB
rappeler

I'll call back at six o'clock.
Je rappellerai à six heures.

call centre NOUN
le **centre d'appels** *masc*
My sister works in a call centre in London.
Ma sœur travaille dans un centre d'appels à Londres.

calm ADJECTIVE
calme

calm down VERB
se calmer
Calm down, Hugo!
Calme-toi, Hugo!
Calm down, children!
Calmez-vous, les enfants!

calorie NOUN
la **calorie** *fem*

camcorder NOUN
le **caméscope** *masc*

came VERB ▷*see* **come**

camera NOUN
1 l' **appareil photo** *masc*
I've got a new camera.
J'ai un nouvel appareil photo.
2 la **caméra** *fem* (for filming, TV)

camera phone NOUN
le **portable appareil photo** *masc*

camp NOUN
le **camp** *masc*
a cub camp
un camp de louveteaux

camping NOUN
le **camping** *masc*
to go camping
faire du camping
We're going camping.
Nous allons faire du camping.

campsite NOUN
le **terrain de camping** *masc*

can

can *can be a noun or a verb.*

A NOUN
la **boîte** *fem*
a can of coke
une boîte de coca
B VERB
1 **pouvoir** *(be able to)*
I can't come.
Je ne peux pas venir.
Can I help you?
Est-ce que je peux vous aider?

Language tip

can *is sometimes not translated into English.*

I can't see it.
Je ne le vois pas.
Can you speak French? — No, I can't.
Parlez-vous français? — Non.

I can.
Je peux.
I can't.
Je ne peux pas.
Can you?
Tu peux?

2 **savoir** *(know how to)*
I can swim.
Je sais nager.
I can make pancakes.
Je sais faire les crêpes.

Canada NOUN
le **Canada** *masc*

Canada Day NOUN *(Canada)*
la **Fête du Canada** *fem*

canal NOUN
le **canal** *masc* (PL les **canaux**)

cancel VERB
annuler
The match was cancelled.
Le match a été annulé.

cancer NOUN
le **cancer** *masc*
He's got cancer.
Il a le cancer.

candle NOUN
la **bougie** *fem*

candyfloss NOUN
la **barbe à papa** *fem*

canoe NOUN
le **canoë** *masc*

canoeing NOUN
to go canoeing
faire du canoë
We're going canoeing.
Nous allons faire du canoë.

can-opener NOUN
l' **ouvre-boîte** *masc*
a can-opener
un ouvre-boîte

can't VERB ▷ *see* **can**

canteen NOUN
la **cantine** *fem*
I eat in the canteen.
Je mange à la cantine.

cap NOUN
la **casquette** *fem*

capital NOUN
1 la **capitale** *fem (city)*
Cardiff is the capital of Wales.
Cardiff est la capitale du pays
de Galles.
2 la **majuscule** *fem (letter)*
Write your address in capitals.
Écris ton adresse en majuscules.

captain NOUN
le **capitaine** *masc*
**She's captain of the hockey
team.**
Elle est capitaine de l'équipe
de hockey.

caption NOUN
la **légende** *fem*

car NOUN
la **voiture** *fem*
We've got a new car.
Nous avons une nouvelle voiture.
by car
en voiture
We're going there by car.
Nous y allons en voiture.

caravan NOUN
la **caravane** *fem*

caravan site NOUN
le **camping pour caravanes**
masc

car-boot sale NOUN
la **brocante** *fem*

car crash NOUN
l' **accident de voiture** *masc*

card NOUN
1 la **carte** *fem (playing card)*
2 la **carte de vœux** *fem (for
birthday, Christmas etc)*
I got lots of cards.
J'ai reçu beaucoup de cartes de
vœux.

cardboard NOUN
le **carton** *masc*

card game NOUN
le **jeu de cartes** *masc*

cardigan NOUN
le **cardigan** *masc*
a green cardigan
un cardigan vert

care

care can be a noun or a verb.

A NOUN
le **soin** *masc*
with care
avec soin
B VERB
I don't care!
Ça m'est égal!

careful ADJECTIVE
Be careful, Gordon!
Fais attention, Gordon!

Be careful, children!
Faites attention, les enfants!

carefully ADVERB
Think carefully, Annick!
Réfléchis bien, Annick!
Listen carefully, children!
Écoutez bien, les enfants!

careless ADJECTIVE
a careless mistake
une faute d'inattention

caretaker NOUN
le **gardien** *masc*
la **gardienne** *fem*

My father's a caretaker.
Mon père est gardien.

Language tip
You do not translate a when you say what someone's job is in French.

car-ferry NOUN
le **ferry** *masc*

carol NOUN
a Christmas carol
un chant de Noël

car park NOUN
le **parking** *masc*

carpet NOUN
la **moquette** *fem*
My bedroom carpet is blue.
La moquette de ma chambre est bleue.

carriage NOUN
la **voiture** *fem*

carrier bag NOUN
le **sac en plastique** *masc*

carrot NOUN
la **carotte** *fem*

Language tip
The French word has only one r, but two ts.

carry VERB
porter
I'll carry your bag.
Je vais porter ton sac.

Language tip

*The French word **porter** is related to the English word 'portable', which describes something you can carry.*

carry on VERB
continuer
Carry on, Cécile!
Continue, Cécile!

carton NOUN
la **brique** *fem*

cartoon NOUN
le **dessin animé** *masc*
I watch cartoons on Saturdays.
Je regarde les dessins animés le samedi.

case NOUN
la **valise** *fem*
That's my case!
C'est ma valise!

casserole NOUN
le **ragoût** *masc*
I can make a casserole.
Je sais faire le ragoût.

cassette NOUN
la **cassette** *fem*
Listen to the cassette, children.
Écoutez la cassette, les enfants.

cassette player NOUN
le **lecteur de cassettes** *masc*

castle NOUN
le **château** *masc*
(PL les **châteaux**)
Dover Castle
le château de Douvres

Language tip

A few other British towns have French names. Can you recognize these: **Édimbourg**, **Cantorbéry**, **Londres***?*

casual ADJECTIVE
décontracté *masc*
décontractée *fem*
I prefer casual clothes.
Je préfère les vêtements décontractés.

cat NOUN
le **chat** *masc*
la **chatte** *fem*
Have you got a cat?
Est-ce que tu as un chat?

catch VERB
1 **attraper**
Catch!
Attrape!
My cat catches birds.
Mon chat attrape des oiseaux.
2 **prendre** *(bus, train)*
Which bus do you catch?
Quel bus prends-tu?

cathedral NOUN
la **cathédrale** *fem*

Catholic

Catholic *can be an adjective or a noun.*

A ADJECTIVE
catholique
B NOUN
le/la **catholique** *masc/fem*
I'm a Catholic.
Je suis catholique.

> *Language tip*
> **catholique** *is not spelled with a capital letter.*

cauliflower NOUN
le **chou-fleur** *masc*
two cauliflowers
deux choux-fleurs

cave NOUN
la **grotte** *fem*

CD NOUN
le **CD** *masc* (PL les **CD**)

CD player NOUN
la **platine laser** *fem*

CD-ROM NOUN
le **CD-ROM** *masc*

ceiling NOUN
le **plafond** *masc*

celebrate VERB
fêter
Let's celebrate!
Il faut fêter ça!

celery NOUN
le **céleri** *masc*
I don't like celery.
Je n'aime pas le céleri.

cellar NOUN
la **cave** *fem*

a wine cellar
une cave à vins

> *Language tip*
> **une cave** *is dark and underground, like an English* **cave**, *but often contains bottles of wine.*

cello NOUN
le **violoncelle** *masc*
I play the cello.
Je joue du violoncelle.

cemetery NOUN
le **cimetière** *masc*

cent NOUN
le **centime** *masc*
two euros and twenty cents
deux euros vingt centimes

centigrade ADJECTIVE
centigrade
twenty degrees centigrade
vingt degrés centigrade

centimetre NOUN
le **centimètre** *masc*

central heating NOUN
le **chauffage central** *masc*

centre NOUN
le **centre** *masc*
in the centre
au centre
a sports centre
un centre sportif
The office is in the centre of town.
Le bureau est en centre-ville.

century NOUN
le **siècle** *masc*
the twenty-first century
le vingt et unième siècle

cereal NOUN
les **céréales** *fem pl*

I have cereal for breakfast.
Je prends des céréales au petit déjeuner.

certain ADJECTIVE
certain *masc*
certaine *fem*
  a certain person
  une certaine personne
  I'm not certain.
  Je n'en suis pas certain.

certainly ADVERB
  Certainly not!
  Certainement pas!

certificate NOUN
  le **certificat** *masc*

chain NOUN
  la **chaîne** *fem*

chair NOUN
  1 la **chaise** *fem*
  There's a table and four chairs in the kitchen.
  Il y a une table et quatre chaises dans la cuisine.
  2 le **fauteuil** *masc* (armchair)
  There are two chairs and a sofa in the lounge.
  Il y a deux fauteuils et un canapé dans le salon.

chalk NOUN
  la **craie** *fem*
  a stick of chalk
  une craie

champagne NOUN
  le **champagne** *masc*
  a glass of champagne
  un verre de champagne

champion NOUN
  le **champion** *masc*
  la **championne** *fem*

Anaïs is the champion!
Anaïs est la championne!

> **Language tip**
> Anaïs is a girl's name. How can you tell from this example?

championship NOUN
  le **championnat** *masc*

chance NOUN
  No chance!
  Pas question!
  You're taking a chance!
  Tu prends un risque!

change

> **change** can be a verb or a noun.

A VERB
  1 **changer**
  I'd like to change £50.
  Je voudrais changer cinquante livres.
  2 **changer de**

> **Language tip**
> Use **changer de** when you change one thing for another.

  Change places!
  Changez de place!
  I want to change my cards.
  Je veux changer de cartes.
  I've changed my mind.
  J'ai changé d'avis.
B NOUN
  la **monnaie** *fem* (money)
  I haven't got any change.
  Je n'ai pas de monnaie.
  Keep the change!
  Gardez la monnaie!

changeable
ADJECTIVE
variable
  The weather is changeable.
  Le temps est variable.

changing room NOUN
le **vestiaire** *masc*

Channel NOUN
la **Manche** *fem*

> **Language tip**
>
> **manche** *means 'sleeve' in French. Do you think the Channel is sleeve-shaped?*

channel NOUN
la **chaîne** *fem*
There's football on the other channel.
Il y a du football sur l'autre chaîne.

Channel Islands PL NOUN
les **îles Anglo-Normandes** *fem pl*

Channel Tunnel NOUN
le **tunnel sous la Manche** *masc*

chapter NOUN
le **chapitre** *masc*

character NOUN
le **personnage** *masc*
Harry is the main character.
Harry est le personnage principal.

charge NOUN
an extra charge
un supplément
There's no charge.
C'est gratuit.
to be in charge
être responsable
Who is in charge?
Qui est responsable?

charity NOUN
l' **association caritative** *fem*
We give the money to charity.
Nous donnons l'argent à une association caritative.

chart NOUN
le **tableau** *masc* (PL les **tableaux**)
We're making a chart.
Nous faisons un tableau.

charter flight NOUN
le **charter** *masc*

chase VERB
pourchasser
My dog chases cats.
Mon chien pourchasse les chats.

chat VERB
bavarder
Pauline chats a lot.
Pauline bavarde beaucoup.

cheap ADJECTIVE
bon marché *masc, fem, pl*
cheap T-shirts
des T-shirts bon marché

cheaper ADJECTIVE
moins cher *masc*
moins chère *fem*
It's cheaper by bus.
C'est moins cher en bus.

cheat

> **cheat** *can be a verb or a noun.*

A VERB
tricher
You're cheating!
Tu triches!
Don't cheat, children!
Ne trichez pas, les enfants!

B NOUN
le **tricheur** *masc*
la **tricheuse** *fem*

Isabelle, you're a cheat!
Isabelle, tu es une tricheuse!

check VERB
vérifier
Check the spelling.
Vérifiez l'orthographe.

check in VERB
**se présenter à
l'enregistrement** *(at airport)*
**What time do I have to
check in?**
À quelle heure je dois me
présenter à l'enregistrement?

checked ADJECTIVE
à carreaux *masc, fem, pl*
a checked shirt
une chemise à carreaux

checkout NOUN
la **caisse** *fem*
at the checkout
à la caisse

cheek NOUN
la **joue** *fem*
Yvette has got red cheeks.
Yvette a les joues rouges.

cheeky ADJECTIVE
effronté *masc*
effrontée *fem*
Don't be cheeky, Hugo!
Ne sois pas effronté, Hugo!

cheer

cheer *can be a noun or a verb.*

A NOUN
Cheers!
À la vôtre!
B VERB
applaudir
Cheer your team!
Applaudissez votre équipe!

cheerful ADJECTIVE
gai *masc*
gaie *fem*

cheerio EXCLAMATION
salut!

cheese NOUN
le **fromage** *masc*
**a cheese
sandwich**
un sandwich
au fromage

chef NOUN
le **chef** *masc*

chemist NOUN
la **pharmacie** *fem*
You get it from the chemist.
Ça s'achète en pharmacie.

Did you know…?
Chemists in France have a big
green cross on a sign outside the
shop.

chemistry NOUN
la **chimie** *fem*
the chemistry lab
le laboratoire de chimie

cherry NOUN
la **cerise** *fem*
I love cherries.
J'adore les cerises.

chess NOUN
les **échecs** *masc pl*
I can play chess.
Je sais jouer aux échecs.

chest NOUN
la **poitrine** *fem*

chest of drawers NOUN
la **commode** *fem*

chewing gum NOUN
le **chewing-gum** *masc*
Put your chewing gum in the bin!
Mets ton chewing-gum à la poubelle!

chick NOUN
le **poussin** *masc*
a hen and her chicks
une poule et ses poussins

chicken NOUN
le **poulet** *masc*
Chicken and chips, please.
Un poulet frites, s'il vous plaît.

chickenpox NOUN
la **varicelle** *fem*
Thibault has got chickenpox.
Thibault a la varicelle.

child NOUN
l' **enfant** *masc/fem*
a child
un enfant
all the children
tous les enfants

child minder NOUN
la **nourrice** *fem*

children PL NOUN
les **enfants** *masc pl*
Goodbye children!
Au revoir, les enfants!

chilly ADJECTIVE
froid *masc*
froide *fem*
It's chilly today.
Il fait froid aujourd'hui.

China NOUN
la **Chine** *fem*

Chinese

Chinese can be an adjective or a noun.

A ADJECTIVE
chinois *masc*
chinoise *fem*
a Chinese restaurant
un restaurant chinois
a Chinese man
un Chinois
a Chinese woman
une Chinoise
Chinese people
les Chinois

Language tip

chinois *is not spelled with a capital letter except when it means a Chinese person.*

B NOUN
the Chinese
les Chinois

chinook wind NOUN
(Canada)
le **chinook** *masc*

chip NOUN
la **frite** *fem*
I'd like some chips.
Je voudrais des frites.

chocolate NOUN
le **chocolat** *masc*
I love chocolate.
J'adore le chocolat.

Language tip

*Use **au chocolat** when something is chocolate-flavoured.*

a chocolate cake
un gâteau au chocolat
a chocolate ice cream
une glace au chocolat

choice NOUN
le **choix** *masc*
There's lots of choice.
Il y a beaucoup de choix.

choir NOUN
la **chorale** *fem*
I sing in the school choir.
Je chante dans la chorale de
l'école.

choose VERB
choisir
It's difficult to choose.
C'est difficile de choisir.
Choose the right answer.
Choisissez la bonne réponse.

chop NOUN
la **côte** *fem*
a pork chop
une côte de porc

chopsticks PL NOUN
les **baguettes** *fem pl*

christening NOUN
le **baptême** *masc*

Christian name NOUN
le **prénom** *masc*

Christmas NOUN
Noël *masc*
at Christmas
à Noël

Happy Christmas!
Joyeux Noël!

Christmas cake NOUN
le **gâteau de Noël** *masc*

Did you know...?

*In France, people often eat
Christmas log (**la bûche de Noël**)
instead of Christmas cake.*

Christmas card NOUN
la **carte de Noël** *fem*

Did you know...?

*Christmas cards are not as common
in France as they are in Britain.
Instead, people sometimes send New
Year cards in January.*

Christmas Day NOUN
le **jour de Noël** *masc*
**Christmas Day is the twenty-
fifth of December.**
Le jour de Noël est le vingt-cinq
décembre.

Christmas dinner NOUN
le **repas de Noël** *masc*

Did you know...?

*In France, most people also have a
Christmas meal (**réveillon de
Noël**) on Christmas Eve.*

Christmas Eve NOUN
la **veille de Noël** *fem*
**Christmas Eve is the twenty-
fourth of December.**
La veille de Noël est le vingt-
quatre décembre.

Christmas tree NOUN
le **sapin de Noël** *masc*
**a big Christmas
tree**
un grand sapin
de Noël

church NOUN
l' **église** *fem*
**I don't go to church every
Sunday.**
Je ne vais pas à l'église tous les
dimanches.

cider NOUN
le **cidre** *masc*

English French

a
b
c
d
e
f
g
h
i
j
k
l
m
n
o
p
q
r
s
t
u
v
w
x
y
z

cigarette NOUN
la **cigarette** *fem*

cinema NOUN
le **cinéma** *masc*
I'm going to the cinema this evening.
Je vais au cinéma ce soir.

circle NOUN
le **cercle** *masc*
Stand in a cicle.
Mettez-vous en cercle.

circumflex NOUN
l' **accent circonflexe** *masc*
'Tête' has a circumflex.
'Tête' a un accent circonflexe.

circus NOUN
le **cirque** *masc*

citizenship NOUN
la **citoyenneté** *fem*

city NOUN
la **grande ville** *fem*
I live in a city.
J'habite dans une grande ville.
the city centre
le centre-ville
It's in the city centre.
C'est au centre-ville.

clap

clap *can be a verb or a noun.*

A VERB
frapper dans ses mains
Sing and clap!
Chantez et frappez dans vos mains!

B NOUN
Give Delphine a clap.
Applaudissez Delphine!

clarinet NOUN
la **clarinette** *fem*
I play the clarinet.
Je joue de la clarinette.

class NOUN
1 la **classe** *fem (group)*
Hermione is in my class.
Hermione est dans ma classe.
2 le **cours** *masc (lesson)*
I go to dancing classes.
Je vais à des cours de danse.

classroom NOUN
la **classe** *fem*

classroom assistant NOUN
l' **aide-éducateur** *masc*
l' **aide-éducatrice** *fem*

clean

clean *can be an adjective or a verb.*

A ADJECTIVE
propre
a clean shirt
une chemise propre
B VERB
nettoyer
Clean the board please!
Nettoie le tableau s'il te plaît!

cleaner NOUN
1 la **femme de ménage** *fem (woman)*
2 l' **agent d'entretien** *masc (man)*

clear ADJECTIVE
clair *masc*
claire *fem*
a clear explanation
une explication claire

368

English French

a
b
c
d
e
f
g
h
i
j
k
l
m
n
o
p
q
r
s
t
u
v
w
x
y
z

clementine NOUN
la **clémentine** fem

clever ADJECTIVE
intelligent masc
intelligente fem
Sylvie is very clever.
Sylvie est très intelligente.

click VERB
cliquer
Click on the icon!
Clique sur l'icône!

climate NOUN
le **climat** masc
We have a terrible climate.
Nous avons un climat terrible.

cloakroom NOUN
1 le **vestiaire** masc (for coats)
2 les **toilettes** fem pl (toilet)

clock NOUN
1 l' **horloge** fem (big)
the station clock
l'horloge de la gare
2 la **pendule** fem (smaller)
Look at the clock.
Regardez la pendule.

close

close can be a verb, an adjective or
an adverb.

A VERB
fermer
Please close the door.
Ferme la porte, s'il te plaît.
Close your books, children.
Fermez vos livres, les enfants.
What time does the pool close?
La piscine ferme à quelle heure?
B ADJECTIVE
proche (near)
**My house is close to the
school.**
Ma maison est proche de l'école.

C ADVERB
Come closer, Pierre.
Rapproche-toi, Pierre.

Language tip

The verb, adjective, and adverb
close *have the same spelling, but
one of them is pronounced 'cloze'.
Which one?*

closed ADJECTIVE
fermé masc
fermée fem
The door's closed.
La porte est fermée.

clothes PL NOUN
les **vêtements** masc pl
I'd like some new clothes.
Je voudrais de nouveaux
vêtements.

cloud NOUN
le **nuage** masc
There are black clouds.
Il y a des nuages noirs.

cloudy ADJECTIVE
It's cloudy today.
Il fait gris aujourd'hui.

Language tip

gris *means 'grey'. It is rather grey
when it's cloudy.*

clown
NOUN
le **clown**
masc

club NOUN
1 le **club** masc
a football club
un club de football

369

2 *(in cards)*
clubs
le trèfle
the ace of clubs
l'as de trèfle

coach NOUN
le **car** *masc*
by coach
en car
We're going by coach.
Nous y allons en car.

> **Language tip**
>
> *Be careful! The French word* **car**
> *doesn't mean the same as the*
> *English word* **car**.

coach station NOUN
la **gare routière** *fem*

coal NOUN
le **charbon** *masc*

coast NOUN
la **côte** *fem*
It's on the west coast of
Scotland.
C'est sur la côte ouest de
l'Écosse.

coat NOUN
le **manteau** *masc*
(PL les **manteaux**)
I'm wearing a warm coat.
Je porte un manteau chaud.

cocoa NOUN
le **cacao** *masc*

coconut NOUN
la **noix de coco** *fem*

coffee NOUN
le **café** *masc*
I like coffee.
J'aime le café.
A cup of coffee, please.
Un café, s'il vous plaît.

coffee table NOUN
la **table basse** *fem*

coin NOUN
la **pièce de monnaie** *fem*
a two euro coin
une pièce de deux euros

Coke® NOUN
le **coca** *masc*
a can of Coke®
une boîte de coca

cold

> **cold** *can be an adjective or a noun.*

A ADJECTIVE
froid *masc*
froide *fem*
The water's
cold.
L'eau est
froide.

It's cold today.
Il fait froid aujourd'hui.
I'm cold.
J'ai froid.
I'm not cold.
Je n'ai pas froid.
Are you cold?
Tu as froid?

B NOUN
le **rhume** *masc (illness)*
I've got a cold.
J'ai un rhume.
Ron's got a cold.
Ron a un rhume.

coleslaw NOUN
la **salade de chou cru à la**
mayonnaise *fem*

collar NOUN
le **col** *masc*

English French

a white collar
un col blanc

collect VERB
1 **ramasser** (pick up)
   Collect the books please, Natasha.
   Ramasse les livres s'il te plaît, Natasha.
2 **faire collection de** (as hobby)
   I collect stamps.
   Je fais collection de timbres.

collection NOUN
la **collection** fem

college NOUN
le **lycée** masc
   a technical college
   un lycée technique

colour

colour can be a noun or a verb.

A NOUN
la **couleur** fem
What colour eyes has he got?
Il a les yeux de quelle couleur?

What colour is it?
C'est de quelle couleur?

B VERB
colorier
Colour it blue, children.
Coloriez en bleu, les enfants.

comb NOUN
le **peigne** masc

come VERB
1 **venir**
   Come with me, Jean.
   Viens avec moi, Jean.

Can I come too?
Est-ce que je peux venir aussi?
I'll come with you.
Je viens avec toi.
2 **arriver** (arrive)
   The bus is coming.
   Le bus arrive.
   The letter came this morning.
   La lettre est arrivée ce matin.

I'm coming!
J'arrive!
Come on!
Allez!

come back VERB
revenir
   Come back, Louise!
   Reviens, Louise!

come from VERB
venir de
   Where do you come from?
   Tu viens d'où?

come in VERB
entrer
   Can I come in?
   Je peux entrer?

Come in!
Entrez!

comfortable ADJECTIVE
1 **à l'aise** (person)
   Are you comfortable?
   Tu es à l'aise?
2 **confortable** (bed, chair)
   a comfortable bed
   un lit confortable

comic NOUN
l' **illustré** masc
   a comic
   un illustré

a b c d e f g h i j k l m n o p q r s t u v w x y z

English French

a b c d e f g h i j k l m n o p q r s t u v w x y z

comma NOUN
la **virgule** *fem*

common ADJECTIVE
courant *masc*
courante *fem*
'Smith' is a very common surname.
'Smith' est un nom de famille très courant.

communion NOUN
la **communion** *fem*
my First Communion
ma première communion

compared ADJECTIVE
Oxford is small compared with London.
Oxford est une petite ville en comparaison de Londres.

competition
NOUN
le **concours**
masc

competitor NOUN
le **concurrent** *masc*
la **concurrente** *fem*

complete

complete can be an adjective or a verb.

A ADJECTIVE
complet *masc*
complète *fem*
B VERB
finir
You must complete your homework by Friday.
Il faut finir vos devoirs pour vendredi.

completely ADVERB
complètement

complicated ADJECTIVE
compliqué *masc*
compliquée *fem*

comprehension NOUN
l' **exercice de compréhension** *masc*
(exercise)

comprehensive school
NOUN
1 le **collège** *masc* (for pupils 11–15)
2 le **lycée** *masc* (for pupils 15–18)

Did you know…?
In France, pupils go to a **collège** between the ages of 11 and 15, and then to a **lycée** until the age of 18.

computer NOUN
l' **ordinateur** *masc*

computer game NOUN
le **jeu électronique** *masc*
I like computer games.
J'aime les jeux électroniques.

computer room NOUN
la **salle d'informatique** *fem*

concert NOUN
le **concert** *masc*

cone NOUN
le **cornet** *masc*
an ice-cream cone
un cornet de glace

congratulations PL NOUN
les **félicitations** *fem pl*
Congratulations!
Félicitations!

conjurer NOUN
le **prestidigitateur** *masc*

conservatory NOUN
le **jardin d'hiver** *masc*

constant ADJECTIVE
constant *masc*
constante *fem*

contact lenses PL NOUN
les **verres de contact** *masc pl*

container NOUN
le **récipient** *masc*
   a plastic container
   un récipient en plastique

contest NOUN
le **concours** *masc*

contestant NOUN
le **concurrent** *masc*
la **concurrente** *fem*

continent NOUN
le **continent** *masc*
   How many continents are there?
   Il y a combien de continents?
   the Continent
   l'Europe
   on the Continent
   en Europe

continental breakfast NOUN
le **petit déjeuner à la française** *masc*

continue VERB
continuer
   Continue with your work, children!
   Continuez à travailler, les enfants!

convent school NOUN
le **couvent** *masc*
   She goes to a convent school.
   Elle va au couvent.

conversation NOUN
la **conversation** *fem*

cook

> **cook** *can be a verb or a noun.*

A VERB
1 cuisiner
   I can cook.
   Je sais cuisiner.
   I can't cook.
   Je ne sais pas cuisiner.
2 faire cuire *(potatoes, rice etc)*
   Cook the pasta for ten minutes.
   Faites cuire les pâtes pendant dix minutes.
B NOUN
   le **cuisinier** *masc*
   la **cuisinière** *fem*
   Matthew's an excellent cook.
   Matthew est un excellent cuisinier.

cookbook NOUN
le **livre de cuisine** *masc*

cooked ADJECTIVE
cuit *masc*
cuite *fem*
   I don't like cooked tomatoes.
   Je n'aime pas les tomates cuites.

cooker NOUN
la **cuisinière** *fem*
   a gas cooker
   une cuisinière à gaz

cooking NOUN
la **cuisine** *fem*
   I like cooking.
   J'aime bien cuisiner.

a
b
c
d
e
f
g
h
i
j
k
l
m
n
o
p
q
r
s
t
u
v
w
x
y
z

cool ADJECTIVE
1 **frais** *masc*
fraîche *fem (quite cold)*
a cool place
un endroit frais
2 **super** *(great)*

copy

> **copy** *can be a noun or a verb.*

A NOUN
la **copie** *fem*
Make a copy.
Faites une copie.
B VERB
copier
Copy the words off the board.
Copiez les mots au tableau.

cork NOUN
le **bouchon** *masc*

corkscrew NOUN
le **tire-bouchon** *masc*

corner NOUN
le **coin** *masc*
in a corner of the room
dans un coin de la pièce

cornflakes PL NOUN
les **corn-flakes** *masc pl*

Cornwall NOUN
la **Cornouailles** *fem*

correct

> **correct** *can be an adjective or a verb.*

A ADJECTIVE
exact *masc*
exacte *fem*
That's correct.
C'est exact.
the correct answer
la bonne réponse

B VERB
corriger
Correct the spelling.
Corrigez l'orthographe.

correction NOUN
la **correction** *fem*

correctly ADVERB
correctement

corridor NOUN
le **couloir** *masc*
in the corridor
dans le couloir

Corsica NOUN
la **Corse** *fem*

cost VERB
coûter
A coke costs two euros.
Un coca coûte deux euros.

> **How much does it cost?**
> Ça coûte combien?

costume
NOUN
le **costume**
masc

cottage NOUN
le **cottage** *masc*

cotton NOUN
le **coton** *masc*
a cotton shirt
une chemise en coton

> ***Language tip***
> *The French word only has one **t**.*

couch NOUN
le **canapé** *masc*

cough

cough *can be a noun or a verb.*

A NOUN
la **toux** *fem*
a bad cough
une mauvaise toux
I've got a cough.
Je tousse.

B VERB
tousser
I can't stop coughing.
Je n'arrête pas de tousser.

could VERB

Could I have a glass of water?
Je peux avoir un verre d'eau?
Could you move a bit?
Tu peux te pousser un peu?
Could you move a bit, boys?
Vous pouvez vous pousser un peu, les garçons?

Could I ...?
Je peux ...?
Could you ...?
Tu peux ...?

count VERB
compter
Count from one to twenty!
Comptez de un à vingt!

counter NOUN
1 le **comptoir** *masc (in shop)*
2 le **jeton** *masc (in game)*

country NOUN
1 le **pays** *masc (France, Britain etc)*
France is a big country.
La France est un grand pays.
2 la **campagne** *fem (countryside)*
I live in the country.
J'habite à la campagne.

country dancing NOUN
la **danse folklorique** *fem*

countryside NOUN
la **campagne** *fem*
in the countryside
à la campagne

couple NOUN
a couple of days
deux jours
a couple of hours
deux heures
a young couple
un jeune couple

courgette NOUN
la **courgette** *fem*

course NOUN
1 le **plat** *masc (of meal)*
the main course
le plat principal
the first course
l'entrée
2 le **cours** *masc (lessons)*
a French course
un cours de français
**Do you love me? —
Of course I do!**
Tu m'aimes? — Bien sûr que oui!

of course
bien sûr

court NOUN
le **court** *masc*
There are tennis courts.
Il y a des courts de tennis.

cousin NOUN
le **cousin** *masc*
la **cousine** *fem*
Jo is my favourite cousin.
Jo est ma cousine préférée.

a
b
c
d
e
f
g
h
i
j
k
l
m
n
o
p
q
r
s
t
u
v
w
x
y
z

cover NOUN
la **couverture** *fem*

cow NOUN
la **vache** *fem*
a big black cow
une grosse vache noire

crab NOUN
le **crabe** *masc*

cracker NOUN
1 le **cracker** *masc* (biscuit)
2 la **papillote** *fem* (Christmas cracker)

Did you know...?

papillotes *are different from crackers in Britain. They consist of a sweet with a joke and a banger wrapped round it, covered in foil. You unwrap them and pull the banger.*

crash NOUN
l' **accident** *masc*
a crash
un accident

crawl NOUN
le **crawl** *masc*
I can do the crawl.
Je sais nager le crawl.

crazy ADJECTIVE
fou *masc*
folle *fem*

cream

cream *can be a noun or an adjective.*

A NOUN
la **crème** *fem*
strawberries and cream
les fraises à la crème
B ADJECTIVE
crème *masc, fem, pl* (colour)
a cream shirt
une chemise crème

Language tip

Colour adjectives come after the noun in French.

cream cake NOUN
le **gâteau à la crème** *masc*
two cream cakes
deux gâteaux à la crème

credit card NOUN
la **carte de crédit** *fem*

cress NOUN
le **cresson** *masc*
I'm growing cress.
Je fais pousser du cresson.

crew cut NOUN
les **cheveux en brosse** *masc pl*
He's got a crew cut.
Il a les cheveux en brosse.

cricket NOUN
le **cricket** *masc*
I play cricket.
Je joue au cricket.

Did you know...?

Cricket *is not played in France.*

cricket bat NOUN
la **batte de cricket** *fem*

crisps PL NOUN
les **chips** *fem pl*
a bag of crisps
un paquet de chips

English **French**

a
b
c
d
e
f
g
h
i
j
k
l
m
n
o
p
q
r
s
t
u
v
w
x
y
z

cross

> **cross** can be a verb, a noun or an adjective.

A VERB
traverser
Cross the road at the lights.
Traversez la rue aux feux.

B NOUN
la **croix** _fem_
Put a tick or a cross.
Cochez ou mettez une croix.

C ADJECTIVE
pas content _masc_
pas contente _fem_
She is cross.
Elle n'est pas contente.

crossing NOUN
la **traversée** _fem_
the crossing from Dover to Calais
la traversée de Douvres à Calais

crossroads NOUN
le **carrefour** _masc_
at the crossroads
au carrefour

crossword NOUN
les **mots croisés** _masc pl_
I like doing crosswords.
J'aime faire les mots croisés.

crowd NOUN
la **foule** _fem_

crowded ADJECTIVE
bondé _masc_
bondée _fem_
The pool is crowded on Saturdays.
La piscine est bondée le samedi.

crown NOUN
la **couronne** _fem_

crutch NOUN
la **béquille** _fem_

cry VERB
pleurer
Why are you crying?
Pourquoi tu pleures?

cub NOUN
1 le **louveteau** _masc_
(PL les **louveteaux**) _(scout)_

> **_Did you know...?_**
> Cubs and scouts are not as common in France as they are in Britain.

2 le **petit** _masc (young animal)_

cube NOUN
le **cube** _masc_

cucumber NOUN
le **concombre** _masc_

cup NOUN
la **tasse** _fem_
a cup of tea
une tasse de thé
a cup of coffee
un café

cupboard NOUN
le **placard** _masc_
What's in the cupboard?
Qu'est-ce qu'il y a dans le placard?

curious ADJECTIVE
curieux *masc*
curieuse *fem*

curly ADJECTIVE
1 **bouclé** *masc*
bouclée *fem (wavy)*
2 **frisé** *masc*
frisée *fem (tightly curled)*

currant NOUN
le **raisin sec** *masc*
I don't like currants.
Je n'aime pas les raisins secs.

Language tip
raisin sec *means 'dried grape',
which is what a currant is.*

curriculum NOUN
le **programme** *masc*

curry NOUN
le **curry** *masc*

curtain NOUN
le **rideau** *masc* (PL les **rideaux**)
**The curtains are green and
white.**
Les rideaux sont verts et blancs.
Draw the curtains, please.
Tirez les rideaux, s'il vous plaît.

cushion NOUN
le **coussin** *masc*

custard NOUN
la **crème anglaise** *fem*

custom NOUN
la **coutume** *fem*
It's an old custom.
C'est une ancienne coutume.

customer NOUN
le **client** *masc*
la **cliente** *fem*

cut VERB
couper
I'll cut the cake.
Je vais couper le gâteau.
Mind you don't cut yourself!
Attention à ne pas te couper!

cutlery NOUN
les **couverts** *masc pl*

cycle VERB
faire du vélo
I like cycling.
J'aime faire du vélo.
I cycle to school.
Je vais à l'école à vélo.

cycle lane NOUN
la **piste cyclable** *fem*

cycling NOUN
le **cyclisme** *masc*

cyclist NOUN
le/la **cycliste** *masc/fem*

D d

dad NOUN
1 le **père** *masc*
my dad
mon père
his dad
son père
2 le **papa** *masc (used as a name)*
Dad!
Papa!
Let's ask Dad.
On va demander
à papa.

daddy NOUN
le **papa** *masc*
Hello Daddy!
Bonjour Papa!

daffodil NOUN
la **jonquille** *fem*

daily ADVERB
tous les jours
**The pool is open daily from
9 a.m. to 6 p.m.**
La piscine est ouverte tous les
jours de neuf heures à dix-huit
heures.

damn EXCLAMATION
Zut!

damp ADJECTIVE
humide

dance

> **dance** *can be a noun or a verb.*

A NOUN
1 la **danse** *fem*
It's a new dance.
C'est une nouvelle danse.
2 le **bal** *masc*
**Are you going to the dance
tonight, Marie-Thérèse?**
Tu vas au bal ce soir, Marie-
Thérèse?
B VERB
danser
Can you dance?
Tu sais danser?
I like dancing.
J'aime danser.

dancer NOUN
le **danseur** *masc*
la **danseuse** *fem*

dandelion NOUN
le **pissenlit** *masc*

danger NOUN
le **danger** *masc*
in danger
en danger
His life is in danger.
Sa vie est en danger.

dangerous ADJECTIVE
dangereux *masc*
dangereuse *fem*

dark

> **dark** *can be an adjective or a noun.*

A ADJECTIVE
1 **foncé** *masc*
foncée *fem (colour)*
a dark green sweater
un pull vert foncé
She's got dark hair.
Elle a les cheveux bruns.

2 *(at night)*
It's dark at six o'clock.
Il fait nuit à six heures.
It's getting dark.
Il commence à faire nuit.
B NOUN
le **noir** *masc*
I'm afraid of the dark.
J'ai peur du noir.

darling NOUN
le **chéri** *masc*
la **chérie** *fem*
Thank you, darling!
Merci, chéri!

dart NOUN
la **fléchette** *fem*
Do you want to play darts?
Tu veux jouer aux fléchettes?

date NOUN
la **date** *fem*
my date of birth
ma date de naissance
What date is your birthday?
Quelle est la date de ton
anniversaire?

What's the date today?
Quelle est la date aujourd'hui?

daughter NOUN
la **fille** *fem*

day NOUN

Language tip
There are two words for **day***: un*
jour *is the whole 24 hours,* **une**
journée *is the time you're awake.*

1 le **jour** *masc*
**I am going to Paris for three
days.**
Je vais à Paris pour trois jours.
2 la **journée** *fem*
during the day
dans la journée
Marc watches TV all day.
Marc regarde la télé toute la
journée.
the day before my birthday
la veille de mon anniversaire
**It's Richard's birthday the
day after tomorrow.**
C'est l'anniversaire de Richard
après-demain.
It's my day off.
C'est mon jour de congé.

the days of the week
les jours de la semaine
every day
tous les jours
all day
toute la journée
What day is it today?
Quel jour sommes-nous?
the day after tomorrow
après-demain

dead ADJECTIVE
mort *masc*
morte *fem*

deaf ADJECTIVE
sourd *masc*
sourde *fem*

deal

deal *can be a noun or a verb.*

A NOUN
le **marché** *masc*
It's a deal!
Marché conclu!
a great deal
beaucoup
a great deal of money
beaucoup d'argent

B VERB
donner *(cards)*
It's your turn to deal.
C'est à toi de donner.

dear ADJECTIVE
cher *masc*
chère *fem*
Dear Mrs Duval
Chère Madame Duval

death NOUN
la **mort** *fem*
after his death
après sa mort

Language tip
mort *is related to the words 'mortal' and 'mortality' in English.*

December NOUN
décembre *masc*
December or January?
Décembre ou janvier?
My birthday's in December.
Mon anniversaire est en décembre.

in December
en décembre
the fifth of December
le cinq décembre

Language tip
The months are not spelled with capital letters in French.

decide VERB
décider
I have decided to go to the party.
J'ai décidé d'aller à la fête.
I can't decide.
Je n'arrive pas à me décider.

decision NOUN
la **décision** *fem*
What's your decision?
Quelle est ta décision?
We need to make a decision.
On doit prendre une décision.

deck NOUN
le **pont** *masc*
on deck
sur le pont

deckchair NOUN
la **chaise longue** *fem*

decorate VERB
1 décorer
We decorate the classroom for Christmas.
Nous décorons la classe pour Noël.
2 peindre et tapisser
(a room)
Mum's going to decorate my bedroom.
Maman va peindre et tapisser ma chambre.

Language tip
*Use **peindre** alone, if you just mean 'paint'. Use **tapisser** alone, if you just mean 'wallpaper'.*

English French

a b c **d** e f g h i j k l m n o p q r s t u v w x y z

decorations PL NOUN
les **décorations** *fem pl*
Christmas decorations
les décorations de Noël

deep ADJECTIVE
1 **profond** *masc*
profonde *fem (water, hole, cut)*
Is it deep?
Est-ce que c'est profond?
2 **épais** *masc*
épaisse *fem (snow, mud)*
The snow is deep.
La neige est épaisse.
Take a deep breath, girls!
Respirez à fond, les filles!

deer NOUN
1 le **cerf** *masc*
(red deer)
2 le **daim** *masc*
(fallow deer)
3 le **chevreuil**
masc (roe deer)

Language tip

In French, you have to say which kind of deer you are talking about!

---

defence NOUN
la **défense** *fem*
I play in defence.
Je joue en défense.

Language tip

What are the two differences in spelling between the French word and the English word?

---

defender NOUN
le **défenseur** *masc*

definite ADJECTIVE
1 **précis** *masc*
précise *fem (precise)*
I haven't got any definite plans.
Je n'ai pas de projets précis.
2 **sûr** *masc*
sûre *fem (certain)*
Maybe, it's not definite.
Peut-être, ce n'est pas sûr.

definitely ADVERB
vraiment
He's definitely the best player.
C'est vraiment lui le meilleur joueur.
Definitely!
C'est sûr!

degree NOUN
1 le **degré** *masc (measurement)*
a temperature of thirty degrees
une température de trente degrés
2 la **licence** *fem (qualification)*
a degree in English
une licence d'anglais

delayed ADJECTIVE
retardé *masc*
retardée *fem*
All flights are delayed.
Tous les vols sont retardés.

delicatessen NOUN
l' **épicerie fine** *fem*
a delicatessen
une épicerie fine

delicious ADJECTIVE
délicieux *masc*
délicieuse *fem*
The chocolate mousse is delicious!
La mousse au chocolat est délicieuse!

deliver VERB
1 **livrer**
I deliver newspapers.
Je livre les journaux.
2 **distribuer** (letters)
The postman delivers our mail.
Le facteur distribue notre courrier.

denim NOUN
le **jean** masc
a denim jacket
une veste en jean

Denmark NOUN
le **Danemark** masc

dentist NOUN
le/la **dentiste** masc/fem
I'm going to the dentist.
Je vais chez le dentiste.
Catherine is a dentist.
Catherine est dentiste.

Language tip

*You do not translate '**a**' when you say what someone's job is in French.*

---

department NOUN
1 le **rayon** masc (in shop)
the shoe department
le rayon chaussures
2 le **département** masc (of university, school)
He works in the English department.
Il travaille dans le département d'anglais.

department store NOUN
le **grand magasin** masc

departure NOUN
le **départ** masc

departure lounge NOUN
le **hall des départs** masc

depend VERB
It depends.
Ça dépend.
depending on the weather
selon le temps

deposit NOUN
1 les **arrhes** fem pl (part payment)
You have to pay a deposit when you book.
Il faut verser des arrhes lors de la réservation.
2 la **caution** fem (when hiring something)
You get the deposit back when you return the bike.
On vous remboursera la caution quand vous ramènerez le vélo.

depressed ADJECTIVE
déprimé masc
déprimée fem
I feel depressed.
Je suis déprimé.

deputy head NOUN
le **directeur adjoint** masc
la **directrice adjointe** fem

describe VERB
décrire
Describe yourself.
Décris-toi.

description NOUN
la **description** fem

desert NOUN
le **désert** *masc*

desert island NOUN
l' **île déserte** *fem*

deserve VERB
mériter
You deserve a prize, Marie.
Tu mérites un prix, Marie.

design

> *design can be a noun or a verb.*

A NOUN
le **motif** *masc (pattern)*
a simple design
un motif simple

B VERB
dessiner
We're going to design a birthday card.
On va dessiner une carte d'anniversaire.

designer clothes PL NOUN
les **vêtements griffés** *masc pl*

desk NOUN
1 le **pupitre** *masc (in school)*
my desk
mon pupitre
2 le **bureau** *masc*
(PL les **bureaux**) *(in office)*

dessert NOUN
le **dessert** *masc*
for dessert
comme dessert

destination NOUN
la **destination** *fem*

detached house NOUN
le **pavillon** *masc*

detail NOUN
le **détail** *masc*
in detail
en détail

detective NOUN
l' **inspecteur de police** *masc*
He's a detective.
Il est inspecteur de police.

> *Language tip*
> *When you say what someone's job is in French, you do not translate* a.

detective story NOUN
le **roman policier** *masc*

detention NOUN
You'll get a detention!
Tu vas avoir une retenue!

develop VERB
développer
I want to get this film developed.
Je veux faire développer ce film.

> *Language tip*
> *The French word* **développer** *has double* p.

diabetic NOUN
le/la **diabétique** *masc/fem*
I'm a diabetic.
Je suis diabétique.

diagonal ADJECTIVE
diagonal *masc*
diagonale *fem*

diagram NOUN
le **diagramme** *masc*

dial VERB
composer

Dial the number.
Composez le numéro.

dialogue NOUN
le **dialogue** masc

diamond NOUN
1 le **diamant** masc
   a diamond ring
   une bague en diamant
2 (cards) **diamonds**
   le carreau
   the ace of diamonds
   l'as de carreau

diary NOUN
1 l' **agenda** masc
   I've got her phone number in my diary.
   J'ai son numéro de téléphone dans mon agenda.
2 le **journal** masc
   (PL les **journaux**)
   I keep a diary.
   Je tiens un journal.

Language tip

*The French word **journal** is related to the word 'jour', which means 'day'. **Journal** also means 'newspaper'. Newspapers come out every day, and people write in their diaries every day.*

dice NOUN
le **dé** masc
   Throw the dice, Leah.
   Jette le dé, Leah.

dictionary NOUN
le **dictionnaire** masc

Look in the dictionary.
Cherchez dans le dictionnaire.

Language tip

*The French word **dictionnaire** has a double **n**.*

did VERB ▷ see **do**

die VERB
mourir
   He died last year.
   Il est mort l'année dernière.
   She died in 2002.
   Elle est morte en deux mille deux.

diesel NOUN
1 le **gazole** masc (fuel)
2 la **voiture diesel** fem (car)

diet

diet can be a noun or a verb.

A NOUN
1 l' **alimentation** fem
   a healthy diet
   une alimentation saine
2 le **régime** masc (for slimming)
   My dad's on a diet.
   Mon père est au régime.
   Are you on a diet?
   Tu es au régime?
B VERB
faire un régime
   My mum's dieting.
   Ma mère fait un régime.

difference NOUN
la **différence** fem
   What's the difference?
   Quelle est la différence?

different ADJECTIVE
différent masc
différente fem

English French

a b c **d** e f g h i j k l m n o p q r s t u v w x y z

We are very different.
Nous sommes très différents.
Paris is different from London.
Paris est différent de Londres.

difficult ADJECTIVE
difficile
It's difficult.
C'est difficile.

difficulty NOUN
la **difficulté** fem
without difficulty
sans difficulté

dig VERB
creuser
My rabbit digs lots of holes.
Mon lapin creuse beaucoup de trous.

digital camera NOUN
l'**appareil photo numérique** masc

digital radio NOUN
la **radio numérique** fem

digital television NOUN
la **télévision numérique** fem

dinghy NOUN
a rubber dinghy
un canot pneumatique

dining room NOUN
la **salle à manger** fem

Language tip

manger means 'to eat', so the French literally means 'the room for eating'.

dinner NOUN
1 le **déjeuner** masc (midday meal)
2 le **dîner** masc (evening meal)

dinner lady NOUN
la **dame de service** fem

dinner time NOUN
1 l' **heure du déjeuner** fem (midday meal)
2 l' **heure du dîner** fem (evening meal)

dinosaur NOUN
le **dinosaure** masc

direct ADJECTIVE
direct masc
directe fem
the most direct route
le chemin le plus direct

direction NOUN
la **direction** fem
You're going in the wrong direction.
Vous allez dans la mauvaise direction.

dirty ADJECTIVE
sale
My shoes are dirty.
Mes chaussures sont sales.

disabled ADJECTIVE
handicapé masc
handicapée fem
disabled people
les handicapés

disagree VERB
I disagree!
Je ne suis pas d'accord!

disappointed ADJECTIVE
déçu masc
déçue fem

disappointment NOUN
la **déception** *fem*

disaster NOUN
le **désastre** *masc*
It's a disaster!
C'est un désastre!

discipline NOUN
la **discipline** *fem*

disc jockey NOUN
le **disc-jockey** *masc*

disco NOUN
la **soirée disco** *fem*
There's a disco at the school tonight.
Il y a une soirée disco à l'école ce soir.

discussion NOUN
la **discussion** *fem*

disguise VERB
déguiser
He was disguised as a policeman.
Il était déguisé en policier.

Language tip

Which consonant is different from the English in the French word **déguiser**?

---

disgusting ADJECTIVE
dégoûtant *masc*
dégoûtante *fem*
It looks disgusting.
Ça a l'air dégoûtant.

dish NOUN
le **plat** *masc*
a vegetarian dish
un plat végétarien

I always do the dishes.
Je fais toujours la vaisselle.

dishwasher NOUN
le **lave-vaisselle** *masc*

disk NOUN
le **disque** *masc*

dislike NOUN
my likes and dislikes
ce que j'aime et ce que je n'aime pas

distance NOUN
la **distance** *fem*
a distance of ten kilometres
une distance de dix kilomètres
in the distance
au loin

distract VERB
distraire
Don't distract him, Lulu.
Ne le distraie pas, Lulu.

district NOUN
1 le **quartier** *masc* (of town)
2 la **région** *fem* (of country)

disturb VERB
déranger
I'm sorry to disturb you.
Je suis désolé de vous déranger.

dive VERB
plonger
I like diving.
J'aime plonger.

Language tip

plonger *is related to the English word 'plunge'. When you dive, you plunge into the pool.*

---

divide VERB
diviser
Divide the pastry in half.
Divisez la pâte en deux.

Twelve divided by three is
four.
Douze divisé par trois égale
quatre.
Divide into two groups!
Divisez-vous en deux groupes!

diving board NOUN
le **plongeoir** masc

divorced ADJECTIVE
divorcé masc
divorcée fem
My parents are divorced.
Mes parents sont divorcés.

Diwali NOUN
le **Dipavali** masc

DIY NOUN
le **bricolage** masc
He likes doing DIY.
Il aime faire du bricolage.

dizzy ADJECTIVE
I feel dizzy.
J'ai la tête qui tourne.

DJ NOUN
le **disc-jockey** masc

do VERB

Language tip

Look carefully through the entry for
do to find what you want to say.

faire
**I do a lot of
cycling.**
Je fais beaucoup
de vélo.
**What are you
doing this
evening?**
Qu'est-ce
que tu fais
ce soir?

My brother does judo.
Mon frère fait du judo.
Do the actions.
Faites les gestes!
I haven't done my homework.
Je n'ai pas fait mes devoirs.
Who did that?
Qui a fait ça?
That'll do, thanks.
Ça ira, merci.

Language tip

In English, **do** is often used to make
questions. In French, questions are
made either with **est-ce que**.

Do you like French food?
Est-ce que vous aimez la cuisine
française?
Where does he live?
Où est-ce qu'il habite?
**What do you do in your free
time?**
Qu'est-ce que vous faites
pendant vos loisirs?

Language tip

... or by reversing the order of verb
and subject ...

Do you speak English?
Parlez-vous anglais?

Language tip

... or by adding a question mark.

Do you speak French, Kevin?
Tu parles français, Kevin?

Language tip

Use **ne ... pas** in negative sentences.

I don't understand.
Je ne comprends pas.
She doesn't like dogs.
Elle n'aime pas les chiens.
**You go swimming on Fridays,
don't you?**

Tu fais de la natation le vendredi, n'est-ce pas?

What are you doing?
Qu'est-ce que tu fais?
I'm not doing anything.
Je ne fais rien.
... don't you?
... n'est-ce pas?

do up VERB
1 **lacer** *(tie)*
Do up your shoes!
Lace tes chaussures!
2 **boutonner** *(button up)*
Do up your coat!
Boutonne ton manteau!
Do up your zip! *(on trousers)*
Ferme ta braguette!

doctor NOUN
le **médecin** *masc*
I'm going to the doctor.
Je vais chez le médecin.
I'd like to be a doctor.
Je voudrais être médecin.
She's a doctor.
Elle est médecin.

Language tip
You do not translate 'a' when you say what someone's job is in French.

dodgems PL NOUN
les **autos tamponneuses** *fem pl*

does VERB ▷ *see* **do**

dog NOUN
le **chien** *masc*
la **chienne** *fem*
Have you got a dog?
Tu as un chien?

doll NOUN
la **poupée** *fem*

dolphin
NOUN
le **dauphin**
masc

dominoes PL NOUN
Let's have a game of dominoes.
Faisons une partie de dominos.

done VERB ▷ *see* **do**

donkey NOUN
l' **âne** *masc*
Pin the tail on the donkey!
Accroche la queue à l'âne.

door NOUN
1 la **porte** *fem*
the first door on the right
la première porte à droite
2 la **portière** *fem (of car, train)*

dormitory NOUN
le **dortoir** *masc*

Language tip
dormitory *is related to the verb* **dormir**, *which means 'to sleep'. A* **dormitory** *is a place where you sleep.*

dot NOUN
le **point** *masc*

double ADJECTIVE
double
a double helping
une double portion

double bed NOUN
le **grand lit** *masc*

English French

a
b
c
d
e
f
g
h
i
j
k
l
m
n
o
p
q
r
s
t
u
v
w
x
y
z

double room NOUN
la **chambre pour deux personnes** fem

double-decker bus NOUN
le **bus à impériale** masc

doubt VERB
I doubt it.
J'en doute.

doughnut NOUN
le **beignet** masc
a jam doughnut
un beignet à la confiture

Dover NOUN
Douvres
from Dover to Boulogne
de Douvres à Boulogne
in Dover
à Douvres

down

down can be an adverb, a preposition, or an adjective.

A ADVERB
en bas
Don't look down!
Ne regarde pas en bas!
It's down in the cellar.
C'est dans la cave.
It's down there.
C'est là-bas.
B PREPOSITION
I live just down the road.
J'habite tout à côté.
C ADJECTIVE
I'm feeling a bit down.
J'ai un peu le cafard.
The computer's down.
L'ordinateur est en panne.

download VERB
télécharger
You can download the file.
Tu peux télécharger le fichier.

downstairs ADVERB
au rez-de-chaussée
The bathroom's downstairs.
La salle de bain est au rez-de-chaussée.
I'm downstairs!
Je suis en bas!

dozen NOUN
la **douzaine** fem
two dozen
deux douzaines
a dozen eggs
une douzaine d'œufs

Language tip

douzaine *is related to the French word* **douze**, *which means 'twelve'. A* **dozen** *means twelve.*

dragon NOUN
le **dragon** masc

drama NOUN
l' **art dramatique** masc
Drama is my favourite subject.
Ma matière préférée, c'est l'art dramatique.

drank VERB ▷ see drink

draughts NOUN
les **dames** fem pl
Do you want to play draughts?
Tu veux jouer aux dames?

draw

draw can be a verb or a noun.

A VERB
1 dessiner *(with pencil)*

I can't draw.
Je ne sais pas dessiner.
Draw a house, everyone.
Dessinez une maison, tout le monde.
Draw a picture.
Faites un dessin.
2 faire match nul *(in game)*
We drew 2-2.
Nous avons fait match nul deux à deux.
B NOUN
le **match nul** *masc (in game)*
It's a draw between the boys and the girls.
Match nul entre les garçons et les filles.

drawer NOUN
le **tiroir** *masc*

Language tip

You see **'Tirez'** *on doors in France. It means 'pull'.* **Un tiroir** *is something you pull out.*

---

drawing NOUN
le **dessin** *masc*

drawing pin NOUN
la **punaise** *fem*

dream NOUN
le **rêve** *masc*

Sweet dreams, darling!
Fais de beaux rêves, chérie!
a bad dream
un cauchemar

dress

---

dress *can be a noun or a verb.*

A NOUN
la **robe** *fem*
Élodie is wearing a white dress.
Élodie porte une robe blanche.
B VERB
to get dressed
s'habiller
I'm getting dressed.
Je m'habille.
Go and get dressed.
Va t'habiller.

dress up VERB
se déguiser
I'm going to dress up as a princess.
Je vais me déguiser en princesse.

dressed ADJECTIVE
habillé *masc*
habillée *fem*
I'm not dressed yet.
Je ne suis pas encore habillé.
How was she dressed?
Comment est-ce qu'elle était habillée?
She was dressed in a green sweater and jeans.
Elle portait un pull vert et un jean.

drew VERB ▷*see* **draw**

drink

---

drink *can be a verb or a noun.*

A VERB
boire
What would you like to drink?
Qu'est-ce que vous voulez boire?
She drank three cups of tea.
Elle a bu trois tasses de thé.

B NOUN

1 la **boisson** *fem*
   a cold drink
   une boisson fraîche

   a hot drink
   une boisson chaude
2 le **verre** *masc (alcoholic)*
   Would you like a drink?
   Vous prenez un verre?

drive

> **drive** *can be a noun or a verb.*

A NOUN

1 le **tour en voiture** *masc*
   Let's go for a drive.
   Allons faire un tour en voiture.
2 l' **allée** *fem (of house)*
   You can park your car in the drive.
   Vous pouvez garer votre voiture dans l'allée.

B VERB

1 **conduire** *(car)*
   She's learning to drive.
   Elle apprend à conduire.
   Can you drive?
   Tu sais conduire?
2 **aller en voiture** *(go by car)*
   Are you going by train? — No, we're driving.
   Vous prenez le train? — Non, nous y allons en voiture.
3 **emmener en voiture** *(take by car)*
   My mother drives me to school.
   Ma mère m'emmène à l'école en voiture.

driver NOUN

1 le **conducteur** *masc*
   la **conductrice** *fem (of car)*
   She's an excellent driver.
   C'est une excellente conductrice.
2 le **chauffeur** *masc (of taxi, bus)*

driving licence NOUN
le **permis de conduire** *masc*

drop

> **drop** *can be a noun or a verb.*

A NOUN
   la **goutte** *fem*
   a drop of water
   une goutte d'eau

B VERB
   laisser tomber
   Drop the ball!
   Laisse tomber la balle!

drug NOUN

1 le **médicament** *masc*
   (medicine)
   They need food and drugs.
   Ils ont besoin de nourriture et de médicaments.
2 la **drogue** *fem (illegal)*
   hard drugs
   les drogues dures
   Don't take drugs.
   Ne vous droguez pas.

drum NOUN
le **tambour** *masc*
   an African drum
   un tambour africain
   I play drums.
   Je joue de la batterie.

drum kit NOUN
la **batterie** *fem*

drummer NOUN
le **batteur** *masc*
la **batteuse** *fem*

English French
a b c d e f g h i j k l m n o p q r s t u v w x y z

drunk ADJECTIVE
ivre

dry

> **dry** can be an adjective or a verb.

A ADJECTIVE
1 **sec** masc
sèche fem (not wet)
The paint isn't dry yet.
La peinture n'est pas encore
sèche.
2 **sans pluie** (weather)
a long dry period
une longue période sans pluie
B VERB
sécher
Let the glue dry.
Laissez sécher la colle.
I need to dry my hair.
Je dois me sécher les cheveux.

duck NOUN
le **canard** masc

due ADJECTIVE
**The plane's due in half an
hour.**
L'avion doit arriver dans une
demi-heure.
When's the baby due?
Le bébé est prévu pour quand?

dull ADJECTIVE
It's dull today.
Il fait gris aujourd'hui.

dummy NOUN
la **tétine** fem

dump NOUN
It's a real dump!
C'est un endroit minable!

dungarees PL NOUN
la **salopette** fem

> **Language tip**
> **salopette** is a singular word.

dungeon NOUN
le **cachot** masc

during PREPOSITION
pendant
during the day
pendant la journée

dustbin NOUN
la **poubelle** fem

duty-free shop NOUN
la boutique hors taxes fem

duvet NOUN
la **couette** fem

DVD NOUN
le **DVD** masc
I've got that film on DVD.
J'ai ce film en DVD.

DVD player NOUN
le **lecteur de DVD** masc

dwarf NOUN
le **nain** masc
la **naine** fem

English
French

a
b
c
d
e
f
g
h
i
j
k
l
m
n
o
p
q
r
s
t
u
v
w
x
y
z

E e

each

> **each** *can be an adjective or a pronoun.*

A ADJECTIVE
chaque
each day
chaque jour

B PRONOUN
chacun *masc*
chacune *fem*
They have ten points each.
Ils ont dix points chacun.
The plates cost £5 each.
Les assiettes coûtent cinq livres chacune.
Take one card each.
Prenez une carte chacun.
We write to each other.
Nous nous écrivons.

ear NOUN
l' **oreille** *fem*

earache NOUN
I've got earache.
J'ai mal aux oreilles.

early ADVERB
1 **tôt** *(early in the day)*
I get up early.
Je me lève tôt.
I go to bed early.
Je me couche tôt.
2 **en avance** *(ahead of time)*
Come early to get a good seat.
Venez en avance pour avoir une bonne place.

earn VERB
gagner
She earns £5 an hour.
Elle gagne cinq livres de l'heure.

earring NOUN
la **boucle d'oreille** *fem*
diamond earrings
des boucles d'oreille en diamant

earth NOUN
la **terre** *fem*

east

> **east** *can be an adjective or a noun.*

A ADJECTIVE
est *masc, fem, pl*
the east coast
la côte est

B NOUN
l' **est** *masc*
in the east
dans l'est

Easter NOUN
Pâques *fem pl*
at Easter
à Pâques
the Easter holidays
les vacances de Pâques

> **Happy Easter!**
> Joyeuses Pâques!

Easter egg NOUN
l' **œuf de Pâques** *masc*
a big Easter egg
un gros œuf de Pâques

English **French**

easy ADJECTIVE
facile
> It's easy!
> C'est facile!

eat VERB
manger
> I eat a lot of sweets.
> Je mange beaucoup de bonbons.
> Would you like something to eat?
> Est-ce que tu veux manger quelque chose?

edge NOUN
le **bord** *masc*
> on the edge of the table
> au bord de la table

Edinburgh NOUN
Édimbourg
> Andrew lives in Edinburgh.
> Andrew habite à Édimbourg.

education NOUN
l' **éducation** *fem*

effect NOUN
l' **effet** *masc*

> special effects
> les effets spéciaux

effort NOUN
l' **effort** *masc*
> You have to make an effort.
> Tu dois faire un effort.

e.g. ABBREVIATION
p. ex.

egg NOUN
l' **œuf** *masc*
> a hard-boiled egg
> un œuf dur
> a soft-boiled egg
> un œuf à la coque
> a fried egg
> un œuf sur le plat
> scrambled eggs
> les œufs brouillés

Eiffel Tower NOUN
la **tour Eiffel** *fem*

eight NUMBER
huit
> eight euros
> huit euros

> She's eight.
> Elle a huit ans.

eighteen NUMBER
dix-huit
> eighteen euros
> dix-huit euros

> He is eighteen.
> Il a dix-huit ans.

Language tip
In English, you can say **eighteen** or
eighteen years old. In French,
you can only say **dix-huit ans**.

eighteenth ADJECTIVE
dix-huitième
   on the eighteenth floor
   au dix-huitième étage

the eighteenth of August
le dix-huit août

eighth ADJECTIVE
huitième
   on the eighth floor
   au huitième étage

the eighth of August
le huit août

eighty NUMBER
quatre-vingts

Language tip
quatre-vingts is made up of two
words. What does each one mean?

Eire NOUN
   la **République d'Irlande** *fem*

either ADVERB, CONJUNCTION,
PRONOUN
non plus
   **I don't like milk, and I don't
   like eggs either.**
   Je n'aime pas le lait, et je n'aime
   pas les œufs non plus.
   **I haven't got any money. —
   I haven't either.**
   Je n'ai pas d'argent. — Moi non
   plus.
   I don't like either of them.
   Je n'aime ni l'un ni l'autre.
   either ... or ...
   soit ... soit ...
   You can have either ice

cream or yoghurt.
Tu peux prendre soit une glace
soit un yaourt.

elastic band NOUN
   l' **élastique** *masc*
   an elastic band
   un élastique

elder ADJECTIVE
aîné *masc*
aînée *fem*
   my elder sister
   ma sœur aînée

elderly ADJECTIVE
âgé *masc*
âgée *fem*
   the elderly
   les personnes âgées

eldest ADJECTIVE
aîné *masc*
aînée *fem*
   my eldest sister
   ma sœur aînée
   He's the eldest.
   C'est l'aîné.

election NOUN
   l' **élection** *fem*
   an election
   une élection

electric
ADJECTIVE
électrique
   **an electric
   guitar**
   une guitare
   électrique

electricity NOUN
   l' **électricité** *fem*

electronic ADJECTIVE
électronique

English French

elegant
ADJECTIVE
élégant *masc*
élégante *fem*

elephant
NOUN
l' **éléphant** *masc*

Language tip
What is the difference in spelling between the French word and the English word?

eleven NUMBER
onze
eleven euros
onze euros

I'm eleven.
J'ai onze ans.

Language tip
In English, you can say **eleven** or **eleven years old**. In French, you can only say **onze ans**.

eleventh ADJECTIVE
onzième
on the eleventh floor
au onzième étage

the eleventh of August
le onze août

else ADVERB
d'autre
somebody else
quelqu'un d'autre
nobody else
personne d'autre
nothing else

rien d'autre
anything else
autre chose
Would you like anything else?
Désirez-vous autre chose?
I don't want anything else.
Je ne veux rien d'autre.

email

email *can be a noun or a verb.*

A NOUN
l' **e-mail** *masc*
by email
par e-mail
Send your penfriend an email.
Envoie un e-mail à ton correspondant.
B VERB
envoyer un e-mail à
I'll email you.
Je vais t'envoyer un e-mail.

email address NOUN
l' **adresse e-mail** *fem*
My email address is: ...
Mon adresse e-mail, c'est: ...

Language tip
adresse in French has one **d**, **address** in English has two **d**s.

embarrassed ADJECTIVE
gêné *masc*
gênée *fem*
I was really embarrassed.
J'étais vraiment gêné.

emergency NOUN
l' **urgence** *fem*
This is an emergency!
C'est une urgence!
in an emergency
en cas d'urgence

a b c d e f g h i j k l m n o p q r s t u v w x y z

emergency exit NOUN
la **sortie de secours** *fem*

empty

empty can be an adjective or a verb.

A ADJECTIVE
vide
The bottle is empty.
La bouteille est vide.

B VERB
vider
Empty your pockets!
Vide tes poches!

encourage VERB
encourager
Encourage your team!
Encouragez votre équipe!

Language tip
Some French words are very like English words!

encyclopedia NOUN
l' **encyclopédie** *fem*

end

end can be a noun or a verb.

A NOUN
1 la **fin** *fem (final part)*
the end of the lesson
la fin du cours
2 le **bout** *masc (of place)*
at the end of the street
au bout de la rue
B VERB
finir

What time does the lesson end?
À quelle heure est-ce que le cours finit?

Language tip
fin and **finir** in French and **finish** and **final** in English are related words. What do they have in common?

ending NOUN
la **fin** *fem*
It's a great film, especially the ending.
C'est un film génial, surtout la fin.

enemy NOUN
l' **ennemi** *masc*
l' **ennemie** *fem*

Language tip
*The French word has double **n**.*

energetic ADJECTIVE
énergique

energy NOUN
l' **énergie** *fem*

engaged ADJECTIVE
1 **occupé** *masc*
occupée *fem (busy)*
Her phone is always engaged.
Son téléphone est toujours occupé.
2 **fiancé** *masc*
fiancée *fem (to be married)*
My brother is engaged.
Mon frère est fiancé.
My sister is engaged.
Ma sœur est fiancée.
She's engaged to Ron.
Elle est fiancée à Ron.

engagement NOUN
les **fiançailles** *fem pl*

engagement ring
la **bague de fiançailles** *fem*

engine NOUN
le **moteur** *masc*

Language tip

Be careful not to translate **engine**
by the French word **engin***, which is
a slang word for 'thing'.*

England NOUN
l' **Angleterre** *fem*
　I live in England.
　J'habite en Angleterre.

to England
en Angleterre
Are you coming to England?
Tu viens en Angleterre?

English

English *can be an adjective or a
noun.*

A ADJECTIVE
　anglais *masc*
　anglaise *fem*
　I am English.
　Je suis anglais.
　English food is different.
　La cuisine anglaise est
　différente.
　English people
　les Anglais
B NOUN
　l' **anglais** *masc (language)*
　Do you speak English?
　Est-ce que vous parlez anglais?
　the English
　les Anglais

He's English.
Il est anglais.
She's English.
Elle est anglaise.

Language tip

anglais *is not spelled with a capital
letter except when it means an
English person.*

Englishman NOUN
l' **Anglais** *masc*
　an Englishman
　un Anglais

Englishwoman NOUN
l' **Anglaise** *fem*
　a Englishwoman
　une Anglaise

enjoy VERB
aimer
　I enjoy learning French.
　J'aime apprendre le français.
　Did you enjoy the film?
　Est-ce que vous avez aimé le film?

enjoyable ADJECTIVE
agréable

enormous ADJECTIVE
énorme
　**Benoît has got enormous
　feet.**
　Benoît a des pieds énormes.

enough

enough *can be an adjective or a
pronoun.*

A ADJECTIVE
　assez de
　enough time
　assez de temps
　I haven't got enough money.
　Je n'ai pas assez d'argent.

English French

a b c d **e** f g h i j k l m n o p q r s t u v w x y z

B PRONOUN
assez
Have you got enough?
Tu en as assez?
I've had enough!
J'en ai assez!

That's enough.
Ça suffit.

enter VERB
I'm going to enter the competition.
Je vais m'inscrire à la compétition.

enthusiasm NOUN
l' **enthousiasme** masc

Language tip
Which letters does the French word have that the English word doesn't?

enthusiastic ADJECTIVE
enthousiaste

entrance NOUN
l' **entrée** fem
by the entrance
à l'entrée

entrance exam NOUN
le **concours d'entrée** masc

entry NOUN
'no entry'
'défense d'entrer'

entry phone NOUN
l' **interphone** masc

envelope NOUN
l' **enveloppe** fem

Language tip
The English word has one **p**, and the French word has two **p**s.

envious ADJECTIVE
envieux masc
envieuse fem

environment NOUN
l' **environnement** masc

Language tip
What are the differences in spelling between the French word and the English word?

episode NOUN
l' **épisode** masc

equal

equal can be an adjective or a verb.

A ADJECTIVE
égal masc
égale fem
Divide the map into six equal squares.
Divisez la carte en six carrés égaux.
B VERB
égaler
Two times three equals six.
Deux fois trois égalent six.

equality NOUN
l' **égalité** fem

Language tip
What letter does the French word have instead of **qu**?

equalize VERB
égaliser
Thierry Henry has equalized.
Thierry Henry a égalisé.

equipment NOUN
l' **équipement** masc

lots of equipment
beaucoup d'équipement

error NOUN
l' **erreur** *fem*
   a small error
   une petite erreur

escalator NOUN
l' **escalier roulant** *masc*
   Is there an escalator?
   Est-ce qu'il y a un escalier roulant?

escape VERB
s'échapper
   A lion has escaped.
   Un lion s'est échappé.

especially ADVERB
surtout
   It's very hot there, especially in summer.
   Il fait très chaud là-bas, surtout en été.

essay NOUN
le **devoir** *masc*
   a history essay
   un devoir d'histoire

essential ADJECTIVE
essentiel *masc*
essentielle *fem*
   It's essential to bring warm clothes.
   Il est essentiel d'apporter des vêtements chauds.

euro NOUN
l' **euro** *masc*
   one euro
   un euro

Europe NOUN
l' **Europe** *fem*

even

A ADVERB
même
   I like all animals, even snakes.
   J'aime tous les animaux, même les serpents.

B ADJECTIVE
   an even number
   un nombre pair

evening NOUN
le **soir** *masc*
   at seven o'clock in the evening
   à sept heures du soir

this evening
ce soir
in the evening
le soir
yesterday evening
hier soir
tomorrow evening
demain soir
Good evening!
Bonsoir!

English French

a b c d **e** f g h i j k l m n o p q r s t u v w x y z

evening class NOUN
le **cours du soir** *masc*
> **My mother goes to an evening class.**
> Ma mère va à un cours du soir.

event NOUN
l' **événement** *masc*
> **an important event**
> un événement important

ever ADVERB
> **Have you ever been to France?**
> Est-ce que tu es déjà allé en France?
> **for the first time ever**
> pour la première fois

every ADJECTIVE
chaque
> **every pupil**
> chaque élève
> **every time**
> chaque fois
> **I talk to her every day.**
> Je parle avec elle tous les jours.
> **I do judo every week.**
> Je fais du judo toutes les semaines.

every day
tous les jours
every night
tous les soirs
every week
toutes les semaines

everybody PRONOUN
tout le monde
> **Good morning everybody!**
> Bonjour tout le monde!
> **Everybody likes sweets.**
> Tout le monde aime les bonbons.

everyone PRONOUN
tout le monde
> **Is everyone here?**
> Tout le monde est là?

Language tip
everyone *is the same as* **everybody**.

everything PRONOUN
tout
> **Everything's fine!**
> Tout va bien!
> **Is that everything?**
> C'est tout?

everywhere ADVERB
partout
> **There are cats everywhere!**
> Il y a des chats partout!

exact ADJECTIVE
exact *masc*
exacte *fem*

exactly ADVERB
exactement
> **Our trainers are exactly the same.**
> Nos baskets sont exactement les mêmes.
> **not exactly**
> pas exactement

Language tip
In English, -ly is added to **exact**. *What is added to* **exact** *in French?*

> **It's exactly 1 o'clock.**
> Il est une heure précise.

exam NOUN
l' **examen** *masc*
a French exam
un examen de français

example NOUN
l' **exemple** *masc*
an example
un exemple
for example
par exemple

Language tip
What is the difference in spelling between the French word and the English word?

excellent ADJECTIVE
excellent *masc*
excellente *fem*
Excellent!
Excellent!
It was excellent fun.
C'était vraiment super.

except PREPOSITION
sauf
everyone except me
tout le monde sauf moi

exchange VERB
échanger
I want to exchange the book for a video.
Je veux échanger le livre contre une vidéo.

exchange rate NOUN
le **taux de change** *masc*

excited
ADJECTIVE
excité *masc*
excitée *fem*

exciting ADJECTIVE
passionnant *masc*
passionnante *fem*

an exciting film
un film passionnant

excuse VERB

Excuse me!
Pardon!

exercise NOUN
l' **exercice** *masc*
an exercise
un exercice

Language tip
What is the difference in spelling between the French word and the English word?

exercise book NOUN
le **cahier** *masc*

exhausted ADJECTIVE
épuisé *masc*
épuisée *fem*
Fabrice is exhausted.
Fabrice est épuisé.

Language tip
Fabrice is a boy's name. How can you tell that by looking at the example sentence?

exhibition NOUN
l' **exposition** *fem*
an exhibition
une exposition

exit NOUN
la **sortie** *fem*
Where is the exit?
Où est la sortie?

English French

a
b
c
d
e
f
g
h
i
j
k
l
m
n
o
p
q
r
s
t
u
v
w
x
y
z

expect VERB
1 **attendre** *(wait for)*
I'm expecting a phone call.
J'attends un coup de téléphone.
She's expecting a baby.
Elle attend un enfant.
2 **supposer** *(suppose)*
I expect he wants a coke.
Je suppose qu'il veut un coca.

expedition NOUN
l' **expédition** *fem*
an expedition
une expédition

expensive ADJECTIVE
cher *masc*
chère *fem*
It's too expensive.
C'est trop cher.

experience NOUN
l' **expérience** *fem*
an interesting experience
une expérience intéressante

experiment NOUN
l' **expérience** *fem*

expert NOUN
le **spécialiste** *masc*
la **spécialiste** *fem*
She's a computer expert.
C'est une spécialiste en
informatique.
Matthew is an expert cook.
Matthew cuisine très bien.

explain VERB
expliquer
I'll explain in English.
Je vais expliquer en Anglais.

explanation NOUN
l' **explication** *fem*

a clear explanation
une explication claire

explode VERB
exploser
It's going to explode!
Ça va exploser!

explosion NOUN
l' **explosion** *fem*
an explosion
une explosion

extension NOUN
1 l' **annexe** *fem (of a public building)*
2 le **poste** *masc (phone)*
Extension 3137, please.
Poste 3137, s'il vous plaît.

Language tip

In France, phone numbers are broken into pairs, so a French person would say this example as 'trente et un, trente-sept'.

extra ADJECTIVE, PRONOUN, ADVERB
supplémentaire
an extra blanket
une couverture supplémentaire
Breakfast is extra.
Il y a un supplément pour le
petit déjeuner.
to pay extra
payer un supplément
It costs extra.
Il y a un supplément.

extremely ADVERB
extrêmement

Language tip

In English, -ly is added to extreme. What is added to extrême in French?

eye NOUN

l' **œil** *masc* (PL les **yeux**)

I've got blue eyes.
J'ai les yeux bleus.

She's got green eyes.
Elle a les yeux verts.

What colour eyes has he got?
Il a les yeux de quelle couleur?

eyesight NOUN

la **vue** *fem*

F f

fabulous ADJECTIVE
formidable
   A fabulous show.
   Un spectacle formidable.

face NOUN
   la **figure** *fem*
     **His face
     is red.**
     Il a la
     figure
     rouge.

face cloth NOUN
   le **gant de toilette** *masc*

> **Language tip**
>
> **gant** *means 'glove'. A* **gant de
> toilette** *is a glove-shaped face
> cloth.*

facilities PL NOUN
   l' **équipement** *masc*

> **Language tip**
>
> **équipement** *is a singular word.*

factory NOUN
   l' **usine** *fem*
     My mum works in a factory.
     Ma mère travaille dans une
     usine.

fail VERB
   rater
     She's going to fail her exams.
     Elle va rater ses examens.

fair

> **fair** *can be an adjective or a noun.*

A ADJECTIVE
1 **juste**
   That's not fair.
   Ce n'est pas juste.
2 **blond** *masc*
   blonde *fem*
   He's got fair hair.
   Il a les cheveux blonds.
B NOUN
   la **foire** *fem*
   Are you going to the fair?
   Est-ce que tu vas à la foire?

fairground NOUN
   le **champ de foire** *masc*

fair-haired ADJECTIVE
   Hélène is fair-haired.
   Hélène a les cheveux blonds.

fairly ADVERB
   assez
     That's fairly good.
     C'est assez bien.

fairy
   NOUN
   la **fée**
   fem

fairy tale NOUN
   le **conte de fées** *masc*

fall VERB
   tomber
     Mind you don't fall!
     Fais attention de ne pas tomber!

fall off VERB
   tomber de
     He's going to fall off the wall.
     Il va tomber du mur.

English French

a b c d e f g h i j k l m n o p q r s t u v w x y z

false ADJECTIVE
True or false?
Vrai ou faux?

family NOUN
la **famille** *fem*
my family
ma famille
the whole family
toute la famille
the Cooke family
la famille Cooke

Language tip
family *has one* **l**, *how many has* **famille** *got?*

famous ADJECTIVE
célèbre

Language tip
There are two different accents for two different sounds in this word.

fan NOUN
le/la **supporter** *masc/fem*
football fans
les supporters de football

fantastic ADJECTIVE
fantastique

far

far *can be an adjective or an adverb.*

A ADJECTIVE
loin *(a long way)*
It's not very far.
Ce n'est pas très loin.
far from
loin de
It's not far from here.
Ce n'est pas loin d'ici.
B ADVERB
beaucoup *(much)*

That's far better!
C'est beaucoup mieux!

Is it far?
C'est loin?
No, it's not far.
Non, ce n'est pas loin.
It's too far.
C'est trop loin.

farm NOUN
la **ferme** *fem*

farmer NOUN
l' **agriculteur** *masc*
l' **agricultrice** *fem*
He's a farmer.
Il est agriculteur.

Language tip
When you say what someone's job is in French, you do not translate **a**.

farmhouse NOUN
la **ferme** *fem*

fashion NOUN
la **mode** *fem*

fashionable ADJECTIVE
à la mode *masc, fem, pl*
Jane wears fashionable clothes.
Jane porte des vêtements à la mode.

fashion show NOUN
le **défilé** *masc*

fast

fast *can be an adverb or an adjective.*

A ADVERB
vite
You walk fast.
Tu marches vite.

B ADJECTIVE
rapide
a fast car
une voiture rapide

fat ADJECTIVE
gros *masc*
grosse *fem*
   They're both fat.
   Ils sont gros tous les deux.

father NOUN
le **père** *masc*
   my father
   mon père
   your father
   ton père

Father Christmas NOUN
le **père Noël** *masc*

Father's Day NOUN
la **fête des pères** *fem*

favourite ADJECTIVE
préféré *masc*
préférée *fem*
   David is my
   favourite cousin.
   David est mon
   cousin préféré.
   Blue's my favourite colour.
   Ma couleur préférée, c'est le bleu.

February NOUN
février *masc*
   next February
   en février

in February
en février
the fifth of February
le cinq février

Language tip

The months are not spelled with a
capital letter in French.

feed VERB
donner à manger à
   I'm going to feed the
   cat.
   Je vais donner à manger
   au chat.

feel VERB
se sentir
   I don't feel well.
   Je ne me sens pas bien.
   I feel like ...
   J'ai envie de ...
   Do you feel like an ice
   cream?
   Tu as envie d'une glace?

feet PL NOUN
les **pieds** *masc pl*
   My feet are cold.
   J'ai froid aux pieds.

felt-tip pen NOUN
le **stylo-feutre** *masc*
   Can I borrow your felt-tip
   pens?
   Je peux emprunter tes stylos-
   feutres?

female NOUN
la **femelle** *fem*
   Is it a male or a female?
   C'est un mâle ou une
   femelle?

feminine ADJECTIVE
féminin *masc*
féminine *fem*

fence NOUN
la **barrière** *fem*

ferret NOUN
le **furet** *masc*

ferry NOUN
le **ferry** *masc*

fetch VERB
aller chercher
Can you fetch my bag?
Tu peux aller chercher mon sac?

few

few can be an adjective or a pronoun.

A ADJECTIVE
a few
quelques
a few hours
quelques heures
quite a few people
pas mal de monde
B PRONOUN
a few
quelques-uns *masc pl*
quelques-unes *fem pl*
How many chips do you want? — Just a few.
Tu veux combien de frites? — Seulement quelques-unes.

fiancé NOUN
le **fiancé** *masc*
He's her fiancé.
C'est son fiancé.

fiancée NOUN
la **fiancée** *fem*
She's his fiancée.
C'est sa fiancée.

field NOUN
1 le **champ** *masc (in countryside)*
a field of wheat
un champ de blé
2 le **terrain** *masc (for sport)*
a football field
un terrain de football

fifteen NUMBER
quinze
fifteen euros
quinze euros

I am fifteen.
J'ai quinze ans.

Language tip
In English, you can say **fifteen** *or* **fifteen years old**. *In French, you can only say* **quinze ans**.

fifteenth ADJECTIVE
quinzième
on the fifteenth floor
au quinzième étage

the fifteenth of August
le quinze août

fifth ADJECTIVE
cinquième
on the fifth floor
au cinquième étage

the fifth of August
le cinq août

fifty NUMBER
cinquante
My aunt is fifty.
Ma tante a cinquante ans.

Language tip
In English, you can say **fifty** *or* **fifty years old**. *In French, you can only say* **cinquante ans**.

fight

fight can be a noun or a verb.

A NOUN
la **bagarre** *fem*
B VERB
se battre
Two boys are fighting.
Deux garçons se battent.

figure NOUN
le **chiffre** *masc*

English French

a
b
c
d
e
f
g
h
i
j
k
l
m
n
o
p
q
r
s
t
u
v
w
x
y
z

Write down the figures.
Écrivez les chiffres.

file NOUN

1 la **chemise** *fem (folder)*
Keep the leaflets in your files.
Gardez les brochures dans vos chemises.

2 le **fichier** *masc (on computer)*

fill VERB
remplir
Can you fill the glasses?
Tu peux remplir les verres?

fill in VERB
remplir
Fill in the gaps in the sentences.
Remplissez les blancs dans les phrases.

film NOUN

1 le **film** *masc*
Is it a good film?
C'est un bon film?

2 la **pellicule** *fem (for camera)*

film star NOUN
la **vedette de cinéma** *fem*
Johnny Depp is a film star.
Johnny Depp est une vedette de cinéma.

final

final *can be an adjective or a noun.*

A ADJECTIVE
dernier *masc*
dernière *fem*
the final minutes
les dernières minutes

B NOUN
la **finale** *fem*
The final is tomorrow.
Demain, c'est la finale.

find VERB
trouver
My brother wants to find a job.
Mon frère veut trouver du travail.
Find page fifteen.
Trouvez la page quinze.

fine ADJECTIVE

That's fine, thanks.
C'est très bien, merci.
How are you? — I'm fine.
Comment ça va? — Ça va bien.

finger NOUN

le **doigt** *masc*
my little finger
mon petit doigt

My finger is hurting.
J'ai mal au doigt.

finish

finish *can be a verb or a noun.*

A VERB
finir
I've got to finish my homework.
Je dois finir mes devoirs.
I've finished!
J'ai fini!
Is it finished?
Ça y est?

Language tip

finir *and* **finish** *are related words. What do they have in common?*

B NOUN
la case 'Arrivée' *(in board game)*

fire NOUN

1 le **feu** *masc* (PL les **feux**)
There's a nice fire in the sitting room.
Il y a un bon feu dans le salon.

2 l' **incendie** *masc* (accidental)
There's a fire in the wood.
Il y a un incendie dans le bois.

fire engine NOUN
la **voiture de pompiers** *fem*
two fire engines
deux voitures de pompiers

fire fighter NOUN
le **pompier** *masc*
He's a fire fighter.
Il est pompier.

Language tip

*You do not translate **a** when you say what someone's job is in French.*

fire station NOUN
la **caserne de pompiers** *fem*

fireworks PL NOUN
le **feu d'artifice** *masc*
There are fireworks this evening.
Il y a un feu d'artifice ce soir.

first

first *can be an adjective, a noun or an adverb.*

A ADJECTIVE
premier *masc*
première *fem*
the first day
le premier jour

the first time
la première fois
to come first
arriver premier
Who came first?
Qui est arrivé premier?
Who wants to be first?
Qui veut commencer?
Who's first?
Qui commence?
Me first!
C'est moi qui commence!

B NOUN
at first
au début
It's easy at first.
Au début c'est facile.

the first of September
le premier septembre

C ADVERB
d'abord
First write your names.
D'abord écrivez vos noms.
first of all
tout d'abord

first aid NOUN
les **premiers secours** *masc pl*

fir tree NOUN
le **sapin** *masc*

fish

fish *can be a noun or a verb.*

A NOUN
le **poisson** *masc*
I don't like fish.
Je n'aime pas le poisson.

B VERB
to go fishing
aller à la pêche
Let's go fishing.
On va à la pêche?

English French

a b c d **e** **f** g h i j k l m n o p q r s t u v w x y z

fish fingers PL NOUN
les **bâtonnets de poisson**
masc pl

fishing NOUN
la **pêche** *fem*
I like fishing.
J'aime la pêche.

fishing boat NOUN
le **bateau de pêche** *masc*

fish tank NOUN
l' **aquarium** *masc*

fit

> **fit** *can be a verb or an adjective.*

A VERB
être la bonne taille
It doesn't fit.
Ce n'est pas la bonne taille.

B ADJECTIVE
en forme
She's fit.
Elle est en forme.

five NUMBER
cinq
five euros
cinq euros

> **She is five.**
> Elle a cinq ans.

> *Language tip*
>
> In English, you can say **five** or **five years old**. In French, you can only say **cinq ans**.

fix VERB
réparer
Can you fix my bike?
Vous pouvez réparer mon vélo?

fizzy ADJECTIVE
gazeux *masc*
gazeuse *fem*
I don't like fizzy drinks.
Je n'aime pas les boissons gazeuses.

flag NOUN
le **drapeau** *masc*
(PL les **drapeaux**)

flame NOUN
la **flamme** *fem*

flan NOUN
1 la **tarte** *fem (sweet)*
a raspberry flan
une tarte aux framboises
2 la **quiche** *fem (savoury)*
a cheese and onion flan
une quiche au fromage et aux oignons

flannel NOUN
le **gant de toilette** *masc*

> *Language tip*
>
> **gant** means 'glove'. A **gant de toilette** is a glove-shaped face cloth.

flash NOUN
le **flash** *masc* (PL les **flashes**)
Has your camera got a flash?
Est-ce que ton appareil photo a un flash?
a flash of lightning
un éclair

flask NOUN
le **thermos** *masc*

flat

flat can be an adjective or a noun.

A ADJECTIVE
1 **plat** *masc*
  plate *fem (level)*
  a flat roof
  un toit plat
  flat shoes
  des chaussures plates
2 **crevé** *masc*
  crevée *fem (tyre)*
  I've got a flat tyre.
  J'ai un pneu crevé.
B NOUN
  l' **appartement** *masc*
  She lives in a flat.
  Elle habite un appartement.

Language tip

*The English word **apartment** has one **p**, how many has **appartement** got?*

flavour NOUN
le **parfum** *masc*
  Which flavour of ice cream would you like?
  Quel parfum de glace est-ce que tu veux?

flight NOUN
le **vol** *masc*
  What time is the flight to Paris?
  À quelle heure est le vol pour Paris?

flippers PL NOUN
les **palmes** *fem pl*

floor NOUN
1 le **sol** *masc*

  a tiled floor
  un sol carrelé
  on the floor
  par terre
  Sit on the floor.
  Asseyez-vous par terre.
2 l' **étage** *masc (storey)*
  the first floor
  le premier étage
  the ground floor
  le rez-de-chaussée
  on the third floor
  au troisième étage

floppy disk NOUN
la **disquette** *fem*

florist NOUN
le/la **fleuriste** *masc/fem*

flour NOUN
la **farine** *fem*

flower NOUN
la **fleur** *fem*

flu NOUN
la **grippe** *fem*
  Jean-Louis has got flu.
  Jean-Louis a la grippe.

fluent ADJECTIVE
  My sister speaks fluent French.
  Ma sœur parle couramment le français.

flute NOUN
la **flûte** *fem*
  I play the flute.
  Je joue de la flûte.

Language tip

There's an extra word in the French example sentence. What is it?

fly

fly can be a verb or a noun.

A VERB
aller en avion *(go by plane)*
I'm going to fly to Florida.
Je vais aller en Floride
en avion.

B NOUN
la **mouche**
fem (insect)

fog NOUN
le **brouillard** *masc*

foggy ADJECTIVE
a foggy day
un jour de brouillard

It's foggy.
Il y a du brouillard.

fold VERB
plier
Fold the paper in half.
Pliez la feuille en deux.

folder NOUN
la **chemise** *fem*

follow VERB
suivre
Follow me.
Suivez-moi.

food NOUN
I like French food.
J'aime la cuisine française.
Bring some food.
Apportez à manger.
We need to buy some food.
Nous devons acheter à manger.

food processor NOUN
le **robot** *masc*

foot NOUN
le **pied** *masc*

My feet are hurting.
J'ai mal aux pieds.
on foot
à pied
Richard is 6 foot tall.
Richard mesure un mètre
quatre-vingt.

Did you know...?
*In France, measurements are always
in metres and centimetres, rather
than feet and inches.*

football NOUN
1 le **football** *masc (game)*
I like playing football.
J'aime jouer au football.

Language tip
You can also say **J'aime jouer au
foot,** *which is more slang.*

**Do you want to play football,
Pascal?**
Tu veux jouer au foot, Pascal?
**Do you want to play football,
boys?**
Vous voulez jouer au foot, les
garçons?
2 le **ballon de foot** *masc (ball)*
Jason's got a new football.
Jason a un nouveau ballon de
foot.

football boots PL NOUN
les **chaussures de foot** *fem pl*

footballer NOUN
le **footballeur** *masc*
la **footballeuse** *fem*

football player NOUN
le **joueur de football** *masc*
la **joueuse de football** *fem*
**David Beckham is a famous
football player.**
David Beckham est un joueur de
football célèbre.

a b c d e f g h i j k l m n o p q r s t u v w x y z

football shirt NOUN
le **maillot de foot** *masc*

footpath NOUN
le **sentier** *masc*

for PREPOSITION
pour
> **a present for me**
> un cadeau pour moi
> **I'll do it for you.**
> Je vais le faire pour toi.
> **What's it for?**
> Ça sert à quoi?
> **What's the French for 'lion'?**
> Comment dit-on 'lion' en français?
> **I have been learning French for six months.**
> J'apprends le français depuis six mois.

forbidden ADJECTIVE
défendu *masc*
défendue *fem*

forecast NOUN
> **the weather forecast**
> la météo
> **What's the forecast for today?**
> Il va faire quel temps aujourd'hui?

foreign ADJECTIVE
étranger *masc*
étrangère *fem*

foreigner NOUN
l' **étranger** *masc*
l' **étrangère** *fem*
> **He's a foreigner.**
> C'est un étranger.

forest NOUN
la **forêt** *fem*

forget VERB
oublier
> **Don't forget!**
> N'oubliez pas!

fork NOUN
la **fourchette** *fem*

form NOUN
le **formulaire** *masc*
> **You have to fill in the form.**
> Vous devez remplir le formulaire.

fortnight NOUN
> **a fortnight**
> quinze jours
> **I'm going on holiday for a fortnight.**
> Je pars en vacances pendant quinze jours.

Language tip

quinze jours *actually means 15 days.*

forty NUMBER
quarante
> **My father is forty.**
> Mon père a quarante ans.

Language tip

In English, you can say **forty** *or* **forty years old**. *In French, you can only say* **quarante ans**.

forward ADVERB
en avant
> **a step forward**
> un pas en avant
> **to move forward**
> avancer
> **Move forward two spaces.**
> Avancez de deux cases.

foster child NOUN
l' **enfant adoptif** *masc*
l' **enfant adoptive** *fem*

a b c d e **f** g h i j k l m n o p q r s t u v w x y z

fountain NOUN
la **fontaine** *fem*

four NUMBER
quatre
four euros
quatre euros

He is four.
Il a quatre ans.

Language tip

In English, you can say **four** *or* **four years old**. *In French, you can only say* **quatre ans**.

fourteen NUMBER
quatorze
fourteen euros
quatorze euros

I'm fourteen.
J'ai quatorze ans.

Language tip

In English, you can say **fourteen** *or* **fourteen years old**. *In French, you can only say* **quatorze ans**.

fourteenth ADJECTIVE
quatorzième
on the fourteenth floor
au quatorzième étage

the fourteenth of August
le quatorze août

fourth ADJECTIVE
quatrième
on the fourth floor
au quatrième étage

the fourth of July
le quatre juillet

fox NOUN
le **renard** *masc*

France NOUN
la **France** *fem*
I like France.
J'aime la France.
Cannes is in France.
Cannes est en France.
We're going to France.
Nous allons en France.

to France
en France
He lives in France.
Il habite en France.
They are from France.
Ils sont français.

freckles PL NOUN
les **taches de rousseur** *fem pl*

free ADJECTIVE
1 **gratuit** *masc*
gratuite *fem* (*free of charge*)
a free brochure
une brochure gratuite
2 **libre** (*not taken*)
Excuse me, is this seat free?
Excusez-moi, la place est libre?

freezer NOUN
le **congélateur** *masc*

freezing ADJECTIVE
I'm freezing!
Je suis gelé!
It's absolutely freezing!
Il fait un froid de canard!

French

French *can be an adjective or a noun.*

A ADJECTIVE
français *masc*
française *fem*

English French
a b c d e f g h i j k l m n o p q r s t u v w x y z

a French name
un nom français
a French school
une école française
our French friends
nos amis français
our French teacher
notre professeur de français
my French book
mon livre de français
French people
les Français

He's French.
Il est français.
She's French.
Elle est française.

B NOUN
le **français** *masc (language)*
Do you speak French?
Est-ce que tu parles français?
the French
les Français

Language tip

français *is not spelled with a capital letter except when it means a French person.*

French beans PL NOUN
les **haricots verts** *masc pl*

French fries PL NOUN
les **frites** *fem pl*

Frenchman NOUN
le **Français** *masc*

Frenchwoman NOUN
la **Française** *fem*

Friday NOUN
le **vendredi** *masc*
It's Friday today.
Aujourd'hui c'est vendredi.

on Friday
vendredi
on Fridays
le vendredi
every Friday
tous les vendredis
last Friday
vendredi dernier
next Friday
vendredi prochain

Language tip

Days of the week are not spelled with a capital letter in French.

fridge NOUN
le **frigo** *masc*

friend NOUN
l' **ami** *masc*
l' **amie** *fem*
my friend Paul
mon ami Paul
my friend Gaëlle
mon amie Gaëlle

friendly ADJECTIVE
gentil *masc*
gentille *fem*
She's very friendly.
Elle est très gentille.

frightened ADJECTIVE
to be frightened
avoir peur
Anna's frightened of spiders.
Anna a peur des araignées.

I'm frightened!
J'ai peur!

fringe NOUN
la **frange** *fem*
She's got a fringe.
Elle a une frange.

Frisbee® NOUN
le **Frisbee**® *masc*

frog NOUN
la **grenouille**
fem
frogs' legs
les cuisses
de grenouille

from PREPOSITION
de
She comes from Perth.
Elle vient de Perth.
a letter from my penfriend
une lettre de mon
correspondant
from ... to ...
de ... à ...
from London to Paris
de Londres à Paris
the numbers from 1 to 39
les nombres de un à trente-neuf

Where do you come from?
Tu viens d'où?
I come from Birmingham.
Je viens de Birmingham.

front

front *can be a noun or an
adjective.*

A NOUN
le **devant** *masc*
the front of the house
le devant de la maison
in front of
devant
in front of the house
devant la maison

B ADJECTIVE
de devant
the front row
la rangée de devant

front door NOUN
la **porte d'entrée** *fem*

frost NOUN
le **gel** *masc*

frosty ADJECTIVE
a frosty morning
un matin glacial

It's frosty today.
Il gèle aujourd'hui.

frozen ADJECTIVE
1 **gelé** *masc*
gelée *fem (fingers, lake)*
2 **surgelé** *masc*
surgelée *fem (food)*

fruit NOUN
I like fruit.
J'aime les fruits.
a piece of fruit
un fruit

fruit juice NOUN
le **jus de fruits** *masc*

fruit salad NOUN
la **salade de fruits** *fem*

frying pan NOUN
la **poêle** *fem*

full ADJECTIVE
plein *masc*
pleine *fem*
The bottle's full.
La bouteille est pleine.
I'm full.
J'ai bien mangé.

full stop NOUN
le **point** *masc*

fun NOUN
to have fun
s'amuser
Are you having fun?
Tu t'amuses?

It's fun!
C'est chouette!
Have fun!
Amuse-toi bien!

funfair NOUN
la **fête foraine** *fem*

funny ADJECTIVE
drôle
It was very funny.
C'était très drôle.

fur NOUN
1 la **fourrure** *fem*
a fur coat
un manteau de fourrure
2 le **poil** *masc*
the dog's fur
le poil du chien

furious ADJECTIVE
furieux *masc*
furieuse *fem*
Dad was furious with me.
Papa était furieux contre moi.
The girls are furious.
Les filles sont furieuses.

furniture NOUN
les **meubles** *masc pl*
We've got new furniture.
Nous avons de nouveaux
meubles.
a piece of furniture
un meuble

future NOUN
l' **avenir** *masc*
Be more careful in future.
Sois plus prudent à l'avenir.

G g

a
b
c
d
e
f
g
h
i
j
k
l
m
n
o
p
q
r
s
t
u
v
w
x
y
z

game NOUN

1 le **jeu** *masc* (PL les **jeux**)
(*hangman, marbles, bingo etc*)
It's a new game.
C'est un nouveau jeu.
Let's play a game.
On joue à un jeu?

2 le **match** *masc* (*match*)
The game is tomorrow.
Le match, c'est demain.
a game of football
un match de foot

games PL NOUN
le **sport** *masc* (*at school*)
I like games.
J'aime le sport.

gang NOUN
la **bande** *fem*

garage NOUN
le **garage** *masc*

garden NOUN
le **jardin** *masc*
We haven't got a garden.
Nous n'avons pas de jardin.

garden centre NOUN
la **jardinerie** *fem*

gardening NOUN
le **jardinage** *masc*

garlic NOUN
l' **ail** *masc*
I don't like garlic.
Je n'aime pas l'ail.

gas NOUN
le **gaz** *masc*

gas cooker NOUN
la **cuisinière à gaz** *fem*

gate NOUN

1 le **portail** *masc* (*of garden, of school*)
Please close the gate.
Fermez le portail s'il vous plaît.

2 la **barrière** *fem* (*of field*)
There's a cow by the gate.
Il y a une vache près de la barrière.

gave VERB ▷ see **give**

GCSE NOUN
le **brevet des collèges** *masc*

Did you know...?

Exams in France are different from exams in Britain. **Le brevet des collèges** *is an exam you take at the end of the fourth year in secondary school.*

geese PL NOUN
les **oies** *fem pl*

general knowledge
NOUN
les **connaissances générales** *fem pl*
a general knowledge quiz
un quiz de connaissances générales

generous ADJECTIVE
　généreux *masc*
　généreuse *fem*
　　That's very generous of you.
　　C'est très généreux de ta part.

genius NOUN
　le **génie** *masc*
　　She's a genius!
　　C'est un génie!

gents NOUN
　les **toilettes**
　　fem pl
　　Where is the gents, please?
　　Où sont les toilettes, s'il vous
　　plaît?

geography NOUN
　la **géographie** *fem*
　　I like geography.
　　J'aime la géographie.

gerbil NOUN
　la **gerbille** *fem*

German

> **German** *can be an adjective or a
> noun.*

　A ADJECTIVE
　　allemand *masc*
　　allemande *fem*
　　a German car
　　une voiture allemande
　　German people
　　les Allemands
　B NOUN
　　l' **allemand** *masc*

I can speak German.
Je parle allemand.

> ***Language tip***
>
> **allemand** *is not spelled with a
> capital letter except when it means a
> German person.*

German measles NOUN
　la **rubéole** *fem*
　　He's got German measles.
　　Il a la rubéole.

Germany NOUN
　l' **Allemagne** *fem*

get VERB
　1 avoir *(receive)*
　　**He always gets lots of
　　presents.**
　　Il a toujours plein de cadeaux.
　　**What did you get for your
　　birthday?**
　　Qu'est-ce que tu as eu pour ton
　　anniversaire?
　　I got lots of presents.
　　J'ai eu beaucoup de cadeaux.
　　**How much pocket money do
　　you get?**
　　Tu reçois combien d'argent de
　　poche?
　　I get £5 a week.
　　Je reçois cinq livres par semaine.

> ***Language tip***
>
> *When **I've got** means **I have** it is
> translated by the verb **avoir**.*

　　I've got a dog and two cats.
　　J'ai un chien et deux chats.

English French

a
b
c
d
e
f
g
h
i
j
k
l
m
n
o
p
q
r
s
t
u
v
w
x
y
z

I haven't got a mobile phone.
Je n'ai pas de portable.
Marie hasn't got long hair.
Marie n'a pas les cheveux longs.
How many have you got?
Combien en avez-vous?

2 **acheter** *(buy)*
Can you get me a coke?
Tu peux m'acheter un coca?
Mum's getting me a playstation.
Maman m'achète une play station.

3 **aller chercher** *(fetch)*
Get your coats.
Allez chercher vos manteaux.

4 **aller** *(go)*
How do you get to the castle, please?
Pour aller au château, s'il vous plaît?

5 **arriver** *(arrive)*
What time do we get there?
À quelle heure est-ce qu'on arrive?

Language tip

When I've got to means I must, it is translated by the verb **devoir**.

I've got to go to the dentist.
Je dois aller chez le dentiste.
You've got to take a card, Michel.
Tu dois prendre une carte, Michel.
You've got to be careful, children.
Vous devez faire attention, les enfants.

I've got a cat.
J'ai un chat.
I haven't got a dog.
Je n'ai pas de chien.

Have you got a sister?
Tu as une sœur?
She's got long hair.
Elle a les cheveux longs.

get away VERB
s'échapper
Quick! He's getting away!
Vite! Il s'échappe!

get back VERB
rentrer
What time will you get back?
Tu rentres à quelle heure?

get in VERB
monter
Get in, boys!
Montez, les garçons!
Get in the car, Charlotte.
Monte dans la voiture, Charlotte.

get off VERB
descendre de
Where do we get off the train?
Où est-ce que nous descendons du train?

get on VERB
1 **prendre** *(bus, train)*
I get on the bus at the station.
Je prends le bus à la gare.
2 **monter sur** *(bike)*
I got on my bike.
Je suis monté sur mon vélo.

How are you getting on?
Comment ça marche?

get out VERB
sortir
Get out!
Sortez!
Get your book out, André.
Sors ton livre, André.

Get your things out!
Sortez vos affaires!

get up VERB
se lever
What time do you get up?
Tu te lèves à quelle heure?
I get up early.
Je me lève tôt.

ghost NOUN
le **fantôme** *masc*

giant NOUN
le **géant** *masc*
la **géante** *fem*

gift NOUN
le **cadeau** *masc* (PL les **cadeaux**)
Christmas gifts
les cadeaux
de Noël

gift shop NOUN
la **boutique de cadeaux** *fem*

gigantic ADJECTIVE
gigantesque

ginger ADJECTIVE
I've got ginger hair.
J'ai les cheveux roux.

giraffe NOUN
la **girafe** *fem*

girl NOUN
1 la **fille** *fem*
Come on girls!
Allez les filles!
2 la **petite fille** *fem* (little girl)
a five-year-old girl
une petite fille de cinq ans

3 la **jeune fille** *fem* (teenager)
a sixteen-year-old girl
une jeune fille de seize ans

girlfriend NOUN
la **copine** *fem*
She's his girlfriend.
C'est sa copine.

give VERB
1 **donner**
Give me the book, please.
Donne-moi le livre, s'il te plaît.
Give the books to Adam.
Donne les livres à Adam.
2 **offrir** (gift)
What are you giving Luc?
Qu'est-ce que tu vas offrir à Luc?
My parents gave me a bike.
Mes parents m'ont offert un vélo.

give out VERB
distribuer
Will you give out the books, please, Christine?
Tu peux distribuer les livres, s'il te plaît, Christine?

glad ADJECTIVE
content *masc*
contente *fem*
I was glad to get your letter.
J'étais content de recevoir ta lettre.

glass NOUN
le **verre** *masc*
I'd like a glass of milk.
Je voudrais un verre de lait.

glasses PL NOUN
les **lunettes** *fem pl*
I wear glasses.
Je porte des
lunettes.

English French

a
b
c
d
e
f
g
h
i
j
k
l
m
n
o
p
q
r
s
t
u
v
w
x
y
z

globe NOUN
le **globe** *masc*
We've got a globe in the classroom.
Nous avons un globe dans la classe.

glove NOUN
le **gant** *masc*
I've got red gloves.
J'ai des gants rouges.

glue NOUN
la **colle** *fem*

go

go *can be a noun or a verb.*

A NOUN
le **tour** *masc*
It's my go.
C'est mon tour.
Whose go is it?
À qui le tour?
B VERB
1 **aller**
I don't want to go to school.
Je ne veux pas aller à l'école.
I don't go to school on Saturday.
Je ne vais pas à l'école le samedi.
Where are you going?
Où vas-tu?
2 *(talking about the future)*
I'm going to win.
Je vais gagner.
We're going to visit our cousins on Friday.
On va rendre visite à nos cousins vendredi.
I'm not going to play.
Je ne vais pas jouer.
3 *(talking about the past)*
I went to London.
Je suis allé à Londres.

Where did you go yesterday?
Où es-tu allé hier?
I went to Luc's house.
Je suis allé chez Luc.
He's gone.
Il est parti.
She's gone.
Elle est partie.

go away VERB
s'en aller
Go away, Sophie!
Va-t'en, Sophie!
Go away!
Allez-vous-en!

go back VERB
1 *(in game)*
Go back three spaces.
Recule de trois cases.
2 **retourner** *(return)*
Go back to your seat, Colette!
Retourne à ta place, Colette!
Go back to your seats, boys!
Retournez à vos places, les garçons!
Let's go back to the beginning.
Recommençons.

go down VERB
descendre
Let's go down to the cellar.
Descendons à la cave.

go forward VERB
Go forward three spaces, Alain.
Avance de trois cases, Alain.

go in VERB
entrer
Let's go in.
Entrons.

go on VERB
1 **continuer** *(continue)*

Shall I go on?
Je continue?
Go on, don't stop.
Vas-y, ne t'arrête pas.
2 se passer *(happen)*
What's going on?
Qu'est-ce qui se passe?

go out VERB
sortir
Are you going out tonight?
Tu sors ce soir?
Melanie's going out with Matt.
Melanie sort avec Matt.

go past VERB
passer devant
We're going past the cathedral.
Nous passons devant la cathédrale.
Go past the post office and turn right.
Passe devant la poste et tourne à droite.

go up VERB
monter
I'm going up to my room.
Je monte dans ma chambre.

goal NOUN
le **but** *masc*
It's a goal!
C'est un but!
He's scored a goal!
Il a marqué un but!

goalkeeper NOUN
le **gardien de but** *masc*
He's the goalkeeper.
C'est le gardien de but.

goat NOUN
la **chèvre** *fem*

God NOUN
Dieu *masc*

godfather NOUN
le **parrain** *masc*
my godfather
mon parrain

godmother NOUN
la **marraine** *fem*
my godmother
ma marraine

goggles PL NOUN
les **lunettes de plongée** *fem pl*
I've got new goggles.
J'ai de nouvelles lunettes de plongée.

gold ADJECTIVE
a gold necklace
un collier en or

goldfish NOUN
le **poisson rouge** *masc*
I've got five goldfish.
J'ai cinq poissons rouges.

golf NOUN
le **golf** *masc*
My dad plays golf.
Mon père joue au golf.

golf club NOUN
le **club de golf** masc

golf course NOUN
le **terrain de golf** masc

gone VERB ▷see **go**

good ADJECTIVE
1 **bon** masc
bonne fem (great)
It's a very good film.
C'est un très bon film.
We've got a good teacher.
Nous avons une bonne
maîtresse.
That's a good idea.
C'est une bonne idée.
Jane's very good at French.
Jane est très bonne en français.
2 **sage** (not naughty)
Marcel is always good.
Marcel est toujours sage.

It's good.
C'est bon.
Good morning!
Bonjour!
Good morning everyone!
Bonjour tout le monde!
Good afternoon!
Bonjour!
Good evening!
Bonsoir!
Good night!
Bonne nuit!
Good luck!
Bonne chance!
Be good, André!
Sois sage, André!

goodbye
EXCLAMATION
au revoir!

Good Friday NOUN
le **Vendredi saint** masc

good-looking ADJECTIVE
beau masc
belle fem
Yann is very good-looking.
Yann est très beau.

Language tip

When **beau** comes before a vowel
sound, it changes to **bel**.

a good-looking man
un bel homme

goose NOUN
l' **oie** fem

gorgeous ADJECTIVE
1 **beau** masc
belle fem (person)
Isn't she gorgeous!
Qu'elle est belle!
2 **splendide** (weather)
The weather's gorgeous.
Il fait un temps splendide.

got VERB ▷see **get**

gradually ADVERB
peu à peu

graffiti PL NOUN
les **graffiti** masc pl
There's a lot of graffiti.
Il y a beaucoup de graffiti.

gram NOUN
le **gramme** masc
two hundred grams of cheese
deux cents grammes de fromage

grammar NOUN
la **grammaire** *fem*
I like grammar.
J'aime la grammaire.

grandchildren PL NOUN
les **petits-enfants** *masc pl*
her grandchildren
ses petits-enfants

granddad NOUN
le **papi** *masc*
my granddad
mon papi

granddaughter NOUN
la **petite-fille** *fem*
He has two granddaughters.
Il a deux petites-filles.

grandfather NOUN
le **grand-père** *masc*
my grandfather
mon grand-père

grandma NOUN
la **mamie** *fem*
her grandma
sa mamie

grandmother NOUN
la **grand-mère** *fem*
his grandmother
sa grand-mère

grandpa NOUN
le **papi** *masc*
my grandpa
mon papi

grandparents PL NOUN
les **grands-parents** *masc pl*
my grandparents
mes grands-parents

grandson NOUN
le **petit-fils** *masc*
her grandsons
ses petits-fils

granny NOUN
la **mamie** *fem*
my granny
ma mamie

grapefruit NOUN
le **pamplemousse** *masc*
I don't like grapefruit.
Je n'aime pas le pamplemousse.

grapefruit juice NOUN
le **jus de pamplemousse**
masc

grapes PL NOUN
le **raisin** *masc*
a kilo of grapes
un kilo de raisin

Language tip

raisin *is a singular word. In English,*
raisins *are dried grapes.*

---

grass NOUN
l' **herbe** *fem*
**The children are playing on
the grass.**
Les enfants jouent dans l'herbe.

grated ADJECTIVE
râpé *masc*
râpée *fem*
grated cheese
du fromage râpé

gravy NOUN
I'd like some gravy.
Je voudrais de la sauce.

great ADJECTIVE
génial *masc*
géniale *fem*
**We're going to France. —
Great!**
Nous allons en France. —
Génial!

That's great!
C'est génial!

Great Britain NOUN
la **Grande-Bretagne** *fem*
We live in Great Britain.
Nous habitons en Grande-Bretagne.

greedy ADJECTIVE
gourmand *masc*
gourmande *fem*
Don't be so greedy Émmeline.
Ne sois pas si gourmande, Émmeline!

green

> **green** *can be an adjective or a noun.*

A ADJECTIVE
vert *masc*
verte *fem*
a green sweater
un pull vert

a green car
une voiture verte
I've got green eyes.
J'ai les yeux verts.

> *Language tip*
>
> *Colour adjectives come after the noun in French.*

B NOUN
le **vert** *masc*
Green is my favourite colour.
Ma couleur préférée, c'est le vert.

greengrocer's NOUN
le **marchand de fruits et légumes** *masc*
at the greengrocer's
chez le marchand de fruits et légumes

greenhouse NOUN
la **serre** *fem*

greetings card NOUN
la **carte de vœux** *fem*

grey

> **grey** *can be an adjective or a noun.*

A ADJECTIVE
gris *masc*
grise *fem*
a grey sweater
un pull gris
a grey skirt
une jupe grise
She's got grey hair.
Elle a les cheveux gris.

> *Language tip*
>
> *Colour adjectives come after the noun in French.*

B NOUN
le **gris** *masc*
He is dressed in grey.
Il est habillé en gris.

grin VERB
sourire
Why are you grinning like that?
Pourquoi tu souris comme ça?

grocer's NOUN
l' **épicerie** *fem*
I'm going to the grocer's.
Je vais à l'épicerie.

groom NOUN
le **marié** *masc*

ground NOUN

1 la **terre** *fem*
   We sat on the ground.
   Nous nous sommes assis par
   terre.

2 le **sol** *masc (earth)*
   The ground is wet.
   Le sol est mouillé.

3 le **terrain** *masc (sports ground)*
   Where's the football ground?
   Où est le terrain de football?

on the ground
par terre

ground floor NOUN
le **rez-de-chaussée** *masc*
   This is the ground floor.
   C'est le rez-de-chaussée.
   **The toilets are on the ground
   floor.**
   Les toilettes sont au rez-de-
   chaussée.

on the ground floor
au rez-de-chaussée

group NOUN
le **groupe** *masc*
   Get into groups of four.
   Mettez-vous en groupes de
   quatre.

grow VERB

1 **pousser** *(plant)*
   Grass grows fast.
   L'herbe pousse vite.

2 **faire pousser** *(gardener)*
   I'm growing a sunflower.
   Je fais pousser un tournesol.

3 **grandir** *(get bigger)*
   My feet have grown.
   Mes pieds ont grandi.

grow up VERB
   **What do you want to be
   when you grow up, Samir?**
   Samir, qu'est ce que tu veux
   faire quand tu seras grand?
   **What do want to be when
   you grow up, Céline?**
   Céline, qu'est ce que tu veux
   faire quand tu seras grande?

Language tip

*One example question is to a boy,
the other to a girl. How can you tell?*

growl VERB
grogner
   My dog growls a lot.
   Mon chien grogne beaucoup.

grown VERB ▷*see* grow

grown-up NOUN
la **grande personne** *fem*
   the grown-ups
   les grandes personnes

guard dog NOUN
le **chien de garde** *masc*

guess VERB
deviner
   Guess what this is!
   Devine ce que c'est!

guest NOUN
l' **invité** *masc*
l' **invitée** *fem*
   our French guests
   nos invités français

guide NOUN

1 le **guide** *masc*
   la **guide** *fem (tourist guide)*

He works as a guide at the castle.
Il travaille comme guide au château.
2 l' **éclaireuse** *fem (girl guide)*
I'm a guide.
Je suis éclaireuse.

guidebook NOUN
le **guide** *masc*

guide dog NOUN
le **chien d'aveugle** *masc*

guinea pig NOUN
le **cochon d'Inde** *masc*
I've got a guinea pig.
J'ai un cochon d'Inde.

guitar NOUN
la **guitare** *fem*
I play the guitar.
Je joue de la guitare.

gun NOUN
le **pistolet** *masc*

guy NOUN
you guys
les gars
Hurry up you guys!
Dépêchez-vous les gars!

gym NOUN
1 la **gym** *fem (school subject)*
We've got gym today.
On a gym aujourd'hui.
2 la **salle de gym** *fem (place)*
My mum goes to the gym.
Ma mère va à la salle de gym.

gymnastics NOUN
la **gymnastique** *fem*
I like gymnastics.
J'aime la gymnastique.
I do gymnastics.
Je fais de la gymnastique.

H h

had VERB ▷see **have**

hadn't = had not ▷see **have**

hail

> **hail** *can be a noun or a verb.*

A NOUN
   la **grêle** *fem*
B VERB
   grêler
   It's hailing.
   Il grêle.

hair NOUN
   1 les **cheveux** *masc pl*

> **cheveux** *is a plural word, so you have to use a plural adjective with it.*

   He's got black hair.
   Il a les cheveux noirs.
   I've got long hair.
   J'ai les cheveux longs.
   I want to wash my hair.
   Je veux me laver les cheveux.
   You've had your hair cut!
   Tu t'es fait couper les cheveux!
   2 le **poil** *masc (fur)*
   My cat has long hair.
   Mon chat a le poil long.

hairbrush NOUN
   la **brosse à cheveux** *fem*

hairdresser NOUN
   le **coiffeur** *masc*
   la **coiffeuse** *fem*
   He's a hairdresser.
   Il est coiffeur.

> *You do not translate '**a**' when you say what someone's job is in French.*

hairdresser's NOUN
   le **coiffeur** *masc*
   at the hairdresser's
   chez le coiffeur

hairstyle NOUN
   la **coiffure** *fem*
   You've got a new hairstyle.
   Tu as une nouvelle coiffure.

hairy ADJECTIVE
   poilu *masc*
   poilue *fem*

half

> **half** *can be a noun, an adjective or an adverb.*

A NOUN
   1 la **moitié** *fem (fraction)*
   half of the class
   la moitié de la classe
   to cut something in half
   couper quelque chose en deux
   2 le **billet demi-tarif** *masc (ticket)*
   A half single to York, please.
   Un billet aller simple demi-tarif pour York, s'il vous plaît.

   two and a half
   deux et demi
   half an hour
   une demi-heure
   half past ten
   dix heures et demie

half a kilo
un demi kilo

B ADJECTIVE
a half portion
une demi-portion

C ADVERB
à moitié
I'm half Scottish.
Je suis à moitié écossais.

half-brother NOUN
le **demi-frère** masc
my half-brother
mon demi-frère

half-sister NOUN
la **demi-sœur** fem
my half-sister
ma demi-sœur

half-term NOUN
les **vacances** fem pl
What are you doing at half-term?
Qu'est-ce que tu fais pendant les vacances?

> ### Did you know...?
> There are two half-term holidays in France: **les vacances de la Toussaint** (in October/November) and **les vacances de février** (in February).

half-time NOUN
la **mi-temps** fem

hall NOUN
1 le **hall** masc (of school)
We have gym in the hall.
On a gym dans le hall.
2 l' **entrée** fem (entrance hall)

Hallowe'en NOUN
la **veille de la Toussaint** fem

> ### Did you know...?
> The French means 'Eve of All Saints' Day'. **Hallowe'en** is not traditionally celebrated in France, but All Saints' Day (the first of November) is a public holiday, and is the day when people often visit family graves.

ham NOUN
le **jambon** masc
a ham sandwich
un sandwich au jambon

hamburger NOUN
le **hamburger** masc

hamster NOUN
le **hamster**
masc

hand NOUN
1 la **main** fem (of person)
Put up your hands.
Levez la main.
Can you give me a hand?
Tu peux me donner un coup de main?
2 l' **aiguille** fem (of clock)

hand in VERB
rendre
Hand in your books.
Rendez vos cahiers.

hand out VERB
distribuer
Hand out the books, Ahmed.
Distribue les livres, Ahmed.

handbag NOUN
le **sac à main** masc

handball NOUN
le **handball** *masc*
Can we play handball?
On peut jouer au handball?

handkerchief NOUN
le **mouchoir** *masc*
Have you got a handkerchief?
Tu as un mouchoir?

handle NOUN
la **poignée** *fem*

handlebars PL NOUN
le **guidon** *masc*

Language tip
guidon *is a singular word.*

handsome ADJECTIVE
beau *masc*
belle *fem*
Gaston is very handsome.
Gaston est très beau.

Language tip
beau *changes to* **bel** *before a vowel sound.*

a handsome man
un bel homme

handwriting NOUN
l' **écriture** *fem*
He has nice handwriting.
Il a une belle écriture.

Language tip
écriture *is related to the French verb* **écrire**, *which means 'to write'.*

hangman NOUN
le **pendu** *masc*

hang on VERB
patienter
Hang on a minute please.
Patientez une minute, s'il vous plaît.

happen VERB
se passer
What's happening?
Qu'est-ce qui se passe?

happy ADJECTIVE
heureux *masc*
heureuse *fem*
Joséphine is happy.
Joséphine est heureuse.
The children are happy.
Les enfants sont heureux.

Happy birthday!
Bon anniversaire!
Happy Mother's Day!
Bonne Fête Maman!
Happy Christmas!
Joyeux Noël!
Happy New Year!
Bonne année!

Happy Families NOUN
le **jeu des sept familles** *masc*

harbour NOUN
le **port** *masc*

hard

hard *can be an adjective or an adverb.*

A ADJECTIVE
1 difficile *(difficult)*
This question's too hard for me.
Cette question est trop difficile pour moi.
2 dur *masc*
dure *fem (not soft)*

This cheese is very hard.
Ce fromage est très dur.

B ADVERB
dur
Colette works hard.
Colette travaille dur.

has VERB ▷ *see* **have**

hasn't = has not ▷ *see* **have**

hat NOUN
le **chapeau** *masc*
(PL les **chapeaux**)

hate VERB
détester
I hate maths.
Je déteste les maths.

Language tip
*There is an extra word in the French
example sentence. What is it?*

have VERB
1 avoir
I've got a bike.
J'ai un vélo.
Have you got a sister?
Tu as une sœur?
No, I haven't got a sister.
Non, je n'ai pas de sœur.
He's got blue eyes.
Il a les yeux bleus.

I have ...
J'ai ...
I have got ...
J'ai ...

Language tip
have *and* **have got** *are the same
in French.*

2 prendre *(eat)*
**What time do you have
breakfast?**
À quelle heure tu prends le petit
déjeuner?
What are you going to have?
Qu'est-ce que tu prends?

3 devoir *(must)*
You have to be careful.
Tu dois faire attention.
Do I have to choose a card?
Est-ce que je dois choisir une carte?
Do I have to?
Est-ce que je suis vraiment
obligé?
You have to ...
Tu dois ...
You have got to ...
Tu dois ...

Language tip
have *and* **have got** *are the same
in French.*

haven't = have not ▷ *see* **have**

hay fever NOUN
le **rhume des foins** *masc*

he PRONOUN
il
He loves dogs.
Il aime les chiens.

head NOUN
1 la **tête** *fem (of person)*
Mind your head!
Attention à la tête!
Heads or tails? — Heads.
Pile ou face? — Face.
2 le **directeur** *masc*
la **directrice** *fem (headteacher)*

headache NOUN
I've got a headache.
J'ai mal à la tête.

headmaster NOUN
le **directeur** *masc*

headmistress NOUN
la **directrice** *fem*

health NOUN
la **santé** *fem*

healthy ADJECTIVE
sain *masc*
saine *fem*
   a healthy diet
   une alimentation saine

hear VERB
entendre
   I can't hear.
   Je n'entends pas.
   I can't hear you.
   Je ne vous entends pas.
   Can you hear the difference?
   Vous entendez la différence?

heart NOUN
1 le **cœur** *masc*
2 *(in cards)*
   hearts
   le cœur
   the ace of hearts
   l'as de cœur

heater NOUN
le **radiateur** *masc*
   an electric heater
   un radiateur électrique

heather NOUN
la **bruyère** *fem*

heavy ADJECTIVE
lourd *masc*
lourde *fem*
   This bag's very heavy.
   Ce sac est très lourd.

hedgehog NOUN
le **hérisson** *masc*

height NOUN
la **taille** *fem*

held VERB ▷ *see* **hold**

helicopter NOUN
l' **hélicoptère** *masc*

hello EXCLAMATION
bonjour!

helmet NOUN
le **casque** *masc*

help

help *can be a verb or a noun.*

A VERB
aider
   Can you help me?
   Vous pouvez m'aider?
   Help yourself!
   Servez-vous!

Help!
Au secours!

B NOUN
l' **aide** *fem*
   Do you need any help?
   Vous avez besoin d'aide?

hen NOUN
la **poule** *fem*

her

her can be an adjective or a pronoun.

A ADJECTIVE

Language tip
*When you want to say something like 'her name', 'her house', or 'her hair' in French, you need to know if 'name', 'house', and 'hair' are masculine, feminine, or plural, because there are three possible words for **her**.*

son *masc*
her name
son nom
sa *fem*
her house
sa maison
ses *pl*
her hair
ses cheveux

Language tip
sa *changes to* **son** *before a vowel sound.*

her address
son adresse
B PRONOUN *(object of the verb)*
1 la
I hate her.
Je la déteste.
Do you know her?
Tu la connais?
Look at her!
Regarde-la!

Language tip
la *changes to* **l'** *before a vowel sound.*

I love her.
Je l'aime.
2 elle
I'm going with her.
Je vais avec elle.

It's for her.
C'est pour elle.
He's next to her.
Il est à côté d'elle.
I'm older than her.
Je suis plus âgé qu'elle.

here ADVERB
ici
I live here.
J'habite ici.
Here's Helen.
Voici Helen.

Here are the books.
Voici les livres.
Here he is!
Le voici!

here is ...
voici ...
here are ...
voici ...

Language tip
here is *and* **here are** *are the same in French.*

hers PRONOUN
à elle
Is this hers?
C'est à elle?
This book is hers.
Ce livre est à elle.
Whose is this? — It's hers.
C'est à qui? — À elle.

herself PRONOUN
se
My cat washes herself a lot.
Ma chatte se lave beaucoup.
She lives by herself.
Elle habite toute seule.

by herself
toute seule

he's = he is, he has ▷ see **have**

hi EXCLAMATION
salut!

hide VERB
se cacher
   Daniel is hiding under the bed.
   Daniel se cache sous le lit.
   Hide!
   Cache-toi!
   Mum hides the biscuits.
   Maman cache les biscuits.

hide-and-seek NOUN
cache-cache *masc*

high ADJECTIVE
haut *masc*
haute *fem*
   It's too high.
   C'est trop haut.
   Higher!
   Plus haut!

high jump NOUN
le **saut en hauteur** *masc*

high-rise NOUN
la **tour** *fem*
   I live in a high-rise.
   J'habite dans une tour.

high school NOUN
   1 le **collège** *masc (for pupils 11–15)*
   2 le **lycée** *masc (for pupils 15–18)*

Did you know...?

*In France, pupils go to a **collège** between the ages of 11 and 15, and then to a **lycée** until the age of 18.*

hiking NOUN
   We're going to go hiking.
   Nous allons faire une randonnée.

hill NOUN
la **colline** *fem*

him PRONOUN
   1 **le** *(object of the verb)*
   I hate him.
   Je le déteste.
   Look at him!
   Regarde-le!

Language tip

le *changes to* **l'** *before a vowel sound.*

   I love him.
   Je l'aime.
   2 **lui**
   I'm going with him.
   Je vais avec lui.
   It's for him.
   C'est pour lui.
   She's next to him.
   Elle est à côté de lui.
   I'm older than him.
   Je suis plus âgé que lui.

himself PRONOUN
se
   The cat is washing himself.
   Le chat se lave.
   He lives by himself.
   Il habite tout seul.

by himself
tout seul

hippo NOUN
l' **hippopotame** *masc*

hire VERB
  louer
    You can hire bikes.
    On peut louer des vélos.

his

his can be an adjective or a pronoun.

A ADJECTIVE

> **Language tip**
>
> *When you want to say something like 'his name', 'his house', or 'his hair' in French, you need to know if 'name', 'house', 'hair' are masculine, feminine or plural, because there are three possible words for* **his**.

  son *masc*
  his name
  son nom
  sa *fem*
  his house
  sa maison
  ses *pl*
  his hair
  ses cheveux

> **Language tip**
>
> *sa changes to* **son** *before a vowel sound.*

  his address
  son adresse
B PRONOUN
  à lui
  Is this his?
  C'est à lui?
  This book is his.
  Ce livre est à lui.
  Whose is this? — It's his.
  C'est à qui? — À lui.

history NOUN
  l' **histoire** *fem*

hit

hit can be a verb or a noun.

A VERB
  frapper
  Don't hit Luc, Pascal!
  Ne frappe pas Luc, Pascal!
B NOUN
  le **tube** *masc (song)*
  Westlife's latest hit
  le dernier tube de Westlife

hobby NOUN
  le **passe-temps** *masc*
  What are your favourite hobbies?
  Quels sont tes passe-temps favoris?

hockey NOUN
  le **hockey** *masc*
  I play hockey.
  Je joue au hockey.

hold VERB
  tenir
  Can you hold the baby?
  Tu peux tenir le bébé?
  Hold hands!
  Donnez-vous la main!

hold on VERB
  Hold on a minute!
  Attends un peu!

hold up VERB
  Hold up your hands.
  Levez la main.

hole NOUN
  le **trou** *masc*

holiday NOUN
  1 les **vacances** *fem pl*
  our holiday in France
  nos vacances en France
  When are you going on holiday?
  Quand pars-tu en vacances?
  We are on holiday.
  Nous sommes en vacances.

in the school holidays
pendant les vacances scolaires

on holiday
en vacances
the school holidays
les vacances scolaires

2 le **jour férié** *masc (public holiday)*
Monday is a holiday.
Lundi, c'est un jour férié.

holiday home NOUN
la **résidence secondaire** *fem*

Holland NOUN
la **Hollande** *fem*

holly NOUN
le **houx** *masc*
a sprig of holly
un brin de houx

home NOUN
la **maison** *fem*
Is Charlotte at home?
Est-ce que Charlotte est à la maison?
What time do you get home?
Tu rentres à quelle heure?
I get home at five o'clock.
Je rentre à cinq heures.
to go home
rentrer à la maison
I want to go home.
Je veux rentrer à la maison.

at home
à la maison

homeless PL NOUN
the homeless
les sans-abri

home page NOUN
la **page d'accueil** *fem*

homework NOUN
les **devoirs** *masc pl*

We have too much homework.
Nous avons trop de devoirs.
my geography homework
mes devoirs de géographie

honey NOUN
le **miel** *masc*

honeymoon NOUN
la **lune de miel** *fem*

hood NOUN
la **capuche** *fem*

hooray EXCLAMATION
hourra!

hop VERB
sauter à cloche-pied
Hop!
Sautez à cloche-pied!

hope VERB
espérer
I hope that's okay.
J'espère que ça ira.
I'm hoping to go to France.
J'espère aller en France.

I hope so.
Je l'espère.
I hope not.
J'espère que non.

hopeless ADJECTIVE
nul *masc*
nulle *fem*
I'm hopeless at maths.
Je suis nul en maths.

You're hopeless, Martine!
Martine, tu es nulle!

horrible ADJECTIVE
horrible

horror film NOUN
le **film d'horreur** *masc*

horse NOUN
le **cheval** *masc* (PL les **chevaux**)

hospital NOUN
l' **hôpital** *masc* (PL les **hôpitaux**)
My grandmother is in hospital
Ma grand-mère est à l'hôpital.

hot ADJECTIVE
1 **chaud** *masc*
chaude *fem (very warm)*
a hot bath
un bain chaud
I'm too hot.
J'ai trop chaud.
It's very hot today.
Il fait très chaud aujourd'hui.

I'm hot.
J'ai chaud.
It's hot.
Il fait chaud.

2 **épicé** *masc*
épicée *fem (spicy)*
a very hot curry
un curry très épicé

hot chocolate NOUN
le **chocolat chaud** *masc*

hot dog NOUN
le **hot-dog** *masc*

hotel NOUN
l' **hôtel** *masc*

hour NOUN
l' **heure** *fem*
an hour and ten minutes
une heure dix

a quarter of an hour
un quart d'heure
half an hour
une demi-heure
two and a half hours
deux heures et demie

house NOUN
1 la **maison** *fem (building)*
You've got a nice house.
Vous avez une belle maison.
Do you want to play at my house?
Tu veux jouer chez moi?

at my house
chez moi

2 le **groupe** *masc (at school)*
Skye house has 180 points.
Le groupe Skye a 180 points.

housewife NOUN
la **femme au foyer** *fem*
She's a housewife.
Elle est femme au foyer.

Language tip
*You do not translate '**a**' when you say what someone's job is in French.*

how ADVERB
comment
How do you say 'apple' in French?
Comment dit-on 'apple' en français?
How many ...?
Combien de ...?

How many pupils are there in the class?
Il y a combien d'élèves dans la classe?
How much is it?
C'est combien?
How old is your brother?
Ton frère a quel âge?

How are you?
Comment allez-vous?
How old are you?
Tu as quel âge?
How many?
Combien?
How much?
Combien?

huge ADJECTIVE
immense

humidex NOUN (Canada)
l' **humidex** masc

hundred NUMBER
a hundred
cent
a hundred euros
cent euros

Language tip

cent is spelled with an **s** when there are two or more hundreds, but not when it is followed by another number, as in 'six hundred and two'.

five hundred
cinq cents
five hundred and one
cinq cent un
hundreds of people
des centaines de personnes

hungry
ADJECTIVE
Are you hungry?
Tu as faim?

I'm hungry.
J'ai faim.
I'm not hungry.
Je n'ai pas faim.

hunting NOUN
la **chasse** fem
I'm against hunting.
Je suis contre la chasse.
fox-hunting
la chasse au renard

hurry up VERB
Hurry up, Gavin!
Dépêche-toi, Gavin!
Hurry up, children!
Dépêchez-vous, les enfants!

hurt VERB
You're hurting me!
Tu me fais mal!
My leg hurts.
J'ai mal à la jambe.
Have you hurt yourself?
Tu t'es fait mal?
That hurts. Ça fait mal.

husband NOUN
le **mari** masc

hydro NOUN (Canada)
l' **électricité** fem

hymn NOUN
le **cantique** masc

hyphen NOUN
le **trait d'union** masc

I i

I PRONOUN
1 je
  I speak French.
  Je parle français.

Language tip

je *changes to* j' *before a vowel sound.*

  I love cats.
  J'aime les chats.
2 moi
  Ann and I
  Ann et moi

ice NOUN
  la **glace** *fem*
  There is ice on the lake.
  Il y a de la glace sur le lac.

ice cream NOUN
  la **glace** *fem*
  Would you like an ice cream?
  Tu veux une glace?
  vanilla ice cream
  la glace à la vanille
  chocolate ice cream
  la glace au chocolat

Language tip

The French is 'à la vanille' because **vanille** *is feminine, and 'au chocolat' because* **chocolat** *is masculine.*

ice cube NOUN
  le **glaçon** *masc*

ice lolly NOUN
  la **glace à l'eau** *fem*

  two ice lollies
  deux glaces à l'eau

ice rink NOUN
  la **patinoire** *fem*

ice-skating NOUN
  le **patin à glace** *masc*
  I go ice-skating.
  Je fais du patin à glace.

ICT PL NOUN
  les **TIC** *fem pl*

icy ADJECTIVE
  The roads are icy.
  Il y a du verglas sur les routes.

idea NOUN
  l' **idée** *fem*
  Good idea!
  Bonne idée!

identical ADJECTIVE
  identique
  The twins are identical.
  Ces jumeaux sont identiques.

if CONJUNCTION
  si
  You can have it if you like.
  Tu peux le prendre si tu veux.

Language tip

si *changes to* s' *before* il *and* ils.

  Do you know if he's there?
  Savez-vous s'il est là?

ill ADJECTIVE
  malade
  Christelle is ill.
  Christelle est malade.

imagination NOUN
  l' **imagination** *fem*

imagine VERB
imaginer
Imagine you have lots of money.
Imagine que tu as beaucoup d'argent.

imitate VERB
imiter
Imitate the sound.
Imitez le son.

immediately ADVERB
immédiatement
I'll do it immediately.
Je vais le faire immédiatement.

immigrant NOUN
l' **immigré** *masc*
l' **immigrée** *fem*

impatient ADJECTIVE
impatient *masc*
impatiente *fem*
Don't be so impatient, Édith.
Ne sois pas si impatiente Édith.

important ADJECTIVE
important *masc*
importante *fem*
This is an important letter.
C'est une lettre importante.
Today's an important day.
Aujourd'hui est un grand jour.

impossible ADJECTIVE
impossible
Sorry, it's impossible.
Désolée, c'est impossible.

in

> *in can be a preposition or an adverb.*

A PREPOSITION

> ***Language tip***
> *There are several ways of translating **in**. Scan the examples for one that is similar to what you want to say.*

1 dans
in the house
dans la maison
in my bag
dans mon sac
What can you see in the picture?
Que voyez-vous sur l'image?

2 à
in the country
à la campagne
in school
à l'école
in hospital
à l'hôpital
in London
à Londres
the boy in the blue shirt
le garçon à la chemise bleue

3 en
in English
en anglais
in summer
en été
in May
en mai
in 2008
en deux mille huit

English French

a
b
c
d
e
f
g
h
i
j
k
l
m
n
o
p
q
r
s
t
u
v
w
x
y
z

in England
en Angleterre
in Portugal
au Portugal
in the United States
aux États-Unis

4 **de**
the tallest person in the family
le plus grand de la famille
at 6 o'clock in the morning
à six heures du matin
She's the oldest in the class.
C'est la plus vieille de la classe.

in my class
dans ma classe
in Paris
à Paris
in France
en France
in French
en français

B ADVERB
to be in
être là
He isn't in.
Il n'est pas là.

inch NOUN
6 inches
quinze centimètres

incident NOUN
l' **incident** *masc*
an incident
un incident

included ADJECTIVE
compris *masc*
comprise *fem*
Service is not included.
Le service n'est pas compris.

incredible ADJECTIVE
incroyable
That's incredible!
C'est incroyable!

indeed ADVERB
Thank you very much indeed!
Merci beaucoup!

Indian ADJECTIVE
indien *masc*
indienne *fem*
an Indian restaurant
un restaurant indien

indoor ADJECTIVE
an indoor swimming pool
une piscine couverte

indoors ADVERB
à l'intérieur
They're indoors.
Ils sont à l'intérieur.

inexpensive ADJECTIVE
bon marché *masc, fem, pl*
  an inexpensive hotel
  un hôtel bon marché

infant school NOUN
  He's going to start at infant school.
  Il va entrer en cours préparatoire.

Did you know...?

CP (cours préparatoire) *is the equivalent of first-year infants, and* CE1 (cours élémentaire de première année) *is the equivalent of second-year infants in schools in the UK.*

infection NOUN
  an ear infection
  une otite
  a throat infection
  une angine

information NOUN
les **renseignements** *masc pl*
  I need some information.
  J'ai besoin de renseignements.
  important information
  des renseignements importants
  information about France
  des renseignements sur la France

Language tip

information *is a singular word in English, but a plural word in French.*

ingredient NOUN
l' **ingrédient** *masc*
  a list of ingredients
  une liste d'ingrédients

inhabitant NOUN
l' **habitant** *masc*
l' **habitante** *fem*

inhaler NOUN
l'**inhalateur** *masc*

initials PL NOUN
les **initiales** *fem pl*
  My initials are GAC.
  Mes initiales sont GAC.

injection NOUN
la **piqûre** *fem*

injure VERB
blesser
  Was anyone injured?
  Est-ce que quelqu'un a été blessé?

injury NOUN
la **blessure** *fem*
  a serious injury
  une blessure grave

ink NOUN
l' **encre** *fem*

inquire VERB
  to inquire about something
  se renseigner sur quelque chose
  I'm going to inquire about train times.
  Je vais me renseigner sur les horaires des trains.

inquiries PL NOUN
les **renseignements** *masc pl*

inquisitive ADJECTIVE
curieux *masc*
curieuse *fem*

English French

a
b
c
d
e
f
g
h
i
j
k
l
m
n
o
p
q
r
s
t
u
v
w
x
y
z

English   French

a
b
c
d
e
f
g
h
i
j
k
l
m
n
o
p
q
r
s
t
u
v
w
x
y
z

insect NOUN
l' **insecte** masc

in-service day NOUN
la **journée de formation** fem

inside

> **inside** can be an adverb or a preposition.

A ADVERB
à l'intérieur
They're inside.
Ils sont à l'intérieur.
Do you want a table inside or outside?
Vous voulez une table à l'intérieur ou à l'extérieur?

B PREPOSITION
à l'intérieur de
inside the house
à l'intérieur de la maison

inspector NOUN
le **contrôleur** masc

instance NOUN
for instance
par exemple

instantly ADVERB
tout de suite

instead ADVERB
à la place
There's no coke. Do you want orange juice instead?
Il n'y a pas de coca. Tu veux du jus d'orange à la place?
instead of
au lieu de
Eat fruit instead of sweets.
Mangez des fruits au lieu de bonbons.

instead of me
à ma place
instead of Manon
à la place de Manon

instructions PL NOUN
les **instructions** fem pl
Follow the instructions.
Suivez les instructions.

instructor NOUN
le **moniteur** masc
la **monitrice** fem
a skiing instructor
un moniteur de ski

instrument NOUN
l' **instrument** masc
Do you play an instrument?
Est-ce que tu joues d'un instrument?

intelligent ADJECTIVE
intelligent masc
intelligente fem
You're very intelligent.
Tu es très intelligente.

> **Language tip**
>
> *The person being spoken to in the example is a girl. How can you tell?*

interest NOUN
My main interest is music.
Ce qui m'intéresse le plus c'est la musique.

interested ADJECTIVE
I'm not interested.
Ça ne m'intéresse pas.
I'm not interested in football.
Le football ne m'intéresse pas.
Are you interested?
Ça t'intéresse?

interesting ADJECTIVE
intéressant masc
intéressante fem
It's a very interesting story.
C'est une histoire très intéressante.

international ADJECTIVE
international masc
internationale fem
an international school
une école internationale

internet NOUN
l' **Internet** masc
on the internet
sur Internet

Language tip

There's one more word in the English example sentence than there is in the French sentence. What is it?

---

internet café NOUN
le **cybercafé** masc

interrupt VERB
interrompre
Don't interrupt Hugues!
N'interromps pas, Hugues!

interval NOUN
1 l' **entracte** masc (cinema, theatre)
during the interval
pendant l'entracte
2 la **récréation** fem (school)

interview NOUN
l' **interview** fem

interviewer NOUN
l' **interviewer** masc

into PREPOSITION
1 **en**
I'm going into town.
Je vais en ville.
Translate it into French.
Traduisez ça en français.
Divide into two groups.
Répartissez-vous en deux groupes.
2 **dans** (inside)
He got into the car.
Il est monté dans la voiture.

introduce VERB
présenter
Introduce yourselves.
Présentez-vous.
I'd like to introduce Michelle Davies.
Je vous présente Michelle Davies.

Inuit

Inuit can be an adjective or a noun.

A ADJECTIVE
inuit masc
inuite fem
B PL NOUN
les **Inuits** masc pl

invalid NOUN
le/la **malade** masc/fem

inventor NOUN
l' **inventeur** masc
l' **inventrice** fem

invisible ADJECTIVE
invisible

invitation NOUN
l' **invitation** fem
Thank you for the invitation.
Merci pour l'invitation.

invite VERB
inviter
   I'm going to invite Léon to my party.
   Je vais inviter Léon à ma fête.

iPod® NOUN
   l'**iPod**® *masc*

Ireland NOUN
   l' **Irlande** *fem*
   I live in Ireland.
   J'habite en Irlande.
   When are you coming to Ireland?
   Quand est-ce que tu viens en Irlande?
   I'm from Ireland.
   Je suis irlandaise.

   in Ireland
   en Irlande
   I'm going to Ireland.
   Je vais en Irlande.

Irish

   Irish *can be an adjective or a noun.*

   A ADJECTIVE
   irlandais *masc*
   irlandaise *fem*
   I am Irish.
   Je suis irlandais.

   Language tip
   Is a boy or a girl speaking in the example sentence? How can you tell?

   I like Irish music.
   J'aime la musique irlandaise.
   Irish people
   les Irlandais

   He's Irish.
   Il est irlandais.
   She's Irish.
   Elle est irlandaise.

   B NOUN
   l' **irlandais** *masc* *(language)*
   Do you speak Irish?
   Est-ce que tu parles irlandais?
   the Irish
   les Irlandais

   Language tip
   irlandais *is not spelled with a capital letter except when it means an Irish person.*

Irishman NOUN
   l' **Irlandais** *masc*

Irishwoman NOUN
   l' **Irlandaise** *fem*

iron

   iron *can be a noun or a verb.*

   A NOUN
   1 le **fer** *masc (metal)*
   an iron gate
   un portail en fer
   2 le **fer à repasser** *masc* *(for clothes)*
   B VERB
   repasser
   I can iron a shirt.
   Je sais repasser une chemise.

irritating ADJECTIVE
   irritant *masc*
   irritante *fem*

is VERB ▷*see* **be**

Islam NOUN
   l' **Islam** *masc*

English French

island NOUN
l' **île** *fem*

isle NOUN
the Isle of Man
l'île de Man
the Isle of Wight
l'île de Wight

it PRONOUN

Language tip
You need to know if **it** *stands for a masculine noun or a feminine noun, so that you can choose* **il** *or* **elle**.

il
Where's my book? —
It's on the table.
Où est mon livre? —
Il est sur la table.

elle
Where's my pencil case? —
It's in your bag.
Où est ma trousse? —
Elle est dans ton sac.

Language tip
Use **le** *or* **la** *when* **it** *is the object of the sentence.* **le** *and* **la** *change to* **l'** *before a vowel sound.*

le
There's a croissant left. Do you want it?
Il reste un croissant. Tu le veux?

la
I don't want this apple.
You can have it.
Je ne veux pas de cette pomme.
Tu peux la prendre.

l'
This is my new jumper.
Do you like it?
C'est mon nouveau pull.
Tu l'aimes?

It's me.
C'est moi.
It's you.
C'est toi.
It's expensive.
C'est cher.
It's delicious.
C'est délicieux.

Italian

Italian *can be an adjective or a noun.*

A ADJECTIVE
italien *masc*
italienne *fem*
an Italian restaurant
un restaurant italien
B NOUN
l' **italien** *masc (language)*

Language tip
italien *is not spelt with a capital letter except when it means an Italian person.*

Italy NOUN
l' **Italie** *fem*

item NOUN
l' **article** *masc*

its ADJECTIVE

Language tip
To say something like 'its name', 'its place', or 'its hair' in French, you need to know if 'name', 'place', and 'hair' are masculine, feminine or plural, because there are three possible words for **its**.

a b c d e f g h **i** j k l m n o p q r s t u v w x y z

449

son *masc*
What's its name?
Quel est son nom?
sa *fem*
Everything is in its place.
Chaque chose est à sa place.

ses *pl*
The dog is losing its hair.
Le chien perd ses poils.

J j

jab NOUN
la **piqûre** *fem*

jack NOUN
le **valet** *masc*
the jack of hearts
le valet de cœur

jacket NOUN
la **veste** *fem*
a white jacket
une veste blanche

jacket potato NOUN
la **pomme de terre cuite au four** *fem*
There are chips and jacket potatoes.
Il y a des frites et des pommes de terre cuites au four.

jam NOUN
la **confiture** *fem*
strawberry jam
la confiture de fraises

jam jar NOUN
le **pot à confiture** *masc*

janitor NOUN
le **concierge** *masc*
He's a janitor.
Il est concierge.

Language tip
You do not translate 'a' when you say what someone's job is in French.

January NOUN
janvier *masc*
January or February?
Janvier ou février?
My birthday's in January.
Mon anniversaire est en janvier.

in January
en janvier
the fifth of January
le cinq janvier

Language tip
The months are not spelled with a capital letter in French.

jealous ADJECTIVE
jaloux *masc*
jalouse *fem*
Aline is jealous.
Aline est jalouse.

jeans PL NOUN
le **jean** *masc*
I've got new jeans.
J'ai un jean neuf.

Language tip
jeans *is plural in English, but the French word is singular.*

jelly NOUN
la **gelée** *fem*

jersey NOUN
le **pull-over** *masc*

Jew NOUN
le **Juif** *masc*
la **Juive** *fem*

jewellery NOUN
les **bijoux** *masc pl*

Jewish ADJECTIVE
juif *masc*
juive *fem*

> **Language tip**
> **Jewish** *has a capital letter, but* **juif**
> *does not.*

jigsaw NOUN
le **puzzle** *masc*
   I like doing jigsaws.
   J'aime faire des puzzles.

job NOUN
l' **emploi** *masc*
   She's looking for a job.
   Elle cherche un emploi.
   I've got a Saturday job.
   Je travaille le samedi.

jogging NOUN
   She goes jogging.
   Elle fait du jogging.

joke NOUN
la **plaisanterie** *fem*

jotter NOUN
le **cahier** *masc*

journey NOUN
le **voyage** *masc*
   I don't like long journeys.
   Je n'aime pas les longs
   voyages.

judge

> **judge** *can be a noun or a verb.*

A NOUN
le **juge** *masc*
   She's a judge.
   Elle est juge.

> **Language tip**
> *You do not translate* **'a'** *when you*
> *say what someone's job is in French.*

B VERB
juger
   Who's going to judge the
   competition?
   Qui va juger le concours?

judo NOUN
le **judo** *masc*
   I do judo.
   Je fais du judo.

juggler NOUN
le **jongleur** *masc*
la **jongleuse** *fem*

juice NOUN
le **jus** *masc*
   I'd like some orange juice.
   Je voudrais du jus d'orange.

July NOUN
juillet *masc*
   July or August?
   Juillet ou août?
   My birthday is in July.
   Mon anniversaire est en juillet.

in July
en juillet
the fourteenth of July
le quatorze juillet

> **Language tip**
> *Months are not written with a*
> *capital letter in French.*

English

French

a
b
c
d
e
f
g
h
i
j
k
l
m
n
o
p
q
r
s
t
u
v
w
x
y
z

Did you know…?
*The fourteenth of July (**la fête nationale**) is the French national holiday. There's a firework display and a military parade in Paris.*

jump VERB
sauter
> **Jump!**
> Saute!

jumper NOUN
le **pull** *masc*
> **a dark green jumper**
> un pull vert foncé

June NOUN
juin *masc*
> **June or July?**
> Juin ou juillet?
> **My birthday is in June.**
> Mon anniversaire est en juin.

> **in June**
> en juin
> **the fourth of June**
> le quatre juin

Language tip
Months are not written with a capital letter in French.

junior NOUN
> **the juniors**
> les élèves des petites classes

junior school NOUN
l' **école primaire** *fem*

just ADVERB
juste
> **just after Christmas**
> juste après Noël
> **just now**
> en ce moment
> **I'm busy just now.**
> Je suis occupé en ce moment.
> **I'm just coming!**
> J'arrive!
> **Just a moment, please.**
> Un moment, s'il vous plaît.

453

K k

karaoke NOUN
le **karaoké** *masc*

karate NOUN
le **karaté** *masc*
I do karate.
Je fais du karaté.

keen ADJECTIVE
enthousiaste
He's not very keen.
Il n'est pas très enthousiaste.

keep VERB
1 **garder** *(have)*
You can keep it.
Tu peux le garder.
2 **rester** *(stay)*
Keep still!
Reste tranquille!
Keep quiet!
Tais-toi!

keep on VERB
continuer
Keep on singing.
Continuez de chanter.

keep-fit NOUN
The keep-fit class is on Tuesday.
Le cours de gym, c'est mardi.

key NOUN
la **clé** *fem*
Where are my keys?
Où sont mes clés?

kick

kick *can be a noun or a verb.*

A NOUN
le **coup de pied** *masc*

B VERB
donner un coup de pied
He kicked me!
Il m'a donné un coup de pied!

kid NOUN
le/la **gosse** *masc/fem (child)*
the kids
les gosses

kill VERB
tuer
My cat kills birds.
Mon chat tue les oiseaux.

kilo NOUN
le **kilo** *masc*
two euros a kilo
deux euros le kilo

kilometre NOUN
le **kilomètre** *masc*

kilt NOUN
le **kilt** *masc*

kind

kind *can be an adjective or a noun.*

A ADJECTIVE
gentil *masc*
gentille *fem*
That's very kind of you.
C'est très gentil.

B NOUN
la **sorte** *fem*
**'Saucisson' is a kind of
sausage.**
Le saucisson est une sorte de
saucisse.

kindergarten NOUN
l' **école maternelle** *fem*

king NOUN
le **roi** *masc*
the king of hearts
le roi de cœur

kiss

kiss can be a noun or a verb.

A NOUN
le **baiser** *masc*
Give me a kiss.
Donne-moi un baiser.

Language tip
bisou and **bise** are two other words
meaning **kiss**. At the end of a letter
to a friend you could write **Bisous**
or **Grosses bises**.

B VERB
embrasser
Kiss me.
Embrasse-moi.

Did you know...?
*Between girls and boys, and
between girls, the normal French
way of saying hello and goodbye is
with kisses, usually one on each
cheek. Boys shake hands with each
other instead.*

kit NOUN
les **affaires** *fem pl*
Don't forget your gym kit.
N'oublie pas tes affaires de gym.

kitchen NOUN
la **cuisine** *fem*
She's in the kitchen.
Elle est dans la cuisine.

kite NOUN
le **cerf-volant**
masc
two kites
deux
cerfs-volants

kitten NOUN
le **chaton** *masc*

knee NOUN
le **genou** *masc* (PL les **genoux**)

knickers PL NOUN
la **culotte** *fem*
I can see your knickers!
Je vois ta culotte!
a pair of knickers
une culotte

Language tip
culotte *is a singular word.*

knife NOUN
le **couteau** *masc*
(PL les **couteaux**)

knit VERB
tricoter
I can knit.
Je sais tricoter.

knives PL NOUN
les **couteaux** *masc pl*
knives, forks and spoons
les couteaux, les fourchettes
et les cuillères

knob NOUN
le **bouton** *masc*

knock VERB
frapper
> **Someone's knocking at the door.**
> Quelqu'un frappe à la porte.

know VERB
1 **savoir** *(know something)*
> **It's a long way. — Yes, I know.**
> C'est loin. — Oui, je sais.
> **Who knows the answer?**
> Qui sait la réponse?

> **I don't know.**
> Je ne sais pas.

2 **connaître** *(know someone)*
> **I know her.**
> Je la connais.
> **I don't know him.**
> Je ne le connais pas.
> **Do you know Louise?**
> Tu connais Louise?

Koran NOUN
le Coran *masc*

L l

label NOUN
l' **étiquette** *fem*

lace NOUN
le **lacet** *masc*

lacrosse NOUN
la **crosse** *fem*
a lacrosse stick
une crosse

Did you know…?
lacrosse *is Canada's official summer sport.*

ladder NOUN
l' **échelle** *fem*

lady NOUN
la **dame** *fem*
a young lady
une jeune fille
Ladies and gentlemen …
Mesdames et messieurs …
Where is the 'ladies'?
Où sont les toilettes?

lake NOUN
le **lac** *masc*

lamb NOUN
l' **agneau** *masc* (PL les **agneaux**)
a lamb chop
une côtelette d'agneau

land

land *can be a verb or a noun.*

A NOUN
la **terre** *fem*
on land
sur terre

B VERB
atterrir
The plane lands at nine o'clock.
L'avion atterrit à neuf heures.

lane NOUN
le **chemin** *masc*
a country lane
un chemin de campagne
the fast lane
la voie rapide

language NOUN
la **langue** *fem*
French isn't a difficult language.
Le français n'est pas une langue difficile.

language laboratory NOUN
le **laboratoire de langues** *masc*

lap NOUN
on my lap
sur mes genoux

laptop NOUN
l' **ordinateur portable** *masc*

large ADJECTIVE
1 **grand** *masc*
grande *fem* (size, glass, plate, garden)
a large house
une grande maison
2 **gros** *masc*
grosse *fem* (car, animal, book, parcel)
a large dog
un gros chien

last

last *can be an adjective or an adverb.*

a b c d e f g h i j k l m n o p q r s t u v w x y z

A ADJECTIVE
dernier *masc*
dernière *fem*
the last time
la dernière fois
tonight and last night
ce soir et hier soir

last Friday
vendredi dernier
last week
la semaine dernière
last summer
l'été dernier
last night
hier soir
at last
enfin

B ADVERB
en dernier
He always comes last.
Il arrive toujours en dernier.

late ADJECTIVE, ADVERB
1 en retard
You're going to be late!
Tu vas être en retard!
I'm late for school.
Je suis en retard pour l'école.

Sorry I'm late!
Désolé d'être en retard!
2 tard *(late at night)*
I go to bed late.
Je me couche tard.

later ADVERB
plus tard
I'll do it later.
Je ferai ça plus tard.

See you later!
À tout à l'heure!

latest ADJECTIVE
dernier *masc*
dernière *fem*
their latest album
leur dernier album

Latin NOUN
le **latin** *masc*
I do Latin.
Je fais du latin.

laugh VERB
rire
Why are you laughing?
Pourquoi tu ris?

lawn NOUN
la **pelouse** *fem*

lawnmower NOUN
la **tondeuse à gazon** *fem*

lawyer NOUN
l' **avocat** *masc*
l' **avocate** *fem*
My mother's a lawyer.
Ma mère est avocate.

Language tip
*You do not translate '**a**' when you
say what someone's job is in French.*

lay VERB
poser
Lay your cards on the table
Posez vos cartes sur la table.
to lay the table
mettre la table
**It's André's turn to lay the
table.**
C'est à André de mettre la table.

lazy ADJECTIVE
paresseux *masc*
paresseuse *fem*

My sister is very lazy.
Ma sœur est très paresseuse.

lead

> **lead** can be a noun or a verb.

A NOUN
to be in the lead
être en tête
Our team is in the lead.
Notre équipe est en tête.

B VERB
mener
This street leads to the station.
Cette rue mène à la gare.

leaf NOUN
la **feuille**
fem

lean out VERB
se pencher
Don't lean out of the window.
Ne te penche pas par la fenêtre.

lean over VERB
se pencher
Don't lean over too far.
Ne te penche pas trop.

leap year NOUN
l' **année bissextile** *fem*

learn VERB
apprendre
I'm learning to ski.
J'apprends à skier.
We're learning a lot.
Nous apprenons beaucoup.

I'm learning French.
J'apprends le français.

least ADVERB, ADJECTIVE, PRONOUN
the least
le moins de
Who's got the least cards?
Qui a le moins de cartes?

Language tip
When **the least** *is followed by an adjective, it is translated as* **le moins**, **la moins**, *or* **les moins**, *depending on the following noun.*

the least expensive hotel
l'hôtel le moins cher
the least expensive seat
la place la moins chère
the least expensive hotels
les hôtels les moins chers
It'll cost at least £200.
Ça va coûter au moins deux cents livres.

at least
au moins

leather NOUN
le **cuir** *masc*
It's made of leather.
C'est en cuir.

leave VERB
1 laisser (on purpose)
Don't leave your bag in the car.
Ne laisse pas ton sac dans la voiture.
2 oublier (by mistake)
I've left my book at home.
J'ai oublié mon livre à la maison.
3 partir (depart)
The bus leaves at 8.
Le car part à huit heures.

leaves PL NOUN
les **feuilles** *fem pl*

English French

a b c d e f g h i j k l m n o p q r s t u v w x y z

leek NOUN
le **poireau** *masc*
(PL les **poireaux**)

left VERB ▷see **leave**

left

left *can be an adjective, an adverb or a noun.*

A ADJECTIVE
1 **gauche** *(not right)*
my left hand
ma main gauche
on the left side of the road
sur le côté gauche de la route
2 *(remaining)*
How many cards have you got left?
Il te reste combien de cartes?
I haven't got any money left.
Il ne me reste plus d'argent.
B ADVERB
à gauche
Turn left.
Tournez à gauche.
Take the next left.
Prenez la prochaine à gauche.
C NOUN
la **gauche** *fem*
on the left
à gauche
the house on the left
la maison à gauche

left-hand ADJECTIVE
the left-hand side
la gauche
It's on the left-hand side.
C'est à gauche.

left-handed ADJECTIVE
gaucher *masc*
gauchère *fem*
Annick is left-handed.
Annick est gauchère.

Language tip
Annick is a girl's name. How can you tell from the translation in the example sentence?

left-luggage office NOUN
la **consigne** *fem*

leg NOUN
la **jambe** *fem*
She has a broken leg.
Elle a une jambe cassée.
a chicken leg
une cuisse de poulet

leisure centre NOUN
le **centre de loisirs** *masc*

lemon NOUN
le **citron** *masc*

lemonade NOUN
la **limonade** *fem*

lend VERB
prêter
Can you lend me a pencil?
Tu peux me prêter un crayon?

less

less *can be an adjective or a pronoun.*

A ADJECTIVE
moins de
Less noise, please!
Moins de bruit, s'il vous plaît!
B PRONOUN
moins
A bit less, please.
Un peu moins, s'il vous plaît.
I've got less than him!
J'en ai moins que lui!

English French

Language tip

When **less than** *is followed by a number, the translation is* **moins de**.

It costs less than £10.
Ça coûte moins de dix livres.

lesson NOUN
1 la **leçon** *fem*
   a French lesson
   une leçon de français
2 le **cours** *masc (class)*
   Each lesson lasts forty minutes.
   Chaque cours dure quarante minutes.

let VERB
1 **laisser** *(allow)*
   Let me have a look.
   Laisse-moi voir.
2 *(shall we)*
   Let's go to the park!
   Allons au parc!

Let's go!
Allons-y!
Let's start now!
Commençons maintenant!

letter NOUN
la **lettre** *fem*
I'm writing a letter to my penfriend.
J'écris une lettre à ma correspondante.
It's a ten-letter word.
C'est un mot en dix lettres.

letterbox NOUN
la **boîte à lettres** *fem*

Did you know…?

In France, people don't usually have letterboxes in their front doors. More often, they have a box outside or, in a block of flats, on the ground floor.

lettuce NOUN
la **salade** *fem*

liar NOUN
le **menteur** *masc*
la **menteuse** *fem*

library NOUN
la **bibliothèque** *fem*

licence NOUN
le **permis** *masc*
   a driving licence
   un permis de conduire

lick VERB
lécher
   The dog is licking me.
   Le chien me lèche.

lid NOUN
le **couvercle** *masc*

lie VERB

lie *can be a verb or a noun.*

A VERB
1 **mentir** *(tell lies)*
   She's lying.
   Elle ment.
2 *(lie down)*
   He is lying on the sofa.
   Il est allongé sur le canapé.
B NOUN
le **mensonge** *masc*

English · **French**

a b c d e f g h i j k **l** m n o p q r s t u v w x y z

That's a lie!
C'est un mensonge!

life NOUN
la **vie** *fem*

life-saving NOUN
le **sauvetage** *masc*
I'm doing a course in life-saving.
Je prends des cours de sauvetage.

lift

> **lift** *can be a verb or a noun.*

A VERB
soulever
It's too heavy, I can't lift it.
C'est trop lourd, je ne peux pas le soulever.

B NOUN
l' **ascenseur** *masc*
The lift isn't working.
L'ascenseur est en panne.

light

> **light** *can be an adjective, a noun or a verb.*

A ADJECTIVE
1 **léger** *masc*
légère *fem (not heavy)*
as light as a feather
léger comme une plume
2 **clair** *masc, fem, pl (colours)*
light blue socks
des chaussettes bleu clair

B NOUN
la **lumière** *fem*
Switch on the light.
Allume la lumière.
Switch off the light.
Éteins la lumière.

C VERB
allumer

Let's light the fire.
Allumons le feu.

light bulb NOUN
l' **ampoule** *fem*

lightning NOUN
les **éclairs** *masc pl*
a flash of lightning
un éclair

like

> **like** *can be a verb or a preposition.*

A VERB
1 **aimer** *(enjoy)*
I like cherries.
J'aime les cerises.

> ### Language tip
> There's an extra word in the French example sentence that isn't in the English. What is it?

I don't like mustard.
Je n'aime pas la moutarde.
I like riding.
J'aime faire du cheval.
2 **bien aimer** *(be fond of)*
I like Paul.
J'aime bien Paul.
3 **vouloir** *(want)*
Yes, if you like.
Oui, si tu veux.

> ### Language tip
> If you want to say that you'd like something, use **je voudrais**.

I'd like an orange juice, please.
Je voudrais un jus d'orange, s'il vous plaît.
I'd like some chips.
Je voudrais des frites.

What would you like, Miss?
Qu'est-ce que vous voulez, Madame?
What would you like, dear?
Qu'est-ce que tu veux, mon chéri?
Would you like some tea, Miss?
Vous voulez du thé, Madame?
Would you like a coke, Louis?
Tu veux un coca, Louis?

Would you like a coke?
Veux-tu un coca?

I'd like ...
Je voudrais ...

B PREPOSITION
comme
a city like Paris
une ville comme Paris
I look like my brother.
Je ressemble à mon frère.
What's the weather like?
Quel temps fait-il?

likely ADJECTIVE
probable
That's not very likely.
C'est peu probable.

lily of the valley NOUN
le **muguet** masc

line NOUN
la **ligne** fem
a straight line
une ligne droite
to draw a line
tirer un trait
Draw a line under each answer.
Tirez un trait après chaque réponse.

lion NOUN
le **lion** masc

lip NOUN
la **lèvre** fem

lipstick NOUN
le **rouge à lèvres** masc

liquid NOUN
le **liquide** masc

list

A NOUN
la **liste** fem
a shopping list
une liste de courses
B VERB
faire une liste de

a b c d e f g h i j k **l** m n o p q r s t u v w x y z

List your hobbies!
Fais une liste de tes hobbies!

listen VERB
écouter
    Are you listening, Gaëlle?
    Tu écoutes, Gaëlle?
    Listen to this, everybody!
    Écoutez ça, tout le monde!

> **Listen to me, children!**
> Écoutez-moi, les enfants!

litre NOUN
    le **litre** masc

litter NOUN
    les **détritus** masc pl
    Don't leave litter.
    Ne laissez pas de détritus.

litter bin NOUN
    la **poubelle** fem

little ADJECTIVE
petit masc
petite fem
    a little girl
    une petite fille
    very little
    très peu
    We've got very little time.
    Nous avons très peu de temps.
    a little
    un peu
    How much would you like? — Just a little.
    Combien en voulez-vous? — Juste un peu.

> **Language tip**
> The word **en** means 'of it'.

live VERB
1 habiter

Where do you live?
Où est-ce que tu habites?
I live here.
J'habite ici.
I live in Edinburgh.
J'habite à Édimbourg.
2 vivre
    I live with my grandmother.
    Je vis avec ma grand-mère.
    to live together
    vivre ensemble
    My parents don't live together anymore.
    Mes parents ne vivent plus ensemble.

living room NOUN
    la **salle de séjour** fem

load NOUN
    loads of
    un tas de
    loads of people
    un tas de gens
    loads of money
    un tas d'argent

loaf NOUN
    le **pain** masc
    a loaf of bread
    un pain

loaves PL NOUN
    les **pains** masc pl

lock

> **lock** can be a noun or a verb.

A NOUN
    la **serrure** fem
    The lock is broken.
    La serrure est cassée.
B VERB
    fermer à clé
    Lock your door.
    Fermez votre porte à clé.

locker NOUN
le **casier** *masc*
Leave your books in your locker.
Laissez vos livres dans votre casier.

log NOUN
la **bûche** *fem*

log in VERB
se **connecter**
I can't log in.
Je n'arrive pas à me connecter.

log off VERB
se **déconnecter**
I've forgotten how to log off.
J'ai oublié comment on se déconnecte.

log on VERB
se **connecter**
Have you logged on yet?
Ça y est, tu t'es connecté?

log out VERB
se **déconnecter**
Please log out now.
Déconnectez-vous maintenant, s'il vous plaît.

lollipop NOUN
la **sucette** *fem*

lollipop lady NOUN
la **dame qui aide à traverser** *fem*

London NOUN
Londres

in London
à Londres
to London
à Londres
I'm from London.
Je suis de Londres.

Language tip

A few British towns have French names. Can you recognize these: **Douvres**, **Cantorbéry**, **Édimbourg***?*

lonely ADJECTIVE
seul *masc*
seule *fem*
to feel lonely
se sentir seul
She feels lonely.
Elle se sent seule.

long ADJECTIVE
long *masc*
longue *fem*
There's a long queue.
Il y a une longue queue.
She's got long hair.
Elle a les cheveux longs.

Language tip

Hair is plural in French so the adjective has to be plural too.

How long is the flight?
Combien de temps dure le vol?

how long?
combien de temps?
It takes a long time.
Ça prend du temps.

loo NOUN
les **toilettes** *fem pl*
Where's the loo?
Où sont les toilettes?
May I go to the loo?
Je peux aller aux toilettes?

look

> **look** *can be a noun or a verb.*

A NOUN
  to have a look
  regarder
  Have a look at this!
  Regardez ça!
B VERB
1 regarder
  Look, children!
  Regardez, les enfants!
  Look Olivier, you've broken it.
  Regarde Olivier, tu l'as cassé.

> *Language tip*
> **to look at** *is also* **regarder**.

  Look at the picture.
  Regardez cette image.
  Look at me, Stéphane.
  Regarde-moi, Stéphane.
2 avoir l'air *(seem)*
  That cake looks nice.
  Ce gâteau a l'air bon.

> **Look!**
> Regarde!
> **Look at the board.**
> Regardez le tableau.
> **Look out!**
> Attention!

look after VERB
s'occuper de
  I look after my little sister.
  Je m'occupe de ma petite sœur.

look for VERB
chercher
  I'm looking for my rubber.
  Je cherche ma gomme.
  What are you looking for?
  Qu'est-ce que tu cherches?

look up VERB
chercher

  Look up the words in the dictionary.
  Cherchez les mots dans le dictionnaire.

loonie NOUN *(Canada)*
le **huard** *masc*

lorry NOUN
le **camion** *masc*

lorry driver NOUN
le **routier** *masc*
  He's a lorry driver.
  Il est routier.

> *Language tip*
> *When you say what someone's job is in French, you do not translate* **a**.

lose VERB
perdre

  I've lost my purse.
  J'ai perdu mon porte-monnaie.
  Our team always loses.
  Notre équipe perd toujours.

loser NOUN
le **perdant** *masc*
la **perdante** *fem*

lost VERB ▷ *see* **lose**

lost property office NOUN
les **objets trouvés** *masc pl*

> *Language tip*
> *The French word literally means 'things that have been found'.*

lot NOUN
a lot
beaucoup
not a lot
pas beaucoup
That's a lot.
C'est beaucoup.
a lot of
beaucoup de
She has a lot of books.
Elle a beaucoup de livres.
lots of
un tas de
He's got lots of friends.
Il a un tas d'amis.

lottery NOUN
le **loto** masc
I hope I win the lottery.
J'espère que je vais gagner au loto.

loud ADJECTIVE
fort masc
forte fem
The television is too loud.
La télévision est trop forte.
Speak louder!
Parle plus fort!

lounge NOUN
le **salon** masc

love

love can be a noun or a verb.

A NOUN
l' **amour** masc
She's in love.
Elle est amoureuse.
She's in love with Paul.
Elle est amoureuse de Paul.

Give Delphine my love.
Embrasse Delphine pour moi.
Love, Rosemary.
Amitiés, Rosemary.
B VERB
1 **aimer**
Do you love me?
Tu m'aimes?
2 **beaucoup aimer** (be very fond of)
Everybody loves her.
Tout le monde l'aime beaucoup.
3 **adorer** (enjoy)
I love chocolate.
J'adore le chocolat.

Language tip
There is an extra word in the French sentence that isn't in the English. What is it?

I love skiing.
J'adore le ski.

I love you.
Je t'aime.
Love from ...
Amitiés ...

lovely ADJECTIVE
It's a lovely day.
Il fait très beau aujourd'hui.
They've got a lovely house.
Ils ont une très belle maison.
Have a lovely time!
Amusez-vous bien!

low ADJECTIVE
bas masc
basse fem
a low price
un prix bas

lower sixth NOUN
la **première** fem
He's in the lower sixth.
Il est en première.

English French

a b c d e f g h i j k l m n o p q r s t u v w x y z

English French

a b c d e f g h i j k **l** m n o p q r s t u v w x y z

luck NOUN
la **chance** *fem*
She doesn't have much luck.
Elle n'a pas beaucoup de chance.

Good luck!
Bonne chance!
Bad luck!
Pas de chance!

luckily ADVERB
heureusement

lucky ADJECTIVE
You're lucky!
Tu as de la chance!
Leah is lucky, she's going to France.
Leah a de la chance, elle va en France.

Language tip
*When you talk about things that are lucky, use **porter bonheur**.*

Black cats are lucky.
Les chats noirs portent bonheur.
a lucky horseshoe
un fer à cheval porte-bonheur

luggage NOUN
les **bagages** *masc pl*
Have you got any luggage?
Vous avez des bagages?

lump NOUN
la **bosse** *fem*
He's got a lump on his forehead.
Il a une bosse sur le front.

lunch NOUN
le **déjeuner** *masc*
I go home for lunch.
Je rentre à la maison pour le déjeuner.
It's time for lunch.
C'est l'heure du déjeuner.
to have lunch
déjeuner
We have lunch at 12.30.
Nous déjeunons à midi et demi.

Luxembourg NOUN
le **Luxembourg** *masc*

lying VERB ▷*see* **lie**

M m

machine NOUN
la **machine** *fem*

mad ADJECTIVE
1 **fou** *masc*
  folle *fem (insane)*
  You're mad!
  Tu es fou!
  He's mad about football.
  Il est dingue de foot.
  She's mad about horses.
  Elle adore les chevaux.
2 **furieux** *masc*
  furieuse *fem (angry)*
  If you don't invite her she'll be mad.
  Elle sera furieuse si tu ne l'invites pas.

madam NOUN
madame *fem*
  Would you like to order, Madam?
  Désirez-vous commander, Madame?

made VERB ▷ *see* **make**

magazine NOUN
le **magazine** *masc*

magic

> **magic** *can be an adjective or a noun.*

A ADJECTIVE
1 **magique** *(magical)*
  a magic wand
  une baguette magique
  a magic trick
  un tour de magie
2 **super** *(brilliant)*
  It was magic!
  C'était super!

B NOUN
  la **magie** *fem*
  by magic
  par magie

magician NOUN
le **prestidigitateur** *masc*

magnifying glass NOUN
la **loupe** *fem*

mail

> **mail** *can be a noun or a verb.*

A NOUN
  le **courrier** *masc*
  You've got some mail.
  Tu as du courrier.
B VERB
  envoyer un e-mail à
  I'll mail my friend.
  Je vais envoyer un e-mail à mon copain.

main ADJECTIVE
principal *masc*
principale *fem*
  the main problem
  le principal problème

main road NOUN
la **grande route** *fem*
  The hotel is on the main road.
  L'hôtel est sur la grande route.

Majorca NOUN
Majorque *fem*

make

> **make** *can be a noun or a verb.*

A NOUN
la **marque** *fem*
What make is that car?
De quelle marque est cette voiture?

B VERB
1 **faire**
I'm going to make a cake.
Je vais faire un gâteau.

Make a sentence, everyone.
Faites une phrase, tout le monde.
I make my bed every morning.
Je fais mon lit tous les matins.
2 and 2 make 4.
Deux et deux font quatre.
4 take away 2, what does that make?
Quatre moins deux, ça fait combien?
He made it himself.
Il l'a fait lui-même.
2 **fabriquer** *(manufacture)*
made in France
fabriqué en France
3 **gagner** *(earn)*
He makes a lot of money.
Il gagne beaucoup d'argent.
4 **préparer** *(prepare)*
She's making lunch.
Elle prépare le déjeuner.

make up VERB
inventer
You're making it up!
Tu inventes!

make-up NOUN
le **maquillage** *masc*

male ADJECTIVE
1 **mâle** *(animal)*
a male kitten
un chaton mâle
2 **masculin** *(person, on official forms)*
Sex: male.
Sexe: masculin.

man NOUN
l' **homme** *masc*
an old man
un vieil homme

manage VERB
se débrouiller
It's okay, I can manage.
Ça va, je me débrouille.
I can't manage all that.
C'est trop pour moi.

manager NOUN
1 le **directeur** *masc*
la **directrice** *fem (of company)*
2 le **gérant** *masc*
la **gérante** *fem (of shop, restaurant)*
3 le **manager** *masc (of team)*

manageress NOUN
la **gérante** *fem*

manners PL NOUN
les **manières** *fem pl*
good manners
les bonnes manières
Her manners are appalling.
Elle a de très mauvaises manières.
It's bad manners to speak with your mouth full.
Ce n'est pas poli de parler la bouche pleine.

English French

a
b
c
d
e
f
g
h
i
j
k
l
m
n
o
p
q
r
s
t
u
v
w
x
y
z

many ADJECTIVE, PRONOUN
  beaucoup de
    He hasn't got many friends.
    Il n'a pas beaucoup d'amis.

  Are many people absent?
    Est-ce qu'il y a beaucoup d'absents?
  How many?
    Combien?

Language tip

When **how many** is followed by a noun, it is translated by **combien de**.

  How many sisters have you got?
    Tu as combien de sœurs?
  How many girls are there?
    Il y a combien de filles?
  How many euros do you get for £10?
    Combien d'euros a-t-on pour dix livres?
  How many do you want?
    Combien en veux-tu?

Language tip

en means 'of them'.

  That's too many.
    C'est trop.
  You ask too many questions!
    Tu poses trop de questions!

How many?
Combien?
Not many.
Pas beaucoup.
too many
trop

map NOUN
  1 la **carte** *fem (of country, area)*
    a map of France
    une carte de France
  2 le **plan** *masc (of town)*
    a map of Paris
    un plan de Paris

marathon NOUN
  le **marathon** *masc*
    the London marathon
    le marathon de Londres

marbles NOUN
  les **billes** *fem pl*
    Do you want to play marbles?
    Tu veux jouer aux billes?

March NOUN
  mars *masc*
    March or April?
    Mars ou avril?
    My birthday's in March
    Mon anniversaire est en mars.

in March
en mars
the fifth of March
le cinq mars

Language tip

The months in French are not spelled with a capital letter.

margarine NOUN
  la **margarine** *fem*

margin NOUN
  la **marge** *fem*
    Write notes in the margin.
    Écrivez vos notes dans la marge.

mark

mark *can be a noun or a verb.*

A NOUN
la **note** *fem (in school)*
I get good marks for French.
J'ai de bonnes notes en français.
B VERB
corriger
She's got books to mark.
Elle a des cahiers à corriger.

market NOUN
le **marché** *masc*

marmalade NOUN
la **confiture d'oranges** *fem*

marriage NOUN
le **mariage** *masc*

Language tip

The English word has one more
letter than the French word. What
is it?

married ADJECTIVE
marié *masc*
mariée *fem*
They are not married.
Ils ne sont pas mariés.
a married couple
un couple marié

marry VERB
épouser
He wants to marry her.
Il veut l'épouser.
They want to get married.
Ils veulent se marier.
**My sister's getting married in
June.**
Ma sœur se marie en juin.

marvellous ADJECTIVE
1 excellent *masc*
excellente *fem*
She's a marvellous cook.
C'est une excellente cuisinière.
2 superbe
**The weather was
marvellous.**
Il a fait un temps superbe.

masculine ADJECTIVE
masculin *masc*
masculine *fem*

mashed potatoes PL NOUN
la **purée** *fem*
**sausages and mashed
potatoes**
des saucisses avec de la purée

Language tip

purée *is a singular word.*

mask NOUN
le **masque**
masc

mass NOUN
1 la **multitude** *fem*
a mass of books and papers
une multitude de livres et de
papiers
2 la **messe** *fem (in church)*
We go to mass on Sunday.
Nous allons à la messe le
dimanche.

massive ADJECTIVE
énorme

masterpiece NOUN
le **chef-d'œuvre** *masc*

mat NOUN
le **paillasson** *masc*
a table mat
un set de table

match

match can be a noun or a verb.

A NOUN

1 l' **allumette** *fem*
a box of matches
une boîte d'allumettes

2 le **match** *masc* (PL les **matchs**)
(game)
a football match
un match de foot

B VERB

1 **être assorti à** *(go with)*
The jacket matches the trousers.
La veste est assortie au pantalon.

2 **faire correspondre à**
(put with)
Match the names to the pictures.
Faites correspondre les noms aux images.

matching ADJECTIVE
assorti *masc*
assortie *fem*
My bedroom has matching wallpaper and curtains.
Ma chambre a du papier peint et des rideaux assortis.

mate NOUN
le **pote** *masc*
He's my mate.
C'est mon pote.

material NOUN
le **tissu** *masc*
It's made of red material.
C'est fait en tissu rouge.

maths NOUN
les **maths**
fem pl

matter

matter can be a noun or a verb.

A NOUN
What's the matter? Why are you crying?
Qu'est-ce que tu as? Pourquoi tu pleures?
What's the matter with him?
Qu'est-ce qu'il a?

B VERB
It doesn't matter.
Ça ne fait rien.

mattress NOUN
le **matelas** *masc*

maximum ADJECTIVE
maximum *masc, fem, pl*

May NOUN
mai *masc*
May or June?
Mai ou juin?
My birthday's in May.
Mon anniversaire est en mai.

in May
en mai
the fifth of May
le cinq mai

Language tip
The months in French are not spelled with a capital letter.

May Day NOUN
le **Premier Mai** *masc*

Did you know...?
*In France, people give friends little bunches of lily of the valley (**muguet**) on May Day.*

maybe ADVERB
peut-être

maybe not
peut-être pas
Maybe she's at home.
Elle est peut-être chez elle.

mayonnaise NOUN
la **mayonnaise** *fem*

mayor NOUN
le **maire** *masc*

maze NOUN
le **labyrinthe** *masc*

me PRONOUN
1 me
Could you lend me your pen, Rachid?
Tu peux me prêter ton stylo, Rachid?
Are you looking for me?
Tu me cherches?

Language tip

me *changes to* **m'** *before a vowel sound.*

Do you love me?
Tu m'aimes?
Can you help me?
Est-ce que tu peux m'aider?
2 moi

Language tip

The French word **me** *cannot come at the end of a sentence. Use* **moi** *instead.*

Wait for me!
Attends-moi!
Look at me, children!
Regardez-moi, les enfants!
You're after me.
Tu es après moi.
Is it for me?
C'est pour moi?

Me too!
Moi aussi!
Excuse me!
Excusez-moi!

meal NOUN
le **repas**
masc

mean

mean *can be a verb or an adjective.*

A VERB
vouloir dire
What does 'complet' mean?
Qu'est-ce que 'complet' veut dire?
I don't know what it means.
Je ne sais pas ce que ça veut dire.
What do you mean?
Qu'est que vous voulez dire?
That's not what I meant.
Ce n'est pas ce que je voulais dire.

What does it mean?
Qu'est-ce que ça veut dire?

B ADJECTIVE
1 radin *masc*
radine *fem (with money)*
He's too mean to buy presents.
Il est trop radin pour acheter des cadeaux.
2 méchant *masc*
méchante *fem (unkind)*
You're being mean to me.
Tu es méchant avec moi.

meaning NOUN
le **sens** *masc*

measles NOUN
la **rougeole** *fem*

English French

measure VERB
mesurer
> **Measure the length.**
> Mesurez la longueur.

meat NOUN
la **viande** *fem*
> **I don't eat meat.**
> Je ne mange pas de viande.

Mecca NOUN
La Mecque *fem*

medal NOUN
la **médaille** *fem*
> **the gold medal**
> la médaille d'or

medical

> **medical** *can be an adjective or a noun.*

> **A** ADJECTIVE
> **She's a medical student.**
> Elle est étudiante en médecine.
> **B** NOUN
> **You have to have a medical.**
> Tu dois passer une visite médicale.

medicine NOUN
le **médicament** *masc*

> **I need some medicine.**
> J'ai besoin d'un médicament.

Mediterranean NOUN
> **the Mediterranean**
> la Méditerranée

medium ADJECTIVE
moyen *masc*
moyenne *fem*
> **a man of medium height**
> un homme de taille moyenne

medium-sized ADJECTIVE
de taille moyenne
> **a medium-sized town**
> une ville de taille moyenne

meet VERB
1 retrouver *(by arrangement)*
> **I'm meeting my friends at the swimming pool.**
> Je retrouve mes amis à la piscine.
> **Let's meet in front of the tourist office.**
> Retrouvons-nous devant l'office de tourisme.
2 rencontrer *(by chance)*
> **I met some French people.**
> J'ai rencontré des Français.

3 aller chercher *(pick up)*
> **I'll meet you at the station.**
> J'irai te chercher à la gare.

meeting NOUN
1 la **rencontre** *fem*
> **their first meeting**
> leur première rencontre
2 la **réunion** *fem*
> **There's a meeting at school tonight.**
> Il y a une réunion à l'école ce soir.

melon NOUN
le **melon** *masc*

melt VERB
fondre
> **The snow is melting.**
> La neige est en train de fondre.

a
b
c
d
e
f
g
h
i
j
k
l
m
n
o
p
q
r
s
t
u
v
w
x
y
z

member NOUN
le **membre** *masc*
a member of our club
un membre de notre club

memory NOUN
la **mémoire** *fem*
I haven't got a good memory.
Je n'ai pas une bonne mémoire.

memory game NOUN
le **jeu de mémoire** *masc*

men PL NOUN ▷*see* **man**
les **hommes** *masc pl*

mend VERB
réparer
Can you mend it?
Vous pouvez le réparer?

mention VERB
Thank you! — Don't mention it!
Merci! — Il n'y a pas de quoi!

menu NOUN
le **menu** *masc*

merry ADJECTIVE

Merry Christmas!
Joyeux Noël!

merry-go-round NOUN
le **manège** *masc*

mess NOUN
le **bazar** *masc*
My bedroom's in a mess.
C'est le bazar dans ma chambre.

message NOUN
le **message** *masc*

met VERB ▷*see* **meet**

metal NOUN
le **métal** *masc* (PL les **métaux**)

method NOUN
la **méthode** *fem*

metre NOUN
le **mètre** *masc*
I'm one metre thirty tall.
Je mesure un mètre trente.

Did you know...?
In France, measurements are always
in metres and centimetres, rather
than feet and inches.

metric ADJECTIVE
métrique

Mexican wave NOUN
la **hola** *fem*

mice PL NOUN
les **souris** *fem pl*

microphone NOUN
le **microphone** *masc*

microwave NOUN
le **four à micro-ondes** *masc*

midday NOUN
le **midi** *masc*
It's midday.
Il est midi.

at midday
à midi

middle NOUN
le **milieu** *masc*
Come into the middle, Hugo.
Viens au milieu, Hugo.

in the middle of the road
au milieu de la route
in the middle of the night
au milieu de la nuit

middle-aged ADJECTIVE
d'un certain âge
a middle-aged man
un homme d'un certain âge

middle name NOUN
le **deuxième prénom** *masc*
It's my middle name.
C'est mon deuxième prénom.

midge NOUN
le **moucheron** *masc*

midnight NOUN
minuit *masc*
It's midnight.
Il est minuit.

> **at midnight**
> à minuit

might VERB
I might, I might not.
Peut-être, peut-être pas.

> *Language tip*
> **peut-être** means 'maybe'. You're
> really saying 'maybe, maybe not'.

migraine NOUN
la **migraine** *fem*
I've got a migraine.
J'ai la migraine.

mild ADJECTIVE
doux *masc*
douce *fem*
The winters are quite mild.
Les hivers sont assez doux.

mile NOUN

> *Did you know...?*
> In France, distances are always
> measured in kilometres. A mile is
> about 1.6 kilometres.

It's five miles from here.
C'est à huit kilomètres d'ici.
We walked miles!
Nous avons marché pendant
des kilomètres!

milk NOUN
le **lait** *masc*
tea with milk
du thé au lait

milkman NOUN
He's a milkman.
Il livre le lait à domicile.

milk shake NOUN
le **milk-shake** *masc*

millimetre NOUN
le **millimètre** *masc*

million NOUN
le **million** *masc*
two million
deux millions

millionaire NOUN
le **millionnaire** *masc*

mince NOUN
la **viande hachée** *fem*

mince pie NOUN
la **tartelette de Noël** *fem*

a
b
c
d
e
f
g
h
i
j
k
l
m
n
o
p
q
r
s
t
u
v
w
x
y
z

Did you know...?

Mince pies *are not eaten in France, instead French people eat* **papillotes**, *which are chocolates wrapped in foil.*

mind

mind *can be a verb or a noun.*

A VERB

Do you mind if I open the window?
Est-ce que je peux ouvrir la fenêtre?
Mind the step!
Attention à la marche!

I don't mind.
Ça ne me dérange pas.
Never mind!
Ça ne fait rien!

B NOUN

I've changed my mind.
J'ai changé d'avis.

mine

mine *can be a pronoun or a noun.*

A PRONOUN

This book is mine.
Ce livre est à moi.

It's mine.
C'est à moi.

B NOUN
la **mine** *fem*
a coal mine
une mine de charbon

mineral water

NOUN
l' **eau minérale** *fem*

minibus NOUN
le **minibus** *masc*

Minidisc® NOUN
le **minidisque** *masc*

minimum ADJECTIVE
minimum *masc, fem, pl*

miniskirt NOUN
la **mini-jupe** *fem*

minister NOUN
1 le **pasteur** *masc*
(of church)
2 le **ministre** *masc*
(in government)

minor ADJECTIVE
mineur *masc*
mineure *fem*
a minor problem
un problème mineur

mint NOUN
1 le **bonbon à la menthe** *masc* (sweet)
2 la **menthe** *fem* (plant)
mint sauce
la sauce à la menthe

minus PREPOSITION
moins
16 minus 3 is 13.
Seize moins trois égale treize.
It's minus two degrees outside.
Il fait moins deux dehors.

minute NOUN
la **minute** *fem*
Wait a minute!
Attends une minute!

mirror NOUN
le **miroir** *masc*

misbehave VERB
Don't misbehave, Pierre!
Sois sage, Pierre!

mischief NOUN
les **bêtises** *fem pl*
My little sister's always up to mischief.
Ma petite sœur fait constamment des bêtises.

miserable ADJECTIVE
1 **malheureux** *masc*
malheureuse *fem (person)*
You're looking miserable.
Tu as l'air malheureux.
2 **épouvantable** *(weather)*
The weather was miserable.
Il faisait un temps épouvantable.

Miss NOUN
1 **maîtresse** *fem (teacher)*
Yes, Miss.
Oui, maîtresse.
2 **Mademoiselle** *fem*
Miss Jones
Mademoiselle Jones

Language tip
In addresses, **Miss** is **Mlle**.

miss VERB
rater

Hurry or you'll miss the bus.
Dépêche-toi ou tu vas rater le bus.
I miss you.
Tu me manques.

Miss a turn.
Passe un tour.

missing ADJECTIVE
manquant *masc*
manquante *fem*
the missing piece
la pièce manquante
My rucksack is missing.
Mon sac à dos a disparu.
Two children are missing.
Deux enfants ont disparu.

mist NOUN
la **brume** *fem*

mistake NOUN
la **faute** *fem*
Only one mistake!
Une faute seulement!
a spelling mistake
une faute d'orthographe
Be careful not to make any mistakes, Luc.
Fais attention à ne pas faire de fautes, Luc.
by mistake
par erreur
I took his bag by mistake.
J'ai pris son sac par erreur.

mistletoe NOUN
le **gui** *masc*

misty ADJECTIVE
brumeux *masc*
brumeuse *fem*
a misty morning
un matin brumeux

English French

a
b
c
d
e
f
g
h
i
j
k
l
m
n
o
p
q
r
s
t
u
v
w
x
y
z

It's misty.
Le temps est brumeux.

mix VERB
mélanger
Mix the flour with the sugar.
Mélangez la farine au sucre.

mix up VERB
confondre
He always mixes me up with my sister.
Il me confond toujours avec ma sœur.

mixed ADJECTIVE
a mixed salad
une salade composée
a mixed school
une école mixte

mixture NOUN
le **mélange** *masc*

mix-up NOUN
la **confusion** *fem*

mobile NOUN
le **portable** *masc*
I haven't got a mobile.
Je n'ai pas de portable.

mobile phone NOUN
le **portable** *masc*
Have you got a mobile phone?
Tu as un portable?

model

model *can be a noun or an adjective.*

A NOUN
1 la **maquette** *fem (small version)*
I'm making a model of the castle.

Je fais une maquette du château.
2 le **mannequin** *masc (person)*
She's a famous model.
C'est un mannequin célèbre.
B ADJECTIVE
a model plane
un modèle réduit d'avion
a model railway
un modèle réduit de voie ferrée

modern ADJECTIVE
moderne

Language tip

What is the difference in spelling between the French word and the English word?

moment NOUN
l' **instant** *masc*
Wait a moment, Alain.
Attends un instant, Alain.
Could you wait a moment?
Pouvez-vous attendre un instant?
in a moment
dans un instant

Just a moment!
Un instant!
at the moment
en ce moment

Monday NOUN
le **lundi** *masc*
It's Monday today.
Aujourd'hui c'est lundi.

on Monday
lundi
on Mondays
le lundi
every Monday
tous les lundis

last Monday
lundi dernier
next Monday
lundi prochain

Language tip

*Days of the week are not written
with a capital letter in French.*

money NOUN
l' **argent** *masc*
I haven't got enough money.
Je n'ai pas assez d'argent.
**I need to change some
money.**
J'ai besoin de changer de
l'argent.

monitor NOUN
le **moniteur** *masc*

monk NOUN
le **moine** *masc*

monkey NOUN
le **singe** *masc*

monster NOUN
le **monstre** *masc*

month NOUN
le **mois** *masc*
two months
deux mois
at the end of the month
à la fin du mois

this month
ce mois-ci
next month
le mois prochain
last month
le mois dernier
every month
tous les mois
What month is it?
Quel mois sommes-nous?

mood NOUN
l' **humeur** *fem*
She's in a bad mood.
Elle est de mauvaise
humeur.

moon NOUN
la **lune** *fem*
the moon and the stars
la lune et les étoiles

moped NOUN
le **cyclomoteur** *masc*

more ADJECTIVE, PRONOUN,
ADVERB
1 plus

Language tip

*When comparing one thing
with another, you usually use*
plus.

more difficult
plus difficile
**This model is more
expensive.**
Ce modèle est plus cher.

Could you speak more slowly?
Vous pourriez parler plus lentement?
more than me
plus que moi
more than that
plus que ça
He's more intelligent than me.
Il est plus intelligent que moi.

There are more girls in the class.
Il y a plus de filles dans la classe.
I've got more than 50 euros.
J'ai plus de cinquante euros.
There isn't any more.
Il n'y en a plus.

a bit more
un peu plus
more ... than
plus ... que

2 encore

Do you want some more, André?
Tu en veux encore, André?
Would you like some more, Mr Gautier?
Vous en voulez encore, M. Gautier?
Two minutes more!
Encore deux minutes!

Could I have some more chips?
Est-ce que je pourrais avoir encore des frites?
Do you want some more tea?
Voulez-vous encore du thé?

morning NOUN
le **matin** *masc*
on Saturday morning
le samedi matin
all morning
toute la matinée
Are they staying all morning?
Est-ce qu'ils vont rester toute la matinée?

this morning
ce matin
tomorrow morning
demain matin
every morning
tous les matins
in the morning
le matin
at 7 o'clock in the morning
à sept heures du matin

mosque NOUN
la **mosquée** *fem*

mosquito NOUN
le **moustique** *masc*
a mosquito bite
une piqûre de moustique

most ADVERB, ADJECTIVE, PRONOUN

most of my friends
la plupart de mes amis
most of the time
la plupart du temps
most French people
la plupart des Français
most of the class
la majeure partie de la classe
the most
le plus
Chantal talks the most.
C'est Chantal qui parle le plus.

Language tip

When **the most** *is followed by an adjective, it is translated* **le plus**, **la plus**, *or* **les plus**, *depending on the following noun.*

the most expensive restaurant
le restaurant le plus cher
the most expensive seat
la place la plus chère
the most expensive restaurants
les restaurants les plus chers
the most expensive seats
les places les plus chères
at the most
au maximum
two hours at the most
deux heures au maximum

motel NOUN
le **motel** *masc*

moth NOUN
le **papillon de nuit** *masc*

Language tip

The French word for moth literally means 'butterfly of the night'.

mother NOUN
la **mère** *fem*

my mother
ma mère
your mother
ta mère

Mother's Day NOUN
la **fête des Mères** *fem*
It's Mother's Day on Sunday.
Dimanche, c'est la fête des Mères.

Happy Mother's Day!
Bonne Fête, Maman!

Did you know…?

Mother's Day is usually on the last Sunday of May in France.

motor NOUN
le **moteur** *masc*

motorbike NOUN
la **moto** *fem*

motorboat NOUN
le **bateau à moteur** *masc*

motorcycle NOUN
le **vélomoteur** *masc*

motorcyclist NOUN
le **motard** *masc*

motorist NOUN
l' **automobiliste** *masc/fem*

motorway NOUN
l' **autoroute** *fem*
on the motorway
sur l'autoroute

mountain NOUN
la **montagne** *fem*

mountain bike NOUN
le **VTT** *masc*
  I've got a mountain bike.
  J'ai un VTT.

mouse NOUN
la **souris** *fem*
  two white mice
  deux souris blanches

mouse mat NOUN
le **tapis de souris** *masc*

mousse NOUN
la **mousse** *fem*
  chocolate mousse
  la mousse au chocolat

moustache NOUN
la **moustache** *fem*
  He's got a moustache.
  Il a une moustache.

mouth NOUN
la **bouche** *fem*

move

> **move** can be a noun or a verb.

A NOUN
  le **tour** *masc*
  It's your move.
  C'est ton tour.
  Get a move on, Marcel!
  Remue-toi, Marcel!
B VERB
  bouger
  Don't move!
  Ne bouge pas!

You moved!
Tu as bougé!
Could you move your stuff please?
Tu peux pousser tes affaires, s'il te plaît?
Move forward two spaces!
Avance de deux cases!

move over VERB
se **pousser**
  Could you move over a bit?
  Tu peux te pousser un peu?

movement NOUN
le **mouvement** *masc*

MP NOUN
le **député** *masc*
  She's an MP.
  Elle est député.

> **Language tip**
> You do not translate '**a**' when you say what someone's job is in French.

MP3 player NOUN
le **baladeur numérique** *masc*

mph ABBREVIATION
km/h

> **Did you know...?**
> In France, speed is measured in kilometres per hour, so 50 mph is about 80 km/h.

Mr NOUN
Monsieur *masc*

> **Language tip**
> In addresses, **Mr** is **M.**

Mrs NOUN
Madame *fem*

> **Language tip**
> In addresses, **Mrs** is **Mme.**

Ms NOUN
Madame *fem*

Language tip
*In addresses, **Ms** is **Mme**.*

Did you know...?
*There isn't a specific word for **Ms** in French. If you are writing to somebody and don't know whether she is married, use **Madame**.*

much ADJECTIVE, ADVERB, PRONOUN
1 beaucoup *(a lot)*
not much
pas beaucoup
I don't like sport much.
Je n'aime pas beaucoup le sport.
I don't want much.
Je n'en veux pas beaucoup.

Language tip
*You can also use **beaucoup** to say 'very much'.*

I like France very much.
J'aime beaucoup la France.
2 beaucoup de *(a lot of)*
I haven't got much money.
Je n'ai pas beaucoup d'argent.

Language tip
*You can also use **beaucoup de** to say 'very much'.*

I don't want very much rice.
Je ne veux pas beaucoup de riz.
How much?
Combien?
How much does it cost?
C'est combien?
How much do you want?
Tu en veux combien?
How much is it all together?
Ça fait combien en tout?

Language tip
*When **how much** is followed by a noun, it is translated by **combien de**.*

How much money have you got?
Tu as combien d'argent?
too much
trop
That's too much!
C'est trop!
It costs too much.
Ça coûte trop cher.

How much?
Combien?
not much
pas beaucoup
too much
trop
Thank you very much.
Merci beaucoup.

mud NOUN
la **boue** *fem*

muesli NOUN
le **muesli** *masc*

mug NOUN
la **grande tasse** *fem*
Do you want a cup or a mug?
Est-ce que vous voulez une tasse normale ou une grande tasse?

multiply VERB
multiplier
Multiply six by three.
Multipliez six par trois.

English French

a b c d e f g h i j k l **m** n o p q r s t u v w x y z

Two multiplied by three is six.
Deux multiplié par trois égale six.

mum NOUN
1 la **mère** fem
my mum
ma mère
2 la **maman** fem (used as a name)
Mum!
Maman!
I'll ask Mum.
Je vais demander à maman.

mummy NOUN
la **maman** fem
Hello Mummy!
Bonjour maman!

mumps NOUN
les **oreillons** masc pl
Thérèse has got mumps.
Thérèse a les oreillons.

murder NOUN
le **meurtre** masc

muscle NOUN
le **muscle** masc

museum NOUN
le **musée** masc

mushroom NOUN
le **champignon** masc

music NOUN
la **musique** fem

I like listening to music.
J'aime écouter de la musique.

musical ADJECTIVE
a musical instrument
un instrument de musique

musician NOUN
le **musicien** masc
la **musicienne** fem

Muslim NOUN
le **musulman** masc
la **musulmane** fem
He's a Muslim.
Il est musulman.

Language tip
The French word is not spelled with a capital letter.

---

mussel NOUN
la **moule** fem

must VERB
You must be careful, Gaëlle.
Tu dois faire attention, Gaëlle.
You must listen, children.
Vous devez écouter, les enfants.

mustard NOUN
la **moutarde** fem

my ADJECTIVE

Language tip
When you want to say something like 'my name', 'my house', or 'my hair' in French, you need to know if 'name', 'house', 'hair' are masculine, feminine, or plural, because there are three possible words for **my**.

---

mon masc
my father
mon père
ma fem
my aunt
ma tante

mes *pl*
my parents
mes parents

English French

a
b
c
d
e
f
g
h
i
j
k
l
m
n
o
p
q
r
s
t
u
v
w
x
y
z

Language tip

ma *changes to* **mon** *before a vowel sound.*

my friend Alice
mon amie Alice

Language tip

my *is not always* **mon**, **ma**, *or* **mes**. *Notice how* **my** *is translated in the next example.*

I wash my face in the morning.
Je me lave le visage le matin.

myself PRONOUN
1 me
I've hurt myself.
Je me suis fait mal.
I like to look at myself in the mirror.
J'aime me regarder dans la glace.

Language tip

me *changes to* **m'** *before a vowel sound.*

I'm enjoying myself.
Je m'amuse.
2 moi

Language tip

After a preposition, use **moi** *instead of* **me**.

I'll tell you about myself.
Je vais te parler de moi.
3 moi-même
I made it myself.
Je l'ai fait moi-même.
by myself
tout seul

Language tip

Use **toute seule** *if you are a girl.*

I don't like travelling by myself.
Je n'aime pas voyager toute seule.

mystery NOUN
le **mystère** *masc*

N n

nail NOUN
1 l' **ongle** masc
Don't bite your nails!
Ne te ronge pas les ongles!
2 le **clou** masc
a hammer and some nails
un marteau et des clous

nailfile NOUN
la **lime à ongles** fem

nail varnish NOUN
le **vernis à ongles** masc

naked ADJECTIVE
nu masc
nue fem

name NOUN
le **nom** masc
What's your cat's name?
Comment s'appelle ton chat?
His name's Max.
Il s'appelle Max.
What's your name?
Comment tu t'appelles?

Language tip

There are two other ways of asking this question: **Tu t'appelles comment?** *and* **Comment t'appelles-tu?**

What's her name?
Comment elle s'appelle?
What are their names?
Ils s'appellent comment?

What's your name?
Comment tu t'appelles?
My name is Natasha.
Je m'appelle Natasha.

nanny NOUN
la **garde d'enfants** fem
She's a nanny.
C'est une garde d'enfants.

napkin NOUN
la **serviette** fem

narrow ADJECTIVE
étroit masc
étroite fem
a narrow street
une rue étroite

nasty ADJECTIVE
1 **mauvais** masc
mauvaise fem (unpleasant)
a nasty cold
un mauvais rhume
a nasty smell
une mauvaise odeur
2 **méchant** masc
méchante fem (evil)
He's a nasty man.
C'est un homme méchant.

nationality NOUN
la **nationalité** fem

natural ADJECTIVE
naturel masc
naturelle fem

nature NOUN
la **nature** fem

naughty ADJECTIVE
vilain masc
vilaine fem
Naughty girl!
Vilaine!

navy NOUN
la **marine** fem

a
b
c
d
e
f
g
h
i
j
k
l
m
n
o
p
q
r
s
t
u
v
w
x
y
z

He's in the navy.
Il est dans la marine.

navy-blue

navy-blue can be an adjective or a noun.

A ADJECTIVE
bleu marine *masc, fem, pl*
a navy-blue skirt
une jupe bleu marine

Language tip

Colour adjectives come after the noun in French.

B NOUN
le **bleu marine** *masc*

near

near can be an adjective or a preposition.

A ADJECTIVE
proche
It's fairly near.
C'est assez proche.

Language tip

the nearest can be translated by **le plus proche**, **la plus proche** *or* **les plus proches**, *depending on the following noun.*

the nearest village
le village le plus proche
Where's the nearest service station?
Où est la station-service la plus proche?
The nearest shops are three kilometres away.
Les magasins les plus proches sont à trois kilomètres.

B PREPOSITION
près de
I live near Liverpool.
J'habite près de Liverpool.

near my house
près de chez moi
near here
près d'ici
Is there a bank near here?
Est-ce qu'il y a une banque près d'ici?

nearby ADVERB
à proximité
There's a supermarket nearby.
Il y a un supermarché à proximité.

nearly ADVERB
presque
Dinner's nearly ready.
Le dîner est presque prêt.
I'm nearly ten.
J'ai presque dix ans.

neat ADJECTIVE
soigné *masc*
soignée *fem*
She has very neat writing.
Elle a une écriture très soignée.

necessary ADJECTIVE
nécessaire

neck NOUN
le **cou** *masc*

necklace NOUN
le **collier** *masc*

need VERB
avoir besoin de
I need a rubber.
J'ai besoin d'une gomme.

needle NOUN
l' **aiguille** *fem*

neighbour NOUN
le **voisin** *masc*
la **voisine** *fem*
the neighbours' garden
le jardin des voisins

neighbourhood NOUN
le **quartier** *masc*

neither PRONOUN, CONJUNCTION, ADVERB
aucun des deux *masc*
aucune des deux *fem*
Carrots or peas? — Neither, thanks.
Des carottes ou des petits pois? — Aucun des deux merci.
neither ... nor ...
ni ... ni ...
Neither Sarah nor Tamsin is coming to the party.
Ni Sarah ni Tamsin ne vient à la soirée.

Neither do I.
Moi non plus.
Neither have I.
Moi non plus.

nephew NOUN
le **neveu** *masc* (PL les **neveux**)
her nephew
son neveu

nerve NOUN
le **nerf** *masc*
She gets on my nerves.
Elle me tape sur les nerfs.

Net NOUN
le **Net** *masc*
I like to surf the Net.
J'aime surfer sur le Net.

netball NOUN
le **netball** *masc*

Did you know...?
Netball is not played in France. Both boys and girls play basketball or volleyball instead.

Netherlands PL NOUN
les **Pays-Bas** *masc pl*

never ADVERB
1 **jamais**
When are you going to phone him? — Never!
Quand est-ce que tu vas l'appeler? — Jamais!
2 **ne ... jamais**

Language tip
Add **ne** *if the sentence contains a verb.*

I never go to the cinema.
Je ne vais jamais au cinéma.

new ADJECTIVE
1 **nouveau** *masc*
nouvelle *fem*
a new jumper
un nouveau pull
a new dress
une nouvelle robe
2 **neuf** *masc*
neuve *fem (brand new)*
We've got a new car.
Nous avons une voiture neuve.

news NOUN
1 les **nouvelles** *fem pl*
good news
de bonnes nouvelles
2 la **nouvelle** *fem (single piece of news)*
That's wonderful news!
Quelle bonne nouvelle!
3 les **informations** *fem pl (on TV)*

It was on the news.
C'était aux informations.

newsagent NOUN
le **marchand de journaux**
masc

newspaper
NOUN
le **journal**
masc
(PL les
journaux)

New Year NOUN
New Year's Day
le premier de l'An
New Year's Eve
la Saint-Sylvestre

Happy New Year!
Bonne Année!

next

next *can be an adjective, an adverb or a preposition.*

A ADJECTIVE
prochain *masc*
prochaine *fem (in time)*
the next time
la prochaine fois
Who's next?
C'est à qui, maintenant?
I'm next.
C'est à moi, maintenant.
next door
à côté
They live next door.
Ils habitent à côté.

next Saturday
samedi prochain
next year
l'année prochaine
next summer
l'été prochain

B ADVERB
ensuite *(after this)*
What shall I do next?
Qu'est-ce que je fais ensuite?
C PREPOSITION
next to
à côté de
next to the bank
à côté de la banque
I sit next to my friend.
Je m'asseois à côté de mon
copain.

Language tip

To get the accents right in **à côté de**, remember that they form a W: `` ` ^ ´ ``.

nice ADJECTIVE
1 **gentil** *masc*
gentille *fem (kind)*
Your parents are very nice.
Tes parents sont très gentils.
2 **joli** *masc*
jolie *fem (pretty)*
Aix is a nice town.
Aix est une jolie ville.
3 **bon** *masc*
bonne *fem (food)*
The soup is very nice.
La soupe est très bonne.

Have a nice time!
Amuse-toi bien!
Have a nice time, girls!
Amusez-vous bien, les filles!
It's a nice day.
Il fait beau.

English   French

a
b
c
d
e
f
g
h
i
j
k
l
m
n
o
p
q
r
s
t
u
v
w
x
y
z

niece NOUN
la **nièce** fem
   his niece
   sa nièce

night NOUN
1 la **nuit** fem
   I want a room for two nights.
   Je veux une chambre pour deux nuits.
2 le **soir** masc (evening)
   What are you doing tonight?
   Qu'est-ce que tu fais ce soir?

last night
hier soir

nightie NOUN
la **chemise de nuit** fem

nightmare NOUN
le **cauchemar** masc
   I have nightmares.
   Je fais des cauchemars.

nightshirt NOUN
la **chemise de nuit** fem

nil NOUN
le **zéro** masc
   We won one-nil.
   Nous avons gagné un à zéro.

nine NUMBER
neuf
   nine euros
   neuf euros

She's nine.
Elle a neuf ans.

Language tip

In English, you can say **nine** or **nine years old**. In French, you can only say **neuf ans**.

nineteen NUMBER
dix-neuf

nineteen euros
dix-neuf euros

She's nineteen.
Elle a dix-neuf ans.

Language tip

In English, you can say **nineteen** or **nineteen years old**. In French, you can only say **dix-neuf ans**.

nineteenth ADJECTIVE
dix-neuvième
   on the nineteenth floor
   au dix-neuvième étage

the nineteenth of August
le dix-neuf août

ninety NUMBER
quatre-vingt-dix
   My gran is ninety.
   Ma grand-mère a quatre-vingt-dix ans.

Language tip

quatre-vingt-dix is made up of three words in French. What do you think they mean?

ninth ADJECTIVE
neuvième
   on the ninth floor
   au neuvième étage

the ninth of August
le neuf août

no ADVERB
1 **non**
   Are you coming? — No.
   Est-ce que tu viens? — Non.
2 **pas de** (not any)
   There are no trains on Sundays.
   Il n'y a pas de trains le dimanche.

'no smoking'
'défense de fumer'

nobody PRONOUN
1 **personne**
Who's going with you? —
Nobody.
Qui t'accompagne? —
Personne.
2 **ne ... personne**

Language tip

Add **ne** *if the sentence contains a verb.*

There's nobody in the classroom.
Il n'y a personne dans la classe.

noise NOUN
le **bruit** *masc*
Please make less noise.
Faites moins de bruit s'il vous plaît.

noisy ADJECTIVE
bruyant *masc*
bruyante *fem*

none PRONOUN
aucun *masc*
aucune *fem*
How many girls? — None.
Combien de filles? — Aucune.
There's none left.
Il n'y en a plus.
There are none left.
Il n'y en a plus.

nonsense NOUN
les **bêtises** *fem pl*
She talks a lot of nonsense.
Elle dit beaucoup de bêtises.

noodles PL NOUN
les **nouilles** *fem pl*

noon NOUN
le **midi** *masc*
It's noon.
Il est midi.

at noon
à midi

no one PRONOUN
1 **personne**
Who's going with you? —
No one.
Qui t'accompagne? — Personne.
2 **ne ... personne**

Language tip

Add **ne** *if the sentence contains a verb.*

There's no one in the classroom.
Il n'y a personne dans la classe.

nor CONJUNCTION
neither ... nor
ni ... ni
neither Pascal nor Yann
ni Pascal, ni Yann

Nor do I.
Moi non plus.
Nor have I.
Moi non plus.

normal ADJECTIVE
habituel *masc*
habituelle *fem*
at the normal time
à l'heure habituelle

493

English **French**

a
b
c
d
e
f
g
h
i
j
k
l
m
n
o
p
q
r
s
t
u
v
w
x
y
z

Normandy NOUN
la **Normandie** *fem*
in Normandy
en Normandie
to Normandy
en Normandie
Alain is from Normandy.
Alain vient de la Normandie.

north

> **north** *can be an adjective or a noun.*

A ADJECTIVE
nord *masc, fem, pl*
the north coast
la côte nord
B NOUN
le **nord** *masc*
in the north
dans le nord

Northern Ireland NOUN
l' **Irlande du Nord** *fem*
in Northern Ireland
en Irlande du Nord
to Northern Ireland
en Irlande du Nord
I'm from Northern Ireland.
Je viens de l'Irlande du Nord.

North Pole NOUN
le **pôle Nord** *masc*

North Sea NOUN
la **mer du Nord** *fem*

nose NOUN
le **nez** *masc*
(PL les **nez**)

nosy ADJECTIVE
fouineur *masc* (FEM **fouineuse**)

not ADVERB
1 pas
Are you coming or not?
Est-ce que tu viens ou pas?

not really
pas vraiment
Do you like him? — Not at all.
Tu l'aimes bien? — Pas du tout.
Have you finished? — Not yet.
As-tu fini? — Pas encore.
2 ne ... pas

> *Language tip*
> *Add* **ne** *if* **not** *comes before a verb.*

It's not raining.
Il ne pleut pas.

not yet
pas encore
not you
pas toi

note NOUN
le **mot** *masc*
I'll write her a note.
Je vais lui écrire un mot.

notebook NOUN
le **carnet** *masc*

notepad NOUN
le **bloc-notes** *masc*

notepaper NOUN
le **papier à lettres** *masc*

nothing NOUN
1 rien *masc*
What's wrong? — Nothing.
Qu'est-ce qui ne va pas? — Rien.
2 ne ... rien
He does nothing.
Il ne fait rien.

notice NOUN
l' **affiche** *fem*

notice board NOUN
le **panneau d'affichage** *masc*

novel NOUN
le **roman** *masc*

November NOUN
novembre *masc*
October or November?
Octobre ou novembre?
My birthday's in November.
Mon anniversaire est en novembre.

in November
en novembre
the fifth of November
le cinq novembre

now ADVERB
maintenant
What are you doing now?
Qu'est-ce que tu fais maintenant?
I'm rather busy just now.
Je suis très occupé en ce moment.

not now
pas maintenant
just now
en ce moment

nowhere ADVERB
nulle part

number NOUN
1 le **nombre** *masc*
a large number of people
un grand nombre de gens
2 le **numéro** *masc (of house, telephone)*
They live at number 5.
Ils habitent au numéro cinq.
What's your phone number?
Quel est votre numéro de téléphone?
3 le **chiffre** *masc (figure)*
the second number
le deuxième chiffre

nun NOUN
la **religieuse** *fem*
I want to be a nun.
Je veux être religieuse.

nurse NOUN
l' **infirmier** *masc*
l' **infirmière** *fem*
She's a nurse.
Elle est infirmière.

nursery NOUN
la **crèche** *fem*
My sister goes to nursery.
Ma sœur va à la crèche.

nursery school NOUN
l' **école maternelle** *fem*
My little sister goes to nursery school.
Ma petite sœur va à l'école maternelle.

Did you know...?
The **école maternelle** *is a state school for children between the ages of three and six.*

Language tip
You have to say which kind of nut you mean, because there is no general word for **nut** *in French.*

nut NOUN
1 la **cacahuète** *fem (peanut)*
2 la **noisette** *fem (hazelnut)*
3 la **noix** *fem* (PL les **noix**)
  (walnut)

O o

oats NOUN
l' **avoine** fem

obedient ADJECTIVE
obéissant *masc*
obéissante *fem*

obey VERB
   You must obey the rules of the game.
   Vous devez respecter les règles du jeu.

object NOUN
l' **objet** *masc*
   classroom objects
   les objets de la classe

obvious ADJECTIVE
évident *masc*
évidente *fem*
   That's obvious!
   C'est évident!

occasion NOUN
l' **occasion** *fem*
   a special occasion
   une occasion spéciale
   on several occasions
   à plusieurs reprises

occasionally ADVERB
de temps en temps

occupation NOUN
la **profession** *fem*

ocean NOUN
l' **océan** *masc*

o'clock ADVERB
   at four o'clock
   à quatre heures

It's five o'clock.
Il est cinq heures.

October NOUN
octobre *masc*
   October or November?
   Octobre ou novembre?
   My birthday's in October.
   Mon anniversaire est en octobre.

in October
en octobre
the fifth of October
le cinq octobre

odd ADJECTIVE
bizarre
   That's odd!
   C'est bizarre!

of PREPOSITION
de
   some photos of my family
   des photos de ma famille

a boy of ten
un garçon de dix ans
a picture of the school
une photo de l'école
a friend of mine
un de mes amis

a
b
c
d
e
f
g
h
i
j
k
l
m
n
o
p
q
r
s
t
u
v
w
x
y
z

That's very kind of you.
C'est très gentil de votre part.

Language tip
de *changes to* **d'** *before a vowel sound.*

a kilo of oranges
un kilo d'oranges

Language tip
de + **le** *changes to* **du**, *and* **de** +
les *changes to* **des**.

the end of the film
la fin du film
the end of the holidays
la fin des vacances

Language tip
of it, of that *and* **of them** *is translated by* **en**.

Do you want half of it?
Tu en veux la moitié?
Can I have half of that?
Je peux en avoir la moitié?
Do you want some of them?
Tu en veux?

off

off *can be an adjective, a preposition or an adverb.*

A ADJECTIVE
1 éteint *masc*
éteinte *fem (switched off)*
The light is off.
La lumière est éteinte.
2 fermé *masc*
fermée *fem (turned off)*
Is the tap off?
Est-ce que le robinet est fermé?
3 annulé *masc*
annulée *fem (cancelled)*
The match is off.
Le match est annulé.

4 absent *masc*
absente *fem (absent)*
He's off today.
Il est absent aujourd'hui.
B PREPOSITION
She's off school today.
Elle n'est pas à l'école aujourd'hui.
C ADVERB
Off you go, Jack!
Vas-y, Jack!

offer VERB
offrir
Offer Melanie something to drink.
Offre quelque chose à boire à Melanie.

office NOUN
le **bureau** *masc*
(PL les **bureaux**)
She works in an office.
Elle travaille dans un bureau.

often ADVERB
souvent
We often go to London.
Nous allons souvent à Londres.
It often rains.
Il pleut souvent.

oil NOUN
l' **huile** *fem*

okay EXCLAMATION, ADJECTIVE
1 **d'accord** *(in agreement)*
I'll come tomorrow. — Okay!
Je viens demain. — D'accord!
Is that okay?
C'est d'accord?
2 **pas mal** *(not bad)*
**Do you like school? —
It's okay.**
Tu aimes l'école? —
C'est pas mal.
I'm okay thanks.
Ça va, merci.
Is everything okay?
Tout va bien?

Okay!
D'accord!
Are you okay?
Ça va?

old ADJECTIVE
vieux *masc*
vieille *fem*
an old dog
un vieux chien
an old house
une vieille maison
old clothes
des vieux vêtements
old shoes
des vieilles chaussures

Language tip
*In the singular, **vieux** changes to
vieil before a vowel sound.*

an old man
un vieil homme

Language tip
âgé *and* **âgée** *are more polite than*
vieux *and* **vieille**.

old people
les personnes âgées

I am older than you.
Je suis plus âgée que toi.
Léa is older than Richard.
Léa est plus âgée que Richard.
**She's two years older than
me.**
Elle a deux ans de plus que moi.
How old are you, Max?
Tu as quel âge, Max?

Language tip
*Another way of asking this question
is* **Quel âge as-tu, Max?**

How old are you?
Quel âge as-tu?
How old are you, Miss?
Quel âge avez-vous, Maîtresse?
He's ten years old.
Il a dix ans.

old age pensioner NOUN
le **retraité** *masc*
la **retraitée** *fem*
She's an old age pensioner.
Elle est retraitée.

oldest ADJECTIVE
aîné *masc*
aînée *fem*
my oldest brother
mon frère aîné

Language tip
To say that someone is the oldest use
le plus âgé *for a boy and* **la plus
âgée** *for a girl.*

**Hugo's the oldest in the
class.**
Hugo est le plus âgé de la classe.
She's the oldest.
C'est la plus âgée.

Olympic ADJECTIVE
olympique

the Olympics
les Jeux olympiques

omelette NOUN
l' **omelette** *fem*

on

> **on** *can be an adjective or a preposition. There are a lot of translations. Skim down the page for the one you need.*

A ADJECTIVE
1 **allumé** *masc*
  allumée *fem (switched on)*
  The light is on.
  La lumière est allumée.
2 **ouvert** *masc*
  ouverte *fem (turned on)*
  The tap is on.
  Le robinet est ouvert.
B PREPOSITION
1 **à**
  on the left
  à gauche
  I go to school on my bike.
  Je vais à l'école à vélo.
  on TV
  à la télé

Language tip

à + le *changes to* **au**.

  on the phone
  au téléphone
  on the 2nd floor
  au deuxième étage
2 **sur** *(on top of)*
  on the table
  sur la table
3 **en**
  They're on holiday.
  Ils sont en vacances.

Language tip

Notice how **on** *is translated in days and dates.*

on Christmas Day
le jour de Noël
on my birthday
le jour de mon anniversaire

on Friday
vendredi
on Fridays
le vendredi
on the twentieth of June
le vingt juin
on holiday
en vacances

once ADVERB
une fois
  once a week
  une fois par semaine
  only once
  juste une fois
  at once
  tout de suite

once more
encore une fois

one NUMBER

Language tip

Use **un** *for masculine nouns and* **une** *for feminine nouns.*

un *masc*
  one day
  un jour
une *fem*
  one minute
  une minute

I've got one brother and one sister.
J'ai un frère et une sœur.

onion NOUN
l' **oignon** *masc*

only

> **only** *can be an adjective or an adverb.*

A ADJECTIVE
seul *masc*
seule *fem*
my only clean T-shirt
mon seul tee-shirt propre
my only dress
ma seule robe
I'm an only child.
Je suis fils unique.
Danielle is an only child.
Danielle est fille unique.

B ADVERB
1 seulement
only ten euros
seulement dix euros
2 ne ... que *(with a verb)*
I've only got two cards.
Je n'ai que deux cartes.
He's only three.
Il n'a que trois ans.

open

> **open** *can be an adjective or a verb.*

A ADJECTIVE
ouvert *masc*
ouverte *fem*
The baker's is open on Sunday morning.
La boulangerie est ouverte le dimanche matin.

B VERB
ouvrir
Can I open the window?
Est-ce que je peux ouvrir la fenêtre?
Open your books.
Ouvrez vos livres.

opening hours PL NOUN
les **heures d'ouverture** *fem pl*

opinion NOUN
l' **avis** *masc*
in my opinion
à mon avis
What's your opinion?
Qu'est-ce que vous en pensez?

opinion poll NOUN
le **sondage** *masc*

opponent NOUN
l' **adversaire** *masc/fem*

opportunity NOUN
l' **occasion** *fem*
It's a good opportunity.
C'est une bonne occasion.

opposite

> **opposite** *can be an adjective, an adverb or a preposition.*

A ADJECTIVE
opposé *masc*
opposée *fem*
It's in the opposite direction.
C'est dans la direction opposée.

B ADVERB
en face
They live opposite.
Ils habitent en face.

C PREPOSITION
en face de
the girl sitting opposite me
la fille assise en face de moi

optimistic ADJECTIVE
  optimiste

or CONJUNCTION
 1 ou
   Would you like tea or coffee?
   Tu veux du thé ou du café?
 2 ni … ni

> *Language tip*
> *Use **ni … ni** in negative sentences.*

   I don't eat meat or fish.
   Je ne mange ni viande, ni
   poisson.
 3 sinon *(otherwise)*
   Hurry up or you'll miss the
   bus.
   Dépêche-toi, sinon tu vas rater
   le bus.

oral NOUN
  l' **oral** *masc* (PL les **oraux**)
   I've got my French oral soon.
   Je vais bientôt passer mon oral
   de français.

orange

> *orange can be a noun or an*
> *adjective.*

 A NOUN
 1 l' **orange** *fem*
   a big orange
   une grosse orange

 2 l' **orange** *masc*
   Orange is my favourite colour.
   Ma couleur préférée, c'est
   l'orange.
 B ADJECTIVE
   orange *masc, fem, pl*

   orange curtains
   des rideaux orange

> *Language tip*
> *Colour adjectives come after the*
> *noun in French.*

orange juice NOUN
  le **jus d'orange** *masc*

orchard NOUN
  le **verger** *masc*

orchestra NOUN
  l' **orchestre** *masc*
   I play in the school
   orchestra.
   Je joue dans l'orchestre de
   l'école.

order

> *order can be a noun or a verb.*

 A NOUN
 1 l' **ordre** *masc (sequence)*
   Put the words in alphabetical
   order, children.
   Rangez ces mots par ordre
   alphabétique, les enfants.
   The words are not in the
   right order.
   Les mots ne sont pas dans le
   bon ordre.
 2 la **commande** *fem*
   (in restaurant)
   The waiter took our order.
   Le serveur a pris notre
   commande.

> **'out of order'**
> 'en panne'

 B VERB
   commander
   Are you ready to order?
   Vous êtes prêt à
   commander?

ordinary ADJECTIVE
 ordinaire
  an ordinary day
  une journée ordinaire

organ NOUN
 l' **orgue** masc
  I play the organ.
  Je joue de l'orgue.

organize VERB
 organiser
  Could you help to organize the party?
  Vous pouvez aider à organiser la fête?

original ADJECTIVE
 original masc
 originale fem
  It's a very original idea.
  C'est une idée très originale.

Orkneys PL NOUN
 les **Orcades** fem pl

orphan NOUN
 l' **orphelin** masc
 l' **orpheline** fem

other

other can be an adjective or a pronoun.

A ADJECTIVE
  autre
  on the other side of the street
  de l'autre côté de la rue
  the other day
  l'autre jour
  the other one
  l'autre
  This one? — No, the other one.
  Celui-ci? — Non, l'autre.
B PRONOUN
 l' **autre** masc/fem

  Get into twos, one behind the other.
  Mettez-vous par deux, l'un derrière l'autre.
  Where are the others?
  Où sont les autres?

our ADJECTIVE
 notre masc/fem (PL nos)
  Our house is quite big.
  Notre maison est plutôt grande.
  They are our friends.
  Ce sont nos amis.

ours PRONOUN
 à nous
  Is this ours?
  C'est à nous?
  Whose is this? — It's ours.
  C'est à qui? — À nous.

out

out can be an adverb or an adjective.

A ADVERB
1 sorti masc
  sortie fem (not at home)
  Gaston's out.
  Gaston est sorti.
  I'm going out.
  Je sors.
2 éliminé masc
  éliminée fem (in game)
  You're out Lucie!
  Tu es éliminée, Lucie!

'way out'
'sortie'

B ADJECTIVE
  éteint masc
  éteinte fem (turned off)
  All the lights are out.
  Toutes les lumières sont éteintes.

outdoor ADJECTIVE
en plein air
an outdoor swimming pool
une piscine en plein air
outdoor activities
les activités de plein air

outdoors ADVERB
au grand air

outer space NOUN
l' **espace** *masc*
a monster from outer space
un monstre de l'espace

outside

> **outside** *can be an adverb or a preposition.*

A ADVERB
dehors
It's very cold outside.
Il fait très froid dehors.

B PREPOSITION
en dehors de
outside the school
en dehors de l'école

oven NOUN
le **four** *masc*

over

> **over** *can be a preposition or an adjective.*

A PREPOSITION
1 **plus de** *(more than)*
Are you over ten?
Tu as plus de dix ans?
**The temperature is over
30 degrees.**
Il fait une température de plus
de trente degrés.
2 **pendant** *(during)*
over Christmas
pendant les fêtes de Noël
3 **de l'autre côté de**
(across)
The baker's is over the road.
La boulangerie est de l'autre
côté de la rue.

> **over here**
> ici
> **over there**
> là-bas
> **all over Scotland**
> dans toute l'Écosse

B ADJECTIVE
terminé *masc*
terminée *fem (finished)*
The match is over.
Le match est terminé.

overcast ADJECTIVE
couvert *masc*
couverte *fem*
The sky was overcast.
Le ciel était couvert.

overhead projector
NOUN
le **rétroprojecteur** *masc*

owl NOUN
le **hibou** masc
(PL les **hiboux**)

own ADJECTIVE
propre
> **I've got my own bathroom.**
> J'ai ma propre salle de bain.
> **I'd like a room of my own.**
> J'aimerais avoir une chambre à
> moi.

on his own
tout seul
on her own
toute seule

owner NOUN
le/la **propriétaire** masc/fem

Pp

pack

pack can be a verb or a noun.

A VERB
faire ses bagages
I need to pack.
Je dois faire mes bagages.

B NOUN
a pack of cards
un jeu de cartes

packed lunch NOUN

le **casse-croûte** *masc*
I take a packed lunch to school.
J'apporte un casse-croûte à l'école pour le déjeuner.

Did you know…?
French schoolchildren do not take packed lunches to school. They either eat at the canteen or go home for lunch.

packet NOUN

le **paquet** *masc*
a packet of crisps
un paquet de chips

page NOUN

la **page** *fem*
on page ten
page dix
Look at page six, everyone.
Regardez page six, tout le monde.

paid VERB ▷ *see* pay

pain NOUN

la **douleur** *fem*
a terrible pain
une douleur insupportable

I've got a pain in my stomach.
J'ai mal à l'estomac.
2 le/la **casse-pieds** *masc/fem*
(*a nuisance*)
My little sister is a pain.
Ma petite sœur est casse-pieds.

paint

paint can be a noun or a verb.

A NOUN
la **peinture** *fem*
'wet paint'
'attention, peinture fraîche'

B VERB
peindre
I'm going to paint it green.
Je vais le peindre en vert.

painting NOUN

le **tableau** *masc*
(PL les **tableaux**)
a painting by Picasso
un tableau de Picasso
I like painting.
J'aime faire de la peinture.

pair NOUN

la **paire** *fem*
a pair of shoes
une paire de chaussures
a pair of trousers
un pantalon
a pair of jeans
un jean
in pairs
deux par deux
We work in pairs.
Nous travaillons deux par deux.

Pakistan NOUN

le **Pakistan** *masc*

Pakistani

Pakistani can be a noun or an adjective.

A NOUN
le **Pakistanais** *masc*
la **Pakistanaise** *fem*

B ADJECTIVE
pakistanais *masc*
pakistanaise *fem*

Language tip

pakistanais *is not spelled with a capital letter when it is an adjective.*

pal NOUN
le **copain** *masc*
la **copine** *fem*
my pal Ronan
mon copain Ronan
my pal Elsa
ma copine Elsa
You're my best pal.
Tu es mon meilleur copain.

Language tip

This 'best pal' in the example sentence is a boy. How can you tell?

palace NOUN
le **palais** *masc*

pale ADJECTIVE
pâle
a pale blue shirt
une chemise bleu pâle

pan NOUN
1 la **casserole** *fem* (saucepan)
2 la **poêle** *fem* (frying pan)

pancake NOUN
la **crêpe** *fem*

Pancake Day NOUN
le **mardi gras** *masc*

Did you know…?

Pancake Day *is celebrated in France as well. Children dress up and eat pancakes (**crêpes**).*

panic VERB
Don't panic!
Pas de panique!

pantomime NOUN
le **spectacle de Noël pour enfants** *masc*

Did you know…?

There is no such thing as a **pantomime** *in France.*

pants PL NOUN
le **slip** *masc*
a pair of pants
un slip

paper NOUN
1 le **papier** *masc*
Have you got a pencil and some paper?
Tu as un crayon et du papier?
a piece of paper
du papier
a paper towel
une serviette en papier
2 le **journal** *masc* (PL les **journaux**) (newspaper)

paper boy NOUN
le **livreur de journaux** *masc*

English French

a b c d e f g h i j k l m n o **p** q r s t u v w x y z

paper girl NOUN
la **livreuse de journaux** *fem*

paper round NOUN
la **tournée de distribution de journaux** *fem*

parade NOUN
le **défilé** *masc*

paragraph NOUN
le **paragraphe** *masc*

parcel NOUN
le **colis** *masc*

pardon NOUN
Pardon?
Pardon?

parent NOUN
parent *masc*
my parents
mes parents

Paris NOUN
Paris
in Paris
à Paris
to Paris
à Paris
Gilles is from Paris.
Gilles est parisien.
Inès is from Paris.
Inès est parisienne.

Parisian NOUN
le **Parisien** *masc*
la **Parisienne** *fem*

park

> **park** *can be a noun or a verb.*

A NOUN
le **parc** *masc*

There's a nice park.
Il y a un beau parc.
B VERB
se garer
It's difficult to park.
C'est difficile de se garer.

parking NOUN
'no parking'
'stationnement interdit'

parrot NOUN
le **perroquet**
masc

part NOUN
la **partie** *fem*
The first part is easy.
La première partie est facile.

partly ADVERB
en partie

partner NOUN
1 le/la **partenaire** *masc/fem*
(in game, role play)
2 le **cavalier** *masc*
la **cavalière** *fem* (in dance)

part-time ADJECTIVE, ADVERB
à temps partiel
a part-time job
un travail à temps partiel
She works part-time.
Elle travaille à temps partiel.

party NOUN
1 la **fête** *fem*
a birthday party
une fête d'anniversaire

> ### *Language tip*
> *In France, a children's birthday party held in the afternoon is called* **un goûter d'anniversaire**.

a Christmas party
une fête de Noël

English French

a
b
c
d
e
f
g
h
i
j
k
l
m
n
o
p
q
r
s
t
u
v
w
x
y
z

a New Year party
une fête du Nouvel An
2 la **soirée** *fem (more formal)*
I'm going to a party on Saturday.
Je vais à une soirée samedi.

pass VERB
1 passer *(hand)*
Pass the ball, Nina!
Passe le ballon, Nina!
Could you pass me the salt?
Vous pouvez me passer le sel?
2 passer devant *(go)*
You pass the post office.
Vous passez devant la poste.

passenger NOUN
le **passager** *masc*
la **passagère** *fem*

Passover NOUN
la **Pâque juive** *fem*
at Passover
à la Pâque juive

passport NOUN
le **passeport** *masc*

password NOUN
le **mot de passe** *masc*

past

> *past can be a preposition or a noun.*

A PREPOSITION
1 après *(after)*
It's on the right, just past the station.
C'est sur la droite, juste après la gare.
2 *(with times)*
It's half past ten exactly.
Il est exactement dix heures et demie.
It's quarter past nine.
Il est neuf heures et quart.

It's ten past eight.
Il est huit heures dix.

> **half past eight**
> huit heures et demie
> **quarter past ten**
> dix heures et quart

B NOUN
le **passé** *masc*
in the past
dans le passé

pasta NOUN
les **pâtes** *fem pl*
Pasta is easy to cook.
Les pâtes sont faciles à préparer.

pâté NOUN
le **pâté** *masc*

path NOUN
1 le **chemin** *masc (footpath)*
Follow the path.
Suivez le chemin.
2 l' **allée** *fem (in garden, park)*

patience NOUN
1 la **patience** *fem*
He hasn't got much patience.
Il n'a pas beaucoup de patience.
2 la **réussite** *fem (card game)*
I sometimes play patience.
Quelquefois je fais une réussite.

patient

> *patient can be a noun or an adjective.*

A NOUN
le **patient** *masc*
la **patiente** *fem*
B ADJECTIVE
patient *masc*
patiente *fem*
The teacher is very patient.
La maîtresse est très patiente.

patio NOUN
le **patio** *masc*

pattern NOUN
le **motif** *masc*
a simple pattern
un motif simple

pause NOUN
la **pause** *fem*

pavement NOUN
le **trottoir** *masc*
on the pavement
sur le trottoir

paw NOUN
la **patte** *fem*

pay

pay can be a noun or a verb.

A NOUN
le **salaire** *masc*
What is the pay?
Le salaire est de combien?

B VERB
payer
Who's going to pay?
Qui va payer?
Where do I pay?
Où est-ce que je dois payer?

Language tip

pay for is also translated by **payer**.

I've paid for my ticket.
J'ai payé mon billet.
I paid ten euros for it.
Je l'ai payé dix euros.

Pay attention, Christophe!
Fais attention, Christophe!
Pay attention, everybody!
Faites attention, tout le monde!

PC NOUN
le **PC** *masc*

I have a PC at home.
J'ai un PC chez moi.

PE NOUN
l' **EPS** *fem*
We do PE twice a week.
Nous avons EPS deux fois par
semaine.

pea NOUN
le **petit pois** *masc*
Peas or beans?
Des petits pois
ou des haricots?

peach NOUN
la **pêche** *fem*
a kilo of peaches
un kilo de pêches

peanut NOUN
la **cacahuète** *fem*
a packet of peanuts
un paquet de cacahuètes

peanut butter NOUN
le **beurre de cacahuètes**
masc
a peanut-butter sandwich
un sandwich au beurre de
cacahuètes

pear NOUN
la **poire** *fem*
**Which would you like, a pear
or an apple?**
Qu'est-ce que tu veux: une poire
ou une pomme?

pebble NOUN
le **galet** *masc*
a pebble beach
une plage de galets

pedal NOUN
la **pédale** *fem*

pedigree ADJECTIVE
de race
  a pedigree dog
  un chien de race

peg NOUN
  1 le **portemanteau** *masc*
    (PL les **portemanteaux**) *(for coats)*
  2 l' **épingle à linge** *fem (clothes peg)*

pen NOUN
  le **stylo** *masc*
    Can I borrow your pen?
    Je peux emprunter ton stylo?

pencil NOUN
  le **crayon** *masc*
    in pencil
    au crayon
    coloured pencils
    les crayons de couleur

pencil case NOUN
  la **trousse** *fem*

pencil sharpener NOUN
  le **taille-crayon** *masc*

penfriend NOUN
  le **correspondant** *masc*
  la **correspondante** *fem*
    I'm Emma, your English penfriend.
    Je suis Emma, ta correspondante anglaise.

Language tip

What is the difference between the English word **correspondent** and the French word **correspondant**?

penknife NOUN
  le **canif** *masc*

pensioner NOUN
  le **retraité** *masc*
  la **retraitée** *fem*

people PL NOUN
  1 les **gens** *masc pl*
    The people are nice.
    Les gens sont sympathiques.
    a lot of people
    beaucoup de gens

  2 les **personnes** *fem pl (individuals)*
    Four people can play.
    Quatre personnes peuvent jouer.
    How many people are there in your family?
    Vous êtes combien dans votre famille?

Language tip

In English, you usually say 'tall people', 'rich people', etc. In French, you say 'the tall', 'the rich', etc.

    tall people
    les grands
    French people
    les Français

pepper NOUN
  1 le **poivre** *masc (spice)*
    Pass the pepper, please.
    Passez-moi le poivre, s'il vous plaît.
  2 le **poivron** *masc (vegetable)*
    a green pepper
    un poivron vert

per PREPOSITION
  par
    per day
    par jour

per cent ADVERB
pour cent
   fifty per cent
   cinquante pour cent

perfect ADJECTIVE
parfait *masc*
parfaite *fem*
   Chantal speaks perfect English.
   Chantal parle un anglais parfait.

performance NOUN
   le **spectacle** *masc (show)*
   **The performance starts at
   two o'clock.**
   Le spectacle commence à deux
   heures.

perfume NOUN
   le **parfum** *masc*

perhaps ADVERB
peut-être
   Perhaps he's ill.
   Il est peut-être malade.

period NOUN
   la **période** *fem*
   the holiday period
   la période des vacances

permission NOUN
   la **permission** *fem*
   Have you got permission?
   Tu as la permission?

person NOUN
   la **personne** *fem*
   She's a very nice person.
   C'est une personne très
   sympathique.

Language tip

*There are two more letters in the
French word. What are they?*

personality NOUN
   la **personnalité** *fem*

personal stereo NOUN
   le **walkman**® *masc*

pessimistic ADJECTIVE
pessimiste

pet NOUN
   l' **animal** *masc* (PL les **animaux**)
   Have you got a pet?
   Tu as un animal?

petrol NOUN
   l' **essence** *fem*
   unleaded petrol
   l'essence sans plomb

phone

phone *can be a noun or a verb.*

A NOUN
   le **téléphone** *masc*
   Where's the phone?
   Où est le téléphone?
   by phone
   par téléphone
   on the phone
   au téléphone
   Can I use the phone, please?
   Je peux téléphoner, s'il vous
   plaît?
B VERB
   téléphoner à
   I have to phone my Mum.
   Je dois téléphoner à ma mère.

phone box NOUN
   la **cabine téléphonique** *fem*

phone call NOUN
   l' **appel** *masc*
   She gets lots of phone calls.
   Elle reçoit beaucoup d'appels.
   Can I make a phone call?
   Est-ce que peux téléphoner?

phonecard NOUN
   la **carte de téléphone** *fem*

phone number NOUN
le **numéro de téléphone** *masc*
What's your phone number?
Quel est ton numéro de
téléphone?

photo NOUN
la **photo** *fem*
This is a photo of my family.
Voici une photo de ma famille.
I want to take some photos.
Je veux prendre des photos.
I want to take a photo of you.
Je veux te prendre en photo.

photocopier NOUN
la **photocopieuse** *fem*

photocopy

photocopy *can be a noun or a verb.*

A NOUN
la **photocopie** *fem*
It's only a photocopy.
Ce n'est qu'une photocopie.
B VERB
photocopier
You can photocopy it.
Vous pouvez le photocopier.

photograph NOUN
la **photo** *fem*

phrase book NOUN
le **guide de conversation** *masc*

physics NOUN
la **physique** *fem*
She teaches physics.
Elle enseigne la physique.

pianist
NOUN
le/la **pianiste** *masc/fem*

piano NOUN
le **piano** *masc*

I play the piano.
Je joue du piano.
**I have piano
lessons.**
Je prends
des leçons
de piano.

pick

pick *can be a noun or a verb.*

A NOUN
Take your pick!
Faites votre choix!
B VERB
1 **choisir** *(choose)*
Pick a card, Jean!
Choisis une carte, Jean.
**Pick three girls and three
boys.**
Choisis trois filles et trois
garçons.
2 **cueillir** *(fruit, flowers)*
I like picking strawberries.
J'aime bien cueillir des fraises.

pick up VERB
1 **venir chercher** *(collect)*
**We can come to the airport
to pick you up.**
Nous pouvons venir vous
chercher à l'aéroport.
2 **tirer**
**Pick up another card,
Susie!**
Tire une autre carte, Susie!
3 **apprendre** *(learn)*
**I hope I'll pick up some
French.**
J'espère apprendre quelques
mots de français.

picnic NOUN
le **pique-nique** *masc*
I like picnics.
J'aime les pique-niques.

to have a picnic
pique-niquer
We had a picnic on the beach.
Nous avons pique-niqué sur la plage.

picture NOUN
1 l' **image** fem
Look at the picture.
Regarde l'image.
There are pictures in this dictionary.
Il a des images dans ce dictionnaire.
2 la **photo** fem
This is a picture of my family.
Voici une photo de ma famille.
3 le **tableau** masc
(PL les **tableaux**) (painting)
a famous picture
un tableau célèbre
4 le **dessin** masc (drawing)
I'll draw a picture.
Je vais faire un dessin.
Draw a picture of your pet, Lisa.
Dessine ton animal, Lisa.

pie NOUN
la **tourte** fem
an apple pie
une tourte aux pommes

piece NOUN
le **morceau** masc
(PL les **morceaux**)
A small piece, please.
Un petit morceau, s'il vous plaît.

pierced ADJECTIVE
percé masc
percée fem
I've got pierced ears.
J'ai les oreilles percées.

pig NOUN
le **cochon** masc

pigeon NOUN
le **pigeon** masc

piggy bank NOUN
la **tirelire** fem

pigtail NOUN
la **natte** fem
She's got pigtails.
Elle a des nattes.

pile NOUN
la **pile** fem

pill NOUN
la **pilule** fem

pillow NOUN
l' **oreiller** masc
a pillow
un oreiller

pilot NOUN
le **pilote** masc

pinball NOUN
le **flipper** masc
Do you want to play pinball?
Tu veux jouer au flipper?

pineapple NOUN
l' **ananas** masc

pink

pink can be an adjective or a noun.

A ADJECTIVE
rose
a pink blouse
un chemisier rose

Language tip
Colour adjectives come after the noun in French.

B NOUN
le **rose** *masc*
Pink is my favourite colour.
Ma couleur préférée, c'est le rose.

pint NOUN
a pint of milk
un demi-litre de lait

Did you know…?
In France, measurements are always in litres and centilitres. A pint is about 0.6 litres.

pipe NOUN
la **pipe** *fem*
He smokes a pipe.
Il fume la pipe.

pirate NOUN
le **pirate** *masc*

pitch NOUN
le **terrain** *masc*
a football pitch
un terrain de football

pity NOUN
What a pity she can't come!
Quel dommage! Elle ne peut pas venir.

What a pity!
Quel dommage!

pizza NOUN
la **pizza** *fem*

place NOUN
1 l' **endroit** *masc (location)*
It's a quiet place.
C'est un endroit tranquille.
There are a lot of interesting places to visit.
Il y a beaucoup d'endroits intéressants à visiter.

2 la **place** *fem (position)*
Can I change places?
Je peux changer de place?
Léon, change places with Nina!
Léon, change de place avec Nina!

plain ADJECTIVE
simple
a plain white blouse
un chemisier blanc simple

plain chocolate NOUN
le **chocolat à croquer** *masc*

plait NOUN
la **natte** *fem*
She wears her hair in a plait.
Elle a une natte.

plan

plan can be a noun or a verb.

A NOUN
1 le **projet** *masc*
Have you got plans for the holidays?
Tu as des projets pour les vacances?
2 le **plan** *masc (map)*
a plan of the school
un plan de l'école
B VERB
préparer
We're planning a trip to France.
Nous préparons un voyage en France.

plane NOUN
l' **avion** *masc*
by plane
en avion

plant NOUN
la **plante** *fem*

plastic ADJECTIVE
en plastique
   a plastic bag
   un sac en plastique

plate NOUN
l' **assiette** *fem*

platform NOUN
le **quai** *masc*
   on platform 7
   sur le quai numéro sept

play

> **play** *can be a noun or a verb.*

A NOUN
la **pièce** *fem*
   a play by Shakespeare
   une pièce de Shakespeare
B VERB
1 jouer
   He's playing with his friends.
   Il joue avec ses amis.
   What sort of music do they play?
   Quel genre de musique jouent-ils?
2 jouer à *(sport, game)*
   I play hockey.
   Je joue au hockey.
   Can you play chess?
   Tu sais jouer aux échecs?
3 jouer de *(instrument)*
   I play the guitar.
   Je joue de la guitare.

player NOUN
le **joueur** *masc*
la **joueuse** *fem*

   a football player
   un joueur de football

playground NOUN
1 la **cour de récréation** *fem*
   (at school)
2 l' **aire de jeux** *fem (in park)*

playgroup NOUN
la **garderie** *fem*

playing card NOUN
la **carte à jouer** *fem*
   (PL les **cartes à jouer**)

playing field NOUN
le **terrain de sport** *masc*

playtime NOUN
la **récréation** *fem*
   at playtime
   à la récréation

please EXCLAMATION
1 s'il vous plaît *(polite form)*
   Two coffees, please.
   Deux cafés, s'il vous plaît.
2 s'il te plaît *(familiar form)*
   Please write back soon.
   Réponds vite, s'il te plaît.

> **Yes please!**
> Oui, merci.

pleased ADJECTIVE
content *masc*
contente *fem*
   My mother's not pleased.
   Ma mère n'est pas contente.

pleasure NOUN
le **plaisir** masc
with pleasure
avec plaisir

plenty NOUN
largement assez
I've got plenty.
J'en ai largement assez.
You've got plenty of time.
Vous avez largement le temps.

That's plenty, thanks.
Ça suffit largement, merci.

plug in VERB
brancher
Is it plugged in?
Est-ce que c'est branché?
It's not plugged in.
Ce n'est pas branché.

plum NOUN
la **prune** fem
plum jam
la confiture de prunes

plump ADJECTIVE
dodu masc
dodue fem

plural NOUN
le **pluriel** masc

plus PREPOSITION
plus
Four plus three equals seven.
Quatre plus trois égalent sept.

p.m. ABBREVIATION
at 8 p.m.
à huit heures du soir
at 2 p.m.
à quatorze heures

Did you know...?
In France, times are often given using the 24-hour clock.

poached egg NOUN
l' **œuf poché** masc
a poached egg
un œuf poché

pocket NOUN
la **poche** fem

pocket calculator NOUN
la **calculette** fem

pocket money NOUN
l' **argent de poche** masc
I get £2 a week pocket money.
Je reçois deux livres d'argent de poche par semaine.

poem NOUN
le **poème** masc

point

point can be a noun or a verb.

A NOUN
1 le **point** masc (in game)
You've got five points.
Vous avez cinq points.
What's the point?
À quoi bon?
What's the point of leaving so early?
À quoi bon partir si tôt?
2 la **virgule** fem (in decimal numbers)
two point five (2.5)
deux virgule cinq (2,5)

Did you know...?
In decimal numbers, the French use a comma instead of a point.

B VERB
Which cake? You can point to it.
Quel gâteau? Vous pouvez le montrer du doigt.

517

a
b
c
d
e
f
g
h
i
j
k
l
m
n
o
p
q
r
s
t
u
v
w
x
y
z

The guide pointed out Notre-Dame to us.
Le guide nous a montré Notre-Dame.

poison NOUN
le **poison** masc

poisonous ADJECTIVE
1 **venimeux** masc
venimeuse fem (snake)
a poisonous snake
un serpent
venimeux

2 **vénéneux** masc
vénéneuse fem (mushroom,
berry)
Don't eat it, it's poisonous!
Ne mange pas ça, c'est
vénéneux!

police PL NOUN
la **police** fem

Language tip
police is a singular word in French.

police car NOUN
la **voiture de police** fem

policeman NOUN
le **policier** masc

policewoman NOUN
la **femme policier** fem

polite ADJECTIVE
poli masc
polie fem
He's a very polite boy.
C'est un garçon très poli.

politely ADVERB
poliment

polluted ADJECTIVE
pollué masc
polluée fem

pollution NOUN
la **pollution** fem

polo shirt NOUN
le **polo** masc

pond NOUN
le **bassin** masc
There's a pond in our garden.
Il y a un bassin dans notre jardin.

pony
NOUN
le **poney**
masc

Language tip
The French word has one more letter
than the English word. What is it?

ponytail NOUN
la **queue de cheval** fem
I've got a ponytail.
J'ai une queue de cheval.

pony trekking NOUN
I go pony trekking.
Je fais des randonnées à dos
de poney.

poodle NOUN
le **caniche** masc

pool NOUN
1 la **piscine** fem (swimming pool)
There's a pool.
Il y a une piscine.
2 le **billard américain** masc
(game)
Can you play pool?
Tu sais jouer au billard
américain?

poor ADJECTIVE
pauvre
> **Poor David, he's very unlucky!**
> Le pauvre David, il n'a vraiment pas de chance!

pop NOUN
la **boisson gazeuse** *fem* (drink)

popcorn NOUN
le **pop-corn** *masc*

pope NOUN
le **pape** *masc*

pop group NOUN
le **groupe pop** *masc*
> **What's your favourite pop group?**
> Quel est ton groupe pop préféré?

pop music NOUN
la **musique pop** *fem*

poppy NOUN
le **coquelicot** *masc*

pop song NOUN
la **chanson pop** *fem*

popular ADJECTIVE
populaire
> **She's a very popular girl.**
> C'est une fille très populaire.

porch NOUN
le **porche** *masc*

pork NOUN
le **porc** *masc*
> **a pork chop**
> une côtelette de porc
> **I don't eat pork.**
> Je ne mange pas de porc.

port NOUN
le **port** *masc*

portable ADJECTIVE
portable

> **a portable TV**
> un téléviseur portable

Language tip
If something is **portable**, *you can carry it. The French for 'to carry' is* **porter**.

portion NOUN
la **portion** *fem*
> **a large portion of chips**
> une grosse portion de frites

Portugal NOUN
le **Portugal** *masc*

posh ADJECTIVE
chic *masc, fem, pl*
> **a posh hotel**
> un hôtel chic

positive ADJECTIVE
certain *masc*
certaine *fem*
> **Are you positive, Joëlle?**
> Tu en es certaine, Joëlle?

possibility NOUN
> **It's a possibility.**
> C'est possible.

possible ADJECTIVE
possible
> **as soon as possible**
> aussitôt que possible

post

> **post** *can be a noun or a verb.*

A NOUN
le **courrier** *masc* (letters)

Is there any post for me?
Est-ce qu'il y a du courrier pour
moi?
B VERB
poster
I've got some cards to post.
J'ai quelques cartes à poster.

postbox NOUN
la **boîte aux lettres** *fem*

Did you know…?
French postboxes are yellow.

postcard NOUN
la **carte postale** *fem*
**Thank you for the postcard,
Charlotte.**
Merci pour la carte postale,
Charlotte.

postcode NOUN
le **code postal** *masc*
What is your postcode?
Quel est ton code postal?

poster NOUN
le **poster** *masc*
**I've got posters on my
bedroom walls.**
J'ai des posters sur les murs de
ma chambre.

Language tip
In French, you pronounce **poster** *as
'post-air'.*

postman NOUN
le **facteur** *masc*
**He's a
postman.**
Il est
facteur.

Language tip
You do not translate **'a'** *when you
say what someone's job is in French.*

post office NOUN
la **poste** *fem*
**Where's the post office,
please?**
Où est la poste, s'il vous plaît?

potato NOUN
la **pomme de terre** *fem*
Rice or potatoes?
Du riz ou des pommes de terre?
mashed potatoes
la purée
boiled potatoes
les pommes vapeur
a baked potato
une pomme de terre cuite au
four

potato salad NOUN
la **salade de pommes de
terre** *fem*

pottery NOUN
la **poterie** *fem*

pound NOUN
la **livre** *fem*
**How many euros do you get
for a pound?**
Combien d'euros a-t-on pour
une livre?
a pound of potatoes
une livre de pommes de terre

pour VERB
pleuvoir à verse

It's pouring.
Il pleut à verse.

powerful ADJECTIVE
puissant *masc*
puissante *fem*

practically ADVERB
  pratiquement
      It's practically impossible.
      C'est pratiquement impossible.

practice NOUN
  l' **entraînement** *masc* (for sport)
      football practice
      l'entraînement de foot
      I've got to do my piano practice.
      Je dois travailler mon piano.

practise VERB
  1 **travailler** (instrument)
      I practise my flute every evening.
      Je travaille ma flûte tous les soirs.
  2 **pratiquer** (language)
      I like practising my French.
      J'aime pratiquer mon français.
  3 **s'entraîner** (sport)
      The team practises on Thursdays.
      L'équipe s'entraîne le jeudi.

prawn NOUN
  la **crevette** *fem*

pray VERB
  prier
      Let us pray.
      Prions.

prayer NOUN
  la **prière** *fem*

precisely ADVERB
      at 10 a.m. precisely
      à dix heures précises

prefer VERB
  préférer
      Which would you prefer?
      Lequel préfères-tu?

Which do you prefer, tennis or football?
Tu préfères le tennis ou le football?
I prefer French to geography.
Je préfère le français à la géographie.

pregnant ADJECTIVE
  enceinte
      She's six months pregnant.
      Elle est enceinte de six mois.

prep NOUN
  les **devoirs** *masc pl*
      history prep
      les devoirs d'histoire

prepare VERB
  préparer
      She has to prepare lessons in the evening.
      Elle doit préparer ses cours le soir.

prep school NOUN
  l' **école primaire privée** *fem*

present

> **present** *can be an adjective or a noun.*

A ADJECTIVE
  présent *masc*
  présente *fem*
      Ten present, two absent.
      Dix présents, deux absents.
      the present tense
      le présent
B NOUN
  1 le **cadeau** *masc*
      (PL les **cadeaux**) (gift)
      I'm going to give Julie a present.
      Je vais offrir un cadeau à Julie.

I got lots of presents.
J'ai eu beaucoup de cadeaux.

2 le **présent** *masc (time)*
the present and the future
le présent et le futur

president NOUN
le **président** *masc*
la **présidente** *fem*

pretend VERB
Pretend you are in a café.
Imagine que tu es dans un café.

pretty

pretty can be an adjective or an adverb.

A ADJECTIVE
joli *masc*
jolie *fem*
She's very pretty.
Elle est très jolie.
B ADVERB
plutôt
It's pretty old.
C'est plutôt vieux.
The weather was pretty awful.
Il faisait un temps minable.

previous ADJECTIVE
précédent *masc*
précédente *fem*
the previous day
le jour précédent

price NOUN
le **prix** *masc*

priest NOUN
le **prêtre** *masc*
He's a priest.
Il est prêtre.

Language tip

You do not translate 'a' when you say what someone's job is in French.

primary NOUN
I am in primary seven.
Je suis au CM2.

primary school NOUN
l' **école primaire** *fem*
I am at primary school.
Je suis à l'école primaire.

Did you know…?

*In France, children start primary school at the age of six. The first year is **CP**, followed by **CE1** and **CE2**. The last two years are **CM1** and **CM2**.*

prince NOUN
le **prince** *masc*
the Prince of Wales
le prince de Galles

Did you know…?

There are no princes in France, because France is a republic, not a monarchy like Britain.

princess NOUN
la **princesse** *fem*
Princess Anne
la princesse Anne

print VERB
écrire en majuscules
Print your name.
Écris ton nom en majuscules.

prison NOUN
la **prison** *fem*

English French

a
b
c
d
e
f
g
h
i
j
k
l
m
n
o
p
q
r
s
t
u
v
w
x
y
z

in prison
en prison

private ADJECTIVE
privé *masc*
privée *fem*
  a private school
  une école privée
  I have private lessons.
  Je prends des cours particuliers.

private school NOUN
l' **école privée** *fem*

prize NOUN
le **prix** *masc*
  The prize is one hundred
  euros.
  C'est un prix de cent euros.
  You can win a prize.
  Tu peux gagner un prix.

prize-giving NOUN
la **distribution des prix** *fem*

prizewinner NOUN
le **gagnant**
  masc
la **gagnante**
  fem

probably ADVERB
probablement
  probably not
  probablement pas

problem NOUN
le **problème** *masc*
  Is there a problem?
  Il y a un problème?
  What's the problem?
  Qu'est-ce qui ne va pas?

No problem!
Pas de problème!

procession NOUN
la **procession** *fem*

profession NOUN
la **profession** *fem*

professor NOUN
le **professeur d'université**
masc

profit NOUN
le **bénéfice** *masc*

program NOUN
le **programme** *masc*
  a computer program
  un programme informatique

programme NOUN
1 l' **émission** *fem (on TV, radio)*
  my favourite programme
  mon émission préférée
2 le **programme** *masc (booklet)*
  Would you like a
  programme?
  Tu veux un programme?

progress NOUN
le **progrès** *masc*
  You're making progress, Éric!
  Tu fais des progrès, Éric!

projector NOUN
le **projecteur** *masc*

promise

promise can be a noun or a verb.

A NOUN
la **promesse** *fem*
I'll make you a promise.
Je te fais une promesse.
That's a promise!
C'est promis!
B VERB
promettre
I promise!
Je te le promets!

English
French

a b c d e f g h i j k l m n o **P** q r s t u v w x y z

I'll write, I promise!
J'écrirai, c'est promis!

prompt

> **prompt** *can be an adjective or an adverb.*

A ADJECTIVE
rapide
a prompt reply
une réponse rapide

B ADVERB
at one o'clock prompt
à une heure précise

pronoun NOUN
le **pronom** *masc*

pronounce VERB
prononcer
How do you pronounce that word?
Comment on prononce ce mot?

pronunciation NOUN
la **prononciation** *fem*
Your pronunciation is good!
Tu as une bonne prononciation!

> *Language tip*
>
> Which vowel is different in the French word?

proper ADJECTIVE
vrai *masc*
vraie *fem*
proper French bread
du vrai pain français

properly ADVERB
comme il faut
I can't pronounce it properly.
Je n'arrive pas à le prononcer comme il faut.

Protestant

> **Protestant** *can be an adjective or a noun.*

A ADJECTIVE
protestant *masc*
protestante *fem*

B NOUN
le **protestant** *masc*
la **protestante** *fem*
I'm a Protestant.
Je suis protestant.

> *Language tip*
>
> In French, **protestant** *is not spelled with a capital letter.*

proud ADJECTIVE
fier *masc*
fière *fem*
Her parents are proud of her.
Ses parents sont fiers d'elle.

prune NOUN
le **pruneau** *masc*
(PL les **pruneaux**)

> *Language tip*
>
> Be careful! There is a word **prune** *in French, but it means 'plum'. A* **prune** *in English is a dried plum.*

PTO ABBREVIATION
T.S.V.P.

> *Language tip*
>
> T.S.V.P. *stands for* **'tournez, s'il vous plaît'**. *What does PTO stand for?*

pub NOUN
le **pub** *masc*

public

public can be a noun or an adjective.

A NOUN
le **public** *masc*
The castle is open to the public.
Le château est ouvert au public.

B ADJECTIVE
public *masc*
publique *fem*
a public swimming pool
une piscine publique

publicity NOUN
la **publicité** *fem*

public school NOUN
l' **école privée** *fem*

public transport NOUN
les **transports en commun** *masc pl*
by public transport
en transports en commun

pudding NOUN
le **dessert** *masc*
Would you like a pudding?
Tu veux un dessert?
What's for pudding?
Qu'est-ce qu'il y a comme dessert?

pull VERB
tirer
Pull!
Tirez!

pullover NOUN
le **pull** *masc*
What colour is your pullover?
De quelle couleur est ton pull?

pump NOUN
1 la **pompe** *fem* (for bike)

a bicycle pump
une pompe à vélo
2 le **chausson de danse** *masc* (shoe)
Have you got your pumps?
Tu as tes chaussons de danse?

pump up VERB
gonfler
Pump up your tyres!
Gonfle tes pneus!

punch VERB
1 **donner un coup de poing à** (hit)
He punched me!
Il m'a donné un coup de poing!
2 **composter** (in ticket machine)
Punch your ticket before you get on the train.
Compostez votre billet avant de monter dans le train.

Did you know…?
In France, you have to punch your ticket before you get on the train. If you don't, you can be fined.

punctual ADJECTIVE
Be punctual!
Soyez à l'heure!

punctuation NOUN
la **ponctuation** *fem*

Language tip
There is a different vowel in the French word. What is it?

punishment NOUN
la **punition** *fem*

pupil NOUN
l' **élève** *masc/fem*
There are 22 pupils in my class.
Il y a vingt-deux élèves dans ma classe.

a b c d e f g h i j k l m n o **p** q r s t u v w x y z

puppet NOUN
la **marionnette** *fem*

puppy NOUN
le **chiot** *masc*

pure ADJECTIVE
pur *masc*
pure *fem*
It's pure orange juice.
C'est du jus d'orange pur.

purple

> *purple can be an adjective or a noun.*

A ADJECTIVE
violet *masc*
violette *fem*
a purple skirt
une jupe violette

Language tip

Colour adjectives come after the noun in French.

B NOUN
le **violet** *masc*
Purple is my favourite colour.
Ma couleur préférée, c'est le violet.

purpose NOUN
on purpose
exprès
You're doing it on purpose.
Tu le fais exprès.

purr VERB
ronronner
The cat is purring.
Le chat ronronne.

purse NOUN
le **porte-monnaie** *masc*

I've lost my purse.
J'ai perdu mon porte-monnaie.

pursuit NOUN
l' **activité** *fem*
outdoor pursuits
les activités de plein air

push VERB
pousser
Don't push, boys!
Arrêtez de pousser, les garçons!
Push!
Poussez!

pushchair NOUN
la **poussette** *fem*

put VERB
1 **mettre** *(place)*
Put your chewing gum in the bin.
Mets ton chewing-gum à la poubelle.
Where shall I put my things?
Où est-ce que je peux mettre mes affaires?
She's putting the baby to bed.
Elle met le bébé au lit.
2 **écrire** *(write)*
Don't forget to put your name on the paper.
N'oubliez pas d'écrire votre nom sur la feuille.

put away VERB
ranger
Put your things away, children.
Rangez vos affaires, les enfants.

put back VERB
remettre en place
Don't forget to put it back.
N'oublie pas de le remettre en place.

put down VERB
poser
Put down a card.
Pose une carte.
Put down your hands.
Baissez la main.

put off VERB
1 **éteindre** (switch off)
Shall I put the light off?
Est-ce que j'éteins la lumière?
2 **déranger** (distract)
Stop putting me off!
Arrête de me déranger!

put on VERB
1 **mettre** (clothes)
I'll put my coat on.
Je vais mettre mon manteau.
2 **allumer** (switch on)
Shall I put the light on?
J'allume la lumière?

put up VERB
1 **mettre** (pin up)
I'll put the poster up on the wall.
Je vais mettre le poster au mur.
2 **lever** (raise)
Put up your hands.
Levez la main.
3 **augmenter** (increase)
They've put up the price.
Ils ont augmenté le prix.

puzzle
NOUN
le puzzle
masc

puzzled ADJECTIVE
perplexe
You look puzzled!
Tu as l'air perplexe!

pyjamas PL NOUN
le pyjama *masc*
my pyjamas
mon pyjama
I've got new pyjamas.
J'ai un nouveau pyjama.
a pair of pyjamas
un pyjama

Language tip
*In French, **pyjama** is a singular word.*

Pyrenees PL NOUN
les Pyrénées *fem pl*
in the Pyrenees
dans les Pyrénées
We went to the Pyrenees.
Nous sommes allés dans les Pyrénées.

quad bike NOUN
le **quad** *masc*

quality NOUN
la **qualité** *fem*

quantity NOUN
la **quantité** *fem*

quarrel VERB
se **disputer**
   Don't quarrel!
   Ne vous disputez pas!

quarter NOUN
le **quart** *masc*
   a quarter of the class
   un quart de la classe
   It's quarter past six.
   Il est six heures et quart.
   at quarter to eight
   à huit heures moins le quart

> **three quarters**
> trois quarts
> **a quarter of an hour**
> un quart d'heure
> **three quarters of an hour**
> trois quarts d'heure
> **a quarter past ten**
> dix heures et quart
> **a quarter to eleven**
> onze heures moins le quart

quarter final
NOUN
le **quart de finale** *masc*

queen
NOUN
1 la **reine**
fem

Queen Elizabeth
la reine Élisabeth
2 la **dame** *fem (card)*
   the queen of hearts
   la dame de cœur

question NOUN
la **question** *fem*
   Can I ask a question?
   Est-ce que je peux poser une
   question?
   Are there any questions?
   Vous avez des questions?
   That's a difficult question.
   C'est une question difficile.

questionnaire NOUN
le **questionnaire** *masc*

queue

> **queue** *can be a noun or a verb.*

A NOUN
la **queue** *fem*
   There's a long queue.
   Il y a une longue queue.
B VERB
faire la queue
   You have to queue.
   Il faut faire la queue.

quick ADJECTIVE
rapide
   a quick lunch
   un déjeuner rapide
   It's quicker by train.
   C'est plus rapide en train.

> **Be quick, Laurent!**
> Dépêche-toi, Laurent!
> **Be quick, girls!**
> Dépêchez-vous les filles!

quickly ADVERB
vite
> **Am I speaking too quickly?**
> Je parle trop vite?

quiet ADJECTIVE
1 **silencieux** *masc*
silencieuse *fem (not chatty)*
> **You're very quiet, Daphne.**
> Tu es bien silencieuse, Daphne.
2 **tranquille** *(peaceful)*
> **a quiet little town**
> une petite ville tranquille

> **a quiet weekend**
> un week-end tranquille
> **Be quiet, I'm thinking!**
> Tais-toi, je réfléchis!

Quiet!
Silence!

quietly ADVERB
doucement
> **Talk quietly.**
> Parlez doucement.
> **Shut the door quietly.**
> Fermez doucement la porte.

quilt NOUN
la **couette** *fem*

quite ADVERB
1 **assez** *(rather)*
> **It's quite warm today.**
> Il fait assez chaud aujourd'hui.
> **It's quite a long way.**
> C'est assez loin.
> **It's quite expensive.**
> C'est assez cher.
> **quite a lot of money**
> pas mal d'argent
2 **tout à fait** *(completely)*
> **I'm quite sure he's coming.**
> Je suis tout à fait sûr qu'il va venir.
> **Are you ready, Lola? —**
> **Not quite.**
> Tu es prête, Lola? —
> Pas tout à fait.

quite good
pas mal

quiz NOUN
le **jeu-concours** *masc*

R r

rabbi NOUN
le **rabbin** *masc*

rabbit NOUN
le **lapin** *masc*

race NOUN
la **course** *fem*
a cycle race
une course cycliste
Let's have a race!
On fait la course?

racer NOUN
le **vélo de course** *masc*
I've got a new racer.
J'ai un nouveau vélo de course.

racing car NOUN
la **voiture de course** *fem*
two racing cars
deux voitures de course

racket NOUN
la **raquette** *fem*
my tennis racket
ma raquette de tennis

radiator NOUN
le **radiateur** *masc*
My coat's on the radiator.
Mon manteau est sur le radiateur.

radio NOUN
la **radio** *fem*
on the radio
à la radio

radio cassette NOUN
le **radiocassette** *masc*

radio-controlled ADJECTIVE
téléguidé *masc*
téléguidée *fem*

raffle NOUN
la **tombola** *fem*

raffle ticket NOUN
le **billet de tombola** *masc*
Do you want to buy a raffle ticket?
Tu veux acheter un billet de tombola?

rage NOUN
to be in a rage
être furieux
She's in a rage.
Elle est furieuse.

rail NOUN
by rail
en train

railway NOUN
le **chemin de fer** *masc*

railway line NOUN
le **chemin de fer** *masc*

railway station NOUN
la **gare** *fem*

rain

rain *can be a noun or a verb.*

A NOUN
la **pluie** *fem*
in the rain
sous la pluie
B VERB
pleuvoir
It's going to rain.
Il va pleuvoir.

It rains a lot here.
Il pleut beaucoup par ici.

It's raining.
Il pleut.

rainbow NOUN
l' **arc-en-ciel** *masc*

raincoat NOUN
l' **imperméable** *masc*

rainy ADJECTIVE
pluvieux *masc*
pluvieuse *fem*
a rainy day
une journée pluvieuse

raise VERB
lever
Raise your right arm, everyone.
Levez le bras droit, tout le monde.
to raise money
collecter des fonds
We're raising money for a new gym.
Nous collectons des fonds pour un nouveau gymnase.

raisin NOUN
le **raisin sec** *masc*

Language tip

raisin in French means 'grape'.
An English **raisin** is a dried grape,
which is what **raisin sec** means.

Ramadan NOUN
le **ramadan** *masc*

ramp NOUN
la **rampe d'accès** *fem*

ran VERB ▷*see* **run**

random ADJECTIVE
at random
au hasard
Pick a card at random.
Choisis une carte au hasard.

rang VERB ▷*see* **ring**

range NOUN
le **choix** *masc*
There's a wide range of colours.
Il y a un grand choix de coloris.

rap NOUN
le **rap** *masc*

rare ADJECTIVE
rare

rasher NOUN
la **tranche** *fem*
an egg and two rashers of bacon
un œuf et deux tranches de bacon

raspberry NOUN
la **framboise** *fem*
raspberry jam
la confiture de framboises

rat NOUN
le **rat** *masc*

rather ADVERB
plutôt
£20! That's rather expensive!
Vingt livres! C'est plutôt cher!
I'd rather ...
J'aimerais mieux ...

I'd rather stay in tonight.
J'aimerais mieux rester à la maison ce soir.
Would you like a sweet? — I'd rather have an apple.
Tu veux un bonbon? — J'aimerais mieux une pomme.
Which would you rather have?
Qu'est-ce que tu préfères?
Would you rather have water or coke?
Tu préfères boire de l'eau ou du coca?

ravenous ADJECTIVE
I'm ravenous!
J'ai une faim de loup!

Language tip

un loup *is a wolf, so literally this means 'I'm as hungry as a wolf'.*

raw ADJECTIVE
cru *masc*
crue *fem*

razor NOUN
le **rasoir** *masc*

RE NOUN
l' **éducation religieuse** *fem*

reach

reach *can be a noun or a verb.*

A NOUN
Mum keeps the biscuits out of reach.
Maman garde les biscuits hors de portée.
The hotel is within easy reach of the town centre.
L'hôtel se trouve à proximité du centre-ville.
B VERB
arriver à *(get to)*

We hope to reach Paris tomorrow evening.
Nous espérons arriver à Paris demain soir.
I can't reach the top shelf.
Je n'arrive pas à atteindre l'étagère du haut.

read VERB
lire
I don't read much.
Je ne lis pas beaucoup.
Have you read 'The Prisoner of Azkaban'?
Est-ce que tu as lu 'le Prisonnier d'Azkaban'?

read out VERB
lire
I'll read out the names.
Je vais lire les noms.

reading NOUN
la **lecture** *fem*
Reading is one of my hobbies.
La lecture est l'un de mes passe-temps.

ready ADJECTIVE
prêt *masc*
prête *fem*
Lunch is ready.
Le déjeuner est prêt.
She's nearly ready.
Elle est presque prête.
Are you ready, children?
Vous êtes prêts, les enfants?

Ready, steady, go!
À vos marques, prêts, partez!

real ADJECTIVE

1 **vrai** *masc*
vraie *fem (true)*
Her real name is Cordelia.
Son vrai nom, c'est Cordelia.

2 **véritable**
It's real leather.
C'est du cuir véritable.

really ADVERB
vraiment
She's really nice.
Elle est vraiment sympa.
**Do you want to go? —
Not really.**
Tu veux y aller? — Pas vraiment.

reason NOUN
la **raison** *fem*

reasonable ADJECTIVE
raisonnable
Be reasonable, Marie!
Sois raisonnable, Marie!

receipt NOUN
le **ticket de caisse** *masc*
Take your receipt.
Prenez votre ticket de caisse.

receive VERB
recevoir
**I received your letter
yesterday.**
J'ai reçu ta lettre hier.

recent ADJECTIVE
récent *masc*
récente *fem*

recently ADVERB
ces derniers temps
He's been ill a lot recently.
Il est souvent malade ces
derniers temps.

reception NOUN
la **réception** *fem*

**Please leave your key at
reception.**
Merci de laisser votre clé à la
réception.
**The reception will be at a big
hotel.**
La réception aura lieu dans un
grand hôtel.

receptionist NOUN
le/la **réceptionniste**
masc/fem

Language tip

*In French, **réceptionniste** has
double **n**.*

recipe NOUN
la **recette** *fem*

reckon VERB
penser
What do you reckon?
Qu'est-ce que tu en penses?

recognize VERB
reconnaître
Do you recognize this boy?
Tu reconnais ce garçon?

recommend VERB
conseiller
What do you recommend?
Qu'est-ce que vous me
conseillez?
I recommend the soup.
Je vous conseille la soupe.

record

record can be a noun or a verb.

A NOUN
le **record** *masc (sport)*
the world record
le record du monde
B VERB
enregistrer

We'll record the song.
On va enregistrer la chanson.

recorder NOUN
la **flûte à bec** *fem*
I play the recorder.
Je joue de la flûte à bec.

rectangle NOUN
le **rectangle** *masc*

red

> **red** *can be an adjective or a noun.*

A ADJECTIVE
1 **rouge**
a red rose
une rose rouge
The lights are red.
Le feu est au rouge.
2 **roux** *masc*
rousse *fem* (hair)
Tamsin's got red hair.
Tamsin a les cheveux roux.

Language tip

Colour adjectives come after the noun in French.

B NOUN
le **rouge** *masc*
Red is my favourite colour.
Ma couleur préférée, c'est le rouge.

redecorate VERB
1 **retapisser** (with wallpaper)
Mum is helping me redecorate my room.
Maman m'aide à retapisser ma chambre.
2 **refaire les peintures**
(with paint)
Mum is helping me redecorate my room.
Maman m'aide à refaire les peintures de ma chambre.

red-haired ADJECTIVE
roux *masc*
rousse *fem*

redhead NOUN
le **roux** *masc*
la **rousse** *fem*

redo VERB
refaire
I need to redo my homework.
Je dois refaire mes devoirs.

reduced ADJECTIVE
at a reduced price
à prix réduit

reduction NOUN
la **réduction** *fem*
a 5% reduction
une réduction de cinq pour cent

referee NOUN
l' **arbitre** *masc*

reflexive ADJECTIVE
a reflexive verb
un verbe réfléchi

refreshments PL NOUN
les **rafraîchissements** *masc pl*

refrigerator NOUN
le **réfrigérateur** *masc*

refugee NOUN
le **réfugié** *masc*
la **réfugiée** *fem*

refuse VERB
refuser
He refuses to help.
Il refuse d'aider.

regards PL NOUN
Give my regards to Luc.
Transmets mon bon souvenir à Luc.
Jean-Louis sends his regards.
Vous avez le bonjour de Jean-Louis.

region NOUN
la **région** *fem*
in this region
dans cette région

register NOUN
I'm going to call the register.
Je vais faire l'appel.

registration NOUN
l' **appel** *masc*
after registration
après l'appel

regular ADJECTIVE
1 **régulier** *masc*
régulière *fem*
at regular intervals
à intervalles réguliers
a regular verb
un verbe régulier
You should take regular exercise.
Il faut faire régulièrement de l'exercice.
2 **normal** *masc*
normale *fem* (*medium*)
a regular portion of fries
une portion de frites normale

rehearsal NOUN
la **répétition** *fem*

reindeer NOUN
le **renne** *masc*

relation NOUN
my relations
ma famille
I've got relations in London.
J'ai de la famille à Londres.

relative NOUN
all her relatives
toute sa famille
I've got relatives in Manchester.
J'ai de la famille à Manchester.

relax VERB
Relax! Everything's fine.
Ne t'en fais pas! Tout va bien.

relaxed ADJECTIVE
détendu *masc*
détendue *fem*

relaxing ADJECTIVE
reposant *masc*
reposante *fem*
I find cooking relaxing.
Cela me détend de faire la cuisine.

relay race NOUN
la **course de relais** *fem*
We won the relay race.
Nous avons gagné la course de relais.

reliable ADJECTIVE
fiable
a reliable car
une voiture fiable
He's not very reliable.
Il n'est pas très fiable.

a
b
c
d
e
f
g
h
i
j
k
l
m
n
o
p
q
r
s
t
u
v
w
x
y
z

religion NOUN
la **religion** *fem*
What religion are you?
Quelle est votre religion?

religious ADJECTIVE
religieux *masc*
religieuse *fem*
a religious school
une école religieuse
My parents are very religious.
Mes parents sont très croyants.

remark NOUN
la **remarque** *fem*

remember VERB
se souvenir de
Who remembers this word?
Qui se souvient de ce mot?
Do you remember the rules of the game?
Tu te souviens des règles du jeu?
I can't remember his name.
Je ne me souviens pas de son nom.

Language tip
In French, you often say 'don't forget' instead of **remember**.

Remember your passport!
N'oublie pas ton passeport!
Remember this word is feminine.
N'oublie pas que ce mot est féminin.
Remember to write your name on the form, children.
N'oubliez pas d'écrire votre nom sur le formulaire, les enfants.

Sorry, I can't remember.
Désolé, je ne m'en souviens pas.

Remembrance Day NOUN
le **jour de l'Armistice** *masc*
on Remembrance Day
le jour de l'Armistice

remind VERB
rappeler
Remind me to speak to Daniel.
Rappelle-moi de parler à Daniel.

remote ADJECTIVE
isolé *masc*
isolée *fem*
a remote village
un village isolé

remote control NOUN
la **télécommande** *fem*

remove VERB
enlever
Please remove your bag from my seat.
Est-ce que vous pouvez enlever votre sac de mon siège?

rent

rent can be a noun or a verb.

A NOUN
le **loyer** *masc*
She has to pay the rent.
Elle doit payer le loyer.
B VERB
louer
We are going to rent a car.
Nous allons louer une voiture.

repair VERB
réparer
Can you repair them?
Vous pouvez les réparer?

repeat VERB
répéter

Repeat after me, everyone.
Répétez après moi, tout le monde.

reply

reply can be a noun or a verb.

A NOUN
la **réponse** *fem*
I got no reply to my letter.
Je n'ai pas eu de réponse à ma lettre.

B VERB
répondre
I hope you will reply soon.
J'espère que tu vas vite répondre.

report NOUN
le **bulletin scolaire** *masc*
I usually get a good report.
D'habitude, j'ai un bon bulletin scolaire.

republic NOUN
la **république** *fem*
France is a republic.
La France est une république.

request NOUN
la **demande** *fem*
another request
une autre demande

reservation NOUN
la **réservation** *fem*
I've got a reservation.
J'ai une réservation.
I'd like to make a reservation for this evening.
J'aimerais faire une réservation pour ce soir.

reserve

reserve can be a noun or a verb.

A NOUN
le **remplaçant** *masc*

la **remplaçante** *fem*
I was reserve in the game last Saturday.
J'étais remplaçant dans le match de samedi dernier.

B VERB
réserver
I'd like to reserve a table for tomorrow evening.
J'aimerais réserver une table pour demain soir.

reserved ADJECTIVE
réservé *masc*
réservée *fem*
a reserved seat
une place réservée

resolution NOUN
la **résolution** *fem*
Have you made any new year's resolutions?
Tu as pris de bonnes résolutions pour l'année nouvelle?

resort NOUN
la **station balnéaire** *fem*
It's a resort on the Costa del Sol.
C'est une station balnéaire sur la Costa del Sol.
a ski resort
une station de ski

responsibility NOUN
la **responsabilité** *fem*
It's your responsibility.
C'est ta responsabilité.

English French

a b c d e f g h i j k l m n o p q r s t u v w x y z

Language tip

What are the differences in spelling between the French and the English word?

responsible ADJECTIVE
responsable
> **He's responsible for booking the tickets.**
> Il est responsable de la réservation des billets.
> **It's a responsible job.**
> C'est un poste à responsabilités.

Language tip

The i in **responsible** *becomes an a in the French word* **responsable***.*

rest

rest can be a noun or a verb.

A NOUN
1 le **repos** *masc*
> **five minutes' rest**
> cinq minutes de repos
> **Can we have a rest?**
> On peut se reposer?
> **I need a rest.**
> J'ai besoin de me reposer.
2 *(remainder)*
> **the rest**
> le reste
> **I'll do the rest.**
> Je ferai le reste.
> **the rest of the money**
> le reste de l'argent

B VERB
se reposer
> **She's resting in her room.**
> Elle se repose dans sa chambre.

restaurant NOUN
le **restaurant** *masc*
> **We don't often go to restaurants.**
> Nous n'allons pas souvent au restaurant.

restaurant car NOUN
le **wagon-restaurant** *masc*

result NOUN
le **résultat** *masc*
> **my exam results**
> mes résultats d'examen
> **What was the result? — One-nil.**
> Quel a été le résultat? — Un à zéro.

retire VERB
prendre sa retraite
> **He's going to retire.**
> Il va prendre sa retraite.

retired ADJECTIVE
retraité *masc*
retraitée *fem*
> **She's retired.**
> Elle est retraitée.

retirement NOUN
la **retraite** *fem*

return

return can be a noun or a verb.

A NOUN
1 le **retour** *masc*
> **after our return**
> à notre retour
> **the return journey**
> le voyage de retour
2 l' **aller retour** *masc (ticket)*
> **A return to Avignon, please.**
> Un aller retour pour Avignon, s'il vous plaît.

Many happy returns!
Bon anniversaire!

B VERB
1 **revenir** *(come back)*

I've just returned from holiday.

Je viens de revenir de vacances.

2 rendre (give back)

I've got to return this book to the library.

Je dois rendre ce livre à la bibliothèque.

reverse ADJECTIVE
inverse

in reverse order

dans l'ordre inverse

revise VERB
réviser

I haven't started revising yet.

Je n'ai pas encore commencé à réviser.

revision NOUN
les **révisions** fem pl

Have you done a lot of revision?

Est-ce que tu as fait beaucoup de révisions?

revolution NOUN
la **révolution** fem

the French Revolution

la Révolution française

reward NOUN
la **récompense** fem

There's a €1000 reward.

Il y a une récompense de 1000€.

rewind VERB
rembobiner

Can you rewind the tape?

Tu peux rembobiner la cassette?

rhubarb NOUN
la **rhubarbe** fem

a rhubarb tart

une tarte à la rhubarbe

rhythm NOUN
le **rythme** masc

Language tip

Which consonant is missing in the French word?

rib NOUN
la **côte** fem

ribbon NOUN
le **ruban** masc

rice NOUN
le **riz** masc

Would you like some rice?

Vous voulez du riz?

rich ADJECTIVE
riche

rid VERB

to get rid of

se débarrasser de

I need to get rid of my chewing gum.

Je dois me débarrasser de mon chewing gum.

ride

ride *can be a noun or a verb.*

A NOUN
la **promenade à cheval** *fem* (on horse)

Would you like to go for a ride?

Tu veux faire une promenade à cheval?

English French

a bike ride
un tour en vélo
I'm going to go for a bike ride.
Je vais faire un tour en vélo.

B VERB
monter à cheval *(on horse)*
I'm learning to ride.
J'apprends à monter à cheval.
to ride a bike
faire du vélo
Can you ride a bike?
Tu sais faire du vélo?

rider NOUN
le **cavalier** *masc*
la **cavalière** *fem*
She's a good rider.
C'est une bonne cavalière.

ridiculous ADJECTIVE
ridicule
Don't be ridiculous, Fiona!
Ne sois pas ridicule, Fiona!

riding NOUN
l' **équitation** *fem*
I like riding.
J'aime l'équitation.
to go riding
faire de l'équitation
I'd like to go riding.
Je voudrais faire de l'équitation.

riding school NOUN
l' **école d'équitation** *fem*

right

> **right** *can be an adjective, an adverb or a noun.*

A ADJECTIVE
1 **bon** *masc*
  bonne *fem (correct)*
  That's the right answer!
  C'est la bonne réponse!
  It isn't the right size.
  Ce n'est pas la bonne taille.
  We're on the right train.
  Nous sommes dans le bon train.
2 **vrai** *masc*
  vraie *fem (true)*
  That's right!
  C'est vrai!
3 **droit** *masc*
  droite *fem (not left)*
  my right hand
  ma main droite

B ADVERB
1 **correctement** *(correctly)*
  Am I pronouncing it right?
  Est-ce que je prononce ça correctement?
2 **à droite** *(to the right)*
  Turn right at the traffic lights.
  Tournez à droite aux prochains feux.

C NOUN *(not left)*
  on the right
  à droite
  a step to the right
  un pas à droite

You're right, Léa.
Tu as raison, Léa.
You're right, sir.
Vous avez raison, monsieur.
Right! Let's get started.
Bon! On commence.
Go right.
Allez à droite.

right-hand ADJECTIVE
   the right-hand side
   la droite
   It's on the right-hand side.
   C'est à droite.

right-handed ADJECTIVE
   droitier *masc*
   droitière *fem*

ring

> *ring can be a noun or a verb.*

A NOUN
1 la **bague** *fem (jewellery)*
   a gold ring
   une bague
   en or
   **a diamond
   ring**
   une bague
   de diamants
   **a wedding
   ring**
   une alliance
2 le **cercle** *masc (circle)*
   Stand in a ring.
   Mettez-vous en cercle.
B VERB
1 **appeler** *(phone)*
   You can ring me at home.
   Tu peux m'appeler à la maison.
2 **sonner** *(make sound)*
   The phone's ringing.
   Le téléphone sonne.

ring tone NOUN
   la **sonnerie** *fem*

rink NOUN
1 la **patinoire** *fem (for ice-skating)*
2 la **piste** *fem (for roller-skating)*

ripe ADJECTIVE
   mûr *masc*
   mûre *fem*

   a ripe peach
   une pêche mûre

risk NOUN
   le **risque** *masc*
   It's a big risk.
   C'est un gros risque.

rival

> *rival can be a noun or an adjective.*

A NOUN
   le **rival** *masc*
   la **rivale** *fem*
   our rivals
   nos rivaux
B ADJECTIVE
   rival *masc*
   rivale *fem*
   a rival gang
   une bande rivale

river NOUN
   la **rivière** *fem*
   across the river
   de l'autre côté de la rivière

> ### Language tip
> **fleuve** is the French word for major rivers that flow into the sea. The five **fleuves** in France are the Seine, the Rhine, the Rhône, the Loire, and the Garonne.

   the river Amazon
   le fleuve Amazone

Riviera NOUN
   the French Riviera
   la Côte d'Azur

road NOUN
1 la **route** *fem*
   There's traffic on the roads.
   Il y a de la circulation sur les routes.
   the main road
   la grande route

2 la **rue** *fem* (street)
They live across the road.
Ils habitent de l'autre côté de la rue.

road sign NOUN
le **panneau** *masc*
(PL les **panneaux**)

roadworks PL NOUN
les **travaux** *masc pl*

roast ADJECTIVE
rôti *masc*
rôtie *fem*
roast chicken
le poulet rôti
roast potatoes
les pommes de terre rôties
roast pork
le rôti de porc
roast beef
le rôti de bœuf

robber NOUN
le **voleur** *masc*
a bank robber
un cambrioleur de banques

robbery NOUN
le **vol** *masc*
a bank robbery
un hold-up

robot NOUN
le **robot** *masc*

rock NOUN
1 le **rocher** *masc* (boulder)
Shall we sit on this rock?
On s'asseoit sur ce rocher?
2 le **rock** *masc* (music)

a rock concert
un concert de rock
He's a rock star.
C'est une rock star.
3 le **sucre d'orge** *masc* (sweet)
a stick of rock
un bâton de sucre d'orge

rocket NOUN
la **fusée** *fem*

rod NOUN
la **canne à pêche** *fem*

role play NOUN
le **jeu de rôle** *masc*
We're going to do a role play.
Nous allons faire un jeu de rôle.

roll

> **roll** *can be a noun or a verb.*

A NOUN
le **petit pain** *masc* (bread)
B VERB
rouler
Roll the truffles in cocoa powder.
Roulez les truffes dans la poudre de cacao.

> **Roll the dice.**
> Lance le dé.

roll call NOUN
l' **appel** *masc*

Rollerblade® NOUN
le **roller** *masc*
a pair of Rollerblades
une paire de rollers

rollercoaster NOUN
les **montagnes russes** *fem pl*

roller skates PL NOUN
les **patins à roulettes** *masc pl*

English French

roller-skating NOUN
le **patin à roulettes** *masc*
Do you want to go roller-skating?
Tu veux faire du patin à roulettes?

Roman NOUN
the Romans
les Romains

Roman Catholic NOUN
le/la **catholique** *masc/fem*
He's a Roman Catholic.
Il est catholique.

Language tip

catholique *is not spelled with a capital letter.*

romantic ADJECTIVE
romantique

roof NOUN
le **toit** *masc*

room NOUN
1 la **pièce** *fem*
the biggest room in the house
la plus grande pièce de la maison

2 la **chambre** *fem (bedroom)*
My room is the smallest.
Ma chambre est la plus petite.
a single room
une chambre pour une personne
a double room
une chambre pour deux personnes

3 la **salle** *fem (in school)*
the music room
la salle de musique
4 la **place** *fem (space)*
Is there room for me?
Est-ce qu'il y a de la place pour moi?

rope NOUN
la **corde** *fem*

rose NOUN
la **rose** *fem*
a bunch of roses
un bouquet de roses

rotten ADJECTIVE
rotten weather
un temps pourri

rough ADJECTIVE
violent *masc*
violente *fem*

roughly ADVERB
à peu près
It weighs roughly 20 kilos.
Ça pèse à peu près vingt kilos.

round

round *can be an adjective, a preposition or a noun.*

A ADJECTIVE
rond *masc*
ronde *fem*
a round table
une table ronde
B PREPOSITION
autour de
Sit round the table.
Asseyez-vous autour de la table.
It's just round the corner.
C'est tout près.
round here
près d'ici

a b c d e f g h i j k l m n o p q **r** s t u v w x y z

English French

a
b
c
d
e
f
g
h i j
k
l
m
n o p
q
r
s
t u v
w
x y
z

Is there a chemist's round here?
Il y a une pharmacie près d'ici?
C NOUN
la **manche** *fem*
(of tournament)
the next round
la prochaine manche
a round of golf
une partie de golf

roundabout NOUN
le **manège** *masc*

rounders NOUN
Rounders is a bit like baseball.
Le 'rounders' ressemble un peu au base-ball.

Did you know…?
Rounders is not played in France.

row

row *can be a noun or a verb.*

A NOUN
la **rangée** *fem*
a row of houses
une rangée de maisons
2 le **rang** *masc (of seats)*
Our seats are in the front row.
Nos places se trouvent au premier rang.
3 le **vacarme** *masc (noise)*
What a row!
Quel vacarme!
B VERB
ramer
I can row.
Je sais ramer.

Language tip
row can be pronounced in two different ways. Be careful to pick the right translation!

rowing boat NOUN
le **bateau à rames** *masc*

royal ADJECTIVE
royal *masc*
royale *fem*
the royal family
la famille royale

rubber NOUN
la **gomme** *fem*
Can I borrow your rubber?
Je peux emprunter ta gomme?

rubber band NOUN
l' **élastique** *masc*

rubbish

rubbish *can be a noun or an adjective.*

A NOUN
1 les **ordures** *fem pl (garbage)*
Where shall I put the rubbish?
Où est-ce que je mets les ordures?
2 les **bêtises** *fem pl (nonsense)*
Don't talk rubbish!
Ne dis pas de bêtises!
B ADJECTIVE
nul *masc*
nulle *fem (useless)*
They're a rubbish team!
Cette équipe est nulle!
The film was rubbish.
Le film était nul.

rubbish bin NOUN
la **poubelle** *fem*

rucksack NOUN
le **sac à dos** *masc*

rude ADJECTIVE
impoli *masc*
impolie *fem*
>**Don't be rude!**
>Ne sois pas impoli!
>**a rude word**
>un gros mot

rug NOUN
1 le **tapis** *masc (carpet)*
>**a Persian rug**
>un tapis persan
2 la **couverture** *fem*
(blanket)
>**a travel rug**
>une couverture de voyage
>**a tartan rug**
>un plaid écossais

rugby NOUN
le **rugby** *masc*
>**I play rugby.**
>Je joue au rugby.

ruin

>*ruin can be a noun or a verb.*

A NOUN
>la **ruine** *fem*
>**the ruins of the castle**
>les ruines du château
B VERB
>**abîmer**
>**You'll ruin your shoes.**
>Tu vas abîmer tes chaussures.

rule NOUN
1 la **règle** *fem (of game)*
>**the rules of the game**
>les règles du jeu

2 *(regulations)*
>**the rules**
>le règlement
>**It's against the rules.**
>C'est contre le règlement.

ruler NOUN
la **règle** *fem*
>**Can I borrow your ruler?**
>Je peux emprunter ta règle?

run

>*run can be a noun or a verb.*

A NOUN
>**Do you want to go for a run?**
>Tu veux courir?
>**I go for a run every morning.**
>Je cours tous les matins.
>**I did a ten-kilometre run.**
>J'ai couru dix kilomètres.

B VERB
1 **courir**
>**Run!**
>Cours!
>**I ran two kilometres.**
>J'ai couru deux kilomètres.
2 **organiser** *(organize)*
>**They run French courses.**
>Ils organisent des cours de français.

runner NOUN
le **coureur** *masc*
la **coureuse** *fem*

runner-up NOUN
le **second** *masc*
la **seconde** *fem*

running NOUN
la **course** *fem*
Running is my favourite sport.
Mon sport préféré, c'est la course.

rush

> **rush** *can be a noun or a verb.*

A NOUN
la **hâte** *fem*
in a rush.
à la hâte

B VERB
se **dépêcher**
There's no need to rush.
Ce n'est pas la peine de se dépêcher.

rush hour NOUN
les **heures de pointe** *fem pl*
in the rush hour
aux heures de pointe

S s

Sabbath NOUN
1 le **dimanche** *masc (Christian)*
2 le **sabbat** *masc (Jewish)*

sack NOUN
le **sac** *masc*

sad ADJECTIVE
triste

saddle NOUN
la **selle** *fem*

sadly ADVERB
tristement

safe ADJECTIVE
1 **sans danger** *masc, fem, pl*
   (not dangerous)
   Don't worry, it's perfectly safe.
   Ne vous inquiétez pas, c'est
   absolument sans danger.
2 **sûr** *masc*
   sûre *fem (secure)*
   Put it in a safe place.
   Mets-le en lieu sûr.

safely ADVERB
The parcel arrived safely.
Le paquet est bien arrivé.

safety NOUN
la **sécurité** *fem*

said VERB ▷ *see* **say**

sailing NOUN
la **voile** *fem*
   His hobby is sailing.
   Son passe-temps, c'est la voile.

   to go sailing
   faire de la voile
   I'd like to go sailing.
   J'aimerais faire de la voile.

sailing boat NOUN
le **voilier** *masc*

saint NOUN
le **saint** *masc*
la **sainte** *fem*

salad NOUN
la **salade** *fem*
   Would you like some salad?
   Tu veux de la salade?

salad cream NOUN
la **mayonnaise** *fem*

salad dressing NOUN
la **vinaigrette** *fem*

salary NOUN
le **salaire** *masc*

sale NOUN
   'for sale'
   'à vendre'

salmon NOUN
le **saumon** *masc*

salt NOUN
le **sel** *masc*

same

same *can be an adjective or a pronoun.*

A ADJECTIVE
même
   the same class
   la même classe
   at the same time
   en même temps

English French

a
b
c
d
e
f
g
h
i
j
k
l
m
n
o
p
q
r
s
t
u
v
w
x
y
z

We've got the same colour T-shirts.
Noun avons des T-shirts de la même couleur.

B PRONOUN
the same
pareil
They're exactly the same.
Ils sont exactement pareils.
It's not the same.
Ça n'est pas pareil.

Language tip
Use **pareille** for something feminine.

Our trainers are the same.
Nos baskets sont pareilles.

sand NOUN
le **sable** masc

sandal NOUN
la **sandale** fem
a pair of sandals
une paire de sandales

sand castle NOUN
le **château de sable** masc

sandwich
NOUN
le **sandwich** masc
a cheese sandwich
un sandwich au fromage

sang VERB ▷see **sing**

Santa Claus NOUN
le **père Noël** masc

Did you know…?
In France, children don't leave anything for Santa to eat!

satchel NOUN
le **cartable** masc
My satchel is black.
Mon cartable est noir.

satisfied ADJECTIVE
satisfait masc
satisfaite fem

sat nav NOUN
la **navigation par satellite** fem

Saturday NOUN
le **samedi** masc
It's Saturday today.
Aujourd'hui c'est samedi.
I've got a Saturday job.
Je travaille le samedi.

on Saturday
samedi
on Saturdays
le samedi
every Saturday
tous les samedis
last Saturday
samedi dernier
next Saturday
samedi prochain

Language tip
Days of the week are not written with a capital letter in French.

sauce NOUN
la **sauce** fem

saucepan NOUN
la **casserole** fem

saucer NOUN
la **soucoupe** fem

English French

a b c d e f g h i j k l m n o p q r **s** t u v w x y z

sausage NOUN
  la **saucisse** *fem*
    sausage and chips
    une saucisse-frites
    a sausage roll
    un friand à la saucisse

save VERB
  1 **mettre de l'argent de côté** *(save up)*
    I'm saving for a new bike.
    Je mets de l'argent de côté pour un nouveau vélo.
  2 **sauver** *(rescue)*
    He saved my life.
    Il m'a sauvé la vie.
  3 **sauvegarder** *(on computer)*
    I saved the file.
    J'ai sauvegardé le fichier.
    to save time
    gagner du temps
    It'll save time.
    Ça nous fera gagner du temps.

save up VERB
  mettre de l'argent de côté
    I'm saving up for a new bike.
    Je mets de l'argent de côté pour un nouveau vélo.

savoury ADJECTIVE
  salé *masc*
  salée *fem*
    Is it sweet or savoury?
    C'est sucré ou salé?

saw VERB ▷ *see* **see**

say VERB
  dire
    I don't know how to say it in French.
    Je ne sais pas comment ça se dit en français.
    Say hello, Donald.
    Dis bonjour, Donald.

Say hello, children.
Dites bonjour, les enfants.
What did you say?
Qu'est-ce que tu as dit?
I said no.
J'ai dit non.

How do you say 'Sorry' in French?
Comment est-ce qu'on dit 'Sorry' en français?
Say the words again, children.
Répétez ces mots, les enfants.
Say it after me, Aurélie.
Répète après moi, Aurélie.
Could you say that again, please?
Pourriez-vous répéter s'il vous plaît?

scampi PL NOUN
  les **scampi** *masc pl*

scared ADJECTIVE
    to be scared
    avoir peur
    I'm scared of dogs.
    J'ai peur des chiens.

I'm scared!
J'ai peur!

scarf NOUN
  l' **écharpe** *fem*
    a hat and scarf
    un bonnet et une écharpe

scary ADJECTIVE
  effrayant *masc*
  effrayante *fem*

It was really scary.
C'était vraiment effrayant.

scenery NOUN
le **paysage** masc

school NOUN
l' **école** fem
I love school.
J'adore l'école.
the school library
la bibliothèque de l'école
I go to school with Marc.
Je vais à l'école avec Marc.

at school
à l'école

schoolbag NOUN
le **cartable** masc

schoolboy NOUN
l' **écolier** masc

schoolchildren NOUN
les **écoliers** masc pl

schoolgirl NOUN
l' **écolière** fem

school holidays PL NOUN
les **vacances scolaires** fem pl

school uniform NOUN
l' **uniforme scolaire** masc

Did you know...?
French children don't wear school uniform.

science NOUN
la **science** fem

scientist NOUN
le **chercheur** masc
la **chercheuse** fem

scissors PL NOUN
les **ciseaux** masc pl
a pair of scissors
une paire de ciseaux

scooter NOUN
1 la **trottinette** fem (for children)
2 le **scooter** masc (motorbike)

score

score can be a noun or a verb.

A NOUN
le **score** masc
What's the score?
Quel est le score?
The score is three-nil.
Le score est de trois à zéro.
B VERB
1 **marquer** (goal, point)
He scores lots of goals.
Il marque beaucoup de buts.
I scored a goal.
J'ai marqué un but.
2 **compter les points** (keep score)
Who's going to score?
Qui va compter les points?

Scot NOUN
l' **Écossais** masc
l' **Écossaise** fem

Scotland NOUN
l' **Écosse** fem
Stirling is in Scotland.
Stirling est en Écosse.
When are you coming to Scotland?
Quand est-ce que tu viens en Écosse?
Tommy is from Scotland.
Tommy est écossais.
Elspeth is from Scotland.
Elspeth est écossaise.

in Scotland
en Écosse
to Scotland
en Écosse
I'm from Scotland.
Je suis écossais.

Scotsman NOUN
l' **Écossais** masc

Scotswoman NOUN
l' **Écossaise** fem

Scottish ADJECTIVE
écossais masc
écossaise fem
    a Scottish accent
    un accent écossais

Language tip

Scottish *always has a capital letter,*
but **écossais** *doesn't.*

Scout NOUN
le **scout** masc
    I'm in the Scouts.
    Je suis scout.

Did you know…?

Guides and scouts are not as
common in France as they are in
Britain.

scrambled eggs PL NOUN
les **œufs brouillés** masc pl

scrapbook NOUN
l' **album** masc

scream VERB
hurler
    Simon says 'Scream!'
    Jacques a dit 'Hurlez!'

screen NOUN
l' **écran** masc

sea NOUN
la **mer** fem
    I live by the sea.
    J'habite au bord de la mer.

seafood NOUN
les **fruits de mer** masc pl

seagull NOUN
la **mouette** fem

seashore NOUN
le **bord de la mer** masc
    on the seashore
    au bord de la mer

seasick ADJECTIVE
    I get seasick.
    J'ai le mal de mer.

seaside NOUN
le **bord de la mer** masc
    at the seaside
    au bord de la mer

season NOUN
la **saison** fem
    What's your favourite
    season?
    Quelle est ta saison préférée?

season ticket NOUN
la **carte d'abonnement** fem

seat NOUN
le **siège** masc
    I'd like a seat by the window.
    Je voudrais un siège côté
    fenêtre.
    Go back to your seat, Michel!
    Retourne à ta place, Michel!

second

> **second** *can be an adjective or a noun.*

A ADJECTIVE
deuxième
on the second page
à la deuxième page
I came second.
Je suis arrivé deuxième.

B NOUN
la **seconde** *fem*
It'll only take a second.
Ça va prendre juste une seconde.

> **the second of March**
> le deux mars

secondary school NOUN

1 le **collège** *masc (for pupils 11–15)*
2 le **lycée** *masc (for pupils 15–18)*

> **Did you know…?**
> In France, pupils go to a **collège** between the ages of 11 and 15, and then to a **lycée** until the age of 18.

secret

> **secret** *can be a noun or an adjective.*

A NOUN
le **secret** *masc*
It's a secret.
C'est un secret.
Can you keep a secret?
Tu sais garder un secret?
in secret
en secret

B ADJECTIVE
secret *masc*
secrète *fem*
a secret passage
un passage secret

secretary NOUN
le/la **secrétaire** *masc/fem*
She's a secretary.
Elle est secrétaire.

> **Language tip**
> When you say what someone's job is in French, you do not translate **a**.

secretly NOUN
secrètement

see VERB
voir
I can see her car.
Je vois sa voiture.

Can you see the difference?
Est-ce que tu vois la différence?
We're going to see Granny and Grandpa.
On va voir Papi et Mamie.
I saw Denis yesterday.
J'ai vu Denis hier.
Have you seen Pascal?
Est-ce que tu as vu Pascal?

> **See you!**
> Salut!
> **See you tomorrow!**
> À demain!
> **See you soon!**
> À bientôt!

seed NOUN
la **graine** *fem*
sunflower seeds
des graines de tournesol

seem VERB
There seems to be a problem.
Il semble y avoir un problème.

seen VERB ▷ *see* **see**

seesaw NOUN
le **tapecul** *masc*

Language tip

tapecul *is made up of the words*
tape *(meaning 'bang') and* **cul**
(meaning 'bottom'). This is what a
seesaw sometimes does to you.

selfish ADJECTIVE
égoïste
Don't be so selfish, Charles.
Ne sois pas si égoïste, Charles.

self-service ADJECTIVE
The café is self-service.
Le café est un self-service.
a self-service restaurant
un self

sell VERB
vendre
He's selling his car.
Il vend sa voiture.
The tickets are all sold out.
Il ne reste plus de billets.

Language tip

The English word 'vendor' is related
to the French word **vendre***. A vendor*
is someone who is selling something.

Sellotape® NOUN
le **scotch**® *masc*

semicircle NOUN
le **demi-cercle** *masc*
Get into a semicircle.
Mettez-vous en demi-cercle.

semi-final NOUN
la **demi-finale** *fem*

send VERB
envoyer
**I'm going to send Magali a
postcard.**
Je vais envoyer une carte postale
à Magali.
Send me an email.
Envoie-moi un e-mail.

**My penfriend has sent me
some photos.**
Ma correspondante m'a envoyé
des photos.

senior ADJECTIVE
senior school
le lycée

sense NOUN
sense of humour
le sens de l'humour
**Our teacher has a sense of
humour.**
Notre prof a le sens de l'humour.
He's got no sense of humour.
Il n'a aucun sens de l'humour.

sensible ADJECTIVE
raisonnable
Be sensible, Brigitte!
Sois raisonnable, Brigitte!
Be sensible, children!
Soyez raisonnables, les enfants!

Language tip

raisonnable *is similar to the*
English word 'reasonable', but it has
two **n***s. Can you see another*
difference?

sent VERB ▷ *see* **send**

sentence NOUN
la **phrase** *fem*
What does this sentence mean?
Que veut dire cette phrase?

separate ADJECTIVE
a separate piece of paper
une feuille différente
Put the green cards in a separate pile.
Fais une pile à part avec les cartes vertes.

September NOUN
septembre *masc*
September or October?
Septembre ou octobre?
My birthday's in September.
Mon anniversaire est en septembre.

in September
en septembre
the fifth of September
le cinq septembre

Language tip
The months in French are not spelled with a capital letter.

sequence NOUN
l' **ordre** *masc*
Put the pictures in sequence, Paul.
Mets les images dans l'ordre, Paul.

series NOUN
la **série** *fem*
a TV series
une série télévisée

serious ADJECTIVE
sérieux *masc*
sérieuse *fem*

You look very serious.
Tu as l'air sérieux.
Are you serious?
Sérieusement?

serve VERB
servir
They're serving lunch now.
On sert le déjeuner en ce moment.
It serves you right.
C'est bien fait pour toi.

service NOUN
1 le **service** *masc (in restaurant)*
Service is included.
Le service est compris.
2 l' **office** *masc (in church)*

service charge NOUN
le **service** *masc*
There's no service charge.
Le service est compris.

service station NOUN
la **station-service** *fem*

serviette NOUN
la **serviette** *fem*

set VERB
se coucher
The sun is setting.
Le soleil se couche.
to set the table
mettre la table
Could you set the table?
Tu peux mettre la table?

set off VERB
partir
> **What time are you setting off?**
> À quelle heure tu pars?

settee NOUN
le **canapé** *masc*

settle down VERB
> **Settle down, children!**
> Du calme, les enfants!

seven NUMBER
sept
> **seven euros**
> sept euros

She's seven.
Elle a sept ans.

Language tip
In English, you can say **seven** *or* **seven years old**. *In French, you can only say* **sept ans**.

seventeen NUMBER
dix-sept
> **seventeen euros**
> dix-sept euros

He's seventeen.
Il a dix-sept ans.

Language tip
In English, you can say **seventeen** *or* **seventeen years old**. *In French, you can only say* **dix-sept ans**.

seventeenth ADJECTIVE
dix-septième
> **on the seventeenth floor**
> au dix-septième étage

the seventeenth of August
le dix-sept août

seventh ADJECTIVE
septième

> **on the seventh floor**
> au septième étage

the seventh of August
le sept août

seventy NUMBER
soixante-dix

Language tip
The French word consists of two numbers, what are they?

several PRONOUN
plusieurs
> **Several children are absent.**
> Plusieurs enfants sont absents.

sewing NOUN
la **couture** *fem*
> **I like sewing.**
> J'aime faire de la couture.

shade NOUN
l' **ombre** *fem*
> **It was 35 degrees in the shade.**
> Il faisait trente-cinq à l'ombre.

shadow NOUN
l' **ombre** *fem*

shake VERB
> **to shake hands with somebody**
> serrer la main à quelqu'un
> **Simon says 'Shake hands with your best friend!'**
> Jacques a dit 'Serrez la main à votre meilleur ami!'
> **French people shake hands a lot.**
> Les Français se serrent beaucoup la main.

---

shall VERB
Shall I shut the window?
Je ferme la fenêtre?
Shall I go first?
Je commence?
Shall I put the light on?
J'allume?

shame NOUN
What a shame! She can't come!
Quel dommage! Elle ne peut pas venir!

shampoo NOUN
le **shampooing** *masc*
a bottle of shampoo
une bouteille de shampooing

shape NOUN
la **forme** *fem*

share VERB
partager
I share a room with Léa.
Je partage ma chambre avec Léa.

sharp ADJECTIVE
coupant *masc*
coupante *fem*
Be careful, it's sharp.
Attention, c'est coupant.

she PRONOUN
elle

She's very nice.
Elle est très gentille.

sheep NOUN
le **mouton** *masc*

sheet NOUN
le **drap** *masc*
clean sheets
des draps propres
a sheet of paper
une feuille de papier

shelf NOUN
l' **étagère** *fem*

shell NOUN
le **coquillage** *masc*

shelves PL NOUN
les **étagères** *fem pl*

she's = she is, she has

Shetland Islands
PL NOUN
les **îles Shetland** *fem pl*

shine VERB
briller
The sun is shining.
Le soleil brille.

ship NOUN
le **bateau** *masc* (PL les **bateaux**)

shirt NOUN
  1 la **chemise** *fem (man's)*
    a white shirt
    une chemise blanche
  2 le **maillot** *masc (footballer's)*

shocking ADJECTIVE
  choquant *masc*
  choquante *fem*
    It's shocking!
    C'est choquant!

shoe NOUN
  la **chaussure** *fem*
    I've got new shoes.
    J'ai de nouvelles chaussures.

shoe shop NOUN
  le **magasin de chaussures**
  masc

shooting NOUN
  la **chasse** *fem*
    He goes shooting.
    Il va à la chasse.

shop NOUN
  le **magasin** *masc*
    The shop is shut.
    Le magasin est fermé.
    a sports shop
    un magasin de sports

shop assistant NOUN
  le **vendeur** *masc*
  la **vendeuse** *fem*
    She's a shop assistant.
    Elle est vendeuse.

Language tip

*You do not translate '**a**' when you
say what someone's job is in French.*

shopkeeper NOUN
  le **commerçant** *masc*
  la **commerçante** *fem*

shopping NOUN
  les **courses** *fem pl*

**Can you get the shopping
from the car?**
Tu peux aller chercher les
courses dans la voiture?

Language tip

*If you're shopping for food, you say
Je fais les courses. If you're
looking round the shops, you say **Je
fais les magasins**.*

Did you know...?

*In Quebec, you can say **Je magasine**
whether you are shopping for food
or looking round the shops.*

  **I do the shopping for my
  granny.**
  Je fais les courses pour ma
  grand-mère.
  I go shopping with my friends.
  Je fais les magasins avec mes
  amies.

shopping bag NOUN
  le **sac à provisions** *masc*

shopping centre NOUN
  le **centre commercial** *masc*

short ADJECTIVE
  1 **court** *masc*
    courte *fem (in length)*
    a short skirt
    une jupe courte
    short hair
    les cheveux courts
  2 **petit** *masc*
    petite *fem (in time)*
    a short walk
    une petite promenade

shorts PL NOUN
  le **short** *masc*
    My shorts are green.
    Mon short est vert.
    a pair of shorts
    un short

English French

a
b
c
d
e
f
g
h
i
j
k
l
m
n
o
p
q
r
s
t
u
v
w
x
y
z

Language tip
short *is a singular word in French.*

short-sighted
ADJECTIVE
myope

shoulder NOUN
l' **épaule** *fem*

should VERB
You should try it.
Tu devrais essayer.
You shouldn't do that.
Tu ne devrais pas faire ça.

shout VERB
crier
Don't shout, children!
Ne criez pas, les enfants!

show VERB
montrer
Show me!
Montrez-moi!
Shall I show you the photos?
Je te montre les photos?

shower NOUN
la **douche** *fem*
I'm going to have a shower.
Je vais prendre une douche.

Shrove Tuesday NOUN
le **mardi gras** *masc*

Did you know…?
Shrove Tuesday *is the same as*
Pancake Day *and is celebrated in*
France as well. French children dress
up and eat pancakes (**crêpes** *).*

shrug VERB
Simon says 'Shrug your
shoulders!'
Jacques a dit 'Haussez les
épaules!'

shuffle VERB
You have to shuffle the cards.
Il faut battre les cartes.

shut

shut *can be a verb or an adjective.*

A VERB
fermer
Shut your books, children.
Fermez vos livres, les enfants.
Open your mouth and shut
your eyes.
Ouvre la bouche et ferme les yeux.
What time do the shops shut?
Les magasins ferment à quelle
heure?

Shut up!
Tais-toi!

B ADJECTIVE
fermé *masc*
fermée *fem*
The door is shut.
La porte est fermée.
The shop is shut.
Le magasin est fermé.

shutters PL NOUN
les **volets** *masc pl*

shy ADJECTIVE
timide

sick ADJECTIVE
malade
He is sick.
Il est malade.
to be sick
vomir
I'm going
to be sick.
Je vais vomir.
I feel sick.
J'ai envie de vomir.

English French

a
b
c
d
e
f
g
h
i
j
k
l
m
n
o
p
q
r
s
t
u
v
w
x
y
z

side NOUN
1 le **côté** masc (of object, building, car)
on this side
de ce côté
It's on this side of the street.
C'est de ce côté de la rue.
It's on the other side.
C'est de l'autre côté.
2 l' **équipe** fem (team)
He's on my side.
Il est dans mon équipe.

sightseeing
NOUN
le **tourisme**
masc
We're going to go sightseeing.
Nous allons faire du tourisme.

sign

sign can be a noun or a verb.

A NOUN
a road sign
un panneau
B VERB
signer
Sign here, please.
Signez ici, s'il vous plaît.

signal NOUN
le **signal** masc
(PL les **signaux**)

signature NOUN
la **signature** fem

sign language NOUN
le **langage des signes**
masc

silence NOUN
le **silence** masc

silent ADJECTIVE
silencieux masc
silencieuse fem

silk ADJECTIVE
en soie
a silk scarf
un foulard en soie

silly ADJECTIVE
bête
Don't be silly, Nadège!
Ne sois pas bête, Nadège!

silver

silver can be a noun or an adjective.

A NOUN
l' **argent** masc
gold and silver
l'or et l'argent
B ADJECTIVE
en argent
a silver chain
une chaîne en argent
a silver medal
une médaille d'argent

Simon says NOUN
Jacques a dit

simple ADJECTIVE
simple
It's very simple.
C'est très simple.

since PREPOSITION
depuis
since Christmas
depuis Noël
since then
depuis ce moment-là

sincerely
  Yours sincerely ...
  Cordialement ...

sing VERB
chanter
  I sing in the choir.
  Je chante dans la chorale.
  Sing everyone!
  Allez, chantez!

singer NOUN
  le **chanteur** *masc*
  la **chanteuse** *fem*

single

single *can be an adjective or a noun.*

  A ADJECTIVE
  a single room
  une chambre pour une personne
  B NOUN
  l' **aller simple** *masc (ticket)*
  A single to Toulouse, please.
  Un aller simple pour Toulouse, s'il vous plaît.

singular NOUN
  le **singulier** *masc*
  in the singular
  au singulier

sink NOUN
  l' **évier** *masc*

sir NOUN
  monsieur *masc*
  Yes sir.
  Oui, monsieur.

sister NOUN
  la **sœur** *fem*
  my little sister
  ma petite sœur
  I've got one sister.
  J'ai une sœur.

I haven't got a sister.
Je n'ai pas de sœur.

Have you got any brothers or sisters?
Tu as des frères et sœurs?

sit VERB
s'asseoir
  I want to sit beside my friend.
  Je veux m'asseoir à côté de mon amie.
  Can I sit here?
  Je peux m'asseoir ici?
  Jean-Pierre sits next to Christelle.
  Jean-Pierre s'assoit à côté de Christelle.

sit down VERB
s'asseoir
  Sit down, Mathilde.
  Assieds-toi, Mathilde.
  You can sit down now, Mathieu.
  Tu peux t'asseoir maintenant, Mathieu.

Sit down, children.
Asseyez-vous, les enfants.

site NOUN
  1 le **camping** *masc (campsite)*
  2 le **site web** *masc (website)*

sitting room NOUN
  le **salon** *masc*

situation NOUN
  la **situation** *fem*

six NUMBER
six
  six euros
  six euros

She's six.
Elle a six ans.

Language tip
In English, you can say **six** *or* **six
years old***. In French, you can only
say* **six ans***.*

sixteen NUMBER
seize
sixteen euros
seize euros

He's sixteen.
Il a seize ans.

Language tip
In English, you can say **sixteen** *or*
sixteen years old*. In French, you
can only say* **seize ans***.*

sixteenth ADJECTIVE
seizième
on the sixteenth floor
au seizième étage

the sixteenth of August
le seize août

sixth ADJECTIVE
sixième
on the sixth floor
au sixième étage

the sixth of August
le six août

sixth form NOUN
le **lycée** *masc*

sixty NUMBER
soixante

My aunt is sixty.
Ma tante a soixante ans.

Language tip
In English, you can say **sixty** *or*
sixty years old*. In French, you can
only say* **soixante ans***.*

size NOUN
la **taille** *fem*
**It's the
right size.**
C'est la
bonne taille.

skate VERB
faire du patin à glace
I like to skate.
J'aime faire du patin à glace.

skateboard NOUN
le **skateboard** *masc*

skateboarding NOUN
le **skateboard** *masc*
I like skateboarding.
J'aime le skateboard.
**I go skateboarding with
Kieran.**
Je fais du skateboard avec
Kieran.

skating NOUN
le **patin à glace** *masc*
I like skating.
J'aime le patin à glace.
I go skating.
Je fais du patin à glace.

skeleton NOUN
le **squelette** *masc*

ski

ski *can be a verb or a noun.*

A VERB
skier
Can you ski?
Tu sais skier?
B NOUN
le **ski** *masc*

ski boots PL NOUN
les **chaussures de ski** *fem pl*

ski lift NOUN
le **remonte-pente** *masc*

ski slope NOUN
la **piste de ski** *fem*

skiing NOUN
le **ski** *masc*
Do you like skiing?
Tu aimes le ski?
I'd like to go skiing.
J'aimerais faire du ski.
I'm going on a skiing holiday.
Je vais aux sports d'hiver.

skin NOUN
la **peau** *fem*

skinny ADJECTIVE
maigre

skipping rope NOUN
la **corde à sauter** *fem*

skirt NOUN
la **jupe** *fem*
a black skirt
une jupe noire

sky NOUN
le **ciel** *masc*
The sky is blue.
Le ciel est bleu.

slam VERB
claquer
Don't slam the door.
Ne claque pas la porte.

sledge NOUN
la **luge** *fem*

sledging NOUN
Let's go sledging!
Allons faire de la luge!

sleep VERB
dormir
My cat sleeps in a box.
Mon chat dort dans une boîte.
Did you sleep well, Cyril?
Tu as bien dormi, Cyril?

sleeping bag NOUN
le **sac de couchage** *masc*

sleepover NOUN
**My friend is coming for a
sleepover tonight.**
Mon amie vient dormir chez moi
ce soir.
**We're going to Jasmine's for
a sleepover.**
On va dormir chez Jasmine.

sleepy ADJECTIVE
I'm sleepy.
J'ai sommeil.

sleeve NOUN
la **manche** *fem*
a shirt with long sleeves
une chemise à manches longues
a shirt with short sleeves
une chemise à manches courtes

slice NOUN
la **tranche** *fem*

slide NOUN
1 le **toboggan** *masc (in
playground)*

2 la **barrette** *fem (hair slide)*

3 la **diapositive** *fem (photo)*

slight ADJECTIVE
léger *masc*
légère *fem*
a slight problem
un léger problème

slightly ADVERB
légèrement

slim

> **slim** *can be an adjective or a verb.*

A ADJECTIVE
mince
You're slim!
Tu es mince!

B VERB
faire un régime
(be on a diet)
I'm slimming.
Je fais un régime.

slipper NOUN
le **chausson** *masc*
a pair of slippers
des chaussons

slow ADJECTIVE
lent *masc*
lente *fem*
The music is too slow.
La musique est trop lente.

slowly ADVERB
lentement
Could you speak more slowly?
Vous pouvez parler plus
lentement?

smack NOUN
la **tape** *fem*

small ADJECTIVE
petit *masc*
petite *fem*

smart ADJECTIVE
1 **chic** *masc, fem, pl*
smart clothes
des vêtements chic

2 **intelligent** *masc*
intelligente *fem (clever)*
She's very smart.
Elle est très intelligente.

smart phone NOUN
le **smartphone** *masc*

smell

> **smell** *can be a noun or a verb.*

A NOUN
l' **odeur** *fem*
a nice smell
une bonne odeur

B VERB
sentir
Mmm, that smells nice!
Mmm, ça sent bon!

smile

> **smile** *can be a noun or a verb.*

A NOUN
le **sourire** *masc*
a beautiful smile
un beau sourire

B VERB
sourire
Why are you smiling?
Pourquoi tu souris?

smiley NOUN
le **smiley** *masc*

smoke VERB
fumer
I don't smoke.
Je ne fume pas.

smoking NOUN
Smoking is bad for you.
Le tabac est mauvais pour
la santé.

'no smoking'
'défense de fumer'

smoothie NOUN
la **boisson frappée aux fruits** *fem*

snack NOUN
le **casse-croûte** *masc*
You can get a snack in the canteen.
On peut s'acheter un casse-croûte à la cantine.

snack bar NOUN
le **snack-bar** *masc*

snail NOUN
l' **escargot** *masc*

snake NOUN
le **serpent** *masc*

snooker NOUN
le **billard** *masc*
I play snooker.
Je joue au billard.

snow

snow *can be a noun or a verb.*

A NOUN
la **neige** *fem*
B VERB
neiger
It's going to snow.
Il va neiger.
It snows a lot in the mountains.
Il neige beaucoup à la montagne.

It's snowing.
Il neige.

snowball NOUN
la **boule de neige** *fem*
lots of snowballs
beaucoup de boules de neige

snowboarding NOUN
le **snowboard** *masc*
I like snowboarding.
J'aime faire du snowboard.

snowflake NOUN
le **flocon de neige** *masc*

snowman
NOUN
le **bonhomme de neige** *masc*
I'm going to make a snowman.
Je vais faire un bonhomme de neige.

so

so *can be an adverb or a conjunction.*

A ADVERB
1 si
Don't eat so fast!
Ne mange pas si vite!
2 tellement *(too)*
You talk so fast.
Tu parles tellement vite.
It's so difficult.
C'est tellement difficile.
I love you so much.
Je t'aime tellement.
B CONJUNCTION
alors
It's Luc's birthday, so I've got him a present.
C'est l'anniversaire de Luc, alors je lui ai acheté un cadeau.

so do I
moi aussi
so have I
moi aussi
so am I
moi aussi
I think so.
Je crois.
I hope so.
J'espère bien.

soap NOUN
le **savon** masc

soccer NOUN
le **football** masc

sock NOUN
la **chaussette** fem
I'm wearing white socks.
Je porte des chaussettes
blanches.

sofa NOUN
le **canapé** masc

soft ADJECTIVE
1 **doux** masc
douce fem (voice, texture)
2 **mou** masc
molle fem (pillow, bed, ball)

soft drink NOUN
la **boisson non alcoolisée**
fem

soil NOUN
la **terre** fem

sold ADJECTIVE
vendu masc
vendue fem

soldier NOUN
le **soldat** masc
He's a soldier.
Il est soldat.

> **Language tip**
> *You do not translate 'a' when you
> say what someone's job is in French.*

some

> **some** *can be an adjective or a
> pronoun.*

A ADJECTIVE
1 *(a certain amount of)*

> **Language tip**
> **Some** *can be* **du, de la, de l'** *and*
> **des** *in the same way that* **the** *can
> be* **le, la, l'** *or* **les.**

du
Would you like some bread?
Voulez-vous du pain?
de la
Would you like some soup?
Voulez-vous de la soupe?
de l'
**Have you got some mineral
water?**
Avez-vous de l'eau minérale?
des
I've got some sweets.
J'ai des bonbons.
2 des *(certain)*
Some children are absent.
Il y a des enfants absents.
B PRONOUN
1 certains masc pl
certaines fem pl *(certain ones)*
some of my friends
certains de mes amis
**Have you got all her books?
— I've got some.**
Tu as tous ses livres? — J'en ai
certains.

a
b
c
d
e
f
g
h
i
j
k
l
m
n
o
p
q
r
s
t
u
v
w
x
y
z

2 quelques-uns *masc pl*
quelques-unes *fem pl (some, not all)*
I've got some, but not many.
J'en ai quelques-uns, mais pas beaucoup.

3 en

> **Language tip**
>
> *The word **en** can mean 'some of them', or 'some of it'. Notice its position in sentences.*

Chips? — No thanks, I've got some.
Des frites? — Non merci, j'en ai déjà.
I've got a bar of chocolate. Do you want some?
J'ai une barre de chocolat. Tu en veux?

I've got some.
J'en ai.
Would you like some?
Tu en veux?

somebody PRONOUN
quelqu'un
Somebody is going to win £100!
Quelqu'un va gagner cent livres!

someone PRONOUN
quelqu'un
Someone is going to win £100!
Quelqu'un va gagner cent livres!

something PRONOUN
quelque chose
Are you looking for something?
Tu cherches quelque chose?
something special
quelque chose de spécial
something hot
quelque chose de chaud

I can see something green.
Je vois quelque chose de vert.

sometimes ADVERB
quelquefois
sometimes, but not very often
quelquefois, mais pas très souvent

somewhere ADVERB
quelque part
It's somewhere in the classroom.
C'est quelque part dans la classe.

son NOUN
le **fils** *masc*
her son
son fils

song NOUN
la **chanson** *fem*
We're going to sing a song.
Nous allons chanter une chanson.
I know some French songs.
Je connais des chansons françaises.

soon ADVERB
bientôt
It'll soon be lunchtime.
C'est bientôt l'heure du déjeuner.
very soon
très bientôt

as soon as possible
aussitôt que possible
Write soon!
Écris-moi vite!

sorcerer NOUN
le **sorcier** *masc*

sore ADJECTIVE
It's sore.
Ça fait mal.
My head is sore.
J'ai mal à la tête.

sorry ADJECTIVE
désolé *masc*
désolée *fem*
I'm really sorry.
Je suis vraiment désolé.
I'm sorry I'm late.
Je suis désolé d'être en retard.
I'm sorry, I can't.
Je suis désolé, je ne peux pas.

sorry!
pardon!

sort NOUN
la **sorte** *fem*
What sort of bike have you got?
Quelle sorte de vélo as-tu?

sound

sound *can be a noun or a verb.*

A NOUN
1 le **bruit** *masc (noise)*
Don't make a sound!
Pas un bruit!
2 le **son** *masc (volume)*
Can I turn the sound down?
Je peux baisser le son?
B VERB
That sounds interesting.
Ça a l'air intéressant.
That sounds like a good idea.
C'est une bonne idée.

soup NOUN
la **soupe** *fem*

vegetable soup
la soupe aux légumes

sour ADJECTIVE
aigre

south

south *can be an adjective or a noun.*

A ADJECTIVE
sud *masc, fem, pl*
the south coast
la côte sud
B NOUN
le **sud** *masc*
in the south
dans le sud
the South of France
le sud de la France
Arles is in the South of France.
Arles est dans le sud de la France.

southern ADJECTIVE
Southern England
le sud de l'Angleterre

South Pole NOUN
le **pôle Sud** *masc*

South Wales NOUN
le **sud du Pays de Galles** *masc*

souvenir NOUN
le **souvenir** *masc*
a souvenir shop
une boutique de souvenirs

space NOUN
1 la **place** *fem (room)*
There's lots of space.
Il y a beaucoup de place.
2 l' **espace** *masc (gap)*
Leave a space for a picture.
Laissez un espace pour le dessin.

3 la **case** *fem (in game)*
Go back three spaces.
Recule de trois cases.
4 l' **espace** *masc (outer space)*

spaceship NOUN
le **vaisseau spatial** *masc*

spade NOUN
1 la **pelle** *fem (shovel)*
a bucket and spade
un seau et une pelle
2 *(in cards)*
spades
le pique
the ace of spades
l'as de pique

Spain NOUN
l' **Espagne** *fem*

Spanish

> **Spanish** *can be an adjective or a noun.*

A ADJECTIVE
espagnol *masc*
espagnole *fem*
He's Spanish.
Il est espagnol.
She's Spanish.
Elle est espagnole.
B NOUN
l' **espagnol** *masc (language)*

> **Language tip**
> **Spanish** *always has a capital letter, but* **espagnol** *doesn't.*

spare room NOUN
la **chambre d'amis** *fem*

spare time NOUN
le **temps libre** *masc*
What do you do in your spare time?
Qu'est-ce que tu fais pendant ton temps libre?

sparkling ADJECTIVE
pétillant *masc*
pétillante *fem*
a bottle of sparkling water
une bouteille d'eau pétillante
sparkling wine
le mousseux

speak VERB
parler
Please could you speak more slowly.
Vous pouvez parler plus lentement, s'il vous plaît?

> **I speak French.**
> Je parle français.
> **Do you speak English?**
> Est-ce que vous parlez anglais?

special ADJECTIVE
spécial *masc*
spéciale *fem*

speciality NOUN
la **spécialité** *fem*

specially ADVERB
surtout
It rains a lot, specially in winter.
Il pleut beaucoup, surtout en hiver.

spectator NOUN
le **spectateur** *masc*
la **spectatrice** *fem*

speech NOUN
le **discours** *masc*

speed NOUN
la **vitesse** *fem*
a ten-speed bike
un vélo à dix vitesses

speedboat NOUN
la **vedette** *fem*

spell VERB
1 **écrire** *(in writing)*
How do you spell that?
Comment ça s'écrit?

Language tip
You can also say Ça s'écrit
comment? *or* Comment est-ce
que ça s'écrit?

2 **épeler** *(out loud)*
Can you spell that please?
Est-ce que vous pouvez l'épeler,
s'il vous plaît?

spelling NOUN
l' **orthographe** *fem*
a spelling mistake
une faute d'orthographe

spend VERB
1 **dépenser** *(money)*
I spent £20 on presents.
J'ai dépensé vingt livres en
cadeaux.
2 **passer** *(time)*
**We are going to spend two
weeks in France.**
Nous allons passer deux
semaines en France.

spicy ADJECTIVE
épicé *masc*
épicée *fem*

spider NOUN
l' **araignée** *fem*

spinach NOUN
les **épinards** *masc pl*

spite NOUN
in spite of
malgré
in spite of the weather
malgré le temps

split VERB
1 **se séparer** *(divide)*
Split into two groups.
Séparez-vous en deux groupes.
2 **partager** *(share)*
**Let's split the money
between us.**
Partageons l'argent entre nous.

spoiled ADJECTIVE
gâté *masc*
gâtée *fem*
a spoiled child
un enfant gâté

spoilsport NOUN
le/la **trouble-fête** *masc, fem, pl*
Don't be a spoilsport!
Ne joue pas les trouble-fête!

spoilt ADJECTIVE
gâté *masc*
gâtée *fem*
a spoilt child
un enfant gâté

sponge NOUN
l' **éponge** *fem*

sponge bag NOUN
la **trousse de toilette** *fem*

sponge cake NOUN
le **biscuit de Savoie** masc

sponsor VERB
parrainer
Twenty people are sponsoring me.
Vingt personnes me parrainent.

Did you know…?
Getting sponsored for charity is not very common in France.

spoon NOUN
la **cuillère** fem
I haven't got a spoon.
Je n'ai pas de cuillère.

sport NOUN
le **sport** masc
What's your favourite sport?
Quel est ton sport préféré?
It's my favourite sport.
C'est mon sport préféré.
What sports do you play?
Qu'est-ce que tu fais comme sport?

sports bag NOUN
le **sac de sport** masc

sports car NOUN
la **voiture de sport** fem

spot

spot can be a noun or a verb.

A NOUN
1 le **pois** masc (dot)
a red dress with white spots
une robe rouge à pois blancs

2 le **bouton** masc (pimple)
He's covered in spots.
Il est couvert de boutons.
B VERB
trouver
Can you spot the odd one out?
Trouvez-vous l'intrus?

spring NOUN
le **printemps** masc
It's the first day of spring.
C'est le premier jour du printemps.

in spring
au printemps

springtime NOUN
le **printemps** masc

in springtime
au printemps

sprouts PL NOUN
les **choux de Bruxelles** masc pl

square NOUN
1 le **carré** masc (shape)
a square and a triangle
un carré et un triangle
2 la **place** fem (in town)
There's a statue in the middle of the square.
Il y a une statue au centre de la place.

squash NOUN
1 (drink) **orange squash**
l'orangeade fem
2 le **squash** masc (sport)
I play squash.
Je joue au squash.

squirrel NOUN
l' **écureuil** masc

stable NOUN
l' **écurie** fem

English French

a
b
c
d
e
f
g
h
i
j
k
l
m
n
o
p
q
r
s
t
u
v
w
x
y
z

stack NOUN
la **pile** *fem*
a stack of books
une pile de livres

stadium NOUN
le **stade** *masc*

staff NOUN
1 les **profs** *masc pl* (in school)

staffroom NOUN
la **salle des profs** *fem*

staircase NOUN
l' **escalier** *masc*

stairs PL NOUN
l' **escalier** *masc*
Go down the stairs.
Descends l'escalier.

Language tip
escalier *is a singular word.*

stamp

stamp can be a noun or a verb.

A NOUN
le **timbre** *masc*
a French stamp
un timbre français
My hobby is stamp collecting.
Je collectionne les timbres.

B VERB
taper du pied
Stamp your feet, everybody!
Tapez des pieds, tout le monde!

stamp album NOUN
l' **album de timbres** *masc*

stamp collection NOUN
la **collection de timbres** *fem*

stand VERB
Stand in a line.
Mettez-vous en rang.

Stand over there, Alain.
Mets-toi là, Alain.

stand for VERB
être l'abréviation de
'SVP' stands for 's'il vous plaît'.
'SVP' est l'abréviation de 's'il vous plaît'.

Language tip
What are the two differences in the spelling of the French word **abréviation** *and the English word* **abbreviation**?

stand up VERB
se lever
Stand up, Élodie!
Lève-toi, Élodie!
Stand up, children!
Levez-vous, les enfants!

star NOUN
1 l' **étoile** *fem* (in sky)
the moon and the stars
la lune et les étoiles

2 la **vedette** *fem* (person)
He's a TV star.
C'est une vedette de la télé.

start

start can be a verb or a noun.

A VERB
1 **commencer** (begin)

571

What time does it start?
Ça commence à quelle heure?
It starts with a P.
Ça commence par un P.
I'll start again.
Je recommence.

Language tip

When **start** is followed by another
verb it is translated by **commencer à**.

Let's start playing.
On commence à jouer.
You can start writing now.
Vous pouvez commencer à
écrire maintenant.
Don't start being silly, Anne.
Ne commence pas à faire
l'imbécile, Anne.

Let's start.
On commence.
Start now, children.
Commencez maintenant,
les enfants.
Fleur, you start.
Commence, Fleur.

2 créer *(set up)*
We want to start a French club.
On veut créer un club de français.
B NOUN
1 le **début** *masc*
at the start of December
début décembre
Shall we make a start?
On commence?
2 le **départ** *masc (of race)*

starter NOUN
l' **entrée** *fem*

starve VERB
I'm starving!
Je meurs de faim!

station NOUN
la **gare** *fem*

Where is the station?
Où est la gare?

statue NOUN
la **statue** *fem*

stay

stay *can be a verb or a noun.*

A VERB
1 rester *(remain)*
Stay here, Michelle!
Reste ici, Michelle!
Stay in the garden, children.
Restez dans le jardin, les enfants.
2 loger *(spend the night)*
**We're going to stay with
friends.**
Nous allons loger chez des amis.
Where are you staying?
Où est-ce que vous logez?
**We stayed in Paris for three
days.**
Nous avons passé trois jours à
Paris.
B NOUN
le **séjour** *masc*
my stay in France
mon séjour en France

stay in VERB
rester à la maison
I'm staying in tonight.
Ce soir je reste à la maison.

steak NOUN
le **steak** *masc*
I'd like steak and chips.
Je voudrais un steak frites.

steal VERB
voler
Who's stolen my pencil case?
Qui a volé ma trousse?

step NOUN
1 le **pas** *masc (pace)*
   a step backwards
   un pas en arrière
   Take a step forward, boys.
   Faites un pas en avant, les garçons.
2 la **marche** *fem (stair)*
   Mind the step.
   Attention à la marche.

stepbrother NOUN
le **demi-frère** *masc*
   his stepbrother
   son demi-frère

stepfather NOUN
le **beau-père** *masc*
   my stepfather
   mon beau-père

stepmother NOUN
la **belle-mère** *fem*
   my stepmother
   ma belle-mère

stepsister NOUN
la **demi-sœur** *fem*
   her stepsister
   sa demi-sœur

stew NOUN
le **ragoût** *masc*

stewardess NOUN
l' **hôtesse de l'air** *fem*

stick VERB
coller
   Stick the stamps on the envelope.
   Collez les timbres sur l'enveloppe.

stick out VERB
   Don't stick out your tongue!
   Ne tire pas la langue!

sticker NOUN
l' **autocollant** *masc*

still

> *still can be an adverb or an adjective.*

A ADVERB
encore
   You've still got two cards.
   Tu as encore deux cartes.
   I'm still hungry.
   J'ai encore faim.
B ADJECTIVE
   Keep still, Charlotte!
   Ne bouge pas, Charlotte!
   Sit still, David!
   Reste tranquille, David!

stitch NOUN
le **point de suture** *masc*
   I've got five stitches.
   J'ai cinq points de suture.

stomach NOUN
l' **estomac** *masc*

stomachache NOUN
   I've got stomachache.
   J'ai mal au ventre.

stone NOUN
1 la **pierre** *fem (rock)*
   a stone wall
   un mur en pierre
2 *(in weight)*
   I weigh five stone.
   Je pèse trente kilos.

> **Did you know…?**
> *In France, weight is always given in kilos. A stone is about 6.3 kg.*

stool NOUN
le **tabouret** *masc*

stop

> *stop can be a verb or a noun.*

English French

a b c d e f g h i j k l m n o p q r s t u v w x y z

A VERB
arrêter
Stop, that's enough!
Arrête, ça suffit!
Stop talking, children.
Arrêtez de parler, les enfants.

Stop it!
Arrête!

B NOUN
l' **arrêt** masc
a bus stop
un arrêt de bus

storey NOUN
l' **étage** masc
a three-storey building
un immeuble à trois étages

storm NOUN
1 la **tempête** fem (with strong winds)
2 l' **orage** masc (thunderstorm)

stormy ADJECTIVE
stormy weather
un temps orageux

story NOUN
l' **histoire** fem
I'm going to tell you a story.
Je vais vous raconter une histoire.

stove NOUN
la **cuisinière** fem

straight

straight can be an adjective or an adverb.

A ADJECTIVE
droit masc
droite fem
a straight line
une ligne droite
2 **raide** (hair)
I've got straight hair.
J'ai les cheveux raides.
B ADVERB
straight away
tout de suite
straight on
tout droit

Go straight on.
Allez tout droit.

strange ADJECTIVE
bizarre
That's strange!
C'est bizarre!

stranger NOUN
l' **inconnu** masc
l' **inconnue** fem
Don't talk to strangers.
Ne parle pas aux inconnus.
I'm a stranger here.
Je ne suis pas d'ici.

strap NOUN
le **bracelet** masc
I need a new strap for my watch.
J'ai besoin d'un nouveau bracelet pour ma montre.

straw NOUN
la **paille** fem

strawberry NOUN
la **fraise** fem

strawberry jam
la confiture de fraises
a strawberry ice cream
une glace à la fraise

stream NOUN
le **ruisseau** *masc*
(PL les **ruisseaux**)

street NOUN
la **rue** *fem*
in the street
dans la rue

stretch VERB
Stretch up high!
Étirez-vous!
Stretch out your arms!
Tendez les bras!

strict ADJECTIVE
strict *masc*
stricte *fem*

strike NOUN
la **grève** *fem*
They are on strike.
Ils sont en grève.

striker NOUN
le **buteur** *masc* *(footballer)*

string NOUN
1 la **ficelle** *fem*
a piece of string
un bout de ficelle
2 la **corde** *fem* *(of violin, guitar)*

stripe NOUN
la **rayure** *fem*

stripy ADJECTIVE
rayé *masc*
rayée *fem*
a stripy shirt
une chemise rayée

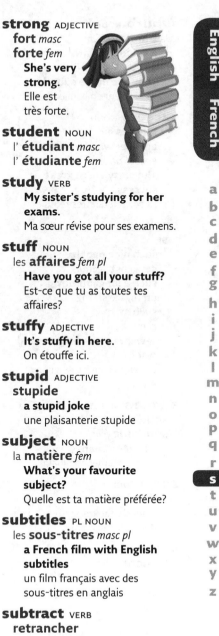

strong ADJECTIVE
fort *masc*
forte *fem*
She's very strong.
Elle est très forte.

student NOUN
l' **étudiant** *masc*
l' **étudiante** *fem*

study VERB
My sister's studying for her exams.
Ma sœur révise pour ses examens.

stuff NOUN
les **affaires** *fem pl*
Have you got all your stuff?
Est-ce que tu as toutes tes affaires?

stuffy ADJECTIVE
It's stuffy in here.
On étouffe ici.

stupid ADJECTIVE
stupide
a stupid joke
une plaisanterie stupide

subject NOUN
la **matière** *fem*
What's your favourite subject?
Quelle est ta matière préférée?

subtitles PL NOUN
les **sous-titres** *masc pl*
a French film with English subtitles
un film français avec des sous-titres en anglais

subtract VERB
retrancher
Subtract three from five.
Retranchez trois à cinq.

suburb NOUN
la **banlieue** *fem*
a suburb of Paris
une banlieue de Paris
They live in the suburbs.
Ils habitent en banlieue.

success NOUN
le **succès** *masc*
another wonderful success
encore un formidable succès
The party was a great success.
La soirée était très réussie.

such ADVERB
si
such nice people
des gens si gentils
such a long journey
un voyage si long
such as
comme
towns such as Avignon and Arles
des villes comme Avignon et Arles

sudden ADJECTIVE
soudain *masc*
soudaine *fem*
a sudden change
un changement soudain

suede NOUN
le **daim** *masc*
a suede jacket
une veste en daim

sugar NOUN
le **sucre** *masc*
Do you take sugar?
Est-ce que vous prenez du sucre?
More sugar?
Encore un peu de sucre?

suggestion NOUN
la **suggestion** *fem*
Have you got any suggestions?
Vous avez des suggestions?

suit

suit *can be a noun or a verb.*

A NOUN
1 le **costume** *masc (man's)*
2 le **tailleur** *masc (woman's)*
B VERB
That dress suits you.
Cette robe te va bien.

suitcase NOUN
la **valise** *fem*

summer NOUN
l' **été** *masc*
We're going to France this summer.
Nous allons en France cet été.

in summer
en été
this summer
cet été
last summer
l'été dernier

summer holidays PL NOUN
les **vacances d'été** *fem pl*
in the summer holidays
pendant les vacances d'été

summertime NOUN
l' **été** *masc*

in summertime
en été

summit NOUN
le **sommet** *masc*

sums PL NOUN
le **calcul** *masc*
She's good at sums.
Elle est bonne en calcul.

Language tip
calcul *is a singular word.*

sun NOUN
le **soleil** *masc*
in the sun
au soleil

sunbathe VERB
se faire bronzer
I like sunbathing.
J'aime me faire bronzer.

sunburnt ADJECTIVE
I got sunburnt.
J'ai attrapé un coup de soleil.

sun cream NOUN
la **crème solaire** *fem*

Sunday NOUN
le **dimanche** *masc*
It's Sunday today.
Aujourd'hui, c'est dimanche

on Sunday
dimanche
on Sundays
le dimanche

every Sunday
tous les dimanches
last Sunday
dimanche dernier
next Sunday
dimanche prochain

Language tip
Days of the week are not written with a capital letter in French.

Sunday school NOUN
le **catéchisme** *masc*

Did you know…?
In France, **le catéchisme** *is on Wednesday mornings, when most children don't have ordinary school.*

sunflower NOUN
le **tournesol** *masc*

sunglasses PL NOUN
les **lunettes de soleil** *fem pl*
a pair of sunglasses
une paire de lunettes de soleil

sunny ADJECTIVE
It's a sunny day.
C'est une belle journée.

It's sunny.
Il fait du soleil.

sunset NOUN
le **coucher du soleil** *masc*
at sunset
au coucher du soleil

sunshine NOUN
le **soleil** *masc*
lots of sunshine
beaucoup de soleil

super ADJECTIVE
formidable

a b c d e f g h i j k l m n o p q r s t u v w x y z

577

supermarket NOUN
le **supermarché** *masc*

supper NOUN
le **dîner** *masc*

supply teacher NOUN
le **suppléant** *masc*
la **suppléante** *fem*
She's a supply teacher.
Elle est suppléante.

Language tip
You do not translate **'a'** *when you say what someone's job is in French.*

support VERB
être supporter de
I support Manchester United.
Je suis supporter de Manchester United.
What team do you support?
Tu es supporter de quelle équipe?

supporter NOUN
le **supporter** *masc*
a Liverpool supporter
un supporter de Liverpool

suppose VERB
imaginer
I suppose he's late.
J'imagine qu'il est en retard.
You're not supposed to do that, Thérèse.
Tu n'es pas censée faire ça, Thérèse.

sure ADJECTIVE
sûr *masc*
sûre *fem*
Are you sure, Inès?
Tu es sûre, Inès?

I'm not sure.
Je ne suis pas sûr.

surface NOUN
la **surface** *fem*

surfboard NOUN
la **planche de surf** *fem*

surfing NOUN
le **surf** *masc*
I go surfing.
Je fais du surf.

surname NOUN
le **nom de famille** *masc*
What's your surname?
Quel est votre nom de famille?

surprise NOUN
la **surprise** *fem*
What a surprise!
Quelle surprise!

survey NOUN
le **sondage** *masc*
We're doing a survey on pets.
On fait un sondage sur les animaux domestiques.

suspend VERB
He's been suspended.
Il s'est fait exclure.

swam VERB ▷*see* **swim**

swan NOUN
le **cygne** *masc*

swap VERB
échanger
Do you want to swap?
Tu veux échanger?
Let's swap places.
Changeons de place.

sweater NOUN
le **pull** *masc*
a white sweater
un pull blanc

sweatshirt NOUN
le **sweat** *masc*
a dark green sweatshirt
un sweat vert foncé

sweet

> **sweet** *can be a noun or an adjective.*

A NOUN
1 le **bonbon** *masc (candy)*
a bag of sweets
un paquet de bonbons
2 le **dessert** *masc (pudding)*
Sweets: ice cream or chocolate mousse
Desserts: glace ou mousse au chocolat
B ADJECTIVE
1 **sucré** *masc*
sucrée *fem (sugary)*
It's too sweet.
C'est trop sucré.
2 **gentil** *masc*
gentille *fem (kind)*
She's a sweet person.
Elle est gentille.
3 **mignon** *masc*
mignonne *fem (cute)*
Isn't she sweet?
Comme elle est mignonne!

sweetcorn NOUN
le **maïs doux** *masc*

sweetie NOUN
le **bonbon** *masc*

swim

> **swim** *can be a verb or a noun.*

A VERB
nager
Can you swim?
Tu sais nager?

I can swim.
Je sais nager.
I can't swim.
Je ne sais pas nager.
B NOUN
I want to go for a swim.
Je veux aller me baigner.

swimmer NOUN
le **nageur** *masc*
la **nageuse** *fem*
She's a good swimmer.
C'est une bonne nageuse.

swimming NOUN
la **natation** *fem*
Do you like swimming?
Tu aimes la natation?
I go swimming on Wednesdays.
Je vais à la piscine le mercredi.

swimming costume NOUN
le **maillot de bain** *masc*

swimming pool NOUN
la **piscine** *fem*

swimming trunks PL NOUN
le **maillot de bain** *masc*
I've got new swimming trunks.
J'ai un nouveau maillot de bain.

> *Language tip*
> **maillot de bain** *is a singular word.*

swimsuit NOUN
le **maillot de bain** *masc*

swing NOUN
la **balançoire** *fem*

Swiss ADJECTIVE
suisse
Sabine is Swiss.
Sabine est suisse.

English French

a b c d e f g h i j k l m n o p q r **s** t u v w x y z

Language tip
Swiss *is always written with a capital letter,* **suisse** *is not.*

switch

switch can be a noun or a verb.

A NOUN
le **bouton** *masc*
Where's the switch?
Où est le bouton?

B VERB
changer de
Switch partners!
Changez de partenaire!

switch off VERB
éteindre
Switch off the computer, Nina.
Éteins l'ordinateur, Nina.

switch on VERB
allumer
Switch on the light, Pierre.
Allume la lumière, Pierre.

Switzerland NOUN
la **Suisse** *fem*

swop VERB
échanger
Do you want to swop?
Tu veux échanger?
Let's swop places.
Changeons de place.

symbol NOUN
le **symbole** *masc*

sympathetic ADJECTIVE
compréhensif *masc*
compréhensive *fem*

T t

table NOUN
la **table** *fem*
> **It's on the table.**
> C'est sur la table.
> **the three times table**
> la table de trois

tablecloth NOUN
la **nappe** *fem*

tablespoon NOUN
la **grande cuillère** *fem*

table tennis NOUN
le **ping-pong** *masc*

tail NOUN
la **queue** *fem*
> **Pin the tail on the donkey.**
> Accroche la queue à l'âne.

Language tip

la **queue** *also has the same meaning as 'queue' in English. Queues are often long and thin, like a tail.*

Heads or tails?
Pile ou face?

---

take
1 prendre *(thing)*
> **Take a card, Luc.**
> Prends une carte, Luc.

Take one card each.
Prenez une carte chacun.
I don't take sugar.
Je ne prends pas de sucre.
It takes about an hour.
Ça prend environ une heure.
Who's taken my ruler?
Qui a pris ma règle?

2 emmener *(person)*
> **Mum's going to take me to the fair.**
> Maman va m'emmener à la fête foraine.

take away VERB
> **30 take away 9 is 21.**
> Trente moins neuf égale vingt et un.

take back VERB
rapporter
> **I'm going to take this book back to the library.**
> Je vais rapporter ce livre à la bibliothèque.

take down VERB
enlever
> **Take the posters down.**
> Enlève les posters.

taken VERB ▷ *see* **take**

take off VERB
enlever
> **Take your coats off.**
> Enlevez vos manteaux.

takeoff NOUN
le **décollage** *masc*

take out VERB
sortir
> **I take the dog out at about six o'clock.**
> Je sors le chien vers six heures.

a
b
c
d
e
f
g
h
i
j
k
l
m
n
o
p
q
r
s
t
u
v
w
x
y
z

talk

talk can be a verb or a noun.

A VERB
parler
You talk too much.
Tu parles trop.
Today we're going to talk about Paris.
Aujourd'hui nous allons parler de Paris.

B NOUN
Let's have a talk about it.
Parlons-en.

talkative ADJECTIVE
bavard *masc*
bavarde *fem*

tall ADJECTIVE
1 **grand** *masc*
grande *fem* (person, tree)
Clément is tall.
Clément est grand.
Yvette is tall.
Yvette est grande.
2 **haut** *masc*
haute *fem*
(building)
a very tall building
un très haut immeuble

How tall are you?
Tu mesures combien?
I'm one metre thirty tall.
Je mesure un mètre trente.

tan NOUN
le **bronzage** *masc*
She's got an amazing tan.
Elle a un bronzage superbe.

tangerine NOUN
la **mandarine** *fem*

tap NOUN
le **robinet** *masc*
Turn on the tap.
Ouvre le robinet.

tap-dancing NOUN
les **claquettes** *fem pl*
I do tap-dancing.
Je fais des claquettes.

tape

tape can be a verb or a noun.

A VERB
enregistrer
I'm going to tape the song.
Je vais enregistrer la chanson.
B NOUN
la **cassette** *fem*
a tape of Kylie Minogue
une cassette de Kylie Minogue

tape recorder NOUN
le **magnétophone** *masc*

target NOUN
la **cible** *fem*

tart NOUN
la **tarte** *fem*
an apple tart
une tarte aux pommes

tartan ADJECTIVE
écossais *masc*
écossaise *fem*
a tartan scarf
une écharpe écossaise

Language tip
écossais *can also mean Scottish.*

taste

taste can be a noun or a verb.

A NOUN
le **goût** masc
It's got a strange taste.
Ça a un goût bizarre.
Would you like a taste?
Tu veux goûter?

B VERB
goûter
Would you like to taste it?
Vous voulez y goûter?

tasty ADJECTIVE
savoureux masc
savoureuse fem

tattoo NOUN
le **tatouage** masc

taxi NOUN
le **taxi** masc
by taxi
en taxi

taxi driver NOUN
le **chauffeur de taxi**
masc

tea

1 NOUN
le **thé** masc (drink)
a cup of tea
une tasse de thé
tea with milk
du thé au lait

Did you know…?

In France, it is more common to
have lemon with your tea.

2 le **dîner** masc (evening meal)
We were having tea.
Nous étions en train de dîner.

tea bag NOUN
le **sachet de thé** masc

teach VERB
1 **enseigner** (in school)
**Mrs Morrison teaches us
French.**
Madame Morrison nous
enseigne le français.
2 **apprendre**
**My cousin is teaching me the
guitar.**
Ma cousine m'apprend la
guitare.

teacher NOUN
1 le **professeur des écoles**
masc (in primary school)
Mr Price is our teacher.
Mr Price est notre professeur.
2 le **professeur** masc (in
secondary school)
a maths teacher
un professeur de maths
She's a teacher.
Elle est professeur.

Language tip

When you say what someone's job is
in French, you do not translate **a**.

team NOUN
l' **équipe** fem
a football team
une équipe de football
She's in my team.
Elle est dans mon équipe.
**We're going to divide the
class into two teams.**
On va diviser la classe en deux
équipes.

teaspoon NOUN
la **petite cuillère** fem

teatime NOUN
l' **heure du dîner** fem
at teatime
à l'heure du dîner

tea towel NOUN
le **torchon** *masc*

technology NOUN
la **technologie** *fem*

teddy bear
NOUN
le **nounours**
masc

teenager NOUN
l' **adolescent** *masc*
l' **adolescente** *fem*

teens PL NOUN
She's in her teens.
C'est une adolescente.
He's in his teens.
C'est un adolescent.

tee-shirt NOUN
le **tee-shirt** *masc*

teeth PL NOUN
les **dents** *fem pl*
I clean my teeth three times a day.
Je me brosse les dents trois fois par jour.

telephone NOUN
le **téléphone** *masc*
on the telephone
au téléphone

telephone call NOUN
le **coup de téléphone** *masc*

telephone number NOUN
le **numéro de téléphone** *masc*

television NOUN
la **télévision** *fem*
on television
à la télévision

television programme
NOUN
l' **émission de télévision** *fem*

tell VERB
1 dire
Tell me why, Marc.
Dis-moi pourquoi, Marc.
Tell me your names.
Dites-moi vos noms.
I'm going to tell my mum.
Je vais le dire à ma maman.
I told you to wait.
Je t'ai dit d'attendre.
2 parler *(talk about)*
I'll tell you about myself.
Je vais te parler de moi.
Tell your penfriends about yourselves.
Parlez de vous à vos correspondants.
3 raconter *(story)*
I'm going to tell you a story.
Je vais vous raconter une histoire.

tell off VERB
gronder
She tells me off if I'm late.
Elle me gronde si je suis en retard.

telly NOUN
la **télé** *fem*
I watch telly a lot.
Je regarde beaucoup la télé.
on telly
à la télé

temperature NOUN
I've got a temperature.
J'ai de la fièvre.

ten NUMBER
dix
ten euros
dix euros

It's ten to three.
Il est trois heures moins dix.
It's ten past two.
Il est deux heures dix.

I'm ten.
J'ai dix ans.

Language tip

*In English, you can say **ten** or **ten years old**. In French, you can only say **dix ans**.*

tennis NOUN
le **tennis** *masc*
I play tennis.
Je joue au tennis.

tennis ball NOUN
la **balle de tennis** *fem*

tennis court NOUN
le **court de tennis** *masc*

tennis racket NOUN
la **raquette de tennis** *fem*

tennis player NOUN
le **joueur de tennis** *masc*
la **joueuse de tennis** *fem*

tenpin bowling NOUN
le **bowling** *masc*
Do you want to go tenpin bowling?
Tu veux jouer au bowling?

tent NOUN
la **tente** *fem*

Language tip

What extra vowel does the French word have that the English word doesn't?

tenth ADJECTIVE
dixième
on the tenth floor
au dixième étage

the tenth of August
le dix août

term NOUN
le **trimestre** *masc*
It'll soon be the end of term.
C'est bientôt la fin du trimestre.

terrible ADJECTIVE
épouvantable
My French is terrible.
Mon français est épouvantable.

terrified ADJECTIVE
terrifié *masc*
terrifiée *fem*
I was terrified!
J'étais terrifié!

test NOUN
l' **interrogation** *fem*
I've got a test tomorrow.
J'ai une interrogation demain.

text

text can be a noun or a verb.

A NOUN
le **SMS** *masc*
Send me a text.
Envoie-moi un SMS.
B VERB
envoyer un SMS à
J'ai envoyé un SMS à Lara.
I texted Lara.

textbook NOUN
le **manuel** *masc*
a French textbook
un manuel de français

English French

a b c d e f g h i j k l m n o p q r **s** t u v w x y z

text message NOUN
le **SMS** *masc*

than CONJUNCTION
que
   She's taller than me.
   Elle est plus grande que moi.
   Are you older than him?
   Tu es plus vieux que lui?

thank you EXCLAMATION
merci!

Thank you very much.
Merci beaucoup.

thanks EXCLAMATION
merci!
   No thanks.
   Non merci.

that

that *can be a pronoun, an adjective or a conjunction.*

A PRONOUN
ça
Do you see that?
Tu vois ça?
That's my brother.
C'est mon frère.
That's my friend Bernadette.
C'est mon amie Bernadette.
That's right! Well done.
C'est ça! Bravo!

What's that?
Qu'est-ce que c'est?
How much is that?
C'est combien?
Who's that?
C'est qui?
I know that.
Je le sais.
Is that him?
C'est lui?
Is that her?
C'est elle?

B ADJECTIVE
ce *masc*
cette *fem*
that dog
ce chien
that woman
cette femme

Language tip

Ce *changes to* **cet** *with masculine nouns starting with a vowel sound.*

that man
cet homme
that bird
cet oiseau

Language tip

When you say **that one** *when you are pointing, use* **celui-là** *if the French noun is masculine, and* **celle-là** *if it is feminine.*

This man? — No, that one.
Cet homme-ci? — Non, celui-là.
This colour? — No, that one.
Cette couleur? — Non, celle-là.

C CONJUNCTION
que
I think that you're right.
Je pense que tu as raison.
I think that it's raining.
Je crois qu'il pleut.

I think that Henri is ill.
Je crois qu'Henri est malade.

the ARTICLE

> *Language tip*
> Use **le** with a masculine noun, and
> **la** with a feminine noun. Use **l'**
> before a vowel sound. For plural
> nouns always use **les**.

le
　the boy
　le garçon
l'
　the man
　l'homme
　the orange
　l'orange

la
　the girl
　la fille
les
　the children
　les enfants

theatre NOUN
　le **théâtre** *masc*

their ADJECTIVE
　leur *masc, fem* (PL **leurs**)
　their house
　leur maison
　their parents
　leurs parents

theirs PRONOUN
　à eux *masc pl* (FEM PL **à elles**)
　This car is theirs.
　Cette voiture est à eux.
　Whose is this? — It's theirs.
　C'est à qui? — À eux.

them PRONOUN
　1 les

I can't see them.
Je ne les vois pas.
Do you want them?
Tu les veux?
2 leur *(for them, to them)*
　**I'm going to buy them a
　present.**
　Je vais leur acheter un cadeau.
　Can you give them a message?
　Tu peux leur donner un message?
3 eux *masc pl*
　elles *fem pl (after a preposition)*
　It's not for you, it's for them.
　Ce n'est pas pour toi, c'est pour
　eux.
　**Ann and Sophie are here,
　and Graham's with them.**
　Ann et Sophie sont là,
　et Graham est avec elles.

theme park NOUN
　le **parc d'attractions** *masc*

themselves PRONOUN
　1 se
　They're enjoying themselves.
　Ils s'amusent.
　2 eux-mêmes *masc pl*
　elles-mêmes *fem pl (by
　themselves)*
　They did it themselves.
　Ils l'ont fait eux-mêmes.

then CONJUNCTION
　ensuite
　**I get dressed. Then I have
　breakfast.**
　Je m'habille. Ensuite je prends
　mon petit déjeuner.

there ADVERB
　1 là
　Put it there, on the table.
　Mets-le là, sur la table.
　up there
　là-haut

English French

down there
là-bas
2 y *(to there)*
I'm going there on Friday.
J'y vais vendredi.

Language tip

To say either **there is** or **there are**
use **il y a**.

There's a new boy in the class.
Il y a un nouveau dans la classe.
There are five people in my
family.
Il y a cinq personnes dans ma
famille.
How many biscuits are there?
Il y a combien de biscuits?
There are lots.
Il y en a beaucoup.
There aren't many.
Il n'y en a pas beaucoup.

over there
là-bas
There he is!
Le voilà!
There they are!
Les voilà!
There is ...
Il y a ...
There are ...
Il y a ...

these

these *can be an adjective or a*
pronoun.

A ADJECTIVE
ces
these shoes
ces chaussures

B PRONOUN
ceux-ci *masc pl*
celles-ci *fem pl*
Which sweets do you want?
— These.
Quels bonbons veux-tu?
— Ceux-ci.
Which seats are free?
— These.
Quelles places sont libres?
— Celles-ci.

they PRONOUN

Language tip

Check if **they** stands for a masculine
or feminine noun; **ils** is used for
masculine nouns and **elles** for
feminine nouns.

ils *masc pl*
Where are your friends? —
They're over there.
Où sont tes amis? —
Ils sont là-bas.
elles *fem pl*
Are your socks white? —
No, they're grey.
Tes chaussettes sont blanches?
— Non, elles sont grises.

thief NOUN
le **voleur** *masc*
la **voleuse** *fem*

thin ADJECTIVE
1 mince *(person, slice)*
I'm quite thin.
Je suis assez mince.
2 maigre *(skinny)*
She's got very thin legs.
Elle a les jambes très maigres.

thing NOUN
1 la **chose** *fem*
I've got lots of things to do.
J'ai beaucoup de choses à faire.

English French

a
b
c
d
e
f
g
h
i
j
k
l
m
n
o
p
q
r
s
t
u
v
w
x
y
z

There are beautiful things in the museum.
Il y a de belles choses au musée.

2 *(belongings)*
my things
mes affaires

think

1 **penser** *(believe)*
I think he's here.
Je pense qu'il est là.

I think so.
Oui, je crois.
I don't think so.
Je ne crois pas.

2 **réfléchir** *(spend time thinking)*
Think carefully, Jason.
Réfléchis bien, Jason.
Think carefully, children.
Réfléchissez bien, les enfants.
I'll think about it.
Je vais y réfléchir.

third ADJECTIVE
troisième
It's the third time.
C'est la troisième fois.
I came third.
Je suis arrivé troisième.

the third of March
le trois mars

thirsty ADJECTIVE
Are you thirsty?
Tu as soif?

I'm not thirsty.
Je n'ai pas soif.

I'm thirsty.
J'ai soif.

thirteen NUMBER
treize
thirteen euros
treize euros

I'm thirteen.
J'ai treize ans.

Language tip

*In English, you can say **thirteen** or **thirteen years old**. In French, you can only say **treize ans**.*

thirteenth ADJECTIVE
treizième
on the thirteenth floor
au treizième étage

the thirteenth of August
le treize août

thirty NUMBER
trente
My aunt is thirty.
Ma tante a trente ans.

Language tip

*In English, you can say **thirty** or **thirty years old**. In French, you can only say **trente ans**.*

this

this *can be an adjective or a pronoun.*

A ADJECTIVE
ce *masc*
cette *fem*
this book
ce livre

589

this time
cette fois

> **Language tip**
> Use **cet** with masculine nouns starting with a vowel sound.

this man
cet homme

> **Language tip**
> For **this one** use **celui-ci** if the French noun it refers to is masculine, and **celle-ci** if it is feminine.

Which T-shirt do you want?
— This one.
Quel tee-shirt veux-tu?
— Celui-ci.
That card? — No, this one.
Cette carte-là? — Non, celle-ci.

B PRONOUN
ça
Look at this.
Regarde ça.

> **this morning**
> ce matin
> **this year**
> cette année
> **this afternoon**
> cet après-midi
> **What's this?**
> Qu'est-ce que c'est?

those

> **those** can be an adjective or a pronoun.

A ADJECTIVE
ces
those shoes
ces chaussures
B PRONOUN
ceux-là masc pl
celles-là fem pl

Which sweets do you want?
— Those.
Quels bonbons veux-tu?
— Ceux-là.
Which seats are free?
— Those.
Quelles places sont libres?
— Celles-là.

thousand NUMBER
a thousand
mille
a thousand euros
mille euros
thousands of people
des milliers de personnes

three NUMBER
trois
three euros
trois euros

> **She's three.**
> Elle a trois ans.

> **Language tip**
> In English, you can say **three** or **three years old**. In French, you can only say **trois ans**.

throat NOUN
la **gorge** fem
I've got a sore throat.
J'ai mal à la gorge.

through PREPOSITION
par
> **through the window**
> par la fenêtre

throw VERB
lancer
> **Throw me the ball.**
> Lance-moi la balle.

throw away VERB
jeter
> **Don't throw it away!**
> Ne le jette pas!

thumb NOUN
le **pouce** *masc*

thunder NOUN
le **tonnerre** *masc*
> **There was thunder and lightning.**
> Il y avait du tonnerre et des éclairs.

thunderstorm NOUN
l' **orage** *masc*

Thursday NOUN
le **jeudi** *masc*
> **It's Thursday today.**
> Aujourd'hui c'est jeudi.

> **on Thursday**
> jeudi
> **on Thursdays**
> le jeudi
> **every Thursday**
> tous les jeudis
> **last Thursday**
> jeudi dernier
> **next Thursday**
> jeudi prochain

Language tip

Days of the week are not written with a capital letter in French.

tick

tick *can be a noun or a verb.*

A NOUN
> **Put a tick or a cross.**
> Cochez ou mettez une croix.

B VERB
cocher
> **Tick the right box.**
> Cochez la bonne case.

ticket NOUN
1 le **ticket** *masc (for bus, tube, cinema, museum)*
> **a bus ticket**
> un ticket de bus
2 le **billet** *masc (for plane, train, concert)*

ticket office NOUN
le **guichet** *masc*

tidy

tidy *can be an adjective or a verb.*

A ADJECTIVE
bien rangé *masc*
bien rangée *fem (place)*
> **My room is tidy.**
> Ma chambre est bien rangée.

B VERB
ranger
> **Go and tidy your room.**
> Va ranger ta chambre.

tidy up VERB
ranger
> **Don't forget to tidy up afterwards, children.**
> N'oubliez pas de ranger après, les enfants.

tie

tie *can be a noun or a verb.*

A NOUN
la **cravate** *fem*

English French

a
b
c
d
e
f
g
h
i
j
k
l
m
n
o
p
q
r
s
t
u
v
w
x
y
z

B VERB
nouer
Tie your laces.
Noue tes lacets.

tiger NOUN
le **tigre** *masc*

tight ADJECTIVE
1 **moulant** *masc*
moulante *fem (tight-fitting)*
a tight skirt
une jupe moulante
2 **juste** *(too tight)*
This dress is a bit tight.
Cette robe est un peu juste.

tights PL NOUN
le **collant** *masc*
I'm wearing black tights.
Je porte un collant noir.

> **Language tip**
> **collant** *is a singular word.*

till

> **till** *can be a noun or a preposition.*

A NOUN
la **caisse** *fem*
at the till
à la caisse
B PREPOSITION
1 **jusqu'à**
He's staying till Monday.
Il reste jusqu'à lundi.
2 **avant** *(with 'not')*
not until tomorrow
pas avant demain

3 **à**
from nine till five
de neuf heures à cinq heures

> **from Monday till Friday**
> du lundi au vendredi

time NOUN
1 l' **heure** *fem (on clock)*
What time is it?
Quelle heure est-il?

> **Language tip**
> *You can also say:* **Il est quelle heure?**

What time?
À quelle heure?
What time do you get up?
À quelle heure tu te lèves?
What time does the train arrive?
Le train arrive à quelle heure?
2 le **temps** *masc (amount of time)*
I'm sorry, I haven't got time.
Je suis désolé, je n'ai pas le temps.
It's time to go.
Il est temps de partir.
3 la **fois** *fem (occasion)*
this time
cette fois
next time
la prochaine fois
the first time
la première fois
two at a time
deux à la fois
two times two is four
deux fois deux égalent quatre

> **What time is it?**
> Quelle heure est-il?
> **It's lunch time.**
> C'est l'heure du déjeuner.

English French

How many times?
Combien de fois?
Have a good time, girls!
Amusez-vous bien, les filles!
Have a good time, Léa!
Amuse-toi bien, Léa!

timetable NOUN
 1 l' **emploi du temps** *masc*
   (at school)
 2 l' **horaire** *masc* (for train, bus)

tin NOUN
 la **boîte** *fem*
   a tin of soup
   une boîte de soupe

tin opener NOUN
 l' **ouvre-boîte** *masc*

tinsel NOUN
 les **guirlandes de Noël** *fem pl*

tiny ADJECTIVE
 minuscule

tip NOUN
 le **pourboire** *masc*
   It's a tip for the waiter.
   C'est un pourboire pour le serveur.

tiptoe NOUN
 on tiptoe
 sur la pointe des pieds

tired ADJECTIVE
 fatigué *masc*
 fatiguée *fem*
   I'm tired.
   Je suis fatigué.

tiring ADJECTIVE
 fatigant *masc*
 fatigante *fem*

tissue NOUN
 le **kleenex**® *masc*
   Have you got a tissue?
   Tu as un kleenex?

title NOUN
 le **titre** *masc*

to PREPOSITION

Language tip
à + **le** *changes to* **au**. à + **les**
changes to **aux**.

 1 **à**
   We're going to London.
   Nous allons à Londres.
   **I go to school with my
   friend.**
   Je vais à l'école avec mon amie.
   We're ready to start.
   Nous sommes prêts à
   commencer.
   **from nine o'clock to half past
   three**
   de neuf heures à trois heures et
   demie
   au
   We're going to a restaurant.
   Nous allons au restaurant.
   aux
   Can I go to the toilet?
   Je peux aller aux toilettes?

Language tip
*To talk about going to a country,
use* **au** *if the country is masculine,*
en *if the country is feminine, and*
aux *if the country is plural.*

   We're going to Wales.
   Nous allons au pays de Galles.
   I'm going to Scotland.
   Je vais en Écosse.
   **We're going to the United
   States.**
   Nous allons aux États-Unis.

a b c d e f g h i j k l m n o p q r s **t** u v w x y z

2 de
the train to London
le train de Londres
the plane to Paris
l'avion pour Paris

3 chez *(to someone's house)*
I'm going to Anne's house.
Je vais chez Anne.
Let's go to mine.
Allons chez moi.
I'm going to the doctor.
Je vais chez le docteur.

4 jusqu'à *(up to)*
Count to ten, everyone.
Comptez jusqu'à dix, tout le monde.

to Paris
à Paris
to France
en France
to Portugal
au Portugal
to the swimming pool
à la piscine
to the supermarket
au supermarché
to my house
chez moi

toad NOUN
le **crapaud** *masc*

toast NOUN
le **pain grillé** *masc*
a piece of toast
une tranche de pain grillé

toastie NOUN
le **sandwich chaud** *masc*

today ADVERB
aujourd'hui
What's the date today?
Quelle est la date aujourd'hui?
It's Monday today.
Aujourd'hui c'est lundi.

toe NOUN
le **doigt de pied** *masc*

Language tip

doigt also means 'finger'. The French **doigt de pied** actually means 'foot finger'!

toffee NOUN
le **caramel** *masc*

together ADVERB
ensemble

toilet NOUN
les **toilettes** *fem pl*
Can I go to the toilet?
Je peux aller aux toilettes?

token NOUN
a gift token
un bon-cadeau

told VERB ▷ *see* **tell**

tomato NOUN
la **tomate**
fem
tomato soup
la soupe
à la tomate

tomorrow ADVERB
demain
Let's go swimming tomorrow.
Allons nager demain.

tomorrow morning
demain matin
the day after tomorrow
après-demain
tomorrow night
demain soir
See you tomorrow.
À demain.

English French

a b c d e f g h i j k l m n o p q r s **t** u v w x y z

tongue NOUN
la **langue** *fem*

> **Language tip**
>
> **la langue** *is related to the word 'language'. You use your tongue to speak a language.*

tonight ADVERB
ce soir
> **Are you going out tonight?**
> Tu sors ce soir?

tonsillitis NOUN
l' **angine** *fem*

too ADVERB
1 **aussi** *(as well)*
> **My sister is coming too.**
> Ma sœur vient aussi.
2 **trop** *(very)*
> **The water's too hot.**
> L'eau est trop chaude.
> **You're too late.**
> Tu arrives trop tard.

> **Language tip**
>
> *You can use* **trop** *with a verb to mean* **too much**.

> **Danielle, you talk too much.**
> Danielle, tu parles trop.
> **It costs too much.**
> Ça coûte trop cher.

> **Language tip**
>
> *You can use* **trop de** *with a noun, to mean* **too much** *or* **too many**.

> **too much noise**
> trop de bruit
> **too many mistakes**
> trop d'erreurs

Me too.
Moi aussi.

toonie NOUN *(Canada)*
le **deux dollars** *masc*

tooth NOUN
la **dent** *fem*

> **Language tip**
>
> **la dent** *is related to the word 'dentist'. A dentist looks after your teeth.*

toothache NOUN
> **I've got toothache.**
> J'ai mal aux dents.

toothbrush NOUN
la **brosse à dents** *fem*

toothpaste NOUN
le **dentifrice** *masc*

top

> **top** *can be a noun or an adjective.*

A NOUN
1 le **haut** *masc*
> **a black skirt and a white top**
> une jupe noire et un haut blanc
> **at the top of the page**
> en haut de la page
2 le **sommet** *masc (of mountain)*
> **the top of Snowdon**
> le sommet de Snowdon
> **on top of**
> sur
> **on top of the fridge**
> sur le frigo
B ADJECTIVE
> **He always gets top marks in French.**
> Il a toujours d'excellentes notes en français.
> **the top floor**
> le dernier étage

595

on the top floor
au dernier étage

torch NOUN
la **lampe de poche** *fem*

tortoise
NOUN
la **tortue**
fem

total NOUN
le **total** *masc* (PL les **totaux**)

touch VERB
toucher
Don't touch that!
N'y touche pas!

tour NOUN
la **visite** *fem*
a tour of the museum
une visite du musée

tourism NOUN
le **tourisme** *masc*

tourist NOUN
le **touriste** *masc*
la **touriste** *fem*
There are lots of tourists.
Il y a beaucoup de touristes.

tourist information office NOUN
l' **office du tourisme** *masc*

towards PREPOSITION
vers
Come towards me.
Viens vers moi.

towel NOUN
la **serviette** *fem*

tower NOUN
la **tour** *fem*
a tower block
une tour

town NOUN
la **ville** *fem*
I'm going into town.
Je vais en ville.
the town centre
le centre-ville

toy NOUN
le **jouet** *masc*

Language tip
The noun **le jouet** *is related to the*
verb **jouer**, *which means 'to play'.*

toy shop NOUN
le **magasin de jouets** *masc*

tracksuit NOUN
le **jogging** *masc*

tractor NOUN
le **tracteur** *masc*

tradition NOUN
la **tradition** *fem*

traffic NOUN
la **circulation** *fem*
There's a lot of traffic.
Il y a beaucoup de circulation.

traffic lights PL NOUN
les **feux** *masc pl*

train NOUN
le **train** *masc*
by train
en train
We're going by train.
Nous y allons en train.

trainers PL NOUN
les **baskets** *fem pl*
a pair of trainers
une paire de baskets

tram NOUN
le **tramway** *masc*

trampoline NOUN
le **trampoline** *masc*

translate VERB
traduire
I can translate the menu into English.
Je sais traduire le menu en anglais.

translation NOUN
la **traduction** *fem*

travel agent's NOUN
l' **agence de voyages** *fem*

travelling NOUN
I love travelling.
J'adore les voyages.

treasure NOUN
le **trésor** *masc*

tree NOUN
l' **arbre** *masc*

triangle NOUN
le **triangle** *masc*

trick NOUN
le **tour** *masc*
I can do magic tricks.
Je sais faire des tours de magie.

trip NOUN
le **voyage** *masc*
We're going on a trip to London.
Nous faisons un voyage à Londres.

Have a good trip!
Bon voyage!

trolley NOUN
le **chariot** *masc*

trouble NOUN
le **problème** *masc*
The trouble is, it's too expensive.
Le problème, c'est que c'est trop cher.
Éric is always getting into trouble.
Éric fait tout le temps des bêtises.

trousers PL NOUN
le **pantalon** *masc*
I'm wearing black trousers.
Je porte un pantalon noir.

Language tip
pantalon *is a singular word.*

trout NOUN
la **truite** *fem*

truck NOUN
le **camion** *masc*

true ADJECTIVE
vrai *masc*
vraie *fem*
That's true.
C'est vrai.
That's not true.
Ce n'est pas vrai.

True or false?
Vrai ou faux?

trumpet NOUN
la **trompette** *fem*
She plays the trumpet.
Elle joue de la trompette.

trunks PL NOUN
le maillot de bain masc
I've got new trunks.
J'ai un nouveau maillot de bain.

Language tip
maillot de bain *is a singular word.*

truth NOUN
la **vérité** fem
Tell me the truth.
Dis-moi la vérité.

try

try can be a verb or a noun.

A VERB
1 essayer (attempt)
I'm going to try.
Je vais essayer.
Try to remember.
Essaie de te souvenir.
Try again, everyone.
Encore une fois, toute la classe.
You're not trying, Éric.
Tu ne fais pas d'effort, Éric.
2 goûter (taste)
Would you like to try some?
Voulez-vous goûter?
B NOUN
l' **essai** masc
his third try
son troisième essai

Good try!
Pas mal!
Can I have a try?
Je peux essayer?

try on VERB
essayer
Can I try it on?
Je peux l'essayer?

T-shirt NOUN
le **tee-shirt** masc

tube NOUN
the Tube
le métro

Tuesday NOUN
le **mardi** masc
It's Tuesday today.
Aujourd'hui c'est mardi.

on Tuesday
mardi
on Tuesdays
le mardi
every Tuesday
tous les mardis
last Tuesday
mardi dernier
next Tuesday
mardi prochain

Language tip
Days of the week are not written with a capital letter in French.

tummy NOUN
le **ventre** masc

tummy ache NOUN
I've got tummy ache.
J'ai mal au ventre.

tuna NOUN
le **thon** masc
a tuna salad
une salade de thon

tune NOUN
l' **air** masc
I know the tune.
Je connais l'air.

tunnel NOUN
le **tunnel** masc
the Channel Tunnel
le tunnel sous la Manche

tuque NOUN (Canada)
la **tuque** fem

turkey NOUN
1 la **dinde** *fem (meat)*
2 le **dindon** *masc (bird)*

turn

> **turn** *can be a noun or a verb.*

A NOUN
le **tour** *masc (go)*
You miss a turn.
Passe ton tour.

> **Whose turn is it?**
> C'est à qui le tour?
> **It's my turn!**
> C'est mon tour!

B VERB
tourner
Turn right at the lights.
Tournez à droite aux feux.

turn off VERB
éteindre
Could you turn off the light?
Tu peux éteindre?

turn on VERB
allumer
Could you turn on the light?
Tu peux allumer?

turn over VERB
retourner
Turn over the cards, everyone.
Retournez les cartes, tout le monde.

turn round VERB
se retourner
Turn round, children!
Retournez-vous, les enfants!

turquoise

> **turquoise** *can be an adjective or a noun.*

A ADJECTIVE
turquoise *masc, fem, pl*
a turquoise top
un haut turquoise

> **Language tip**
> *Colour adjectives come after the noun in French.*

B NOUN
le **turquoise** *masc*
Turquoise is my favourite colour.
Ma couleur préférée, c'est le turquoise.

TV NOUN
la **télé** *fem*
on TV
à la télé

twelfth ADJECTIVE
douzième
on the twelfth floor
au douzième étage

> **the twelfth of August**
> le douze août

twelve NUMBER
douze
twelve euros
douze euros
I have lunch at twelve o'clock.
Je déjeune à midi.

It is twelve thirty.
Il est midi et demi.

twelve o'clock
midi
twelve o'clock at night
minuit
I'm twelve.
J'ai douze ans.

Language tip

In English, you can say **twelve** *or* **twelve years old**. *In French, you can only say* **douze ans**.

twentieth ADJECTIVE
vingtième
    the twentieth time
    la vingtième fois

the twentieth of May
le vingt mai

twenty NUMBER
vingt
    twenty euros
    vingt euros
    It's twenty to two.
    Il est deux heures moins vingt.

    It's twenty past eleven.
    Il est onze heures vingt.

He's twenty.
Il a vingt ans.

Language tip

In English, you can say **twenty** *or* **twenty years old**. *In French, you can only say* **vingt ans**.

twice ADVERB
deux fois

twin NOUN
le **jumeau** *masc*
    (PL les **jumeaux**)
la **jumelle** *fem* (PL les **jumelles**)
    my twin brother
    mon frère jumeau
    her twin sister
    sa sœur jumelle
    identical twins
    les vrais jumeaux

twin room NOUN
la **chambre à deux lits** *fem*

twinned ADJECTIVE
jumelé *masc*
jumelée *fem*
    Stroud is twinned with Châteaubriant.
    Stroud est jumelée avec Châteaubriant.

two NUMBER
deux
    two euros
    deux euros
    Get into twos.
    Mettez-vous deux par deux.

She's two.
Elle a deux ans.

Language tip

In English, you can say **two** *or* **two years old**. *In French, you can only say* **deux ans**.

type NOUN
le **type** *masc*
    What type of camera have you got?
    Quel type d'appareil photo as-tu?

tyre NOUN
le **pneu** *masc*

U u

UFO NOUN
l' **OVNI** masc

ugly ADJECTIVE
laid masc
laide fem

UK NOUN
le **Royaume-Uni** masc
in the UK
au Royaume-Uni
to the UK
au Royaume-Uni
I live in the UK.
J'habite au Royaume-Uni.

Ulster NOUN
l' **Irlande du Nord** fem
in Ulster
en Irlande du Nord

umbrella NOUN
1 le **parapluie** masc

Language tip

The French for rain is 'pluie'. **un parapluie** is something that keeps the rain off you.

2 le **parasol** masc (sunshade)

umpire NOUN
1 le **juge de chaise** masc (in tennis)
2 l' **arbitre** masc (in cricket)

unbeatable ADJECTIVE
imbattable

unbelievable ADJECTIVE
incroyable
That's unbelievable!
C'est incroyable!

uncle NOUN
l' **oncle** masc
my uncle
mon oncle

uncomfortable ADJECTIVE
pas confortable
The seats are rather uncomfortable.
Les sièges ne sont pas très confortables.

under PREPOSITION
1 **sous** (beneath)
The cat's under the table.
Le chat est sous la table.

The tunnel goes under the Channel.
Le tunnel passe sous la Manche.
under there
là-dessous
What's under there?
Qu'est-ce qu'il y a là-dessous?
2 **moins de** (less than)
It costs under £10.
Ça coûte moins de dix livres.
children under ten
les enfants de moins de dix ans

underground

underground can be a noun, an adjective or an adverb.

A NOUN
le **métro** *masc*
by underground
en métro

B ADJECTIVE
souterrain *masc*
souterraine *fem*
an underground car park
un parking souterrain

C ADVERB
sous terre
Moles live underground.
Les taupes vivent sous terre.

underneath

> **underneath** *can be a preposition or an adverb.*

A PREPOSITION
sous
underneath the carpet
sous la moquette

B ADVERB
dessous
Look underneath, Pierre!
Regarde dessous, Pierre!

understand VERB
comprendre

> **Language tip**
>
> *The English words 'comprehend' and 'comprehension' are related to* **comprendre***. Comprehension exercises test your understanding of something.*

Do you all understand?
Vous comprenez tous?
Do you understand, Richard?
Tu comprends, Richard?
I don't understand this word.
Je ne comprends pas ce mot.
I understood almost everything.
J'ai presque tout compris.

It's easy to understand.
C'est facile à comprendre.

> **I don't understand.**
> Je ne comprends pas.
> **Did you understand, Claire?**
> Tu as compris, Claire?
> **Did you understand, children?**
> Vous avez compris, les enfants?

understood VERB ▷*see*
understand

underwear NOUN
les **sous-vêtements** *masc pl*

undone ADJECTIVE
défait *masc*
défaite *fem*
Your laces are undone.
Tes lacets sont défaits.

undressed ADJECTIVE
to get undressed
se déshabiller
I'm getting undressed.
Je me déshabille.

> **Language tip**
>
> **Je m'habille** *means 'I'm getting dressed'. By adding* **dés** *to the start of the French verb, you make the opposite.*

unemployed ADJECTIVE
au chômage
He's unemployed.
Il est au chômage.

unfair ADJECTIVE
injuste
That's unfair!
C'est injuste!

unfashionable ADJECTIVE
démodé *masc*
démodée *fem*

unfold VERB
déplier
> **Unfold the map.**
> Déplie la carte.

unforgettable ADJECTIVE
inoubliable

unfortunately ADVERB
malheureusement
> **Unfortunately it's too late.**
> Malheureusement, c'est trop tard.
> **Unfortunately not.**
> Malheureusement, non.

unhappy ADJECTIVE
malheureux *masc*
malheureuse *fem*
> **He's unhappy at school.**
> Il est malheureux à l'école.
> **You look unhappy.**
> Tu as l'air triste.

uni NOUN
la **fac** *fem*
> **She's at uni.**
> Elle est à la fac.

uniform NOUN
l' **uniforme** *masc*
> **We wear school uniform.**
> Nous portons un uniforme scolaire.

Did you know…?

French children don't wear school uniform.

Union Jack NOUN
le **drapeau du Royaume-Uni** *masc*

Did you know…?

le drapeau tricolore is the French flag: its three colours are blue, white and red.

United Kingdom NOUN
le **Royaume-Uni** *masc*
> **to the United Kingdom**
> au Royaume-Uni
> **in the United Kingdom**
> au Royaume-Uni

United States NOUN
les **États-Unis** *masc pl*
> **in the United States**
> aux États-Unis
> **to the United States**
> aux États-Unis

universe NOUN
l' **univers** *masc*

university NOUN
l' **université** *fem*
> **She's at university.**
> Elle va à l'université.
> **Do you want to go to university?**
> Tu veux aller à l'université?
> **Lancaster University**
> l'université de Lancaster

unless CONJUNCTION
> **Don't do it unless I say 'Simon says'.**
> Ne le faites pas si je ne dis pas 'Jacques a dit'.
> **I'll have that biscuit, unless you want it.**
> Je veux bien ce biscuit si tu n'en veux pas.

unlikely ADJECTIVE
peu probable
> **It's possible, but unlikely.**
> C'est possible, mais peu probable.

unlucky ADJECTIVE
1 *(person)*
> **If you are unlucky, try again.**
> Si tu n'as pas de chance, recommence.
> **I'm always unlucky.**
> Je n'ai jamais de chance.
2 *(number, animal)*
> **Thirteen is an unlucky number.**
> Le nombre treize porte malheur.
> **It's unlucky to walk under a ladder.**
> Ça porte malheur de passer sous une échelle.

> *Did you know...?*
> French people think black cats are unlucky.

unnecessary ADJECTIVE
inutile

unpack VERB
défaire
> **I'm going to unpack my suitcase.**
> Je vais défaire ma valise.

> *Language tip*
> **Je fais ma valise** means 'I'm packing my case'. By adding **dé** to the start of the French verb, you give it the opposite meaning. In English, you add **un** to make the opposite.

unpleasant ADJECTIVE
désagréable

unpopular ADJECTIVE
impopulaire

unpredictable ADJECTIVE
imprévisible
> **The weather is unpredictable.**
> Le temps est imprévisible.

unreliable ADJECTIVE
pas fiable
> **Our car is unreliable.**
> Notre voiture n'est pas fiable.

unsuitable ADJECTIVE
inapproprié *masc*
inappropriée *fem*

untidy ADJECTIVE
en désordre
> **My bedroom's always untidy.**
> Ma chambre est toujours en désordre.
> **My writing is untidy.**
> J'écris mal.

until PREPOSITION
1 **jusqu'à**
> **He's here until tomorrow.**
> Il est là jusqu'à demain.
> **The supermarket is open until ten.**
> Le supermarché reste ouvert jusqu'à dix heures du soir.
2 **avant** *(with 'not')*
> **not until tomorrow**
> pas avant demain
> **When will it be ready? — Not until next week.**
> Quand est-ce que ça sera prêt? — Pas avant la semaine prochaine.
3 **à**
> **from nine until five**
> de neuf heures à cinq heures

> **from Monday until Friday**
> du lundi jusqu'au vendredi

unusual ADJECTIVE
  peu courant *masc*
  peu courante *fem*
    It's an unusual name.
    C'est un nom peu courant.

up

> **up** *can be an adverb, an adjective or a preposition.*

A ADVERB
  en haut
  up on the hill
  en haut de la colline
  up to
  jusqu'à
  Let's count up to fifty.
  Comptons jusqu'à cinquante.
  up to now
  jusqu'à présent

> **up here**
> ici
> **up there**
> là-haut
> **It's up to you.**
> C'est à vous de décider.

B ADJECTIVE
  levé *masc*
  levée *fem (person)*
  I'm always up before eight.
  Je suis toujours levé avant huit heures.
  He's not up yet.
  Il n'est pas encore levé.
C PREPOSITION
  The post office is up the road.
  La poste est en haut de la rue.

The cat is up on the roof.
Le chat est en haut sur le toit.

upper ADJECTIVE
  supérieur *masc*
  supérieure *fem*
    on the upper floor
    à l'étage supérieur

upper sixth NOUN
    She's in the upper sixth.
    Elle est en terminale.

> **Did you know...?**
> In French secondary schools, the years are counted from the **sixième** (youngest) to **première** and **terminale** (oldest).

upset

> **upset** *can be an adjective or a verb.*

A ADJECTIVE
  secoué *masc*
  secouée *fem*
  She's still a bit upset.
  Elle est encore un peu secouée.
  I had an upset stomach.
  J'avais l'estomac dérangé.
B VERB
  faire de la peine
  I don't want to upset my granny.
  Je ne veux pas faire de peine à ma grand-mère.

upside down ADVERB

à l'envers
    That painting is upside down.
    Ce tableau est à l'envers.

English French

a b c d e f g h i j k l m n o p q r s t u v w x y z

English French

a b c d e f g h i j k l m n o p q r s t **u** v w x y z

upstairs ADVERB
en haut
   Where's your coat? —
   It's upstairs.
   Où est ton manteau? —
   Il est en haut.

up-to-date ADJECTIVE
moderne

upwards ADVERB
vers le haut

urgent ADJECTIVE
urgent *masc*
urgente *fem*
   Is it urgent?
   C'est urgent?

US NOUN
les **USA** *masc pl*
   in the US
   aux USA
   to the US
   aux USA
   from the US
   des USA

us PRONOUN
nous
   Come with us.
   Viens avec nous.
   Tell us the story.
   Raconte-nous l'histoire.

USA NOUN
les **USA** *masc pl*
   in the USA
   aux USA
   to the USA
   aux USA
   from the USA
   des USA

use

> **use** *can be a verb or a noun.*

A VERB
utiliser
   You can use a spoon or a
   fork.
   Tu peux utiliser une cuillère ou
   une fourchette.
   Can we use a dictionary in
   the exam?
   Est-ce qu'on peut utiliser un
   dictionnaire à l'examen?
   Can I use your phone?
   Je peux téléphoner?
   Can I use the toilet?
   Je peux aller aux toilettes?
B NOUN
   It's no use.
   Ça ne sert à rien.

use up VERB
finir
   We've used up all the paint.
   Nous avons fini la peinture.

used ADJECTIVE
   I'm used to getting up early.
   J'ai l'habitude de me lever tôt.

> **I'm used to it.**
> J'ai l'habitude.
> **I'm not used to it.**
> Je n'ai pas l'habitude.

useful ADJECTIVE
utile

useless ADJECTIVE
nul *masc*
nulle *fem*
This map is useless.
Cette carte est nulle.
You're useless!
Tu es nul!

usual ADJECTIVE
habituel *masc*
habituelle *fem*
my usual seat
ma place habituelle

as usual
comme d'habitude

usually ADVERB
en général
I usually wear trousers.
En général, je porte un pantalon.

utility room NOUN
la **buanderie** *fem*

English French

a
b
c
d
e
f
g
h
i
j
k
l
m
n
o
p
q
r
s
t
u
v
w
x
y
z

V v

vacancy NOUN
'no vacancies'
'complet'

vacuum cleaner NOUN
l' **aspirateur** *masc*

vague ADJECTIVE
vague

Valentine card NOUN
la **carte de la Saint-Valentin** *fem*

Valentine's Day NOUN
la **Saint-Valentin** *fem*

valley NOUN
la **vallée** *fem*

valuable ADJECTIVE
de valeur
    a valuable picture
    un tableau de valeur

van NOUN
la **camionnette** *fem*

> ***Language tip***
> *'Un camion' is a lorry. The ending*
> *-ette shows that **une camionnette***
> *is smaller than a lorry.*

vandal NOUN
le/la **vandale** *masc/fem*

vandalism NOUN
le **vandalisme** *masc*

vanilla NOUN
la **vanille** *fem*
    vanilla
    ice cream
    la glace à
    la vanille

varied ADJECTIVE
varié *masc*
variée *fem*

variety NOUN
la **variété** *fem*
    There's lots of variety.
    Il y a beaucoup de
    variété.

various ADJECTIVE
plusieurs
    There are various
    possibilities.
    Il y a plusieurs
    possibilités.

vase NOUN
le **vase** *masc*

VDU NOUN
la **console** *fem*

vegan NOUN
le **végétalien** *masc*
la **végétalienne** *fem*
    I'm a vegan.
    Je suis végétalienne.

vegetable NOUN
le **légume** *masc*
    vegetable soup
    la soupe aux légumes
    Would you like some
    vegetables?
    Vous voulez des légumes?

vegetarian

> **vegetarian** *can be an adjective or*
> *a noun.*

A ADJECTIVE
végétarien *masc*
végétarienne *fem*

vegetarian lasagne
les lasagnes végétariennes
B NOUN
le **végétarien** *masc*
la **végétarienne** *fem*
I'm a vegetarian.
Je suis végétarien.
Susie's a vegetarian.
Susie est végétarienne.

verb NOUN
le **verbe** *masc*

very ADVERB
très
very tall
très grand
not very interesting
pas très intéressant

very much
beaucoup
very soon
très bientôt
I'm very sorry.
Je suis vraiment désolé.

vest NOUN
le **maillot de corps** *masc*

vet NOUN
le/la **vétérinaire** *masc/fem*
She's a vet.
Elle est
vétérinaire.

Language tip
When you say what someone's job is
in French, you do not translate **a**.

vicar NOUN
le **pasteur** *masc*
My uncle's a vicar.
Mon oncle est pasteur.

Language tip
When you say what someone's job is
in French, you do not translate **a**.

video

video can be a noun or a verb.

A NOUN
1 la **vidéo** *fem* (film)
**We're going to watch a
video.**
Nous allons regarder une vidéo.
2 la **cassette vidéo** *fem*
(cassette)
I've got the video.
J'ai la cassette vidéo.
3 le **magnétoscope** *masc*
(video recorder)
Can you switch on the video?
Tu peux allumer le
magnétoscope?
B VERB
filmer
**We're going to video the
concert.**
On va filmer le concert.

video game NOUN
le **jeu vidéo** *masc*
I like playing video games.
J'aime les jeux vidéo.

video recorder NOUN
le **magnétoscope** masc

video shop NOUN
le **vidéoclub** masc

view NOUN
la **vue** fem
There's an amazing view.
Il y a une vue extraordinaire.

villa NOUN
la **villa** fem

village NOUN
le **village** masc
in the village
dans le village

vinegar NOUN
le **vinaigre** masc

vineyard NOUN
le **vignoble** masc

violent ADJECTIVE
violent masc
violente fem

violin NOUN
le **violon** masc
I play the violin.
Je joue du violon.

virus NOUN
le **virus** masc

visit

> **visit** can be a noun or a verb.

A NOUN
1 la **visite** fem (to tourist
attraction)
a visit to Edinburgh castle
une visite du château
d'Édimbourg
2 le **séjour** masc (to country)
**Did you enjoy your visit to
France?**
Ton séjour en France s'est bien
passé?

B VERB
1 **rendre visite à** (person)
I'm going to visit friends.
Je vais rendre visite à des amis.
2 **visiter** (place)
**We're going to visit the
castle.**
Nous allons visiter le
château.

visitor NOUN
l' **invité** masc
l' **invitée** fem
**Today we've got a French
visitor.**
Aujourd'hui, nous avons un
invité français.

vitamin NOUN
la **vitamine** *fem*

Language tip

What extra vowel does the French word have?

vocabulary NOUN
le **vocabulaire** *masc*

voice NOUN
la **voix** *fem* (PL les **voix**)

volleyball NOUN
le **volley-ball** *masc*
We sometimes play volleyball.
Quelquefois nous jouons au volley-ball.

volunteer NOUN
le/la **volontaire** *masc/fem*

English French

a
b
c
d
e
f
g
h
i
j
k
l
m
n
o
p
q
r
s
t
u
v
w
x
y
z

W w

waist NOUN
la **taille** *fem*

wait VERB
attendre
> **Wait Mathieu, it's not your turn.**
> Attends Mathieu, ce n'est pas ton tour.
> **Wait boys, I'm coming.**
> Attendez les garçons, j'arrive.

> **Wait for me!**
> Attends-moi!
> **Wait a minute!**
> Attends!
> **Wait a minute, children!**
> Attendez, les enfants!

waiter NOUN
le **serveur** *masc*

waiting room NOUN
la **salle d'attente** *fem*

waitress NOUN
la **serveuse** *fem*

wake up VERB
se réveiller
> **Wake up, Marie!**
> Réveille-toi, Marie!

Wales NOUN
le **pays de Galles** *masc*
> **Swansea is in Wales.**
> Swansea est au pays de Galles.

> **When are you coming to Wales?**
> Quand est-ce que tu viens au pays de Galles?
> **Bronwen is from Wales.**
> Bronwen est galloise.

Language tip
How can you tell that Bronwen is a girl's name in this example sentence?

> **the Prince of Wales**
> le prince de Galles

walk

walk *can be a verb or a noun.*

A VERB
1 **marcher**
> **He walks fast.**
> Il marche vite.
> **Walk faster, Serge.**
> Marche plus vite, Serge.
> **Walk faster, children.**
> Marchez plus vite, les enfants.
2 **aller à pied** *(go on foot)*
> **Are you walking or going by bus?**
> Tu y vas à pied ou en bus?
> **I walked 10 kilometres.**
> J'ai fait dix kilomètres à pied.

B NOUN
la **promenade** *fem*
> **Would you like to go for a walk?**
> Tu veux faire une promenade?

Language tip
promenade *is used in English to mean a road by the sea where you can go for a walk.*

English   French
a b c d e f g h i j k l m n o p q r s t u v **w** x y z

612

walking NOUN
la **marche** *fem*
> **My parents like walking.**
> Mes parents aiment la marche.

Walkman® NOUN
le **walkman**® *masc*

wall NOUN
le **mur** *masc*
> **There are posters on the wall.**
> Il y a des posters au mur.

wallet NOUN
le **portefeuille** *masc*

want VERB
vouloir
> **Do you want some cake?**
> Tu veux du gâteau?
> **I don't want to play.**
> Je ne veux pas jouer.
> **What do you want to do tomorrow?**
> Qu'est-ce que tu veux faire demain?

> **What do you want, Marie?**
> Qu'est-ce que tu veux, Marie?
> **What do you want, boys?**
> Qu'est-ce que vous voulez, les garçons?

war NOUN
la **guerre** *fem*

wardrobe NOUN
l' **armoire** *fem*

warm ADJECTIVE
chaud *masc*
chaude *fem*
> **warm water**
> l'eau chaude
> **It's warm.**
> Il fait chaud.
> **I'm warm.**
> J'ai chaud.

was VERB ▷ *see* **be**

wash VERB
1 laver *(thing)*
> **I'll wash the grapes.**
> Je vais laver le raisin.
2 se laver *(oneself)*
> **At seven I get up, wash and get dressed.**
> À sept heures je me lève, je me lave et je m'habille.

Language tip
Notice how **my** *is translated in the next two examples.*

> **I'm going to wash my hands.**
> Je vais me laver les mains.
> **I want to wash my hair.**
> Je veux me laver les cheveux.

Wash your hands!
Lave-toi les mains!

washbasin NOUN
le **lavabo** *masc*

washing machine NOUN
la **machine à laver** *fem*

washing-up NOUN
> **Who's going to do the washing-up?**
> Qui va faire la vaisselle?
> **I often do the washing-up.**
> Je fais souvent la vaisselle.

washroom NOUN *(Canada)*
les **toilettes** *fem pl*

wasn't (= was not) VERB
▷ *see* **be**

wasp NOUN
la **guêpe** *fem*

waste NOUN
> It's a waste of time.
> C'est une perte de temps.

wastepaper basket NOUN
> la **corbeille à papier** *fem*
> Put your chewing gum in the wastepaper basket.
> Mets ton chewing gum dans la corbeille à papier.

watch

> watch *can be a noun or a verb.*

A NOUN
> la **montre** *fem*
> I haven't got a watch.
> Je n'ai pas de montre.

B VERB
> **regarder**
> I watch television on Saturday mornings.
> Je regarde la télévision le samedi matin.

> Watch me, Mum!
> Regarde-moi, maman!

watch out VERB
> **faire attention**
> You need to watch out.
> Il faut faire attention.

> Watch out!
> Attention!

water NOUN
> l' **eau** *fem*
> a glass of water
> un verre d'eau

wave NOUN
> la **vague** *fem*

> There are sometimes big waves.
> Il y a parfois des grosses vagues.

wavy ADJECTIVE
> wavy hair
> les cheveux ondulés

way NOUN
> **1** le **chemin** *masc (to place)*
> I don't know the way.
> Je ne connais pas le chemin.
> Ask the way.
> Demande le chemin.
> Can you tell me the way to the station?
> Vous pouvez me dire comment aller à la gare?

> It's a long way.
> C'est loin.
> Which way is it?
> C'est par où?
> It's this way.
> C'est par ici.

> **2** la **façon** *fem (manner)*
> What's the best way to learn French?
> Quelle est la meilleure façon d'apprendre le français?
> Do it this way, Sophie.
> Fais-le comme ça, Sophie.

way in NOUN
> l' **entrée** *fem*

way out NOUN
> la **sortie** *fem*
> Where's the way out?
> Où est la sortie?

we PRONOUN

> ***Language tip***
> *There are two ways of saying 'we'. In spoken French, **on** is used more often than **nous**.*

English French

1 nous
We're staying here for a week.
Nous restons une semaine ici.
2 on
Shall we start?
On commence?

wear VERB
porter
She's wearing a hat.
Elle porte un chapeau.
I wear glasses.
Je porte des lunettes.

weather NOUN
le **temps** *masc*
because of the weather
à cause du temps
What's the weather like today?
Quel temps fait-il aujourd'hui?
The weather's not very nice.
Il ne fait pas très beau.

What's the weather like?
Quel temps fait-il?
The weather's nice.
Il fait beau temps.

weather forecast NOUN
la **météo** *fem*

webcam NOUN
la **webcam** *fem*

website NOUN
le **site web** *masc*

wedding NOUN
le **mariage** *masc*
It's my cousin's wedding today.
Aujourd'hui, c'est le mariage de ma cousine.

wedding anniversary
NOUN
l' **anniversaire de mariage**
masc

Wednesday NOUN
le **mercredi** *masc*
It's Wednesday today.
Aujourd'hui c'est mercredi.

on Wednesday
mercredi
on Wednesdays
le mercredi
every Wednesday
tous les mercredis
last Wednesday
mercredi dernier
next Wednesday
mercredi prochain

Language tip
Days of the week are not written with a capital letter in French.

week NOUN
la **semaine** *fem*
two weeks
deux semaines

this week
cette semaine
last week
la semaine dernière
every week
toutes les semaines
next week
la semaine prochaine
in a week's time
dans une semaine

a b c d e f g h i j k l m n o p q r s t u v **w** x y z

a b c d e f g h i j k l m n o p q r s t u v **w** x y z

weekday NOUN
on weekdays
en semaine

weekend NOUN
le **week-end** *masc*
What are you doing at the weekend?
Qu'est-ce que tu fais ce week-end?

at weekends
le week-end
last weekend
le week-end dernier
next weekend
le week-end prochain

Did you know…?
In Quebec, **la fin de semaine** *is used instead of* **le week-end**.

welcome ADJECTIVE
Welcome!
Bienvenue!

Welcome to Scotland!
Bienvenue en Écosse!

Thank you! — You're welcome!
Merci! — De rien!

well

well can be an adverb or an adjective.

A ADVERB
bien
The team is playing well.
L'équipe joue bien.
as well
aussi
We're going to Chartres as well as Paris.

Nous allons à Paris et aussi à Chartres.
B ADJECTIVE *(in good health)*
He's not well.
Il ne va pas bien.
I'm not very well at the moment.
Je ne vais pas très bien en ce moment.

Well done!
Bravo!
Get well soon!
Remets-toi vite!

well-behaved ADJECTIVE
sage

wellies PL NOUN
les **bottes en caoutchouc** *fem pl*

wellingtons PL NOUN
les **bottes en caoutchouc** *fem pl*

well-known ADJECTIVE
célèbre
a well-known film star
une vedette de cinéma célèbre

Welsh

Welsh *can be an adjective or a noun.*

A ADJECTIVE
gallois *masc*
galloise *fem*
She's Welsh.
Elle est galloise.
Welsh people
les Gallois

Language tip
gallois *is not spelled with a capital letter except when it means a Welsh person.*

B NOUN
le **gallois** *masc (language)*

Welshman NOUN
le **Gallois** *masc*

Welshwoman NOUN
la **Galloise** *fem*

went VERB ▷*see* **go**

were VERB ▷*see* **be**

weren't (= were not) VERB
▷*see* **be**

west

> **west** *can be an adjective or a noun.*

A ADJECTIVE
ouest *masc, fem, pl*
the west coast
la côte ouest
B NOUN
l' **ouest** *masc*
in the west
dans l'ouest

West Country NOUN
le **sud-ouest de l'Angleterre** *masc*

western NOUN
le **western** *masc*
I like westerns.
J'aime les westerns.

West Indian ADJECTIVE
antillais *masc*
antillaise *fem*
She's West Indian.
Elle est antillaise.

> **Language tip**
> The adjective **West Indian** is spelled with a capital letter, but **antillais** is not.

West Indies PL NOUN
les **Antilles** *fem pl*

wet ADJECTIVE
mouillé *masc*
mouillée *fem*
wet clothes
des vêtements mouillés
I'm wet.
Je suis mouillé.
It's wet today.
Il pleut aujourd'hui.

whale NOUN
la **baleine** *fem*

what

> **what** *can be a pronoun or an adjective.*

A PRONOUN
1 qu'est-ce que
What are you doing, children?
Qu'est-ce que vous faites, les enfants?
What's happening?
Qu'est-ce qu'il se passe?
What's the matter?
Qu'est-ce qu'il y a?
Take a card and tell your partner what it is.
Prends une carte, et dis à ton partenaire ce que c'est.
2 quel *masc*
quelle *fem*
What's your phone number?
Quel est ton numéro de téléphone?
What's the capital of Belgium?
Quelle est la capitale de la Belgique?

English French

a b c d e f g h i j k l m n o p q r s t u v **w** x y z

English French

a b c d e f g h i j k l m n o p q r s t u v **w** x y z

B ADJECTIVE
quel *masc*
quelle *fem (which)*
What letter does it start with?
Ça commence par quelle lettre?
What colour is it?
C'est de quelle couleur?

What?
Comment?
What is it?
Qu'est-ce que c'est?
What do you want?
Qu'est-ce que tu veux?
What's the weather like?
Quel temps fait-il?
What's your name?
Comment tu t'appelles?
What time is it?
Quelle heure est-il?
What day is it today?
Quel jour sommes-nous?

wheel NOUN
la **roue** *fem*

wheelchair NOUN
le **fauteuil roulant** *masc*

when ADVERB
quand
When it rains we stay in the classroom.
Quand il pleut nous restons dans la classe.
When's your birthday?
C'est quand, ton anniversaire?

Language tip
You can also say: **Ton anniversaire, c'est quand?**

where ADVERB, CONJUNCTION
où

Language tip
où *can come first or last in a sentence.*

Where's Emma today?
Où est Emma aujourd'hui?
Where are you going?
Tu vas où?

Where do you live?
Où habites-tu?

which

which *can be an adjective or a pronoun.*

A ADJECTIVE
quel *masc*
quelle *fem*
Which flavour do you want?
Quel parfum est-ce que tu veux?
Which number is it?
C'est quel numéro?
B PRONOUN
lequel *masc*
laquelle *fem*
Which would you like?
Vous voulez lequel?
Which is your car?
C'est laquelle, ta voiture?
Which do you prefer, cricket or football?
Qu'est-ce que tu préfères, le cricket ou le football?

while CONJUNCTION
pendant que
While you're here we can do some sightseeing.
On peut faire du tourisme pendant que tu es là.

whipped cream NOUN
la **crème fouettée** *fem*

whiskers PL NOUN
les **moustaches** *fem pl*

white

white can be an adjective or a noun.

A ADJECTIVE
blanc *masc*
blanche *fem*
He's wearing white trousers.
Il porte un pantalon blanc.
My shirt is white.
Ma chemise est blanche.

Language tip

Colour adjectives come after the noun in French.

B NOUN
le **blanc** *masc*
The bride is wearing white.
La mariée est vêtue de blanc.

whiteboard NOUN
le **tableau blanc** *masc*
(PL les **tableaux blancs**)
an interactive whiteboard
un tableau interactif

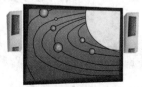

white coffee NOUN
le **café au lait** *masc*

Whitsun NOUN
la **Pentecôte** *fem*

who PRONOUN
qui
Who wants to start?
Qui veut commencer?
Who's that?
C'est qui?

Language tip
You can also say: **Qui est-ce?**

whole ADJECTIVE
tout *masc*
toute *fem*
the whole class
toute la classe
the whole afternoon
tout l'après-midi
the whole world
le monde entier

whose PRONOUN, ADJECTIVE
à qui
Whose pencil case is this?
À qui est cette trousse?
Whose turn is it?
C'est à qui le tour?

Whose is this?
C'est à qui?

why ADVERB
pourquoi
Why are you crying?
Pourquoi tu pleures?
That's why I can't come.
Voilà pourquoi je ne peux pas venir.
Why not?
Pourquoi pas?

wide ADJECTIVE
large
a wide road
une route large

widow NOUN
la **veuve** *fem*

widower NOUN
le **veuf** *masc*

wife NOUN
la **femme** *fem*
She's his wife.
C'est sa femme.

wifi NOUN
le **wifi** *masc*

wild ADJECTIVE
  sauvage
    a wild animal
    un animal sauvage

will VERB
    It will soon be my birthday.
    C'est bientôt mon anniversaire.
    It'll soon be the holidays.
    C'est bientôt les vacances.
    I'll come with you.
    Je vais venir avec toi.
    Do you think he will come?
    Tu crois qu'il va venir?
    Colette won't come.
    Colette ne viendra pas.
    Will you help me?
    Est-ce que tu peux m'aider?

win VERB
  gagner
    I've won!
    J'ai gagné!

wind NOUN
  le **vent** masc
    There is a lot of wind.
    Il y a beaucoup de vent.

window NOUN
  la **fenêtre** fem
    Look out of the window, boys.
    Regardez par la fenêtre, les garçons.
    a shop window
    une vitrine

windy ADJECTIVE
    a windy day
    un jour de grand vent

    It's windy.
    Il y a du vent.

wine NOUN
  le **vin** masc
    a bottle of wine
    une bouteille de vin
    a glass of wine
    un verre de vin
    white wine
    le vin blanc
    red wine
    le vin rouge

winner NOUN
  le **gagnant** masc
  la **gagnante** fem

winning ADJECTIVE
    the winning team
    l'équipe gagnante

winter NOUN
  l' **hiver** masc
    last winter
    l'hiver dernier

    in winter
    en hiver

winter sports PL NOUN
  les **sports d'hiver** masc pl

winter time NOUN
  l' **hiver** masc

    in wintertime
    en hiver

wish

    wish can be a noun or a verb.

A NOUN
    le **vœu** masc (PL les **vœux**)
    Make a wish!
    Fais un vœu!

with best wishes, Kathy
bien amicalement, Kathy

'best wishes'
'meilleurs vœux'

B VERB
I wish I could!
Si je pouvais!

witch NOUN
la **sorcière** *fem*

with PREPOSITION
1 avec
Come with me.
Venez avec moi.
Tea with milk?
Du thé avec du lait?
It begins with 'b'.
Ça commence par un 'b'.
2 chez *(at the home of)*
We're going to stay with friends.
Nous allons loger chez des amis.
I live with my dad.
J'habite chez mon père.

without PREPOSITION
sans
I drink coffee without sugar.
Je bois mon café sans sucre.
without a coat
sans manteau
without speaking
sans parler

wives PL NOUN
les **femmes** *fem pl*

wolf NOUN
le **loup** *masc*

woman NOUN
la **femme** *fem*
three women and two men
trois femmes et deux hommes

won VERB ▷*see* **win**

wonder VERB
se demander
I wonder where Caroline is.
Je me demande où est Caroline.

won't (= will not) VERB ▷*see* **will**

wonderful ADJECTIVE
formidable

wood NOUN
le **bois** *masc*

wool NOUN
la **laine** *fem*
It's made of wool.
C'est en laine.

word NOUN
le **mot** *masc*
Repeat the words, everyone.
Répétez les mots, tout le monde.
I've forgotten the word.
J'ai oublié le mot.
What's the word for 'shop' in French?
Comment dit-on 'shop' en français?

I don't know the word.
Je ne connais pas le mot.
the words *(lyrics)*
les paroles
We're going to learn the words of a song.
Nous allons apprendre les paroles d'une chanson.

work

work *can be a verb or a noun.*

A VERB

1 travailler *(person)*

She works in a shop.
Elle travaille dans un magasin.

2 marcher *(machine, plan)*
The heating isn't working.
Le chauffage ne marche pas.

B NOUN

le **travail** *masc*
He's at work at the moment.
Il est au travail en ce moment.
I've got a lot of work to do.
J'ai beaucoup de travail à faire.

at work
au travail

worker NOUN
She's a good worker.
Elle travaille bien.

worksheet NOUN
la **feuille d'exercices** *fem*
Have you got a worksheet Max?
Max, tu as une feuille d'exercices?

world NOUN
le **monde** *masc*
the whole world
le monde entier
He's the world champion.
Il est champion du monde.

worried ADJECTIVE
inquiet *masc*
inquiète *fem*
She's very worried.
Elle est très inquiète.

worry VERB
s'inquiéter
Don't worry, Mum!
Ne t'inquiète pas, Maman!

worse

worse can be an adjective or an adverb.

A ADJECTIVE
pire
The weather is worse in Scotland.
Le temps est pire en Écosse.

B ADVERB
plus mal
I'm feeling worse.
Je me sens plus mal.

worst ADJECTIVE
the worst
le plus mauvais

Language tip

Use **la plus mauvaise** *if the noun is feminine.*

I always get the worst mark.
J'ai toujours la plus mauvaise note.
Ten! My worst score.
Dix! Mon plus mauvais score.
Maths is my worst subject.
Je suis vraiment nul en maths.

would VERB
1 *(in offers)*
Would you like to play with me?
Tu veux jouer avec moi?

Would you like coffee, sir?
Vous voulez du café, monsieur?

2 (in requests)
I'd like a hot chocolate, please.
Je voudrais un chocolat chaud, s'il vous plaît.
My friend would like a coke.
Mon ami voudrait un coca.
What would you like, sir?
Vous désirez, monsieur?
What would you like, dear?
Qu'est-ce que tu veux, ma chérie?

Language tip

You can also say: **Que veux-tu, ma chérie?**

---

3 (in polite orders)
Would you give out the books, Hugues?
Tu peux distribuer les cahiers, Hugues?
Would you close the door please?
Vous pouvez fermer la porte, s'il vous plaît?

wrapping paper NOUN
le **papier cadeau** masc

write VERB
écrire
Write your names.
Écrivez vos noms.
Write to me soon, Roxanne.
Écris-moi vite, Roxanne.
I'm going to write to my penfriend.
Je vais écrire à ma correspondante.

Write soon!
Écris-moi vite!

write down
noter
I'll write down the address.
Je vais noter l'adresse.
Can you write it down for me, please?
Vous pouvez me l'écrire, s'il vous plaît?

writing NOUN
l' **écriture** fem
I can't read your writing.
Je n'arrive pas à lire ton écriture.

wrong

wrong can be an adjective or an adverb.

A ADJECTIVE
Number two is right, but number three is wrong.
Le numéro deux est juste, mais le numéro trois est faux.
I got three questions wrong.
J'ai eu trois questions fausses.
You're looking at the wrong page.
Tu n'es pas à la bonne page.
That's the wrong answer.
Ce n'est pas la bonne réponse.

B ADVERB
mal
You're saying it wrong.
Tu le dis mal.
Have I spelled it wrong?
Je l'ai mal écrit?

What's wrong?
Qu'est-ce qui ne va pas?
What's wrong with you?
Qu'est-ce que tu as?

Xx

Xmas NOUN
  Noël *masc*

X-ray

X-ray *can be a verb or a noun.*

A VERB
  faire une radio de
  They're going to X-ray my leg.
  Ils vont faire une radio de ma jambe.
  They X-rayed my arm.
  Ils ont fait une radio de mon bras.
B NOUN
  la **radio** *fem*
  I'm going to have an X-ray.
  Je vais passer une radio.

Y y

yacht NOUN
1 le **voilier** *masc (sailing boat)*
2 le **yacht** *masc (luxury motorboat)*

yard NOUN
la **cour** *fem*
in the yard
dans la cour

year NOUN
l' **année** *fem*
next year
l'année prochaine

> ***Language tip***
> There are two words for **year**: **année** and **an**. Use **an** with numbers.

a hundred years
cent ans
an eight-year-old child
un enfant de huit ans

this year
cette année
I'm ten years old.
J'ai dix ans.
I'm in Year 6.
Je suis au CM2.
She's in Year 5.
Elle est au CM1.

> ***Did you know…?***
> In France, children start primary school at the age of six. The first year is **CP**, followed by **CE1** and **CE2**. The last two years are **CM1** and **CM2**.

yellow

> **yellow** *can be an adjective or a noun.*

A ADJECTIVE
jaune
I'm wearing yellow shorts.
Je porte un short jaune.

> ***Language tip***
> Colour adjectives come after the noun in French.

B NOUN
le **jaune** *masc*
Yellow is my favourite colour.
Ma couleur préférée, c'est le jaune.

yes ADVERB
oui
Do you like it? — Yes.
Tu aimes ça? — Oui.
Answer yes or no.
Réponds par oui ou par non.

yesterday ADVERB
hier
When? — Yesterday.
Quand? — Hier.
I was absent yesterday.
Hier, j'étais absente.

yesterday morning
hier matin
yesterday afternoon
hier après-midi

yesterday evening
hier soir

yet ADVERB
encore
   I haven't finished yet.
   Je n'ai pas encore fini.
   Have you finished yet, children?
   Vous avez fini, les enfants?

Not yet.
Pas encore.

yoghurt NOUN
   le **yaourt** masc

you PRONOUN

> **Language tip**
>
> Only use **tu** when you're talking to your family or to someone of your own age, or younger. Use **vous** when you're talking to several people, or to an adult you don't know very well. The teacher calls you '**tu**', but you call the teacher '**vous**'.

1 tu (singular and subject of verb)
   Do you like football, Nina?
   Tu aimes le football, Nina?
   Do you understand, Michelle?
   Tu comprends, Michelle?
2 te (singular and object of verb)
   I know you.
   Je te connais.

> **Language tip**
>
> **te** changes to **t'** before a vowel sound.

   I love you.
   Je t'aime.

3 toi (singular and after a preposition)
   I'll come with you.
   Je viens avec toi.
   It's for you, Xavier.
   C'est pour toi, Xavier.
   She's younger than you.
   Elle est plus jeune que toi.
4 vous (polite form or plural)
   Do you understand, children?
   Vous comprenez, les enfants?
   Are you listening, Gaëlle and Richard?
   Vous écoutez, Gaëlle et Richard?
   Could you move out of the way please, miss?
   Vous pouvez vous pousser s'il vous plaît, madame?
   Can I help you?
   Est-ce que je peux vous aider?
   It's for you, children.
   C'est pour vous, les enfants.

young ADJECTIVE
jeune
   You're too young.
   Tu es trop jeune.

younger ADJECTIVE
plus jeune
   He's younger than me.
   Il est plus jeune que moi.

youngest ADJECTIVE
plus jeune
   my youngest brother
   mon plus jeune frère

> **Language tip**
>
> To say that someone is **the youngest**, use **le plus jeune** for a boy and **la plus jeune** for a girl.

   Hugo's the youngest.
   Hugo est le plus jeune.

She's the youngest in the class.
C'est la plus jeune de la classe.

your ADJECTIVE

Language tip

*When you want to say something like 'your name', 'your house', or 'your hair' in French, you need to know if 'name', 'house', 'hair' are masculine, feminine, or plural, because there are three possible words for **your**.*

1 ton *masc (to someone you call 'tu')*
Is that your brother?
C'est ton frère?
ta *fem*
Is that your sister?
C'est ta sœur?
tes *pl*
your parents
tes parents

Language tip

ta *changes to* **ton** *before a vowel sound.*

your friend Éléonore
ton amie Éléonore
2 votre *(to people you call 'vous')*
your house
votre maison
When's your birthday, miss?
Quelle est la date de votre anniversaire, madame?
vos *pl*
Take your things out.
Sortez vos affaires.

Language tip

*Notice how **your** is translated in the next two examples.*

Wash your hands, Laura.
Lave-toi les mains, Laura.
Wash your hands, children.
Lavez-vous les mains, les enfants.

yours PRONOUN
1 à toi *(to someone you call 'tu')*
Is this yours, Frank?
C'est à toi, Frank?
Whose is this? —
It's yours, dear.
C'est à qui? — À toi, chéri.
2 à vous *(to people you call 'vous')*
Is this yours, sir?
C'est à vous, monsieur?
These tickets are yours.
Ces billets sont à vous.
Whose is this? — It's yours.
C'est à qui? — À vous.

yourself PRONOUN
1 te *(to someone you call 'tu')*
You'll make yourself sick!
Tu vas te rendre malade!

Language tip

te *changes to* **t'** *before a vowel sound.*

Are you enjoying yourself?
Tu t'amuses bien?
2 toi

Language tip

*After a preposition, use **toi** instead of **te**.*

Tell me about yourself!
Parle-moi de toi!
3 vous *(to someone you call 'vous')*
Help yourself, Mrs Day!
Servez-vous, Madame Day!
Tell me about yourself!
Parlez-moi de vous!

a
b
c
d
e
f
g
h
i
j
k
l
m
n
o
p
q
r
s
t
u
v
w
x
y
z

yourselves PRONOUN
  1 **vous**
    Did you enjoy yourselves?
    Vous vous êtes bien amusés?
  2 **vous-mêmes**
    Do it yourselves!
    Faites-le vous-mêmes!

youth club NOUN
  le **centre de jeunes** *masc*
    at the youth club
    au centre de jeunes

youth hostel NOUN
  l' **auberge de jeunesse** *fem*
    We're going to stay at a youth hostel.
    Nous allons loger dans une auberge de jeunesse.

Z z

zebra NOUN
  le **zèbre** *masc*

zero NOUN
  le **zéro** *masc*

zoo NOUN
  le **zoo** *masc*
    We went to the zoo on Saturday.
    Samedi, nous sommes allésau zoo.